Library of Congress Cataloging in Publication Data

BARKER, LUCIUS JEFFERSON, comp.
  Civil liberties and the Constitution.

  Includes bibliographies.
  1. Civil rights—United States. I. Barker, Twiley
Wendell, joint comp. II. Title.
KF4748.B2 1975   342'.73'085   74-34364
ISBN 0-13-134817-5
ISBN 0-13-134809-4 pbk.

To RUTH, VALERIE, SHERI, MAUD, TRACEY, and HEIDI

Printed in the United States of America

10 9 8 7 6 5 4 3

Prentice-Hall International, Inc., *London*
Prentice-Hall of Australia, Pty., Ltd., *Sydney*
Prentice-Hall of Canada, Ltd., *Toronto*
Prentice-Hall of India Private Limited, *New Delhi*
Prentice-Hall of Japan, Inc., *Tokyo*

Civil Liberties and the Constitution

CASES AND COMMENTARIES

Second Edition

LUCIUS J. BARKER

Edna Gellhorn University Professor of Public Affairs and Political Science,
Washington University, St. Louis

TWILEY W. BARKER, JR.

Professor of Political Science,
University of Illinois at Chicago Circle

PRENTICE-HALL, INC., Englewood Cliffs, New Jersey

Contents

Preface to the Second Edition

This second edition is evidence that the assumption implicit in *Civil Liberties and The Constitution* has been borne out. That basic assumption was that the increasing sensitivity of Americans to the importance of civil liberties and civil rights in the overall operation of the political system warrants and indeed requires a systematic study of the issues involved in such problems. We continue to believe that this systematic study should include the "basic stuff" from one of the most important sources upon which much of our civil liberty/civil rights policy depends—the decisions of the United States Supreme Court.

In this way, students and others are able to see and interpret for themselves what the Court decides, and its reasons for doing so. Equally important is that they will be in a better position to gauge how the *law as doctrine* (e.g., court decisions) squares or does not square with the *law in practice* (e.g., behavior of policemen). This in turn focuses attention on the more basic question of the role and limitations of courts and law in coping with such problems in the context of the political system.

However, this volume, just as the first edition, does not attempt to cover the wide range of concerns with respect to the study of civil rights and liberties. Rather, its central purpose is to provide, in a coherent fashion, a collation of leading Supreme Court cases that focus on particular topics. These cases are edited in such a way as to promote a general, rather than a technically legal, understanding of the issues involved. With this in mind, and wherever possible, an attempt is made to give major arguments from majority, concurring, and dissenting opinions. In addition, extensive commentaries (introducing each chapter) are designed to place these leading cases in historical perspective. This context allows us to see more clearly continuity and/or changes in the posture of the Court. For example, we are able to show in this revision how the transition from the Warren Court to the Burger Court seems to be producing change in the tone and substance of Supreme Court decisions. This may particularly be seen in cases involving racial discrimination and rights of persons accused of crime. Moreover, in this revision, special attention is directed to cases and commentaries that deal with freedom and security, women's rights, rights of the poor and other minorities.

We reemphasize here that our focus on Supreme Court decisions should not, and we are certain will not, lead readers to minimize or overlook the range of activities and actors (including lower courts, legislators, executives, and interest groups) in the formation of civil liberties and civil rights policy. Moreover, as we stated in the first edition, we are "keenly aware and deeply sensitive to the political, social, psychological, and economic dimensions of civil liberties problems," and our hope was that the volume would be supplemented by appropriate materials. This continues to be our hope. The general response to the first edition gives us reason to believe that readers appreciate a volume that is free from rigid interpretations of authors and is thus more adaptable to a variety of learning situations.

We are grateful for the helpful suggestions passed along to us by users of the first edition. We are also immensely appreciative of the valuable research and collating assistance of Marc Schnall and Michael Mulkey, and the typing assistance of Margaret Kennedy, Beatrice Villar, and Anita Worthington. The errors that invariably have a way of showing up later are our misdeeds, not theirs.

L.J.B.
T.W.B.

1 Nationalizing the Bill of Rights

Barron v. *Baltimore*   *Palko* v. *Connecticut*   *Adamson* v. *California*   *Duncan* v. *Louisiana*

The framers of the Bill of Rights considered federal power the major threat to individual liberties. The injunction of the First Amendment, "Congress shall make no law . . . ," is indicative of that concern. But there were others who viewed the Bill of Rights as restricting state power as well. This view was urged in *Barron* v. *Baltimore,* [1] but the Supreme Court rejected such a construction. Speaking for a unanimous Court, Chief Justice John Marshall said:

> The Constitution was ordained and established by the people of the United States for themselves, for their own government, and not for the government of the individual states. . . . The powers they conferred on this government were to be exercised by itself; and the limitations on power, if expressed in general terms are . . . necessarily applicable to the government created by the instrument. They are limitations of power granted in the instrument itself; not of distinct governments framed by different persons and for different purposes.

He concluded that if his propositions are correct, then the Fifth Amendment (and hence the Bill of Rights) must be understood as restraining the power of the national government and not that of the states.

This principle was reaffirmed in a number of cases prior to the Civil War and continued to be a guide for the Court in decisions following the adoption of the

[1] Complete citations for decisions reprinted in this book appear at the beginning of each decision.

Fourteenth Amendment in 1868. Indeed, the Court heard several cases in which counsel argued that the Fourteenth Amendment had as one of its objectives the incorporation of the Bill of Rights. But the Court steadfastly refused to interpret the Fourteenth Amendment in this way.

Then in 1925, in a historic decision, *Gitlow* v. *New York* (268 U.S. 652, 1925), the Court said:

> For present purposes we may and do assume that freedom of speech and of the press which are protected by the First Amendment from abridgement by Congress are among the fundamental personal rights and liberties protected by the due process clause of the Fourteenth Amendment from impairment by the States.

Gitlow v. *New York* was a case of major, almost revolutionary, significance, which turned the tide in favor of those who saw the provisions of the Bill of Rights as effective limitations on the states through the Fourteenth Amendment. Two years after *Gitlow*, for example, the Court reversed a conviction under a Kansas criminal syndicalism act, saying that the application of the act imposed "an arbitrary and unreasonable exercise of the police power of the State . . . in violation of the due process clause of the Fourteenth Amendment."[2] Four years later in *Near* v. *Minnesota* (283 U.S. 679, 1931), the Court struck down a Minnesota statute as an abridgement of freedom of the press. Chief Justice Charles Evans Hughes asserted in the opinion for the Court that "it is no longer open to doubt that the liberty of the press, and of speech, is within the liberty safeguarded by the due process clause of the Fourteenth Amendment from invasion by state action."

The Court continued this erosion of the *Barron* rule, at least as far as First Amendment freedoms were concerned, when in *De Jonge* v. *Oregon* it held peaceable assembly a right cognate to those of free speech and free press and hence protected against state impairment by the due process clause of the Fourteenth Amendment.

But any notion that this trend of decisions would lead to a reversal of *Barron* v. *Baltimore* and the total incorporation of the first eight amendments into the Fourteenth Amendment was dispelled by Justice Benjamin Cardozo in a decision handed down just 11 months after *De Jonge*. In *Palko* v. *Connecticut* the Court refused to apply the double jeopardy provision of the Fifth Amendment to a state criminal prosecution. Justice Cardozo argued that only those guarantees of the first eight amendments which are "implicit in the concept of ordered liberty" are to be construed as valid restrictions on state power through the Fourteenth Amendment. In effect, he enunciated a doctrine of "selective incorporation" of specific Bill of Rights guarantees into the Fourteenth Amendment based on the test of their essentiality to his concept of "ordered liberty."

In 1940 the "selective incorporation" process resulted in the Court's holding in *Cantwell* v. *Connecticut* (310 U.S. 296, 1940) that the free exercise of religion clause of the First Amendment is applicable to the states. In this case the Court struck down a state statute which allowed officials unfettered discretion in

---

[2] *Fiske* v. *Kansas* (274 U.S. 380, 1927).

regulating religious advocacy and solicitation. In his opinion for a unanimous Court, Justice Owen Roberts contended:

> The fundamental concept of liberty embodied in that [the Fourteenth] Amendment embraces the liberties guaranteed by the First Amendment . . . , [which] declares that Congress shall make no law respecting an establishment of religion or prohibiting the free exercise thereof. The Fourteenth Amendment has rendered the legislatures of the states as incompetent as Congress to enact such laws.

This expansive interpretation of the scope of the Fourteenth Amendment was followed by an application of the establishment clause of the First Amendment to the states in *Everson* v. *Board of Education.* In that case the Court considered the troublesome issues of public aid to parochial schools and held that the due process clause of the Fourteenth Amendment enjoins the states from rendering such aid just as the First Amendment restrains Congress.

The most comprehensive arguments supporting the total incorporation theory were made in *Adamson* v. *California.* Here the Court's five-man majority refused to upset a state conviction where the appellant argued that the state procedure infringed the Fifth Amendment guarantee against compulsory self-incrimination, which was made applicable to the states through the Fourteenth Amendment. The four dissenters—Justices Hugo Black, William O. Douglas, Frank Murphy, and Wiley B. Rutledge—contended that all the specific guarantees of the first eight amendments should be read into the due process clause of the Fourteenth Amendment and made applicable to the states. Justice Black's dissenting opinion is most often cited in support of this thesis. He maintained that the legislative history of the Fourteenth Amendment, as well as the debates in the state legislatures ratifying it, clearly revealed that the Fourteenth Amendment was designed to make the Bill of Rights applicable to the states. In effect, his position was that the framers of the Fourteenth Amendment intended for the due process clause to be a shorthand restatement of the specific guarantees of the Bill of Rights, *but no more.*

In a concurring opinion, Justice Felix Frankfurter not only questioned Black's reading and interpretation of history but contended that incorporation of the specific guarantees of the Bill of Rights into the due process clause would import to it a far more expansive meaning than intended in some cases and a more restricted meaning than intended in others. To him, such a construction would also do violence to the principle of federalism upon which the Republic was founded. As he put it:

> A construction which gives to due process no independent function but turns it into a summary of the specific provisions of the Bill of Rights would . . . tear up the fabric of law in the several States, and would deprive the States of the opportunity for reforms in legal process designed for extending the area of freedom. It would assume that no other abuses would reveal themselves in the course of time than those which had become manifest in 1791.

On the other hand, two of Black's fellow dissenters did not share his view of the limited protection afforded by the due process clause. It was their view that restricting the scope of the clause only to the Bill of Rights guarantees and *no more* fails to include enough. As Murphy contended in a separate opinion in which Rutledge joined:

Occasions may arise where a proceeding falls so far short of conforming to fundamental standards of procedure as to warrant constitutional condemnation in terms of lack of due process despite the absence of a specific provision in the Bill of Rights.

In subsequent cases, Justice Black reaffirmed his total incorporation position and continued to urge a "narrow" or "strict" interpretation of the specific guarantees of the Bill of Rights. In *Wolf* v. *Colorado*, for example, he concurred in the Court's action "selectively incorporating" the Fourth Amendment into the Fourteenth *without* the exclusionary rule. He contended that the rule, which holds that evidence obtained in violation of the Fourth Amendment is inadmissible in criminal prosecutions, "is not a command of the Fourth Amendment" but instead is a "judicially created" one. Justices Murphy and Rutledge were joined this time by Justice Douglas in taking issue with Black's narrow construction of the Fourth Amendment. In their view, not only does the Fourteenth Amendment incorporate the guarantees of the Fourth, but the exclusionary rule must be construed as embraced in the Amendment if its command is to be an effective sanction against the evil to which it is directed.

Though the "total incorporation" theory has never gained majority support, its proponents have virtually accomplished their goal. Note the forward thrust of incorporation since 1961: *Mapp* v. *Ohio,* where the exclusionary rule was made obligatory on the states, thereby making the Fourth Amendment an effective restraint on state action; *Malloy* v. *Hogan* and *Benton* v. *Maryland,* making the Fifth Amendment's self-incrimination and double jeopardy provisions applicable to the states; *Gideon* v. *Wainwright, Pointer* v. *Texas, Klopfer* v. *North Carolina,* and *Duncan* v. *Louisiana,* in which the Court incorporated into the Fourteenth Amendment the Sixth Amendment guarantees of counsel, confrontation, a speedy trial, and trial by jury for serious criminal offenses; and *Robinson* v. *California,* tying to the Fourteenth Amendment the Eighth Amendment's protection against cruel and unusual punishment.

As the Court ended its 1973 term, only a few provisions of the Bill of Rights had not been incorporated into the Fourteenth Amendment. These include the Second and Third Amendments (which have no practical significance for the states), the grand jury indictment requirement of the Fifth Amendment, the jury trial provision for civil suits guaranteed by the Seventh Amendment, and the provision prohibiting excessive bail and the imposition of excessive fines of the Eighth Amendment. For all practical purposes, however, imposition of excessive bail and fines by a state would violate the due process clause of the Fourteenth Amendment.

The opponents of the incorporation theory did not allow the gradual process of undermining *Barron* to proceed uncontested. To them it was just as offensive as total incorporation. For example, Justice John Harlan contended in *Malloy* v. *Hogan* (1964) that this approach "is in fact nothing more or less than 'incorporation' in snatches." Furthermore, it was his contention there that "if the Due Process Clause of the Fourteenth Amendment is something more than a reference to the Bill of Rights and protects only those rights which derive from fundamental principles . . . , it is just as contrary to precedent and just as illogical to incorporate the provisions of the Bill of Rights one at a time as it is to incorporate them all at once." Harlan echoed this same theme in *Pointer* v. *Texas* (1965) one year later while concurring in the Court's decision guaranteeing the right of confrontation in state cases. To him the confrontation guarantee was "implicit in the concept of ordered liberty," and the majority opinion incorporating the guarantee into the Fourteenth Amendment was simply "another step in the onward march of the long-since discredited 'incorporation' doctrine. . . ."

In *Duncan* v. *Louisiana* (1968), Justice Harlan launched another full-scale attack on the "total incorporation" doctrine. Here, the Court incorporated the Sixth Amendment guarantee of trial by jury and in doing so revised the *Palko* test. Instead of asking whether a particular guarantee is essential for a civilized society, the Court *now* asks whether such a guarantee is "necessary to an Anglo-American regime of ordered liberty."[3] Harlan argued that "the Court's approach [to the case] and its reading of history are altogether topsy-turvy." Hence, he rejected the view that it was the intention of those who drafted the Fourteenth Amendment to incorporate the first eight amendments. To him Black's interpretation of the legislative history of the Fourteenth Amendment (as set forth in *Adamson* in support of the "total incorporation" doctrine) had been thoroughly discredited by Charles Fairman.[4] He noted that the evidence marshalled by Professor Fairman convincingly demonstrates that the Congressmen who drafted, and the state legislators who ratified, the Fourteenth Amendment did not think they were making the first eight amendments applicable to the states. "In short," he concluded, "neither history, nor sense, supports using the Fourteenth Amendment to put the states in a constitutional straight-jacket with respect to their own development in the administration of criminal or civil law." For Harlan, the "only one method of analysis that has any internal logic . . . is to start with the words 'liberty' and 'due process' and attempt to define them in a way that accords with American traditions and our system of government."

Justice Black could not let this opportunity pass without defending and clarifying his historical analysis, which supported the incorporation theory advanced in *Adamson*. In a concurring opinion (primarily a rejoinder to Professor Fairman's attack), Black caustically referred to Fairman's emphasis on "what was *not* said in the Congress which proposed, and the state legislatures that passed on,

---

[3] Such a "test" appears to further strengthen the supports upon which the incorporation decisions since 1961 stand, for, as Justice Black noted, it could well be argued that the limitations embraced in the Bill of Rights may not be essential to fundamental fairness in any and every criminal system, but they are essential in the context of the criminal system in operation in the American states.

[4] Charles Fairman, "Does the Fourteenth Amendment Incorporate the Bill of Rights? The Original Understanding," 2 *Stanford Law Review* 5 1949).

the Fourteenth Amendment" as a kind of "negative pregnant." (Emphasis added.) Reemphasizing the correctness of his reading of history, he contended that his appraisal followed ten years of experience in the United States Senate which prepared him "to learn the value of what *is* said in legislative debates, committee discussions, committee reports, and various other steps taken in the course of passage of . . . proposed constitutional amendments." (Emphasis added.) In essence, what Black seems to imply is that because of his Senate experience his history is better than Professor Fairman's. Apart from the historical issue, Black was critical of Harlan's restatement of the *Twining* concept of due process—a concept which Black contends allows the Court "boundless power under 'natural law' periodically to expand and contract constitutional standards to conform to the Court's conception of what at a particular time constitutes 'civilized decency' and 'fundamental liberty and justice' "[5] Black noted that such a view of due process was too loose and shifting, since its meaning would be "in accordance with judges' predilections and understandings of what is best for the country."

Whether, as a general rule, the provisions of the Bill of Rights which have been incorporated into the Fourteenth Amendment operate with equal force and impose the same standards upon the states as upon the federal government is still an unsettled question. Justices supporting total incorporation (never a majority) have, at one time or another, argued that the standard should be the same. For example, Justice Black in his dissenting opinion in *Adamson* referred to the "literal application" of the Bill of Rights to the states, and Justice Douglas, dissenting in *Beauharnis* v. *Illinois* (343 U.S. 250, 288, 1952), contended that there is no exception in the command of the First Amendment when applied to limit states via the Fourteenth Amendment. Douglas has also contended that the rights incorporated in the Fourteenth Amendment are not "watered-down versions" of what the Bill of Rights guarantees. Likewise, Justice Brennan, dissenting in *Cohen* v. *Hurley* (336 U.S. 117, 1961), argued that the "full sweep" of the privilege against self-incrimination is applicable to the states through the Fourteenth Amendment. And Justice Tom Clark declared in *Mapp* v. *Ohio* that the Fourth Amendment's provisions are enforceable against the states "by the same sanction of exclusion as issued against the Federal Government." Furthermore, Justice Clark wrote an opinion in *Ker* v. *California* (374 U.S. 23, 1963), in which all the justices except Harlan agreed that the "standard of reasonableness of a search and seizure is the same under the Fourth and Fourteenth Amendments." And Justice Thurgood Marshall echoed the same theme in *Benton* v. *Maryland* when he asserted that "[o]nce it is decided that a particular Bill of Rights guarantee is 'fundamental to the American scheme of justice,' the same constitutional standards apply against both the State and Federal governments."

On the other hand, some of justices have rejected this kind of congruence argument. For example, Justice Jackson, while dissenting in *Beauharnis,* rejected the notion that the liberty which the Fourteenth Amendment protects against state

---

[5] In *Twining* v. *New Jersey* (211 U.S. 78, 1908), the Supreme Court rejected a self-incrimination claim and upheld a state criminal procedure which permitted the courts in their instructions to the jury to comment on the accused's failure to testify and contradict evidence presented against him. Justice Moody concluded, after extensive historical analysis, that the self-incrimination privilege was not inherent in due process of law.

impairment is the "literal and identical freedom of speech or of the press" which the First Amendment protects against federal abridgement. Justice John Harlan II has offered the most vigorous opposition to the "equivalence" position. In his dissent in *Mapp,* in which he was supported by Justices Frankfurter and Whittaker, he contended that it would be improper to impose "any precise equivalence, either as regards the scope of the right or the means of its implementation, between the requirements of the Fourth and Fourteenth Amendment."

The cases that follow examine the rationale for the *Barron* rule, the modification of it by the *Palko* doctrine, and leading arguments on incorporation of the Bill of Rights into the Fourteenth Amendment.

BARRON v. BALTIMORE
7 Peters 242; 8 L. Ed. 672 (1833)

CHIEF JUSTICE MARSHALL *delivered the opinion of the Court.*

[This case was instituted by the plaintiff in error against the city of Baltimore . . . to recover damages for injuries to the wharf-property of the plaintiff, arising from the acts of the corporation. Craig and Barron, of whom the plaintiff is survivor, were owners of an extensive and highly productive wharf in the eastern section of Baltimore, enjoying, at the period of their purchase of it, the deepest water in the harbour.

[The city, in the asserted exercise of its corporate authority over the harbour, the paving of streets, and regulating grades for paving, and over the health of Baltimore, directed from their accustomed and natural course, certain streams of water which flow from the range of hills bordering the city, and diverted them. . . . These streams becoming very full and violent in rains, carried down with them from the hills and the soil over which they ran, large masses of sand and earth, which they deposited along, and widely in front of the wharf of the plaintiff. The alleged consequence was, that the water was rendered so shallow that it ceased to be useful for vessels of any important burthen, lost its income, and became of little or no value as a wharf.

[At the trial of the cause . . . the decision of Baltimore county court was against the defendants, and a verdict for four thousand five hundred dollars was rendered for the plaintiff. An appeal was taken to the court of appeals, which reversed the judgment of Baltimore county court and did not remand the case to that court for a further trial. From this judgment the defendant in the court of appeals, prosecuted a writ of error to this court.]

The plaintiff in error contends that it comes within that clause in the fifth amendment to the Constitution, which inhibits the taking of private property for public use, without just compensation. He insists that this amendment, being in favor of the liberty of the citizen, ought to be so construed as to restrain the legislative power of a State, as well as that of the United States. If this proposition be untrue, the court can take no jurisdiction of the cause.

The question thus presented is, we think, of great importance, but not of much difficulty.

The Constitution was ordained and established by the people of the United States for themselves, for their own government, and not for the government of the individual States. Each State established a Constitution for itself, and, in that Constitution, provided such limitations and restrictions on the powers of its particular government as its judgment dictated. The people of the United States framed such a government for the United States as they supposed best adapted to their situation, and best calculated to promote their interests. The powers they conferred on this government were to be exercised by itself; and the limitations on power, if expressed in general terms, are naturally, and, we think, necessarily applicable to the government created by the instrument. They are limitations of power granted in the instrument itself; not of distinct governments, framed by different persons and for different purposes.

If these propositions be correct, the fifth amendment must be understood as restraining the power of the general government, not as applicable to the states. In their several constitutions, they had imposed such restrictions on their respective governments, as their own wisdom suggested; such as they deemed most proper for themselves. It is a subject on which they judge exclusively. . . .

The counsel for the plaintiff in error insists, that the constitution was intended to secure the people of the several states against the undue exercise of power by their respective state governments; as well as against that which might be attempted by their general government. In support of this argument he relies on the inhibitions contained in the tenth section of the first article. We think that section affords a strong, if not a conclusive, argument in support of the court. The preceding section contains restrictions which are obviously intended for the exclusive purpose of restraining the exercise of power by the departments of the general government. Some of them use language applicable only to congress; others are expressed in general terms. The third clause, for example, declares, that "no bill of attainder or *ex post facto* law shall be passed." No language can be more general; yet the demonstration is complete, that it applies solely to the government of the United States. In addition to the general arguments furnished by the instrument itself, some of which have been already suggested, the succeeding section, the avowed purpose of which is to restrain state legislation, contains in terms the very prohibition. It declares, that "no State shall pass any bill of attainder or *ex post facto* law." This provision, then of the ninth section, however comprehensive its language, contains no restrictions on state legislation.

The ninth section having enumerated, in the nature of a bill of rights, the limitations intended to be imposed on the powers of the general government, the tenth proceeds to enumerate those which were to operate on the state legislatures. These restrictions are brought together in the same section, and are by express words applied to the states. "No state shall enter into any treaty," etc. Perceiving that in a constitution framed by the people of the United States for the government of all, no limitation of the action of government on the people would apply to the state government, unless expressed in terms, the restrictions contained in the tenth section are in direct words so applied to the states.

It is worthy of remark, too, that these inhibitions generally restrain state legislation on subjects intrusted to the general government, or in which the people of all the states feel an interest. A state is forbidden to enter into any treaty, alliance, or confederation. If these compacts are with foreign nations, they interfere with the treaty-making power, which is conferred entirely on the general government; if with each other, for political purposes, they can scarcely fail to interfere with the general purpose and intent of the constitution. To grant letters of marque and reprisal, would lead directly to war; the power of declaring which is expressly given to congress. To coin money is also the exercise of a power conferred on congress. It would be tedious to recapitulate the several limitations on the powers of the states which are contained in this section. They will be found, generally, to restrain state legislation on subjects intrusted to the government of the Union, in which the citizens of all the states are interested. In these alone were the whole people concerned. The question of their application to states is not left to construction. It is averred in positive words.

If the original constitution, in the ninth and tenth sections of the first article, draws this plain and marked line of discrimination between the limitations it imposes on the powers of the general government, and on those of the states; if in every inhibition intended to act on state power, words are employed, which directly express that intent; some strong reason must be assigned for departing from this safe and judicious course, in framing the amendments, before that departure can be assumed. We search in vain for that reason.

Had the people of the several states, or any of them, required changes in their constitutions; had they required additional safeguards to liberty from the apprehended encroachments of their particular governments; the remedy was in their own hands, and could have been applied by themselves. A convention could have been assembled by the discontented state, and the required improvements could have been made by itself. The unwieldy and cumbrous machinery of procuring a recommendation from two-thirds of congress, and the assent of three-fourths of their sister states, could never have occurred to any human being, as a mode of doing that which might be effected by the state itself. Had the framers of these amendments intended them to be limitations on the powers of the state governments, they would have imitated the framers of the original constitution, and have expressed that intention. Had congress engaged in the extraordinary occupation of improving the constitutions of the several states by affording the people additional protection from the exercise of power by their own governments, in matters which concerned themselves alone, they

would have declared this purpose in plain and intelligible language.

But it is universally understood, it is a part of the history of the day, that the great revolution which established the constitution of the United States was not effected without immense opposition. Serious fears were extensively entertained that those powers which the patriot statesmen, who then watched over the interests of our country, deemed essential to union, and to the attainment of those invaluable objects for which union was sought, might be exercised in a manner dangerous to liberty. In almost every convention by which the constitution was adopted, amendments to guard against the abuse of power were recommended. These amendments demanded security against the apprehended encroachments of the general government, not against those of the local governments. In compliance with a sentiment thus generally expressed, to quiet fears thus extensively entertained, amendments were proposed by the required majority in congress, and adopted by the states. These amendments contained no expression indicating an intention to apply them to the state governments. This court cannot so apply them.

We are of opinion, that the provision in the fifth amendment to the constitution, declaring that private property shall not be taken for public use without just compensation, is intended solely as a limitation on the exercise of power by the government of the United States, and is not applicable to the legislation of the states. We are therefore, of [the] opinion, that there is no repugnancy between the several Acts of the General Assembly of Maryland, given in evidence by the defendants at the trial of this cause, in the court of that state, and the constitution of the United States. This court, therefore, has no jurisdiction of the cause, and it is dismissed.

PALKO v. CONNECTICUT

302 U.S. 319; 82 L. Ed. 288; 58 S. Ct. 149 (1937)

MR. JUSTICE CARDOZO *delivered the opinion of the Court.*

A statute of Connecticut permitting appeals in criminal cases to be taken by the state is challenged by appellant as an infringement of the Fourteenth Amendment of the Constitution of the United States. . . .

Appellant was indicted . . . for the crime of murder in the first degree. A jury found him guilty of murder in the second degree, and he was sentenced to confinement in the state prison for life. Thereafter the State of Connecticut, with the permission of the judge presiding at the trial, gave notice of appeal to the Supreme Court of Errors. This it did pursuant to an act adopted in 1886 which [provides that appeals from the rulings and decisions of the superior court or of any criminal court of common pleas, upon all questions of law arising on the trial of criminal cases, may be taken by the state, with the permission of the presiding judge, to the supreme court of errors, in the same manner and to the same effect as if made by the accused]. Upon such appeal, the Supreme Court of Errors reversed the judgment and ordered a new trial. . . . It found that there had been error of law to the prejudice of the state (1) in excluding testimony as to a confession by defendant; (2) in excluding testimony upon cross-examination of defendant to impeach his credibility; and (3) in the instructions to the jury as to the difference between first and second degree murder.

Pursuant to the mandate of the Supreme Court of Errors, defendant was brought to trial again. Before a jury was impaneled and also at later stages of the case he made the objection that the effect of the new trial was to place him twice in jeopardy for the same offense, and in so doing to violate the Fourteenth Amendment of the Constitution of the United States. . . . The jury returned a verdict of murder in the first degree, and the court sentenced the defendant to

the punishment of death. The Supreme Court of Errors affirmed the judgment of conviction. . . .

1. The execution of the sentence will not deprive appellant of his life without the process of law assured to him by the Fourteenth Amendment of the Federal Constitution.

The argument for appellant is that whatever is forbidden by the Fifth Amendment is forbidden by the Fourteenth also. The Fifth Amendment, which is not directed to the states, but solely to the federal government, creates immunity from double jeopardy. No person shall be "subject for the same offense to be twice put in jeopardy of life or limb." The Fourteenth Amendment ordains, "nor shall any State deprive any person of life, liberty, or property, without due process of law." To retry a defendant, though under one indictment and only one, subjects him, it is said, to double jeopardy in violation of the Fifth Amendment, if the prosecution is one on behalf of the United States. From this the consequence is said to follow that there is a denial of life or liberty without due process of law, if the prosecution is one on behalf of the People of a State.

We have said that in appellant's view the Fourteenth Amendment is to be taken as embodying the prohibitions of the Fifth. His thesis is even broader. Whatever would be a violation of the original bill of rights (Amendment I to VIII) if done by the federal government is now equally unlawful by a state. There is no such general rule.

The Fifth Amendment provides, among other things, that no person shall be held to answer for a capital or otherwise infamous crime unless on presentment or indictment of a grand jury. This court has held that, in prosecutions by a state, presentment or indictment by a grand jury may give way to informations at the instance of a public officer. *Hurtado* v. *California,* 110 U.S. 516. . . . The Fifth Amendment provides also that no person shall be compelled in any criminal case to be a witness against himself. This court has said that, in prosecutions by a state, the exemption will fail if the state elects to end it. *Twining* v. *New Jersey*, 211 U.S. 78, 106, 111, 112. . . . The Sixth Amendment calls for a jury trial in criminal cases and the Seventh for a jury trial in civil cases at common law where the value in controversy shall exceed twenty dollars. This court has ruled that consistent with those amendments trial by jury may be modified by a state or abolished altogether. *Walker* v. *Sauvinet*, 92 U.S. 90; *Maxwell* v. *Dow*, 176 U.S. 581. . . .

On the other hand, the due process clause of the Fourteenth Amendment may make it unlawful for a state to abridge by its statutes the freedom of speech which the First Amendment safeguards against encroachment by the Congress, *De Jonge* v. *Oregon*, 299 U.S. 353, 364; *Herndon* v. *Lowry*, 301 U.S. 242, 259; or the like freedom of the press, *Grosjean* v. *American Press Co.*, 297 U.S. 233; *Near* v. *Minnesota ex rel. Olson*, 283 U.S. 697, 707; or the free exercise of religion, *Hamilton* v. *Regents*, 293 U.S. 245, 262 . . . ; or the right of peaceable assembly, without which speech would be unduly trammeled . . . ; or the right of one accused of crime to the benefit of counsel, *Powell* v. *Alabama*, 287 U.S. 45. In these and other situations immunities that are valid as against the federal government by force of the specific pledges of particular amendments have been found to be implicit in the concept of ordered liberty, and thus, through the Fourteenth Amendment, become valid as against the states.

The line of division may seem to be wavering and broken if there is a hasty catalogue of the cases on the one side and the other. Reflection and analysis will induce a different view. There emerges the perception of a rationalizing principle which gives to discrete instances a proper order and coherence. The right to trial by jury and the immunity from prosecution except as the result of an indictment may have value and importance. Even so, they are not of the very essence of a scheme of ordered liberty. To abolish them is not to violate a "principle of justice so rooted in the traditions and conscience of our people as to be ranked as fundamental." . . . Few would be so narrow or provincial as to maintain that a fair and enlightened system of justice would be impossible without them. What is true of jury trials and indictments is true also, as the cases show, of the immunity from compulsory self-incrimination. *Twining* v. *New Jersey, supra*. This too might be lost, and justice still be done. Indeed, today as in the past there are students of our penal system who look upon the immunity as a mischief rather than a benefit, and who would limit its scope, or destroy it altogether. No doubt there would remain the need to give protection against torture, physical or mental. . . . Justice, however, would not perish if the accused were subject to a duty to respond to orderly inquiry. The exclusion of these immunities and privileges from the privileges and immunities protected against the action of the states has not been arbitrary or casual. It has been dictated by a study and appreciation of the meaning, the essential implications, of liberty itself.

We reach a different plane of social and moral values when we pass to the privileges and immunities that have been taken over from the earlier articles of the federal bill of rights and brought within the Fourteenth Amendment by a process of absorption. These in their origin were effective against the federal government alone. If the Fourteenth Amendment has absorbed them the process of absorption has had its source in the belief that neither liberty nor justice would exist if they were sacrificed. . . . This is true, for illustration, of freedom of thought, and speech. Of that freedom one may say that it is the matrix, the indispensable condition, of nearly every other form of freedom. With rare aberrations a pervasive recognition of that truth can be traced in our history, political and legal. So it has come about that the domain of liberty, withdrawn by the Fourteenth Amendment from encroachment by the states, has been enlarged by latter-day judgments to include liberty of the mind as well as liberty of action. The extension became, indeed, a logical imperative when once it was recognized, as long ago it was, that liberty is something more than exemption from physical restraint, and that even in the field of substantive rights and duties the legislative judgment, if oppressive and arbitrary, may be overridden by the courts. . . .

Our survey of the cases serves, we think, to justify the statement that the dividing line between them, if not unfaltering throughout its course, has been true for the most part to a unifying principle. On which side of the line the case made out by the appellant has appropriate location must be the next inquiry and the final one. Is that kind of double jeopardy to which the statute has subjected him a hardship so acute and shocking that our polity will not endure it? Does it violate those "fundamental principles of liberty and justice which lie at the base of all our civil and political institutions"? . . . The answer surely must be "no." What the answer would have to be if the state were permitted after a trial free from error to try the accused over again or to bring another case against him, we have no occasion to consider. We deal with the statute before us and no other. The state is not attempting to wear the accused out by a multitude of cases with accumulated trials. It asks no more than this, that the case against him shall go on until there shall be a trial free from the corrosion of substantial legal error. . . . This is not cruelty at all, nor even vexation in any immoderate degree. If the trial had been infected with error adverse to the accused, there might have been review at this instance, and as often as necessary to purge the vicious taint. A reciprocal privilege, subject at all times to the discretion of the presiding judge . . . has now been granted to the state. There is here no seismic innovation. The edifice of justice stands, its symmetry, to many, greater than before.

2. The conviction of appellant is not in derogation of any privileges or immunities that belong to him as a citizen of the United States. . . .

The judgment is

Affirmed.

MR. JUSTICE BUTLER *dissents.*

ADAMSON v. CALIFORNIA
332 U.S. 46; 91 L. Ed. 1903; 67 S. Ct. 1672 (1947)

MR. JUSTICE REED *delivered the opinion of the Court.*

The appellant . . . was convicted, without recommendation for mercy, by a jury in a Superior Court of the State of California of murder in the first degree. . . . [T] he sentence of death was affirmed by the Supreme Court of the state. . . . The provisions of California law which were challenged in the state proceedings as invalid under the Fourteenth Amendment of the Federal Constitution . . . permit the failure of a defendant to explain or to deny evidence against him to be commented upon by court and by counsel and to be considered by court and jury. The defendant did not testify. As the trial court gave its instructions and the District Attorney argued the case in accordance with the constitutional and statutory provisions just referred to, we have for decision the question of their constitutionality in these circumstances under the limitations of Section I of the Fourteenth Amendment. . . .

The appellant was charged in the information with former convictions for burglary, larceny and robbery . . . [and] answered that he had suffered the previous convictions. This answer barred allusion to these charges of convictions on the trial. Under, California's interpretation of [the statute], however, if the defendant, after answering affirmatively charges alleging prior convictions, takes the witness stand to deny or explain away other evidence that has been introduced "the commission of these crimes could have been revealed to the jury on cross-examination to impeach his testimony." ... This forces an accused who is a repeated offender to choose between the risk of having his prior offenses disclosed to the jury or of having it draw harmful inferences from uncontradicted evidence that can only be denied or explained by the defendant.

In the first place, appellant urges that the provision of the Fifth Amendment that no person "shall be compelled in any criminal case to be a witness against himself" is a fundamental national privilege or immunity protected against state abridgement by the Fourteenth Amendment or a privilege or immunity secured, through the Fourteenth Amendment, against deprivation by state action because it is a personal right, enumerated in the federal Bill of Rights.

Secondly, appellant relies upon the due process of law clause of the Fourteenth Amendment to invalidate the provisions of the California law ... and as applied (a) because comment on failure to testify is permitted, (b) because appellant was forced to forego testimony in person because of danger of disclosure of his past convictions through cross-examination and (c) because the presumption of innocence was infringed by the shifting of the burden of proof to appellant in permitting comment on his failure to testify.

We shall assume, but without any intention thereby of ruling upon the issue, that permission by law to the court, counsel and jury to comment upon and consider the failure of defendant "to explain or to deny by his testimony any evidence or facts in the case against him" would infringe defendant's privilege against self-incrimination under the Fifth Amendment if

this were a trial in a court of the United States under a similar law. Such an assumption does not determine appellant's rights under the Fourteenth Amendment. It is settled law that the clause of the Fifth Amendment, protecting a person against being compelled to be a witness against himself, is not made effective by the Fourteenth Amendment as a protection against state action on the ground that freedom from testimonial compulsion is a right of national citizenship, or because it is a personal privilege or immunity secured by the Federal Constitution as one of the rights of man that are listed in the Bill of Rights.

The reasoning that leads to those conclusions starts with the unquestioned premise that the Bill of Rights, when adopted, was for the protection of the individual against the federal government and its provisions were inapplicable to similar actions done by the states. ... The power to free defendants in state trials from self-incrimination was specifically determined to be beyond the scope of the privileges and immunities clause of the Fourteenth Amendment in *Twining* v. *New Jersey*. ... This Court held that the inclusion in the Bill of Rights of this protection against the power of the national government did not make the privilege a federal privilege or immunity secured to citizens by the Constitution against state action. ... After declaring that state and national citizenship coexist in the same person, the Fourteenth Amendment forbids a state from abridging the privileges and immunities of citizens of the United States. As a matter of words, this leaves a state free to abridge, within the limits of the due process clause, the privileges and immunities flowing from state citizenship. This reading of the Federal Constitution has heretofore found favor with the majority of this Court as a natural and logical interpretation. It accords with the constitutional doctrine of federalism by leaving to the states the responsibility of dealing with the privileges and immunities of their citizens except those inherent in their national citizenship. It is the construction placed upon the amendment by justices whose own experience had given them contemporaneous knowledge of the purposes that led to the adoption of the Fourteenth Amendment. This construction has become embedded in our federal system as a functioning element in preserving the balance between national and state power. We reaffirm the conclusion of the Twining and Palko Cases that protection against self-incrimination is not a privilege or immunity of national citizenship.

Appellant secondly contends that if the privilege against self-incrimination is not a right protected by the privileges and immunities clause of the Fourteenth Amendment against state action, this privilege, to its full scope under the Fifth Amendment, inheres in the right to a fair trial. A right to a fair trial is a right admittedly protected by the due process clause of the Fourteenth Amendment. Therefore, appellant argues, the due process clause of the Fourteenth Amendment protects his privilege against self-incrimination. The due process clause of the Fourteenth Amendment, however, does not draw all the rights of the federal Bill of Rights under its protection. That contention was made and rejected in *Palko* v. *Connecticut*... Nothing has been called to our attention that either the framers of the Fourteenth Amendment or the states that adopted it intended its due process clause to draw within its scope the earlier amendments to the Constitution....

Specifically, the due process clause does not protect, by virtue of its mere existence, the accused's freedom from giving testimony by compulsion in state trials that is secured to him against federal interference by the Fifth Amendment....

MR. JUSTICE FRANKFURTER, *concurring.*

For historical reasons a limited immunity from the common duty to testify was written into the Federal Bill of Rights, and I am prepared to agree that, as part of that immunity, comment on the failure of an accused to take the witness stand is forbidden in federal prosecutions. It is so, of course, by explicit act of Congress.... But to suggest that such a limitation can be drawn out of "due process" in its protection of ultimate decency in a civilized society is to suggest that the Due Process Clause fastened fetters of unreason upon the State....

Between the incorporation of the Fourteenth Amendment into the Constitution and the beginning of the present membership of the Court—a period of seventy years—the scope of that Amendment was passed upon by forty-three judges. Of all these judges, only one, who may respectfully be called an eccentric exception, ever indicated the belief that the Fourteenth Amendment was a shorthand summary of the first eight Amendments theretofore limiting only the federal Government, and that due process incorporated those eight Amendments as restrictions upon the powers of the States. Among these judges were not only those who would have to be included among the greatest in the history of the Court, but—it is especially relevant to note—they included those whose services in the cause of human rights and the spirit of freedom are the most conspicuous in our history. It is not invidious to single out Miller, Davis, Bradley, Waite, Matthews, Gray, Fuller, Holmes, Brandeis, Stone and Cardozo (to speak only of the dead) as judges who were alert in safeguarding and promoting the interests of liberty and human dignity through law. But they were also judges mindful of the relation of our federal system to a progressively democratic society and therefore duly regardful of the scope of authority that was left to the States even after the Civil War. And so they did not find that the Fourteenth Amendment, concerned as it was with matters fundamental to the pursuit of justice, fastened upon the States procedural arrangements which, in the language of Mr. Justice Cardozo, only those who are "narrow or provincial" would deem essential to "a fair and enlightened system of justice." ...

The short answer to the suggestion that the provision of the Fourteenth Amendment, which ordains "nor shall any State deprive any person of life, liberty, or property, without due process of law," was a way of saying that every State must thereafter initiate prosecutions through indictment by a grand jury, must have a trial by a jury of twelve in criminal cases, and must have trial by such a jury in common law suits where the amount in controversy exceeds twenty dollars, is that it is a strange way of saying it. It would be extraordinarily strange for a Constitution to convey such specific commands in such a roundabout and inexplicit way. After all, an amendment to the Constitution should be read in a " 'sense most obvious to the common understanding at the time of its adoption.' . . . For it was for public adoption that it was proposed." See Mr. Justice Holmes in *Eisner* v. *Macomber*, 252 U.S. 189, 220. Those reading the English language with the meaning which it ordinarily conveys, those conversant with the political and legal history of the concept of due process, those sensitive to the relations of the States to the central government as well as the relation of some of the provisions of the Bill of Rights to the process of justice, would hardly recognize the Fourteenth Amendment as a cover for the various explicit provisions of the first eight Amendments. . . . The notion that the Fourteenth Amendment was a covert way of imposing upon the States all the rules which it seemed important to Eighteenth Century statesmen to write into the Federal Amendments, was rejected by judges who were themselves witnesses of the process by which the Fourteenth Amendment became part of the Constitution. Arguments that may now be adduced to prove that the first eight Amendments were concealed within the historic phrasing of the Fourteenth Amendment were not unknown at the time of its adoption. A surer estimate of their bearing was possible for judges at the time than distorting distance is likely to vouchsafe. Any evidence of design or purpose not contemporaneously known could hardly have influenced those who ratified the Amendment. . . . Thus, at the time of the ratification of the Fourteenth Amendment the constitutions of nearly half of

the ratifying States did not have the rigorous requirements of the Fifth Amendment for instituting criminal proceedings through a grand jury. It could hardly have occurred to these States that by ratifying the Amendment they uprooted their established methods for prosecuting crime and fastened upon themselves a new prosecutorial system.

It may not be amiss to restate the pervasive function of the Fourteenth Amendment in exacting from the States observance of basic liberties. . . . The Amendment neither comprehends the specific provisions by which the founders deemed it appropriate to restrict the federal government nor is it confined to them. The Due Process Clause of the Fourteenth Amendment has an independent potency, precisely as does the Due Process Clause of the Fifth Amendment in relation to the Federal Government. It ought not to require argument to reject the notion that due process of law meant one thing in the Fifth Amendment and another in the Fourteenth. . . . Are Madison and his contemporaries in the framing of the Bill of Rights to be charged with writing into it a meaningless clause? To consider "due process of law" as merely a shorthand statement of other specific clauses in the same amendment is to attribute to the authors and proponents of this Amendment ignorance of, or indifference to, a historic conception which was one of the great instruments in the arsenal of constitutional freedom which the Bill of Rights was to protect and strengthen.

A construction which gives to due process no independent function but turns it into a summary of the specific provisions of the Bill of Rights would, as has been noted, tear up by the roots much of the fabric of law in the several States, and would deprive the States of opportunity for reforms in legal process designed for extending the area of freedom. It would assume that no other abuses would reveal themselves in the course of time than those which had become manifest in 1791. Such a view not only disregards the historic meaning of "due process." It leads inevitably to a warped construction of specific provisions of the Bill of Rights to bring within their scope conduct clearly condemend by due process but not easily fitting into the pigeon-holes of the specific provisions. It seems pretty late in the day to suggest that a phrase so laden with historic meaning should be given an improvised content consisting of some but not all of the provisions of the first eight Amendments, selected on an undefined basis, with improvisation of content for the provisions so selected.

MR. JUSTICE BLACK, *dissenting.*

This decision reasserts a constitutional theory spelled out in *Twining* v. *New Jersey* . . . that this Court is endowed by the Constitution with boundless power under "natural law" periodically to expand and contract constitutional standards to conform to the Court's conception of what at a particular time constitutes "civilized decency" and "fundamental liberty and justice." Invoking this *Twining* rule, the Court concludes that although comment upon testimony in a federal court would violate the Fifth Amendment, identical comment in a state court does not violate today's fashion in civilized decency and fundamentals and is therefore not prohibited by the Federal Constitution as amended.

. . . But I would not reaffirm the *Twining* decision. I think that decision and the "natural law" theory of the Constitution upon which it relies degrade the constitutional safeguards of the Bill of Rights and simultaneously appropriate for this Court a broad power which we are not authorized by the Constitution to exercise. . . .

My study of the historical events that culminated in the Fourteenth Amendment, and the expressions of those who sponsored and favored, as well as those who opposed its submission and passage, persuades me that one of the chief objects that the provisions of the Amendment's first section, and as a whole, were intended to accomplish was to make the Bill of Rights applicable to the states. With full knowledge of the import of the *Barron* decision, the framers and backers of the Fourteenth Amendment

proclaimed its purpose to be to overturn the constitutional rule that case had announced. This historical purpose has never received full consideration or exposition in any opinion of this Court interpreting the Amendment. . . .

. . . In my judgment [the legislative history of the Fourteenth Amendment] conclusively demonstrates that the language of [its] first section . . . taken as a whole, was thought by those responsible for its submission to the people, and by those who opposed its submission, sufficiently explicit to guarantee that thereafter no state could deprive its citizens of the privileges and protections of the Bill of Rights. Whether this Court ever will, or whether it now should, in the light of past decisions, give full effect to what the Amendment was intended to accomplish is not necessarily essential to a decision here. However that may be, our prior decisions, including *Twining*, do not prevent our carrying out that purpose, at least to the extent of making applicable to the states, not a mere part, as the Court has, but the full protection of the Fifth Amendment's provision against compelling evidence from an accused to convict him of crime. And I further contend that the "natural law" formula which the Court uses to reach its conclusion in this case should be abandoned as an incongruous excrescence on our Constitution. I believe that formula to be itself a violation of our Constitution, in that it subtly conveys to courts, at the expense of legislatures, ultimate power over public policies in fields where no specific provision of the Constitution limits legislative power. And my belief seems to be in accord with the views expressed by this Court, at least for the first two decades after the Fourteenth Amendment was adopted. . . .

I cannot consider the Bill of Rights to be an outworn 18th Century "strait-jacket" as the *Twining* opinion did. Its provisions may be thought outdated abstractions by some. And it is true that they were designed to meet ancient evils. But they are the same kind of human evils that have emerged from century to century wherever excessive power is sought by the few at the expense of the many. In my judgment the people of no nation can lose their liberty so long as a Bill of Rights like ours survives and its basic purposes are conscientiously interpreted, enforced and respected so as to afford continuous protection against old, as well as new, devices and practices which might thwart those purposes. I fear to see the consequences of the Court's practices of substituting its own concepts of decency and fundamental justice for the language of the Bill of Rights as its point of departure in interpreting and enforcing that Bill of Rights. If the choice must be between the selective process of the *Palko* decision applying some of the Bill of Rights to the States, or the *Twining* rule applying none of them, I would choose the *Palko* selective process. But rather than accept either of these choices, I would follow what I believe was the original purpose of the Fourteenth Amendment—to extend to all the people of the nation the complete protection of the Bill of Rights. To hold that this Court can determine what, if any, provisions of the Bill of Rights will be enforced, and if so to what degree, is to frustrate the great design of a written Constitution.

. . .

It is an illusory apprehension that literal application of some or all of the provisions of the Bill of Rights to the States would unwisely increase the sum total of the powers of this Court to invalidate state legislation. The Federal Government has not been harmfully burdened by the requirement that enforcement of federal laws affecting civil liberty conform literally to the Bill of Rights. Who would advocate its repeal? It must be conceded, of course, that the natural-law-due-process formula, which the Court today reaffirms, has been interpreted to limit substantially this Court's power to prevent state violations of the individual civil liberties guaranteed by the Bill of Rights. But this formula also has been used in the past, and can be used in the future, to license this Court, in considering regulatory legislation, to roam at large in the broad expanses of policy and morals and to trespass, all too freely, on the legislative domain of the States as well as the Federal Government.

DUNCAN v. LOUISIANA
391 U.S. 145; 20 L. Ed. 2d 491; 88 S. Ct. 1444 (1968)

[The concurring and dissenting opinions below focus on the last full-scale debate within the Supreme Court on the issue of total incorporation of the Bill of Rights into the due process clause of the Fourteenth Amendment.]

MR. JUSTICE BLACK, *with whom* MR. JUSTICE DOUGLAS *joins, concurring.*

The Court today holds that the right to trial by jury guaranteed defendants in criminal cases in federal courts by Art. III of the United States Constitution and by the Sixth Amendment is also guaranteed by the Fourteenth Amendment to defendants tried in state courts. With this holding I agree for reasons given by the Court. I also agree because of reasons given in my dissent in *Adamson* v. *California,* 332 U.S. 46, 68. In that dissent . . . I took the position, contrary to the holding in *Twining* v. *New Jersey,* 211 U.S. 78, that the Fourteenth Amendment made all of the provisions of the Bill of Rights applicable to the States. This Court in *Palko* v. *Connecticut,* 302 U.S. 319 . . . [said] "there is no such general rule," . . . [and was of the opinion] that certain Bill of Rights' provisions were made applicable to the States by bringing them "within the Fourteenth Amendment by a process of absorption."

Thus *Twining* v. *New Jersey* ... refused to hold that any one of the Bill of Rights' provisions was made applicable to the States by the Fourteenth Amendment, but *Palko*, which must be read as overruling *Twining* on this point, concluded that the Bill of Rights' Amendments that are "implicit in the concept of ordered liberty" are "absorbed" by the Fourteenth as protections against state invasion. In this situation I said in *Adamson* v. *California*, 332 U.S., at 89, that while "I would extend to all the people of the nation the complete protection of the Bill of Rights," that "[i] f the choice must be between the selective process of the *Palko* decision applying some of the Bill of Rights to the States, or the *Twining* rule applying none of them, I would choose the *Palko* selective process." And I am very happy to support this selective process through which our Court has since the *Adamson* case held most of the specific Bill of Rights' protections applicable to the States to the same extent they are applicable to the Federal Government. . . .

... The dissent in this case ... makes a spirited and forceful defense of that now discredited doctrine. I do not believe that it is necessary for me to repeat the historical and logical reasons for my challenge to the *Twining* holding contained in my *Adamson* dissent and Appendix to it. What I wrote there in 1947 was the product of years of study and research. My appraisal of the legislative history followed 10 years of legislative experience as a Senator of the United States, not a bad way, I suspect, to learn the value of what is said in legislative debates, committee discussions, committee reports, and various other steps taken in the course of passage of bills, resolutions, and proposed constitutional amendments. My Brother Harlan's objections to my *Adamson* dissent history, like that of most of the objections, relies most heavily on a criticism written by Professor Charles Fairman and published in the Stanford Law Review, 2 Stan. L. Rev. 5 (1949). I have read and studied this article extensively, including the historical references, but am compelled to add that in my view it has completely failed to refute the inferences and

arguments that I suggested in my *Adamson* dissent. Professor Fairman's "history" relies very heavily on what was not said in the state legislatures that passed on the Fourteenth Amendment. Instead of relying on this kind of negative pregnant, my legislative experience has convinced me that it is far wiser to rely on what was said, and most importantly, said by the men who actually sponsored the Amendment in the Congress. I know from my years in the United States Senate that it is to men like Congressman Bingham, who steered the Amendment through the House, and Senator Howard, who introduced it in the Senate, that members of Congress look when they seek the real meaning of what is being offered. And they vote for or against a bill based on what the sponsors of that bill and those who oppose it tell them it means. The historical appendix to my *Adamson* dissent leaves no doubt in my mind that both its sponsors and those who opposed it believed the Fourteenth Amendment made the first eight Amendments of the Constitution (The Bill of Rights) applicable to the States.

In addition to the adoption of Professor Fairman's "history," the dissent states that "the great words of the four clauses of the first section of the Fourteenth Amendment would have been an exceedingly peculiar way to say that The rights heretofore guaranteed against federal intrusion by the first eight amendments are henceforth guaranteed against State intrusion as well.' " ... In response to this I can say only that the words "No State shall make or enforce any law which shall abridge the privileges or immunities of citizens of the United States" seems to me an eminently reasonable way of expressing the idea that henceforth the Bill of Rights shall apply to the States.† What more

---

†My view has been and is that the Fourteenth Amendment, *as a whole*, makes the Bill of Rights applicable to the States. This would certainly include the language of the Privileges and Immunities Clause, as well as the Due Process Clause.

precious "privilege" of American citizenship could there be than that privilege to claim the protection of our great Bill of Rights? I suggest that any reading of "privileges and immunities of citizens of the United States" which excludes the Bill of Rights' safeguards renders the words of this section of the Fourteenth Amendment meaningless. . . .

While I do not wish at this time to discuss at length my disagreement with Brother Harlan's forthright and frank restatement of the now discredited *Twining* doctrine, I do want to point out what appears to me to be the basic difference between us. His view, as was indeed the view of *Twining,* is that "due process is an evolving concept" and therefore that it entails a "gradual process of judicial inclusion and exclusion" to ascertain those "immutable principles of free government which no member of the Union may disregard." Thus the Due Process Clause is treated as prescribing no specific and clearly ascertainable constitutional command that judges must obey in interpreting the Constitution, but rather as leaving judges free to decide at any particular time whether a particular rule or judicial formulation embodies an "immutable principle of free government" [or "is implicit in the concept of ordered liberty," or whether certain conduct "shocks the judge's conscience"] or runs counter to some other similar, undefined and undefinable standard. Thus due process, according to my Brother Harlan, is to be a word with no permanent meaning, but one which is found to shift from time to time in accordance with judges' predilections and understandings of what is best for the country. If due process means this, the Fourteenth Amendment, in my opinion, might as well have been written that "no person shall be deprived of life, liberty or property except by laws that the judges of the United States Supreme Court shall find to be consistent with the immutable principles of free government." It is impossible for me to believe that such unconfined power is given to judges in our Constitution that is a written one in order to limit governmental power.

Another tenet of the *Twining* doctrine as restated by my Brother Harlan is that "due process of law requires only fundamental fairness." But the "fundamental fairness" test is one on a par with that of shocking the conscience of the Court. Each of such tests depends entirely on the particular judge's idea of ethics and morals instead of requiring him to depend on the boundaries fixed by the written words of the Constitution. Nothing in the history of the phrase "due process of law" suggests that constitutional controls are to depend on any particular judge's sense of values. . . . [T]he Due Process Clause gives all Americans, whoever they are and wherever they happen to be, the right to be tried by independent and unprejudiced Courts using established procedures and applying valid preexisting laws. There is not one word of legal history that justifies making the term "due process of law" mean a guarantee of a trial free from laws and conduct which the courts deem at the time to be "arbitrary," "unreasonable," "unfair," or "contrary to civilized standards." The due process of law standard for a trial is one tried in accordance with the Bill of Rights and laws passed pursuant to constitutional power, guaranteeing to all alike a trial under the general law of the land.

Finally I want to add that I am not bothered by the argument that applying the Bill of Rights to the States, "according to the same standards that protect those rights against Federal encroachment," interferes with our concept of federalism in that it may prevent States from trying novel social and economic experiments. I have never believed that under the guise of federalism the States should be able to experiment with the protections afforded our citizens through the Bill of Rights. . . .

In closing I want to emphasize that I believe as strongly as ever that the Fourteenth Amendment was intended to make the Bill of Rights applicable to the States. I have been willing to support the selective incorporation doctrine, however, as an alternative, although perhaps less historically supportable than complete incorporation. The selective incorporation process, if used properly, does limit the Supreme Court in the Fourteenth Amendment field to specific Bill of Rights' protection only and keeps judges from roaming at will in their own notions of what policies outside the Bill of Rights are desirable and what are not. And, most importantly for me, the selective incorporation process has the virtue of having already worked to make most of the Bill of Rights' protections applicable to the States.

MR. JUSTICE HARLAN, *whom* MR. JUSTICE STEWART *joins, dissenting.*

Every American jurisdiction provides for trial by jury in criminal cases. The question before us is not whether jury trial is an ancient institution, which it is; nor whether it plays a significant role in the administration of criminal justice, which it does; nor whether it will endure, which it shall. The question in this case is whether the State of Louisiana, which provides trial by jury for all felonies, is prohibited by the Constitution from trying charges of simple battery to the court alone. In my view, the answer to that question, mandated alike by our constitutional history and by the longer history of a trial by jury, is clearly "no."

The States have always borne primary responsibility for operating the machinery of criminal justice within their borders, and adapting it to their particular circumstances. In exercising this responsibility, each State is compelled to conform its procedures to the requirements of the Federal Constitution. The Due Process Clause of the Fourteenth Amendment requires that those procedures be fundamentally fair in all respects. It does not, in my view, impose or encourage nationwide uniformity for its own sake; it does not command adherence to forms that happen to be old; and it does not impose on the States the rules that may be in force in the federal courts except where such rules are also found to be essential to basic fairness.

The Court's approach to this case is an uneasy and illogical compromise among the views of various Justices on how the Due Process Clause should be interpreted. The Court does not say that those who framed the Fourteenth Amendment intended to make the Sixth Amendment applicable to the States. And the Court concedes that it finds nothing unfair about the procedure by which the present appellant was tried. Nevertheless, the Court reverses his conviciton: it holds, for some reason not apparent to me, that the Due Process Clause incorporates the particular clause of the Sixth Amendment that requires trial by jury in federal criminal cases—including, as I read its opinion, the sometimes trivial accompanying baggage of judicial interpretation in federal contexts. I have raised my voice many times before against the Court's continuing undiscriminating insistence upon fastening on the States federal notions of criminal justice, and I must do so again in this instance. With all respect, the Court's approach and its reading of history are altogether topsy-turvy.

I believe I am correct in saying that every member of the Court for at least the last 135 years has agreed that our Founders did not consider the requirements of the Bill of Rights so fundamental that they should operate directly against the States. They were wont to believe rather that the security of liberty in America rested primarily upon the dispersion of governmental power across a federal system. The Bill of Rights was considered unnecessary by some but insisted upon by others in order to curb the possibility of abuse of power by the strong central government they were creating.

The Civil War Amendments dramatically altered the relation of the Federal Government to the States. The first section of the Fourteenth Amendment imposes highly significant restrictions on state action. But the restrictions are couched in very broad and general terms: citizenship, privileges and immunities; due process of law; equal protection of the laws. Consequently, for 100 years this Court has engaged in the difficult process Professor Jaffe has well called "the search for intermediate premises." . . .

A few members of the Court have taken the position that the intention of those who drafted the first section of the Fourteenth Amendment was simply, and exclusively, to make the provisions of the first eight amendments applicable to state action. This view has never been accepted by this Court. In my view, often expressed elsewhere, the first section of the Fourteenth Amendment was meant neither to incorporate, nor to be limited to, the specific guarantees of the first eight amendments. The overwhelming historical evidence marshalled by Professor Fairman demonstrates, to me conclusively, that the Congressmen and state legislators who wrote, debated, and ratified the Fourteenth Amendment did not think they were "incorporating" the Bill of Rights and the very breadth and generality of the Amendment's provisions suggests that its authors did not suppose that the Nation would always be limited to mid-19th-century conceptions of "liberty" and "due process of law" but that the increasing experience and evolving conscience of the American people would add new "intermediate premises." In short, neither history, nor sense, supports using the Fourteenth Amendment to put the States in a constitutional straitjacket with respect to their own development in the administration of criminal or civil law.

Although I therefore fundamentally disagree with the total incorporation view of the Fourteenth Amendment, it seems to me that such a position does at least have the virtue lacking in the Court's selective incorporation approach, of internal consistency; we look to the Bill of Rights, word for word, clause for clause, precedent for precedent because, it is said, the men who wrote the Amendment wanted it that way. For those who do not accept this "history," a different source of "intermediate premises" must be found. The Bill of Rights is not necessarily irrelevant to the search for guidance in interpreting the Fourteenth Amendment, but the

reason for and the nature of its relevance must be articulated.

Apart from the approach taken by the absolute incorporationists, I can see only one method of analysis that has any internal logic. This is to start with the words "liberty" and "due process of law" and attempt to define them in a way that accords with American traditions and our system of government. This approach, involving a much more discriminating process of adjudication than does "incorporation," is, albeit difficult, the one that was followed throughout the Nineteenth and most of the present century. It entails a "gradual process of judicial inclusion and exclusion," seeking, with due recognition of constitutional tolerance for state experimentation and disparity, to ascertain those "immutable principles of free government which no member of the Union may disregard." Due process was not restricted to rules fixed in the past, for that "would be to deny every quality of the law but its age, and to render it incapable of progress or improvement." . . .

Through this gradual process, this Court sought to define "liberty" by isolating freedoms that Americans of the past and of the present considered more important than any suggested countervailing public objective. The Court also, by interpretation of the phrase "due process of law," enforced the Constitution's guarantee that no State may imprison an individual except by fair and impartial procedures.

The relationship of the Bill of Rights to this "gradual process" seems to me to be twofold. In the first place it has long been clear that the Due Process Clause imposes some restrictions on state action that parallel Bill of Rights restrictions on federal action. Second, and more important than this accidental overlap, is the fact that the Bill of Rights is evidence, at various points, of the content Americans find in the term "liberty" and of American standards of fundamental fairness.

An example, both of the phenomenon of parallelism and the use of the first eight amendments as evidence of a historic commitment, is found in the partial definition of "liberty" offered by Mr. Justice Holmes, dissenting in *Gitlow* v. *New York*, 268 U.S. 652.

> The general principle of free speech ... must be taken to be included in the Fourteenth Amendment, in view of the scope that has been given to the word "liberty" as there used, although perhaps it may be accepted with a somewhat larger latitude of interpretation than is allowed to Congress by the sweeping language that governs or ought to govern the laws of the United States. *Id.,* at 672. ...

The Court has also found among the procedural requirements of "due process of law" certain rules paralleling requirements of the first eight amendments. For example, in *Powell* v. *Alabama*, 287 U.S. 45, the Court ruled that a State could not deny counsel to an accused in a capital case. ... Later, the right to counsel was extended to all felony cases. The Court has also ruled, for example, that "due process" means a speedy process, so that liberty will not be long restricted prior to an adjudication, and evidence of fact will not become stale; that in a system committed to the resolution of issues of fact by adversary proceedings the right to confront opposing witnesses must be guaranteed; and that if issues of fact are tried to a jury, fairness demands a jury impartially selected. ...

In all these instances, the right guaranteed against the States by the Fourteenth Amendment was one that had also been guaranteed against the Federal Government by one of the first eight amendments. The logically critical thing, however, was not that the rights had been found in the Bill of Rights, but that they were deemed, in the context of American legal history, to be fundamental. ...

Today's Court still remains unwilling to accept the total incorporationists' view of the history of the Fourteenth Amendment. This, if accepted, would afford a cogent reason for applying the Sixth Amendment to the States.

The Court is also, apparently, unwilling to face the task of determining whether denial of trial by jury in the situation before us, or in other situations, is fundamentally unfair. Consequently, the Court has compromised on the ease of the incorporationist position, without its internal logic. It has simply assumed that the question before us is whether the Jury Trial Clause of the Sixth Amendment should be incorporated into the Fourteenth, jot-for-jot and case-for-case, or ignored. Then the Court merely declares that the clause in question is "in" rather than "out."

The Court has justified neither its starting place nor its conclusion. If the problem is to discover and articulate the rules of fundamental fairness in criminal proceedings, there is no reason to assume that the whole body of rules developed in this Court constituting Sixth Amendment jury trial must be regarded as a unit. The requirement of trial by jury in federal criminal cases has given rise to numerous subsidiary questions respecting the exact scope and content of the right. It surely cannot be that every answer the Court has given, or will give, to such a question is attributable to the Founders; or even that every rule announced carries equal conviction of this Court; still less can it be that every such subprinciple is equally fundamental to ordered liberty.

. . .

Even if I could agree that the question before us is whether Sixth Amendment jury trial is totally "in" or totally "out," I can find in the Court's opinion no real reasons for concluding that it should be "in." The basis for differentiating among clauses in the Bill of Rights cannot be that only some clauses are in the Bill of Rights or that only some are old and much praised, or that only some have played an important role in the development of federal law. These things are true of all. The Court says that some clauses are more "fundamental" than others, but it turns out to be using this word in a sense that would have astonished Mr. Justice Cardozo and which, in addition, is of no help. The word does not mean "analytically critical to procedural fairness" for no real analysis of the role of the jury in making procedures fair is even attempted. Instead, the word turns out to mean "old," "much praised," and "found in the Bill of Rights." The definition of "fundamental" thus turns out to be circular. . . .

This Court, other courts, and the political process are available to correct any experiments in criminal procedure that prove fundamentally unfair to defendants. That is not what is being done today: instead, and quite without reason, the Court has chosen to impose upon every State one means of trying criminal cases; it is a good means, but it is not the only fair means, and it is not demonstrably better than the alternatives States might devise. . . .

I would affirm the judgment of the Supreme Court of Louisiana.

SELECTED REFERENCES

Fairman, Charles, "Does the Fourteenth Amendment Incorporate the Bill of Rights? The Original Understanding," 2 *Stanford Law Review* 5 (1949).

Flack, Horace, *The Adoption of the Fourteenth Amendment.* (Baltimore: The Johns Hopkins University Press, 1908), especially Chaps. 2 and 5.

Frankfurter, Felix, "Memorandum on 'Incorporation' of the Bill of Rights into the Due Process Clause of the 14th Amendment," 78 *Harvard Law Review* 746 (1965).

Green, John R., "The Bill of Rights, the Fourteenth Amendment and the Supreme Court," 46 *Michigan Law Review* 869 (1948).

Henkin, Louis, "Selective Incorporation in the Fourteenth Amendment," 73 *Yale Law Journal* 74 (1963).

Mendelson, Wallace, "Mr. Justice Black's Fourteenth Amendment," 53 *Minnesota Law Review* 711 (1969).

Morrison, Stanley, "Does the Fourteenth Amendment Incorporate the Bill of Rights? The Judicial Interpretation," 2 *Stanford Law Review* 140 (1949).

Walker, Frank H., Jr., "Was It Intended That the Fourteenth Amendment Incorporate the Bill of Rights?" 42 *N. Carolina Law Review* 925 (1964).

2 Religious Liberty

The framers of the Bill of Rights guaranteed religious liberty in the United States by proclaiming in the First Amendment that "Congress shall make no law respecting an establishment of religion, or abridging the free exercise thereof. . . ." Despite the potential for litigation in this area, only a few controversies raising issues under these provisions reached the Supreme Court in the century following the Amendment's adoption. For the most part, these cases were concerned with the scope and meaning of the free exercise clause. But in the twentieth century, particularly after 1930, there has been a fairly constant flow of cases to the Supreme Court raising both free exercise and establishment clause claims. And, as we move deeper into the 1970s, many of the policy issues which gave rise to the religious liberty cases of the 40s, 50s, 60s, e.g., religious instruction and observances in public schools, public support of sectarian schools, tax exemption for religious institutions and activities, and conscientious objection to compulsory military service, are still hotly debated in the political arena. Such controversy will undoubtedly present the Burger and future courts with a range of complex cases through which to reexamine the meaning of religious liberty as guaranteed in the First Amendment.

FREE EXERCISE OF RELIGION

Watson v. *Jones* (13 Wall, 670, 1872) was one of the earliest cases in which the Supreme Court discussed the nature of the religious liberty guaranteed by the First

Amendment. It involved a factional dispute within a Presbyterian church congregation over control of church property. The Court disclaimed any power to decide independently which of the two factions represented the church. Rather, it held that the dispute would have to be settled by church authority and that such a decision, under the constitutional guarantee of religious liberty, would be binding on the courts. In his opinion for the Court, Justice Samuel Miller expressed the prevailing view on the religious liberty protected by the First Amendment:

> In this country the full and free right to entertain any religious belief, to practice any religious principle and to teach any religious doctrine which does not violate the laws of morality and property, and which does not infringe personal rights, is conceded to all. The laws know no heresy, and are committed to the support of no dogma, the establishment of no sect. The right to organize voluntary religious associations to assist in the expression, and the dissemination of any religious doctrine . . . is unquestioned.

The free exercise issue was squarely before the Court for the first time six years later in *Reynolds* v. *United States* (98 U.S. 145, 1878). At issue was the validity of a federal law prohibiting polygamy in the territories of the United States. Reynolds was convicted for violating the law, but he argued for reversal on the ground that as a member of the Mormon Church he was required by its religious tenets to engage in polygamous relationships. Hence, he maintained that the law impaired his free exercise of religion as guaranteed by the First Amendment. In rejecting this contention and affirming the conviction, the Court made a distinction between religious beliefs and the actions based on such beliefs. The former were considered inviolable and beyond the reach of Congress by the First Amendment; the latter, however, could be regulated by Congress consistent with the First Amendment in restraining antisocial conduct. Chief Justice Morrison R. Waite said in his opinion for the Court: "Laws are made for the government of actions, and while they cannot interfere with mere religious beliefs and opinions, they may with practices." The Chief Justice concluded that to allow a man to excuse his illegal actions because of his religious beliefs "would be to make the professed doctrines of religious beliefs superior to the law of the land. . . ."

There was no appreciable increase in the number of religious liberty cases decided by the Supreme Court during the first four decades of the twentieth century. Among the problems considered in the few cases that did reach the Court were the constitutional status of parochial schools, military obligations of conscientious objectors, and the use of public funds to provide books for children attending parochial schools.

The Court considered the first problem in *Pierce* v. *Society of Sisters of the Holy Name* (268 U.S. 510, 1925). At issue was the constitutionality of an Oregon statute which required all children to attend public schools for the first eight grades. The Society argued that the statute threatened the continued existence of its educational operations and the destruction of its property. It was further argued that the statute infringed the right of parents to choose schools where their children will receive appropriate mental and religious training. The Court agreed with these claims and struck down the statute. Although this case involved a religious order challenging governmental action alleged to be harmful to its activities, the religious liberty issue was neither raised by the Society nor considered by the Court. Rather, Justice James McReynolds declared that the "liberty" guaranteed by the Fourteenth Amendment protects the Society's business and property (its schools) from destruction by the state's actions.

But the conflict of state compulsory school policy and the free exercise of religion was at issue in *Wisconsin* v. *Yoder* (406 U.S. 205, 1972) almost a half century later. Members of two Amish religious orders claimed that the Wisconsin compulsory school attendance statute as applied to their minor children abridged their free exercise of religion protected by the First and Fourteenth Amendments. The desire not to expose their teenage children to the complex cultural currents alien to their simple mode of living was considered by the Amish as a valid justification for keeping them out of public or private schools beyond the eighth grade. Specifically, they argued that the values taught in high schools and higher education in general are markedly different from Amish values and that the "worldly influences" to which their children would be exposed at that level would seriously conflict with their religious beliefs. Expert testimony at the trial revealed that compulsory high school attendance could possibly be psychologically damaging to the Amish children, and could well lead to the ultimate destruction of the Old Order Amish church community as it existed in the country.

Recognizing some responsibility for the educational needs of their children, the Amish had sought unsuccessfully to meet the state requirements by setting up a program based on the Pennsylvania model of community-controlled vocational training. Under this plan, the children would be required to attend an Amish vocational school for three hours per week where they would be given instruction by an Amish teacher in English, mathematics, health, and social studies. The remainder of the week would be devoted to performance of farm and household duties under parental supervision.

A unanimous Court, with Chief Justice Warren Burger applying the "compelling state interest—no alternative means" test, held that the enforcement of the law against the Amish abridged their free exercise of religion. As Burger noted, "only those interests of the highest order and those not otherwise served can overbalance legitimate claims to the free exercise of religion." And the record made clear, he continued, that the Wisconsin law lets loose the very kind of danger that the First Amendment was designed to stifle. In concluding, Burger intimated that the kind of vocational training in their communities to which these teenagers were exposed was a viable alternative to the formal high schooling that the state would compel them to undertake. He implied that Wisconsin might do well to consider it as a means of reconciling the conflict.

Justice William O. Douglas, while supporting the decision that the state had unconstitutionally applied the statute, felt that the Court had focused on the free exercise claims of the wrong people. To him, the matter is not solely "within the dispensation of parents." He held that the rights sought to be vindicated were personal and that children are covered by Bill of Rights guarantees. On the important matter of education, he concluded that the child should be heard for it is his future that is at stake.

The conflict between freedom of conscience and compulsory military conscription was first considered by the Court in the *Selective Draft Law Cases* (245 U.S. 366, 1918). Rejecting the religious liberty claims of several conscientious objectors, the Court held that there was no constitutional right to be relieved of military obligations because of religious convictions. Chief Justice Edward Douglas White observed that the privilege of exemption from such duty is at the discretion of Congress.

Another aspect of this problem was considered in *Hamilton* v. *Regents of the University of California* (293 U.S. 245, 1934). Here the Court rejected the claims of two Methodist students who, because of religious principles, challenged the compulsory military science and tactics requirement of all able-bodied male students. Probably because the religious clauses of the First Amendment had not been made applicable to the states, the case was argued and decided on other issues. However, Justice Benjamin Cardozo, in a concurring opinion, made the point that instruction in a military science and tactics course was too remotely related to the actual bearing of arms in warfare to claim exemption on religious grounds. Significantly, he forecast the trend of the Court's interpretation of the religious clauses when he said: "I assume for present purposes that religious liberty protected by the First Amendment against invasion by the [national government] is protected by the Fourteenth against invasion by the states."

In 1930, the Court was presented with an opportunity to make a significant pronouncement on the scope of restrictions contained in the establishment clause in *Cochran* v. *Louisiana State Board of Education* (281 U.S. 370, 1930). At issue was the constitutionality of a state statute which provided free textbooks for children attending both public and parochial schools. Those attacking the statute alleged that in providing free books for pupils attending parochial schools, the state was expending public funds for private use contrary to the due process clause of the Fourteenth Amendment. The Court rejected that contention, holding the appropriations to be for a public purpose. In taking this approach, the Court simply postponed the day when such problems would be considered as establishment issues.

The most significant decisions by the Supreme Count involving religious liberty issues have been handed down during the last three decades. Many of the cases in the first part of this period were brought by the Jehovah's Witnesses who vigorously contested state and local action which they thought infringed upon their religious liberty. In *Cantwell* v. *Connecticut* (310 U.S. 296, 1940) the Witnesses succeeded in getting the Court to strike down a statute which required persons soliciting or canvassing for religious and philanthropic causes to obtain prior approval from a local administrative official. The local official was also clothed with the authority to determine if the cause was of a bona fide religious nature. Justice Owen Roberts, in announcing the decision for a unanimous Court, maintained that the statute's defectiveness stemmed from the unfettered discretion which it granted the administering official. Such discretion, argued Roberts, "is to lay a forbidden burden upon the exercise of liberty protected by the Constitution." In striking down this regulation, the Court made the "free exercise" clause applicable to the states when Justice Roberts asserted: "Such censorship of religion as a means of determining its right to survive is a denial of liberty protected by the First Amendment and included in the liberty which is within the protection of the Fourteenth."

During the same term, however, Jehovah's Witnesses were rebuffed in their attempt to have the Court strike down the "flag-salute" ceremony of the Minersville, Pennsylvania school district. Essentially, this ceremony required all public school children, as a part of the daily opening exercises, to salute the United States flag and repeat the Pledge of Allegiance. Two children of a member of the Jehovah's Witnesses were expelled from school for refusing to participate in the ceremony. A federal district court agreed with the contention of the Witnesses that compulsory participation in the ceremony infringed upon their free exercise of religion and enjoined the school district from its continued use. Upon appeal the Supreme Court reversed. (*Minersville School District* v. *Gobitis,* 310 U.S. 586, 1940). Justice Felix Frankfurter, speaking for the eight-man majority, rejected the religious liberty claims and, instead, stressed the relationship between such symbolism and national unity. He maintained that "we live by symbols" and that "the flag is a symbol of our national unity, transcending all internal differences, however large, within the framework of the Constitution." In addition, Frankfurter urged judicial restraint in such matters of "educational policy." Justice Harlan F. Stone, the lone dissenter, stressed the need to protect the right of the individual to hold and to express opinions. He contended that the liberty protected by the Constitution from state infringement includes "the freedom of the individual from compulsion as to what he shall think and what he shall say, at least where the compulsion is to bear false witness to his religion."

Three years later, the Court did a complete about-face on the "flag-salute" issue in *West Virginia State Board of Education* v. *Barnette* (319 U.S. 624, 1943). Factors usually cited in explaining this turnabout include: (1) the addition of two new associate justices—Justice Robert H. Jackson filled the vacancy created by the retirement of Chief Justice Charles Evans Hughes in 1941 (Justice Harlan Fiske Stone was elevated to the Chief Justiceship), and Justice Wiley B. Rutledge replaced Justice James C. McReynolds in 1943; and (2) while dissenting in *Jones* v. *Opelika* (316 U.S. 584) a year earlier, the unusual admission of three justices of the *Gobitis* majority that they believed *Gobitis* was wrongly decided.

Justice Jackson's opinion for the six-man majority was not based on the Witnesses' assertions of religious liberty. Rather it stressed freedom of speech and conscience, and the implied right to remain silent. Noting that "the compulsory flag salute and pledge requires affirmation of a belief and an attitude of mind," Jackson argued:

> To sustain the compulsory flag salute we are required to say that a Bill of Rights which guards the individual's right to speak his own mind, left it open to public authorities to compel him to utter what is not in his mind.

In language obviously directed at Frankfurter's "national unity and patriotism" theme expressed in *Gobitis*, Jackson asserted:

> To believe that patriotism will not flourish if patriotic ceremonies are voluntary and spontaneous instead of a compulsory routine is to make an unflattering estimate of the appeal of our institutions to free minds. We can have

intellectual individualism and the rich cultural diversities that we owe to exceptional minds only at the price of occasional eccentricity and abnormal attitudes. When they are so harmless to others or to the State as those we deal with here, the price is not too great. But freedom to differ is not limited to things that do not matter much. That would be a mere shadow of freedom. The test of its substance is the right to differ as to things that touch the heart of the existing order.

In an oft-quoted passage in defense of freedom of expression and conscience, Jackson concluded:

> If there is any fixed star in our constitutional constellation, it is that no official, high or petty, can prescribe what shall be orthodox in politics, nationalism, religion, or other matters of opinion or force citizens to confess by word or act their faith therein. . . .

Cases initiated by Jehovah's Witnesses also led to the Court's rejection of local ordinances levying license fees on the distribution of literature. In *Murdock* v. *Pennsylvania* (319 U.S. 105, 1943), the Court reversed its decision in *Jones* v. *Opelika* and struck down a local ordinance requiring payment of a license fee by those selling literature. The Court reasoned that in applying the law to Jehovah's Witnesses, government was in reality taxing the dissemination of religious doctrines. Speaking for a 5-4 majority, Justice William O. Douglas said that "the hand distribution of religious tracts is an age-old form of missionary evangelism [which] occupies the same high estate under the First Amendment as do worship in the churches and preaching from the pulpit." Applying the ordinance to this kind of activity was patently unconstitutional because of its restraint on freedom of the press and the free exercise of religion.

In recent years members of the Black Muslims, a militant black separatist group, on several occasions during the 1960s, encountered official restrictions which they alleged infringed their free exercise of religion. While operating within the framework of a religious ritual embracing many of the traditional elements of orthodox religious groups, the Muslims advocate political, economic, and social separation from white America. Their religious meetings were often used as a platform for denouncing white America, and their status as a religious sect has frequently been questioned. This was essentially the rationale used by some prison officials to deny to Black Muslim prisoners the privilege of purchasing and using their Bible (the Quran, a modification of the Moslem Koran) and other Muslim literature, including the official organ *Muhammad Speaks*, and of conducting worship services.

The official position that such restrictions are essential to the maintenance of prison discipline has been accepted by several lower courts. In *Williford* v. *California* (217 F. Supp. 245, 1963), for example, a federal district court held that prison officials did not infringe the free exercise of religion of Muslims by denying them the right to conduct services because freedom to act on religious belief can be regulated in the maintenance of prison discipline. Similarly, the California Supreme Court in *In re Ferguson* (361 P2d 417, 1961), held that it is not unreasonable to prohibit the "religious" activities of Black Muslims because the black supremacy doctrines eschewed lead to a reluctance to submit to white authority in prison administration.

Where lower courts have followed the view that the Black Muslim group is not a religious sect and have summarily dismissed free exercise claims, appellate courts have reversed, contending that a constitutional claim of discriminatory action by government based solely on religion requires a hearing on its merits. In *Sewell* v. *Pigelow* (291 F2d 196, 1961), after the Court of Appeals for the Fourth Circuit reversed and remanded with such directions, prison officials lifted the restrictions complained of and the case became moot. Likewise, in *Cooper* v. *Pate* (378 U.S. 546, 1964), the Supreme Court reversed a federal district court ruling (affirmed by the Court of Appeals) which dismissed a claim by a Black Muslim prisoner that Illinois officials, in denying him the privilege of obtaining his Bible and other Muslim literature, and of being visited by Black Muslim ministers and holding religious services, had discriminated against him because of his religious faith. The Court held that such a claim constituted a valid cause of action. Upon remand, the district court held that these restrictions could be constitutionally justified only if exercise of the privileges in question presented a "clear-and-present-danger to prison security."

Undoubtedly one of the most significant and far-reaching decisions of the Supreme Court on the free-exercise issue during the Warren Court era was *Sherbert* v. *Verner.* The case resulted from a ruling of the South Carolina Unemployment Compensation Commission (sustained by the state supreme court) holding that a member of the Seventh-Day Adventist faith was ineligible for benefits because of her unwillingness to accept jobs which required work on Saturdays (her day of worship). In a 7-2 decision, the Court held that the state's action imposed an unconstitutional burden on the free exercise of religion. Justice William J. Brennan's opinion for the majority contained language that indicated a broadening scope of the free exercise guarantee and a more restricted state regulatory authority. Setting forth what has been characterized as the "compelling state interest" rule, Brennan asserted that "no showing merely of a rational relationship to some colorable state interest would suffice [for] in this highly sensitive constitutional area, '[o]nly the gravest abuses, endangering paramount interests, give occasion for permissible limitation.' " In addition, Brennan indicated that in order to justify, constitutionally, a regulation which has such an impact on the free exercise of religion, the state must show that it has "no alternative forms of regulation" to combat the abuse.

Using this "paramount state interest-no alternative means" test, the Court, in *In re Jennison* (375 U.S. 14, 1963), reversed a Minnesota criminal contempt conviction where the petitioner had refused to serve as a juror because of religious scruples. Upon remand, the Minnesota Supreme Court held that the state failed to demonstrate that its interest in obtaining competent jurors would be jeopardized by exempting those opposed to jury service on religious grounds (267 Minn. 136, 125 N.W. 2d 588, 1963).

Pushing religious liberty to the limit, a few groups have asserted religious claims to protect their use of narcotics. These groups contend that certain drugs are as essential to their religious ritual as the bread and wine are to orthodox religious sects. In *People* v. *Woody* (394 P. 2d 813, 1964), for example, a group of Navajo

Indians, members of the Native American Church of California, were convicted in a California court for using the drug peyote (described as a nonaddictive hallucinatory drug). The Supreme Court of California reversed the conviction on the grounds that peyote was central, as a sacramental symbol, to the worship services of the church. Citing *Sherbert* v. *Verner,* the court said the use of peyote under such circumstances did not "frustrate a compelling interest of the state."

Attempts of other groups to use the *Woody* ruling as a precedent have proven unsuccessful. In *State* v. *Bullard* (148 S.E. 2d 565, 1966), for example, the Supreme Court of North Carolina affirmed a conviction for use of peyote by a person who claimed membership in the Neo-American Church, in which "peyote is [considered] most necessary and marijuana . . . most advisable" in the practice of its ritual. However, the court reasoned that in this instance religion was merely a subterfuge for the use of drugs. The court found that the use of drugs under the circumstances constituted a threat to the public safety, morals, peace, and order.

On the issue of use of psychedelics and the free exercise of religion, one of the most widely publicized cases involved Dr. Timothy Leary's conviction by a federal district court for illegal trafficking in marijuana. Dr. Leary, known as the high priest of LSD (League of Spiritual Discovery), has been a prolific publisher on the religious and scientific uses of psychedelic drugs. Leary claims membership in a Hindu sect (Brahmakrishna) in Massachusetts that considers the use of marijuana essential to illumination and meditation. In affirming the lower court ruling, the Court of Appeals for the Fifth Circuit rejected Leary's reliance on *Sherbert* v. *Verner* as misplaced and inapposite on the facts (*Leary* v. *United States*, 383 F.2d 851, 1967). Instead, the court found that trafficking in marijuana poses a "substantial threat to public safety [and] order." Furthermore, the court rejected Leary's attempt to apply the *Woody* decision and reiterated the need to show that a drug plays a "central role" in the religious ceremony and practice. The Supreme Court granted certiorari. However, the Court did not include the free-exercise issue in its review, but reversed the conviction on self-incrimination and due process grounds (395 U.S. 6, 1969).

Opposition to United States participation in the Vietnam War in the 1960s once again brought to the Court the religious liberty-compulsory military service question in which both free-exercise and establishment issues were raised. As draft eligible college students lost their student deferment classification (2-S), a number of them sought the conscientious-objector classification (1-0). Denials of their petitions usually returned them to (1-A) and made them eligible for immediate induction. But some of those rejected refused to submit to induction, thereby precipitating prosecutorial actions that resulted in several constitutional challenges to the conscientious objector provision (Sec. 6j) of the Universal Military Training and Service Act on its face and as applied.

In *United States* v. *Seeger* (380 U.S. 163, 1965) and two companion cases (*United States* v. *Jakobson* and *Peter* v. *United States*), for example, the constitutionality of the clause that defines the term "religious training and belief" was at issue. While the appeals pressed both establishment and free-exercise challenges, the Court chose to sidestep them. Instead, it construed the statute in its most favorable light and held that Congress had not intended to give preference to believers in a conventional God when it employed the term "religious training and belief . . . in relation to a Supreme Being . . . ". Justice Hugo Black, in writing the Court's opinion, noted that with the "vast panoply of beliefs" that abound in our society, construing the phrase to embrace all religions was consistent with long-established Congressional policy "of not picking and choosing among religious beliefs." Consequently, the narrow construction of Section 6(j) applied in rejecting the petitioners' conscientious-objector claims was overturned. In the process, Justice Black provided draft boards and lower courts some guidance for the future by proposing a test to determine if a belief is within the statutory definition of Section 6(j). To qualify, the belief must be "a sincere and meaningful one which occupies in the life of its possessor a place parallel to that filled by the God of those admittedly qualifying for the exemption."

What the Court said in effect was that adherence to formal religious principles was no longer the sole grounds for granting conscientious-objector status. But the possibility that a large number of young men would escape serving their country by claiming conscientious-objector status under this liberal construction was already foreclosed by the provision of the Selective Service Act that authorizes local draft boards, under Presidential regulations, to assign such persons to "civilian work contributing to the maintenance of national health, safety or interest" for a period equivalent to that which is required of military inductees.

Congressional response to the decision was in the form of a 1967 amendment to the selective service law eliminating the clause that defines the term "religious training and belief" in terms of an individual's "belief in relation to a Supreme Being." However, the lawmakers retained the provision that "religious training and belief" does not include political, sociological, or philosophical views and personal moral codes.

Three years later, in *Welsh* v. *United States*, the Court virtually rendered this provision meaningless. In reversing Welsh's conviction for refusing to submit to induction after his request for conscientious-objector status had been denied, Justice Hugo Black spoke for the Court and held that "essentially political, sociological, or philosophical views or a merely personal moral code" should not be read to exclude persons with strong beliefs about the nation's domestic and foreign affairs. Furthermore, Black contended that Section 6(j) does not require exclusion of those whose conscientious objection is grounded to a great degree "in considerations of public policy." Thusly construed, he concluded that exemption must be granted to those "whose consciences, spurred by deeply held *moral, ethical,* or *religious beliefs* would give them no rest or peace if they allowed themselves to become a part of an instrument of war." (Emphasis added.)

Justice John M. Harlan II concurred in the result, but expressed serious concern about the length to which the majority had gone in statutory construction to avoid facing the constitutional issues presented. To him the Court, in the face of compelling legislative history, had interpreted the statute to produce a policy outcome which Congress did not intend—to make conscientious objection exemption available "to all individuals who in good faith opposed all war." He felt that the majority had performed this "lobotomy" to save the statute since it was clear to him that 6(j)'s theistic bias abridged the establishment clause of the First Amendment.

Justice Byron White's dissent, in which Chief Justice Burger and Justice Potter Stewart joined, supported Harlan's attack on the Court's "rewriting" of the statute. Since the First Amendment does not forbid the Congressional policy in this area, he argued, certainly the Court should not "frustrate the legislative will."

In 1971, the Court examined further the meaning of Section 6(j) in the companion cases of *Gillette* v. *United States* and *Negre* v. *Larsen* (401 U.S. 437, 1971). At issue was the question of conscientious exemption based on opposition to a particular war—Vietnam. Petitioner Gillette had refused to report for induction after having been denied conscientious-objector status and Negre instituted proceedings for discharge from the Army as a conscientious objector upon receipt of orders for duty in Vietnam. Essentially, their argument was that the statutory requirement that one must be opposed to participation in all wars rather than to a particular war to be eligible for a (1-0) status results in a discrimination among religions in violation of the Establishment Clause. Hence, even those acting in accordance with "religious training and belief" (such as Negre, a devout Catholic), and who are opposed to participating in only "unjust wars" cannot qualify for exemption.

In rejecting these claims, Justice Thurgood Marshall insisted that there was no religious preference reflected in the statute, but that its underlying purposes were neutral and secular. As an example, Marshall noted "the hopelessness of converting a sincere conscientious objector into an effective fighting man." Certainly, he concluded, such a pragmatic consideration has nothing to do with aiding or fostering any religious sect.

In dissent, Justice William O. Douglas contended that "the law as written is a species of those which show an insidious discrimination in favor of religious persons and against others with like scruples." To him, the Court had failed to come to grips with the basic issue of these cases which was whether a conscientious objector whose objection is rooted either in religion or in moral values can be required to kill.

Can a person who is exempted from the military service as a conscientious objector, but meets his obligation through "alternative civilian service" be denied educational benefits under the Veterans Readjustment Act of 1966? In *Johnson* v. *Robinson* (415 U.S. 361, 1974), an 8 to 1 majority said yes. Justice Brennan's majority opinion emphasized that the distinction which Congress made between the veteran of military service and the conscientious objector performing "alternative service" for purposes of receiving educational benefits was based upon a rational classification scheme and did not deny the latter the equal protection of the laws. In rejecting Robinson's free exercise claim, Brennan had serious doubts that the statutory exclusion of benefits from his class imposed a burden on his free exercise of religion and, at most, if such a burden did result it was only an incidental one.

In dissent Justice William O. Douglas urged that *Sherbert* v. *Verner, supra.* should be controlling. To him this was a simple case of government penalizing those "for asserting their religious scruples."

ESTABLISHMENT CLAUSE PROBLEMS

The various decisions in the Jehovah's Witnesses cases of the 1930s and 1940s gave considerable clarity to the scope of the free-exercise clause of the First Amendment, but the meaning and sweep of the establishment clause remained unclear. As we have noted in the discussion of *Cochran* v. *Louisiana* (1930), the controversial question of public aid to parochial schools was involved, but the establishment issue was neither raised in the statutory challenge nor considered by the Court. Hence, it was not until *Everson* v. *Board of Education* (1947) that the establishment issue was placed squarely before the Supreme Court. At issue was the constitutionality of a New Jersey statute which permitted expenditure of public funds to defray the cost of transporting children to both public and parochial schools. In upholding the law as a valid "public welfare" measure, the Court construed the establishment clause as erecting a "wall of separation between Church and State." As Justice Hugo Black asserted for the 5-4 majority:

> Neither a state nor the Federal Government can set up a church. Neither can pass laws which aid one religion, aid all religions, or prefer one religion over another. Neither can force or influence a person to go to or to remain away from church against his will or force him to profess a belief or disbelief in any religion. No person can be punished for entertaining or professing religious beliefs or disbeliefs, for church attendance or non-attendance. No tax in any amount, large or small, can be levied to support any religious activities or institutions, whatever they may be called, or whatever form they may adopt to teach or practice religion. . . . In the words of Jefferson, the clause against establishment of religion by law was intended to erect "a wall of separation between Church and State."

The financial assistance provided for under the statute would appear to constitute the kind of aid prohibited in this construction of the establishment clause. However, Black felt otherwise. He emphasized the "child benefit" and "public welfare" aspects of the New Jersey legislation and concluded that while state power cannot be used to favor religions, neither can it be used to handicap them.

In his dissenting opinion in *Everson,* Justice Wiley B. Rutledge warned of the drive to introduce religious instruction in the public schools. Just one year after this warning, the Court was asked to determine the constitutionality of a "released time" religious education program in the public schools in *McCollum* v. *Board of Education* (333 U.S. 203, 1948). The program was conducted in the Champaign,

Illinois public school system on a voluntary basis and provided classes for Protestants, Catholics, and Jews. Instruction was the responsibility of the religious authorities and took place during the regular school hours and in the school classrooms. Students not participating in the program were required to leave their regular classrooms and pursue their school activities elsewhere in the school building. On the other hand, students who volunteered to participate in the program were required to attend religious classes. The public school teachers assisted in several routine matters such as distribution of permission slips and keeping attendance records.

Eight members of the Court found this arrangement an outright violation of the strictures of the establishment clause as enunciated in *Everson.* Justice Black, whose opinion was supported by five other justices, maintained that the use of the public school classrooms to conduct religious instruction, the operation of the compulsory school attendance machinery to provide audience for the propagation of sectarian dogma and the close cooperation between religious and school authorities in promoting the program constituted "beyond all question a utilization of the . . . tax-supported public school system to aid religious groups to spread their faith."

Justice Felix Frankfurter wrote a concurring opinion in which he complained about the coercive nature of the program and its separatist impact on children at a highly impressionistic age. To him, the program "sharpen[ed] the consciousness of religious differences . . . among some of the children committed to [the care of the Champaign public school system] ." Justice Jackson agreed with Frankfurter but, in addition, cautioned against too much judicial interference in school policy. He feared such a result could follow from Black's failure to include in the Court's opinion a more specific statement of legal principles to provide guidance in this area of public school policy. Only Justice Reed dissented and it was his contention that the framers of the First Amendment did not intend to exclude religious education from the public schools. Instead, their concern was to prevent the establishment of a state church.

The decision in *McCollum* met with widespread criticism since in communities across the country such programs were commonly accepted. It would appear that a majority of the justices were not oblivious to such reaction when they decided to limit the *McCollum* ruling four years later in *Zorach* v. *Clauson* (343 U.S. 306, 1952).

The only significant difference in the two programs was the place where the religious classes were conducted. In Champaign they were held inside the regular school classrooms; in New York they were conducted off school property. For the six-man majority, however, this difference was sufficient to save New York's program from constitutional infirmity. Justice William O. Douglas, writing the majority opinion, rejected the view of rigid and absolute separation of Church and State. He maintained that the First Amendment does not say that in all respects there must be a separation of Church and State, for if that thesis were accepted, "the state and religion would be alien to each other—hostile, suspicious, and even unfriendly." In an oft-quoted passage, Justice Douglas argued further:

We are a religious people whose institutions presuppose a Supreme Being. . . .
When the state encourages religious instruction or cooperates with religious
authorities by adjusting the schedule of public events to sectarian needs, it
follows the best of our traditions. For it then respects the religious nature of our
people and accommodates the public service to their spiritual needs. To hold
that it may not would be to find in the Constitution a requirement that the
government show a callous indifference to religious groups. That would be
preferring those who believe in no religion over those who do believe.

He concluded that while "government may not finance religious groups . . . or
blend secular and sectarian education," there is nothing in the Constitution that
requires governmental opposition to "efforts to widen the scope of religious
influence."

The dissenters—Justices Black, Frankfurter, and Jackson—saw no significant
difference between the invalid Champaign program and that of New York. To
them, the school authorities were rendering invaluable (and unconstitutional) aid to
religious sects in getting them audiences for the propagation of their dogma. The
element of coercion was too great, and as Justice Black concluded: "Government
should not be allowed, under cover of the soft euphemism 'cooperation,' to steal
into the sacred area of religious choice."

The Court reexamined its *Everson* holding in *Board of Education* v. *Allen* (392
U.S. 236, 1968). At issue was the validity of a 1965 New York statute which
requires local school boards to provide a free loan service of textbooks to students
in grades seven through 12, including those attending parochial and other private
schools. In upholding the law, the Court reaffirmed the "general welfare" and
"secular legislative purpose" doctrines enunciated in *Everson*. In addition, Justice
Byron White, who wrote the Court's opinion, thought the law met the test (the
purpose and primary effect of the enactment) laid down in *School District of
Abington Township* v. *Schempp*. He contended that the purpose of the legislation
was to expand educational opportunity by making available textbooks free of
charge. Ownership of the books remains with the school board and no funds or
books are given to the parochial schools. The financial benefit is to the student and
the parent and not to the school. White conceded that there is a difference between
buses and books, but argued that the control of the public school board over the
books loaned and the statutory requirement that only *secular* books could be
loaned, provided sufficient protection against public funds being used to purchase
sectarian matter.

Both Black and Douglas in their separate dissents felt that the majority's reliance
on *Everson* was grossly misplaced. Black charged that the law "is a flat, flagrant and
open violation" of the establishment clause and does not meet the test that was laid
down in *Everson*. Black warned that it would take "no prophet to foresee" that
similar arguments could be used to support and uphold legislation funding parochial
school construction and teachers' salaries.

Justice Douglas was troubled with the ideological bias possible in the selection of textbooks. He noted that the statute provides that the board may only provide a student with textbooks that he is required to use, "in a particular class in the school he legally attends." Hence, the initial selection is in the hands of those who can exercise an ideological (sectarian) bias and, whatever the subsequent action of the public school board, the church-state problem is aggravated. In distinguishing this case from *Everson*, Douglas concluded that "there is nothing ideological about a bus . . . , a school lunch . . . , a public school nurse, nor a scholarship." But he contended that the textbook had a far more significant impact for "it is the chief . . . instrumentality for propagating a particular religious creed or faith."

Attempts at more extensive public aid (parochaid as some characterize it) to sectarian schools in the form of teacher salary supplements and other instructional costs were rejected by the Court in the companion cases of *Lemon* v. *Kurtzman, Earley* v. *Dicenso*, and *Robinson* v. *Dicenso* (403 U.S. 602, 1971). Challenged were the statutes of Pennsylvania and Rhode Island. Under the provisions of the former, the State Superintendent of Public Instruction was authorized to purchase secular educational services from nonpublic schools and reimburse them for teachers' salaries, textbooks, and instructional materials. The Rhode Island statute provided for a 15 percent salary supplement to be paid to teachers in nonpublic schools where the average per pupil expenditure on secular instruction was below the average in the public schools. Restrictions were included to prevent expenditure of funds that would support the teaching of courses in religion. With only Justice Byron White dissenting in the Rhode Island *Dicenso* cases, the Court found that such parochaid arrangements involved "excessive entanglement" of secular and sectarian activities and authorities. Expanding on the concept of "excessive entanglement" advanced in *Walz* v. *Tax Commission* (discussed *infra*, p. 38) a year earlier, Chief Justice Warren Burger's opinion for the Court condemned the "intimate and continuing relationship[s]" between church and state necessitated in order to accomplish statutory objectives. He noted that not only did the kind of aid afforded infringe the establishment clause, but the kind of state surveillance of parochial school administration to enforce statutory restrictions "is a relationship pregnant with dangers of excessive government direction of church schools and hence of churches" that conflicts with the free-exercise clause.

Justice William O. Douglas's concurring opinion echoed this point when he noted that the supervision required to police the grants effectively would amount to putting "a public investigator in every [nonpublic school] classroom." But if this were not done, he continued, overzealous "religious proselytizers" could very well "make a shambles of the Establishment Clause." In the end, Douglas expressed great impatience with those who, despite the Court's "long and consistent" position against the expenditure of public funds to support religious institutions and activities, still have "the courage to announce that a state may . . . finance the *secular* part of a sectarian school's educational program."

In his partial dissent, Justice Byron White found enough in prior holdings of the Court to sustain the statutes against the establishment clause challenge. For him, the state support of a "separable secular function of overriding importance" was sufficient to sustain the program's constitutionality. Simply because there might be some substantial benefit to the nonpublic interests accruing from the arrangements, he contended, does not make the statutes challenged unconstitutional abridgments of the establishment clause.

On the same day it struck down the Pennsylvania and Rhode Island parochaid programs, the Court stopped short of blocking the federal government's program to aid higher educational institutions (including the nonpublic sector) in the construction of facilities. In *Tilton* v. *Richardson* (403 U.S. 672, 1971), the Court did not feel that enforcement of provisions of the Higher Education Facilities Act of 1963 required the kind of excessive entangling relations between church and state condemned in the Pennsylvania and Rhode Island cases. Chief Justice Warren Burger, speaking for Justices John M. Harlan II, Potter Stewart, and Harry A. Blackmun, noted that the act provided for facilities that were "religiously neutral" and that the "one-shot" grants did not require the continuous surveillance condemned in *Kurtzman* and *Dicenso*. Furthermore, he contended that there was far less danger of religious matter permeating secular education and indoctrinating its recipients at this level than is possible at the elementary and secondary level. However, the Court felt that the provision limiting federal interest in the facility to a period of 20 years did not provide adequate safeguards against impermissible aid to religious establishments. The Chief Justice reasoned that Congress was in error in assuming that such substantial facilities would not have considerable value after 20 years. Consequently, their unrestricted use by religious bodies thereafter would constitute the kind of aid which the establishment clause proscribes. But in the end, Burger held that under the doctrine of separability, this defect was not fatal to the remainder of the statute.

In his dissent, Justice William O. Douglas, with whom Justices Hugo Black and Thurgood Marshall concurred, pointed to President Kennedy's statement in March, 1961, in which he flatly asserted that there was no doubt that "the Constitution clearly prohibits aid to . . . parochial schools" as "the correct constitutional principle for this case." Douglas had no doubt that the statute furthered secular education but the aid accruing to parochial schools therefrom constituted a fatally defective constitutional flaw. Like the Chief Justice, Douglas held that the "reversionary interest" clause would constitute an unconstitutional "gift of taxpayers' funds," but unlike Burger, he contended that the invalidation of that provision was not enough to "cure the constitutional infirmities of the statute as a whole." It was clear to him that "excessive entanglements" of secular and sectarian officials and actions would permeate the entire scheme.

The longstanding policy of exempting church property from public taxation has long been considered by some to be an unconstitutional aid to religious establishments. But when the Supreme Court finally made a definitive pronouncement on the issue in *Walz* v. *Tax Commission*, it found such a policy to be in furtherance of the state's neutrality comprehended by the establishment clause. Chief Justice Burger made it clear that the tax exemption "is neither the advancement nor the inhibition of religion." Furthermore, he contended that New York and other states can, consistent with the establishment clause, establish harmonious relationships with various entities in the community (including sectarian groups) that foster "its moral and mental improvements" and exempt them from the burdens of property taxation in furtherance of such ends. Recognizing the indirect economic benefit derived from a tax exemption, the Chief Justice distinguished it from the direct subsidy that produces the "excessive governmental entanglement" that the establishment clause prohibits. In the end, he concluded, the policy assures that those in the free exercise of religion will not be burdened by the taxation levied on "private profit" entities.

In dissent, Justice William O. Douglas was disturbed by the discriminatory nature of the tax-exemption policy. Nonbelievers must pay the toll, while believers are exempted. This kind of aid, he continued, is even more suspect than the various forms approved for the educational operations of religious bodies because it is rendered directly to the church and is the same as a "subsidy." Citing the vast real estate holdings of religious groups and their lucrative annual income, he concluded that "the extent to which they are feeding from the public trough in a variety of ways is alarming."

The *Tilton* and *Walz* rulings appeared to provide a small ray of hope for those seeking some means through which public resources could be used to shore up the steadily deteriorating financial position of parochial schools. This hope was further buttressed by what was deemed to be a more sympathetic Supreme Court with the four Nixon appointees aware of the President's promise to seek some financial relief for nonpublic schools through federal tax credits for parents of pupils attending those schools.

Such a hope was crushed, however, when the Supreme Court held in 1973 that the New York legislative program which provided for nonpublic school aid through maintenance and repair grants, tuition reimbursements, and tax credits, and a Pennsylvania statute which authorized tuition reimbursements constituted unconstitutional aid to religious establishments. In the New York case (*Committee for Public Education* v. *Nyquist*), Justice Lewis F. Powell, Jr., speaking for the 6-3 majority, noted that the purpose and primary effect of the program was to "advance religion in that it subsidizes directly the religious activities of sectarian elementary and secondary schools." Furthermore, Justice Powell repelled the notion that parents could serve as conduits for such aid by employing tuition reimbursements and tax credits. Rejecting one of the most oft-cited justifications for public aid to parochial schools, Justice Powell concluded:

> However great our sympathy for the burdens of those who must pay public school taxes at the same time that they support other schools because of the constraints of "conscience and discipline," and notwithstanding the "high social importance" of the State's purposes, neither may justify an eroding of the limitations of the Establishment Clause now firmly emplanted.

For similar reasons, the Pennsylvania tuition-reimbursement program was struck down in *Sloan* v. *Lemon* (413 U.S. 825, 1973). Noting that more than 90 percent of the pupils attending nonpublic schools in that state were enrolled in sectarian schools, Justice Powell contended that the program's "intended consequence" was to "preserve and support [such] religion-oriented institutions."

In dissent, Chief Justice Burger, supported by Justices White and Rehnquist, emphasized the secular purpose and general welfare nature of the benefits embraced by the legislative programs. He argued that the *Everson* and *Allen* precedents fully support this attempt to equalize the costs incurred by parents who send their children to nonpublic schools. To him, the establishment clause limitations are attenuated "when the legislation moves away from direct aid to religious institutions and takes on the character of general aid to individual families."

These rulings, along with the *Lemon* and *Dicenso* cases of 1971, could well result in increased efforts to establish more shared-time programs. Basically, shared-time is an arrangement that provides for dual enrollment of pupils in parochial and public schools. The plan rests on the premise that parents have the option of enrolling their children in either public or parochial schools in complying with compulsory school attendance laws. This is coupled with the controversial claim that a child is legally entitled to enroll as a part-time student in the public schools while, at the same time, attending a private (usually parochial) school on a part-time basis.

The plan's merit is twofold. In the first place, a child can receive the desired religious training and instruction in the parochial school, eliminating the need for a makeshift release-time program. Of equal, if not greater importance, is the resulting financial relief to the parochial school. The plan, as a matter of fact, usually provides for the subjects where instruction is most costly (i.e., the natural sciences and industrial arts) to be offered the shared-time pupil in the public school.

Against claims that this kind of arrangement is nothing but a subterfuge (and not a very good one) for public support of sectarian education contrary to the establishment clause, supporters contend that shared-time provides a constitutional means for resolving the continuous policy controversy over public aid to parochial schools. Certainly, the fatal defects of salary supplements, tuition reimbursements, repair and maintenance grants, and tax credits are not found in these programs. In fact, proponents of shared-time point to a number of provisions in the Elementary and Secondary Education Act of 1965 that authorize dual admission (pupils from public and private schools) to special classes for "educationally deprived children" as substantial recognition of the constitutionality of such programs.

Despite the continuing debate over the validity of shared-time, only a few lower courts have considered the issue. In *Commonwealth ex. rel. Wehrle* v. *School District of Altoona* (88 Atl. 481, 1913), the Pennsylvania Supreme Court sustained a lower court decision in which a shared-time plan was upheld against a challenge that it violated the state constitutional provisions that prohibit the expenditure of public funds to support private and sectarian schools. The court said that "the benefits and advantages of [programs embraced in public elementary schools] are not restricted to pupils in regular attendance . . . and pursuing the entire pre-scribed . . . courses, but are intended to be free to all 'persons residing in [the school] district' . . . ." The court concluded that the statutory provision authorizing a pupil to enroll in courses or departments of public schools, although his "academic education" is being received in a nonpublic school, was within the constitutional authority of the legislature. Understandably, coming when it did, a First Amendment issue was neither raised nor considered. Only state issues involving compulsory school attendance laws have been raised in other challenges to shared-time programs in St. Louis, Missouri and Chicago, Illinois.[1] And the Supreme Court of Michigan ruled in 1971 in *In re Proposal C* (185 N.W. 2d 9), that a state constitutional amendment prohibiting the expenditure of public money for parochial and nonpublic schools does not preclude provision for instructional services by public schools to nonpublic schools through shared-time or dual enrollment programs.

Whether shared-time programs breach the First Amendment prohibition of aid to religious establishments has not as yet been considered directly by the United States Supreme Court. But *Flast* v. *Cohen* (392 U.S. 83, 1968) opens the way for establishment clause challenges to such programs now operating in some school districts under the Elementary and Secondary Education Act of 1965 noted above.[2]

ESTABLISHMENT AND FREE EXERCISE IN CONFLICT

Several emotion-packed public questions brought to the Supreme Court during the 1960s have embraced both establishment and free-exercise issues, and the Court's disposition of some of them suggests the difficulty of reconciling the two clauses. Some have contended, as did Justice Potter Stewart in *Sherbert* v. *Verner*, that "a mechanistic" application of the establishment clause may result in a decision which compels government to violate that clause in order to guarantee the free exercise of religion and vice versa. Stewart concluded in the *Sherbert* case that so long as this dilemma is unresolved, "consistent and perceptive" decisions in such cases will be "impeded and impaired."

The school prayer and Bible reading cases are illustrative of the establishment—free-exercise dilemma posed by some types of regulatory action in the religious field. This controversy reached the Supreme Court in *Engel* v. *Vitale* (370 U.S. 471) in 1962. At issue was the constitutionality of the use of a 22-word prayer (composed by the State Board of Regents of New York) in the public school daily opening exercises. Although participation in the "prayer-exercise" was voluntary and the prayer was characterized as nonsectarian, the Court declared its use an infringement of the establishment clause. Justice Hugo Black's opinion for the 6–1 majority stressed that it was not prayer but an "officially prescribed prayer" that was being condemned. He warned that in this country it is not the business of any government to compose official prayers for any group of people.

[1] *Special District for Education and Training of the Handicapped* v. *Wheeler* (408 S.W. 2d 60, 1966); *Morton* v. *Board of Education* (216 N.E. 2d 305, 1966).

[2] In *Flast,* the Court reversed the rule enunciated in *Frothingham* v. *Mellon* (262 U.S. 447, 1923), that prohibited suits challenging the constitutionality of federal statutes where the plaintiff's standing to bring the action rested solely on his status as a federal taxpayer.

In dissent, Justice Potter Stewart focused on the conflict between the two clauses declaring that he could not "see how an 'official religion' is established by letting those who want to say a prayer say it." On the contrary, however, Stewart contended that to deny use of the prayer by children who desire it, "is to deny them the opportunity of sharing in the spiritual heritage of our Nation."

Though Justice Black stressed that it was not prayer but a governmentally prescribed prayer that the Court was condemning, many churchmen, public officials, and laymen were nevertheless outraged and chose to base their condemnation of the Court's action on a more sweeping interpretation of the decision. These critics warned that the Court should be checked now before it struck down other types of activities that are considered a part of our heritage as a religious people. Members of Congress likewise expressed their concern by introducing a variety of proposals to amend the First Amendment and overturn the Court's decision, but these efforts came to naught.

The emotional outbursts in response to the *Engel* decision had hardly subsided when, just one year later, the Court dropped the other shoe in this "two-pronged" controversy. In companion cases arising from school districts in Pennsylvania and Maryland (*School District of Abington Township* v. *Schempp* and *Murray* v. *Curlett*), public school opening exercises utilizing the more traditional Lord's Prayer and readings from the Holy Bible were struck down as unconstitutional infringements of the establishment clause. Justice Tom Clark's opinion for the Court set forth the test of establishment violation in this manner:

> [W]hat are the purpose and primary effect of the enactment? If either is the advancement or inhibition of religion then the enactment exceeds the scope of legislative power as circumscribed by the Constitution. . . .

Clark explained that to save an enactment from condemnation under the establishment clause there must be a showing of "a secular legislative purpose and a primary effect that neither advances nor inhibits religion."

Justice Arthur Goldberg's concurring opinion focused on the difficult and sensitive task [of delineating] the constitutionally permissible relationship between religion and government. Noting that the opening exercises at issue were clearly prohibited by the establishment clause under the doctrine of state neutrality toward religion, Goldberg nevertheless advanced this warning:

> [U]ntutored devotion to the concept of neutrality can lead to invocation or approval of results which partake not simply of that noninterference and noninvolvement with the religious which the Constitution commands, but of a brooding and pervasive devotion to the secular and a passive, or even active, hostility to the religious.

He concluded that the religious commitment of a vast majority of the population cannot be ignored and that "under certain circumstances the First Amendment may require" cognizance of it.

In his dissent, Justice Potter Stewart advanced the view that the free exercise of religion is the central value embodied in the First Amendment. Consequently, he argued that the Court's action striking down the prayer exercises constituted a denial of a substantial free-exercise claim of those desiring the exercises. To him, the statutes authorizing the ceremonies are no more than measures that make possible the free exercise of religion.

There was immediate response to the *Engel* and *Schempp* rulings in the political arena. Scores of legislators brought forth proposals to amend the Constitution to permit various forms of voluntary prayer in the public schools. But from the immediate vigorous efforts mounted by Representative Frank Becker (R., N.Y.) in the House of Representatives in 1963 and followed by those of Senator Everett M. Dirksen (R., Ill.) in 1966 to the most recent proposal of Senator Richard S. Schweiker (R., Pa.) in 1973, Congress has steadfastly refused to provide the necessary constitutional majority required for formal initiation of such an amendment. Hence, the Court's ban of prayer exercises in the public schools remains intact.

The Sunday Closing Law controversy also illustrates the difficult problem of reconciling the establishment and free-exercise requirements of the First Amendment. Challenged in four cases decided by the Court in 1961 were the laws of Pennsylvania (*Two Guys from Harrison-Allentown* v. *McGinley*, 366 U.S. 582; *Braunfeld* v. *Brown*, 366 U.S. 599), Massachusetts (*Gallagher* v. *Crown Kosher Super Market*, 366 U.S. 617), and Maryland (*McGowan* v. *Maryland*, 366 U.S. 420). While upholding the constitutionality of all the statutes against allegations that they infringed upon the establishment, free-exercise, and equal protection clauses of the First and Fourteenth Amendments, the great difficulty the justices had in resolving the issues is revealed by the eight opinions filed in the cases. Chief Justice Earl Warren wrote the majority, or leading, opinion in each of the cases and, while recognizing "the strongly religious origin" of Sunday closing laws, stressed the secular purpose of the present-day legislation. Hence, in *McGowan*, he noted:

> [T]he State seeks to set one day apart from all others as a day of rest, repose, recreation and tranquility—a day which all members of the family and community have the opportunity to spend and enjoy together, a day in which there exists relative quiet and disassociation from the everyday intensity of commercial activities, a day in which people may visit friends and relatives who are not available during working days.

The Chief Justice made it clear that such laws do not infringe the establishment clause merely because the day (Sunday) through which the secular purpose is to be accomplished "happens to coincide or harmonize with the tenets of some or all religions." And, he concluded, since "Sunday is a day apart from all others," it would be unrealistic to require a state to select as its designated day of "rest and relaxation" one different from that to which most people traditionally adhere.

Warren also rejected the free-exercise claim advanced by the Orthodox Jewish merchants challenging the Pennsylvania legislation in *Braunfeld*. They argued that the statutory compulsion to close their business on Sunday places them at an economic disadvantage because they closed their businesses on Saturdays in observance of their Sabbath. Hence, they are penalized because of their religious beliefs. The Chief Justice recognized the operational consequences of the statute as making their religious beliefs and practices "more expensive," but he contended that none of those beliefs and practices are made unlawful. In essense, his argument is that alleged economic injury cannot be translated into a constitutional claim. When a statute regulates conduct, he argued, the imposition of an indirect burden on the exercise of religion does not necessarily render it unconstitutional. It is only when the "purpose and effect" of such a statute is to impede religious observance or is to "discriminate invidiously between religions" that it is constitutionally invalid. The Chief Justice set the constitutional limits of state regulatory power in this area this way:

[I]f the State regulates conduct by enacting a general law within its power, the purpose and effect of which is to advance the State's secular goals, the statute is valid despite its indirect burden on religious observance unless the State may accomplish its purpose by means which do not impose such a burden. . . .

Only Justice William O. Douglas dissented in all four cases, with Justices William J. Brennan and Potter Stewart joining him in the *Gallagher* and *Braunfeld* cases. Essentially, they argued that such laws, in recognizing the Christian sabbath and in putting Sabbatarians to a choice between their religion and economic survival, infringed both the establishment and free-exercise clauses.

Some have charged, including Justices Potter Stewart, John Harlan II, and Byron White, that the Court's action in *Sherbert* v. *Verner* discussed *supra*, constituted a reversal of *Braunfeld*. They could not see any substantial difference between the choice of religion and economic survival to which Verner had been subjected (which the Court condemned) and that to which Braunfeld was put under the Sunday Closing Law which the Court approved. The decisions in these two cases illustrate well the difficulty of obtaining consistent rulings on these kinds of questions under the Court's current construction of the establishment clause. As Justice Stewart pointed out in *Sherbert*, "[t]o require South Carolina to so administer its laws as to pay public money to the appellant is . . . clearly to require the State to violate the establishment clause. . . ."

The cases that follow focus on some of the most significant issues reviewed in this commentary.

EVERSON v. BOARD OF EDUCATION

330 U.S. 1; 91 L. Ed. 711, 67 S. Ct. 504 (1947)

MR. JUSTICE BLACK *delivered the opinion of the Court.*

A New Jersey statute authorizes its local school districts to make rules and contracts for the transportation of children to and from schools. The appellee, a township board of education, acting pursuant to this statute, authorized reimbursement to parents of money expended by them for the bus transportation of their children on regular busses operated by the public transportation system. Part of this money was for the payment of transportation of some school children in the community to Catholic parochial schools. These church schools give their students, in addition to secular education, regular religious instruction conforming to the religious tenets and modes of worship of the Catholic Faith. The superintendent of these schools is a Catholic priest.

The appellant, in his capacity as a district taxpayer, filed suit in a state court challenging the right of the Board to reimburse parents of parochial school students. He contended that the statute and the resolution passed pursuant to it violated both the State and Federal Constitutions. That court held that the legislature was without power to authorize such payments under the state constitution. . . . The New Jersey Court of Errors and Appeals reversed, holding that neither the statute nor the resolution passed pursuant to it was in conflict with the State Constitution or the provisions of the Federal Constitution in issue. . . . The case is here on appeal under 28 U.S.C. sec. 344(a). . . .

The only contention here is that the state statute and the resolution, insofar as they authorize reimbursement to parents of children attending parochial schools, violate the Federal Constitution in these two aspects, which to some extent overlap. *First.* They authorize the State to take by taxation the private property of some and bestow it upon others, to be used for their own private purposes. This, it is alleged, violates the due process clause of the Fourteenth Amendment. *Second.* The statute and the resolution forced inhabitants to pay taxes to help support and maintain schools which are dedicated to, and which regularly teach, the Catholic Faith. This is alleged to be a use of state power to support church schools contrary to the prohibition of the First Amendment which the Fourteenth Amendment made applicable to the states.

First. The due process argument that the state law taxes some people to help others carry out their private purposes is framed in two phases. The first phase is that a state cannot tax A to reimburse B for the cost of transporting his children to church schools. This is said to violate the due process clause because the children are sent to these church schools to satisfy the personal desires of their parents, rather than the public's interest in the general education of all children. This argument, if valid, would apply equally to prohibit state payment for the transportation of children to any non-public school, whether operated by a church or any other non-government individual or group. But, the New Jersey legislature has decided that a public purpose will be served by using tax-raised funds to pay the bus fares of all school children, including those who attend parochial schools. The New Jersey Court of Errors and Appeals has reached the same conclusion. The fact that a state law, passed to satisfy a public need, coincides with the personal desires of the individuals most directly affected is certainly an inadequate reason for us to say that a legislature has erroneously appraised the public need. . . .

It is much too late to argue that legislation intended to facilitate the opportunity of children to get a secular education serves no public purpose. *Cochran* v. *Louisiana State Board of Education*, 281 U.S. 340; Holmes, J., in *Interstate Ry.* v. *Massachusetts*, 207 U.S. 79, 87. See opinion of Cooley, J. in *Stuart* v. *School District No. 1 of Kalamazoo*, 30 Mich. 69 (1874). The same thing is no less true of legislation to reimburse needy parents, or all parents, for payment of the fares of their children so that they can ride in public busses to and from schools rather than run the risk of traffic and other hazards incident to walking or "hitch-hiking." . . . Nor does it follow that a law has a private rather than a public purpose because it provides that tax-raised funds will be paid to reimburse individuals on account of money spent by them in a way which furthers a public program. See *Carmichael* v. *Southern Coal & Coke Co.*, 301 U.S. 495, 518. . . .

Second. The New Jersey statute is challenged as a "law respecting an establishment of religion." The First Amendment, as made applicable to the states by the Fourteenth, *Murdock* v. *Pennsylvania*, 319 U.S. 105, commands that a state "shall make no law respecting an establishment of religion, or prohibiting the free exercise thereof. . . ." These words of the First Amendment reflected in the minds of early Americans a vivid mental picture of conditions and practices which they fervently wished to stamp out in order to preserve liberty for themselves and for their posterity. Doubtless their goal has not been entirely reached; but so far has the Nation moved toward it that the expression "law respecting an establishment of religion," probably does not so vividly remind present-day Americans of the evils, fears, and political problems that caused that expression to be written into our Bill of Rights. . . .

The meaning and scope of the First Amendment, preventing establishment of religion or prohibiting the free exercise thereof, in the light of the history and the evils it was designed forever to suppress, have been several times elaborated by the decisions of this Court prior to the application of the First Amendment to the states by the Fourteenth. The broad meaning given the Amendment by these earlier cases has been accepted by this Court in its decision concerning an individual's religious freedom rendered since the Fourteenth Amendment was interpreted to make the prohibitions of the First applicable to state action abridging religious freedom. There is every reason to give the same application and broad interpretation to the "establishment of religion" clause. The interrelation of these complementary clauses was well summarized in a statement of the Court of Appeals of South Carolina, quoted with approval by this Court in *Watson* v. *Jones*, 13 Wall. 679, 730: "The structure of our government has, for the preservation of civil liberty, rescued the temporal institutions from religious interference. On the other hand, it has secured religious liberty from the invasion of the civil authority."

The "establishment of religion" clause of the First Amendment means at least this: Neither a state nor the Federal Government can set up a church. Neither can pass laws which aid one religion, aid all religions, or prefer one religion over another. Neither can force nor influence a person to go to or to remain away from church against his will or force him to profess a belief or disbelief in any religion. No person can be punished for entertaining or professing religious beliefs or disbeliefs, for church attendance or non-attendance. No tax in any amount, large or small, can be levied to support any religious activities or institutions, whatever they may be called or whatever form they may adopt to teach or practice religion. Neither a state nor the Federal Government can, openly or secretly, participate in the affairs of any religious organizations or groups and *vice versa*. In the words of Jefferson, the clause against establishment of religion by law was intended to erect "a wall of Separation between church and State. . . ."

We must consider the New Jersey statute in accordance with the foregoing limitations imposed by the First Amendment. But we must not strike that state statute down if it is within the State's constitutional power even though it approaches the verge of that power. ... New Jersey cannot consistently with the "establishment of religion" clause of the First Amendment contribute tax-raised funds to the support of an institution which teaches the tenets and faith of any church. On the other hand, other language of the amendment commands that New Jersey cannot hamper its citizens in the free exercise of their own religion. Consequently, it cannot exclude individual Catholics, Lutherans, Mohammedans, Baptists, Jews, Methodists, Non-believers, Presbyterians, or the members of any other faith, because of their faith, or lack of it, from receiving the benefits of public welfare legislation. While we do not mean to intimate that a state could not provide transportation only to children attending public schools, we must be careful, in protecting the citizens of New Jersey against state-established churches, to be sure that we do not inadvertently prohibit New Jersey from extending its general state law benefits to all its citizens without regard to their religious belief.

Measured by these standards, we cannot say that the First Amendment prohibits New Jersey from spending tax-raised funds to pay the bus fares of parochial school pupils as a part of a general program under which it pays the fares of pupils attending public and other schools. It is undoubtedly true that children are helped to get to church schools. There is even a possibility that some of the children might not be sent to the church schools if the parents were compelled to pay their children's bus fares out of their own pockets when transportation to a public school would have been paid for by the State. The same possibility exists where the state requires a local transit company to provide reduced fares to school children including those attending parochial schools, or where a municipally owned transportation system undertakes to carry all school children free of charge. Moreover, state-paid policemen, detailed to protect children going to and from church schools from the very real hazards of traffic, would serve much the same purpose and accomplish much the same result as state provisions intended to guarantee free transportation of a kind which the state deems to be best for the school children's welfare. And parents might refuse to risk their children to the serious danger of traffic accidents going to and from parochial schools, the approaches to which were not protected by the policemen. Similarly, parents might be reluctant to permit their children to attend schools which the state had cut off from such general government services as ordinary police and fire protection, connections for sewage disposal, public highways and sidewalks. Of course, cutting off church schools from these services, so separate and so indisputably marked off from the religious function, would make it far more difficult for the schools to operate. But such is obviously not the purpose of the First Amendment. That Amendment requires the state to be a neutral in its relations with groups of religious believers and non-believers; it does not require the state to be their adversary. State power is no more to be used so as to handicap religions than it is to favor them.

This Court has said that parents may, in the discharge of their duty under state compulsory education laws, send their children to a religious rather than a public school if the school meets the secular educational requirements which the state has power to impose. See *Pierce* v. *Society of Sisters*, 268 U.S. 510. It appears that these parochial schools meet New Jersey's requirement. The State contributes no money to the schools. It does not support them. Its legislation, as applied, does no more than provide a general program to help parents get their children, regardless of their religion, safely and expeditiously to and from accredited schools.

The First Amendment has erected a wall

between church and state. That wall must be kept high and impregnable. We could not approve the slightest breach. New Jersey has not breached it here.

Affirmed.

MR. JUSTICE JACKSON, *dissenting.*

I find myself, contrary to first impressions, unable to join in this decision. I have a sympathy, though it is not ideological, with Catholic citizens who are compelled by law to pay taxes for public schools, and also feel constrained by conscience and discipline to support other schools for their own children. Such relief to them as this case involves is not in itself a serious burden to taxpayers and I had assumed it to be as little serious in principle. Study of this case convinces me otherwise. The Court's opinion marshals every argument in favor of state aid and puts the case in its most favorable light, but much of its reasoning confirms my conclusions that there are no good grounds upon which to support the present legislation. In fact, the undertones of the opinion, advocating complete and uncompromising separation of Church from State, seem utterly discordant with its conclusion yielding support to their commingling in educational matters. The case which irresistibly comes to mind as the most fitting precedent is that of Julia who, according to Byron's reports, "whispering 'I will ne'er consent,'—consented."

The Court sustains this legislation by assuming two deviations from the facts of this particular case; first, it assumes a state of facts the record does not support, and secondly, it refuses to consider facts which are inescapable on the record.

The Court concludes that this "legislation, as applied, does no more than provide a general program to help parents get their children, regardless of their religion, safely and expeditiously to and from accredited schools," and it

draws a comparison between "state provisions intended to guarantee free transportation" for school children with services such as police and fire protection, and implies that we are here dealing with "laws authorizing new types of public services...." This hypothesis permeates the opinion. The facts will not bear that construction.

The Township of Ewing is not furnishing transportation to the children in any form; it is not operating school busses itself or contracting for their operation; and it is not performing any public service of any kind with this taxpayer's money. All school children are left to ride as ordinary paying passengers on the regular busses operated by the public transportation system. What the Township does, and what the taxpayer complains of, is at stated intervals to reimburse parents for the fares paid, provided the children attend either public schools or Catholic Church schools. This expenditure of tax funds has no possible effect on the child's safety or expedition in transit. As passengers on the public busses they travel as fast and no faster, and are as safe and no safer, since their parents are reimbursed as before.

In addition to this assuming a type of service that does not exist, the Court also insists that we must close our eyes to a discrimination which does exist. The resolution which authorizes disbursement of this taxpayer's money limits reimbursement to those who attend public schools and Catholic schools. That is the way the Act is applied to this taxpayer.

The New Jersey Act in question makes the character of the school, not the needs of the children, determine the eligibility of parents to reimbursement. The Act permits payment for transportation to parochial schools or public schools but prohibits it to private schools operated in whole or in part for profit. Children often are sent to private schools because their parents feel that they require more individual instruction than public schools can provide, or because they are backward or defective and need special attention. If all children of the state were objects of impartial solicitude, no reason is obvious for denying transportation reimbursement to students of this class, for these often are as needy and as worthy as those who go to public or parochial schools. Refusal to reimburse those who attend such schools is understandable only in the light of a purpose to aid the schools, because the state might well abstain from aiding a profit-making private enterprise. Thus, under the Act and resolution brought to us by this case, children are classified according to the schools they attend and are to be aided if they attend private secular schools or private religious schools of other faiths. . . .

. . . .[T]his case is not one of a Baptist or a Jew or an Episcopalian or a pupil of a private school complaining of discrimination. It is one of a taxpayer urging that he is being taxed for an unconstitutional purpose. I think he is entitled to have us consider the Act just as it is written. . . .

If we are to decide this case on the facts before us, our question is simply this: Is it constitutional to tax this complainant to pay the cost of carrying pupils of Church schools of one specified denomination?

Whether the taxpayer constitutionally can be made to contribute aid to parents of students because of their attendance at parochial schools depends upon the nature of those schools and their relation to the Church. The Constitution says nothing of education. It lays no obligation on the states to provide schools and does not undertake to regulate state systems of education if they see fit to maintain them. But they cannot, through school policy any more than through other means, invade rights secured to citizens by the Constitution of the United States. *West Virginia State Board of Education* v. *Barnette* 319 U.S. 624. . . . One of our basic rights is to be free of taxation to support a transgression of the constitutional command that the authorities "shall make no law respecting an establishment of religion, or prohibiting the free exercise thereof. . . ."

It is no exaggeration to say that the whole historic conflict in temporal policy between the Cátholic Church and non-Catholics comes to a focus in their respective school policies. The Roman Catholic Church, counseled by experience in many ages and many lands and with all sorts and conditions of men, takes what, from the viewpoint of its own progress and the success of its mission, is a wise estimate of the importance of education to religion. It does not leave the individual to pick up religion by chance. It relies on early and indelible indoctrination in the faith and order of the Church by the word and example of persons consecrated to the task.

Our public school, if not a product of Protestantism, at least is more consistent with it than with the Catholic culture and scheme of values. It is a relatively recent development dating from about 1840. It is organized on the premises that secular education can be isolated from all religious teaching so that the school can inculcate all needed temporal knowledge and also maintain a strict and lofty neutrality as to religion. The assumption is that after the individual has been instructed in worldly wisdom he will be better fitted to choose his religion. Whether such a disjunction is possible, and if possible whether it is wise, are questions I need not try to answer.

I should be surprised if any Catholic would deny that the parochial school is a vital, if not the most vital, part of the Roman Catholic Church. If put to the choice, that venerable institution, I should expect, would forego its whole service for mature persons before it would give up education of the young, and it would be a wise choice. Its growth and cohesion, discipline and loyalty, spring from its schools. Catholic education is the rock on which the whole structure rests, and to render tax aid to its Church school is indistinguishable to me from rendering the same aid to the Church itself. . . .

. . . I agree that this Court has left, and always should leave to each state, great latitude in deciding for itself, in the light of its own conditions, what shall be public purpose in its scheme of things. It may socialize utilities and economic enterprises and make taxpayers' business out of what conventionally had been private business. It may make public business of individual welfare, health, education, entertainment or security. But it cannot make public business of religious worship or instruction, or of attendance at religious institutions of any character. There is no answer to the proposition, more fully expounded by Mr. Justice Rutledge, that the effect of the religious freedom Amendment to our Constitution was to take every form of propagation of religion out of the realm of things which could directly or indirectly be made public business and thereby be supported in whole or in part at taxpayers' expense. That is a difference which the Constitution sets up between religion and almost every other subject matter of legislation, a difference which goes to the very root of religious freedom and which the Court is overlooking today. This freedom was first in the Bill of Rights because it was first in the forefathers' minds; it was set forth in absolute terms, and its strength is its rigidity. It was intended not only to keep the states' hands out of religion, but to keep religion's hands off the state, and, above all, to keep bitter religious controversy out of public life by denying to every denomination any advantage from getting control of public policy or the public purse. Those great ends I cannot but think are immeasurably compromised by today's decision.

This policy of our Federal Constitution has never been wholly pleasing to most religious groups. They all are quick to invoke its protections; they all are irked when they feel its restraints. This Court has gone a long way, if not an unreasonable way, to hold that public business of such paramount importance as maintenance of public order, protection of the privacy of the home, and taxation may not be pursued by a state in a way that even indirectly will interfere with religious proselyting. See dissent in *Douglas* v. *Jeannette* 319 U.S. 157, 186. . . .

But we cannot have it both ways. Religious teaching cannot be a private affair when the state seeks to impose regulations which infringe on it indirectly, and a public affair when it comes to taxing citizens of one faith to aid another, or those of no faith to aid all. If these principles seem harsh in prohibiting aid to Catholic education, it must not be forgotten that it is the same Constitution that alone assures Catholics the right to maintain these schools at all when predominant local sentiment would forbid them. *Pierce* v. *Society of Sisters*, 268 U.S. 510. Nor should I think that those who have done so well without this aid would want to see this separation between Church and State broken down. If the state may aid these religious schools, it may therefore regulate them. Many groups have sought aid from tax funds only to find that it carried political controls with it. Indeed this Court has declared that "It is hardly lack of due process for the Government to regulate that which it subsidizes." *Wickard* v. *Filburn*, 317 U.S. 111, 131.

But in any event, the great purposes of the Constitution do not depend on the approval or convenience of those they restrain. I cannot read this history of the struggle to separate political from ecclesiastical affairs, well summarized in the opinion of Mr. Justice Rutledge in which I generally concur, without a conviction that the Court today is unconsciously giving the clock's hand a backward turn.

MR. JUSTICE FRANKFURTER *joins in this opinion.*

MR. JUSTICE RUTLEDGE, *with whom* MR. JUSTICE FRANKFURTER, MR. JUSTICE JACKSON, *and* MR. JUSTICE BURTON *agree, dissenting.*

This case forces us to determine squarely for the first time what was "an establishment of religion" in the First Amendment's conception; and by that measure to decide whether New Jersey's action violates its command. . . .

I

The Amendment's purpose was not to strike merely at the official establishment of a single sect, creed or religion, outlawing only a formal relation such as had prevailed in England and some of the colonies. Necessarily it was to uproot all such relationships. But the object was broader than separating church and state in this narrow sense. It was to create a complete and permanent separation of the spheres of religious activity and civil authority by comprehensively forbidding every form of public aid or support for religion. In proof the Amendment's wording and history unite with this Court's consistent utterances whenever attention has been fixed directly upon the question. . . . .

II

. . . [T]oday, apart from efforts to inject religious training or exercises and sectarian issues into the public schools, the only serious surviving threat to maintaining that complete and permanent separation of religion and civil power which the First Amendment commands is through use of the taxing power to support religion, religious establishments, or establishments having a religious foundation whatever their form of special religious function.

Does New Jersey's action furnish support for religion by use of the taxing power? Certainly it does, if the test remains undiluted as Jefferson and Madison made it, that money taken by taxation from one is not to be used or given to support another's religious training or belief, or indeed one's own. Today as then the furnishing of "contributions of money for the propagation of opinions which he disbelieves" is the forbidden exaction; and the prohibition is absolute for whatever measure brings that consequence and whatever amount may be sought or given to that end. . . .

Believers of all faiths, and others who do not express their feeling toward ultimate issues of existence in any creedal form, pay the New Jersey tax. When the money so raised is used to pay for transportation to religious schools, the Catholic taxpayer to the extent of his proportionate share pays for the transportation of Lutheran, Jewish, and otherwise religiously affiliated children to receive their non-Catholic religious instruction. Their parents likewise pay proportionately for the transportation of Catholic children to receive Catholic instruction. Each thus contributes to "the propagation of opinions which he disbelieves" in so far as their religions differ, as do others who accept no creed without regard to those differences. Each thus pays taxes also to support the teaching of his own religion, an exaction equally forbidden since it denies "the comfortable liberty" of giving one's contribution to the particular agency of instruction he approves.

New Jersey's action therefore exactly fits the type of exaction and the kind of evil at which Madison and Jefferson struck. Under the test they framed it cannot be said that the cost of transportation is no part of the cost of education or of the religious instruction given. That it is a substantial and a necessary element is shown most plainly by the continuing and increasing demand for the state to assume it. Nor is there pretense that it relates only to the secular instruction given in religious schools or that any attempt is or could be made toward allocating proportional shares as between the secular and the religious instruction. It is precisely because the instruction is religious and relates to a particular faith, whether one or another, that parents send their children to religious schools under the *Pierce* doctrine. And the very purpose of the state's contribution is to defray the cost of conveying the pupil to the place where he will receive not simply secular, but also and primarily religious, teaching and guidance. . . .

Finally, transportation, where it is needed, is as essential to education as any other element. Its cost is as much a part of the total expense, except at times in amount, as the cost of textbooks, of school lunches, of athletic equipment, of writing and other materials; indeed of all other items composing the total burden. . . . Without buildings, without equipment, without library, textbooks and other materials, and without transportation to bring teacher and pupil together in such an effective teaching environment, there can be not even the skeleton of what our times require. Hardly can it be maintained that transportation is the least essential of these items, or that it does not in fact aid, encourage, sustain and support, just as they do, the very process which is its purpose to accomplish. . . .

For me, therefore, the feat is impossible to select so indispensable an item from the composite of total costs, and characterize it as not aiding, contributing to, promoting or sustaining the propagation of beliefs which it is the very end of all to bring about. Unless this can be maintained, and the Court does not maintain it, the aid thus given is outlawed. Payment of transportation is no more, nor is it any the less essential to education, whether religious or secular, than payment for tuitions, for teachers' salaries, for buildings, equipment and necessary materials.

. . .

IV

No one conscious of religious value can be unsympathetic toward the burden which our constitutional separation puts on parents who desire religious instruction mixed with secular for their children. They pay taxes for others'

children's education, at the same time the added cost of instruction for their own. Nor can one happily see benefits denied to children which others receive, because in conscience they or their parents desire for them a different kind of training others do not demand.

But if those feelings should prevail, there would be an end to our historic constitutional policy and command. No more unjust or discriminatory in fact is it to deny attendants at religious schools the cost of their transportation than it is to deny them tuitions, sustenance for their teachers, or any other additional expense which others receive at public cost. Hardship in fact there is which none can blink. But, for assuring to those who undergo it the greater, the most comprehensive freedom, it is one written by design and firm intent into our basic law. . . .

That policy necessarily entails hardship upon persons who forego the right to educational advantages the state can supply in order to secure others it is precluded from giving. Indeed this may hamper the parent and the child forced by conscience to that choice. But it does not make the state unneutral to withhold what the Constitution forbids it to give. On the contrary it is only by observing the prohibition rigidly that the state can maintain its neutrality and avoid partisanship in the dissensions inevitable when sect opposes sect over demands for public moneys to further religious education, teaching or training in any form or degree, directly or indirectly. . . .

The problem then cannot be cast in terms of legal discrimination or its absence. This would be true, even though the state in giving aid should treat all religious instruction alike. Thus, if the present statute and its application were shown to apply equally to all religious schools of whatever faith, yet in the light of our tradition it could not stand. For then the adherent of one creed still would pay for the support of another, the childless taxpayer with others more fortunate. Then, too, there would seem to be no bar to making appropriations for transportation and other expenses of children attending public or other secular schools, after hours in separate places and classes for their exclusively religious instruction. The person who embraces no creed also would be forced to pay for teaching what he does not believe. Again, it was the furnishing of "contributions of money for the propagation of opinions which he disbelieves" that the fathers outlawed. That consequence and effect are not removed by multiplying to all-inclusiveness the sects for which support is exacted. The Constitution requires, not comprehensive identification of state with religion, but complete separation. . . .

Two great drives are constantly in motion to abridge, in the name of education, the complete division of religion and civil authority which our forefathers made. One is to introduce religious education and observances into the public schools. The other, to obtain public funds for the aid and support of various private religious schools. See Johnson, *The Legal Status of Church-State Relationships in the United States* (1934); Thayer, *Religion in Public Education* (1947); Note (1941) 50 Yale L. J. 917. In my opinion both avenues were closed by the Constitution. Neither should be opened by this Court. The matter is not one of quantity, to be measured by the amount of money expended. Now as in Madison's day it is one of principle, to keep separate the separate spheres as the First Amendment drew them; to prevent the first experiment upon our liberties; and to keep the question from becoming entangled in corrosive precedents. We should not be less strict to keep strong and untarnished the one side of the shield of religious freedom than we have been of the other. The judgment should be reversed.

SCHOOL DISTRICT OF ABINGTON TOWNSHIP PENNSYLVANIA v. SCHEMPP
MURRAY v. CURLETT
374 U.S. 203; 10 L. Ed. 2d 844; 83 S. Ct. 1560 (1963)

MR. JUSTICE CLARK *delivered the opinion of the Court.*

Once again we are called upon to consider the scope of the provision of the First Amendment to the United States Constitution which declares that "Congress shall make no law respecting an establishment of religion, or prohibiting the free exercise thereof. . . ." These companion cases present the issues in the context of state action requiring that schools begin each day with readings from the Bible. While raising the basic questions under slightly different factual situations, the cases permit of joint treatment. In light of the history of the First Amendment and of our cases interpreting and applying its requirements, we hold that the practices at issue and the laws respecting them are unconstitutional under the Establishment Clause, as applied to the states through the Fourteenth Amendment. . . . [In] No. 142 [t]he Commonwealth of Pennsylvania by law, 24 Pa. Stat. Sec. 15–1516, as amended, . . . requires that "At least ten verses from the Holy Bible shall be read, without comment, at the opening of each public school on each school day. Any child shall be excused from such Bible reading, or attending such Bible reading, upon the written request of his parent or guardian." The Schempp family, husband and wife and two of their three children, brought suit to enjoin enforcement of the statute, contending that their rights under the Fourteenth Amendment to the

Constitution of the United States are, have been, and will continue to be violated unless this statute be declared unconstitutional as violative of these provisions of the First Amendment. They sought to enjoin the appellant school district ... from continuing to conduct such readings and recitation of the Lord's Prayer in the public schools of the district. ... A three-judge statutory District Court for the Eastern District of Pennsylvania held that the statute is violative of the Establishment Clause of the First Amendment as applied to the States by the Due Process Clause of the Fourteenth Amendment and directed that appropriate injunctive relief issue. ...

The appellees ... are of the Unitarian faith ... [and] they ... regularly attend religious services. ... The ... children attend the Abington Senior High School, which is a public school operated by appellant district.

On each school day at the Abington Senior High School between 8:15 and 8:30 A.M., while the pupils are attending their home rooms or advisory sections, opening exercises are conducted pursuant to the statute. The exercises are broadcast into each room in the school building through an intercommunications system and are conducted under the supervision of a teacher by students attending the school's radio and television workshop. Selected students from this course gather each morning in the school's workshop studio for the exercises, which include readings by one of the students of 10 verses of the Holy Bible, broadcast to each room in the building. This is followed by the recitation of the Lord's Prayer, likewise over the intercommunications system, but also by the students in the various classrooms, who are asked to stand and join in repeating the prayer in unison. The exercises are closed with the flag salute and such pertinent announcements as are of interest to the students. Participation in the opening exercises, as directed by the statute, is voluntary. The student reading the verses from the Bible may select the passages and read from any version he

chooses, although the only copies furnished by the school are the King James version, copies of which were circulated to each teacher by the school district. During the period in which the exercises have been conducted the King James, the Douay and the Revised Standard versions of the Bible have been used, as well as the Jewish Holy Scriptures. There are no prefatory statements, no questions asked or solicited, no comments or explanations made and no interpretations given at or during the exercises. The students and parents are advised that the student may absent himself from the classroom or, should he elect to remain, not participate in the exercises.

It appears from the record that in schools not having an intercommunications system the Bible reading and the recitation of the Lord's Prayer were conducted by the home-room teacher, who chose the text of the verses and read them herself or had students read them in rotation or by volunteers. ...

At the first trial Edward Schempp and the children testified as to specific religious doctrines purveyed by a literal reading of the Bible "which were contrary to the religious beliefs which they held and to their familial teaching." ... Edward Schempp testified at the second trial that he had considered having ... [his children] excused from attendance at the exercises but decided against it for several reasons, including his belief that the children's relationships with their teachers and classmates would be adversely affected.

. . .

The trial court, in striking down the practices and the statute requiring them, made specific findings of fact that the children's attendance at Abington Senior High School is compulsory and that the practice of reading 10 verses from the Bible is also compelled by law. It also found that:

> The reading of the verses, even without comment, possesses a devotional and religious

character and constitutes in effect a religious observance. The devotional and religious nature of the morning exercises is made all the more apparent by the fact that the Bible reading is followed immediately by a recital in unison by the pupils of the Lord's Prayer. . . . The exercises are held in the school buildings and perforce are conducted by and under the authority of the local school authorities and during school sessions. Since the statute requires the reading of the "Holy Bible," a Christian document, the practice . . . prefers the Christian religion. . . .

[The facts in] no. 119 [show that] [i]n 1905 the Board of School Commissioners of Baltimore City adopted a rule pursuant to . . . [state law which] . . . provided for the holding of opening exercises in the schools of the city, consisting primarily of the "reading, without comment, of a chapter in the Holy Bible and/or the use of the Lord's Prayer." The petitioners, Mrs. Madalyn Murray and her son, William J. Murray III, are both professed atheists. Following unsuccessful attempts to have the respondent school board rescind the rule, this suit was filed for mandamus to compel its rescission and cancellation. It was alleged that William was a student in a public school of the city and Mrs. Murray, his mother, was a taxpayer therein; . . . that at petitioners' insistence the rule was amended to permit children to be excused from the exercise on request of the parent and that William had been excused pursuant thereto. . . .

The respondents demurred and the trial court, recognizing that the demurrer admitted all facts well pleaded, sustained it without leave to amend. The Maryland Court of Appeals affirmed, the majority of four justices holding the exercise not in violation of the First and Fourteenth Amendments, with three justices dissenting. . . .

It is true that religion has been closely identified with our history and government. . . . The fact that the Founding Fathers believed devotedly that there was a God and that the unalienable rights of man were rooted in Him is clearly evidenced in their writings, from the Mayflower Compact to the Constitution itself. This background is evidenced today in our public life through the continuance in our oaths of office from the Presidency to the Alderman of the final supplication, "So help me God." Likewise each House of the Congress provides through the Chaplain an opening prayer, and the sessions of this Court are declared open by the crier in a short ceremony, the final phrase of which invokes the grace of God. Again, there are such manifestations in our military forces, where those of our citizens who are under the restrictions of military service wish to engage in voluntary worship. Indeed, only last year an official survey of the country indicated that 64% of our people have church membership . . . while less than 3% profess no religion whatever. . . . It can be truly said, therefore, that today, as in the beginning, our national life reflects a religious people who, in the words of Madison are "earnestly praying, as . . . in duty bound, that the Supreme Lawgiver of the Universe . . . guide them into every measure which may be worthy of his [blessing . . .]"

Almost a hundred years ago in *Minor* v. *Board of Education of Cincinnati*, Judge Alphonzo Taft, father of the revered Chief Justice, in an unpublished opinion stated the ideal of our people as to religious freedom as one of:

absolute equality before the law of all religious opinions and sects. . . . The government is neutral, and while protecting all, it prefers none, and it *disparages* none. . . .

The wholesome "neutrality" of which this Court's cases speak thus stems from a recognition of the teachings of history that powerful sects or groups might bring about a fusion or a concert or dependency of one upon the other to the end that official support of the State or Federal Government would be placed behind the tenets of one or of all orthodoxies. This the Establishment Clause prohibits. And a further reason for neutrality is found in the Free Exercise Clause, which recognizes the value of religious training, teaching and observance and, more particularly, the right of every person to freely choose his own course with reference thereto, free of any compulsion from the state. This the Free Exercise Clause guarantees. Thus, as we have seen, the two clauses may overlap. As we have indicated, the Establishment Clause has been directly considered by this Court eight times in the past score of years and, with only one Justice dissenting on the point, it has consistently held that the clause withdrew all legislative power respecting religious belief or the exercise thereof. The test may be stated as follows: what are the purpose and primary effect of the enactment? If either is the advancement or inhibition of religion then the enactment exceeds the scope of legislative power as circumscribed by the Constitution. That is to say that to withstand the strictures of the Establishment Clause there must be a secular legislative purpose and a primary effect that neither advances nor inhibits religion. . . . The Free Exercise Clause, likewise considered many times here, withdraws from legislative power, state and federal, the exertion of any restraint on the free exercise of religion. Its purpose is to secure religious liberty in the individual by prohibiting any invasions thereof by civil authority. Hence it is necessary in a free exercise case for one to show the coercive effect of the enactment as it operates against him in the practice of his religion. The distinction between the two clauses is apparent—a violation of the Free Exercise Clause is predicated on coercion while the Establishment Clause violation need not be so attended.

Applying the Establishment Clause principles to the cases at bar we find that the States are requiring the selection and reading at the opening of the school day of verses from the Holy Bible and the recitation of the Lord's Prayer by the students in unison. These exercises are prescribed as part of the curricular activities of students who are required by law to attend school. They are held in the school buildings under the supervision and with the participation of teachers employed in those schools. None of these factors, other than compulsory school attendance, was present in the program upheld in *Zorach* v. *Clauson.* The trial court in [*Schempp*] has found that such an opening exercise is a religious ceremony and was intended by the State to be so. We agree with the trial court's finding as to the religious character of the exercises. Given that finding the exercises and the law requiring them are in violation of the Establishment Clause.

There is no such specific finding as to the religious character of the exercises in [*Murray*], and the state contends (as does the state in [*Schempp*]) that the program is an effort to extend its benefits to all public school children without regard to their religious belief. Included within its secular purposes, it says, are the promotion of moral values, the contradiction to the materialistic trends of our times, the perpetuation of our institutions and the teaching of literature. The case came up on demurrer, of course, to a petition which alleged that the uniform practice under the rule had been to read from the King James version of the Bible and that the exercise was sectarian. The short answer, therefore, is that the religious character of the exercise was admitted by the State. But even if its purpose is not strictly religious, it sought to be accomplished through readings, without comment, from the Bible. Surely the place of the Bible as an instrument of religion cannot be gainsaid, and the State's recognition of the pervading religious character of the ceremony is evident from the rule's specific permission of the alternative use of the Catholic Douay version as well as the recent amendment permitting nonattendance at the exercises. None of these factors is consistent with the contention that the Bible is here used either as an instrument for nonreligious moral consideration or as a reference for the teaching of secular subjects.

The conclusion follows that in both cases the

laws require religious exercises and such exercises are being conducted in direct violation of the rights of the appellees and petitioners. Nor are these required exercises mitigated by the fact that individual students may absent themselves upon parental request, for that fact furnishes no defense to a claim of unconstitutionality under the Establishment Clause.... Further, it is no defense to urge that the religious practices here may be relatively minor encroachments on the First Amendment. The breach of neutrality that is today a trickling stream may all too soon become a raging torrent and, in the words of Madison, "it is proper to take alarm at the first experiment on our liberties." ...

It is insisted that unless these religious exercises are permitted a "religion of secularism" is established in the schools. We agree of course that the State may not establish a "religion of secularism" in the sense of affirmatively opposing or showing hostility to religion, thus "preferring those who believe in no religion over those who do believe." ... We do not agree, however, that this decision in any sense has that effect. In addition, it might well be said that one's education is not complete without a study of comparative religion or the history of religion and its relationship to the advancement of civilization. It certainly may be said that the Bible is worthy of study for its literary and historic qualities. Nothing we have said here indicates that such study of the Bible or of religion, when presented objectively as part of a secular program of education, may not be effected consistent with the First Amendment. But the exercises here do not fall into those categories. ...

Finally, we cannot accept that the concept of neutrality, which does not permit a State to require a religious exercise even with the consent of the majority of those affected, collides with the majority's right to free exercise of religion. While the Free Exercise Clause clearly prohibits the use of state action to deny the rights of free exercise to *anyone,* it has never meant that a

majority could use the machinery of the State to practice its beliefs. Such a contention was effectively answered by Mr. Justice Jackson for the Court in *West Virginia Board of Education* v. *Barnette,* 319 U.S. 624, 638, 63 S. Ct. 1178, 1185, 87 L. Ed 1628, (1943):

> The very purpose of a Bill of Rights was to withdraw certain subjects from the vicissitudes of political controversy, to place them beyond the reach of majorities and officials and to establish them as legal principles to be applied by the courts. One's right to ... freedom of worship ... and other fundamental rights may not be submitted to vote; they depend on the outcome of no elections.

The place of religion in our society is an exalted one, achieved through a long tradition of reliance on the home, the church and the inviolable citadel of the individual heart and mind. We have come to recognize through bitter experience that it is not within the power of government to invade that citadel, whether its purpose or effect be to aid or oppose, to advance or retard. In the relationship between man and religion, the State is firmly committed to a position of neutrality....
It is so ordered.

Judgment in [*Schempp*] affirmed; judgment in [*Murray*] reversed and cause remanded with directions.

The *concurring opinions* of MR. JUSTICE DOUGLAS and MR. JUSTICE BRENNAN *are not reprinted here.*

MR. JUSTICE STEWART, *dissenting.*

I think the records in the two cases before us are so fundamentally deficient as to make impossible an informed or responsible determination of the constitutional issues presented. Specifically, I cannot agree that on these records we can say that the Establishment Clause has necessarily been violated. But I think there exist serious questions under both that provision and the Free Exercise Clause ... which require the remand of these cases for the taking of additional evidence.

... It is, I think, a fallacious oversimplification to regard these two provisions as establishing a single constitutional standard of "separation of church and state," which can be mechanically applied in every case to delineate the required boundaries between government and religion. We err in the first place if we do not recognize, as a matter of history and as a matter of the imperatives of our free society, that religion and government must necessarily interact in countless ways. Secondly, the fact is that while in many contexts the Establishment Clause and the Free Exercise Clause fully complement each other, there are areas in which a doctrinaire reading of the Establishment Clause leads to irreconcilable conflict with the Free Exercise Clause.

A single obvious example should suffice to make the point. Spending federal funds to employ chaplains for the armed forces might be said to violate the Establishment Clause. Yet a lonely soldier stationed at some faraway outpost could surely complain that a government which did not provide him the opportunity for pastoral guidance was affirmatively prohibiting the free exercise of his religion. And such examples could readily be multiplied. The short of the matter is simply that the two relevant clauses of the First Amendment cannot accurately be reflected in a sterile metaphor which by its very nature may distort rather than illumine the problems involved in a particular case.

. . .

That the central value embodied in the First Amendment—and, more particularly, in the guarantee of "liberty" contained in the Fourteenth—is the safeguarding of an individual's right to free exercise of his religion has been consistently recognized. . . .

It is this concept of constitutional protection embodied in our decisions which makes the cases before us such difficult ones for me. For there is involved in these cases a substantial free exercise claim on the part of those who affirmatively desire to have their children's school day open with the reading of passages from the Bible.

. . .

It might also be argued that parents who want their children exposed to religious influences can adequately fulfill that wish off school property and outside school time. With all its surface persuasiveness, however, this argument seriously misconceives the basic constitutional justification for permitting the exercises at issue in these cases. For a compulsory state educational system so structures a child's life that if religious exercises are held to be an impermissible activity in schools, religion is placed at an artificial and state created disadvantage. Viewed in this light, permission of such exercises for those who want them is necessary if the schools are truly to be neutral in the matter of religion. And a refusal to permit religious exercises thus is seen, not as the realization of state neutrality, but rather as the establishment of a religion of secularism, or at the least, as government support of the beliefs of those who think that religious exercises should be conducted only in private.

What seems to me to be of paramount importance, then, is recognition of the fact that the claim advanced here in favor of Bible reading is sufficiently substantial to make simple reference to the constitutional phrase of "establishment of religion" as inadequate an analysis of the cases before us as the ritualistic invocation of the nonconstitutional phrase "separation of church and state." What these cases compel, rather, is an analysis of just what the "neutrality" is which is required by the interplay of the Establishment and Free Exercise Clauses of the First Amendment, as imbedded in the Fourteenth.

. . .

I have said that these provisions authorizing religious exercises are properly to be regarded as measures making possible the free exercise of religion. But it is important to stress that, strictly speaking, what is at issue here is a privilege rather than a right. In other words, the question presented is not whether exercises such as those at issue here are constitutionally compelled, but rather whether they are constitutionally invalid. And that issue, in my view, turns on the question of coercion.

It is clear that the dangers of coercion involved in the holding of religious exercises in a schoolroom differ qualitatively from those presented by the use of similar exercises or affirmations in ceremonies attended by adults. Even as to children, however, the duty laid upon government in connection with religious exercises in the public schools is that of refraining from so structuring the school environment as to put any kind of pressure on a child to participate in those exercises; it is not that of providing an atmosphere in which children are kept scrupulously insulated from any awareness that some of their fellows may want to open the school day with prayer, or of the fact that there exist in our pluralistic society differences of religious belief.

. . .

. . . [I]t seems to me clear that certain types of exercises would present situations in which no possibility of coercion on the part of secular officials could be claimed to exist. Thus, if such exercises were held either before or after the official school day, or if the school schedule were such that participation were merely one among a number of desirable alternatives, it could hardly be contended that the exercises did anything more than to provide an opportunity for the voluntary expression of religious belief. On the other hand, a law which provided for religious exercises during the school day and which contained no excusal provision would obviously be unconstitutionally coercive upon those who did not wish to participate. And even under a law containing an excusal provision, if the exercises were held during the school day, and no equally desirable alternative were provided by the school authorities, the likelihood that children might be under at least some psychological compulsion to participate would be great. In a case such as the latter, however, I think we would err if we assumed such coercion in the absence of any evidence.

Viewed in this light, it seems to me clear that the records in both of the cases before us are wholly inadequate to support an informed or responsible decision. Both cases involve provisions which explicitly permit any student who wishes, to be excused from participation in the exercises. There is no evidence in either case as to whether there would exist any coercion of any kind upon a student who did not want to participate. . . .

. . . It is conceivable that these school boards, or even all school boards, might eventually find it impossible to administer a system of religious exercises during school hours in such a way to meet this constitutional standard—in such a way as completely to free from any kind of official coercion those who do not affirmatively want to participate. But I think we must not assume that school boards so lack the qualities of inventiveness and good will as to make impossible the achievement of the goal.

I would remand both cases for further hearings.

SHERBERT v. VERNER

374 U.S. 398; 10 L. Ed. 2d 965; 83 S. Ct. 1790 (1963)

MR. JUSTICE BRENNAN *delivered the opinion of the Court.*

Appellant, a member of the Seventh-day Adventist Church, was discharged by her South Carolina employer because she would not work on Saturday, the Sabbath Day of her faith. When she was unable to obtain other employment because from conscientious scruples she would not take Saturday work, she filed a claim for unemployment compensation benefits under the South Carolina Unemployment Compensation Act. That law provides that, to be eligible for benefits, a claimant must be "able to work and . . . available for work"; and further, that a claimant is ineligible for benefits "[i] f . . . he has failed, without good cause . . . to accept available suitable work when offered him by the employment office or the employer. . . ." The appellee Employment Security Commission, in administrative proceedings under the statute, found that appellant's restriction upon her availability for Saturday work brought her within the provision disqualifying for benefits insured workers who fail, without good cause, to accept "suitable work when offered . . . by the employment office or the employer. . . ." The Commission's finding was sustained by the Court of Common Pleas for Spartanburg County. That court's judgment was in turn affirmed by the South Carolina Supreme Court, which rejected appellant's contention that, as applied to her, the disqualifying provisions of the South Carolina statute abridged her right to the free exercise of her religion secured under the Free Exercise Clause of the First Amendment through the Fourteenth Amendment. . . .

We turn first to the question whether the disqualification for benefits imposes any burden on the free exercise of appellant's religion. We think it is clear that it does. In a sense the consequences of such a disqualification to religious principles and practices may be only an indirect result of welfare legislation within the State's general competence to enact; it is true that no criminal sanctions directly compel appellant to work a six-day week. But this is only the beginning, not the end, of our inquiry. For "[i] f the purpose or effect of a law is to impede the observance of one or all religions or is to discriminate invidiously between religions, that law is constitutionally invalid even though the burden may be characterized as being only indirect." *Braunfeld* v. *Brown* (366 U.S. 607). Here not only is it apparent that appellant's declared ineligibility for benefits derives solely from the practice of her religion, but the pressure upon her to forego that practice is unmistakable. The ruling forces her to choose between following the precepts of her religion and forfeiting benefits, on the one hand, and abandoning one of the precepts of her religion in order to accept work, on the other hand. Governmental imposition of such a choice puts the same kind of burden upon the free exercise of religion as would a fine imposed against appellant for her Saturday worship.

Nor may the South Carolina court's construction of the statute be saved from constitutional infirmity on the ground that unemployment compensation benefits are not appellant's "right" but merely a "privilege." It is too late in the day to doubt that the liberties of religion and expression may be infringed by the denial of or placing of conditions upon a benefit or privilege. . . . In *Spieser* v. *Randall*, 357 U.S. 513, we emphasized that conditions upon public benefits cannot be sustained if they so operate, whatever their purpose, as to inhibit or deter the exercise of First Amendment freedoms. We there struck down a condition which limited the availability of a tax exemption to those members of the exempted class who affirmed their loyalty to the state government granting the exemption. While the State was surely under no obligation to afford such an exemption, we held that the imposition of such a condition upon even a gratuitous benefit inevitably deterred or discouraged the exercise of First Amendment rights of expression and thereby threatened to "produce a result which the State could not command directly." 357 U.S., at 526. "To deny an exemption to claimants who engage in certain forms of speech is in effect to penalize them for such speech." Id. 357 U.S., at 518. Likewise, to condition the availability of benefits upon this appellant's willingness to violate a cardinal principle of her religious faith effectively penalizes the free exercise of her constitutional liberties.

Significantly South Carolina expressly saves the Sunday worshipper from having to make the kind of choice which we here hold infringes the Sabbatarian's religious liberty. When in times of "national emergency" the textile plants are authorized by the State Commissioner of Labor to operate on Sunday, "no employee shall be required to work on Sunday . . . who is conscientiously opposed to Sunday work; and if any employee should refuse to work on Sunday on account of conscientious . . . objections he or she shall not jeopardize his or her seniority by such refusal or be discriminated against in any other manner." S.C. Code, par. 64–4. No question of the disqualification of a Sunday worshipper for benefits is likely to arise, since we cannot suppose that an employer will discharge him in violation of this statute. The unconstitutionality of the disqualification of the Sabbatarian is thus compounded by the religious discrimination which South Carolina's general statutory scheme necessarily effects.

We must next consider whether some compelling state interest enforced in the eligibility provisions of the South Carolina statute justifies the substantial infringement of appellant's First Amendment right. It is basic that no showing merely of a rational relationship to some colorable state interest would suffice; in this highly sensitive constitutional area, "[o]nly the gravest abuses, endangering paramount interests, give occasion for permissible limitation," *Thomas* v. *Collins*, 323 U.S. 516, 530. No such abuse or danger has been advanced in the present case. The appellees suggest no more than a possibility that the filing of fraudulent claims by unscrupulous claimants feigning religious objections to Saturday work might not only dilute the unemployment compensation fund but also hinder the scheduling by employers of necessary Saturday work. But that possibility is not apposite here because no such objection appears to have been made before the South Carolina Supreme Court, and we are unwilling to assess the importance of an asserted state interest without the views of the state court. Nor, if the contention had been made below, would the record appear to sustain it; there is no proof whatever to warrant such fears of malingering or deceit as those which the respondents now advance. . . . . For even if the possibility of spurious claims did threaten to dilute the fund and disrupt the scheduling of work, it would plainly be incumbent upon the appellees to demonstrate that no alternative forms of regulation would combat such abuses without infringing First Amendment rights. . . .

In these respects, then, the state interest asserted in the present case is wholly dissimilar to the interests which were found to justify the less direct burden upon religious practices in *Braunfeld* v. *Brown*. The Court recognized that the Sunday closing law which that decision sustained undoubtedly served "to make the practice of [the Orthodox Jewish merchants'] . . . religious beliefs more expensive," 366 U.S., at 605. But the statute was nevertheless saved by a countervailing factor which finds no equivalent in the instant case—a strong state interest in providing one uniform day of rest for all workers. That secular objective could be achieved, the Court found, only by declaring Sunday to be that day of rest. Requiring exemptions for Sabbatarians, while theoretically possible, appeared to present an administrative problem of such magnitude, or to afford the exempted class so great a competitive advantage, that such a requirement would have rendered the entire statutory scheme unworkable. In the present case no such justifications underlie the determination of the state court that appellant's religion makes her ineligible to receive benefits.

In holding as we do, plainly we are not fostering the "establishment" of the Seventh-day Adventist religion in South Carolina, for the extension of unemployment benefits to Sabbatarians in common with Sunday worshippers reflects nothing more than the governmental obligation of neutrality in the face of religious differences, and does not represent that involvement of religious with secular institutions which it is the object of the Establishment Clause to forestall. ... Nor does the recognition of the appellant's right to unemployment benefits under the state statute serve to abridge any other person's religious liberties. Nor do we, by our decision today, declare the existence of a constitutional right to unemployment benefits on the part of all persons whose religious convictions are the cause of their unemployment. ... Finally, nothing we say today constrains the States to adopt any particular form or scheme of unemployment compensation. Our holding today is only that South Carolina may not constitutionally apply the eligibility provisions so as to constrain a worker to abandon his religious convictions respecting the day of rest. This holding but reaffirms a principle that we announced a decade and a half ago, namely that no State may "exclude individual Catholics, Lutherans, Mohammedans, Baptists, Jews, Meth-odists, Non-believers, Presbyterians, or the members of any other faith, *because of their faith, or lack of it,* from receiving the benefits of public welfare legislation." ...

In view of the result we have reached under the First and Fourteenth Amendments' guarantee of free exercise of religion, we have no occasion to consider appellant's claim that the denial of benefits also deprived her of the equal protection of the laws in violation of the Fourteenth Amendment.

The judgment of the South Carolina Supreme Court is reversed and the case is remanded for further proceedings not inconsistent with this opinion.

It is so ordered.

MR. JUSTICE STEWART *wrote a concurring opinion which is not printed here.* MR. JUSTICE HARLAN, *whom* MR. JUSTICE WHITE *joins, dissenting.*

Today's decision is disturbing both in its rejection of existing precedent and in its implications for the future. The significance of the decision can best be understood after an examination of the state law applied in this case.

South Carolina's Unemployment Compensation Law was enacted in 1936 in response to the grave social and economic problems that arose during the depression of that period. As stated in the statute itself:

> Economic insecurity due to unemployment is a serious menace to health, morals and welfare of the people of this State; *involuntary unemployment* is therefore a subject of general interest and concern ... ; the achievement of social security requires protection against this greatest hazard of our economic life; this can be provided by encouraging the employers to *provide more stable employment and by the systematic accumulation of funds during periods of employment to provide benefits for periods of unemployment,*

thus maintaining purchasing power and limiting the serious social consequences of poor relief assistance. Sec. 68-38 (Emphasis added.)

Thus the purpose of the legislation was to tide people over, and to avoid social and economic chaos, during periods when *work was unavailable*. But at the same time there was clearly no intent to provide relief for those who for purely personal reasons were or became *unavailable for work*. In accordance with this design, the legislature provided, in Sec. 68–113, that "[a]n unemployed insured worker shall be eligible to receive benefits with respect to any week *only* if the Commission finds that . . . [h]e is able to work and is available for work. . . ." (Emphasis added.)

The South Carolina Supreme Court has uniformly applied this law in conformity with its clearly expressed purpose. It has consistently held that one is not "available for work" if his unemployment has resulted not from the inability of industry to provide a job but rather from personal circumstances, no matter how compelling. . . .

In the present case all that the state court has done is to apply these accepted principles. Since virtually all of the mills in the Spartanburg area were operating on a six-day week, the appellant was "unavailable for work," and thus ineligible for benefits, when personal considerations prevented her from accepting employment on a full-time basis in the industry and locality in which she had worked. The fact was wholly without relevance to the state court's application of the law. Thus in no proper sense can it be said that the State discriminated against the appellant on the basis of her religious beliefs or that she was denied benefits *because* she was a Seventh-day Adventist. She was denied benefits just as any other claimant would be denied benefits who was not "available for work" for personal reasons.

With this background, this Court's decision comes into clearer focus. What the Court is holding is that if the State chooses to condition unemployment compensation on the applicant's availability for work, it is constitutionally compelled to *carve out an exemption*—and to provide benefits—for those whose unavailability is due to their religious convictions. Such a holding has particular significance in two respects.

First, despite the Court's protestations to the contrary, the decision necessarily overrules *Braunfeld* v. *Brown* . . . which held that it did not offend the "Free Exercise" clause of the Constitution for a State to forbid a Sabbatarian to do business on Sunday. The secular purpose of the statute before us today is even clearer than that involved in *Braunfeld*. And just as in *Braunfeld*—where exceptions to the Sunday closing laws for Sabbatarians would have been inconsistent with the purpose to acheive a uniform day of rest and would have required case-by-case inquiry into religious beliefs—so here, an exception to the rules of eligibility based on religious convictions would necessitate judicial examination of those convictions and would be at odds with the limited purpose of the statute to smooth out the economy during periods of industrial instability . . . .

Second, the implications of the present decision are far more troublesome than its apparently narrow dimensions would indicate at first glance. The meaning of today's holding, as already noted, is that the State must furnish unemployment benefits to one who is unavailable for work if the unavailability stems from the exercise of religious convictions. The State, in other words, must *single out* for financial assistance those whose behavior is religiously motivated, even though it denies such assistance to others whose identical behavior (in this case, inability to work on Saturdays) is not religiously motivated.

It has been suggested that such singling out of religious conduct for special treatment may violate the constitutional limitations on state action. See Kurland, Of Church and State and the Supreme Court, 29 U of Chi L Rev 1. . . . My own view, however, is that at least under the circumstances of this case it would be a permissible accommodation of religion for the State, if it *chose* to do so, to create an exception to its eligibility requirements for persons like the appellant. The constitutional obligation of "neutrality" . . . is not so narrow a channel that the slightest deviation from an absolutely straight course leads to condemnation. There are too many instances in which no such course can be charted, too many areas in which the pervasive activities of the State justify some special provision for religion to prevent it from being submerged by an all-embracing secularism. . . . [T]here is, I believe, enough flexibility in the Constitution to permit a legislative judgment accommodating an unemployment compensation law to the exercise of religious beliefs such as appellant's.

For very much the same reasons, however, I cannot subscribe to the conclusion that the State is constitutionally *compelled* to carve out an exception to its general rule of eligibility in the present case. Those situations in which the Constitution may require special treatment on account of religion are, in my view, few and far between, and this view is amply supported by the course of constitutional litigation in this area. . . .

For these reasons I respectfully dissent from the opinion and judgment of the Court.

WELSH v. UNITED STATES
398 U.S. 333; 26L. Ed. 2d 308; 90 S. Ct. 1792 (1970)

MR. JUSTICE BLACK *announced the judgment of the Court and delivered an opinion in which* MR. JUSTICE DOUGLAS, MR. JUSTICE BRENNAN, *and* MR. JUSTICE MARSHALL *join.*

The petitioner, Elliott Ashton Welsh, II, was convicted by a United States district judge of refusing to submit to induction into the Armed Forces in violation of 50 U.S.C. App. § 462 (a) and was . . . sentenced to imprisonment for three years. One of petitioner's defenses to the prosecution was that § 6(j) of the Universal Military Training and Service Act exempted him from combat and noncombat service because he was "by reason of religious training and belief . . . conscientiously opposed to participation in war in any form." After finding that there was no religious basis for petitioner's conscientious objector claim, the Court of Appeals . . . affirmed the conviction. . . . We granted certiorari chiefly to review the contention that Welsh's conviction should be set aside on the basis of this Court's decision in *United States* v. *Seeger,* 380 U.S. 163 . . .

The controlling facts in this case are strikingly similar to those in *Seeger.* Both Seeger and Welsh were brought up in religious homes and attended church in their childhood, but in neither case was this church one which taught its members not to engage in war at any time for any reason. Neither Seeger nor Welsh continued his childhood religious ties into his young manhood, and neither belonged to any religious group or adhered to the teachings of any organized religion during the period of his involvement with the Selective Service System. At the time of their registration for the draft, neither had yet come to accept pacifist principles. Their views on war developed only in subsequent years, but when their ideas did fully mature both made application with their local draft boards for conscientious objector exemptions from military service under §

6(j) of the Universal Military Training and Service Act. That section then provided, in part:

> Nothing contained in this title shall be construed to require any person to be subject to combatant training and service in the armed forces of the United States who, by reason of religious training and belief, is conscientiously opposed to participation in war in any form. Religious training and belief in this connection means an individual's belief in a relation to a Supreme Being involving duties superior to those arising from any human relation, but does not include essentially political, sociological, or philosophical views or a merely personal moral code.

In filling out their exemption applications both Seeger and Welsh were unable to sign the statement which, as printed in the Selective Service form, stated "I am, by reason of my religious training and belief, conscientiously opposed to participation in war in any form." Seeger could sign only after striking the words "training and" and putting quotation marks around the word "religious." Welsh could sign only after striking the words "religious training and." On those same applications, neither could definitely affirm or deny that he believed in a "Supreme Being," both stating that they preferred to leave the question open. But both Seeger and Welsh affirmed on those applications that they held deep conscientious scruples against taking part in wars where people were killed. Both strongly believed that killing in war was wrong, unethical, and immoral, and their conscience forbade them to take part in such an evil practice. Their objection to participating in war in any form could not be said to come from a "still, soft voice of conscience"; rather, for them that voice was so loud and insistent that both men preferred to go to jail rather than serve in the Armed Forces. There was never any question about the sincerity and depth of Seeger's convictions as a conscientious objector, and the same is true of Welsh. In this regard the Court of Appeals noted, "[t]he government concedes that (Welsh's) beliefs are held with the strength of more traditional religious convictions." . . . But in both cases the Selective Service System concluded that the beliefs of these men were in some sense insufficiently "religious" to qualify them for conscientious objector exemptions under the terms of § 6(j). Seeger's conscientious objector claim was denied "solely because it was not based upon a 'belief in a relation to a Supreme Being' as required by § 6(j) of the Act" . . . , while Welsh was denied the exemption because his Appeal Board and the Department of Justice hearing officer "could find no religious basis for the registrant's belief, opinions, and convictions." Both Seeger and Welsh subsequently refused to submit to induction into the military and both were convicted of that offense.

In *Seeger* the Court was confronted, first, with the problem that § 6(j) defined "religious training and belief" in terms of a "belief in a relation to a Supreme Being . . . ," a definition which arguably gave a preference to those who believed in a conventional God as opposed to those who did not. Noting the "vast panoply of beliefs" prevalent in our country, the Court construed the congressional intent as being in "keeping with its long-established policy of not picking and choosing among religious beliefs," and accordingly interpreted "the meaning of religious training and belief so as to embrace *all* religions . . . ." But, having decided that all religious conscientious objectors were entitled to the exemption, we faced the more serious problem of determining which beliefs were "religious" within the meaning of the statute. This question was particularly difficult in the case of Seeger himself. Seeger stated that his was a "belief in the devotion to goodness and virtue for their own sakes, and a religious faith in a purely ethical creed." . . . In a letter to his draft board, he wrote:

> My decision arises from what I believe to be considerations of validity from the standpoint

of the welfare of humanity and the preservation of the democratic values which we in the United States are struggling to maintain. I have concluded that war, from the practical standpoint, is futile and self-defeating, and that from the more important moral standpoint, it is unethical. 326 F.2d 846, 848 (2 Cir. 1964).

On the basis of these and similar assertions, the Government argued that Seeger's conscientious objection to war was not "religious" but stemmed from "essentially political, sociological, or philosophical views or a merely personal moral code."

In resolving the question whether Seeger and the other registrants in that case qualified for the exemption, the Court stated that "(the) task is to decide whether the beliefs professed by a registrant are sincerely held and whether they are, *in his own scheme of things,* religious" .... The Court's principal statement of its test for determining whether a conscientious objector's beliefs are religious within the meaning of § 6(j) was as follows:

> The test might be stated in these words: A sincere and meaningful belief which occupies in the life of its possessor a place parallel to that filled by the God of those admittedly qualifying for the exemption comes within the statutory definition.

The Court made it clear that these sincere and meaningful beliefs which prompt the registrant's objection to all wars need not be confined in either source or content to traditional or parochial concepts of religion. It held that § 6(j) "does not distinguish between externally and internally derived beliefs," and also held that "intensely personal" convictions which some might find "incomprehensible" or "incorrect" come within the meaning of "religious belief" in the Act. . . .

In [*Welsh*] the Government seeks to distinguish our holding in *Seeger* on basically two grounds, both of which were relied upon by the Court of Appeals in affirming Welsh's conviction. First, it is stressed that Welsh was far more insistent and explicit than Seeger in denying that his views were religious. For example, in filling out their conscientious objector applications, Seeger put quotation marks around the word "religious," but Welsh struck the word "religious" entirely and later characterized his beliefs as having been formed "by reading in the fields of history and sociology." The Court of Appeals found that Welsh had "denied that his objection to war was premised on religious belief" and concluded that "the Appeal Board was entitled to take him at his word." We think this attempt to distinguish *Seeger* fails for the reason that it places undue emphasis on the registrant's interpretation of his own beliefs. The Court's statement in *Seeger* that a registrant's characterization of his own belief as "religious" should carry great weight does not imply that his declaration that his views are nonreligious should be treated similarly. When a registrant states that his objections to war are "religious," that information is highly relevant to the question of the function his beliefs have in his life. But very few registrants are fully aware of the broad scope of the word "religious" as used in § 6(j), and accordingly a registrant's statement that his beliefs are nonreligious is a highly unreliable guide for those charged with administering the exemption. Welsh himself presents a case in point. Although he originally characterized his beliefs as nonreligious, he later upon reflection wrote a long and thoughtful letter to his Appeal Board in which he declared that his beliefs were "certainly religious in the ethical sense of that word." . . .

The Government also seeks to distinguish *Seeger* on the ground that Welsh's views, unlike Seeger's, were "essentially political, sociological, or philosophical or a merely personal moral code." As previously noted, the Government made the same argument about Seeger, and not without reason, for Seeger's views had a substantial political dimension. In this case, Welsh's conscientious objection to war was undeniably based in part on his perception of world politics. In a letter to his local board, he wrote:

> I can only act according to what I am and what I see. And I see that the military complex wastes both human and material resources, that it fosters disregard for (what I consider a paramount concern) human needs and ends; I see that the means we employ to "defend" our "way of life" profoundly change that way of life. I see that in our failure to recognize the political, social, and economic realities of the world, we, *as a nation,* fail our responsibility *as a nation.*

We certainly do not think that § 6(j)'s exclusion of those persons with "essentially political, sociological, or philosophical views or a merely personal moral code" should be read to exclude those who hold strong beliefs about our domestic and foreign affairs or even those whose conscientious objection to participation in all wars is founded to a substantial extent upon considerations of public policy. The two groups of registrants which obviously do fall within these exclusions from the exemption are those whose beliefs are not deeply held and those whose objection to war does not rest at all upon moral, ethical, or religious principle but instead rests solely upon considerations of policy, pragmatism, or expediency. In applying § 6(j)'s exclusion of those whose views are "essentially political, etc.," it should be remembered that these exclusions are definitional and do not therefore restrict the category of persons who are conscientious objectors "by religious training and belief." Once the Selective Service System has taken the first step and determined under the standards set out here and in *Seeger* that the registrant is a "religious" conscientious objector, it follows that his views cannot be "essentially political, sociological or philosophical." Nor can they be a "merely personal moral code." . . .

The judgment is reversed.

MR. JUSTICE BLACKMUN *took no part in the consideration or decision of this case.*

MR. JUSTICE HARLAN, *concurring in the result.*

Candor requires me to say that I joined the Court's opinion in *Seeger* v. *United States* . . . only with the gravest misgivings as to whether it was a legitimate exercise in statutory construction, and today's decision convinces me that in doing so I made a mistake that I should now acknowledge.

In Seeger the Court construed § 6(j) of the Selective Service Act so as to sustain a conscientious objector claim not founded on the theistic belief. . . . Today the Court makes explicit its total elimination of the statutorily required religious content for a conscientious objector exemption. The Court now says: "If an individual deeply and sincerely holds beliefs which are *purely ethical* or *moral* in source and content but which nevertheless impose on him a duty of conscience to refrain from participating in any war at any time [emphasis added]," he qualifies for a § 6(j) exemption.

In my opinion, the liberties taken with the statute both in *Seeger* and today's decision cannot be justified in the name of the familiar doctrine of construing federal statutes in a manner that will avoid possible constitutional infirmities in them. There are limits to the permissible application of that doctrine, and . . . those limits were crossed in *Seeger*, and even more apparently have been exceeded in the present case. I therefore find myself unable to escape facing the constitutional issue that this case squarely presents: whether § 6(j) in limiting this draft exemption to those opposed to war in general because of theistic beliefs runs afoul of the religious clauses of the First Amendment. . . . I believe it does, and on that basis I concur in the Court's judgment reversing this conviction. . . .

The issue is . . . whether Welsh's opposition to

war is "founded on religious training and belief" and hence "belief in a relation to a Supreme Being" as Congress used those words. It is of course true that certain words are more plastic in meaning than others. "Supreme Being" is a concept of theology and philosophy, not a technical term, and consequently may be, in some circumstances, capable of bearing a contemporary construction as notions of theology and philosophy evolve.... This language appears, however, in a congressional statute; it is not a phrase of the Constitution, like "religion" or "speech," that which this Court is freer to construe in light of evolving needs and circumstances.... Nor is it so broad a statutory directive, like that of the Sherman Act, that we may assume that we are free to adopt and shape policies limited only by the most general statement of purpose.... It is Congress' will that must here be divined. In that endeavor it is one thing to give words a meaning not necessarily envisioned by Congress so as to adapt them to circumstances also uncontemplated by the legislature in order to achieve the legislative policy, ... it is a wholly different matter to define words so as to change policy. The limits of this Court's mandate to stretch concededly elastic congressional language are fixed in all cases by the context of its usage and legislative history, if available, that are the best guides to congressional *purpose* and the lengths to which Congress enacted a policy....

The natural reading of § 6(j), which quite evidently draws a distinction between theistic and nontheistic religions, is the only one that is consistent with the legislative history....

[Here follows an analysis of the legislative history of section 6(j) and lower court interpretation to Seeger.]

Against this legislative history it is a remarkable feat of judicial surgery to remove, as did Seeger, the theistic requirement of § 6(j). The Court today, however, in the name of interpreting the will of Congress, has performed a lobotomy and completely transformed the sta-

tute by reading out of it any distinction between religious acquired beliefs and those deriving from "essentially political, sociological, or philosophical views or a merely personal moral code." ...

Of the five pertinent definitions [in Webster's New International Dictionary, Unabridged, 2d ed., 1934], four include the notion of either a Supreme Being or a cohesive, organized group pursuing a common spiritual purpose together. While, as the Court's opinion in *Seeger* points out, these definitions do not exhaust the almost infinite and sophisticated possibilities for defining "religion," there is strong evidence that Congress restricted, in this instance, the word to its conventional sense....

When the plain thrust of a legislative enactment can only be circumvented by distortion to avert an inevitable constitutional collision, it is only by exalting form over substance that one can justify this veering off the path that has been plainly marked by the statute. Such a course betrays extreme skepticism as to constitutionality, and, in this instance, reflects a groping to preserve the conscientious objector exemption at all cost.

I cannot subscribe to a wholly emasculated construction of a statute to avoid facing a latent constitutional question, in purported fidelity to the salutary doctrine of avoiding unnecessary resolution of constitutional issues, a principle to which I fully adhere.... It is, of course, desirable to salvage by construction legislative enactments whenever there is good reason to believe that Congress did not intend to legislate consequences that are unconstitutional, but it is not permissible, in my judgment, to take a lateral step that robs legislation of all meaning in order to avert the collision between its plainly intended purpose and the commands of the Constitution....

The constitutional question that must be faced in this case is whether a statute that defers to the individual's conscience only when his views emanate from adherence to theistic religious beliefs is within the power of Congress. Congress, of course, could, entirely consistently with the requirements of the Constitution, eliminate *all* exemptions for conscientious objectors. Such a course would be wholly "neutral" and, in my views, would not offend the Free Exercise Clause.... However, having chosen to exempt, it cannot draw the line between theistic or non-theistic religious beliefs on the one hand and secular beliefs on the other. Any such distinctions are not, in my view, compatible with the Establishment Clause of the First Amendment....

The "radius" of this legislation is the conscientiousness with which an individual opposes war in general, yet the statute, as I think it must be construed, excludes from its "circumference" individuals motivated by teachings of non-theistic religions, and individuals guided by an inner ethical voice that bespeaks secular and not "religious" reflection. It not only accords a preference to the "religious" but disadvantages adherents of religions that do not worship a Supreme Being. The constitutional infirmity cannot be cured, moreover, even by an impermissible construction that eliminates the theistic requirement and simply draws the line between religious and nonreligious. This in my view offends the Establishment Clause and is that kind of classification that this Court has condemned.

When a policy has roots so deeply embedded in history, there is a compelling reason for a court to hazard the necessary statutory repairs if they can be made within the administrative framework of the statute and without impairing other legislative goals, even though they entail, not simply eliminating an offending section but rather building upon it. Thus I am prepared to accept the Court's conscientious objector test, not as a reflection of congressional statutory intent but as patchwork of judicial making that cures the defect of underinclusion in § 6(j) and can be administered by local boards in the usual course of business. Like the Court, I also conclude that petitioner's beliefs are held with

the required intensity and consequently vote to reverse the judgment of conviction.

MR. JUSTICE WHITE, *with whom* THE CHIEF JUSTICE *and* MR. JUSTICE STEWART *join, dissenting.*

Whether or not *Seeger* v. *United States* ... accurately reflected the intent of Congress in providing draft exemptions for religious conscientious objectors to war, I cannot join today's construction of § 6(j) extending draft exemption to those who disclaim religious objections to war and whose views about war represent a purely personal code arising not from religious training and belief as the statute requires but from readings in philosophy, history, and sociology. Our obligation in statutory construction cases is to enforce the will of Congress, not our own; and as Mr. Justice Harlan has demonstrated, construing § 6(j) to include Welsh exempts from the draft a class of persons to whom Congress has expressly denied an exemption.

For me that conclusion should end this case. Even if Welsh is quite right in asserting that exempting religious believers is an establishment of religion forbidden by the First Amendment, he nevertheless remains one of those persons whom Congress took pains not to relieve from military duty. Whether or not § 6(j) is constitutional, Welsh had no First Amendment excuse for refusing to report for induction. If it is contrary to the express will of Congress to exempt Welsh, as I think it is, then there is no warrant for saving the religious exemption and the statute by redrafting it in this Court to include Welsh and all others like him. ...

If I am wrong in thinking that Welsh cannot benefit from invalidation of § 6(j) on Establishment Clause grounds, I would nevertheless affirm his conviction; for I cannot hold that Congress violated the Clause in exempting from the draft all those who oppose war by reason of religious training and belief. In exempting religious conscientious objectors, Congress was making one of two judgments, perhaps both. First, § 6(j) may represent a purely practical judgment that religious objectors, however admirable, would be of no more use in combat than many others unqualified for military service. Exemption was not extended to them to further religious belief or practice but to limit military service to those who were prepared to undertake the fighting which the armed services have to do. On this basis, the exemption has neither the primary purpose nor the effect of furthering religion. . . .

Second, Congress may have granted the exemption because otherwise religious objectors would be forced into conduct which their religions forbid and because in the view of Congress to deny the exemption would violate the Free Exercise Clause or at least raise grave problems in this respect. True, this Court has more than once stated its unwillingness to construe the First Amendment, standing alone, as requiring draft exemptions for religious believers. . . . But this Court is not alone in being obliged to construe the Constitution in the course of its work; nor does it even approach having a monopoly on the wisdom and insight appropriate to the task. Legislative exemptions for those with religious convictions against war date from colonial days. . . . However this Court might construe the First Amendment, Congress has regularly steered clear of free exercise problems by granting exemptions to those who conscientiously oppose war on religious grounds. . . .

On the assumption, however, that the Free Exercise Clause of the First Amendment does not by its own force require exemption of devout objectors from military service, it does not follow that § 6(j) is a law respecting an establishment of religion within the meaning of the First Amendment. It is very likely that § 6(j) is a recognition by Congress of free exercise values and its view of desirable or required policy in implementing the Free Exercise Clause. That judgment is entitled to respect. . . .

The Establishment Clause as construed by this Court unquestionably has independent significance; its function is not wholly auxiliary to the Free Exercise Clause. It bans some involvements of the State with religion which otherwise might be consistent with the Free Exercise Clause. But when in the rationally based judgment of Congress free exercise of religion calls for shielding religious objectors from compulsory combat duty, I am reluctant to frustrate the legislative will by striking down the statutory exemption because it does not also reach those to whom the Free Exercise Clause offers no protection whatsoever.

I would affirm the judgment below.

WALZ v. TAX COMMISSION OF CITY OF NEW YORK

397 U.S. 664; 25 L. Ed. 2d 697; 90 S. Ct. 1409 (1970)

MR. CHIEF JUSTICE BURGER *delivered the opinion of the Court.*

Appellant, owner of real estate in Richmond County, New York, sought an injunction in the New York courts to prevent the New York City Tax Commission from granting property tax exemptions to religious organizations for religious properties used solely for religious worship. The exemption from state taxes is authorized by . . . the New York Constitution. . . .

The essence of appellant's contention was that the New York State Tax Commission's grant of an exemption to church property indirectly requires the appellant to make a contribution to religious bodies and thereby violates provisions prohibiting establishment of religion under the First Amendment which under the Fourteenth Amendment is binding on the States.

Appellee's motion for summary judgment was granted and the Appellate Division, New York Supreme Court, and the New York Court of Appeals affirmed. We . . . affirm. . . .

Prior opinions of this Court have discussed the development and historical background of the First Amendment in detail. . . . It would therefore serve no useful purpose to review in detail the background of the Establishment and Free Exercise Clauses of the First Amendment or to restate what the Court's opinions have reflected over the years.

[At the outset, it] is sufficient to note that for the men who wrote the Religious Clauses of the First Amendment the "establishment" of a religion connoted sponsorship, financial support, and active involvement of the sovereign in religious activity. . . .

The Establishment and Free Exercise Clauses of the First Amendment are not the most precisely drawn portions of the Constitution. The sweep of the absolute prohibitions in the Religion Clauses may have been calculated; but the purpose was to state an objective not to write a statute. In attempting to articulate the scope of the two Religious Clauses, the Court's opinions reflect the limitations inherent in formulating general principles on a case-by-case basis. The considerable internal inconsistency in the opinions of the Court derives from what, in retrospect, may have been too sweeping utterances on aspects of these clauses that seemed clear in relation to the particular cases but have limited meaning as general principles.

The Court has struggled to find a neutral course between the two Religion Clauses, both of which are cast in absolute terms, and either of which, if expanded to a logical extreme, would tend to clash with the other. . . .

The course of constitutional neutrality in this area cannot be an absolutely straight line; rigidity could well defeat the basic purpose of these provisions, which is to insure that no religion be sponsored or favored, none commanded, and none inhibited. The general principle deducible from the First Amendment and all that has been said by the Court is this: that we will not tolerate either governmentally established religion or governmental interference with religion. Short of those expressly proscribed governmental acts there is room for play in the joints productive of a benevolent neutrality which will permit religious exercise to exist without sponsorship and without interference.

Each value judgment under the Religion Clauses must therefore turn on whether particular acts in question are intended to establish or interfere with religious beliefs and practices or have the effect of doing so. Adherence to the policy of neutrality that derives from an accommodation of the Establishment and Free Exercise Clauses has prevented the kind of involvement that would tip the balance toward government control of churches or governmental restraint on religious practice.

Adherents of particular faiths and individual churches frequently take strong positions on public issues including, as this case reveals in the several briefs *amici,* vigorous advocacy of legal or constitutional positions. Of course, churches as much as secular bodies and private citizens have that right. No perfect or absolute separation is really possible; the very existence of the Religion Clauses is an involvement of sorts—one which seeks to mark boundaries to avoid excessive entanglement. . . .

In *Everson* the Court declined to construe the religion clauses with a literalness that would undermine the ultimate constitutional objective as illuminated by history. Surely, bus transportation and police protection to pupils who receive religious instruction "aid" that particular religion to maintain schools that plainly tend to assure future adherents to a particular faith by having control of their total education at an early age. No religious body that maintains schools would deny this as an affirmative if not dominant policy of church schools. But if as in *Everson* buses can be provided to carry and policemen to protect church school pupils, we fail to see how a broader range of police and fire protection given equally to all churches along with nonprofit hospitals, art galleries, and libraries receiving the same tax exemption, is different for purposes of the religion clauses.

Similarly, making textbooks available to pupils in parochial schools in common with public schools was surely an "aid" to the sponsoring churches because it relieved those churches of an enormous aggregate cost for those books. Supplying of costly teaching materials was not seen either as manifesting a legislative purpose to aid or as having a primary effect of aid contravening the First Amendment. . . .

With all the risks inherent in programs that bring about administrative relationships between public education bodies and church-sponsored schools, we have been able to chart a course that preserved the autonomy and freedom of religious bodies while avoiding any semblance of established religion. This is a "tight rope" and one we have successfully traversed.

The legislative purpose of a property tax exemption is neither the advancement nor the inhibition of religion; it is neither sponsorship nor hostility. New York, in common with the other States, has determined that certain entities that exist in a harmonious relationship to the community at large, and that foster its "moral or mental improvement," should not be inhibited in their activities by property taxation or the hazard of loss of those properties for non-payment of taxes. It has not singled out one particular church or religious group or even churches as such; rather, it has granted exemption to all houses of religious worship within a broad class of property owned by non-profit, quasi-public corporations which include hospitals, libraries, playgrounds, scientific, professional, historical and patriotic groups. The State has an affirmative policy that considers these groups as beneficial and stabilizing influences in community life and finds this classification useful, desirable, and in the public interest. Qualification for tax exemption is not perpetual or immutable; some tax-exempt groups lose that status when their activities take them outside the classification and new entities can come into being and qualify for exemption.

Governments have not always been tolerant of religious activity, and hostility toward religion has taken many shapes and forms—economic, political, and sometimes harshly oppressive. Grants of exemption historically reflect the concern of authors of constitutions and statutes as to the latent dangers inherent in the imposition of property taxes; exemption constitutes a reasonable and balanced attempt to guard against those dangers. The limits of permissible state accommodation to religion are by no means co-extensive with the noninterference mandated by the Free Exercise Clause. To equate the two would be to deny a national heritage with roots in the Revolution itself. . . . We cannot read New York's statute as attempting to establish religion; it is simply sparing the exercise of religion from the burden of property taxation levied on private profit institutions.

We find it unnecessary to justify the tax exemption on the social welfare services or "good works" that some churches perform for parishioners and others—family counselling, aid to the elderly and the infirm, and to children. Churches vary substantially in the scope of such services; programs expand or contract according to resources and need. As public-sponsored programs enlarge, private aid from the church sector may diminish. The extent of social services may vary, depending on whether the church serves an urban or rural, a rich or poor constituency. To give emphasis to so variable an aspect of the work of religious bodies would introduce an element of governmental evaluation and standards as to the worth of particular social welfare programs, thus producing a kind of continuing day-to-day relationship which the policy of neutrality seeks to minimize. . . .

Determining that the legislative purpose of tax exemption is not aimed at establishing, sponsoring, or supporting religion does not end the inquiry, however. We must also be sure that the end result—the effect—is not an excessive government entanglement with religion. The test is inescapably one of degree. Either course, taxation of churches or exemption, occasions some degree of involvement with religion. Elimination of exemption would tend to expand the involvement of government by giving rise to tax valuation of church property, tax liens, tax foreclosures, and the direct confrontations and conflicts that follow in the train of those legal processes.

Granting tax exemptions to churches necessarily operates to afford an indirect economic benefit and also gives rise to some, but yet a lesser, involvement than taxing them. In analyzing either alternative the questions are whether the involvement is excessive, and whether it is a continuing one calling for official and continuing surveillance leading to an impermissible degree of entanglement. Obviously a direct money subsidy would be a relationship pregnant with involvement and, as with most governmental grant programs, could encompass sustained and detailed administrative relationships for enforcement of statutory or administrative standards, but that is not this case. . . .

The grant of a tax exemption is not sponsorship since the government does not transfer part of its revenue to churches but simply abstains from demanding that the church support the state. No one has ever suggested that tax exemption has converted libraries, art galleries, or hospitals into arms of the state or employees "on the public payroll." There is no genuine nexus between tax exemption and establishment of religion. . . . . The exemption creates only a minimal and remote involvement between church and state and far less than taxation of churches. It restricts the fiscal relationship between church and state, and tends to complement and reinforce the desired separation insulating each from the other.

Separation in this context cannot mean absence of all contact; the complexities of modern life inevitably produce some contact and the fire and police protection received by houses of religious worship are no more than incidental benefits accorded all persons or institutions within a State's boundaries, along with many other exempt organizations. The appellant has not established even an arguable quantitative correlation between the payment of an ad valorem property tax and the receipt of these municipal benefits.

All of the 50 States provide for tax exemption of places of worship, most of them doing so by constitutional guarantees. For so long as federal income taxes have had any potential impact on churches—over 75 years—religious organizations have been expressly exempt from the tax. Such treatment is an "aid" to churches no more and no less in principle than the real estate tax exemption granted by States. Few concepts are more deeply embedded in the fabric of our national life, beginning with pre-Revolutionary colonial times, than for the government to exercise at the very least this kind of benevolent neutrality toward churches and religious exercise generally so long as none was favored over others and none suffered interference. . . .

Nothing in this national attitude toward religious tolerance and two centuries of uninterrupted freedom from taxation has given the remotest sign of leading to an established church or religion and on the contrary it has operated affirmatively to help guarantee the free exercise of all forms of religious beliefs. Thus, it is hardly useful to suggest that tax exemption is but the "foot in the door" or the "nose of the camel in the tent" leading to an established church. If tax exemption can be seen as this first step toward "establishment" of religion, as Mr. Justice Douglas fears, the second step has been long in coming. Any move which realistically "establishes" a church or tends to do so can be dealt with "while this Court sits." . . .

Affirmed.

[*The concurring opinions of* MR. JUSTICE BRENNAN *and* MR. JUSTICE HARLAN *are not reprinted here.*]

MR. JUSTICE DOUGLAS, *dissenting.*

. . . The question in the case . . . is whether believers—organized in church groups—can be made exempt from real estate taxes, merely because they are believers, while non-believers, whether organized or not, must pay the real estate taxes.

My Brother Harlan says he "would suppose" that the tax exemption extends to "groups whose avowed tenets may be antitheological, atheistic and agnostic." . . . If it does, then the line between believers and nonbelievers has not been drawn. But, with all respect, there is not even a suggestion in the present record that the statute covers property used exclusively by organizations for "antitheological purposes," "atheistic purposes" or "agnostic purposes."

In *Torcaso* v. *Watkins,* 367 U.S. 488, . . . we held that a State could not bar an atheist from public office in light of the freedom of belief and religion guaranteed by the First and Fourteenth Amendments. Neither the State nor the Federal Government, we said, "can constitutionally pass laws or impose requirements which aid all religions as against non-believers, and neither can aid those religions based on a belief in the existence of God as against those religions founded on different beliefs." . . .

That principle should govern this case.

There is a line between what a State may do in encouraging "religious" activities . . . and what a State may not do by using its resources to promote "religious" activities . . . or bestowing benefits because of them. Yet that line may not always be clear. Closing public schools on Sunday is in the former category; subsidizing churches, in my view, is in the latter. Indeed I would suppose that in common understanding one of the best ways to "establish" one or more religions is to subsidize them, which a tax exemption does. . . .

In affirming this judgment the Court largely overlooks the revolution initiated by the adoption of the Fourteenth Amendment. That revolution involved the imposition of new and far-reaching constitutional restraints on the States. Nationalization of many civil liberties has been the consequence of the Fourteenth Amendment, reversing the historic position that the foundations of those liberties rested largely in state law. . . .

Hence the question in the present case makes irrelevant the "two centuries of uninterrupted freedom from taxation," referred to by the Court. . . . If history be our guide, then tax exemption of church property in this country is indeed highly suspect, as it arose in the early days when the church was an agency of the state. . . . The question here, though, concerns the meaning of the Establishment Clause and the Free Exercise Clause made applicable to the States for only a few decades at best.

With all due respect the governing principle is not controlled by *Everson* v. *Board of Education, supra*. . . .

This case . . . is quite different. Education is not involved. The financial support rendered here is to the church, the place of worship. A tax exemption is a subsidy. Is my Brother Brennan correct in saying that we would hold that state or federal grants to churches, say, to construct the edifice itself would be unconstitutional? What is the difference between that kind of subsidy and the present subsidy? . . .

State aid to places of worship, whether in the form of direct grants, or tax exemption, takes us back to the *Assessment Bill* and the *Remonstrance.* The church *qua* church would not be entitled to that support from believers and from nonbelievers alike. Yet the church *qua* nonprofit, charitable institution is one of many that receives a form of subsidy through tax exemption. To be sure, the New York statute does not single out the church for grant or favor. It includes churches in a long list of nonprofit organizations. . . . While the beneficiaries cover a wide range, "atheistic," "agnostic," or "anti-theological" groups do not seem to be included. . . .

If believers are entitled to public financial support, so are non-believers. A believer and nonbeliever under the present law are treated differently because of the articles of their faith. Believers are doubtless comforted that the cause of religion is being fostered by this legislation Yet one of the mandates of the First Amendment is to promote a viable, pluralistic society and to keep government neutral, not only between sects but between believers and non-believers. The present involvement of government in religion may seem *de mimimis.* But it is, I fear, a long step down the Establishment path. Perhaps I have been misinformed. But as I have read the Constituiton and its philosophy, I gathered that independence was the price of liberty.

I conclude that this tax exemption is unconstitutional.

COMMITTEE FOR PUBLIC EDUCATION AND RELIGIOUS LIBERTY v. NYQUIST

413 U.S. 756; 37 L. Ed. 2d 948; 93 S.Ct. 2993 (1973)

MR. JUSTICE POWELL *delivered the opinion of the Court.*

This case raises a challenge under the Establishment Clause of the First Amendment to the constitutionality of a recently enacted New York law which provides financial assistance, in several ways, to nonpublic elementary and secondary schools in that state. The case involves an intertwining of societal and constitutional issues of the greatest importance. . . .

The first section of the challenged enact- entitled "Health and Safety Grants for Nonpublic School Children," provides for direct money grants from the State to "qualifying" nonpublic schools to be used for the "maintenance and repair of . . . school facilities and equipment to ensure the health, welfare and safety of enrolled pupils." A "qualifying" school is any nonpublic, nonprofit elementary or secondary school which "has been designated during the [immediately preceding] year as serving a high concentration of pupils from low-income families for purposes of Title IV of the Federal Higher Education Act of 1965. . . . Such schools are entitled to receive a grant of $30 per pupil per year, or $40 per pupil per year if the facilities are more than 25 years old. Each school is required to submit to the Commissioner of Education an audited statement of its expenditures for maintenance and repair during the preceding year. . . .

"Maintenance and repair" is defined by the statute to include "the provision of heat, light, water, ventilation and sanitary facilities, cleaning, janitorial and custodial services; snow removal; necessary upkeep and renovation of buildings, grounds and equipment; fire and accident protection; and such other items as the commissioner may deem necessary to ensure the health, welfare and safety of enrolled pupils." . . .

The remainder of the challenged legislation sections 2 through 5—is a single package captioned the "Elementary and Secondary Education Opportunity Program." It is composed, essentially, of two parts, a tuition grant program and a tax benefit program. Section 2 establishes a limited plan providing tuition reimbursements to parents of children attending elementary or secondary nonpublic schools. To qualify under this section the parent must have an annual taxable income of less than $5,000. The amount of reimbursement is limited to $50 for each grade-school child and $100 for each high-school child. Each parent is required, however, to submit to the Commissioner of Education a verified statement containing a receipted tuition bill, and the amount of state reimbursement may not exceed 50 percent of that figure. No restrictions are imposed on the use of the funds by the reimbursed parents. . . .

The remainder of the "Elementary and Secondary Education Opportunity Program," contained in sections 3, 4, and 5 of the challenged law, is designed to provide a form of tax relief to those who fail to qualify for tuition reimbursement. Under these sections parents may subtract from their adjusted gross income for state income tax purposes a designated amount for each dependent for whom they have paid at least $50 in nonpublic school tuition. If the taxpayer's adjusted gross income is less than $9,000 he may subtract $1,000 for each of as many as three dependents. As the taxpayer's income rises, the amount he may subtract diminishes. Thus, if a taxpayer has adjusted gross income of $15,000 he may subtract only $400 per dependent, and if his income in $25,000 or more, no deduction is allowed. The amount of the deduction is not dependent upon how much the taxpayer actually paid for nonpublic school tuition, and is given in addition to any deductions to which the taxpayer may be entitled for other religious or charitable contributions. . . .

Plaintiffs argued below that because of the substantially religious character of the intended beneficiaries, each of the State's three enactments offended the Establishment Clause. The District Court, in an opinion carefully canvassing this Court's recent precedents, held unanimously that section 1 (maintenance and repair grants) and section 2 (tuition reimbursement grants) were invalid. As to the income tax provisions of sections 3, 4 and 5, however, a majority of the District Court, over the dissent of Circuit Judge Hays, held that the Establishment Clause had not been violated. Finding the provisions of the law severable, it enjoined permanently any further implementation of sections 1 and 2 but declared the remainder of the law independently enforceable. . . . . We affirm the District Court insofar as it struck down sections 1 and 2 and reverse its determination regarding sections 3, 4, and 5.

The history of the Establishment Clause has been recounted frequently and need not be repeated here. . . .

Most of the cases coming to this Court raising Establishment Clause questions have involved the relationship between religion and education. Among these religion-education precedents, two general categories of cases may be identified: those dealing with religious activities within the public schools, and those involving public aid in varying forms to sectarian educational institutions. While the New York legislation places this case in the latter category, its resolution requires consideration not only of the several aid-to-sec-

tarian-education cases but also of our other education precedents and of several important non-education cases. For the now well defined three-part test that has emerged from our decisions is a product of considerations derived from the full sweep of the Establishment Clause cases. Taken together these decisions dictate that to pass muster under the Establishment Clause the law in question, first, must reflect a clearly secular legislative purpose, . . . second, must have a primary effect that neither advances not inhibits religion, . . . and, third, must avoid excessive government entanglement with religion. . .

In applying these criteria to the three distinct forms of aid involved in this case, we need touch only briefly on the requirement of a "secular legislative purpose." As the recitation of legislative purposes appended to New York's law indicates, each measure is adequately supported by legitimate, nonsectarian state interests. We do not question the propriety, and fully secular content, of New York's interest in preserving a healthy and safe educational environment for all of its school children. And we do not doubt— indeed, we fully recognize—the validity of the State's interests in promoting pluralism and diversity among its public and nonpublic schools. Nor do we hesitate to acknowledge the reality of its concern for an already overburdened public school system that might suffer in the event that a significant percentage of children presently attending nonpublic schools should abandon those schools in favor of the public schools.

But the propriety of a legislature's purposes may not immunize from further scrutiny a law which either has a primary effect that advances religion, or which fosters excessive entanglements between Church and State. Accordingly, we must weigh each of the three aid provisions challenged here against these criteria of effect and entanglement.

The "maintenance and repair" provisions of section 1 authorize direct payments to nonpublic schools, virtually all of which are Roman Catholic schools in low income areas. . . . So long as expenditures do not exceed 50 percent of comparable expenses in the public school system, it is possible for a sectarian elementary or secondary school to finance its entire "maintenance and repair" budget from state tax-raised funds. No attempt is made to restrict payments to those expenditures related to the upkeep of facilities used exclusively for secular purposes, nor do we think it possible within the context of these religion-oriented institutions to impose such restrictions. Nothing in the statute, for instance, bars a qualifying school from paying out of state funds the salary of employees who maintain the school chapel, or the cost of renovating classrooms in which religion is taught, or the cost of heating and lighting those same facilities. Absent appropriate restrictions on expenditures for these and similar purposes, it simply cannot be denied that this section has a primary effect that advances religion in that it subsidizes directly the religious activities of sectarian elementary and secondary schools.

The state officials nevertheless argue that these expenditures for "maintenance and repair" are similar to other financial expenditures approved by this Court. Primarily they rely on *Everson* v. *Board of Education, Board of Education* v. *Allen*, and *Tilton* v. *Richardson*. . . . In each of those cases it is true that the Court approved a form of financial assistance which conferred undeniable benefits upon private, sectarian schools. But a close examination of those cases illuminates their distinguishing characteristics. . . .

These cases simply recognize that sectarian schools perform secular, educative functions as well as religious functions, and that some forms of aid may be channelled to the secular without providing direct aid to the sectarian. But the channel is a narrow one, as the above cases illustrate. Of course it is true in each case that the provision of such neutral, nonideological aid, assisting only the secular functions of sectarian schools, served indirectly and incidentally to promote the religious function by rendering it

more likely that children would attend sectarian schools and by freeing the budgets of those schools for use in other nonsecular areas. But an indirect and incidental effect beneficial to religious institutions has never been thought a sufficient defect to warrant the invalidation of a state law. . . .

. . . New York's maintenance and repair provisions violate the Establishment Clause because their effect, inevitably, is to subsidize and advance the religious mission of sectarian schools. We have no occasion, therefore, to consider the further question whether those provisions as presently written would also fail to survive scrutiny under the administrative entanglement aspect of the three-part test because assuring the secular use of all funds requires too intrusive and continuing a relationship between Church and State. . . .

New York's tuition reimbursement program also fails the "effect" test, for much the same reasons that govern its maintenance and repair grants. The state program is designed to allow direct, unrestricted grants of $50 to $100 per child (but no more than 50 percent of tuition actually paid) as reimbursement to parents in low-income brackets who send their children to nonpublic schools. To qualify, a parent must have earned less than $5,000 in taxable income and must present a receipted tuition bill from a nonpublic school, the bulk of which are concededly sectarian in orientation.

There can be no question that these grants could not, consistently with the Establishment Clause, be given directly to sectarian schools, since they would suffer from the same deficiency that renders invalid the grants for maintenance and repair. In the absence of an effective means of guaranteeing that the state aid derived from public funds will be used exclusively for secular, neutral, and nonideological purposes, it is clear from our cases that direct aid in whatever form is invalid. . . . The controlling question here, then, is whether the fact that the grants are delivered to parents rather than schools is of such significance as to compel a contrary result. The State and intervenor-appellees rely on *Everson* and *Allen* for their claim that grants to parents, unlike grants to institutions, respect the "wall of separation" required by the Constitution. It is true that in those cases the Court upheld laws that provided benefits to children attending religious schools and to their parents.... [I]n *Everson* parents were reimbursed for bus fares paid to send children to parochial schools, and in *Allen* textbooks were loaned directly to the children. But those decisions make clear that, far from providing a *per se* immunity from examination of the substance of the State's program, the fact that aid is disbursed to parents rather than to the schools is only one among many factors to be considered....

[In] the tuition grants here... [t]here has been no endeavor "to guarantee the separation between secular and religious educational functions and to ensure that State financial aid supports only the former." ... Indeed, it is precisely the function of New York's law to provide assistance to private schools, the great majority of which are sectarian. By reimbursing parents for a portion of their tuition bill, the State seeks to relieve their financial burdens sufficiently to assure that they continue to have the option to send their children to religion-oriented schools. And while the other purposes for that aid—to perpetuate a pluralistic educational environment and to protect the fiscal integrity of over-burdened public schools—are certainly unexceptionable, the effect of the aid is unmistakably to provide desired financial support for nonpublic, sectarian institutions....

Although we think it clear, for the reasons above stated, that New York's tuition grant program fares no better under the "effect" test than its maintenance and repair program, in view of the novelty of the question we will address briefly the subsidiary arguments made by the state officials and intervenors in its defense.

First, it has been suggested that it is of controlling significance that New York's program calls for *reimbursement* for tuition already paid rather than for direct contributions which are merely routed through the parents to the schools, in advance of or in lieu of payment by the parents. The parent is not a mere conduit, we are told, but is absolutely free to spend the money he receives in any manner he wishes. There is no element of coercion attached to the reimbursement, and no assurance that the money will eventually end up in the hands of religious schools. The absence of any element of coercion is irrelevant to questions arising under the Establishment Clause.... [I]f the grants are offered as an incentive to parents to send their children to sectarian schools by making unrestricted cash payments to them, the Establishment Clause is violated whether or not the actual dollars given eventually find their way into the sectarian institutions. Whether the grant is labeled a reimbursement, a reward or a subsidy, its substantive impact is still the same....

Second, [appellees] argue that it is significant here that the tuition reimbursement grants pay only a portion of the tuition bill, and an even smaller portion of the religious school's total expenses.... Additionally... appellee reasons that the "maximum tuition reimbursement by the State is ... only 15 percent of the educational costs in the nonpublic schools." And, "since compulsory education laws of the State, by necessity require significantly more than 15 percent of school time to be devoted to teaching secular courses," the New York statute provides "a statistical guarantee of neutrality." It should readily be seen that this is simply another variant of the argument we have rejected as to maintenance and repair costs, and it can fare no better here. Obviously, if accepted, this argument would provide the foundation for massive direct subsidization of sectarian elementary and secondary schools. Our cases, however, have long since foreclosed the notion that mere statistical assurances will suffice to sail between the Scylla and Charybdis of "effect" and "entanglement."

Finally, the State argues that its program of

tuition grants should survive scrutiny because it is designed to promote the free exercise of religion. The State notes that only "low-income parents" are aided by this law, and without state assistance their right to have their children educated in a religious environment "is diminished or even denied." It is true, of course, that this Court has long recognized and maintained the right to choose nonpublic over public education. *Pierce* v. *Society of Sisters,* 268 U.S. 510 (1925). It is also true that a state law interfering with a parent's right to have his child educated in a sectarian school would run afoul of the Free Exercise Clause. But this Court repeatedly has recognized that tension inevitably exists between the Free Exercise and the Establishment Clauses, . . . and that it may often not be possible to promote the former without offending the latter. As a result of this tension, our cases require the State to maintain an attitude of "neutrality," neither "advancing" nor "inhibiting" religion. In its attempt to enhance the opportunities of the poor to choose between public and nonpublic education, the State has taken a step which can only be regarded as one "advancing" religion. However great our sympathy . . . for the burdens experienced by those who must pay public school taxes at the same time that they support other schools because of the constraints of "conscience and discipline," . . . and notwithstanding the "high social importance" of the State's purposes, . . . neither may justify an eroding of the limitations of the Establishment Clause now firmly emplanted.

Sections 3, 4, and 5 establish a system for providing income tax benefits to parents of children attending New York's nonpublic schools. In this Court, the parties have engaged in a considerable debate over what label best fits the New York law. Appellants insist that the law is, in effect, one establishing a system of tax "credits." The State and the intervenors reject that characterization and would label it, instead, a system of income tax "modification." The Solicitor General, in an *amicus curiae* brief filed

in this Court, has referred throughout to the New York law as one authorizing tax "deductions." The District Court majority found that the aid was "in effect a tax *credit.*" 350 F. Supp., at 672 (emphasis in original). Because of the peculiar nature of the benefit allowed, it is difficult to adopt any single traditional label lifted from the law of income taxation. It is, at least in its form, a tax deduction since it is an amount subtracted from adjusted gross income, prior to computation of the tax due. Its effect, as the District Court concluded, is more like that of a tax credit since the deduction is not related to the amount actually spent for tuition and is apparently designed to yield a predetermined amount of tax "forgiveness" in exchange for performing a specific act which the State desires to encourage—the usual attribute of a tax credit. We see no reason to select one label over the other, as the constitutionality of this hybrid benefit does not turn in any event on the label we accord it. . . .

In practical terms there would appear to be little difference, for purposes of determining whether such aid has the effect of advancing religion, between the tax benefit allowed here and the tuition grant allowed under section 2. The qualifying parent under either program receives the same form of encouragement and reward for sending his children to nonpublic schools. The only difference is that one parent receives an actual cash payment while the other is allowed to reduce by an arbitrary amount the sum he would otherwise be obliged to pay over to the State. . . .

Appellees defend the tax portion of New York's legislative package on two grounds. First, they contend that it is of controlling significance that the grants or credits are directed to the schools. This is the same argument made in support of the tuition reimbursements and rests on the same reading of the same precedents of this Court, primarily *Everson* and *Allen.* Our treatment of this issue . . . , *supra,* is applicable here and requires rejection of this claim. Second, appellees place their strongest reliance on *Walz* v.

Tax Commission, supra, in which New York's property tax exemption for religious organizations was upheld. We think that *Walz* provides no support for appellees' position. Indeed, its rationale plainly compels the conclusion that New York's tax package violates the Establishment Clause. . . .

We find the *Walz* analogy unpersuasive, and in light of the practical similarity between New York's tax and tuition reimbursement programs, we hold that neither form of aid is sufficiently restricted to assure that it will not have the impermissible effect of advancing the sectarian activities of religious schools.

Because we have found that the challenged sections have the impermissible effect of advancing religion, we need not consider whether such aid would result in entanglement of the State with religion in the sense of "[a] comprehensive, discriminating, and continuing state surveillance." *Lemon* v. *Kurtzman,* 403 U.S. at 619. But the importance of the competing societal interests implicated in this case prompts us to make the further observation that, apart from any specific entanglement of the State in particular religious programs, assistance of the sort here involved carries grave potential for entanglement in the broader sense of continuing political strife over aid to religion.

Few would question most of the legislative findings supporting this statute. We recognized in *Board of Education* v. *Allen,* 392 U.S., at 247, that "private education has played and is playing a significant and valuable role in raising levels of knowledge, competency, and experience," and certainly private parochial schools have contributed importantly to this role. Moreover, the tailoring of the New York statute to channel the aid provided primarily to afford low-income families the option of determining where their children are to be educated is most appealing. There is no doubt that the private schools are confronted with increasingly grave fiscal problems, that resolving these problems by increasing tuition charges forces parents to turn to the

public schools, and that this in turn—as the present legislation recognizes—exacerbates the problems of public education at the same time that it weakens support for the parochial schools.

These, in briefest summary, are the underlying reasons for the New York legislation and for similar legislation in other States. They are substantial reasons. Yet they must be weighed against the relevant provisions and purposes of the First Amendment, which safeguard the separation of Church from State and which have been regarded from the beginning as among the most cherished features of our constitutional system.

One factor of recurring significance in this weighing process is the potentially divisive political effect of an aid program. As Mr. Justice Black's opinion in *Everson* v. *Board of Education, supra,* emphasizes, competition among religious sects for political and religious supremacy has occasioned considerable civil strife, "generated in large part" by competing efforts to gain or maintain the support of government. As Mr. Justice Harlan put it, "[w]hat is at stake as a matter of policy in Establishment Clause cases is preventing that kind and degree of government involvement in religious life that, as history teaches us, is apt to lead to strife and frequently strain a political system to the breaking point." *Walz* v. *Tax Commission,* 397 U.S., at 694 (concurring opinion). . . .

It is so ordered.

MR. CHIEF JUSTICE BURGER, *joined in part by* MR. JUSTICE WHITE, *and joined by* MR. JUSTICE REHNQUIST, *concurring in part and dissenting in part.*

I join in that part of the Court's opinion . . . which hold[s] the New York "maintenance and repair" provision unconstitutional under the Establishment Clause because it is a direct aid to religion. I disagree, however, with the Court's decisions in *Nyquist* and in *Sloan* v. *Lemon* to strike down the New York and Pennsylvania tuition grant programs and the New York tax relief provisions. I believe the Court's decisions on those statutory provisions ignore the teachings of *Everson* v. *Board of Education* . . . and *Board of Education* v. *Allen* . . . and fail to observe what I thought the Court had held in *Walz* v. *Tax Comm'n.* . . . I therefore dissent as to those aspects of the two holdings.

While there is no straight line running through our decisions interpreting the Establishment and Free Exercise clauses of the First Amendment, our cases do, it seems to me, lay down one solid, basic principle: that the Establishment Clause does not forbid governments, state or federal, from enacting a program of general welfare under which benefits are distributed to private individuals, even though many of those individuals may elect to use those benefits in ways that "aid" religious instruction or worship. . . .

The tuition grant and tax relief programs now before us are, in my view, indistinguishable in principle, purpose and effect from the statutes in *Everson* and *Allen*. In the instant cases, as in *Everson* and *Allen*, the States have merely attempted to equalize the costs incurred by parents in obtaining an education for their children. The only discernible difference between the programs in *Everson* and *Allen* and these cases is in the method of the distribution of benefits: here the particular benefits of the Pennsylvania and New York statutes are given only to parents of private school children, while in *Everson* and *Allen* the statutory benefits were made available to parents of both public and private school children. But to regard that difference as constitutionally meaningful is to exalt form over substance. It is beyond dispute that the parents of public school children in New York and Pennsylvania presently receive the "benefit" of having their children educated totally at state expense; the statutes enacted in those States and at issue here merely attempt to equalize that "benefit" by giving to parents of private school children, in the form of dollars or

tax deductions, what the parents of public school children receive in kind. It is no more than simple equity to grant partial relief to parents who support the public schools they do not use. . . .

Since I am unable to discern in the Court's analysis of *Everson* and *Allen* any neutral principle to explain the result reached in these cases, I fear that the Court has in reality followed the unsupportable approach of measuring the "effect" of a law by the percentage of the recipients who choose to use the money for religious, rather than secular, education. Indeed, in discussing the New York tax credit provisions, the Court's opinion argues that "the tax reductions authorized by this law flow primarily to the parents of children attending sectarian, nonpublic schools." While the opinion refrains from "intimating whether this factor alone might have controlling significance in another context in some future case," similar references to this factor elsewhere in the Court's opinion suggest that it has been given considerable weight. Thus, the Court observes as to the New York tuition grant program: "indeed, it is precisely the function of New York's law to provide assistance to private schools, *the great majority of which are sectarian.* . . ."

Such a consideration, it is true, might be relevant in ascertaining whether the *primary legislative purpose* was to advance the cause of religion. But the Court has, and I think correctly, summarily dismissed the contention that either New York or Pennsylvania had an improper purpose in enacting these laws. The Court fully recognizes that the legislatures of New York and Pennsylvania have a legitimate interest in "promoting pluralism and diversity among. . . public and nonpublic schools," . . . in assisting those who reduce the State's expenses in providing public education, and in protecting the already overburdened public school system against a massive influx of private school children. And in light of this Court's recognition of these secular legislative purposes, I fail to see any acceptable resolution to these cases except one favoring constitutionality.

I would therefore uphold these New York and Pennsylvania statutes. However sincere our collective protestations of the debt owed by the public generally to the parochial school systems, the wholesome diversity they engender will not survive on expressions of good will. . . .

SELECTED REFERENCES

Carroll, William A., "The Constitution, the Supreme Court, and Religion," 61 *The American Political Science Review* 657 (1967).

Choper, Jesse H., "Establishment Clause and Aid to Parochial Schools," 56 *California Law Review* 260 (1968).

"Conscientious Objection: the End of the Road," 22 *South Carolina Law Review* 822 (1970).

Fifner, W. R., "Parochiaid and Prayer: A Perplexing Problem," 21 *Cleveland State Law Review* 74 (1972).

Finer, J. J., "Psychedelics and Religious Freedom," 19 *Hastings Law Journal* 667 (1968).

"Free Exercise and the Police Power-Current Developments," 43 *Notre Dame Lawyer* 764 (1968).

Gianella, Donald A., "Lemon and Tilton: The Bitter and Sweet of Church-State Entanglement," 1971 *Supreme Court Review* 147 (1971).

_____, "Religious Liberty, Nonestablishment, and Doctrinal Development," 80 *Harvard Law Review* 1381 (1967).

Griffiths, William E., *Religion, the Courts, and the Public School: A Century of Litigation* (Cincinnati: The W. H. Anderson Co., 1966).

Hochstadt, Theodore, "The Right to Exemption from Military Service of a Conscientious Objector to a Particular War," 3 *Harvard Civil Rights-Civil Liberties Review* 1 (1967).

La Noue, George R., "Child Benefit Theory Revisited: Textbooks, Transportation and Medical Care," 13 *Journal of Public Law* 76 (1964).

Morgan, Richard E., *The Politics of Religious Conflict* (New York: Pegasus, 1968).

Oteri, Joseph, Mitchell Benjoia, and Jonathan Souweine, "Abortion and the Religious Liberty Clauses," 7 *Harvard Civil Rights-Civil Liberties Review* 559 (May, 1972).

Strong, George A., "Liberty, Religion and Flouridation," 8 *Santa Clara Lawyer* 37 (1967).

Taylor, T. R., "Nine Rulings: Three Wins, Three Losses, and Three Remands on Government Aid to Church-Related Institutions," 17 *Catholic Law* 182 (1971).

Winter, Ralph E., "Crumbling Wall: Public Aid to Schools Operated by Churches Increases Despite Foes," 176 *Wall Street Journal* (1970).

3 Freedom of Expression, Assembly, and Association

Feiner v. *New York*   *Edwards* v. *South Carolina*   *NAACP* v. *Alabama*
Lloyd Corporation v. *Tanner*   *United States* v. *O'Brien*   *New York Times* v. *Sullivan*
Miller v. *California*

Speech, press, assembly, and association represent rights that go to the heart of the democratic process. For without these guarantees that process becomes hollow. That process must ensure free exchange of ideas, ensure minorities the opportunity to challenge the majority and its prevailing policies with full opportunity to change those policies and the majority itself. This constant sifting and winnowing process—with constantly shifting majorities and minorities—is premised upon preserving and protecting the First Amendment rights of all of us. To put the matter starkly, this means that to keep the democratic process open and functioning, those we hate must be as fully protected in the exercise of their rights to free speech, press, assembly, and association as those we like. Even in periods of relative calm this is not an easy proposition. And given periods of great controversies, such as those involving civil rights and the Vietnam War—when the pressure on these constitutional rights is severe—the proposition becomes even more difficult to uphold. This applies to those who espouse unpopular causes, who participate in mass demonstrations and parades, who picket, who distribute literature that some think is obscene. Here is where First Amendment guarantees have met and are likely to meet some of their most critical tests. Substantial state interests, such as the preservation of peace and order, invariably collide with paramount constitutional interests, viz. free speech, assembly, and association. The intensity of the civil rights and antiwar movements, coupled with the equally intense determination of law enforcement officials and others to maintain "law and order," has exacerbated the problem.

Moreover, another group of Americans—university and college students—in the last two decades has used ideas and muscle to gain more student power, more freedoms, more relevant curricula and experiences, and more changes in academia. Student activists—seasoned by civil-rights struggles and antiwar drives—have resorted to similar tactics such as demonstrations and sit-ins to achieve these goals. But faculty and administrators, governing boards, state legislatures, and others have resisted this attempted power grab or at the least have rejected what they termed "coercive and disruptive actions" as the proper way to bring about change in the academic community. In any case, it is arguable that such conflicts—be they in or outside the halls of ivy—involve the exercise of First Amendment guarantees, such as freedom of speech and assembly. When these constitutional rights hang in the balance, sooner or later the courts—and ultimately the U.S. Supreme Court—become the arenas for resolving (or accommodating) the disputes. Let us take a look at what the courts, especially the U.S. Supreme Court, have done in these areas.

SOME JUDICIAL GUIDELINES

Although the First Amendment guarantees are couched as absolutes, the Supreme Court has never interpreted them without limitations. The Court has long since tried to distinguish between speech that is protected by the Constitution and speech that is not. In doing so, the Court has developed several tests or doctrines to serve as guidelines. Though judges rather than "tests or doctrines" decide cases that come before them, a brief look at these "tests or doctrines" might help explain how the Court has gone about the difficult task of safeguarding First Amendment freedoms in the face of substantial societal interests, such as the preservation of peace and order.

Perhaps the first test to be adopted by the Court was the "clear-and-present-danger" test. "The question in every case," said Justice Holmes for a unanimous Court in *Schenck* v. *United States* (249 U.S. 47, 1919), "is whether the words used are used in such circumstances and are of such a nature as to create a clear and present danger that they will bring about the substantive evils that Congress has a right to prevent." Though destined to become a sort of "libertarian" test (see *Bridges* v. *California* 314 U.S. 252, 1941), its early effect was to restrict rather than broaden the scope of First Amendment freedoms.[1] Since it was formulated, however, the test has traveled a rather rocky road. This, of course, illustrates the fact that judges rather than doctrines decide cases.

Another judicial guideline used in dealing with free expression problems is the "preferred position" doctrine. Those who adhere to this doctrine believe that the First Amendment freedoms are so important to the democratic process that they occupy—or should occupy—a preferred position in our constitutional hierarchy. Hence, legislation restricting First Amendment freedoms is presumed to be unconstitutional, and courts bear a heavy responsibility to scrutinize such

[1] For the development and early application of clear and present danger, *see* Chapter 4.

legislation with care. While having roots in several cases in the late 1930s and early 40s, perhaps the first clear statement of the preferred position doctrine which commanded support of the Court majority occurred in *Thomas* v. *Collins* (323 U.S. 516, 1945) in which Justice Rutledge, speaking for the majority, stated:

> The case confronts us again with the duty our system places on this Court to say where the individual's freedom ends and the State's power begins. Choice on that border, now as always delicate, is perhaps more so where the usual presumption supporting legislation is balanced by the preferred place given in our scheme to the great, the indispensable democratic freedoms secured by the First Amendment. . . . That priority gives these liberties a sanctity and a sanction not permitting dubious intrusions. And it is the character of the right, not of the limitation, which determines what standard governs the choice. . . .
>
> For these reasons any attempt to restrict those liberties must be justified by clear public interest, threatened not doubtfully or remotely, but by clear and present danger. The rational connection between the remedy provided and the evil to be curbed, which in other contexts might support legislation against attack on due process grounds, will not suffice. These rights rest on firmer foundation. Accordingly, whatever occasion would restrain orderly discussion and persuasion, at appropriate time and place, must have clear support in public danger, actual or impending. Only the gravest abuses, endangering paramount interests, give occasion for permissible limitation.

The "preferred position" doctrine, thus stated, could be considered as an extension of the clear-and-present-danger doctrine to its outermost limits. In fact, of all the doctrines used by the court, it comes closest to an absolutist position with regard to First Amendment freedoms.

"Legislative reasonableness" or "bad tendency" has been the guideline used by the Court in some free speech cases, most notably in *Gitlow* v. *New York, supra.* Here, in effect, was the reasonable man theory, so widely applied in the economic field, now being applied to First Amendment freedoms. This doctrine or test gives great deference to the *legislative* determination that certain kinds of speech have a tendency to lead to substantive evils and therefore do not enjoy constitutional protection. In upholding a New York statute prohibiting certain kinds of utterances, the Court said:

> By enacting the present statute the State has determined, through its legislative body, that utterances advocating the overthrow of organized government by force, violence and unlawful means, are so inimical to the general welfare and involve such danger of substantive evil that they may be penalized in the exercise of its police power. That determination must be given great weight. Every presumption is to be indulged in favor of the validity of the statute. . . . And the case is to be considered "in the light of the principle that the State is primarily the judge of regulations required in the interest of public safety and welfare"; and that its police "statutes may only be declared unconstitutional where they are arbitrary or unreasonable attempts to exercise

authority vested in the State in the public interest." . . . That utterances inciting to the overthrow of organized government by unlawful means present a sufficient danger of substantive evil to bring their punishment within the range of legislative discretion is clear. Such utterances, by their very nature, involve danger to the public peace and to the security of the State. They threaten breaches of the peace and ultimate revolution. And the immediate danger is none the less real and substantial, because the effect of a given utterance cannot be accurately foreseen. The State cannot reasonably be required to measure the danger from every such utterance in the nice balance of a jeweler's scale. A single revolutionary spark may kindle a fire that, smouldering for a time, may burst into a sweeping and destructive conflagration. It cannot be said that the State is acting arbitrarily or unreasonably when in the exercise of its judgment as to the measures necessary to protect the public peace and safety, it seeks to extinguish the spark without waiting until it has enkindled the flame or blazed into the conflagration. It cannot reasonably be required to defer the adoption of measures for its own peace and safety until the revolutionary utterances lead to actual disturbances of the public peace or imminent and immediate danger of its own destruction; but it may, in the exercise of its judgment, suppress the threatened danger in its incipiency.

. . . We cannot hold that the present statute is an arbitrary or unreasonable exercise of the police power of the State unwarrantably infringing the freedom of speech or press; and we must and do sustain its constitutionality.

The effect of *Gitlow* was the adoption of the earlier standard of judicial review, the reasonable-man test, brought it into conflict with the emerging clear-and-present-danger test. The latter gives the judiciary great latitude in determining whether the circumstances warrant restrictions on First Amendment freedoms while the former limits the judiciary to deciding whether a reasonable man could have reached the legistative conclusion that the statute was necessary to prevent substantive evils.

In general, the Court has steadfastly held to the view that the First Amendment forbids *prior restraint* on the exercise of those freedoms. Government cannot prevent a speech or publication *before* the act takes place but can take such action as might be appropriate *after* the act. For example, in *Near* v. *Minnesota* (283 U.S. 697, 1931) the Court declared unconstitutional a state statute that allowed a newspaper to be enjoined from future publication on the ground that it constituted a "public nuisance" by engaging "in the business of regularly and customarily producing . . . a malicious, scandalous and defamatory newspaper, magazine or other periodical. . . ." The paper enjoined was a Minneapolis weekly, *The Saturday Press*, which had directed charges against law enforcement officers including the chief of police, county attorney, and mayor. In effect the paper charged these officials were allowing a "Jewish gangster" to control illegal operations—gambling, bootlegging, racketeering—and were not "energetically performing their duties." Some, principally the chief of police, were charged with "gross neglect of duty, illicit relations with gangsters, and with participation in graft." But by a 5—4 decision, the Court thought the statute authorizing an injunction was an unconstitutional prior restraint on freedom of the press as protected by the First and Fourteenth Amendments. Chief Justice Hughes, speaking for the Court, found that the statute was directed not against publication of scandalous and defamatory statements about private citizens but at the continued publication of such matters against public officials. Moreover, the statute operated not only to suppress the offending publication but to put the publisher under effective censorship as well. The Court found this to be the essence of censorship, which is inconsistent with the constitutional guarantee of liberty of the press. The extent of that constitutional guarantee has been generally, if not universally, considered, said Hughes, to "prevent previous restraints upon publication." He quoted Blackstone with approval: "The liberty of the press is indeed essential to the nature of a free state; but this consists in laying no *previous* [italics theirs] restraints upon publications." Hughes said that "for whatever wrong the appellant has committed or may commit, by his publications, the state appropriately affords both public and private redress by its libel laws." However, the Chief Justice said that the protection against previous restraint is not "absolutely unlimited." "But," he contended, "the limitation has been recognized only in exceptional cases." The Chief Justice said:

> No one would question but that a government might prevent actual obstruction to its recruiting service or the publication of the sailing dates of transports or the number and location of troops. On similar grounds, the primary requirements of decency may be enforced against obscene publications. The security of the community life may be protected against incitements to acts of violence and the overthrow by force of orderly government. . . . These limitations are not applicable here.

In dissent, Justice Butler made two major points. First, he said that the statute did not constitute prior restraint within the proper meaning of that phrase since "it does not authorize administrative control in advance such as was formerly exercised by the licensers and censors, but prescribes a remedy to be enforced by a suit in equity." Moreover, Butler felt that the state was not "powerless to restrain by injunction the business of publishing and circulating among the people malicious, scandalous, and defamatory periodicals that in due course of judicial procedure have been adjudged to be a public nuisance." Butler concluded:

> The doctrine that measures such as the one before us are invalid because they operate as previous restraints to infringe freedom of press exposes the peace and good order of every community and the business and private affairs of every individual to the constant and protracted false and malicious assaults of any insolvent publisher who may have purpose and sufficient capacity to contrive and put into effect a scheme or program for oppression, blackmail or extortion.

Judges weigh a variety of factors in making their decisions. However, when some judges, such as Justices Frankfurter and Harlan, began to articulate the weighing of interests in particular cases, the "balancing doctrine" began to take on a more special meaning. Those who espouse the "balancing doctrine" reject the notion that the First Amendment should be read in absolute terms—that those freedoms should stand on a higher plane or be preferred more than other constitutional freedoms. They view the judge's responsibility regarding the protection of First Amendment freedoms as no more or no less than that in any other area. Justice Frankfurter's concurring opinion in *Dennis* v. *United States* provides a good example of the "balancing doctrine" in operation.[2]

Justices Black and Douglas have been highly critical of "balancing" away First Amendment freedoms. As Black said in his dissent in *Barenblatt* v. *United States* (see Chapter 4, *infra*), applying the balancing test is like reading the First Amendment to say "Congress shall pass no law abridging freedom of speech, press, assembly, and petition unless Congress and the Supreme Court reach the joint conclusion that on balance the interests of the Government in stifling these freedoms is greater than the interest of the people in having them exercised." Instead, when it comes to expression, they have urged an absolutist-literalist view. Justice Black explained the doctrine in *Smith* v. *California, infra,* when he said:

> I read "no law abridging" to mean *no law abridging*. The First Amendment, which is the supreme law of the land, has thus fixed its own value on freedom of speech and press by putting these freedoms wholly "beyond the reach of *federal* power to abridge. No other provision of the Constitution purports to dilute the scope of these unequivocal commands of the First Amendment. Consequently, I do not believe that any federal agencies, including Congress and this Court, have power or authority to subordinate speech and press to what they think are "more important interests." (Italics in original.)

SPEECHMAKING, SOLICITATIONS, AND DEMONSTRATIONS

The street corner speaker, the demonstrator, the distributor of handbills, the labor organizer who solicits members, and the man who uses the sound amplifier are all exercising what they consider their First Amendment freedoms. But sometimes these activities run counter to some state law or local ordinance designed to preserve peace and order or some other societal value. The crucial question then becomes how and under what conditions may a state control speechmaking, solicitation, or demonstrations in public places such as streets and parks.

Permit systems have been one way that state and local governments have attempted to cope with this problem. In *Hague* v. *CIO* (307 U.S. 496, 1939), the Court declared unconstitutional a Jersey City ordinance that prohibited public parades or public assemblies "in or upon the public streets, highways, public parks, or public buildings" without first securing a permit from the director of public safety. Here Jersey City, under Mayor Hague, was preventing members of the CIO from distributing materials and holding a meeting to discuss the National Labor Relations Act. The ordinance enabled the Director of Safety "to refuse a permit on

[2] See Chapter 4. Consider also Justice Harlan's opinions in *Barenblatt* v. *United States* and *NAACP* v. *Alabama, infra.*

his mere opinion that such refusal will prevent riots, disturbances or disorderly assemblage." By investing such uncontrolled authority in the Director of Public Safety, said Justice Roberts, the ordinance can "be made the instrument of arbitrary suppression of free expression of views on national affairs, for the prohibition of all speaking will undoubtedly 'prevent' such eventualities."

It was in *Hague* that Justice Roberts made what has now become a classic comment on the use of public streets and parks for speechmaking, soliciting, and assembly:

> Wherever the title of streets and parks may rest, they have immemorially been held in trust for the use of the public and, time out of mind, have been used for purposes of assembly, communicating thoughts between citizens, and discussing public questions. Such use of the streets and public places has, from ancient times, been a part of the privileges, immunities, rights, and liberties of citizens. The privilege of a citizen of the United States to use the streets and parks for communication of views on national questions may be regulated in the interest of all; it is not absolute, but relative, and must be exercised in subordination to the general comfort and convenience, and in consonance with peace and good order; but it must not, in the guise of regulation, be abridged or denied.

Though there was no majority opinion in *Hague* (some of the majority Justices acted on the due process clause, others on privileges and immunities), it was generally assumed in later decisions that the public had a basic constitutional right to use the streets and parks and other public places in the exercise of First Amendment freedoms subject to reasonable state regulations such as protecting public safety. In *Cox* v. *New Hampshire* (312 U.S. 529, 1941), the Court unanimously upheld convictions of Jehovah's Witnesses who marched along downtown streets of Manchester without first securing a special permit (license) as required by state statute for "parades or processions" on public streets. Here the Court found that the statute as construed by the state supreme court provided for reasonable and non-discriminatory regulations with respect to the use of streets. Chief Justice Charles Evans Hughes, who delivered the opinion of the Court, defined further the problem of maintaining public order vis-à-vis the exercise of civil liberties. The Chief Justice said:

> Civil liberties, as guaranteed by the Constitution, imply the existence of an organized society maintaining public order without which liberty itself would be lost in the excesses of unrestrained abuses. The authority of a municipality to impose regulations in order to assure the safety and convenience of the people in the use of public highways has never been regarded as inconsistent with civil liberties but rather as one of the means of safeguarding the good order upon which they ultimately depend. The control of travel on the streets of cities is the most familiar illustration of the recognition of social need. Where a restriction of the use of highways in that relation is designed to promote the public convenience in the interest of all, it cannot be disregarded by the attempted

exercise of some civil rights which in other circumstances would be entitled to protection. One would not be justified in ignoring the familiar red traffic light because he thought it his religious duty to disobey the municipal command or sought by that means to direct public attention to an announcement of his opinions. As regulation of the use of the streets for parades and processions is a traditional exercise of control by local government, the question in a particular case is whether that control is exerted so as not to deny or unwarrantedly abridge the right of assembly and the opportunities for communication of thought and the discussion of public questions immemorially associated with resort to public places. . . .

In *Thomas* v. *Collins* (323 U.S. 516, 1945) the Court declared unconstitutional a Texas statute which forbade the solicitation of members for labor unions without first obtaining an organizer's card from the Secretary of State. The majority considered the registration device an interference with free speech and assembly because of the conditions imposed before these First Amendment freedoms could be exercised. Justice Rutledge, who spoke for the majority, said:

> If the exercise of the rights of free speech and free assembly cannot be made a crime, we do not think this can be accomplished by the device of requiring previous registration as a condition for exercising them and making such a condition the foundation for restraining in advance their exercise and for imposing a penalty for violating such a restraining order. So long as no more is involved than exercise of the rights of free speech and assembly, it is immune to such a restriction. We think a requirement that one must register before he undertakes to make a public speech is quite incompatible with the requirements of the First Amendment.

During the 1950s the Court continued its close scrutiny of permit and licensing systems. In *Niemotko* v. *Maryland* (34 U.S. 268, 1951), for example, there was no statute or ordinance requiring a permit to use public parks and there were no established standards for granting permits. There was, however, a "custom" that required those desiring to use parks to first obtain permits from the Park Commissioner. In accordance with this practice, Jehovah's Witnesses requested and were refused permission by the commissioner and the city council to use a public park for Bible talks. But the Witnesses used the park anyway and were arrested and convicted of disorderly conduct. However, there was no evidence of disorder; "on the contrary, there was positive testimony by police that each of the appellants had conducted himself beyond reproach." Here the Court was faced with a situation where there was "no ordinance or statute regulating or prohibiting the use of the park; all that is here is an amorphous 'practice' whereby all authority to grant permits . . . is in the Park Commissioner and the City Council." There were no standards; "no narrowly drawn limitations; no circumscribing of this absolute power; and no substantial interests of the community to be served." Moreover, there was evidence that other groups had in the past sought and received permission to use public parks. Under such circumstances, the Court found the practice of obtaining permits a *prior restraint* on the exercise of First Amendment freedoms, and "the completely arbitrary and discriminatory refusal to grant the permits was a denial of equal protection."

Likewise in *Staub* v. *Baxley* (355 U.S. 313, 1958) the Court held a city ordinance unconstitutional on its face as a prior restraint on freedom of speech. Here the ordinance made it unlawful to " 'solicit' citizens of the City (Baxley, Georgia) to become members of any 'organization, union or society' which requires fees or dues from its members without first applying for and receiving from the Mayor and Council a 'permit.' " (A labor union organizer was convicted of violating the ordinance in the instant case.) In determining whether to grant the permit the mayor and city council were to consider "the character of the applicant, the nature of the organization and its effect upon the general welfare." Similarly, in *Cantwell* v. *Connecticut, supra,* and *Kunz* v. *New York* (340 U.S. 395, 1953), the Court found that permit requirements amounted to prior restraints on First Amendment freedoms. By contrast, the Court in *Poulos* v. *New Hampshire* (345 U.S. 395, 1953) upheld a city ordinance providing a permit system for "open air public meetings" on the ground that "by its construction of the ordinance the state left to the licensing officials no discretion as to granting permits, no power to discriminate, no control over speech."

Demonstrations may also be limited by court injunctions. Indeed, when Nobel Peace Prize winner Martin Luther King and his followers deliberately violated a state court injunction forbidding them to participate in or encourage "mass street parades or mass processions" without a permit as required by a Birmingham city ordinance, the Supreme Court affirmed their convictions for criminal contempt (*Walker* v. *Birmingham,* 388 U.S. 307, 1967). Though Justice Stewart, who spoke for the 5–4 court majority, admitted that both the injunction and the city ordinance raised "substantial" constitutional questions, he nevertheless maintained that the petitioners should have followed the orderly procedures of the law rather than ignoring them altogether and carrying "their battle to the streets."[3] "One may sympathize with the petitioners' impatient commitment to their cause," said Stewart, "but respect for judicial process is a small price to pay for the civilizing hand of law, which alone can give abiding meaning to constitutional freedom." However, Justice Brennan, in a dissent joined by Chief Justice Warren, and Justices Douglas and Fortas, bitterly assailed the majority for letting "loose a devastatingly destructive weapon [the injunction] for infringement of freedom. . . ." "Convictions for contempt of court orders which invalidly abridge First Amendment freedoms," said Brennan, "must be condemned equally with convictions for violation of statutes which do the same thing."

An interesting contrast to *Walker* is afforded in *Carroll* v. *President and Commissioners of Princess Anne* (393 U.S. 175, 1968). There a "white suprema-

---

[3]However, in another case growing out of the same factual situation (*Shuttlesworth* v. *Birmingham,* 394 U.S. 147, 1969), the Court reversed a conviction for violating the permit ordinance because of the unfettered discretion allowed administrative officials in its application.

cist" organization called the National States Rights Party was enjoined in *ex parte* proceedings from resuming a rally which had been held the night before. In his opinion for the Court, Justice Fortas described the nature of the first night's rally:

> Petitioners' speeches, amplified by a public address system so that they could be heard for several blocks, were aggressively and militantly racist. Their target was primarily Negroes, and secondarily, Jews. It is sufficient to observe with the court below, that the speakers engaged in deliberately derogatory, insulting, and threatening language, scarcely disguised by disclaimers of peaceful purposes; and that listeners might well have construed their words as both a provocation to the Negroes in the crowd and an incitement to the whites. The rally continued for something more than an hour. . . . The crowd listening to the speeches increased from about 50 at the beginning to about 150 of whom 25% were Negroes.
>
> In the course of the proceedings it was announced that the rally would be resumed the following night. . . .

It was against the resumption of the rally the second night that law enforcement officials in Princess Anne and Somerset County, Maryland, sought and obtained a restraining order in *ex parte* proceedings from the county circuit court. The order, originally issued for ten days and later extended for ten months, sought to restrain petitioners from holding rallies "which . . . tend to disturb and endanger the citizens of the County." No notice was given to the petitioners, and apparently as Justice Fortas observed, no effort was made to otherwise communicate with them as was "expressly contemplated under Maryland law." In any case, the petitioners obeyed the injunction and took their battle to the courts.

The Maryland Court of Appeals subsequently upheld the ten-day injunction but reversed the ten-month order on the ground that "the period of time was unreasonable and that it was arbitrary to assume that a clear and present danger of civil disturbance and riot would persist for ten months." However, on certiorari, Justice Fortas speaking for the U.S. Supreme Court brushed aside the ten-day order "because of a basic infirmity in the procedure by which it was obtained." "There is no place within the area of basic freedoms guaranteed by the First Amendment for [ex parte] orders," said Fortas, "where no showing is made that it is impossible to serve or to notify the opposing parties and to give them an opportunity to participate." Earlier in his opinion Fortas noted that unlike *Walker* the petitioners here had pursued orderly judicial procedures to challenge the injunction.

The Court remains apprehensive of injunctions that restrain the exercise of First Amendment freedoms in public places. For example, in *Organization for a Better Austin* v. *Keefe* (402 U.S. 415, 1971), the Court set aside an Illinois state court injunction that barred a community organization from distributing leaflets. The leaflets alleged that respondent (a real estate broker) was engaged in "blockbusting" and "panic peddling" activities in the Austin area of Chicago. Chief Justice Burger, who spoke for a unanimous Court, observed that the Illinois court "was apparently of the view that petitioners' purpose in distributing their literature was not to inform the public but to force respondent to sign a no-solicitation agreement."

"But even if this coercive impact was intended," Burger continued, "it does not remove the petitioner's expressions [leaflets] from the reach of the First Amendment." Burger concluded that the respondent had not met the "heavy burden of showing justification for the imposition of such a [prior] restraint."

What about political or religious speechmaking in public places with the use of sound amplifiers? This is an attempt by the speechmaker to reach a wider audience, but what about unwilling listeners, those who do not wish to be disturbed? In *Saia* v. *New York* (334 U.S. 558, 1948) the Court was faced with a city ordinance that forbade use of sound amplification devices except "public dissemination through radio loudspeakers of items of news and matters of public concern ... provided that the same be done under permission obtained from the Chief of Police." Here the appellant, a Jehovah's Witness, was refused a new permit since complaints had been received concerning his speeches and sermons delivered under an earlier permit. Nevertheless, the lack of a permit did not keep the appellant from delivering speeches over a loudspeaker in a small public park used primarily for recreational purposes. He was subsequently tried and convicted for violating the ordinance. By a 5-4 majority, the Supreme Court held the ordinance unconstitutional on its face as a prior restraint on freedom of speech. Said Justice William O. Douglas, speaking for the majority:

> Any abuses which loudspeakers create can be controlled by narrowly drawn statutes. When a city allows an official to ban them in his uncontrolled discretion, it sanctions a device for suppression of free communication of ideas. In this case a permit is denied because some persons were said to have found the sound annoying. In the next one a permit may be denied because some people find the ideas annoying. Annoyance at ideas can be cloaked in annoyance at sound. The power of censorship inherent in this type of ordinance reveals its vice.

Justice Felix Frankfurter, joined by Justices Stanley Reed and Harold Burton, dissented. "The native power of human speech," said Frankfurter, "can interfere little with the self-protection of those who do not wish to listen." But modern devices for amplifying the range and volume of the noise, continued Frankfurter, "afford easy, too easy, opportunities for aural aggression," and "if uncontrolled the result is intrusion into cherished privacy."

In a subsequent case (*Kovacs* v. *Cooper,* 336 U.S. 77, 1949), however, the Court retreated and upheld a Trenton, New Jersey, loudspeaker ordinance that prohibited use of sound trucks and similar amplifying devices that emit "loud and raucous noises." Justice Reed announced the judgment of the 5-4 majority and, in an opinion joined by Chief Justice Vinson and Justice Burton, accepted the state supreme court's construction of the ordinance to apply only to vehicles with sound amplifiers emitting "loud and raucous noises." Said Justice Reed:

> City streets are recognized as a normal place for the exchange of ideas by speech or paper. But this does not mean the freedom is beyond all control. We

think it is a permissible exercise of legislative discretion to bar sound trucks with broadcasts of public interest, amplified to a loud and raucous volume, from the public ways of municipalities. On the business streets of cities like Trenton, with its more than 125,000 people, such distractions would be dangerous to traffic at all hours useful for the dissemination of information, and in the residential thoroughfares the quiet and tranquility so desirable for city dwellers would likewise be at the mercy of advocates of particular religious, social or political persuasions. We cannot believe that rights of free speech compel a municipality to allow such mechanical voice amplification on any of its streets. The right of free speech is guaranteed every citizen that he may reach the minds of willing listeners and to do so there must be opportunity to win their attention. This is the phase of freedom of speech that is involved here. We do not think the Trenton ordinance abridges that freedom.

Justices Douglas, Black, Rutledge, and Murphy dissented. Justice Black, in an opinion supported by Douglas and Rutledge, thought the ordinance on its face and as applied constituted "an absolute and unqualified prohibition of amplifying devices on any of Trenton's streets at any time, at any place, for any purpose, and without regard to how noisy they may be." Black said that he was "aware that the 'blare' of this new method of carrying ideas is susceptible of abuse and may under certain circumstances constitute an intolerable nuisance." "But," he continued, "ordinances can be drawn which adequately protect a community from unreasonable use of public speaking devices without absolutely denying to the community's citizens all information that may be disseminated or received through this new avenue for trade in ideas."

What about persons who ride on public streetcars? May music, news announcements, and advertisements be piped in beyond the control of unwilling listeners? How much privacy can one have in public? These questions were raised in *Public Utilities Commission* v. *Pollak* (343 U.S. 451, 1952). Here Capital Transit Company, with the approval of the Public Utilities Commission of the District of Columbia, arranged with an FM station for special programs to be piped in over streetcar radios. The special programs consisted of about 90 percent music, 5 percent news announcements, and 5 percent commercial advertisements. Two passengers thought that this practice infringed upon their constitutional right to privacy under the Fifth Amendment. But Justice Burton, speaking for the Court majority said.

This position wrongly assumes that the Fifth Amendment secures to each passenger on a public vehicle regulated by the Federal Government a right of privacy substantially equal to the privacy to which he is entitled in his own home. However complete his right of privacy may be at home, it is substantially limited by the rights of others when its possessor travels on a public thoroughfare or rides in a public conveyance.

Justice Douglas dissented and Justice Black dissented in part. Justice Frankfurter did not participate in the case since "[his] feelings [were] so strongly engaged as a victim of the practice in controversy. . . ." Justice Douglas' dissent emphasized "the right to be let alone," which he argued, "is . . . the beginning of all freedom." Said Douglas:

> The present case involves a form of coercion to make people listen. The listeners are of course in a public place; they are on streetcars traveling to and from home. In one sense it can be said that those who ride streetcars do so voluntarily. Yet in a practical sense they are forced to ride, since this mode of transportation is today essential for many thousands. Compulsion which comes from circumstances can be as real as compulsion which comes from a command. . . . When we force people to listen to another's ideas, we give the propagandist a powerful weapon. . . . Once a man is forced to submit to one type of radio program, he can be forced to submit to another. It may be but a short step from a cultural program to a political program.

How much privacy can one have in his own home? The door-to-door canvasser has long been a constant irritant to the late sleeper, the night shift worker, the fearful housewife, or the person who just wants to be let alone. Some door-to-door canvassing is protected by the First Amendment, but not all. Noncommercial canvassing, for example, would appear to come within First Amendment guarantees. In *Martin* v. *Struthers* (319 U.S. 141, 1943) the Court was faced with an ordinance that made it unlawful "for any person distributing handbills, circulars or other advertisements to ring the doorbell, sound the doorknocker, or otherwise summon the inmate or inmates to the door for the purpose of receiving such handbills, circulars or other advertisements they or any person with them may be distributing." When a Jehovah's Witness was convicted under this ordinance for distributing advertisements for a religious meeting, the Supreme Court declared the ordinance invalid as a denial of free speech and press. Justice Black, who delivered the opinion for a 5-4 majority, said:

> The ordinance does not control anything but the distribution of literature, and in that respect it substitutes the judgment of the community for the judgment of the individual householder. . . . Freedom to distribute information to every citizen wherever he desires to receive it is so clearly vital to the preservation of a free society that, putting aside reasonable police and health regulations of time and manner of distribution, it must be fully preserved. The dangers of distribution can so easily be controlled by traditional legal methods, leaving to each householder the full right to decide whether he will receive strangers as visitors, that stringent prohibition can serve no purpose but that forbidden by the Constitution, the naked restriction of the dissemination of ideas.

Justice Reed, for himself and Justices Roberts and Jackson, dissented. Reed said:

If the citizens of Struthers desire to be protected from the arrogance of being called to their doors to receive printed matter, there is to my mind no constitutional provision which forbids their municipal council from modifying the rule that anyone may sound a call for the householder to attend his door. It is the council which is entrusted by the citizens with the power to declare and abate the myriad nuisances which develop in a community. Its determination should not be set aside by the Court unless clearly and patently unconstitutional. . . . The ordinance seems a fair adjustment of the privilege of distributors and the rights of householders.

On the other side of the ledger, Court decisions also suggest that commercial canvassing is clearly subject to local regulation (*Green River* v. *Bunger,* 58 P. 2d 456; *Bunger* v. *Green River,* 300 U.S. 638, 1937; and *Breard* v. *Alexandria,* 341 U.S. 622, 1951). The Court held to this view in *Breard* despite the free speech and free press problem raised by an Alexandria, Louisiana, city ordinance against door-to-door commercial canvassing as applied in this instance to magazine solicitors. Justice Reed, who dissented in *Struthers,* now spoke for the Court majority in *Breard.* To Reed, the constitutionality of the ordinance turned on "a balancing of the conveniences between some householders' desires for privacy and the publisher's right to distribute publications in the precise way that those soliciting for him think brings the best results." But Justice Black, in an opinion joined by Justice Douglas, dissented on the strength of the free press guarantee of the First Amendment. Said Black:

The constitutional sanctuary for the press must necessarily include liberty to publish and circulate. In view of our economic system, it must also include freedom to solicit paying subscribers. Of course homeowners can if they wish forbid newsboys, reporters or magazine solicitors to ring their doorbells. But when the homeowner himself has not done this, I believe that the First Amendment interpreted with due regard for the freedoms in guarantees, bars laws like the present ordinance which punish persons who peacefully go from door to door as agents of the press.

In 1970, in *Rowan* v. *United States Post Office Department* (397 U.S. 728, 1970), the "right to be let alone" versus the "right to communicate" (under the First Amendment) was once again before the Court. At issue was a provision of the Postal Revenue and Salary Act of 1967 under which householders could insulate themselves from advertisements that offer for sale "matter which the addressee in his sole discretion believes to be erotically arousing or sexually provocative." The Postmaster General, once an addressee gives notice that he has received ads he believes to be within the statutory category and does not wish to receive them, is obliged to order the sender "to refrain from further mailings" to that addressee.

The Postmaster General must also (1) order the sender to delete the addressee's name from all mailing lists owned or controlled by the sender and (2) prohibit the sender from selling or renting any mailing lists that include the addressee's name.

A federal district court upheld the act, construing it to prohibit future mailings *similar* to those originally sent to the addressee. Chief Justice Burger, speaking for the Court, gave the act a more restrictive scope, but upheld its constitutionality. He found that the act's purpose was "to allow the addressee complete and unfettered discretion in electing whether or not he desired to receive further material from a particular sender." By focusing on prohibition of any *further* mailings rather than of similar mailings, Burger relieved the addressee of the "further burdens of scrutinizing the [sender's] mail for objectionable material" and avoided a situation that "would interpose the Postmaster General between the sender and the addressee and, at the least, create the appearance if not the substance of governmental censorship." Thus, Burger held that the statute did not violate the sender's constitutional right to communicate. "Without doubt," he concluded, "the public postal system is an indispensable adjunct of every civilized society and communication is imperative to a healthy social order. But the right of every person 'to be let alone' must be placed on the scales with the right of others to communicate."

Government also seeks to preserve public peace and order through laws relating to unlawful assembly, breach of the peace, disorderly conduct, and incitement to riot. But the enforcement of these laws may, and sometimes does, collide with the exercise of constitutional guarantees. Governmental restrictions on unpopular speakers, streetcorner preachers, picketers, protesters, and demonstrators have produced an almost endless stream of Supreme Court cases.

Two of the early cases in this area involved Jehovah's Witnesses. In *Cantwell* v. *Connecticut, supra,* a Jehovah's Witness approached two men in the street, asked and received permission to play, and played a phonograph record entitled "Enemies," which contained a vitriolic attack on organized religion and the Catholic Church. Coincidentally, both men were Catholics and were incensed by the contents of the record. They testified that they were tempted to strike Cantwell, but on being told to be on his way he left their presence. There was no evidence that Cantwell was personally offensive or entered into any argument with the persons he stopped. Cantwell was charged with and convicted of inciting a breach of the peace. The Supreme Court reversed the conviction, as Justice Roberts, who wrote the majority opinion, declared:

> The offense known as breach of the peace embraces a great variety of conduct destroying or menacing public order and tranquility. It includes not only violent acts but acts and words likely to produce violence in others. No one would have the hardihood to suggest that the principle of freedom of speech sanctions incitement to riot or that religious liberty connotes the privilege to exhort others to physical attack upon those belonging to another sect. When clear and present danger of riot, disorder, interference with traffic upon the public streets, or other immediate threat to public safety, peace, or order, appears, the power of the State to prevent or punish is obvious. Equally obvious

is it that a State may not unduly suppress free communication of views, religious or other, under the guise of conserving desirable conditions. Here we have a situation analogous to a conviction under a statute sweeping in a great variety of conduct under a general and indefinite characterization, and leaving to the executive and judicial branches too wide a discretion in its application. . . .

Although the contents of the record not unnaturally aroused animosity, we think that, in the absence of a statute narrowly drawn to define and punish specific conduct as constituting a clear and present danger to a substantial interest of the State, the petitioner's communication, considered in the light of the constitutional guarantees, raised no such clear and present menace of public peace and order as to render him liable to conviction of the common law offense in question.

In *Chaplinsky* v. *New Hampshire* (315 U.S. 568, 1942) another Jehovah's Witness was convicted under a state law for calling a city marshal a "God damned racketeer" and a "damned Fascist." The state law made it a crime for any person to address "any offensive, derisive or annoying word" to another person or call him by "any offensive or derisive name. . . ." In an opinion by Justice Murphy, the Supreme Court affirmed the conviction stating that " . . it is well understood that the right of free speech is not absolute at all times and under all circumstances." Said Justice Murphy:

There are certain well-defined and narrowly limited classes of speech, the prevention and punishment of which have never been thought to raise any Constitutional problem. These include the lewd and obscene, the profane, the libelous, and the insulting or "fighting" words—those which by their very utterance inflict injury or tend to incite an immediate breach of the peace. It has been well observed that such utterances are no essential part of any exposition of ideas and are of such slight social value as a step to truth that any benefit that may be derived from them is clearly outweighed by the social interest in order and morality.

Another case that could have extended or clarified the "fighting words" doctrine of *Chaplinsky* was *Terminiello* v. *Chicago* (337 U.S. 1, 1947). However, the Court decided the case on another basis. Terminiello, a defrocked Catholic priest, was well known for his vicious attacks on Jews, Negroes, Communists, and others. The instant case arose when he spoke in a Chicago auditorium to a crowd of about 800. An even larger crowd gathered outside picketing the auditorium, throwing ice picks, stones and bottles, and attempting to storm the doors. In his speech Terminiello condemned the conduct of the crowd outside and bitterly criticized various political, racial, and religious groups whose activities he denounced as "inimical to the welfare of the nation." Terminiello was arrested and convicted under a breach of the peace ordinance. The Supreme Court, however, reversed the conviction on an issue that neither party brought to the Court—the trial judge's charge to the jury. The trial judge charged the jury that "breach of the peace" includes "misbehavior" (or speech) which "stirs the public to anger, invites dispute, brings about a condition of unrest, or creates a disturbance, or if it molests the inhabitants in the enjoyment of peace and quiet by arousing alarm." Justice Douglas, who spoke for the majority, read this construction of the breach of the peace ordinance as "part of the ordinance" itself and binding upon the Court. Consequently, Douglas and the majority of his colleagues ignored completely the facts or circumstances of the situation and rested their decision on the fact that the ordinance, as construed by the trial judge in his charge to the jury, was too broad and might encompass speech that is constitutionally protected. Said Justice Douglas:

> ... [A] function of free speech under our system of government is to invite dispute. It may indeed best serve its high purpose when it induces a condition of unrest, creates dissatisfaction with conditions as they are, or even stirs people to anger. Speech is often provocative and challenging. It may strike at prejudices and preconceptions and have profound unsettling effects as it presses for acceptance of an idea. ... The ordinance as construed by the trial court seriously invaded this province. It permitted conviction of petitioner if his speech stirred people to anger, invited public dispute, or brought about a condition of unrest. A conviction resting on any of those grounds may not stand.

Justice Jackson, in a dissent joined by Justices Frankfurter and Burton, sharply criticized the majority for ignoring the facts of the highly explosive situation that existed in *Terminiello* and for not giving sufficient weight to the importance of order in the enjoyment of liberty. Said Jackson: "The choice is not between order and liberty. It is between liberty with order and anarchy without either. There is danger that, if the Court does not temper its doctrinaire logic with a little practical wisdom, it will convert the constitutional Bill of Rights into a suicide pact."

Though in *Terminiello* the Court avoided the problem of free speech when a threat to public peace and order is imminent, the problem was before the Court again a short time later in *Feiner* v. *New York*. Feiner, a Syracuse University student, spoke from a large box placed on the sidewalk and used loudspeakers fixed on his car. He was protesting the revocation of speaker's permit which his organization, the Young Progressives of America, had obtained, and he was also publicizing the new place where the YPA would hold its public meeting. A crowd gathered to hear him. Two policemen were sent to the scene because there was a "disturbance." In the course of his speech, Feiner made some critically sharp references to the mayor, the city administration, the American Legion, the President of the United States, and others. After listening for about 20 minutes, the two policemen on the scene, upon hearing some angry muttering throughout the crowd of about 75 people, concluded that the situation had become volatile and ordered Feiner to stop speaking. His refusal to do so led to his arrest and eventual conviction under a breach of the peace statute. The conviction was affirmed by the Supreme Court as Chief Justice Fred Vinson, who spoke for the 6-3 majority, declared:

We are well aware that the ordinary murmurings and objections of a hostile audience cannot be allowed to silence a speaker, and are also mindful of the possible danger of giving overzealous police officials complete discretion to break up otherwise lawful public meetings. . . . But we are not faced here with such a situation. It is one thing to say that the police cannot be used as an instrument for the suppression of unpopular views, and another to say that, when as here the speaker passes the bounds of argument or persuasion and undertakes incitement to riot, they are powerless to prevent a breach of the peace. . . .

Justices Black, Douglas, and Minton dissented. Black issued a particularly sharp dissent saying that he was convinced that Feiner was convicted for his unpopular views, nothing more.

The *Feiner* case was only a prelude to a number of cases the Court faced in the 1960s when civil-rights demonstrators and protesters took to the streets and other public places to press their causes. In *Edwards* v. *South Carolina* the Supreme Court reversed breach of peace convictions of 187 black student demonstrators who had marched in small groups to the South Carolina State House grounds to protest segregation practices. A crowd of some 200 onlookers gathered, but there was no disturbance or obstruction of any kind. Accordingly, the Court found insufficient evidence to support breach of the peace convictions. "The Fourteenth Amendment," said Justice Stewart speaking for the majority, "does not permit a state to make criminal the peaceful expression of unpopular views." While Stewart attempted to distinguish *Edwards* from *Feiner* Justice Tom Clark, in dissent, did not see any distinction. Said Clark: "We upheld a breach of the peace in a situation [in *Feiner*] no more dangerous than found here." Nevertheless, the Court continued to support its *Edwards* position in several subsequent cases. (Cf. *Fields* v. *South Carolina,* 375 U.S. 44, 1963; *Henry* v. *Rock Hill,* 376 U.S. 776, 1964; and *Gregory* v. *City of Chicago,* 394 U.S. 111, 1969.)

Far more difficult questions reached the Court in 1965 in two cases (*Cox* v. *Louisiana,* No. 24; and *Cox* v. *Louisiana,* No. 49, 379 U.S. 536, 1965), arising out of the same set of facts. In 1961 over 2,000 Southern University students converged on downtown Baton Rouge, Louisiana, and conducted a protest rally near the Old State Capitol Building in the vicinity of the courthouse. They were protesting against segregation practices generally as well as the arrest the day before of 23 of their fellow students who had been picketing downtown stores that maintained segregated lunch counters. The leader of the group, an ordained Congregational minister, the Reverend Mr. B. Elton Cox, was arrested and convicted on three charges: (1) disturbing the peace under Louisiana's breach of the peace statute; (2) obstructing public passages; and (3) picketing before a courthouse. The Supreme Court reversed convictions on all three charges. The first two charges were heard in *Cox* No. 24, the third in *Cox* No. 49.

The Court voted unanimously to reverse the breach of the peace conviction saying that it infringed on Cox's rights of free speech and free assembly. The Court relied on grounds similar to those in *Edwards,* and as in *Edwards,* found the situation a "far cry from *Feiner.*" The court held that not only was there insufficient evidence to support the breach of the peace charge but also that the statute as interpreted by the Louisiana Supreme Court was unconstitutionally broad in scope.

The Court next considered Cox's conviction on the "obstructing public passages" charge, and voted 7-2 for reversal. The relevant Louisiana statute provided in part:

> No person shall wilfully obstruct the free, convenient and normal use of any public sidewalk, street, highway, bridge, alley, road or other passageway, or the entrance, corridor or passage of any public building, structure, water craft or ferry, by impeding, hindering, stifling, retarding or restraining traffic or passage thereon or therein. Providing however nothing herein contained shall apply to a bona fide legitimate labor organization or to any of its legal activities such as picketing, lawful assembly or concerted activity in the interest of its members for the purpose of accomplishing or securing more favorable wage standards, hours of employment and working conditions.

Speaking for five members of the Court, Justice Goldberg said that "although the statute . . . on its face precludes all street assemblies and parades, it has not been so applied and enforced by the Baton Rouge authorities." Goldberg said that "city officials who testified for the State clearly indicated that certain meetings and parades are permitted in Baton Rouge, even though they have the effect of obstructing traffic, provided prior approval is obtained." Goldberg continued:

> The statute itself provides no standards for the determination of local officials as to which assemblies to permit or which to prohibit. Nor are there any administrative regulations on this subject which have been called to our attention. From all the evidence before us it appears that the authorities in Baton Rouge permit or prohibit parades or street meetings in their completely uncontrolled discretion. The situation is thus the same as if the statute itself expressly provided that there could only be peaceful parades or demonstrations in the unbridled discretion of local officials. The pervasive restraint on freedom of discussion by the practice of authorities under the statute is not any less effective than a statute expressly permitting such selective enforcement. . . .

Consequently Goldberg concluded that the practice of allowing such "unfettered discretion" in local officials in regulating the use of the streets for peaceful parades and meetings [was] an unwarranted abridgement of the appellant's freedom of speech and assembly. . . ." Justices Black and Clark concurred on the ground that the Louisiana statute ran afoul of the equal protection clause of the Fourteenth Amendment by expressly permitting picketing for the publication of labor union views while forbidding picketing for other purposes.

In *Cox* No. 49 the Court, by a narrow 5-4 majority, also reversed the appellant's conviction on the third charge of picketing before a courthouse. The relevant state law prohibited picketing or parading "in or near" a building housing a state court "with the intent of interfering with, obstructing, or impeding the administration of justice or with the intent of influencing any judge, juror, witness, or court officer in the discharge of his duty. . . ." Justice Goldberg again spoke for the majority. He found that the state statute was precise, well drawn and that its purpose of protecting the state's judicial system was wholly within the legitimate interest of the state. In general, Goldberg's opinion supported the proposition that the state had a right to forbid what the demonstrators had done. "There can be no question," said Goldberg, "that a state has a legitimate interest in protecting its judicial system from pressures which picketing near a courthouse might create." Despite the principled rhetoric, however, Goldberg and a majority of his colleagues reversed Cox's conviction on the ground that:

> [T]he highest police officials of the city, in the presence of the Sheriff and Mayor, in effect told the demonstrators that they could meet where they did, 101 feet from the courthouse steps, but could not meet closer to the courthouse. In effect, appellant was advised that a demonstration at the place it was held would not be one "near" the courthouse within the terms of the statute.

Goldberg concluded that "under all the circumstances of this case, after the public officials acted as they did, to sustain appellant's later conviction for demonstrating where they told him he could, would be to sanction an indefensible sort of entrapment by the State—convicting a citizen for exercising a privilege which the State had clearly told him was available to him. The Due Process Clause does not permit convictions to be obtained under such circumstances."

Justice Black, along with Justices Clark, White, and Harlan, dissented. In his dissent, Black said that he could not "understand how the Court can justify the reversal of these convictions [in No. 49] because of a permission which testimony in the record denies was given, which could not have been authoritatively given anyway, and which even if given was soon afterward revoked."

What of mass demonstrations and protest that take place on public properties other than streets? The Court considered this question in two cases decided in 1966. In *Brown* v. *Louisiana* (383 U.S. 131, 1966), the demonstrations did not take place on the streets but in a public library. When the five black demonstrators refused to leave, they were arrested and convicted for violating Louisiana's "breach of the peace" statute, the same statute involved in *Cox*. By a 5-4 decision, the Supreme Court reversed the convictions on the ground that there was, in fact, no violation of the statute. As Justice Abe Fortas said for the majority, there was no disorder, no intent to provoke a breach of the peace and no circumstances indicating a breach might be occasioned by petitioners' actions. They were merely exercising their constitutional right to protest unconstitutional segregation. However, Justice Black, joined by Justices Clark, Harlan, and Stewart issued a strong dissent. Black said that he did not believe that the First Amendment guarantees to any person "the right to use someone else's property, even that owned by government and dedicated to other purposes, as a stage to express dissident ideas," especially in a library where tranquility is of the highest priority.

Black did not have to wait long for his views to gain majority support. In *Adderley* v. *Florida* (385 U.S. 39, 1966), the Court upheld the convictions of student demonstrators under a state trespass statute. The demonstrators, students at Florida A. & M. University, had marched to the jailhouse to protest segregation, including segregation in the jail. But Justice Black, now speaking for the majority, emphasized the significant difference between this case and *Edwards*. In *Edwards*, the demonstrators went to the state capitol grounds whereas in this case they went to the jail. Traditionally state capitol grounds are open to the public, said Black, but jails, built for security purposes, are not. The Constitution does not prevent Florida, Black continued, from "evenhanded enforcement of its general trespass statute . . . to preserve the property under its control for the use to which it is lawfully dedicated." People who wish to propagandize protests or views do not have a constitutional right to do so "whenever and however and wherever they please."

Justice Douglas wrote a dissenting opinion in which Chief Justice Warren and Justices Brennan and Fortas joined. To Douglas, the jailhouse, just as an executive mansion, legislative chamber or a statehouse, is one of the seats of government and when it "houses political prisoners or those whom many think are unjustly held, it is an obvious center for protest."

A number of cases reaching the Court in the early 1970s continued to focus on the scope of constitutional protections afforded speechmaking and demonstrations. In the main, these cases were the outgrowth of state and local governmental actions designed to maintain peace and order. While some of these actions ran afoul of constitutional limitation, others survived constitutional challenges. In *Coates* v. *Cincinnati* (402 U.S. 611, 1971), for example, a city ordinance made it a criminal offense for "three or more persons to assemble. . . on any of the sidewalks . . . and there conduct themselves in a manner annoying to persons passing by." But Justice Stewart, who spoke for the Court, found the ordinance unconstitutional on its face without reaching the merits of the case. Stewart conceded that the ordinance was broad enough to cover many types of conduct clearly within the city's constitutional power to prohibit (e.g., preventing people from blocking sidewalks, obstructing traffic, and littering streets). The city is free to prevent such occurrences, said Stewart, through "ordinances directed with reasonable specificity toward the conduct to be prohibited. It cannot constitutionally do so through the enactment and enforcement of an ordinance whose violation may entirely depend upon whether or not a policeman is annoyed." Continuing, Stewart said that "the vice of the ordinance lies not alone in its violation of the due process standard of vagueness," but it "also violates the constitutional rights of free assembly and association." Stewart was especially disturbed that these constitutional rights may be prohibited because their exercise may be "annoying" to some people. Such a standard, he asserted, "contains an obvious invitation to discriminatory enforcement against those whose association together is 'annoying' because their ideas, their lifestyle, or their physical appearance is resented by the majority of their fellow citizens." Consequently, he concluded:

> ... The ordinance before us makes a crime out of what under the Constitution cannot be a crime. It is aimed directly at activity protected by the Constitution. We need not lament that we do not have before us the details of the conduct found to be annoying. It is the ordinance on its face that sets the standard of conduct and warns against transgression. The details of the offense could no more serve to validate this ordinance than could the details of an offense charged under an ordinance suspending unconditionally the right of assembly and free speech.

Chief Justice Burger and Justices Black, White, and Blackmun dissented. Justice White indicated the thrust of the dissenter's view when he stated that he "would deal with the Cincinnati ordinance as we would with the ordinary criminal statute." Then, said White, "when a criminal charge is based on conduct constitutionally subject to proscription and clearly forbidden by a statute, it is no defense that the law would be unconstitutionally vague if applied to other behavior." White thought the ordinance clearly reaches certain conduct, was not infirm on its face, and in order to reach a decision the Court needed to have more information "as to what conduct was charged against these defendants."

Similarly, in *Police Department of the City of Chicago* v. *Mosley* (408 U.S. 92, 1972), the Court held unconstitutional a Chicago ordinance that banned all picketing within 150 feet of a school building while school was in session except "the peaceful picketing of any school involved in a labor dispute." Mosley had picketed a Chicago school for seven months prior to the enactment of this statute. Mosley, whose activities were conceded by the city to be "always peaceful, orderly and quiet," carried a picket sign reading "Jones High School practices black discrimination. Jones High School has a black quota." After checking with the police and learning that he would be arrested for violation of the new ordinance if he continued picketing, Mosley stopped picketing and sued to enjoin enforcement of the ordinance. Justice Thurgood Marshall, who spoke for the Court, said that the ordinance made an "impermissible distinction between labor picketing and other peaceful picketing." For him the fatal defect of the ordinance was its description of impermissible picketing in terms of subject matter. He put it this way:

> The central problem with Chicago's ordinance is that it describes permissible picketing in terms of its subject matter. Peaceful picketing on the subject of a school's labor-management dispute is permitted, but all other peaceful picketing is prohibited. The operative distinction is the message on a picket sign. But, above all else, the First Amendment means that government has no power to restrict expression because of its message, its ideas, its subject matter, or its content.

Whether because of "permissiveness" or "telling it like it is," the Court has been faced with several so-called offensive-word cases. The charge in such cases is that certain words in and of themselves may be so "offensive" to the community or to individuals that the words alone disturb the peace or provoke others to do so. These are so-called fighting words, which might stir those to whom they are addressed to breach the peace or to react predictably and angrily. However, in *Cohen* v. *California* (403 U.S. 15, 1971), the Court reversed a conviction based on a general state disturbing the peace statute which prohibits "maliciously and willfully disturbing the peace or quiet of any neighborhood or person by offensive conduct." Here Cohen had worn a jacket which plainly bore the words "Fuck the Draft" in a Los Angeles courthouse corridor where women and children were present. Cohen testified that he wore the jacket to demonstrate to the public the intensity of his feelings against the Vietnam War and the military draft. Cohen did not engage in any act of violence, nor did anyone who saw him in the courthouse corridor. There was no evidence that he had "uttered any sound prior to his arrest." Accordingly, said Justice John Marshall Harlan, who spoke for the Court, "the conviction quite clearly rests upon the asserted offensiveness of the *words* Cohen used to convey his message to the public. The only 'conduct' which the State sought to punish is the fact of communication." For the conviction to stand, Harlan said, the state needed to show that the statute sought to preserve "an appropriately decorous atmosphere in the courthouse where Cohen was arrested" or that it falls within the gambit of prior decisions establishing the "power of government to deal more comprehensively with certain forms of individual expression simply upon a showing that such a form was employed." But to Harlan neither of these showings was made. The decorous courthouse atmosphere failed, he noted, because the statute did not put Cohen "on notice that certain kinds of otherwise permissible speech or conduct would nevertheless, under California law, not be tolerated in certain places." As to the "fighting words" doctrine, Harlan said:

> This Court has. . . held that the States are free to ban the simple use, without a demonstration of additional justifying circumstances, of so-called "fighting words," those personally abusive epithets which, when addressed to the ordinary citizen, are, as a matter of common knowledge, inherently likely to provoke violent reaction. *Chaplinsky* v. *New Hampshire*. While the four-letter word displayed by Cohen in relation to the draft is not uncommonly employed in a personally provocative fashion, in this instance it was clearly not "directed to the person of the hearer." *Cantwell* v. *Connecticut*. No individual actually or likely to be present could reasonably have regarded the words on appellant's jacket as a direct personal insult. Nor do we have here an instance of the exercise of the State's police power to prevent a speaker from intentionally provoking a given group to hostile reaction. Cf. *Feiner* v. *New York; Terminiello* v. *Chicago*.

In *Gooding* v. *Wilson* (405 U.S. 518, 1972) the Court found unconstitutionally vague and overbroad a Georgia statute that made the use of "opprobrious words or abusive language" a breach of the peace. Here Wilson, with others, picketed an

Army headquarters building carrying signs opposing the Vietnam War. The demonstrators blocked the door and refused to heed a police request to stop blocking it so that inductees could enter the building. A scuffle ensued during which Wilson said to a policemen attempting to restore access to the building: "White son-of-a-bitch, I'll kill you. You son-of-a-bitch, I'll choke you to death." Wilson was arrested and convicted for violating the aforementioned statute. Justice Brennan, who spoke for a 5-2 Court majority, noted that Georgia courts had not limited the reach of the terms and hence the statute did not have that quality of narrowness and particularity so it could be applied only to unprotected expression. Reemphasizing the constitutional requirement that statutes must be "narrowly drawn and limited to define and punish specific conduct lying within the domain of state power," Brennan concluded that "the separation of legitimate from illegitimate speech calls for more sensitive tools than [Georgia] has supplied." To him, the "fighting words" doctrine of *Chaplinsky* was the constitutional doctrine which the state had failed to follow.

In separate opinions Chief Justice Burger and Justice Blackmun voiced sharp dissents. Describing the Georgia statute, the Chief Justice said:

> [It] does not prohibit language "tending to cause a breach of the peace." Nor does it prohibit the use of "opprobrious words or abusive language" without more. Rather, it prohibits use "to or of another, and in his presence [of] opprobrious words or abusive language, tending to cause a breach of the peace." If words are to bear their common meaning, and are to be considered in context, rather than dissected with surgical precision using a semantic scalpel, this statute has little potential for application outside the realm of "fighting words."

He characterized the result in the case as "bizarre," and concluded that "[i]t is regrettable that one consequence of this holding may be to mislead some citizens to believe that fighting words of this kind may be uttered free of any legal sanctions." Justice Blackmun wondered—since the Georgia statute was voided—just what the state "can do if it seeks to proscribe what the Court says it still may constitutionally proscribe. The natural thing would be to enact a new statute reading just as [the voided statute] reads. But it, too, presumably would be overbroad unless the legislature would add words to the effect that it means only what this Court says it may mean and no more." Blackmun thought that *Chaplinsky* "was good law when it was decided and deserves to remain as good law now." "But," he continued, "I feel that by decisions such as this one and, indeed, *Cohen* v. *California,* the Court, despite its protestations to the contrary, is merely paying lip service to *Chaplinsky.*" As such, Blackmun agreed with Wilson's position that all that the *Chaplinsky* decision means is that the state can punish fighting words and no more. "If this is what the overbreadth doctrine means," concluded Blackmun, "and if this is what it produces, it urgently needs re-examination. The Court has painted itself into a corner from which it, and the States, can extricate themselves only with difficulty."

Similarly, in *Rosenfeld* v. *New Jersey* (408 U.S. 901, 1972) the Court vacated a conviction under a New Jersey statute that provides that "any person who utters loud and offensive or profane or indecent language in any public . . . place . . . or place to which the public is invited . . . is a disorderly person." Here Rosenfeld "addressed a public school board meeting attended by about 150 people, approximately 40 of whom were children and 25 of whom were women. In the course of his remarks he used the adjective 'M●●●●● f●●●●●' [sic] on four occasions, to describe the teachers, the school board, the town and his own country." Without opinion, the Court remanded the case "for reconsideration in light of *Cohen* v. *California* and *Gooding* v. *Wilson.*"

The four *Rosenfeld* dissenters (all Nixon appointees), voted to dismiss the appeal for lack of a substantial Federal question. In one of the three dissenting opinions, Justice Powell, joined by the Chief Justice and Justice Blackmun, reasoned that it was perhaps true that Rosenfeld's language did not constitute "fighting words" within *Chaplinsky*. However, Powell argued that "the exception to the First Amendment protection recognized in *Chaplinsky* is not limited to words whose mere utterance entails a high probability of an outbreak of physical violence. It also extends to the willful use of scurrilous language calculated to offend the sensibilities of an unwilling audience. [A] verbal assault on an unwilling audience may be so grossly offensive and emotionally disturbing as to be the proper subject of criminal proscription." Chief Justice Burger's dissent was sharper: "When we undermine the general belief that the law will give protection against fighting words and profane and abusive language such as the utterances involved [here], we take steps to return to the law of the jungle." Burger concluded that "it does not unduly tax the imagination to think that some justifiably outraged parent whose family were exposed to the foul mouthings of [the speaker] would 'meet him outside' and, either alone or with others, resort to the 19th century's vigorous modes of dealing with such people." Justice Rehnquist also dissented. (Cf. *Lewis* v. *City of New Orleans,* 408 U.S. 913, 1972; *Brown* v. *Oklahoma,* 408 U.S. 914, 1972, and *Hess* v. *Indiana,* 414 U.S. 105, 1973.)

ASSEMBLY AND ASSOCIATION: DEVELOPING THE STANDARDS

In *DeJonge* v. *Oregon* (299 U.S. 353, 1937) the Supreme Court made it clear that the "right of peaceable assembly is a right cognate to those of free speech and free press and equally fundamental." DeJonge was indicted for violating the state criminal syndicalism law. He was charged and convicted with assisting in the conduct of a meeting called under the auspices of the Communist Party. The fact that nothing unlawful took place at the meeting was immaterial, since the indictment was not concerned with conduct at the meeting in question but rather with the fact that DeJonge assisted in the conduct of a public meeting held under the auspices of the Communist Party. The Supreme Court reversed the conviction saying that "peaceable assembly for lawful discussion cannot be made a crime." Chief Justice Hughes, in his strongly worded opinion for the Court, hit hard at the "broad reach" of the statute and said that "the question, if the rights of free speech and peaceable assembly are to be preserved, is not as to the auspices under which the meeting is held but as to its purposes; not as to the relations of the speakers, but whether their utterances transcend the bounds of the freedom of speech which the Constitution protects."

The right of assembly of *DeJonge* was greatly bolstered in 1958 when the Court in *National Association for the Advancement of Colored People* v. *Alabama* clearly recognized that the First Amendment protected freedom of association.[4] Here the Court overturned Alabama's attempt to compel the NAACP to disclose its membership list. Speaking for a unanimous Court, Justice Harlan said:

> Effective advocacy of both public and private points of view, particularly controversial ones, is undeniably enhanced by group association, as this Court has more than once recognized by remarking upon the close nexus between the freedoms of speech and assembly.... It is beyond debate that freedom to engage in association for the advancement of beliefs and ideas is an inseparable aspect of the "liberty" assured by the Due Process Clause of the Fourteenth Amendment, which embraces freedom of speech....

The Court said that the NAACP had uncontrovertedly shown that, in the past, revealing the identity of rank-and-file members had resulted in "economic reprisals, loss of employment, threat of physical coercion, and other manifestations of public hostility." Under such circumstances, the Court thought, compelled disclosure of membership would be likely to adversely affect the petitioner's freedom of association.

Following *NAACP* v. *Alabama,* in *Shelton* v. *Tucker* (364 U.S. 479, 1960) the Court declared unconstitutional an Arkansas statute on the ground that it violated the "associational freedom" of the First Amendment. The statute required every teacher, "as a condition of employment in a state supported school or college, to file annually an affidavit listing without limitation every organization to which he has belonged or regularly contributed within the preceding five years." Unlike the *NAACP* case, the Court acknowledged that Arkansas had a legitimate interest to inquire into the fitness and competence of its teachers. Nevertheless, the Court thought the statute went "far beyond what might be justified in the exercise of the state's legitimate inquiry" and thus greatly interfered with associational freedom. Said Justice Stewart for the 5-4 majority:

> The question is whether the State can ask every one of its teachers to disclose every single organization with which he has been associated over a five-year period. The scope of the inquiry required by [the statute] is completely unlimited. The statute requires a teacher to reveal the church to which he belongs, or to which he has given financial support. It requires him to disclose his political party, and every political organization to which he may have

---

[4] This associational freedom has been quite relevant in the context of cases dealing with the Communist Party and loyalty oaths. See Chapter 4.

contributed over a five-year period. It requires him to list, without number, every conceivable kind of associational tie—social, professional, political, avocational, or religious. Many such relationships could have no possible bearing upon the teacher's occupational competence or fitness.

In a series of decisions this Court has held that, even though the governmental purpose be legitimate and substantial, that purpose cannot be pursued by means that broadly stifle fundamental personal liberties when the end can be more narrowly achieved. The breadth of legislative abridgement must be viewed in the light of less drastic means for achieving the same basic purpose.

Justice Frankfurter, who spoke for himself and the other dissenting justices, thought the statute provided a reasonable means for a school board to inquire into the nature and quality of its teachers' outside activities as these might relate to their school work. If information collected is misused—such as terminating a teacher's employment solely on the basis of membership in "unpopular" organizations—said Frankfurter, "it will be time enough . . . to hold the application of the statute unconstitutional."

Associational freedom for college students was the crucial issue in *Healy* v. *James* (408 U.S. 169, 1972). These students contested college President James' refusal to recognize their chapter of Students for a Democratic Society (SDS) as a campus organization. The students argued that denying them recognition, which precluded use of campus facilities ranging from bulletin boards to meeting rooms, abridged their rights of freedom of expression and association protected by the First and Fourteenth Amendments. Justice Lewis Powell's majority opinion indicated that the "denial of official recognition, without justification" interfered improperly with associational rights and that the courts below erred in characterizing the denial as insubstantial. Furthermore, Powell held that the burden in this dispute was on the college official to justify the refusal of recognition, not on the students to prove entitlement to recognition. In the end, however, the Court remanded the case because one of the reasons given for the denial of recognition was "potentially acceptable."

PICKETING, HANDBILLING, AND SYMBOLIC SPEECH

When Alabama banned all peaceful picketing regardless of purpose, the Supreme Court declared the law unconstitutional as an invasion of freedom of speech. The statute swept too broadly. Speaking for the Court in *Thornhill* v. *Alabama* (310 U.S. 88, 1940), Justice Frank Murphy contended:

> The freedom of speech and of the press guaranteed by the Constitution embraces at the least the liberty to discuss publicly and truthfully all matters of public concern without previous restraint or fear of subsequent punishment. . . . Freedom of discussion, if it would fulfill its historic function in this nation, must embrace all issues about which information is needed or appropriate to enable the members of society to cope with the exigencies of their period.

In the circumstances of our times the dissemination of information concerning the facts of a labor dispute must be regarded as within that area of free discussion that is guaranteed by the Constitution. . . . The merest glance at State and Federal legislation on the subject demonstrates the force of the argument that labor relations are not matters of mere local or private concern.

This glowing language of *Thornhill*, however, has since been narrowed in subsequent Court decisions. Thus, even peaceful picketing can be constitutionally enjoined if it prevents the effectuation of valid state policies. (See, for example, *Hughes* v. *Superior Court of California* 339 U.S. 460, 1950, and *International Brotherhood of Teamsters* v. *Vogt* 354 U.S. 284, 1957.) Indeed picketing, the traditional method used by workers to convey their views to the public, involves more than speech; it involves elements of speech and conduct. And the Court indicated in *Hughes* and *Vogt* that "because of the intermingling of these protected and unprotected elements, picketing can be subjected to controls that would not be constitutionally permissible in the case of pure speech." But in *Amalgamated Food Employees Local 590* v. *Logan Valley Plaza, Inc.* (391 U.S. 308, 1968) Justice Thurgood Marshall rejected the notion that "the nonspeech aspects of peaceful picketing are so great as to render the provisions of the First Amendment inapplicable to it altogether." Here, the Court held that the First Amendment protects peaceful picketing within a privately-owned shopping center "because the shopping center serves as the community business block 'and is freely accessible and open to the people in the area and those passing through.'"

However, the Burger Court apparently is not as scrupulous in protecting those who distribute handbills on private property. In *Lloyd Corp.* v. *Tanner* (407 U.S. 551, 1972) Justice Byron White, for a closely divided 5-4 Court, upheld the right of a privately-owned shopping center, open to the public, to prohibit the distribution of handbills on its property when the handbilling is unrelated to the shopping center's operations. The handbills advertised a meeting to protest the draft and the Vietnam War. The Court distinguished this case from *Logan Valley* by focusing on the "shopping center's operations" language and not on the "community business block" phrase. In a strong defense of private property rights, Justice White reemphasized the basic principle that "the First and Fourteenth Amendments safeguard the rights of free speech and assembly by limitations on state action, not on action by the owner of private property used nondiscriminatorily for private purposes only."

Dissenting, Justice Thurgood Marshall, also speaking for Justices Brennan, Douglas, and Stewart, thought that the majority had strayed from time-honored precedents such as *Marsh* v. *Alabama* (326 U.S. 501, 1946) and *Logan Valley*. In a sharply worded observation, Marshall said:

[O]ne may suspect from reading the opinion of the Court that it is *Logan Valley* itself that the Court finds bothersome. The vote in *Logan Valley* was 6-3, and that decision is only four years old. But I am aware that the composition of this Court has radically changed in four years. The fact remains that *Logan*

Valley is binding unless and until it is overruled. There is no valid distinction between that case and this one. . . .

Noting the increasing reliance of governments on private enterprise, Marshall warned that "only the wealthy may find effective communication possible unless we adhere to *Marsh* v. *Alabama* and continue to hold that '[t]he more an owner, for his advantage, opens up his property for use by the public in general, the more do his rights become circumscribed by the statutory and constitutional rights of those who use it.' "

Is the communication of an idea by conduct protected by the First Amendment? In other words, what about symbolic speech? The issue was raised when four persons stood on the steps of the South Boston Courthouse on March 13, 1966, and burned their draft cards as a way of expressing opposition to the Vietnam War. They were tried and convicted under a 1965 Congressional law which made it a crime to knowingly destroy or mutilate draft cards. But burning draft cards, they argued, was "symbolic speech" or "communication of ideas by conduct," which is protected by the First Amendment. The Supreme Court disagreed. In *United States* v. *O'Brien* the Court by a 7-1 vote said it could not accept the position that an "apparently limitless variety of conduct can be labelled 'speech' whenever the person engaging in the conduct intends thereby to express an idea." Moreover, continued Chief Justice Warren who spoke for the majority, when "speech" and "non-speech" elements are "combined in the same course of conduct, a sufficiently important governmental interest in regulating the non-speech element can justify incidental limitations on First Amendment freedoms." The Court found that the governmental regulation as imposed by the 1965 law was sufficiently justified. Justice Douglas, the lone dissenter, thought that the basic question in the case was "whether conscription is permissible in the absence of a declaration of war." He argued that the Court should make a ruling on it.

Symbolic speech, involving another sort of national symbol, arose in a 1970 case, *Schacht* v. *United States* (398 U.S. 58, 1970). Schacht, who wore part of an Army uniform while participating in an antiwar skit performed in front of an induction center, was convicted under a Federal law (18 U.S.C., Sec. 702) that bars the unauthorized wearing of a United States military uniform. The Court, citing *O'Brien,* upheld the statute's constitutionality, but at the same time reversed Schacht's conviction, citing another statute (10 U.S.C., Sec. 772(f)). That law, authorizing actors portraying members of the armed forces in a "theatrical production" to wear military uniforms "if the portrayal does not tend to discredit that armed force"—was found to "impose an unconstitutional restraint on [Schacht's] right of free speech." Justice Black argued that the antiwar skit, although "crude and amateurish and perhaps unappealing," was a "theatrical production" within the scope of the provision and held that "the final clause of section 772 (f), which leaves Americans free to praise the war in Vietnam but can send persons like Schacht to prison for opposing it, cannot survive in a country which has the First Amendment."

In *Street* v. *New York* (394 U.S. 577, 1969), a case similar to *O'Brien,* the Court skirted the question of whether a person could be punished for burning or defacing an American Flag. After learning that James Meredith had been shot from ambush in Mississippi in 1966, Street, a Brooklyn black, in apparent disgust, burned the American flag that he had always displayed on national holidays. When encountered by a police officer, Street remarked: "We don't need no damn flag." He was convicted under a New York law that makes it a crime to "publicly mutilate, deface, defile or defy, trample upon or cast contempt upon either by word or act" the state or national flag. By a 5-4 majority the Court voted to set aside Street's conviction. Justice John Marshall Harlan delivered the Court's opinion and emphasized the overbreadth of the statute under which Street was convicted. Harlan noted that the judge (Street was tried before a judge without a jury) did not make a distinction between the actual act of burning and the contemptuous remarks about the flag. Consequently, he held that the statute "was unconstitutionally applied [to Street] because it permitted him to be punished merely for [his] defiant or contemptuous words about the flag"—words which, Harlan contended, were constitutionally protected. Even assuming that the conviction could have been based solely on the act of burning the flag, Harlan argued that the conviction should be reversed because a guilty verdict ensued from the indictment, which charged the commission of a crime by use of words and the act of flag burning without elucidation and it is possible that the trial judge could have considered the two acts as "intertwined . . . . . [resting] the conviction on both together." Harlan concluded that while "disrespect for our flag is to be deplored no less in these vexed times than in calmer periods of our history," a conviction that may have been based on a form of expression that the Constitution protects cannot be sustained. For, he continued, "the 'right to differ as to things that touch the heart of the existing order,' encompass[es] the freedom to express publicly one's opinions about our flag, including those opinions which are defiant or contemptuous."

The dissenters took sharp exception to the majority's avoidance of the crucial constitutional issue presented in the case. To them, this case was not one in which constitutionally protected expression had been sacrificed to protect the flag; rather, at issue was whether the deliberate act of burning the American flag is symbolic expression protected by the Constitution. In his dissent, Chief Justice Earl Warren noted that the record below indicated clearly that all parties focused on the "flag burning as symbolic expression" issue and so did the state appellate court. Warren argued that where a constitutional issue is presented to the Court, as this one had been, the Court has the "responsibility to confront [it] squarely and resolve it." He warned that facing the flag burning and desecration issue was particularly pressing because the "flag has increasingly become an integral part of public protests." Indicating his belief that federal and state governments have the power to protect the flag from desecration, he thought that the Court would have concluded likewise if it had faced the issue.

The Court also faced symbolic speech cases focusing on the Vietnam War in a public school setting. Such a situation came before the Court in *Tinker* v. *Des Moines Independent Community School District* (393 U.S. 503, 1969). Here public school officials, under the claim of maintaining orderly processes and decorum, suspended students who persisted in wearing black armbands to express opposition to United States involvement in Vietnam. Justice Fortas, speaking for the Court, viewed the black armbands as peaceful expression of political opinion and thus protected by the First Amendment. The students' behavior did not cause disorder or disruption of school activities, observed Fortas, and "undifferentiated fear or apprehension of disturbance is not enough to overcome the right to freedom of expression." In any event, since school officials had permitted students in Des Moines to wear other symbols, e.g., political campaign buttons, Fortas saw the prohibition against armbands as a method to suppress opposition to the Vietnam War. "In our system," said Fortas, "students may not be regarded as closed-circuit recipients of only that which the state chooses to communicate." Thus, for the first time in its history, the Court ruled that public school students are entitled to free speech guarantees of the First Amendment. However, Fortas was careful to point out that the Court's decision pertained only to "symbolic speech" or speech itself and did not extend to protest demonstrations.

Nonetheless, Justice Hugo Black issued a sharp dissent. He complained that the Court's decision ushers in "a new revolutionary era of permissiveness in this country in which the power of school officials to control pupils is substantially weakened." Black took judicial notice of the timing of the decision and noted that "groups of students all over the land . . . [were] running loose, conducting break-ins, sit-ins, lie-ins, and smash-ins." Decisions like *Tinker,* warned Black, "subject all the public schools in the country to the whims and caprices of their loudest-mouthed, but maybe not their brightest students." He was certain that students were not wise enough to run the public school system.

The *Tinker* ruling prompted numerous constitutional challenges to school dress and hair style codes in the lower Federal courts. However, the Supreme Court has steadfastly refused to review lower court decisions on the enforcement of such regulations by school officials, despite conflicting rulings of several courts of appeals. William O. Douglas, dissenting in one such refusal (*Freeman* v. *Flake,* 405 U.S. 1032, 1972), noted of the eight appeals courts that have ruled on the issue, four upheld school hair regulations, and four rejected them. He felt that because of the widely divergent rationales set forth to support those rulings and their important bearing on First and Ninth Amendment rights, the Court should exercise its discretionary jurisdiction to reconcile the conflicting lower court rulings.

DAMAGE TO REPUTATION

In his opinion in *Near* v. *Minnesota*, Chief Justice Charles Evans Hughes emphasized the need for "a vigilant and courageous press" to focus attention on malfeasance and corruption of unfaithful public officials.[5] But when does comment on official conduct lose its character as constitutionally protected expression and become subject to the sanctions of state libel laws? The Supreme Court supplied the answer in *New York Times* v. *Sullivan* in reversing a half-million dollar judgment against the New York Times Publishing Company which had been awarded to a local public official by an Alabama court. Paradoxically, the allegedly defamatory publication did not deal with the traditional subjects on which there has been criticism of official conduct, e.g., alliances with criminal elements and malfeasance in office. Instead, the publication was an editorial advertisement on the civil-rights movement in the South.

In setting aside the judgment, the Supreme Court applied the brakes to Southern public officials who try to stifle comment critical of their conduct in actions involving race relations. Thus, Sullivan's allegation that the advertisement contained a number of inaccuracies and was injurious to his reputation as a public official was rejected. Justice William J. Brennan, who wrote the opinion of the Court, noted that the case must be considered "against the background of a profound national commitment to the principle that debate on public issues should be uninhibited, robust, and wide open, and that it may well include vehement, caustic, and sometimes unpleasantly sharp attacks . . . on public officials." With this principal in mind, Brennan held that the crucial question is whether the advertisement forfeited its status as constitutionally protected expression because it contained some false statements and allegedly defamed the respondent. Advancing the proposition that "erroneous statement is inevitable in free debate and . . . must be protected if the freedoms of expression are to have the 'breathing space' that they 'need . . . to survive,' " he concluded that "neither factual error nor defamatory content" nor "the combination of the two elements" can justify removal of "the constitutional shield from criticism of official conduct" unless there is proof of "actual malice."

Justice Hugo Black's concurring opinion, supported by Justice William O. Douglas, set forth the absolutist position that the *Times* and the sponsors of the ad had an "unconditional constitutional right to publish . . . their criticisms of the Montgomery agencies and officials."

Later that year, the Court extended its *New York Times* rule to limit state power to impose criminal sanctions for criticism of the official conduct of public officials. In *Garrison* v. *Louisiana* (379 U.S. 64, 1964) a unanimous Court reversed the conviction of District Attorney Jim Garrison of Orleans Parish (County), Louisiana, on a charge of criminal defamation based on his criticism of the official conduct of judges of the parish's Criminal District Court. In an opinion supported by five members of the Court, Justice Brennan rejected the contention that because "criminal libel laws serve distinct interests from those secured by civil libel laws" they should not be subject to the limitations laid down in the *New York Times* case. Said Brennan, "[t]he *New York Times* rule is not rendered inapplicable merely because an official's private reputation, as well as his public reputation, is

---

[5] Probably the most significant rulings on freedom of the press since *Near* were the Pentagon Papers cases decided by the Court in 1972. See Chapter 4 on Internal Security, *infra*.

harmed.... [A]nything which might touch an official's fitness for office is relevant." He concluded that "even where the utterance is false, the great principles of the Constitution ... preclude attaching adverse consequences to any except the knowing or reckless falsehood."

As in *New York Times,* the concurring opinions of Justices Black and Douglas once again emphasized that the absolutist position is the only rule which makes sense.

The Court examined further the scope of the term "public official" and the meaning of "malice" in *Rosenblatt* v. *Baer* (383 U.S. 75, 1966). Here the Court reversed a state libel judgment against a newspaper columnist for using defamatory falsehoods in commentary about the performance of a supervisor of a county recreation area. Justice William J. Brennan held that since the position of "Supervisor of the Belknap County Recreation Area" was embraced within the term "public official" as construed in *New York Times,* the instructions to the jury (which permitted the jury to find that negligent misstatement of fact would abrogate the commentary's privileged status) were defective.

Regarding "malice," Brennan contended that the state court definition, which includes "ill will, evil motive [and] intention to injure," was "constitutionally insufficient where discussion of public affairs is concerned." It did not square with the definition set forth in *New York Times* which requires a showing that the statement was made with knowledge of its falsity or "reckless disregard of whether it was false or not."

In another dimension of the defamation issue, the Court, in *Time, Inc.* v. *Hill* (385 U.S. 374, 1967) applied the *New York Times* rule in holding that a New York "right of privacy" statute was unconstitutionally applied to redress false reports of matters of public interest in the absence of proof of actual malice. The case involved a *Life* magazine article in which the fictionalized play "The Desperate Hours" was portrayed as a reenactment of the ordeal of a family held captive by three escaped convicts. Taking cognizance of the "exposure of one's self to others [as] a concomitant of life in a civilized community," Justice William J. Brennan contended that such a risk "is an essential incident of life in a society which places a primary value on freedom of speech and of press." He argued that "[e]rroneous statement[s]" are just as inevitable in commentary on "newsworthy" private citizens and events as in commentary on "public affairs." Consequently, Brennan concluded, erroneous statements in both categories, "if innocent or merely negligent, ... must be protected if the freedoms of expression are to have the "breathing space" that they 'need ... to survive.' "

In the companion cases of *Curtis Publishing Co.* v. *Butts,* and *Associated Press* v. *Walker* (338 U.S. 130, 1967) the Court considered whether its ruling in *New York Times* extended to libel actions brought by "public figures" who are "involved in issues in which the public has a justified and important interest." The *Butts* case involved a federal district court libel judgment of $460,000 against the Curtis Publishing Company for publication of an article in *Saturday Evening Post* in which Wally Butts, longtime football coach and athletic director of the University of Georgia, was accused of plotting to fix a football game between his school and the University of Alabama. The *Walker* case was an appeal from a state court libel judgment of $500,000 against the Associated Press for publication of news stories describing the role of retired Major General Edwin A. Walker in the campus disorders accompanying the enrollment of James Meredith at the University of Mississippi.

In examining the constitutional issues presented by these cases, Justice Harlan, who wrote the leading opinion, counseled against "blind application" of the *New York Times* rule. He stressed that "none of the particular considerations involved in *New York Times*" were present in *Butts* and *Walker*. Hence, it was necessary to formulate a new rule of libel which he stated as follows:

> [A] "public figure" who is not a public official may . . . recover damages for a defamatory falsehood whose substance makes substantial danger to reputation apparent, on a showing of highly unreasonable conduct constituting an extreme departure from standards of investigation and reporting ordinarily adhered to by responsible publishers.

Applying this new rule to the cases, Harlan concluded that there was enough evidence to support the judgment in *Butts* but that the evidence was insufficient to prove "a severe departure from accepted publishing standards" in *Walker*.

The *New York Times* doctrine was further expanded in a 1971 decision— *Rosenbloom* v. *Metromedia, Inc.* (403 U.S. 29, 1971)—which involved a libel suit brought by a private individual against a radio broadcasting corporation. Rosenbloom, a distributor of nudist magazines, was arrested for possession of obscene literature. One of Metromedia's radio stations, in reports concerning Rosenbloom's subsequent suit alleging that the magazines he distributed were not obscene, described Rosenbloom and the publisher of the magazines involved as "girlie-book peddlers" and as part of the "smut literature racket." Rosenbloom initiated the libel suit against Metromedia after being acquitted of criminal obscenity charges. The Court held that the *New York Times* standard applied to libel suits brought by private individuals as well as to suits brought by "public officials" or "public figures" so long as the subject of the suit was a matter of "public or general concern." Justice Brennan's opinion in which Chief Justice Burger and Justice Blackmun joined, explained that:

> Drawing a distinction between "public" and "private" figures makes no sense in terms of the First Amendment guarantees. The *New York Times* standard was applied to libel of a public official or public figure to give effect to the Amendment's function to encourage ventilation of public issues, not because the public official has any less interest in protecting his reputation than an individual in private life.

The Court's decision in the case indicated that there was no evidence to support the contention that Metromedia's descriptions of Rosenbloom, even if defamatory, were made with knowledge of their falsity or with a reckless disregard therefor.

Dissenting, Justice Harlan, who had defined the "public figure" libel rule only four years earlier, contended that "those special considerations" compelling a different test when public officials or public figures are the plaintiffs "do not obtain where the litigant is a purely private individual." Justice Marshall's dissent was critical of Brennan's "public or general concern" test, arguing that it "threatens society's interest in protecting private individuals from being thrust into the public eye by the distorting light of defamation" since "all human events are arguably within the area of 'public or general concern'."

In *Gertz* v. *Robert Welch, Inc.* (94 S. Ct. 2997, 1974) three years later, the Court eliminated some of the confusion fostered by the five separate opinions in *Rosenbloom* when it held the *New York Times* v. *Sullivan* rule was not applicable in determining media liability for alleged defamation of private persons. In his opinion for the Court, Justice Lewis Powell took notice of the greater access of public officials and public figures to the media for counteracting false statements. Contrariwise, he felt that the private individual is much "more vulnerable to injury and [hence,] the state's interest in protecting him is correspondingly greater." Consequently, states should be accorded "substantial latitude" in fashioning legal remedies for such relief.

In dissent, Chief Justice Burger complained about the Court's departure from the orderly development of the law of defamation since the decision in *New York Times* v. *Sullivan*. He indicated his preference for the development of law as it had up to then with respect to private persons rather than embarking "on a new doctrinal theory which has no jurisprudential ancestry." And Justice Douglas' dissent echoed his familiar theme that the First Amendment prohibits such laws absolutely.

Another dimension of the conflict between a free press and governmental regulation in protecting societal interests was considered by the Court in *Miami Herald Publishing Co.* v. *Tornillo* (94 S. Ct. 2831, 1974). There a Florida "right-to-reply" statute was struck down as offending freedom of the press because of its "intrusion into the functions of editors in choosing what materials they wish to print" and what issues and public officials on which and on whom they wish to comment. Such governmental regulation of editorial control and judgment, Chief Justice Burger concluded, is inconsistent with the First Amendment guarantees of a free press. The practical effect of the decision was to deny to political candidates free space to reply to editorial comment which criticized them.

OBSCENITY

Justice William J. Brennan noted in his opinion in *Ron* v. *United States*, that "sex ... has indisputably been a subject of absorbing interest through the ages ...," and as Professors Lockhart and McClure contend, the subject "has always occupied too important and dominant a place in literature and in human interest to be excluded from the [protection of the] First Amendment. . . ."[6] The portrayal

---

[6] William B. Lockhart and Robert C. McClure, "Literature, the Law of Obscenity, and the Constitution," 38 *Minnesota Law Review* 358-359 (1954).

of sex in books, magazines, motion pictures, the legitimate theater, and television is now commonplace. Sex and obscenity are not synonymous, but the various media have the potential for portraying sex in an obscene manner. Hence, governments have instituted various types of regulatory actions to protect the public morals. Statutes have been enacted to prohibit the publication, production, sale, and exhibition of obscene books, magazines, motion pictures, and other matter. Administrative agencies have been established to review and license motion pictures prior to their exhibition. Postal and customs authorities have exercised regulatory powers in prohibiting dissemination of obscene materials through their channels. Enforcement of such regulations has raised many troublesome questions involving the federal constitutional guarantees of freedom of speech and freedom of the press—questions that have inevitably ended up in the Supreme Court for resolution.

The Court first considered the difficult problem of defining obscenity in 1957. In companion cases arising under the federal obscenity statute (*Roth* v. *United States*, 354 U.S. 476) and the California obscenity code (*Alberts* v. *California*), the Court sustained convictions (in *Roth*) for use of the mails to disseminate obscene matter, and (in *Alberts*) for possession of obscene matter for sale by mail order. In his opinion for the Court, Justice William J. Brennan emphasized that ideas with the "slightest redeeming social importance" must be accorded the full protection of the First Amendment. But since obscene matter is "utterly without redeeming social importance," it is not protected expression. The test, said Brennan, is "whether to the average person, applying contemporary community standards, the dominant theme of the material taken as a whole appeals to prurient interest." While this test was considered an improvement over the earlier *Hicklin* test that allowed material to be judged "by the effect of an isolated [passage] upon particularly susceptible persons," in practice it opened up a Pandora's box of questions for law enforcement officials and the lower courts. What does the term "prurient interest" mean? Who is "the average person"? What is "redeeming social importance"? Who determines "contemporary community standards" and what is the "relevant community"?

In subsequent decisions the Court provided some answers to these questions. In *Manual Enterprises* v. *Day* (370 U.S. 478, 1962), the Court narrowed the sweep of its "prurient interest" test by holding that to be adjudged obscene, material must not only have "prurient interest" appeal but its "patent offensiveness" must be demonstrated. Furthermore, Justice Harlan held that the two elements "must conjoin" to support a finding of obscenity. Applying this test to reverse an obscenity finding of postal authorities, Harlan contended that the magazines in question (containing photographs of nude males), while "dismally unpleasant, uncouth, and tawdry," were not "under any permissible constitutional standard . . . beyond the pale of contemporary notions of rudimentary decency."

Jacobellis v. *Ohio* (378 U.S. 184, 1964) was used by Justice William J. Brennan to expand upon the "redeeming social importance" concept. In that case, a state court obscenity conviction for exhibiting the movie *Les Amants* was reversed by the Court and Justice Brennan stressed that obscene material is that which is "utterly without redeeming social importance." Conversely, he argued, if material "has literary or scientific or any other form of social importance [it] may not be branded as obscenity. . . ." Brennan also focused attention on the "contemporary community standards" concept. The "relevant community," he held, must be construed in the broad sense of "society at large."

The significance of the "redeeming social importance" test is well illustrated in *A Book Named "John Cleland's Memoirs of a Woman of Pleasure"* v. *Attorney General of Massachusetts* (383 U.S. 413, 1966). The controversial novel *Fanny Hill*, in which a prostitute reviews her life's experiences, was adjudged obscene by Massachusetts courts. The Supreme Court reversed that holding and, in the opinion for the Court, Justice Brennan emphasized that, although a book may have "prurient interest" appeal and is "patently offensive," it may not be held obscene unless it is "utterly without redeeming social value." To him, each of these criteria is to be applied independently, but material must have all three qualities to be proscribed as obscene. Hence, because the trial court found that *Fanny Hill* contained at least "a modicum of social value" its obscenity finding was erroneous.

A further criterion for determining obscenity was set forth in *Ginzburg* v. *United States* (383 U.S. 463, 1966). Apparently frowning on the "sordid business" of commercializing sex engaged in by some publishers under the guise of freedom of expression, the Court affirmed a federal obscenity conviction on the basis of the publisher's motives as revealed by his advertising and promotion methods. Conceding that the materials under "a different setting" might not be obscene, Justice Brennan, speaking for the majority, made it clear that "where the purveyor's sole emphasis is on the sexually provocative aspects of his publications, that fact may be decisive in the determination of obscenity." Furthermore, he assumed that the prosecution could not have succeeded otherwise.

The obvious difficulty with Brennan's opinion is that it provides for the evaluation of the substantive content of a work partly on the basis of the use to which it is put. Actually, Brennan was focusing on "pandering" and in doing so, as Justice Harlan pointed out, the conviction was affirmed upon something quite different from that on which Ginzburg was charged and tried. Harlan contended that if there is any validity in adding the "pandering" dimension to the existing obscenity tests, then the least the Court could do would be to remand the case so Ginzburg could "have his day in court" on the "amended" charges.

The Court continued to recognize the need for more legislative flexibility in dealing with obscenity when it held in *Ginsberg* v. *New York* (390 U.S. 629, 1968), that what may be obscene for minors may not be for adults. Speaking for the Court, Justice Brennan accepted the state's "variable obscenity" standard and held that government can impose stricter standards on materials sold to juveniles than on that sold to adults. "The state has an independent interest in the well-being of its youth," said Brennan, and can constitutionally accord them "a more restricted right than that assured to adults." But even the "variable obscenity" doctrine does not give states unfettered discretion to move against minors. In *Interstate Circuit, Inc.* v. *Dallas* (390 U.S. 676, 1968), for example, the Court held void for vagueness a city ordinance that empowered a board to ban from exhibition for persons under sixteen years of age motion pictures in which the portrayal of brutality and sex would tend to incite crime and encourage sexual promiscuity among youth. Justice

Thurgood Marshall, who wrote the Court's opinion, pointed out that the inclusion of such undefined terms as "sacrilegious" and "sexual promiscuity" rendered the ordinance fatally defective. Such loose language, said Marshall, left the censors free to apply their own mores in regulating the film fare of others.

The indefiniteness resulting from these several "tests" had the result of providing publishers, movie-makers, and others wide latitude in the treatment of sexual matters in their works. Consequently, there was a major boom in so-called smut and pornography in the late 1960s and the early 1970s. As never before, motion pictures with "X" ratings for "Adults Only" depicted graphically a wide variety of sexual activities. In addition, "Adults Only" bookstores openly promoted as having "a modicum of redeeming social value" books and magazines that many considered to be hard-core pornography. Alarmed at this trend, many Americans pointed an accusing finger at the Supreme Court as a major causal agent of this crisis in morals. And, to be sure, President Nixon had echoed a similar view in rejecting in 1970 the recommendation of the Commission on Obscenity and Pornography that advocated unrestricted access to sexual materials by consenting adults.

When this latest dimension of the obscenity debate reached the Court in 1973, the four Nixon appointees (Burger, Blackmun, Powell, and Rehnquist) were joined by Warren Court holdover Byron White in a major overhaul of obscenity law which had developed since the 1957 *Roth-Alberts* decision. In *Miller* v. *California,* and four companion cases, the Court emphasized the need for more definitive standards than those employed in the past. Chief Justice Burger, speaking for the Court, set forth the following test:

(a) [W]hether "the average person, applying contemporary community stan-dards" would find that the work taken as a whole, appeals to the prurient interest;
(b) whether the work depicts or describes, in a patently offensive way, sexual conduct specifically defined by the applicable state law; and
(c) whether the work, taken as a whole, lacks serious literary, artistic, political, or scientific value.

Careful examination of this test reveals a major modification of the "contem-porary community" concept and the "redeeming social value" standard. Rejecting the "national standards" concept implicit in Justice Brennan's "society-at-large" language in the 1964 *Jacobellis* case, the Chief Justice emphasized the need for standards to reflect local views. Notwithstanding the national implications of the First Amendment, he held that it was "neither realistic nor constitutionally sound" to demand "that the people of Maine or Mississippi accept public depiction of conduct found tolerable in Las Vegas or New York City."

Under the new test the publishers of controversial works like *Fanny Hill* will no longer be able to protect their works by arguing their "redeeming social value." Instead, the more demanding modification allows authorities to inquire if the work, "taken as a whole, lacks serious literary, artistic, political or scientific value." The trier of facts makes this determination.

That *Miller* marked a more restrictive posture of the Court with regard to the First Amendment and obscenity was underscored by the sharp dissents of Justices Douglas, Brennan, Stewart, and Marshall, all holdovers from the Warren Court. For example, Justice Douglas, after reviewing the Court's major prior decisions on obscenity, asserted:

> Today the Court retreats from the earlier formulations of the constitutional test and undertakes to make new definitions. This effort, like the earlier ones, is earnest and well-intentioned. The difficulty is that we do not deal with constitutional terms, since "obscenity" is not mentioned in the Constitution or Bill of Rights. . . . So there are no constitutional guidelines for deciding what is and what is not "obscene." The Court is at large because we deal with tastes and standards of literature. What shocks me may be sustenance for my neighbor. . . . We deal here with problems of censorship which, if adopted, should be done by constitutional amendment after full debate by the people.

Such an amendment, said Douglas, would give courts "some guidelines." "Now," he concluded, "we have none except our predilections."

In its first application of the *Miller* standards, the Court reversed the obscenity conviction of a theater owner for exhibiting the motion picture "Carnal Knowledge" in *Jenkins* v. *Georgia* (94 S. Ct. 2750, 1974), and in doing so appeared to be continuing a case-by-case adjudication which it had hoped to avoid with its *Miller* decision. Such was suggested by Justice William Rehnquist, who spoke for a unanimous court, when he said that " *our own view* of the film satisfies us" that it is not obscene under the *Miller* standard which requires a finding that sexual conduct is depicted in a "patently offensive way." In a concurring opinion, Justice William J. Brennan put it more bluntly. He charged that the court's actions in *Jenkins* and in *Hamling* v. *United States* (94 S. Ct. 2887, 1974) (where, at the same time, the Court affirmed a conviction of a distributor of a brochure that advertised an illustrated version of the report of the President's Commission on Obscenity and Pornography because a local jury decided that the brochure contained obscene illustrations), "do not extricate us from the mire of case-by-case determinations of obscenity." He concluded that not only does this continue great uncertainty in this area of the law, but it continues "institutional stress upon the judiciary."

Various methods used by state and local government to control dissemination of obscene matter have resulted in considerable litigation producing a number of significant Supreme Court decisions. With regard to books and other printed matter, the Court has: (1) approved a New York statute authorizing limited injunctive proceedings against the sale of obscene books (*Kingsley Books* v. *Brown*, 354 U.S. 436, 1957), reaffirmed in *A Quantity of Copies of Books* v. *Kansas*, (378 U.S. 205, 1964); (2) declared a Michigan statute unconstitutional that made it a crime to sell to the general public materials, which tended to "incite minors to violent or depraved or immoral acts, manifestly tending to the corruption of the morals of youth" (*Butler* v. *Michigan*, 352 U.S. 380, 1957); (3) invalidated a city ordinance because it did not contain "scienter"—a provision that the bookseller knowingly offered an obscene book for sale (*Smith* v. *California,* 361 U.S. 147, 1959); (4) declared the "informal practices" of a Rhode Island statutory Commission to Encourage Morality in Youth unconstitutional as a form of prior restraint abridging freedom of the press (*Bantam Books* v. *Sullivan,* 372 U.S. 58, 1963); and (5) invalidated the search and seizure procedures of a Kansas law because the procedures lacked sufficient safeguards for the protection of non-obscene materials and allowed law enforcement officials too much discretion to determine which publication should be seized (*Marcus* v. *Search Warrant,* 376 U.S. 717, 1961).

The Court has also held that mere possession of obscene matter in the home for personal use is not a crime. In *Stanley* v. *Georgia* (394 U.S. 557, 1969) a unanimous Court overturned a Georgia conviction for possession of obscene matter where law enforcement officers raided Stanley's home searching for gambling paraphernalia and in the process discovered and seized three reels of "stag movies" from a desk drawer in the bedroom. These movies were used as evidence to support the obscenity conviction. In overturning the conviction, Justice Thurgood Marshall emphasized the constitutional right of an individual "to satisfy his intellectual and emotional needs in the privacy of his own home." "If the First Amendment means anything," said Marshall, "it means that a state has no business telling a man sitting alone in his own house, what books he may read or what films he may watch."

Four subsequent rulings, however, severely limit this decision. In two 1971 cases—*United States* v. *Reidel* (402 U.S. 351) and *United States* v. *Thirty-Seven Photographs* (402 U.S. 363)—the Supreme Court indicated that although the Stanley holding remained viable, its extension was unlikely. Justice White's opinion for the Court in *Reidel,* for example, stated:

> ... To extrapolate from Stanley's right to have and peruse obscene material in the privacy of his own home, a First Amendment right in *Reidel* to sell it to him would effectively scuttle *Roth,* the precise result that the *Stanley* opinion abjured. Whatever the scope of the "right to receive" referred to in *Stanley*, it is not so broad as to immunize the dealings in obscenity in which Reidel engaged here—dealings which *Roth* held unprotected by the First Amendment.

Reidel upheld the right of Congress to prevent mail distribution of pornography, while *Thirty-Seven Photographs* sustained its right to prohibit importation of obscene materials. Moreover, the trend indicated in *Reidel* and *Thirty-Seven Photographs* was continued in two 1973 decisions *United States* v. *Orito* (413 U.S. 139) and *United States* v. *12 200-Ft. Reels* (413 U.S. 123). In *Orito* the Court held that the *Stanley* rationale did not go so far as to permit interstate transportation of obscene material by a passenger on a common carrier even if such material was for purely personal use. And in *12 200-Ft. Reels* the Court clarified the *Thirty-Seven Photographs* decision by holding that Congress could prohibit importation of obscene material intended solely for personal use.

Motion pictures, unlike books and other printed matter, were long considered entertainment and not a medium for the communication of ideas protected by the

First Amendment. Justice Joseph McKenna stated the principle in *Mutual Film Corporation* v. *Industrial Commission of Ohio* (236 U.S. 230, 1915) when he said that the production and exhibition of motion pictures is "a business, pure and simple," and is not "to be regarded . . . as part of the press of the country, or as organs of public opinion." As such, and recognizing the medium's "capacity for evil," the Court approved state censorship of motion pictures. By 1948, however, a change in the judicial attitude on the subject was indicated in the antitrust case of *United States* v. *Paramount Pictures, Inc.* (331 U.S. 131, 1948), when Justice Douglas remarked: "We have no doubt that moving pictures like newspapers and radio, are included in the press whose freedom is guaranteed by the First Amendment." Four years later in *Burstyn* v. *Wilson* (343 U.S. 495, 1952), the controversy over New York's banning of the Italian film *The Miracle* put the constitutional issue squarely before the Court. The Court struck down the New York ban and in so doing overruled the *Mutual* precedent. There can be no longer any doubt, said the Court, "that motion pictures are a significant medium for the communication of ideas." However, because the New York statute contained vague and meaningless standards, the Court found it unnecessary to rule on whether censorship would be valid under a narrowly drawn statute directed at obscene films.

The Court reemphasized the need for definitive standards in clearly drawn statutes in *Kingsley International Pictures* v. *Regents of State University of New York* (360 U.S. 684, 1959). In his opinion for the Court, Justice Potter Stewart said that the manner in which the state court construed the movie licensing statute "struck at the very heart of constitutionally protected liberty." The state court had sustained a ban on the movie *Lady Chatterly's Lover* because it advocated the unorthodox idea that adultery may be proper behavior under certain circumstances. While Justice Stewart was careful to indicate that this case was not an occasion to consider the scope of state power to censor movies, two concurring justices—Black and Douglas—did. They expressed the view that prior censorship of motion pictures was just as offensive to the First and Fourteenth Amendments as is prior censorship of newspapers and books.

A full examination of the extent of state movie censorship authority came two years later in *Times Film Corporation* v. *City of Chicago* (365 U.S. 43, 1961). In question was the constitutionality of the Chicago movie censorship ordinance, which required submission of motion pictures to a censorship agency before exhibition. No issue of standards was raised. The distributor applied for a permit, paid the license fee, but refused to submit the film *Don Juan* for screening by the censors. He urged on the Court an absolute privilege against prior restraint, thereby challenging the basic authority of the censor. A closely divided Court (5-4) rejected that claim and held that motion picture censorship per se was not necessarily unconstitutional. Justice Tom Clark's majority opinion recognized the motion picture medium's "capacity for evil" as a relevant factor "in determining the permissible scope of community control." Consequently, he argued, since the Court had held in *Burstyn* that motion pictures were not "necessarily subject to the precise rules governing any other particular method of expression," states should not be limited in the selection of the remedy they considered most effective to deal with the problem. In exercising such authority, however, Justice Clark warned against regulations that allowed censors unfettered discretion.

Chief Justice Earl Warren, writing the major dissent (in which Justices Black, Douglas, and Brennan joined), contended that the majority's action amounted to approval of unlimited motion picture censorship by an administrative agency and could also subject other media—newspapers, books, television, radio—to the same type of unlimited censorship.

Four years later, in *Freedman* v. *Maryland* (380 U.S. 51, 1965), the Court restricted its *Times Film* ruling and outlined certain specific and permissible constitutional standards that must be included in laws calling for prior submission of all films to a review board. They provide that: (1) the burden of proving that the film is unprotected expression must rest on the censor; (2) only a procedure requiring a judicial determination suffices to impose a valid final restraint; and (3) any restraint imposed in advance of a final judicial determination on the merits of the case must be limited to preservation of the status quo for the shortest fixed period compatible with sound judicial resolution. These standards were reaffirmed in *Teitel Film Corporation* v. *Cusak* (390 U.S. 139, 1968), where the Court invalidated the Chicago motion picture censorship ordinance because of the lengthy administrative licensing process (50 to 75 days) required before initiation of judicial proceedings.

Of course, censorship of films and books may be imposed by means other than formal legislative action. Informal actions (sanctions) taken by religious and civic groups prove much more effective (or damaging to free expression) than formal means. (See Selected References at the end of the chapter.)

The cases that follow focus on some of the significant issues reviewed in this commentary.

FEINER v. *NEW YORK*
340 U.S. 315; 95 L. Ed. 295; 71 S. Ct. 303 (1951)

MR. CHIEF JUSTICE VINSON *delivered the opinion of the Court.*

Petitioner was convicted of the offense of disorderly conduct, a misdemeanor under the New York penal laws,* in the court of Special

Sessions of the City of Syracuse and was sentenced to thirty days in the county penitentiary. The conviction was affirmed by the Onondaga

*[Sec. 722 of the Penal Law of New York provides:]

Any person who with intent to provoke a breach of the peace, or whereby a breach of the peace may be occasioned, commits any of the following acts shall be deemed to have committed the offense of disorderly conduct:
1. Uses offensive, disorderly, threatening, abusive or insulting language, conduct or behavior;
2. Acts in such a manner as to annoy, disturb, interfere with, obstruct, or be offensive, to others;
3. Congregates with others on a public street and refuses to move on when ordered by the police; . . . .

County Court and the New York Court of Appeals. . . . The case is here on certiorari, . . . petitioner having claimed that the conviction is in violation of his right of free speech under the Fourteenth Amendment.

In the review of state decisions where First Amendment rights are drawn into question, we of course make an examination of the evidence to ascertain independently whether the right has been violated. Here, the trial judge who heard the case without a jury rendered an oral decision at the end of the trial setting forth his determination of the facts upon which he found the petitioner guilty. His decision indicated generally that he believed the state's witnesses, and his summation of the testimony was used by the two New York courts on review in stating the facts. Our appraisal of the facts is, therefore, based upon the uncontroverted facts and, where the controversy exists, upon that testimony which the trial judge did reasonably conclude to be true.

On the evening of March 8, 1949, petitioner Irving Feiner was addressing an open-air meeting at the corner of South McBride and Harrison Streets in the City of Syracuse. At approximately 6:30 p.m., the police received a telephone complaint concerning the meeting, and two officers were detailed to investigate. One of these officers went to the scene immediately, the other arriving some twelve minutes later. They found a crowd of about seventy-five or eighty people, both Negro and white, filling the sidewalk and spreading out into the street. Petitioner, standing on a large wooden box on the sidewalk, was addressing the crowd through a loud-speaker system attached to an automobile. Although the purpose of his speech was to urge his listeners to attend a meeting to be held that night in the Syracuse Hotel, in its course he was making derogatory remarks concerning President Truman, the American Legion, the Mayor of Syracuse, and other local political officials.

The police officers made no effort to interfere with petitioner's speech, but were first concerned with the effect of the crowd on both pedestrian and vehicular traffic. They observed the situation from the opposite side of the street, noting that some pedestrians were forced to walk in the street to avoid the crowd. Since traffic was passing at the time, the officers attempted to get the people listening to petitioner back on the sidewalk. The crowd was restless and there was some pushing, shoving and milling around. One of the officers telephoned the police station from a nearby store, and then both policemen crossed the street and mingled with the crowd without any intention of arresting the speaker.

At this time, petitioner was speaking in a "loud, high-pitched voice." He gave the impression that he was endeavoring to arouse the Negro people against the whites, urging that they rise up in arms and fight for equal rights. The statements before such a mixed audience "stirred up a little excitement." Some of the onlookers made remarks to the police about their inability to handle the crowd and at least one threatened violence if the police did not act. There were others who appeared to be favoring petitioner's arguments. Because of the feeling that existed in the crowd both for and against the speaker, the officers finally "stepped in to prevent it from resulting in a fight." One of the officers approached the petitioner, not for the purpose of arresting him, but to get him to break up the crowd. He asked petitioner to get down off the box, but the latter refused to accede to his request and continued talking. The officer waited for a minute and then demanded that he cease talking. Although the officer had thus twice requested petitioner to stop over the course of several minutes, petitioner not only ignored him but continued talking. During all this time, the crowd was pressing closer around petitioner and the officer. Finally, the officer told petitioner he was under arrest and ordered him to get down from the box, reaching up to grab him. Petitioner stepped down, announcing over the microphone that "the law has arrived, and I suppose they will take over now." In all, the officer had asked petitioner to get down off the box three times over a space of four or five minutes. Petitioner had been speaking for over a half hour.

. . .

We are not faced here with blind condonation by a state court of arbitrary police action. Petitioner was accorded a full, fair trial. . . . The exercise of the police officers' proper discretionary power to prevent a breach of the peace was . . . approved by the trial court and later by two courts on review. The courts below recognized petitioner's right to hold a street meeting at this locality, to make use of loud-speaking equipment in giving his speech, and to make derogatory remarks concerning public officials and the American Legion. They found that the officers in making the arrest were motivated solely by a proper concern for the preservation of the general welfare, and that there was no evidence which could lend color to a claim that the acts of the police were a cover for suppression of petitioner's views and opinions. Petitioner was thus neither arrested nor convicted for the making or the content of his speech. Rather, it was the reaction which it actually engendered.

. . . The findings of the New York courts as to the condition of the crowd and the refusal of petitioner to obey the police requests, supported as they are by the record of this case, are persuasive that the conviction of petitioner for violation of public peace, order and authority does not exceed the bounds of proper state police action. This Court respects, as it must, the interest of the community in maintaining peace and order on its streets. . . . We cannot say that the preservation of that interest here encroaches on the constitutional rights of this petitioner.

We are well aware that the ordinary murmurings and objections of a hostile audience cannot be allowed to silence a speaker, and are also mindful of the possible danger of giving overzealous police officials complete discretion to break up otherwise lawful public meetings. . . . But we are not faced here with such a situation.

It is one thing to say that the police cannot be used as an instrument for the suppression of unpopular views, and another to say that, when as here the speaker passes the bounds of argument or persuasion and undertakes incitement to riot, they are powerless to prevent a breach of the peace. Nor in this case can we condemn the considered judgment of three New York courts approving the means which the police, faced with a crisis, used in the exercise of their power and duty to preserve peace and order. The findings of the state courts as to the existing situation and the imminence of greater disorder coupled with petitioner's deliberate defiance of the police officers convince us that we should not reverse this conviction in the name of free speech.

Affirmed.

MR. JUSTICE FRANKFURTER *concurs in the result in an opinion which is not printed here.*

MR. JUSTICE BLACK, *dissenting.*

The record before us convinces me that petitioner, a young college student, has been sentenced to the penitentiary for the unpopular views he expressed on matters of public interest while lawfully making a streetcorner speech. . . . Today's decision, however, indicates that we must blind ourselves to this fact because the trial judge fully accepted the testimony of the prosecution witnesses on all important points. Many times in the past this Court has said that despite findings below, we will examine the evidence for ourselves to ascertain whether federally protected rights have been denied; otherwise review here would fail of its purpose in safeguarding constitutional guarantees. Even a partial abandonment of this rule marks a dark day for civil liberties in our Nation.

But still more has been lost today. Even accepting every "finding of fact" below, I think this conviction makes a mockery of the free speech guarantees of the First and Fourteenth

Amendments. The end result of the affirmance here is to approve a simple and readily available technique by which cities and states can with impunity subject all speeches, political or otherwise, on streets or elsewhere, to the supervision and censorship of the local police. I will have no part or parcel in this holding which I view as a long step toward totalitarian authority.

. . .

The Court's opinion apparently rests on this reasoning: The policeman, under the circumstances detailed, could reasonably conclude that serious fighting or even riot was imminent; therefore he could stop petitioner's speech to prevent a breach of peace; accordingly, it was "disorderly conduct" for petitioner to continue speaking in disobedience of the officer's request. As to the existence of a dangerous situation on the street corner, it seems far-fetched to suggest that the "facts" show any imminent threat of riot or uncontrollable disorder. It is neither unusual nor unexpected that some people at public street meetings mutter, mill about, push, shove, or disagree, even violently, with the speaker. Indeed, it is rare where controversial topics are discussed that an outdoor crowd does not do some or all of these things. Nor does one isolated threat to assault the speaker forebode disorder. Especially should the danger be discounted where, as here, the person threatening was a man whose wife and two small children accompanied him and who, so far as the record shows, was never close enough to petitioner to carry out the threat.

Moreover, assuming that the "facts" did indicate a critical situation, I reject the implication of the Court's opinion that the police had no obligation to protect the petitioner's constitutional right to talk. The police of course have power to prevent breaches of the peace. But if, in the name of preserving order, they ever can interfere with a lawful public speaker, they first must make all reasonable efforts to protect him. Here the policeman did not even pretend to try

to protect petitioner. According to the officers' testimony, the crowd was restless but there is no showing of any attempt to quiet it; pedestrians were forced to walk into the street, but there was no effort to clear a path on the sidewalk; one person threatened to assault petitioner but the officers did nothing to discourage this when even a word might have sufficed. Their duty was to protect petitioner's right to talk, even to the extent of arresting the man who threatened to interfere. Instead, they shirked that duty and acted only to suppress the right to speak.

Finally, I cannot agree with the Court's statement that petitioner's disregard of the policeman's unexplained request amounted to such "deliberate defiance" as would justify an arrest or conviction for disorderly conduct. On the contrary, I think that the policeman's action was a "deliberate defiance" of ordinary official duty as well as of the constitutional right of free speech. For at least where time allows, courtesy and explanation of commands are basic elements of good official conduct in a democratic society. Here petitioner was "asked" then "told" then "commanded" to stop speaking, but a man making a lawful address is certainly not required to be silent merely because an officer directs it. Petitioner was entitled to know why he should cease doing a lawful act. Not once was he told. I understand that people in authoritarian countries must obey arbitrary orders. I had hoped that there was no such duty in the United States.

In my judgment, today's holding means that as a practical matter, minority speakers can be silenced in any city. Hereafter, despite the First and Fourteenth Amendments, the policeman's club can take heavy toll of a current administration's public critics. Criticism of public officials will be too dangerous for all but the most courageous. . . .

MR. JUSTICE DOUGLAS, *with whom* MR. JUSTICE MINTON *concurs, dissenting.*

Feiner, a university student, made a speech on

a street corner in Syracuse, New York. . . . The purpose of the speech was to publicize a meeting of the Young Progressives of America to be held that evening. A permit authorizing the meeting to be held in a public school auditorium had been revoked and the meeting shifted to a local hotel.

...

The speech was mainly devoted to publicizing the evening's meeting and protesting the revocation of the permit. It also touched on various public issues. The following are the only excerpts revealed by the record:

"Mayor Costello (of Syracuse) is a champagne-sipping bum; he does not speak for the negro people."

"The 15th Ward is run by corrupt politicians, and there are horse rooms operating there."

"President Truman is a bum."

"Mayor O'Dwyer is a bum."

"The American Legion is a Nazi Gestapo."

"The negroes don't have equal rights; they should rise up in arms and fight for their rights."

There was some pushing and shoving in the crowd and some angry muttering. That is the testimony of the police. But there were no fights and no "disorder" even by the standards of the police. There was not even any heckling of the speaker.

But after Feiner had been speaking about 20 minutes a man said to the police officers, "If you don't get that son of a bitch off, I will go over and get him off myself." It was then that the police ordered Feiner to stop speaking; when he refused, they arrested him.

Public assemblies and public speech occupy an important role in American life. One high function of the police is to protect these lawful gatherings so that the speakers may exercise their constitutional rights. When unpopular causes are sponsored from the public platform there will commonly be mutterings and unrest and heckling from the crowd. When a speaker mounts a platform it is not unusual to find him resorting to exaggeration, to vilification of ideas and men, to the making of false charges. But those extravagances ... do not justify penalizing the speaker by depriving him of the platform or by punishing him for his conduct.

A speaker may not, of course, incite a riot any more than he may incite a breach of the peace by the use of "fighting words." ... But this record shows no such extremes. It shows an unsympathetic audience and the threat of one man to haul the speaker from the stage. It is against that kind of threat that speakers need police protection. If they do not receive it and instead the police throw their weight on the side of those who would break up the meetings, the police become the new censors of speech. Police censorship has all the vices of the censorship from city halls which we have repeatedly struck down. . . .

EDWARDS v. SOUTH CAROLINA
372 U.S. 229; 9 L. Ed. 2d 697; 83 S. Ct. 680 (1963)

MR. JUSTICE STEWART *delivered the opinion of the Court.*

The petitioners, 187 in number, were convicted in a magistrate's court in Columbia, South Carolina, of the common-law crime of breach of the peace. Their convictions were ultimately affirmed by the South Carolina Supreme Court. . . . We granted certiorari . . . to consider the claim that these convictions cannot be squared with the Fourteenth Amendment of the United States Constitution.

There was no substantial conflict in the trial evidence. Late in the morning of March 2, 1961, the petitioners, high school and college students of the Negro race, met at the Zion Baptist Church in Columbia. From there, at about noon, they walked in separate groups of about 15 to the South Carolina State House grounds, an area of two city blocks open to the general public. Their purpose was "to submit a protest to the citizens of South Carolina, along with the Legislative Bodies of South Carolina, our feelings and our dissatisfaction with the present condition of discriminatory actions against Negroes, in general, and to let them know that we were dissatisfied and that we would like for the laws which prohibited Negro privileges in this State to be removed."

Already on the State House grounds when the petitioners arrived were 30 or more law enforcement officers, who had advance knowledge that the petitioners were coming.* Each group of petitioners entered the grounds through a driveway and parking area known in the record as the "horseshoe." As they entered, they were told by the law enforcement officials that "they had a right, as a citizen, to go through the State House grounds, as any other citizen has, as long as they were peaceful." During the next half hour or 45 minutes, the petitioners, in the same small groups, walked single file or two abreast in an orderly way† through the grounds, each group

carrying placards bearing such messages as "I am proud to be a Negro" and "Down with segregation."

During this time a crowd of some 200 to 300 onlookers had collected in the horseshoe area and on the adjacent sidewalks. There was no evidence to suggest that these onlookers were anything but curious, and no evidence at all of any threatening remarks, hostile gestures, or offensive language on the part of any member of the crowd. The City Manager testified that he recognized some of the onlookers, whom he did not identify, as "possible trouble makers," but his subsequent testimony made it clear that nobody among the crowd actually caused or threatened any trouble.‡ There was no obstruction of pedestrian or vehicular traffic within the

---

*The Police Chief of Columbia testified that about 15 of his men were present, and that there were, in addition, "some State Highway Patrolmen; there were some South Carolina Law Enforcement officers present and I believe, I'm not positive, I believe there were about three Deputy Sheriffs."

†The Police Chief of Columbia testified as follows:
"Q. Did you, Chief, walk around the State House Building with any of these persons?
"A. I did not. I stayed at the Horseshoe. I placed men over the grounds.
"Q. Did any of your men make a report that any of these persons were disorderly in walking around the State House Grounds?
"A. They did not.

"Q. Under normal circumstances your men would report to you when you are at the scene?
"A. They should.
"Q. Is it reasonable to assume then that there was no disorderly conduct on the part of these persons, since you received no report from your officers?
"A. I would take that for granted, yes."

‡The City Manager testified:
"Q. Were the Negro college students or other students well demeaned? Were they well dressed and were they orderly?
"A. Yes, they were."
"Q. Who were those persons?
"A. I can't tell you who they were. I can tell you they were present in the group. They were recognized as possible trouble makers.
"Q. Did you and your police chief do anything about placing those people under arrest?
"A. No, we had no occasion to place them under arrest.
"Q. Now, sir, you have stated that there were possible trouble makers and your whole testimony has been that, as City Manager, as supervisor of the City Police, your object is to preserve the peace and law and order?
"A. That's right.
"Q. Yet you took no official action against people who were present and possibly might have done some harm to these people?
"A. We took no official action because there was none to be taken. They were not creating a disturbance, those particular people were not at that time doing anything to make trouble but they could have been."

State House grounds. . . . Although vehicular traffic at a nearby street intersection was slowed down somewhat, an officer was dispatched to keep traffic moving. There were a number of bystanders on the public sidewalks adjacent to the State House grounds, but they all moved on when asked to do so, and there was no impediment of pedestrian traffic. Police protection at the scene was at all times sufficient to meet any foreseeable possibility of disorder.

In the situation and under the circumstances thus described, the police authorities advised the petitioners that they would be arrested if they did not disperse within 15 minutes. Instead of dispersing, the petitioners engaged in what the City Manager described as "boisterous," "loud," and "flamboyant" conduct, which, as his later testimony made clear, consisted of listening to a "religious harangue" by one of their leaders, and loudly singing "The Star Spangled Banner" and other patriotic and religious songs, while stamping their feet and clapping their hands. After 15 minutes had passed, the police arrested the petitioners and marched them off to jail.

Upon this evidence the state trial court convicted the petitioners of breach of the peace, and imposed sentences ranging from a $10 fine or five days in jail, to a $100 fine or 30 days in jail. In affirming the judgments, the Supreme Court of South Carolina said that under the law of that State the offense of breach of the peace "is not susceptible of exact definition," but that the "general definition of the offense is as follows:

> In general terms, a breach of the peace is a violation of public order, a disturbance of the public tranquility, by an act or conduct inciting to violence . . . , it includes any violation of any law enacted to preserve peace and good order. It may consist of an act of violence or an act likely to produce violence. It is not necessary that the peace be actually broken to lay the foundation for a prosecution for this offense. If what is done is unjustifiable and unlawful, tending with sufficient directness to break the peace, no more is

required. Nor is actual personal violence an essential element in the offense. . . .

> By "peace," as used in the law in this connection, is meant the tranquility enjoyed by citizens of a municipality or community where good order reigns among its members, which is the natural right of all persons in political society.

It has long been established that . . . First Amendment freedoms are protected by the Fourteenth Amendment from invasion by the States. . . . The circumstances in this case reflect an exercise of these basic constitutional rights in their most pristine and classic form. The petitioners felt aggrieved by laws of South Carolina which allegedly "prohibited Negro privileges in this State." They peaceably assembled at the site of the State Government and there peaceably expressed their grievances "to the citizens of South Carolina, along with the Legislative Bodies of South Carolina." Not until they were told by police officials that they must disperse on pain of arrest did they do more. Even then, they but sang patriotic and religious songs after one of their leaders had delivered a "religious harangue." There was no violence or threat of violence on their part, or on the part of any member of the crowd watching them. Police protection was "ample."

This, therefore, was a far cry from the situation in *Feiner* v. *New York*. . . . And the record is barren of any evidence of "fighting words." See *Chaplinsky* v. *New Hampshire*, 315 U.S. 568 (1942). . . .

We do not review in this case criminal convictions resulting from the evenhanded application of a precise and narrowly drawn regulatory statute evincing a legislative judgment that certain specific conduct be limited or proscribed. If, for example, the petitioners had been convicted upon evidence that they had violated a law regulating traffic, or had disobeyed a law reasonably limiting the periods during which the State House grounds were open to the public, this would be a different case. . . . These petitioners were convicted of an offense so generalized as to be, in the words of the South Carolina Supreme Court, "not susceptible of exact definition." And they were convicted upon evidence which showed no more than that the opinions which they were peaceably expressing were sufficiently opposed to the views of the majority of the community to attract a crowd and necessitate police protection.

The Fourteenth Amendment does not permit a State to make criminal the peaceful expression of unpopular views. "[A] function of free speech under our system of government is to invite dispute. It may indeed best serve its high purpose when it induces a condition of unrest, creates dissatisfaction with conditions as they are, or even stirs people to anger. Speech is often provocative and challenging. It may strike at prejudices and preconceptions and have profound unsettling effects as it presses for acceptance of an idea. That is why freedom of speech . . . is . . . protected against censorship or punishment, unless shown likely to produce a clear and present danger of a serious substantive evil that rises far above public inconvenience, annoyance, or unrest. . . . There is no room under our Constitution for a more restrictive view. For the alternative would lead to standardization of ideas either by legislatures, courts, or dominant political or community groups." *Terminiello* v. *Chicago*, 337 U.S. 1 (1949). . . . As in the Terminiello case, the courts of South Carolina have defined a criminal offense so as to permit conviction of the petitioners if their speech "stirred people to anger, invited public dispute, or brought about a condition of unrest. A conviction resting on any of these grounds may not stand."

. . .

For these reasons we conclude that these criminal convictions cannot stand.

Reversed.

MR. JUSTICE CLARK, *dissenting.*

. . . Petitioners, of course, had a right to peaceable assembly, to espouse their cause and to petition, but in my view the manner in which they exercised their rights was by no means the passive demonstration which this Court relates; rather, as the City Manager of Columbia testified, "a dangerous situation was really building up" which South Carolina's courts expressly found had created "an actual interference with traffic and an imminently threatened disturbance of the peace of the community." Since the Court does not attack the state courts' findings and accepts the convictions as "binding" to the extent that the petitioners' conduct constituted a breach of the peace, it is difficult for me to understand its understatement of the facts and reversal of the convictions.

. . . [T]he petitioners were arrested, as they apparently planned from the beginning, and convicted on evidence the sufficiency of which the Court does not challenge. The question thus seems to me whether a State is constitutionally prohibited from enforcing laws to prevent breach of the peace in a situation where city officials in good faith believe, and the record shows, that disorder and violence are imminent, merely because the activities constituting that breach contain claimed elements of constitutionally protected speech and assembly. To me the answer under our cases is clearly in the negative.

Beginning, as did the South Carolina courts, with the premise that the petitioners were entitled to assemble and voice their dissatisfaction with segregation, the enlargement of constitutional protection for the conduct here is as fallacious as would be the conclusion that free speech necessarily includes the right to broadcast from a sound truck in the public streets. *Kovacs* v. *Cooper*, 336 U.S. 77. . . . Here the petitioners were permitted without hindrance to exercise their rights of free speech and assembly. Their arrests occurred only after a situation arose in which the law-enforcement officials on the scene considered that a dangerous disturbance was imminent. The County Court found that "the evidence is clear that the officers were motivated solely by a proper concern for the preservation of order and the protection of the general welfare in the face of an actual interference with traffic and an imminently threatened disturbance of the peace of the community." In affirming, the South Carolina Supreme Court said the action of the police was "reasonable and motivated solely by a proper concern for the preservation of order and prevention of further interference with traffic upon the public streets and sidewalks." . . .

In *Cantwell* v. *Connecticut* . . . this Court recognized that "[w]hen clear and present danger of riot, disorder, interference with traffic upon public streets, or other immediate threat to public safety, peace, or order, appears, the power of the State to prevent or punish is obvious." And in *Feiner* v. *New York* . . . we upheld a conviction for breach of the peace in a situation no more dangerous than that found here. There the demonstration was conducted by only one person and the crowd was limited to approximately 80, as compared with the present lineup of some 200 demonstrators and 300 onlookers. There the petitioner was "endeavoring to arouse the Negro people against the whites, urging them that they rise up in arms and fight for equal rights." . . . Only one person—in a city having an entirely different historical background—was exhorting adults. Here 200 youthful Negro demonstrators were being aroused to a "fever pitch" before a crowd of some 300 people who undoubtedly were hostile. Perhaps their speech was not so animated but in this setting their actions, their placards reading "You may jail our bodies but not our souls" and their chanting of "I Shall Not Be Moved," accompanied by stamping feet and clapping hands, created a much greater danger of riot and disorder. It is my belief that anyone conversant with the almost spontaneous combustion in some Southern communities in such a situation will agree that the City Manager's action may well have averted a major catastrophe.

The gravity of the danger here surely needs no further explication. The imminence of that danger has been emphasized at every stage of this proceeding, from the complaints charging that the demonstrations "tended directly to immediate violence" to the State Supreme Court's affirmance on the authority of Feiner. This record, then, shows no steps backward from a standard of "clear and present danger." But to say that the police may not intervene until the riot has occurred is like keeping out the doctor until the patient dies.

. . .

I would affirm the convictions.

NATIONAL ASSOCIATION FOR THE ADVANCEMENT OF COLORED PEOPLE v. STATE OF ALABAMA ex. rel. JOHN PATTERSON
357 U.S. 449; 2 L. Ed. 2d 1488; 78 S. Ct. 1163 (1958)

MR. JUSTICE HARLAN *delivered the opinion of the Court.*

We review from the standpoint of its validity under the Federal Constitution a judgment of civil contempt entered against petitioner, the National Association for the Advancement of Colored People, in the courts of Alabama. The question presented is whether Alabama, consistently with the Due Process Clause of the Fourteenth Amendment, can compel petitioner to reveal to the State's Attorney General the names and addresses of all its Alabama members and agents, with regard to their positions or functions in the Association. The judgment of contempt was based upon petitioner's refusal to comply fully with a court order requiring in part the production of membership lists. Petitioner's claim is that the order, in the circumstances shown by this record, violated rights assured to petitioner and its members under the Constitution.

Alabama has a statute similar to those of many other States which requires a foreign corporation, except as exempted, to qualify before doing business by filing its corporate charter with the Secretary of State.... The statute imposes a fine on a corporation transacting intrastate business before qualifying and provides for criminal prosecution of officers of such a corporation.... The National Association for the Advancement of Colored People is a non-profit membership corporation organized under the laws of New York. Its purposes, fostered on a nationwide basis, are those indicated by its name and it operates through chartered affiliates which are independent unincorporated associations, with membership therein equivalent to membership in petitioner. The first Alabama affiliates were chartered in 1918. Since that time the aims of the Association have been advanced through activities of its affiliates, and in 1951 the Association itself opened a regional office in Alabama, at which it employed two supervisory persons and one clerical worker. The Association has never complied with the qualification statute, from which it considered itself exempt.

In 1956 the Attorney General of Alabama brought an equity suit in the State Circuit Court, Montgomery County, to enjoin the Association from conducting further activities within, and to oust it from, the State. Among other things the bill in equity alleged that the Association had opened a regional office and had organized various affiliates in Alabama; had recruited members and solicited contributions within the State; had given financial support and furnished legal assistance to Negro students seeking ad-

mission to the state university; and had supported a Negro boycott of the bus lines in Montgomery to compel the seating of passengers without regard to race. The bill recited that the Association, by continuing to do business in Alabama without complying with the qualification statute, was "...causing irreparable injury to the property and civil rights of the residents and citizens of the State of Alabama for which criminal prosecution and civil actions of law afford no adequate relief...." On the day the complaint was filed, the Circuit Court issued ex parte an order restraining the Association, *pendente lite*, from engaging in further activities within the State and forbidding it to take any steps to qualify itself to do business therein.

Petitioner demurred to the allegations of the bill and moved to dissolve the restraining order. It contended that its activities did not subject it to the qualification requirements of the statute and that in any event what the State sought to accomplish by its suit would violate rights to freedom of speech and assembly guaranteed under the Fourteenth Amendment to the Constitution of the United States. Before the date set for a hearing on this motion, the State moved for the production of a large number of the Association's records and papers, including bank statements, leases, deeds, and records containing the names and addresses of all Alabama "members" and "agents" of the Association. It alleged that all such documents were necessary for adequate preparation for the hearing, in view of petitioner's denial of the conduct of intrastate business within the meaning of the qualification statute. Over petitioner's objections, the court ordered the production of a substantial part of the requested records, including the membership lists, and postponed the hearing on the restraining order to a date later than the time ordered for production.

Thereafter petitioner filed its answer to the bill in equity. It admitted its Alabama activities substantially as alleged in the complaint and that it had not qualified to do business in the State.

Although still disclaiming the statute's application to it, petitioner offered to qualify if the bar from qualification made part of the restraining order were lifted, and it submitted with the answer an executed set of the forms required by the statute. However petitioner did not comply with the production order, and for this failure was adjudged in civil contempt and fined $10,000. The contempt judgment provided that the fine would be subject to reduction or remission if compliance were forthcoming within five days but otherwise would be increased to $100,000.

At the end of the five-day period petitioner produced substantially all the data called for by the production order except its membership lists, as to which it contended that Alabama could not consitutionally compel disclosure, and moved to modify or vacate the contempt judgment, or stay its execution pending appellate review. This motion was denied. While a similar stay application, which was later denied, was pending before the Supreme Court of Alabama, the Circuit Court made a further order adjudging petitioner in continuing contempt and increasing the fine already imposed to $100,000. Under Alabama law ... the effect of the contempt adjudication was to foreclose petitioner from obtaining a hearing on the merits of the underlying ouster action, or from taking any steps to dissolve the temporary restraining order which had been issued ex parte, until it purged itself of contempt. . . .

The State Supreme Court thereafter twice dismissed petitions for certiorari to review this final contempt judgment.

. . .

The Association both urges that it is constitutionally entitled to resist official inquiry into its membership lists, and that it may assert, on behalf of its members, a right personal to them to be protected from compelled disclosure by the State of their affiliation with the Association as revealed by the membership lists. We think that petitioner argues more appropriately the rights of its members, and that its nexus with them is sufficient to permit that it act as their representative before this Court. In so concluding, we reject respondent's argument that the Association lacks standing to assert here constitutional rights pertaining to the members, who are not of course parties to the litigation.

To limit the breadth of issues which must be dealt with in particular litigation, this Court has generally insisted that parties rely only on constitutional rights which are personal to themselves. . . . This rule is related to the broader doctrine that constitutional adjudication should where possible be avoided. . . . The principle is not disrespected where constitutional rights of persons who are not immediately before the Court could not be effectively vindicated except through an appropriate representative before the Court. . . .

If petitioner's rank-and-file members are constitutionally entitled to withhold their connection with the Association despite the production order, it is manifest that this right is properly assertable by the Association. To require that it be claimed by the members themselves would result in nullification of the right at the very moment of its assertion. Petitioner is the appropriate party to assert these rights, because it and its members are in every practical sense identical. The Association, which provides in its constitution that "[a]ny person who is in accordance with [its] principles and policies . . . " may become a member, is but the medium through which its individual members seek to make more effective the expression of their own views. The reasonable likelihood that the Association itself through diminished financial support and membership may be adversely affected if production is compelled is a further factor pointing towards our holding that petitioner has standing to complain of the production order on behalf of its members. . . .

We thus reach petitioner's claim that the production order in the state litigation trespasses upon fundamental freedoms protected by the Due Process Clause of the Fourteenth Amendment. Petitioner argues that in view of the facts and circumstances shown in the record, the effect of compelled disclosure of the membership lists will be to abridge the rights of its rank-and-file members to engage in lawful association in support of their common beliefs. It contends that governmental action, which although not directly suppressing association, nevertheless carries this consequence, can be justified only upon some overriding valid interest of the State.

Effective advocacy of both public and private points of view, particularly controversial ones, is undeniably enhanced by group association, as this Court has more than once recognized by remarking upon the close nexus between the freedoms of speech and assembly. . . . It is beyond debate that freedom to engage in association for the advancement of beliefs and ideas is an inseparable aspect of the "liberty" assured by the Due Process Clause of the Fourteenth Amendment, which embraces freedom of speech. . . . Of course, it is immaterial whether the beliefs sought to be advanced by association pertain to political, economic, religious or cultural matters, and state action which may have the effect of curtailing the freedom is subject to the closest scrutiny.

. . .

It is hardly a novel perception that compelled disclosure of affiliation with groups engaged in advocacy may constitute as effective a restraint on freedom of association as the forms of governmental action in the cases above were thought likely to produce upon the particular constitutional rights there involved. This Court has recognized the vital relationship between freedom to associate and privacy in one's associations. When referring to the varied forms of governmental action which might interfere with freedom of assembly, it said in *American Communications Assn.* v. *Douds, supra* (339 U.S. 402): "A requirement that adherents of particu-

lar religious faiths or political parties wear identifying arm-bands, for example, is obviously of this nature." Compelled disclosure of membership in an organization engaged in advocacy of particular beliefs is of the same order. Inviolability of privacy in group association may in many circumstances be indispensable to preservation of freedom of association, particularly where a group espouses dissident beliefs. . . .

We think that the production order, in the respects here drawn in question, must be regarded as entailing the likelihood of a substantial restraint upon the exercise by petitioner's members of their right to freedom of association. Petitioner has made an uncontroverted showing that on past occasions revelation of the identity of its rank-and-file members has exposed these members to economic reprisal, loss of employment, threat of physical coercion, and other manifestations of public hostility. Under these circumstances, we think it apparent that compelled disclosure of petitioner's Alabama membership is likely to affect adversely the ability of petitioner and its members to pursue their collective effort to foster beliefs which they admittedly have the right to advocate, in that it may induce members to withdraw from the Association and dissuade others from joining it because of fear of exposure of their beliefs shown through their associations and of the consequences of this exposure.

It is not sufficient to answer, as the State does here, that whatever repressive effect compulsory disclosure of names of petitioner's members may have upon participation by Alabama citizens in petitioner's activities follows not from *state* action but from *private* community pressures. The crucial factor is the interplay of governmental and private action, for it is only after the initial exertion of state power represented by the production order that private action takes hold.

We turn to the final question whether Alabama has demonstrated an interest in obtaining the disclosures it seeks from petitioner which is sufficient to justify the deterrent effect which we have concluded these disclosures may well have on the free exercise by petitioner's members of their constitutionally protected right of association. . . .

It is important to bear in mind that petitioner asserts no right to absolute immunity from state investigation, and no right to disregard Alabama's laws. As shown by its substantial compliance with the production order, petitioner does not deny Alabama's right to obtain from it such information as the State desires concerning the purposes of the Association and its activities within the State. Petitioner has not objected to divulging the identity of its members who are employed by or hold official positions with it. It has urged the rights solely of its ordinary rank-and-file members. This is therefore not analogous to a case involving the interest of a State in protecting its citizens in their dealings with paid solicitors or agents of foreign corporations by requiring identification.

. . .

. . . [W]e think it apparent that *New York* ex. rel. *Bryant* v. *Zimmerman*, 278 U.S. 63 . . . cannot be relied on in support of the State's position, for that case involved markedly different considerations in terms of the interest of the State in obtaining disclosure. There, this Court upheld as applied to a member of a local chapter of the Ku Klux Klan, a New York statute requiring any unincorporated association which demanded an oath as a condition to membership to file with state officials copies of its " . . .

constitution, by-laws, rules, regulations, and oath of membership, together with a roster of its membership and a list of its officers for the current year." NY Laws 1923, ch 664, sections 53, 56. In its opinion, the Court took care to emphasize the nature of the organization which New York sought to regulate. The decision was based on the particular character of the Klan's activities, involving acts of unlawful intimidation and violence, which the Court assumed was before the state legislature when it enacted the statute, and of which the Court itself took judicial notice. Furthermore the situation before us is significantly different from that in *Bryant*, because the organization there had made no effort to comply with any of the requirements of New York's statute but rather had refused to furnish the State with any information as to its local activities.

We hold that the immunity from state scrutiny of membership lists which the Association claims on behalf of its members is here so related to the right of the members to pursue their lawful private interests privately and to associate freely with others in so doing as to come within the protection of the Fourteenth Amendment. And we conclude that Alabama has fallen short of showing a controlling justification for the deterrent effect on the free enjoyment of the right to associate which disclosure of membership lists is likely to have. Accordingly, the judgment of civil contempt and the $100,000 fine which resulted from petitioner's refusal to comply with the production order in this respect must fall.

. . .

Reversed.

LLOYD CORPORATION, LTD. v. TANNER
407 U.S. 551; 32 L. Ed. 2d 131; 92 S. Ct. 2219 (1972)

MR. JUSTICE POWELL *delivered the opinion of the Court.*

This case presents the question reserved by the Court in *Amalgamated Food Employees Union Local 509* v. *Logan Valley Plaza, Inc.* (1968), as to the right of a privately owned shopping center to prohibit the distribution of handbills on its property when the handbilling is unrelated to the shopping center's operations. Relying primarily on *Marsh* v. *Alabama* (1946), and *Logan Valley,* the United States District Court for the District of Oregon sustained an asserted First Amendment right to distribute handbills in petitioner's shopping center, and issued a permanent injunction restraining petitioner from interfering with such right. The Court of Appeals for the Ninth Circuit affirmed. We granted certiorari to consider petitioner's contention that the decision below violates rights of private property protected by the Fifth and Fourteenth Amendments.

Lloyd Corporation, Ltd. (Lloyd), owns a large, modern retail shopping center in Portland, Oregon. Lloyd Center embraces altogether about 50 acres, including some 20 acres of open and covered parking facilities which accommodate more than 1,000 automobiles. It has a perimeter of almost one and one-half miles, bounded by four public streets. It is crossed in varying degrees by several other public streets, all of which have adjacent public sidewalks. Lloyd owns all land and buildings within the Center, except these public streets and sidewalks. There are some 60 commercial tenants, including small shops and several major department stores.

The Center embodies a relatively new concept in shopping center design. The stores are all located within a single large, multi-level building complex sometimes referred to as the "Mall." Within this complex, in addition to the stores, there are parking facilities, malls, private sidewalks, stairways, escalators, gardens, and an auditorium and a skating rink. Some of the stores open directly on the outside public sidewalks, but most open on the interior privately owned malls. Some stores open on both. There are no public streets or public sidewalks within the building complex which is enclosed and entirely covered except for the landscaped portions of some of the interior malls.

The distribution of the handbills occurred in the malls. They are a distinctive feature of the Center, serving both utilitarian and esthetic functions. Essentially, they are private, interior promenades with 10-foot sidewalks serving the stores, and with a center strip 30 feet wide in which flowers and shrubs are planted, and statuary, fountains, benches and other amenities are located. There is no vehicular traffic on the malls. An architectural expert described the purpose of the malls as follows:

> In order to make shopping easier and pleasant, and to help realize the goal of maximum sales [for the Center], the shops are grouped about special pedestrian ways or malls. Here the shopper is isolated from the noise, fumes, confusion and distraction which he normally finds along city streets, and a controlled carefree environment is provided. . . .

Although the stores close at customary hours, the malls are not physically closed, as pedestrian window shopping is encouraged within reasonable hours. Lloyd employs 12 security guards who are commissioned as such by the city of Portland. The guards have police authority within the Center, wear uniforms similar to those worn by city police, and are licensed to carry handguns. They are employed by and subject to the control of Lloyd. Their duties are the customary ones, including shoplifting surveillance and general security.

At a few places within the Center small signs are embedded in the sidewalk which state:

> NOTICE—Areas in Lloyd Center Used By the Public Are Not Public Ways But Are For The Use of Lloyd Center Tenants And The Public Transacting Business With Them. Permission To Use Said Areas May Be Revoked At Any Time. Lloyd Corporation, Ltd.

The Center is open generally to the public, with a considerable effort being made to attract shoppers and prospective shoppers, and to create "customer motivation" as well as customer good will in the community. In this respect the Center pursues policies comparable to those of major stores and shopping centers across the country, although the Center affords superior facilities for these purposes. Groups and organizations are permitted, by invitation and advance arrangement, to use the auditorium and other facilities. Rent is charged for use of the auditorium except with respect to certain civic and charitable organizations, such as the Cancer Society, Boy and Girl Scouts. The Center also allows limited use of the malls by the American Legion to sell "Buddy Poppies" for disabled veterans, and by the Salvation Army and Volunteers of America to solicit Christmas contributions. It has denied similar use to other civic and charitable organizations. Political use is also forbidden, except that presidential candidates of both parties have been allowed to speak in the auditorium.

The Center had been in operation for some eight years when this litigation commenced. Throughout this period it had a policy, strictly enforced, against the distribution of handbills within the building complex and its malls. No exceptions were made with respect to handbilling, which was considered likely to annoy customers, to create litter, potentially to create disorders, and generally to be incompatible with the purpose of the Center and the atmosphere sought to be preserved.

On November 14, 1968, the respondents in this case distributed within the Center handbill invitations to a meeting of the "Resistance Community" to protest the draft and the Vietnam War. The distribution, made in several different places on the mall walkways by five young people, was quiet and orderly, and there was no littering. There was a complaint from one customer. Security guards informed the respondents that they were trespassing and would be arrested unless they stopped distributing the handbills within the Center. The guards suggested that respondents distribute their literature on the public streets and sidewalks adjacent to but outside of the Center complex. Respondents left the premises as requested "to avoid arrest" and continued the handbilling outside. Subsequently this suit was instituted in the District Court seeking declaratory and injunctive relief. . . .

The courts below considered the critical inquiry to be whether Lloyd Center was "the functional equivalent of a public business district." This phrase was first used in *Logan Valley*, but its genesis was in *Marsh*. It is well to consider what *Marsh* actually decided. As noted above, it involved an economic anomaly of the past, "the company town." One must have seen such towns to understand that "functionally" they were no different from municipalities of comparable size. They developed primarily in the deep south to meet economic conditions, especially those which existed following the Civil War. Impoverished States, and especially backward areas thereof, needed an influx of industry and capital. Corporations attracted to the area by natural resources and abundant labor were willing to assume the role of local government. Quite literally, towns were built and operated by private capital with all of the customary services and utilities normally afforded by a municipal or state government: there were streets, sidewalks, sewers, public lighting, police and fire protection, business and residential areas, churches, postal facilities, and sometimes schools. In short, as Mr. Justice Black said, Chickasaw, Alabama, had "all the characteristics of any other American town." The Court simply held that where private interests were substituting for and performing the customary functions of government, First Amendment freedoms could not be denied where exercised in the customary manner on the town's sidewalks and streets. Indeed, as title to the entire town was held privately, there were no publicly owned streets, sidewalks or parks where such rights could be exercised.

Logan Valley extended *Marsh* to a shopping center situation in a different context from the company town setting, but it did so only in a context where the First Amendment activity was related to the shopping center's operations. There is some language in *Logan Valley,* unnecessary to the decision, suggesting that the key focus of *Marsh* was upon the "business district," and that whenever a privately owned business district serves the public generally its sidewalks and streets become the functional equivalents of similar public facilities. . . .

The holding in *Logan Valley* was not dependent upon the suggestion that the privately owned streets and sidewalks of a business district or a shopping center are the equivalent, for First Amendment purposes, of municipally owned streets and sidewalks. No such expansive reading of the opinion for the Court is necessary or appropriate. The opinion was carefully phrased to limit its holding to the picketing involved, where the picketing was "directly related in its purpose to the use to which the shopping center property was being put," and where the store was located in the center of a large private enclave with the consequence that no other reasonable opportunities for the pickets to convey their message to their intended audience were available.

Neither of these elements is present in the case now before the Court.

A

The handbilling by respondents in the malls of Lloyd Center had no relation to any purpose for which the center was built and being used. It is nevertheless argued by respondents that since the Center is open to the public the private owner cannot enforce a restriction against handbilling on the premises. The thrust of this argument is considerably broader than the rationale of *Logan Valley.* It requires no relationship, direct or indirect, between the purpose of the expressive activity and the business of the shopping center. The message sought to be conveyed by respondents was directed to all members of the public, not solely to patrons of Lloyd Center or of any of its operations. Respondents could have distributed these handbills on any public street, on any public sidewalk, in any public park, or in any public building in the city of Portland.

Respondents' argument, even if otherwise meritorious, misapprehends the scope of the invitation extended to the public. The invitation is to come to the Center to do business with the tenants. It is true that facilities at the Center are used for certain meetings and for various promotional activities. The obvious purpose, recognized widely as legitimate and responsible business activity, is to bring potential shoppers to the Center, to create a favorable impression, and to generate goodwill. There is no open-ended invitation to the public to use the Center for any and all purposes, however incompatible with the interests of both the stores and the shoppers whom they serve. . . .

It is noteworthy that respondents' argument based on the Center being "open to the public" would apply in varying degrees to most retail stores and service establishments across the country. They are all open to the public in the sense that customers and potential customers are invited and encouraged to enter. In terms of being open to the public, there are differences only of degree—not of principle—between a free standing store and one located in a shopping center, between a small store and a large one, between a single store with some malls and open areas designed to attract customers and Lloyd Center with its elaborate malls and interior landscaping.

B

A further fact, distinguishing the present case from *Logan Valley,* is that the Union picketers in that case would have been deprived of all reasonable opportunity to convey their message to patrons of the Weis store had they been denied access to the shopping center. The situation at Lloyd Center was notably different. The central building complex was surrounded by public sidewalks, totaling 66 linear blocks. All persons who enter or leave the private areas within the complex must cross public streets and sidewalks, either on foot or in automobiles. When moving to and from the privately owned parking lots, automobiles are required by law to come to a complete stop. Handbills may be distributed conveniently to pedestrians, and also to occupants of automobiles, from these public sidewalks and streets. Indeed, respondents moved to these public areas and continued distribution of their handbills after being requested to leave the interior malls. It would be an unwarranted infringement of property rights to require them to yield to the exercise of First Amendment rights under circumstances where adequate alternative avenues of communication exist. Such an accommodation would diminish property rights without significantly enhancing the asserted right of free speech. In ordering this accommodation the courts below erred in their interpretation of this Court's decisions in *Marsh* and *Logan Valley.*

The basic issue in this case is whether respondents, in the exercise of asserted First Amendment rights, may distribute handbills on Lloyd's private property contrary to its wishes and contrary to a policy enforced against *all* hand-billing. In addressing this issue, it must be remembered that the First and Fourteenth Amendments safeguard the rights of free speech and assembly by limitations on *state* action, not on action by the owner of private property used nondiscriminatorily for private purposes only. The Due Process Clauses of the Fifth and Fourteenth Amendments are also relevant to this case. They provide that "no person shall . . . be deprived of life, liberty, or property, without due process of law." There is the further proscription in the Fifth Amendment against the taking of "private property . . . for public use, without just compensation."

Although accommodations between the values protected by these three Amendments are sometimes necessary, and the courts properly have shown a special solicitude for the guarantees of the First Amendment, this Court has never held that a trespasser or an uninvited guest may exercise general rights of free speech on property privately owned and used nondiscriminatorily for private purposes only. Even where public property is involved, the Court has recognized that it is not necessarily available for speech, pickets, or other communicative activities.

Respondents contend, however, that the property of a large shopping center is "open to the public," serves the same purposes as a "business district" of a municipality, and therefore has been dedicated to certain types of public use. The argument is that such a center has sidewalks, streets, and parking areas which are functionally similar to facilities customarily provided by municipalities. It is then asserted that all members of the public, whether invited as customers or not, have the same right of free speech as they would have on the similar public facilities in the streets of a city or town.

The argument reaches too far. The Constitution by no means requires such an attenuated doctrine of dedication of private property to public use. The closest decision in theory. *Marsh v. Alabama, supra,* involved the assumption by a private enterprise of all of the attributes of a state-created municipality and the exercise by that enterprise of semi-official municipal functions as a delegate of the State. In effect, the owner of the company town was performing the full spectrum of municipal powers and stood in the shoes of the State. In the instant case there is no comparable assumption or exercise of municipal functions or power.

Nor does property lose its private character merely because the public is generally invited to use it for designated purposes. Few would argue that a free standing store, with abutting parking space for customers, assumes significant public attributes merely because the public is invited to shop. Nor is size alone the controlling factor. The essentially private character of a store and its privately owned abutting property does not change by virtue of being large or clustered with other stores in a modern shopping center. This is not to say that no differences may exist with respect to government regulation or rights of citizens arising by virtue of the size and diversity of activities carried on within a privately owned facility serving the public. There will be, for example, problems with respect to public health and safety which vary in degree and in the appropriate government response, depending upon the size and character of a shopping center, an office building, a sports arena or other large facility serving the public for commercial purposes. We do say that the Fifth and Fourteenth Amendment rights of private property owners, as well as the First Amendment rights of all citizens, must be respected and protected. The Framers of the Constitution certainly did not think these fundamental rights of a free society are incompatible with each other. There may be situations where accommodations between them, and the drawing of lines to assure due protection of both, are not easy. But on the facts presented in this case, the answer is clear.

We hold that there has been no such dedication of Lloyd's privately owned and operated shopping center to public use as to entitle respondents to exercise therein the asserted First Amendment rights. Accordingly, we reverse the judgment and remand the case to the Court of Appeals with directions to vacate the injunction.

It is so ordered.

Judgment reversed and case remanded.

MR. JUSTICE MARSHALL, *with whom* MR. JUSTICE DOUGLAS, MR. JUSTICE BRENNAN, *and* MR. JUSTICE STEWART *join, dissenting.*

Donald Tanner, Betsy Wheeler, and Susan Roberts (respondents) brought this action for a declaratory judgment that they have the right under the First and Fourteenth Amendments to the United States Constitution to distribute handbills in a shopping center owned by petitioner and an injunction to enforce that right. Relying primarily on our very recent decision in *Amalgamated Food Employees Union* v. *Logan Valley Plaza, Inc.* (1968), the United States District Court for the District of Oregon granted the relief requested. The United States Court of Appeals for the Ninth Circuit affirmed. Today, this Court reverses the judgment of the Court of Appeals and attempts to distinguish this case from *Logan Valley*. In my view, the distinction that the Court sees between the cases does not exist. As I read the opinion of the Court, it is an attack not only on the rationale of *Logan Valley*, but also on this Court's longstanding decision in *Marsh* v. *Alabama* (1946). Accordingly, I dissent.

The question presented by this case is whether one of the incidents of petitioner's private ownership of the Lloyd Center is the power to exclude certain forms of speech from its property. In other words, we must decide whether ownership of the Center gives petitioner unfettered discretion to determine whether or not it will be used as a public forum.

This Court held in *Marsh* v. *Alabama, supra,* that even though property is privately owned, under some circumstances it may be treated as though it were publicly held, at least for purposes of the First Amendment. In *Marsh*, a member of the Jehovah's Witness religious sect was arrested and convicted of violating Alabama's criminal trespass statute when she undertook to distribute religious literature in the downtown shopping area of a privately owned town without permission of the owner. The Court reasoned that "the more an owner, for his advantage, opens up his property for use by the public in general, the more do his rights become circumscribed by the statutory and constitutional rights of those who use it." ... Noting that the stifling effect produced by any ban on free expression in a community's central business district was the same whether the ban was imposed by public owners, the Court concluded that

When we balance the Constitutional rights of owners of property against those of the people to enjoy freedom of press and religion, as we must here, we remain mindful of the fact that the latter occupy a preferred position. As we have stated before, the right to exercise the liberties safeguarded by the First Amendment "lies at the foundation of free government by free men" and we must in all cases "weigh the circumstances and appraise ... the reasons ... in support of the regulation of [those] rights." ... In our view the circumstance that the property rights to the premises where the deprivation of liberty, here involved, took place, were held by others than the public is not sufficient to justify the State's permitting a corporation to govern a community of citizens so as to restrict their fundamental liberties and the enforcement of such restraint by the application of a State statute.

We relied heavily on *Marsh* in deciding *Logan Valley*. In *Logan Valley,* a shopping center in its formative stages contained a supermarket and department store. The supermarket employed a staff composed of only nonunion employees.

Members of Amalgamated Food Employees Union, Local 590, began to picket the market with signs stating that the market's employees were not receiving union wages or union benefits. The picketing was carried out almost entirely in the parcel pickup area and that portion of the parking lot immediately adjacent thereto.... The supermarket sought and obtained an injunction from a Pennsylvania state court prohibiting the union members from trespassing upon the parking areas or in the store, the effect of which was to prohibit picketing and handbilling on any part of the private property and to relegate the union members to carrying signs on the publicly owned earthern berms that surrounded the shopping center. Finding that the shopping center was the functional equivalent of the business district involved in *Marsh*, we could see "no reason why access to a business district in a company town for the purpose of exercising First Amendment rights should be constitutionally required, while access for the same purpose to property functioning as a business district should be limited simply because the property surrounding the 'business district' is not under the same ownership." Thus, we held that the union activity was constitutionally protected.

In the instant case the District Court found that "the Mall is the functional equivalent of a public business district" within the meaning of *Marsh* and *Logan Valley*. The Court of Appeals specifically affirmed this finding, and it is overwhelmingly supported by the record.

The Lloyd Center is similar to Logan Valley Plaza in several respects: both are bordered by public roads, and the entrances of both lead directly into the public roads; both contain large parking areas and privately owned walkways leading from store to store; and the general public has unrestricted access to both. The principal differences between the two centers are that the Lloyd Center is larger than Logan Valley, that Lloyd Center contains more commercial facilities, the Lloyd Center contains a range of professional and nonprofessional services that were not found in Logan Valley, and the Lloyd Center is much more intertwined with public streets than Logan Valley. Also, as in *Marsh,* Lloyd's private police are given full police power by the city of Portland, even though they are hired, fired, controlled, and paid by the owners of the Center. This was not true in *Logan Valley.*

In 1954, when Lloyd's owners first acquired land for the Center, the City of Portland vacated about eight acres of public streets for their use. The ordinance accomplishing the vacation sets forth the city's view of the Center's function:

> Whereas the Council finds that the reason for these vacations is for general building purposes to be used in the development of a *general retail business district* and the development of an adequate parking area to support said district; ... the Council ... finds that in order to develop a large retail unit such as that contemplated by Lloyd Corporation, Ltd., it is necessary to vacate the streets mentioned, ..." (Emphasis added.)

The 1954 ordinance also indicates that the city of Portland was aware that as Lloyd Center developed, it would be necessary for the city to build new streets and to take other steps to control the traffic flow that the Center would engender. In 1958, an emergency ordinance was passed giving the Lloyd Center an extension of time to meet various conditions on which the 1954 vacations were made. The city council viewed the projected Center as offering an "opportunity for much needed employment" and concluded that the emergency ordinance was "necessary for the immediate preservation of the public health, peace, and safety of the city of Portland."

In sum, the Lloyd Center is an integral part of the Portland community. From its inception, the city viewed it as a "business district" of the city and depended on it to supply much needed employment opportunities. To insure the success of the Center, the city carefully integrated it into the pattern of streets already established and planned future development of streets around the Center. It is plain, therefore, that Lloyd Center is the equivalent of a public "business district" within the meaning of *Marsh* and *Logan Valley.* In fact, the Lloyd Center is much more analogous to the company town in *Marsh* than was the Logan Valley Plaza.

Petitioner agrees with our decision in *Logan Valley* that is proper for courts to treat shopping centers differently from other privately owned property, like private residences. ... Petitioner contends that our decision in *Logan Valley* struck the appropriate balance between First Amendment and private property interests. The argument is made, however, that this case should be distinguished from *Logan Valley,* and this is the argument that the Court accepts.

As I have pointed out above, Lloyd Center is even more clearly the equivalent of a public business district than was Logan Valley Plaza. The First Amendment activity in both *Logan Valley* and the instant case was peaceful and nondisruptive; and both cases involve traditionally acceptable modes of speech. Why then should there be a different result here? The Court's answer is that the speech in this case was directed at topics of general interest—the Vietnam war and the draft—whereas the speech in Logan Valley was directed to the activities of a store in the shopping center, and that this factual difference is of constitutional dimensions. I cannot agree....

... If the property of Lloyd Center is generally open to First Amendment activity, respondents cannot be excluded.

On Veteran's Day, Lloyd Center allows organizations to parade through the Center with flags, drummers, and color guard units and to have a speaker deliver an address on the meaning of Veteran's Day and the valor of American soldiers. Presidential candidates have been permitted to speak without restriction on the issues of the day, which presumably include war and peace. The American Legion is annually given permission to sell poppies in the Mall because

Lloyd Center believes that "veterans . . . deserves [sic] some comfort and support by the people of the United States." In light of these facts, I perceive no basis for depriving respondents of the opportunity to distribute leaflets inviting patrons of the Center to attend a meeting in which different points of view would be expressed than those held by the organizations and persons privileged to use Lloyd Center as a forum for parading their ideas and symbols.

I believe that the lower courts correctly held that respondents' activities were directly related in purpose to the use to which the shopping center was being put. In my view, therefore, this case presents no occasion to consider whether or not *Logan Valley* should be extended. But, the Court takes a different view and concludes that Lloyd Center was never open to First Amendment activity. Even if I could agree with the Court on this point, I would not reach a different result in this case.

If respondents had distributed handbills complaining about one or more stores in Lloyd Center or about the Center itself, petitioner concedes that our decision in *Logan Valley* would insulate that conduct from proscription by the Center. I cannot see any logical reason to treat differently speech that is related to subjects other than the Center and its member stores.

We must remember that it is a balance that we are striking—a balance between the freedom to speak, a freedom that is given a preferred place in our hierarchy of values, and the freedom of a private property-owner to control his property. When the competing interests are fairly weighted, the balance can only be struck in favor of speech.

Members of the Portland community are able to see doctors, dentists, lawyers, bankers, travel agents, and persons offering countless other services in Lloyd Center. They can buy almost anything that they want or need there. For many Portland citizens, Lloyd Center will so completely satisfy their wants that they will have no reason to go elsewhere for goods or services. If speech is to reach these people, it must reach them in Lloyd Center. The Center itself rec-

ognizes this. For example, in 1964 its director of public relations offered candidates for President and Vice-President the use of the center for political speeches, boasting "that our convenient location and setting would provide the largest audience [the candidates] could attract in Oregon."

For many persons who do not have easy access to television, radio, the major newspapers, and the other forms of mass media, the only way they can express themselves to a broad range of citizens on issues of general public concern is to picket, or to handbill, or to utilize other free or relatively inexpensive means of communication. The only hope that these people have to be able to communicate effectively is to be permitted to speak in those areas in which most of their fellow citizens can be found. One such area is the business district of a city or town or its functional equivalent. And this is why respondents have a tremendous need to express themselves within Lloyd Center.

Petitioner's interests, on the other hand, pale in comparison. For example, petitioner urges that respondents' First Amendment activity would disturb the Center's customers. It is undisputed that some patrons will be disturbed by any First Amendment activity that goes on regardless of its object. But, there is no evidence to indicate that speech directed to topics unrelated to the shopping center would be more likely to impair the motivation of customers to buy than speech directed to the uses to which the Center is put, which petitioner concedes is constitutionally protected under *Logan Valley*. On the contrary, common sense would indicate that speech that is critical of a shopping center or one or more of its stores is more likely to deter consumers from purchasing goods or services than speech on any other subject. Moreover, petitioner acknowledges that respondents have a constitutional right to leaflet on any subject on public streets and sidewalks within Lloyd Center. It is difficult for me to understand why leafletting in the Mall would be so much more disturbing to the Center's customers.

I also find patently frivolous petitioner's argument that if handbilling in the Mall is permitted, Lloyd Center would face inordinate difficulties in removing litter from its premises. The District Court found that respondents' activities were litter-free. Assuming *arguendo* that if respondents had been permitted to continue their activities. litter might have resulted, I think that it is immediately apparent that even if respondents confined their activities to the public streets and sidewalks of the Center as Lloyd's private police suggested, litter would have been a problem as the recipients of the handbills carried them to the shopping and parking areas. Petitioner concedes that it would have had to remove this litter. There is no evidence that the amount of litter would have substantially increased if respondents distributed the leaflets within the Mall. But, even assuming that the litter might have increased, that is not a sufficient reason for barring First Amendment activity. See, e.g., *Schneider* v. *State of New Jersey* (1939). If petitioner is truly concerned about litter, it should accept a previous suggestion by this Court and prosecute those who throw handbills away, not those who use them for communicative purposes.

In sum, the balance plainly must be struck in favor of speech.

Petitioner's other grounds for denying respondents access to the Mall can be dealt with quickly. The assertion is made that petitioner had the right to regulate the manner in which First Amendment activity took place on its property, and that because the public streets and sidewalks inside the Center offered sufficient access to the public, it was permissible to deny respondents use of the Mall. The District court found that certain stores in the Center could only be reached by using the private walkways of the Mall. Those persons who drove into the Center, parked in the privately owned parking lots, and who entered the stores accessible only through the Mall could not be safely reached from the public streets and sidewalks. Hence, the District Court properly found that the Mall was the only place where respondents had reasonable access to all of Lloyd Center's patrons. At one point in this litigation, petitioner also attempted to assert that it was entitled to bar respondents' distribution of leaflets on the ground that the leaflets violated the Selective Service laws. The District Court found that this contention was without merit. 308 F. Supp., at 132–133. It seems that petitioner has abandoned the contention in this Court. In any event, it is meritless for the reasons given by the District Court.

In his dissenting opinion in *Logan Valley*, 391 U.S. 308, at 339, 88 S.Ct. 1601, at 1618, 20 L.Ed. 2d. 603, Mr. Justice White said that the rationale of that case would require affirmance of a case like the instant one. Mr. Justice White, at that time, was convinced that our decision in *Logan Valley*, incorrect though he thought it to be, required that all peaceful and nondisruptive speech be permitted on private property that was the functional equivalent of a public business district.

. . . I believe that the earlier view of Mr. Justice White is the correct one, that there is no legitimate way of following *Logan Valley* and not applying it to this case. But, one may suspect from reading the opinion of the Court that it is *Logan Valley* itself that the Court finds bothersome. The vote in *Logan Valley* was 6-3, and that decision is only four years old. But, I am aware that the composition of this Court has radically changed in four years. The fact remains that *Logan Valley* is binding unless and until it is overruled. There is no valid distinction between that case and this one, and, therefore, the results in both cases should be the same. . . .

It would not be surprising in the future to see cities rely more and more on private businesses to perform functions once performed by governmental agencies. The advantage of reduced expenses and an increased tax base cannot be overstated. As governments rely on private enterprise, public property decreases in favor of privately owned property. It becomes harder and harder for citizens to find means to communicate with other citizens. Only the wealthy may find effective communication possible unless we adhere to *Marsh* v. *Alabama* and continue to hold that "the more an owner, for his advantage, opens up his property for use by the public in general, the more do his rights become circum-scribed by the statutory and constitutional rights of those who use it."

When there are no effective means of communication, free speech is a mere shibboleth. I believe that the First Amendment requires it to be a reality. . . .

UNITED STATES v. O'BRIEN
O'BRIEN v. UNITED STATES
391 U.S. 367; 20 L. Ed. 672; 88 S. Ct. 1673 (1968)

MR. CHIEF JUSTICE WARREN *delivered the opinion of the Court.*

On the morning of March 31, 1966, David Paul O'Brien and three companions burned their Selective Service registration certificates on the steps of the South Boston Courthouse. A sizable crowd, including several agents of the Federal Bureau of Investigation, witnessed the event. . . . After he was advised of his right to counsel and to silence, O'Brien stated to FBI agents that he had burned his registration certificate because of his beliefs, knowing that he was violating federal law. He produced the charred remains of the certificate, which, with his consent, were photographed.

For this act, O'Brien was indicted, tried, convicted, and sentenced in the United States District Court for the District of Massachusetts. He did not contest the fact that he had burned the certificate. He stated in argument to the jury that he burned the certificate publicly to influence others to adopt his antiwar beliefs, as he put it, "so that other people would reevaluate their positions with Selective Service, with the armed forces, and reevaluate their place in the culture of today, to hopefully consider my position."

The indictment upon which he was tried charged that he "wilfully and knowingly did mutilate, destroy, and change by burning . . . [his] Registration Certificate (Selective Service System Form No. 2); in violation of Title 50, App., United States Code, Section 462(b)." Section 462(b) is part of the Universal Military Training and Service Act of 1948. Section 462(b)(3) . . . was amended by Congress in 1965, 79 Stat. 586 (adding the words italicized below), so that at the time O'Brien burned his certificate an offense was committed by any person,

> who forges, alters, *knowingly destroys, knowingly mutilates,* or in any manner changes any such certificate. . . . (Italics supplied.)

In the District Court, O'Brien argued that the 1965 Amendment prohibiting the knowing destruction or mutilation of certificates was unconstitutional because it was enacted to abridge free speech, and because it served no legitimate legislative purpose. The District Court rejected these arguments, holding that the statute on its face did not abridge First Amendment rights, that the court was not competent to inquire into the motives of Congress in enacting the 1965 Amendment, and that the Amendment was a reasonable exercise of the power of Congress to raise armies.

On appeal, the Court of Appeals for the First Circuit held the 1965 Amendment unconstitutional as a law abridging freedom of speech. At the time the Amendment was enacted, a regulation of the Selective Service System required registrants to keep their registration certificates in their "personal possession at all times." . . . Wilful violations of regulations promulgated pursuant to the Universal Military Training and Service Act were made criminal by statute. . . . The Court of Appeals, therefore, was of the opinion that conduct punishable under the 1965 Amendment was already punishable under the nonpossession regulation, and consequently that the Amendment served no valid purpose; further, that in light of the prior regulation, the Amendment must have been "directed at public as distinguished from private destruction." On this basis, the Court concluded that the 1965 Amendment ran afoul of the First Amendment by singling our persons engaged in protests for special treatment. The Court ruled, however, that O'Brien's conviction should be affirmed under the statutory provision, 50 U.S.C. App. Sec. 462(b)(6), which in its view made violation of the nonpossession regulation a crime, because it regarded such violation to be a lesser included offense of the crime defined by the 1965 Amendment.*

The Government petitioned for certiorari . . . arguing that the Court of Appeals erred in holding the statute unconstitutional, and that its decision conflicted with decisions by the Court of Appeals for the Second† and Eighth Circuits‡

*The Court of Appeals nevertheless remanded the case to the District Court to vacate the sentence and resentence O'Brien. In the Court's view, the district judge might have considered the violation of the 1965 Amendment as an aggravating circumstance in imposing sentence. The Court of Appeals subsequently denied O'Brien's petition for a rehearing, in which he argued that he had not been charged, tried, or convicted for nonpossession, and that nonpossession was not a lesser included offense of mutilation or destruction. *O'Brien* v. *United States*, 376 F. 2d 538, 542 (C.A. 1st Cir. 1967).

†*United States* v. *Miller*, 367 F. 2d 72 (C.A. 2d Cir. 1966), cert. denied, 386 U.S. 911 (1967).

‡*Smith* v. *United States*, 368 F. 2d 529 (C.A. 8th Cir. 1966).

upholding the 1965 Amendment against identical constitutional challenges. O'Brien cross-petitioned for certiorari, . . . arguing that the Court of Appeals erred in sustaining his conviction on the basis of a crime of which he was neither charged nor tried. We granted the Government's petition to resolve the conflict in the circuits, and we also granted O'Brien's cross-petition. We hold that the 1965 Amendment is constitutional both as enacted and as applied. We therefore vacate the judgment of the Court of Appeals and reinstate the judgment and sentence of the District Court without reaching the issue raised by O'Brien in [his cross-petition].

. . .

. . . We note at the outset that the 1965 Amendment plainly does not abridge free speech on its face, and we do not understand O'Brien to argue otherwise. Amended Sec. 12(b) (3) on its face deals with conduct having no connection with speech. It prohibits the knowing destruction of certificates issued by the Selective Service System, and there is nothing necessarily expressive about such conduct. The Amendment does not distinguish between public and private destruction, and it does not punish only destruction engaged in for the purpose of expressing views. . . . A law prohibiting destruction of Selective Service certificates no more abridges free speech on its face than a motor vehicle law prohibiting the destruction of drivers' licenses, or a tax law prohibiting the destruction of books and records.

O'Brien nonetheless argues that the 1965 Amendment is unconstitutional in its application to him, and is unconstitutional as enacted because what he calls the "purpose" of Congress was "to suppress freedom of speech." We consider these arguments separately.

O'Brien first argues that the 1965 Amendment is unconstitutional as applied to him because his act of burning his registration certificate was protected "symbolic speech" within the First Amendment. His argument is that the freedom of expression which the First Amendment guarantees includes all modes of "communication of ideas by conduct," and that his conduct is within this definition because he did it in "demonstration against the war and against the draft."

We cannot accept the view that an apparently limitless variety of conduct can be labeled "speech" whenever the person engaging in the conduct intends thereby to express an idea. However, even on the assumption that the alleged communicative element in O'Brien's conduct is sufficient to bring into play the First Amendment, it does not necessarily follow that the destruction of a registration certificate is constitutionally protected activity. This Court has held that when "speech" and "non-speech" elements are combined in the same course of conduct, a sufficiently important governmental interest in regulating the nonspeech element can justify incidental limitations on First Amendment freedoms. To characterize the quality of the governmental interest which must appear, the Court has employed a variety of descriptive terms: compelling; substantial; subordinating; paramount; cogent; strong. Whatever imprecision inheres in these terms, we think it clear that a government regulation is sufficiently justified if it is within the constitutional power of the government; if it furthers an important or substantial governmental interest; if the governmental interest is unrelated to the suppression of free expression; and if the incidental restriction on alleged First Amendment freedom is no greater than is essential to the furtherance of that interest. We find that the 1965 Amendment to Sec. 462(b)(3) of the Universal Military Training and Service Act meets all of these requirements, and consequently that O'Brien can be constitutionally convicted for violating it.

The constitutional power of Congress to raise and support armies and to make all laws necessary and proper to that end is broad and sweeping. . . . The power of Congress to classify and conscript manpower for military service is "beyond question." . . . Pursuant to this power, Congress may establish a system of registration for individuals liable for training and service, and may require such individuals within reason to cooperate in the registration system. The issuance of certificates indicating the registration and eligibility classification of individuals is a legitimate and substantial administrative aid in the functioning of this system. And legislation to insure the continuing availability of issued certificates serves a legitimate and substantial purpose in the system's administration.

O'Brien's argument to the contrary is necessarily premised upon his unrealistic characterization of Selective Service certificates. He essentially adopts the position that such certificates are so many pieces of paper designed to notify registrants of their registration or classification, to be retained or tossed in the wastebasket according to the convenience or taste of the registrant. Once the registrant has received notification, according to this view, there is no reason for him to retain the certificates. O'Brien notes that most of the information on a registration certificate serves no notification purpose at all; the registrant hardly needs to be told his address and physical characteristics. We agree that the registration certificate contains much information of which the registrant needs no notification. This circumstance, however, leads not to the conclusion that the certificate serves no purpose but that, like the classification certificate, it serves purposes in addition to initial notification. Many of these purposes would be defeated by the certificates' destruction or mutilation. Among these are:

1. The registration certificate serves as proof that the individual described thereon has registered for the draft. The classification certificate shows the eligibility classification of a named but undescribed individual. Voluntarily displaying the two certificates is an easy and painless way for a young man to dispel a question as to whether he might be delinquent in his Selective Service obligations. Correspondingly, the availability of the certificates for such display relieves the Selective Service System of the administrative burden it would otherwise have in verifying

the registration and classification of all suspected delinquents. . . .

2. The information supplied on the certificates facilitates communication between registrants and local boards, simplifying the system and benefiting all concerned. . . .

3. Both certificates carry continual reminders that the registrant must notify his local board of any change of address, and other specified changes in his status. The smooth functioning of the system requires that local boards be continually aware of the status and whereabouts of registrants, and the destruction of certificates deprives the system of a potentially useful notice device.

4. The regulatory scheme involving Selective Service certificates includes clearly valid prohibitions against the alteration, forgery or similar deceptive misuse of certificates. The destruction or mutilation of certicates increases the difficulty of detecting and tracing abuses such as these. Further, a mutilated certificate might itself be used for deceptive purposes.

The many functions performed by Selective Service certificates establish beyond doubt that Congress has a legitimate and substantial interest in preventing their wanton and unrestrained destruction and assuring their continuing availability by punishing people who knowingly and wilfully destroy or mutilate them. And we are unpersuaded that the preexistence of the nonpossession regulations in any way negates this interest.

. . .

We think it apparent that the continuing availability to each registrant of his Selective Service certificates substantially furthers the smooth and proper functioning of the system that Congress has established to raise armies. We think it also apparent that the Nation has a vital interest in having a system for raising armies that functions with maximum efficiency and is capable of easily and quickly responding to continually changing circumstances. For these reasons, the Government has a substantial interest in assuring the continuing availability of issued Selective Service certificates.

It is equally clear that the 1965 Amendment specifically protects this substantial governmental interest. We perceive no alternative means that would more precisely and narrowly assure the continuing availability of issued Selective Service certificates than a law which prohibits their wilful mutilation or destruction. . . . The 1965 Amendment prohibits such conduct and does nothing more. In other words, both the governmental interest and the operation of the 1965 Amendment are limited to the noncommunicative aspect of O'Brien's conduct. . . . When O'Brien deliberately rendered unavailable his registration certificate, he wilfully frustrated this governmental interest. For this noncommunicative impact of his conduct, and for nothing else, he was convicted.

. . .

O'Brien finally argues that the 1965 Amendment is unconstitutional as enacted because what he calls the "purpose" of Congress was "to suppress freedom of speech." We reject this argument because under settled principles the purpose of Congress, as O'Brien uses the term, is not a basis for declaring this legislation unconstitutional.

It is a familiar principle of constitutional law that this Court will not strike down an otherwise constitutional statute on the basis of an alleged illicit legislative motive.

. . .

Since the 1965 Amendment to Sec. 12(b)(3) of the Universal Military Training and Service Act is constitutional as enacted and as applied, the Court of Appeals should have affirmed the judgment of conviction entered by the District Court. Accordingly, we vacate the judgment of the Court of Appeals, and reinstate the judgment and sentence of the District Court. This disposition makes unnecessary consideration of O'Brien's claim that the Court of Appeals erred in affirming his conviction on the basis of the nonpossession regulation.

It is so ordered.

MR. JUSTICE MARSHALL *took no part in the consideration or decision of these cases.*

MR. JUSTICE HARLAN'S *brief concurring opinion is not reprinted here.*

MR. JUSTICE DOUGLAS, *dissenting.*

. . . The underlying and basic problem in this case . . . is whether conscription is permissible in the absence of a declaration of war. That question has not been briefed nor was it presented in oral argument; but it is, I submit, a question upon which the litigants and the country are entitled to a ruling. . . . It is time that we made a ruling. This case should be put down for reargument and heard with *Holmes* v. *United States* and with *Hart* v. *United States* . . . in which the Court today denies certiorari.

The rule that this Court will not consider issues not raised by the parties is not inflexible and yields in "exceptional cases" . . . to the need correctly to decide the case before the court . . . .

NEW YORK TIMES CO. v. SULLIVAN
376 U.S. 255; 11 L. Ed. 2d 686; 84 S. Ct. 710 (1964)

MR. JUSTICE BRENNAN *delivered the opinion of the Court.*

We are required for the first time in this case to determine the extent to which the constitutional protections for speech and press limit a state's power to award damages in a libel action brought by a public official against critics of his official conduct.

Respondent L. B. Sullivan is one of the three elected Commissioners of the City of Montgomery, Alabama. He testified that he was "Commissioner of Public Affairs and the duties are supervision of the Police Department, Fire Department, Department of Cemetery and Department of Scales." He brought this civil libel action against the four individual petitioners, who are Negroes and Alabama clergymen, and against petitioner the New York Times Company . . . which publishes the New York Times. . . . A jury in the Circuit Court of Montgomery County awarded him damages of $500,000, the full amount claimed, against all the petitioners, and the Supreme Court of Alabama affirmed.

Respondent's complaint alleged that he had been libeled by statements in a full-page advertisement that was carried in the *New York Times* on March 29, 1960. Entitled "Heed Their Rising Voices," the advertisement began by stating that "As the whole world knows by now, thousands of Southern Negro students are engaged in widespread nonviolent demonstrations in positive affirmation of the right to live in human dignity as guaranteed by the U.S. Constitution and the Bill of Rights." It went on to charge that "in their efforts to uphold these guarantees, they are being met by an unprecedented wave of terror by those who would deny and negate that document which the whole world looks upon as setting the pattern for modern freedom. . . ." Succeeding paragraphs purported to illustrate the "wave of terror" by describing certain alleged events. The text concluded with an appeal for funds for three purposes: support of the student movement, "the struggle for the right-to-vote," and the legal defense of Dr. Martin Luther King, Jr., leader of the movement, against a perjury indictment then pending in Montgomery.

The text appeared over the names of 64 persons, many widely known for their activities in public affairs, religion, trade unions, and the performing arts. Below these names, and under a line reading "We in the South who are struggling daily for dignity and freedom warmly endorse this appeal," appeared the names of the four individual petitioners and of 16 other persons, all but two of whom were identified as clergymen in various Southern cities. The advertisement was signed at the bottom of the page by the "Committee to Defend Martin Luther King and the Struggle for Freedom in the South," and the officers of the Committee were listed.

Of the 10 paragraphs of text in the advertisement, the third and a portion of the sixth were the basis of respondent's claim of libel. They read as follows:

Third paragraph:

In Montgomery, Alabama, after students sang "My Country, 'Tis of Thee" on the State Capitol steps, their leaders were expelled from school, and truckloads of police armed with shotguns and teargas ringed the Alabama State College Campus. When the entire student body protested to state authorities by refusing to re-register, their dining hall was padlocked in an attempt to starve them into submission.

Sixth paragraph:

Again and again the Southern violators have answered Dr. King's peaceful protests with intimidation and violence. They have bombed his home almost killing his wife and child. They have assaulted his person. They have arrested him seven times—for "speeding," "loitering" and similar "offenses." And now they have charged him with "perjury"—a *felony* under which they would imprison him for *ten years.* . . .

Although neither of these statements mentions respondent by name, he contended that the word "police" in the third paragraph referred to him as the Montgomery Commissioner who supervised the Police Department, so that he was being accused of "ringing" the campus with police. He further claimed that the paragraph would be read as imputing to the police, and hence to him, the padlocking of the dining hall in order to starve the students into submission. As to the sixth paragraph, he contended that since arrests are ordinarily made by the police, the statement "They have arrested [Dr. King] seven times" would be read as referring to him; he further contended that the "They" who did the arresting would be equated with the "They" who committed the other described acts and with the "Southern violators." Thus, he argued, the paragraph would be read as accusing the Montgomery police, and hence him, of answering Dr. King's protests with "intimidation and violence," bombing his home, assaulting his person, and charging him with perjury. Respondent and six other Montgomery residents testified that they read some or all of the statements as referring to him in his capacity as Commissioner.

It is uncontroverted that some of the statements contained in the two paragraphs were not accurate descriptions of events which occurred in Montgomery. Although Negro students staged a demonstration on the State Capitol steps, they sang the National Anthem and not "My Country, 'Tis of Thee." Although nine students were expelled by the State Board of Education, this was not for leading the demonstration at the Capitol, but for demanding service at a lunch counter in the Montgomery County Courthouse on another day. Not the entire student body, but most of it, had protested the expulsion, not by refusing to register, but by boycotting classes on a single day; virtually all the students did register for the ensuing semester. The campus dining hall was not padlocked on any occasion, and the only students who may have been barred from eating there were the few who had neither signed a preregistration application nor requested temporary meal tickets. Although the police were deployed near the campus in large numbers on three occasions, they did not at any time "ring" the campus, and they were not called to the campus in connection with the demonstration on the State Capitol steps, as the third paragraph implied. Dr. King had not been arrested seven times, but only four; and although he claimed to have been assaulted some years earlier in connection with his arrest for loitering outside a courtroom, one of the officers who made the arrest denied that there was such an assault.

On the premise that the charges in the sixth paragraph could be read as referring to him, respondent was allowed to prove that he had not participated in the events described. Although Dr. King's home had in fact been bombed twice when his wife and child were there, both of these occasions antedated respondent's tenure as Commissioner, and the police were not only not implicated in the bombings, but had made every effort to apprehend those who were. Three of Dr. King's four arrests took place before respondent became Commissioner. Although Dr. King had in fact been indicted (he was subsequently acquitted) on two counts of perjury, each of which carried a possible five-year sentence, respondent had nothing to do with procuring the indictment.

Respondent made no effort to prove that he suffered actual pecuniary loss as a result of the alleged libel.* One of his witnesses, a former employer, testified that if he had believed the statements, he doubted whether he "would want to be associated with anybody who would be a party to such things as are stated in that ad," and that he would not re-employ respondent if he believed "that he allowed the Police Department to do the things that the paper said he did." But neither this witness nor any of the others testified that he had actually believed the state-

ments in their supported reference to respondent.

The cost of the advertisement was approximately $4800, and it was published by the Times upon an order from a New York advertising agency acting for the signatory Committee. The agency submitted the advertisement with a letter from A. Philip Randolph, Chairman of the Committee, certifying that the persons whose names appeared on the advertisement had given their permission. Mr. Randolph was known to the Times' Advertising Acceptability Department as a responsible person, and in accepting the letter as sufficient proof of authorization it followed its established practice. There was testimony that the copy of the advertisement which accompanied the letter listed only the sixty-four names appearing under the text, and that the statement, "We in the South . . . warmly endorse this appeal" and the list of names thereunder, which included those of the individual petitioners, were subsequently added when the first proof of the advertisement was received. Each of the individual petitioners testified that he had not authorized the use of his name, and that he had been unaware of its use until receipt of respondent's demand for a retraction. The manager of the Advertising Acceptability Department testified that he had approved the advertisement for publication because he knew nothing to cause him to believe that anything in it was false, and because it bore the endorsement of "a number of people who are well known and whose reputation" he "had no reason to question." Neither he nor anyone else at the Times made an effort to confirm the accuracy of the advertisement, either by checking it against recent Times news stories relating to some of the described events or by some other means.

Alabama law denies a public officer recovery of punitive damages in a libel action brought on account of a publication concerning his official conduct unless he first makes a written demand for a public retraction and the defendant fails or refuses to comply. Respondent served such a demand upon each of the petitioners. None

*Approximately 394 copies of the edition of the *Times* containing the advertisement were circulated in Alabama. Of these, about 35 copies were distributed in Montgomery County. The total circulation of the *Times* for that day was approximately 650,000 copies.

of the individual petitioners responded to the demand, primarily because each took the position that he had not authorized the use of his name on the advertisement and therefore had not published the statements that respondent alleged to have libeled him. The Times did not publish a retraction in response to the demand, but wrote respondent a letter stating, among other things, that "we . . . are somewhat puzzled as to how you think the statements in any way reflect on you," and "you might, if you desire, let us know in what respect you claim that the statements in the advertisement reflect on you." Respondent filed this suit a few days later without answering the letter. The Times did, however, subsequently publish a retraction of the advertisement upon the demand of Governor John Patterson of Alabama, who asserted that the publication charged him with "grave misconduct and . . . improper actions and omissions as Governor of Alabama and Ex-Officio Chairman of the State Board of Education of Alabama." When asked to explain why there had been a retraction for the Governor but not for respondent, the Secretary of the Times testified: "We did that because we didn't want anything that was published by The Times to be a reflection on the State of Alabama and the Governor was, as far as we could see, the embodiment of the State of Alabama and the proper representative of the State and, furthermore, we had by that time learned more of the actual facts which the ad purported to recite and, finally, the ad did refer to the action of the State authorities and the Board of Education presumably of which the Governor is ex-officio, chairman. . . ." On the other hand, he testified that he did not think that "any of the language in there referred to Mr. Sullivan."

The trial judge submitted the case to the jury under instructions that the statements in the advertisement were "libelous per se" and were not privileged, so that petitioners might be held liable if the jury found that they had published the advertisement and that the statements were made "of and concerning" respondent. The jury was instructed that, because the statements were libelous *per se*, "the law . . . implies legal injury from the bare fact of publication itself," "falsity and malice are presumed," "general damages need not be alleged or proved but are presumed," and "punitive damages may be awarded by the jury even though the amount of actual damages in neither found nor shown." An award of punitive damages—as distinguished from "general" damages, which are compensatory in nature—apparently requires proof of actual malice under Alabama law, and the judge charged that "mere negligence or carelessness is not evidence of actual malice or malice in fact, and does not justify an award of exemplary or punitive damages." He refused to charge, however, that the jury must be "convinced" of malice, in the sense of "actual intent" to harm or "gross negligence and recklessness," to make such an award, and he also refused to require that a verdict for respondent differentiate between compensatory and punitive damages. The judge rejected petitioners' contention that his rulings abridged the freedoms of speech and of the press that are guaranteed by the First and Fourteenth Amendments.

In affirming the judgment, the Supreme Court of Alabama sustained the trial judge's rulings and instructions in all respects. . . . In sustaining the trial court's determination that the verdict was not excessive, the court said that malice could be inferred from the Times' "irresponsibility" in printing the advertisement while "the Times in its own files had articles already published which would have demonstrated the falsity of the allegations in the advertisement"; from the Times' failure to retract for respondent while retracting for the Governor, whereas the falsity of some of the allegations was then known to the Times and "the matter contained in the advertisement was equally false as to both parties"; and from the testimony of the Times' Secretary that, apart from the statement that the dining hall was padlocked, he thought the two paragraphs were "substantially correct.". . .

. . . We reverse the judgment. We hold that the rule of law applied by the Alabama courts is constitutionally deficient for failure to provide the safeguards for freedom of speech and of the press that are required by the First and Fourteenth Amendments in a libel action brought by a public official against critics of his official conduct. We further hold that under the proper safeguards the evidence presented in this case is constitutionally insufficient to support the judgment for respondent.

We may dispose at the outset of two grounds asserted to insulate the judgment of the Alabama courts from constitutional scrutiny. The first is the proposition relied on by the State Supreme Court—that "The Fourteenth Amendment is directed against State action and not private action." That proposition has no application to this case. Although this is a civil lawsuit between private parties, the Alabama courts have applied a state rule of law which petitioners claim to impose invalid restrictions on their constitutional freedoms of speech and press. It matters not that that law has been applied in a civil action and that it is common law only, though supplemented by statute. . . .

The second contention is that the constitutional guarantees of freedom of speech and of the press are inapplicable here, at least so far as the Times is concerned, because the allegedly libelous statements were published as part of a paid, "commercial" advertisement. The argument relies on *Valentine* v. *Chrestensen*, 316 U.S. 52, where the Court held that a city ordinance forbidding street distribution of commercial and business advertising matter did not abridge the First Amendment freedoms, even as applied to a handbill having a commercial message on one side but a protest against certain official action on the other. The reliance is wholly misplaced. The Court in *Chrestensen* reaffirmed the constitutional protection for "the freedom of communicating information and disseminating opinion"; its holding was based upon the factual conclusions that the handbill was "purely commercial advertising" and that the protest against official action had been added only to evade the ordinance.

The publication here was not a "commercial" advertisement in the sense in which the word was used in *Chrestensen*. It communicated information, expressed opinion, recited grievances, protested claimed abuses, and sought financial support on behalf of a movement whose existence and objectives are matters of the highest public interest and concern. That the Times was paid for publishing the advertisement is as immaterial in this connection as is the fact that newspapers and books are sold. Any other conclusion would discourage newspapers from carrying "editorial advertisements" of this type, and so might shut off an important outlet for the promulgation of information and ideas by persons who do not themselves have access to publishing facilities—who wish to exercise their freedom of speech even though they are not members of the press. The effect would be to shackle the First Amendment in its attempt to secure "the widest possible dissemination of information from diverse and antagonistic sources." To avoid placing such a handicap upon the freedoms of expression, we hold that if the allegedly libelous statements would otherwise be constitutionally protected from the present judgment, they do not forfeit that protection because they were published in the form of a paid advertisement.

Under Alabama law as applied in this case, a publication is "libelous per se" if the words "tend to injure a person . . . in his reputation" or to "bring [him] into public contempt"; the trial court stated that the standard was met if the words are such as to injure him in his public office, or impute misconduct to him in his office, or want of official integrity, or want of fidelity to a public trust. . . ." The jury must find that the words were published "of and concerning" the plaintiff, but where the plaintiff is a public official his place in the governmental hierarchy is sufficient evidence to support a finding that his reputation has been affected by statements that reflect upon the agency of which he is in charge. Once "libel per se" has been established, the defendant has no defense as to stated facts unless he can persuade the jury that they were true in all their particulars. His privilege of "fair comment" for expressions of opinion depends on the truth of the facts upon which the comment is based. Unless he can discharge the burden of proving truth, general damages are presumed, and may be awarded without proof of pecuniary injury. A showing of actual malice is apparently a prerequisite to recovery of punitive damages, and the defendant may in any event forestall these by a retraction meeting the statutory requirements. Good motives and belief in truth do not negate an inference of malice, but are relevant only in mitigation of punitive damages if the jury chooses to accord them weight.

The question before us is whether this rule of liability, as applied to an action brought by a public official against critics of his official conduct, abridges the freedom of speech and of the press that is guaranteed by the First and Fourteenth Amendments. . . .

. . . In deciding the question now, we are compelled by neither precedent nor policy to give any more weight to the epithet "libel" than we have to other "mere labels" of state law. Like "insurrection," contempt, advocacy of unlawful acts, breach of the peace, obscenity, solicitation of legal business, and the various other formulae for the repression of expression that have been challenged in this Court, libel can claim no talismanic immunity from constitutional limitations. It must be measured by standards that satisfy the First Amendment. . . .

. . . [W]e consider this case against the background of a profound national commitment to the principle that debate on public issues should be uninhibited, robust, and wide-open, and that it may well include vehement, caustic, and sometimes unpleasantly sharp attacks on government and public officials. The present adver-

tisement, as an expression of grievance and protest on one of the major public issues of our time, would seem clearly to qualify for the constitutional protection. The question is whether it forfeits that protection by the falsity of some of its factual statements and by its alleged defamation of respondent.

Authoritative interpretations of the First Amendment guarantees have consistently refused to recognize an exception for any test of truth, whether administered by judges, juries, or administrative officials—and especially not one that puts the burden of proving truth on the speaker. The constitutional protection does not turn upon "the truth, popularity, or social utility of the ideas and beliefs which are offered." *N.A.A.C.P. v. Button*, 371 U.S. 415, 445. . . .

. . . [E]rroneous statement is inevitable in free debate, and . . . it must be protected if the freedoms of expression are to have the "breathing space" that they "need . . . to survive," *N.A.A.C.P. v. Button.* . . .

Just as factual error affords no warrant for repressing speech that would otherwise be free, the same is true of injury to official reputation. Where judicial officers are involved, this Court has held that concern for the dignity and reputation of the courts does not justify the punishment as criminal contempt of criticism of the judge or his decision. *Bridges* v. *California*, 314 U.S. 252. This is true even though the utterance contains "half-truths" and "misinformation.". . . If judges are to be treated as "men of fortitude, able to thrive in a hardy climate," surely the same must be true of other government officials, such as elected city commissioners.† Criticism of their official conduct does

†The climate in which public officials operate, especially during a political campaign, has been described by one commentator in the following terms: "Charges of gross incompetence, disregard of the public interest, communist sympathies, and the like usually have filled the air; and hints of bribery, embezzlement, and other criminal conduct are not infrequent." Noel, "Defamation of Public Officers and Candidates," 49 *Col. L. Rev.* 875 (1949). . . .

not lose its constitutional protection merely because it is effective criticism and hence diminishes their official reputations.

If neither factual error nor defamatory content suffices to remove the constitutional shield from criticism of official conduct, the combination of the two elements is no less inadequate. This is the lesson to be drawn from the great controversy over the Sedition Act of 1798, 1 Stat. 596, which first crystallized a national awareness of the central meaning of the First Amendment. See Levy, *Legacy of Suppression* (1960), at 258 et seq.; Smith, *Freedom's Fetters* (1956), at 426, 431 and *passim*. . . .

Athough the Sedition Act was never tested in this Court, the attack upon its validity has carried the day in the court of history. Fines levied in its prosecution were repaid by Act of Congress on the ground that it was unconstitutional. . . .

What a State may not constitutionally bring about by means of a criminal statute is likewise beyond the reach of its civil law of libel. The fear of damage awards under a rule such as that invoked by the Alabama courts here may be markedly more inhibiting than the fear of prosecution under a criminal statute. Alabama, for example, has a criminal libel law which subjects to prosecution "any person who speaks, writes, or prints of and concerning another any accusation falsely and maliciously importing the commission by such person of a felony, or any other indictable offense involving moral turpitude," and which allows as punishment upon conviction a fine not exceeding $500 and a prison sentence of six months. Alabama Code, Tit. 14, § 350. Presumably a person charged with violation of this statute enjoys ordinary criminal-law safeguards such as the requirements of an indictment and of proof beyond a reasonable doubt. These safeguards are not available to the defendant in a civil action. The judgment awarded in this case—without the need for any proof of actual pecuniary loss—was one thousand times greater than the maximum fine provided by the Alabama criminal statute, and one hundred times greater than that provided by the Sedition Act. And since there is no double-jeopardy limitation applicable to civil lawsuits, this is not the only judgment that may be awarded against petitioners for the same publication. Whether or not a newspaper can survive a succession of such judgments, the pall of fear and timidity imposed upon those who would give voice to public criticism is an atmosphere in which the First Amendment freedoms cannot survive. Plainly the Alabama law of civil libel is "a form of regulation that creates hazards to protected freedoms markedly greater than those that attend reliance upon the criminal law."

The state rule of law is not saved by its allowance of the defense of truth. A defense for erroneous statements honestly made is no less essential here than was the requirement of proof of guilty knowledge which, in *Smith* v. *California*, 361 U.S. 147, we held indispensable to a valid conviction of a bookseller for possessing obscene writings for sale. . . . A rule compelling the critic of official conduct to guarantee the truth of all his factual assertions—and to do so on pain of libel judgments virtually unlimited in amount—leads to a comparable "self-censorship." Allowance of the defense of truth, with the burden of proving it on the defendant, does not mean that only false speech will be deterred. Even courts accepting this defense as an adequate safeguard have recognized the difficulties of adducing legal proofs that the alleged libel was true in all its factual particulars. Under such a rule, would-be critics of official conduct may be deterred from voicing their criticism, even though it is believed to be true and even though it is in fact true, because of doubt whether it can be proved in court or fear of the expense of having to do so. They tend to make only statements which "steer far wider of the unlawful zone." The rule thus dampens the vigor and limits the variety of public debate. It is inconsistent with the First and Fourteenth Amendments.

The constitutional guarantees require, we think, a federal rule that prohibits a public official from recovering damages for a defamatory falsehood relating to his official conduct unless he proves that the statement was made with "actual malice"—that is, with knowledge that it was false or with reckless disregard of whether it was false or not. . . .

We hold today that the Constitution delimits a State's power to award damages for libel in actions brought by public officials against critics of their official conduct. Since this is such an action, the rule requiring proof of actual malice is applicable. While Alabama law apparently requires proof of actual malice for an award of punitive damages, where general damages are concerned malice is "presumed." Such a presumption is inconsistent with the federal rule. "The power to create presumptions is not a means of escape from constitutional restrictions," *Bailey* v. *Alabama*, 219 U.S. 219, 239; "[t]he showing of malice required for the forfeiture of the privilege is not presumed but is a matter for proof by the plaintiff. . . ." Since the trial judge did not instruct the jury to differentiate between general and punitive damages, it it may be that the verdict was wholly an award of one or the other. But it is impossible to know, in view of the general verdict returned. Because of this uncertainty, the judgment must be reversed and the case remanded. . . .

Since respondent may seek a new trial, we deem that considerations of effective judicial administration require us to review the evidence in the present record to determine whether it could constitutionally support a judgment for respondent. This Court's duty is not limited to the elaboration of constitutional principles; we must also in proper cases review the evidence to make certain that those principles have been constitutionally applied. This is such a case, particularly since the question is one of alleged trespass across "the line between speech uncondi-

tionally guaranteed and speech which may legitimately be regulated." In cases where that line must be drawn, the rule is that we "examine for ourselves the statements in issue and the circumstances under which they were made to see . . . whether they are of a character which the principles of the First Amendment, as adopted by the Due Process Clause of the Fourteenth Amendment, protect." . . .

Applying these standards, we consider that the proof presented to show actual malice lacks the convincing clarity which the constitutional standard demands, and hence that it would not constitutionally sustain the judgment for respondent under the proper rule of law. The case of the individual petitioners requires little discussion. Even assuming that they could constitutionally be found to have authorized the use of their names on the advertisement, there was no evidence whatever that they were aware of any erroneous statements or were in any way reckless in that regard. The judgment against them is thus without constitutional support.

As to the Times, we similarly conclude that the facts do not support a finding of actual malice. The statement by the Times' Secretary that, apart from the padlocking allegation, he thought the advertisement was "substantially correct," affords no constitutional warrant for the Alabama Supreme Court's conclusion that it was a "cavalier ignoring of the falsity of the advertisement [from which], the jury could not have but been impressed with the bad faith of The Times, and its maliciousness inferable therefrom." The statement does not indicate malice at the time of the publication; even if the advertisement was not "substantially correct"—although respondent's own proofs tend to show that it was—that opinion was at least a reasonable one, and there was no evidence to impeach the witness' good faith in holding it. The Times' failure to retract upon respondent's demand, although it later retracted upon the demand of Governor Patterson, is likewise not adequate evidence of malice for constitutional purposes. Whether or not a failure to retract may ever constitute such evidence, there are two reasons why it does not here. *First*, the letter written by the Times reflected a reasonable doubt on its part as to whether the advertisement could reasonably be taken to refer to respondent at all. *Second,* it was not a final refusal, since it asked for an explanation on this point—a request that respondent chose to ignore. Nor does the retraction upon the demand of the Governor supply the necessary proof. It may be doubted that a failure to retract which is not itself evidence of malice can retroactively become such by virtue of a retraction subsequently made to another party. But in any event that did not happen here, since the explanation given by the Times' Secretary for the distinction drawn between respondent and the Governor was a reasonable one, the good faith of which was not impeached.

Finally, there is evidence that the Times published the advertisement without checking its accuracy against the news stories in the Times' own files. The mere presence of the stories in the files does not, of course, establish that the Times "knew" the advertisement was false, since the state of mind required for actual malice would have to be brought home to the persons in the Times' organization having responsibility for the publication of the advertisement. With respect to the failure of those persons to make the check, the record shows that they relied upon their knowledge of the good reputation of many of those whose names were listed as sponsors of the advertisement, and upon the letter from A. Philip Randolph, known to them as a responsible individual, certifying that the use of the names was authorized. There was testimony that the persons handling the advertisement saw nothing in it that would render it unacceptable under the Times' policy of rejecting advertisements containing "attacks of a personal character"; their failure to reject it on this ground was not unreasonable. We think the evidence against the Times supports at most a finding of negligence in failing to discover the misstatements, and is constitutionally insufficient to show the recklessness that is required for a finding of actual malice.

We also think the evidence was constitutionally defective in another respect: it was incapable of supporting the jury's finding that the allegedly libelous statements were made "of and concerning" respondent. Respondent relies on the words of the advertisement and the testimony of six witnesses to establish a connection between it and himself.... There was no reference to respondent in the advertisement, either by name or official position. A number of the allegedly libelous statements—the charges that the dining hall was padlocked and that Dr. King's home was bombed, his person assaulted, and a perjury prosecution instituted against him—did not even concern the police; despite the ingenuity of the arguments which would attach this significance to the word "They," it is plain that these statements could not reasonably be read as accusing respondent of personal involvement in the acts in question. The statements upon which respondent principally relies as referring to him are the two allegations that did concern the police or police functions: that "truckloads of police ... ringed the Alabama State College Campus" after the demonstration on the State Capitol steps, and Dr. King had been "arrested ... seven times." These statements were false only in that the police had been "deployed near" the campus but had not actually "ringed" it and had not gone there in connection with the State Capitol demonstration, and in that Dr. King had been arrested only four times. The ruling that these discrepancies between what was true and what was asserted were sufficient to injure respondent's reputation may itself raise constitutional problems, but we need not consider them here. Although the statements may be taken as referring to the police, they did not on their face make even an oblique reference to respondent as an individual. Support for the asserted reference must, therefore, be sought in the testimony of respondent's witnesses. But none of them suggested any basis for the belief that respondent himself was attacked in the advertisement beyond the bare fact that he was in overall charge of the Police Department and thus bore official responsibility for police conduct; to the extent that some of the witnesses thought respondent to have been charged with ordering or approving the conduct or otherwise being personally involved in it, they based this notion not on any statements in the advertisement, and not on any evidence that he had in fact been so involved, but solely on the unsupported assumption that, because of his official position, he must have been. This reliance on the bare fact of respondent's official position was made explicit by the Supreme Court of Alabama. That court, in holding that the trial court "did not err in overruling the demurrer [of the Times] in the aspect that the libelous matter was not of and concerning the plaintiffs," based its ruling on the proposition that:

We think it common knowledge that the average person knows that municipal agents, such as police and fireman, and others, are under the control and direction of the city governing body, and more particularly under the direction and control of a single commissioner. In measuring the performance or deficiencies of such groups, praise or criticism is usually attached to the offical in complete control of the body.

This proposition has disquieting implications for criticism of governmental conduct. For good reason, "no court of last resort in this country has ever held, or even suggested, that prosecutions for libel on government have any place in the American system of jurisprudence." The present proposition would sidestep this obstacle by transmuting criticism of government, however impersonal it may seem on its face, into personal criticism, and hence potential libel, of the officials of whom the government is composed.

There is no legal alchemy by which a State may thus create the cause of action that would otherwise be denied for a publication which, as respondent himself said of the advertisement, "reflects not only on me but on the other Commissioners and the community." Raising as it does the possibility that a good-faith critic of government will be penalized for his criticism, the proposition relied on by the Alabama courts strikes at the very center of the constitutionally protected area of free expression. We hold that such a proposition may not constitutionally be utilized to establish that an otherwise impersonal attack on governmental operations was a libel of an official responsible for those operations. . . .

The judgment of the Supreme Court of Alabama is reversed and the case is remanded to that court for further proceedings not inconsistent with this opinion.

Reversed and remanded.

MR. JUSTICE BLACK, *with whom* MR. JUSTICE DOUGLAS *joins (concurring).*

. . . I base my vote to reverse on the belief that the First and Fourteenth Amendments not merely "delimit" a State's power to award damages to "a public official against critics of his official conduct" but completely prohibit a State from exercising such a power. . . . Unlike the Court . . . I vote to reverse exclusively on the ground that the Times and the individual defendants had an absolute, unconditional constitutional right to publish in the Times advertisement their criticisms of the Montgomery agencies and officials. I do not base my vote to reverse on any failure to prove that these individual defendants signed the advertisement or that their criticism of the Police Department was aimed at the respondent Sullivan, who was then the Montgomery City Commissioner having supervision of the city's police; for present purposes I assume these things were proved. Nor is my reason for reversal the size of the half-million-dollar judgment, large as it is. If Alabama has constitutional power to use its civil libel law to impose damages on the press for criticizing the way public officials perform or fail to perform their duties, I know of no provision in the Federal Constitution which either expressly or impliedly bars the State from fixing the amount of damages.

The half-million-dollar verdict does give dramatic proof, however, that state libel laws threaten the very existence of an American press virile enough to publish unpopular views on public affairs and bold enough to criticize the conduct of public officials. The factual background of this case emphasizes the imminence and enormity of that threat. One of the acute and highly emotional issues in this country arises out of efforts of many people, even including some public officials, to continue state-commanded segregation of races in the public schools and other public places, despite our several holdings that such a state practice is forbidden by the Fourteenth Amendment. Montgomery is one of the localities in which widespread hostility to desegregation has been manifested. This hostility has sometimes extended itself to persons who favor desegregation, particularly to so-called "outside agitators," a term which can be made to fit papers like the Times. . . . The scarcity of testimony to show that Commissioner Sullivan suffered any actual damages at all suggests that these feelings of hostility had at least as much to do with rendition of this half-million-dollar verdict as did an appraisal of damages. Viewed realistically, this record lends support to an inference that instead of being damaged Commissioner Sullivan's political, social, and financial prestige has likely been enhanced by the Times' publication. Moreover, a second half-million-dollar libel verdict against the Times based on the same advertisement has already been awarded to another Commissioner. There a jury again gave the full amount claimed. There is no reason to believe that there are not more such huge verdicts lurking just around the corner for the Times or any other newspaper or broad-

caster which might dare to crtiicize public officials. In fact, briefs before us show that in Alabama there are now pending eleven libel suits by local and state officials against the Times seeking $5,600,000, and five such suits against the Columbia Broadcasting System seeking $1,700,000. Moreover, this technique for harassing and punishing a free press—now that it has been shown to be possible—is by no means limited to cases with racial overtones; it can be used in other fields where public feelings may make local as well as out-of-state newspapers easy prey for libel verdict seekers.

In my opinion the Federal Constitution has dealt with this deadly danger to the press in the only way possible without leaving the free press open to destruction—by granting the press an absolute immunity for criticism of the way public officials do their public duty. Stopgap measures like those the Court adopts are in my judgment not enough. This record certainly does not indicate that any different verdict would have been rendered here whatever the Court had charged the jury about "malice," "truth," "good motives," "justifiable ends," or any other legal formulas which in theory would protect the press. Nor does the record indicate that any of these legalistic words would have caused the courts below to set aside or to reduce the half-million-dollar verdict in any amount. . . .

We would . . . more faithfully interpret the First Amendment by holding that at the very least it leaves the people and the press free to criticize officials and discuss public affairs with impunity. This Nation of ours elects many of its important officials; so do the States, the municipalities, the counties, and even many precincts. These officials are responsible to the people for the way they perform their duties. . . . [F]reedom to discuss public affairs and public officials is unquestionably . . . the kind of speech the First Amendment was primarily designed to keep within the area of free discussion. To punish the exercise of this right to discuss public affairs or to penalize it through libel judgments is to abridge or shut off discussion of the very kind most needed. This Nation, I suspect, can live in peace without libel suits based on public discussions of public affairs and public officials. But I doubt that a country can live in freedom where its people can be made to suffer physically or financially for criticizing their government, its actions, or its officials. "For a representative democracy ceases to exist the moment that the public functionaries are by any means absolved from their responsibility to their constituents; and this happens whenever the constituent can be restrained in any manner from speaking, writing, or publishing his opinions upon any public measure, or upon the conduct of those who may advise or execute it." An unconditional right to say what one pleases about public affairs is what I consider to be the minimum guarantee of the First Amendment. . . .

MILLER v. CALIFORNIA
413 U.S. 5; 36 L. Ed. 2d 419; 93 S.Ct. 2607 (1973)

MR. CHIEF JUSTICE BURGER *delivered the opinion of the court.*

This is one of a group of "obscenity-pornography" cases being reviewed by the Court in a re-examination of standards enunciated in earlier cases involving what Mr. Justice Harlan called "the intractable obscenity problem." *Interstate Circuit, Inc.* v. *Dallas,* 390 U.S. 676, 704 (concurring and dissenting opinion) (1968).

Appellant conducted a mass mailing campaign to advertise the sale of illustrated books. euphemistically called "adult" material. After a jury trial, he was convicted of violating California Penal Code . . . by knowledgeably distributing obscene matter, and the Appellate Department, Superior Court of California, County of Orange, summarily affirmed the judgment without opinion. Appellant's conviction was specifically based on his conduct in causing five unsolicited advertising brochures to be sent through the mail in an envelope addressed to a restaurant in Newport Beach, California. The envelope was opened by the manager of the restaurant and his mother. They had not requested the brochures; they complained to the police.

The brochures advertise four books entitled "Intercourse," "Man-Woman," "Sex Orgies Illustrated," and "An Illustrated History of Pornography," and a film entitled "Marital Intercourse." While the brochures contain some descriptive printed material, primarily they consist of pictures and drawings very explicitly depicting men and women in groups of two or more engaging in a variety of sexual activities, with genitals often prominently displayed.

This case involves the application of a State's criminal obscenity statute to a situation in which sexually explicit materials have been thrust by aggressive sales action upon unwilling recipients who had in no way indicated any desire to receive such materials. . . .

The dissent of Mr. Justice Brennan reviews the background of the obscenity problem, but since the Court now undertakes to formulate standards more concrete than those in the past, it is useful for us to focus on two of the landmark cases in the somewhat tortured history of the Court's obscenity decisions. In *Roth* v. *United States,* 354 U.S. 476 (1957), the Court sustained a conviction under a federal statute punishing the mailing of "obscene, lewd, lascivious or filthy. . ." materials. The key to that holding was the Court's rejection of the claim that obscene materials were protected by the First Amendment. Five Justices joined in the opinion stating:

All ideas having even the slightest redeeming social importance—unorthodox ideas, controversial ideas, even ideas hateful to the prevailing climate of opinion—have full protection of the First Amendment guarantees, unless excludable because they encroach upon the limited area of more important interests. But implicit in the history of the First Amendment is the rejection of obscenity as utterly without redeeming social importance. . . .

Nine years later in *Memoirs* v. *Massachusetts*, 383 U.S. 413 (1966), the Court veered sharply away from the *Roth* concept and, with only three Justices in the plurality opinion, articulated a new test of obscenity. The plurality held that under the *Roth* definition:

. . . as elaborated in subsequent cases, three elements must coalesce: it must be established that (a) the dominant theme of the material taken as a whole appeals to a prurient interest in sex; (b) the material is patently offensive because it affronts contemporary community standards relating to the description or representation of sexual matters; and (c) the material is utterly without redeeming social value. . . .

The sharpness of the break with *Roth*, represented by the third element of the *Memoirs* test . . . was further underscored when the *Memoirs* plurality went on to state:

The Supreme Judicial Court erred in holding that a book need not be "unqualifiedly worthless before it can be deemed obscene." A book cannot be proscribed unless it is found to be *utterly* without redeeming social value. (Emphasis in original.) 383 U.S., at 419.

While *Roth* presumed "obscenity" to be "utterly without redeeming social value," *Mem-oirs* required that to prove obscenity it must be affirmatively established that the material is "utterly without redeeming social value." Thus, even as they repeated the words of *Roth*, the *Memoirs* plurality produced a drastically altered test that called on the prosecution to prove a negative, i.e., that the material was "*utterly* without redeeming social value"—a burden virtually impossible to discharge under our criminal standards of proof. Such considerations caused Justice Harlan to wonder if the "*utterly* without redeeming social value" test had any meaning at all. . . .

Apart from the initial formulation in the *Roth* case, no majority of the Court has at any given time been able to agree on a standard to determine what constitutes obscene, pornographic material subject to regulation under the States' police power. . . . We have seen "a variety of views among the members of the Court unmatched in any other course of constitutional adjudication. . . ."

The case we now review was tried on the theory that the California Penal Code . . . approximately incorporates the three-stage *Memoirs* test. . . . But now the *Memoirs* test has been abandoned as unworkable by its author [Justice Brennan] and no member of the Court today supports the *Memoirs* formulation.

. . . We acknowledge . . . the inherent dangers of undertaking to regulate any form of expression. State statutes designed to regulate obscene materials must be carefully limited. . . . As a result, we now confine the permissible scope of such regulation to works which depict or describe sexual conduct. That conduct must be specifically defined by the applicable state law, as written or authoritatively construed. A state offense must also be limited to works which, taken as a whole, appeal to the prurient interest in sex, which portray sexual conduct in a patently offensive way, and which, taken as a whole, do not have serious literary, artistic, political, or scientific value.

The basic guidelines for the trier of fact must

be: (a) whether "the average person, applying contemporary community standards" would find that the work, taken as a whole, appeals to the prurient interest, . . . (b) whether the work depicts or describes, in a patently offensive way, sexual conduct specifically defined by the applicable state law, and (c) whether the work, taken as a whole, lacks serious literary, artistic, political, or scientific value. We do not adopt as a constitutional standard the *utterly* without redeeming social value" test of *Memoirs* v. *Massachusetts*; that concept has never commanded the adherence of more than three Justices at one time. If a state law that regulates obscene materials is thus limited, as written or construed, the First Amendment values applicable to the States through the Fourteenth Amendment are adequately protected by the ultimate power of appellate courts to conduct an independent review of constitutional claims when necessary. . . .

We emphasize that it is not our function to propose regulatory schemes for the States. That must await their concrete legislative efforts. It is possible, however, to give a few plain examples of what a state statute could define for regulation under the second part (b), of the standard announced in this opinion, *supra*:

(a) Patently offensive representations or descriptions of ultimate sexual acts, normal or perverted, actual or simulated.

(b) Patently offensive representations or descriptions of masturbation, excretory functions, and lewd exhibition of the genitals.

Sex and nudity may not be exploited without limit by films or pictures exhibited or sold in places of public accommodation any more than live sex and nudity can be exhibited or sold without limit in such public places. At a minimum, prurient, patently offensive depiction or description of sexual conduct must have serious literary, artistic, political, or scientific value to merit First Amendment protection. . . . For example, medical books for the education of physicians and related personnel necessarily use graphic illustrations and descriptions of human anatomy. . . .

Mr. Justice Brennan, author of the opinions of the Court, or the plurality opinions, in *Roth* v. *United States, Jacobellis* v. *Ohio, Ginzburg* v. *United States, Mishkin* v. *New York,* and *Memoirs* v. *Massachusetts* has abandoned his former positions and now maintains that no formulation of this Court, the Congress, or the States can adequately distinguish obscene material unprotected by the First Amendment from protected expression. . . . Paradoxically, Mr. Justice Brennan indicates that suppression of unprotected obscene material is permissible to avoid exposure to unconsenting adults, as in this case, and to juveniles, although he gives no indication of how the division between protected and nonprotected materials may be drawn with greater precision for these purposes than for regulation of commercial exposure to consenting adults only. Nor does he indicate where in the Constitution he finds the authority to distinguish between a willing "adult" one month past the state law age of majority and a willing "juvenile" one month younger.

Under the holdings announced today, no one will be subject to prosecution for the sale or exposure of obscene materials unless these materials depict or describe patently offensive "hard core" sexual conduct specifically defined by the regulating state law, as written or construed. We are satisfied that these specific prerequisites will provide fair notice to a dealer in such materials that his public and commercial activities may bring prosecution. . . . If the inability to define regulated materials with ultimate, god-like precision altogether removes the power of the States or the Congress to regulate, then "hard core" pornography may be exposed without limit to the juvenile, the passerby, and the consenting adult alike, as, indeed Mr. Justice Douglas contends. . . . In this belief, however, Mr. Justice Douglas now stands alone. . . .

It is certainly true that the absence, since *Roth*, of a single majority view of this Court as to proper standards for testing obscenity has placed a strain on both state and federal courts. But today, for the first time since *Roth* was decided in 1957, a majority of this Court has agreed on concrete guidelines to isolate "hard core" pornography from expression protected by the First Amendment. . . .

This may not be an easy road, free from difficulty. But no amount of "fatigue" should lead us to adopt a convenient "institutional" rationale—an absolutist, "anything goes" view of the First Amendment—because it will lighten our burdens. "Such an abnegation of judicial supervision in this field would be inconsistent with our duty to uphold constitutional guarantees. . . ."

Under a national Constitution, fundamental First Amendment limitations on the powers of the States do not vary from community to community, but this does not mean that there are, or should be, fixed, uniform national standards of precisely what appeals to the "prurient interest" or is "patently offensive." These are essentially questions of fact, and our nation is simply too big and diverse for this Court to reasonably expect that such standards could be articulated for all 50 States in a single formulation, even assuming the prerequisite consensus exists. When triers of fact are asked to decide whether "the average person, applying contemporary community standards" would consider certain materials "prurient," it would be unrealistic to require that the answer be based on some abstract formulation. The adversary system, with lay jurors as the usual ultimate factfinders in criminal prosecutions, has historically permitted triers-of-fact to draw on the standards of their community, guided always by limiting instructions on the law. To require a State to structure obscenity proceedings around evidence of a *national* "community standard" would be an exercise in futility. . . .

We conclude that neither the State's alleged failure to offer evidence of "national standards," nor the trial court's charge that the jury consider state community standards, were constitutional

errors. Nothing in the First Amendment requires that a jury must consider hypothetical and unascertainable "national standards" when attempting to determine whether certain materials are obscene as a matter of fact. . . .

It is neither realistic nor constitutionally sound to read the First Amendment as requiring that the people of Maine or Mississippi accept public depiction of conduct found tolerable in Las Vegas, or New York City. . . . People in different States vary in their tastes and attitudes, and this diversity is not to be strangled by the absolutism of imposed uniformity. . . .

In sum we (a) reaffirm the *Roth* holding that obscene material is not protected by the First Amendment, (b) hold that such material can be regulated by the States, subject to the specific safeguards enunciated above, without a showing that the material is "*utterly* without redeeming social value," and (c) hold that obscenity is to be determined by applying "contemporary community standards," . . . not "national standards." The judgment of the Appellate Department of the Superior Court, Orange County, California, is vacated and the case remanded to that court for further proceedings not inconsistent with the First Amendment standards established by this opinion. . . .

Vacated and remanded for further proceedings.

MR. JUSTICE BRENNAN'S *views in dissent are set forth in Paris Adult Theater* v. *Slaton, 413 U.S. 49, decided the same day.*

. . .

The view that, until today, enjoyed the most, but not majority, support was an interpretation of *Roth* (and not, as the Court suggests, a veering "sharply away from the *Roth* concept" and the articulation of "a new test of obscenity," *ante*, at 6) adopted by Mr. Chief Justice Warren, Mr. Justice Fortas, and the author of this opinion in *Memoirs* v. *Massachusetts*, 383 U.S. 413 (1966). We expressed the view that Federal or State

Governments could control the distribution of material where "three elements ... coalesce: it must be established that (a) the dominant theme of the material taken as a whole appeals to a prurient interest in sex; (b) the material is patently offensive because it affronts contemporary community standards relating to the description or representation of sexual matters; and (c) the material is utterly without redeeming social value." Even this formulation, however, concealed differences of opinion. ... Nor, finally, did it ever command a majority of the Court. Aside from the other views described above, Mr. Justice Clark believed that "social importance" could only "be considered together with evidence that the material in question appeals to prurient interest and is patently offensive...." Similarly, Mr. Justice White regarded "a publication to be obscene if its predominant theme appeals to the prurient interest in a manner exceeding customary limits of candor," ...and regarded " 'social importance' ... not [as] an independent test of obscenity, but [as] relevant only to determining the predominant prurient interest of the material. ..."

In the face of this divergence of opinion the Court began the practice in 1967 in *Redrup* v. *New York*, 386 U.S. 767, of *per curiam* reversals of convictions for the dissemination of materials that at least five members of the Court, applying their separate tests, deemed not to be obscene. ...

Our experience with the *Roth* approach has certainly taught us that the outright suppression of obscenity cannot be reconciled with the fundamental principles of the First and Fourteenth Amendments. For we have failed to formulate a standard that sharply distinguishes protected from unprotected speech, and out of necessity, we have resorted to the *Redrup* approach, which resolves cases as between the parties, but offers only the most obscure guidance to legislation, adjudication by other courts, and primary conduct. By disposing of cases

through summary reversal or denial of certiorari we have deliberately and effectively obscured the rationale underlying the decision. It comes as no surprise that judicial attempts to follow our lead conscientiously have often ended in hopeless confusion. ...

I need hardly point out that the factors which must be taken into account are judgmental and can only be applied on "a case-by-case, sight-by-sight" basis. These considerations suggest that no one definition, no matter how precisely or narrowly drawn, can possibly suffice for all situations, or carve out fully suppressible expression from all media without also creating a substantial risk of encroachment upon the guarantees of the Due Process Clause and the First Amendment. ...

The approach requiring the smallest deviation from our present course would be to draw a new line between protected and unprotected speech, still permitting the States to suppress all material on the unprotected side of the line. In my view, clarity cannot be obtained pursuant to this approach except by drawing a line that resolves all doubts in favor of state power and against the guarantees of the First Amendment. We could hold, for example, that any depiction or description of human sexual organs, irrespective of the manner or purpose of the portrayal, is outside the protection of the First Amendment and therefore open to suppression by the States. That formula would, no doubt, offer much fairer notice of the reach of any state statute drawn at the boundary of the State's constitutional power. And it would also, in all likelihood, give rise to a substantial probability of regularity in most judicial determinations under the standard. But such a standard would be appallingly overbroad, permitting the suppression of a vast range of literary, scientific, and artistic masterpieces. Neither the First Amendment nor any free community could possibly tolerate such a standard. Yet short of that extreme it is hard to see how any choice of words could reduce the vagueness problem to tolerable proportions, so long as we remain committed to the view that some class of materials is subject to outright suppression by the State. . . .

Of course, the Court's restated *Roth* test does limit the definition of obscenity to depictions of physical conduct and explicit sexual acts. And that limitation may seem, at first glance, a welcome and clarifying addition to the *Roth-Memoirs* formula. But just as the agreement in *Roth* on an abstract definition of obscenity gave little hint of the extreme difficulty that was to follow in attempting to apply that definition to specific material, the mere formulation of a "physical conduct" test is no assurance that it can be applied with any greater facility. The Court does not indicate how it would apply its test to the materials involved in *California* v. *Miller*, and we can only speculate as to its application. But even a confirmed optimist could find little realistic comfort in the adoption of such a test. Indeed, the valiant attempt of one lower federal court to draw the constitutional line at depictions of explicit sexual conduct seems to belie any suggestion that this approach marks the road to clarity. The Court surely demonstrates little sensitivity to our own institutional problems, much less the other vagueness-related difficulties, in establishing a system that requires us to consider whether a description of human genitals is sufficiently "lewd" to deprive it of constitutional protection; whether a sexual act is "ultimate"; whether the conduct depicted in materials before us fits within one of the categories of conduct whose depiction the state or federal governments have attempted to suppress; and a host of equally pointless inquiries. In addition, adoption of such a test does not, presumably, obviate the need for consideration of the nuances of presentation of sexually oriented material, yet it hardly clarifies the application of those opaque but important factors.

If the application of the "physical conduct" test to pictorial material is fraught with difficulty, its application to textual material carries the potential for extraordinary abuse. Surely we have passed the point where the mere written description of sexual conduct is deprived of First Amendment protection. Yet the test offers no guidance to us, or anyone else, in determining which written descriptions of sexual conduct are protected, and which are not.

Ultimately, the reformulation must fail because it still leaves in this Court the responsibility of determining in each case whether the materials are protected by the First Amendment. The Court concedes that even under its restated formulation, the First Amendment interests at stake require "appellate courts to conduct an independent review of constitutional claims when necessary. . . ." Thus, the Court's new formulation will not relieve us of "the awesome task of making case by case at once the criminal and the constitutional law." And the careful efforts of state and lower federal courts to apply the standard will remain an essentially pointless exercise, in view of the need for an ultimate decision by this Court. . . .

Finally, I have considered the view, urged so forcefully since 1957 by our Brothers Black and Douglas, that the First Amendment bars the suppression of any sexually oriented expression. That position would effect a sharp reduction, although perhaps not a total elimination, of the uncertainty that surrounds our current approach. Nevertheless, I am convinced that it would achieve that desirable goal only by stripping the States of power to an extent that cannot be justified by the commands of the Constitution, at least so long as there is available an alternative approach that strikes a better balance between the guarantee of free expression and the States' legitimate interests.

Our experience since *Roth* requires us not only to abandon the effort to pick our obscene materials on a case-by-case basis, but also to reconsider a fundamental postulate of *Roth*: that there exists a definable class of sexually oriented expression that may be totally suppressed by the Federal and State Governments. Assuming that such a class of expression does in fact exist, I am forced to conclude that the concept of "obscenity" cannot be defined with sufficient specificity and clarity to provide fair notice to persons who create and distribute sexually oriented materials, to prevent substantial erosion of protected speech as a by-product of the attempt to suppress unprotected speech, and to avoid very costly institutional harms. Given these inevitable side-effects of state efforts to suppress what is assumed to be *unprotected* speech, we must scrutinize with care the state interest that is asserted to justify the suppression. For in the absence of some very substantial interest in suppressing such speech, we can hardly condone the ill-effects that seem to flow inevitably from the effort. . . .

If, as the Court today assumes, "a state legislature may . . . act on the . . . assumption that . . . commerce in obscene books, or public exhibitions focused on obscene conduct, have a tendency to exert a corrupting debasing impact leading to antisocial behavior," . . . then it is hard to see how state-ordered regimentation of our minds can ever be forestalled. For if a State may, in an effort to maintain or create a particular moral tone, prescribe what its citizens cannot read or cannot see, then it would seem to follow that in pursuit of that same objective a State could decree that its citizens must read certain books or must view certain films. . . . However laudable its goal—and that is obviously a question on which reasonable minds may differ—the State cannot proceed by means that violate the Constitution. . . .

Recognizing these principles, we have held that so-called thematic obscenity—obscenity which might persuade the viewer or reader to engage in "obscene" conduct—is not outside the protection of the First Amendment. . . . Even a legitimate, sharply focused state concern for the morality of the community cannot, in other words, justify an assault on the protections of the First Amendment. . . . Where the state interest in regulation of morality is vague and ill-defined, interference with the guarantees of the First Amendment is even more difficult to justify.

In short, while I cannot say that the interests of the State—apart from the question of juveniles and unconsenting adults—are trivial or nonexistent, I am compelled to conclude that these interests cannot justify the substantial damage to constitutional rights and to this Nation's judicial machinery that inevitably results from state efforts to bar the distribution even of unprotected material to consenting adults. . . . I would hold, therefore, that at least in the absence of distribution to juveniles or obtrusive exposure to unconsenting adults, the First and Fourteenth Amendments prohibit the state and federal governments from attempting wholly to suppress sexually oriented materials on the bases of their allegedly "obscene" contents. Nothing in this approach precludes those governments from taking action to serve what may be strong and legitimate interests through regulation of the manner of distribution of sexually oriented material. . . .

SELECTED REFERENCES

Comment, "Of Shadows and Substance: Freedom of Speech, Expression and Action," 1971 *Wisconsin Law Review* 1209 (1971).

Emerson, Thomas I., *The System of Freedom of Expression* (New York: Random House, 1970).

Harris, Paul, "Black Power Advocacy: Criminal Anarchy or Free Speech," 56 *California Law Review* 702 (1968).

Kramer, D. C., "Right to Denounce Public Officials in England and the United States," 17 *Journal of Public Law* 78 (1968).

Krislov, Samuel, *The Supreme Court and Political Freedom* (New York: The Free Press, 1968).

Loewy, A. H., "Free Speech: The 'Missing Link' in the Law of Obscenity," 16 *Journal of Public Law* 81 (1967).

Note, "Developments in the Law—Academic Freedom," 81 *Harvard Law Review* 1045 (1968) esp. pp. 1128-1134 on constitutional protection of student speech and association.

Note, "Still More Ado About Dirty Books (and Pictures): *Stanley, Reidel* and *Thirty-Seven Photographs*," 81 *Yale Law Journal* 309 (1971).

Schnall, Marc, "The United States Supreme Court: Definitions of Obscenity," 18 *Crime & Delinquency* 59 (1972).

Schwartz, Herbert, "Students, the University and the First Amendment," 31 *Ohio State Law Journal* 635 (1970).

Shapiro, Martin, *Freedom of Speech: The Supreme Court and Judicial Review* (Englewood Cliffs, N.J.: Prentice-Hall, 1966).

Velvel, Lawrence R., "Freedom of Speech and the Draft Card Burning Cases," 16 *Kansas Law Review* 149 (1968).

4 Freedom and Security – Problems Old and New

Dennis v. *United States*   *Brandenburg* v. *Ohio*   *Barenblatt* v. *United States*
New York Times Co. v. *United States*   *Branzburg* v. *Hayes*

Americans have strong interests in freedom and in national security. But these interests often collide. Some attempt to blunt the collision through the delicate act of balancing the needs of freedom as over and against the needs of security. Others see the needs of liberty and freedom as overriding any other interests, including national security. Still there are others who hold that preserving national security is the hallmark prerequisite for preserving any freedom at all. And undoubtedly there are yet others who fall somewhere in between these positions or who take still other stances. Thus, how Americans divide on the needs of freedom and national security is not at all fixed. Moreover, positions are constantly changing.

Furthermore, the conflict between freedom and security does not end here. We are not at all certain as to what *it* is upon which we divide. Most of us want both freedom and national security. But while pragmatism is our most realistic gauge of freedom, we do not—nor can we—use any such gauge for national security. Our freedoms are dynamic; we exercise them (or at least want to) daily. Preserving national security is much more illusory, invisible and intangible. In short, it is something we simply do not know enough about or of which we are not too sure. This, of course, is quite understandable since national security covers a broad range of subjects. While the central concern of national security is the government's capacity to protect itself from violent overthrow (whether by domestic subversion or by foreign aggression), it involves much more.[1] National security, for example,

---

[1] See reference note to *Harvard Law Review*, p. 194, note 11 *infra*.

includes all that is necessary for the effective functioning of the government. Virtually any government program may fall within this aegis, but, of course, certain governmental programs or activities are much more likely to conflict with political and civil liberties than others. And while Congress plays a role in *defining* national security policy, we primarily look to the President and law enforcement agencies to *protect* this vital interest. Attempts by government to safeguard national security are often manifested through limitations or encroachments on the exercise of political and civil liberties. Accordingly, we know when our freedoms have been restricted, but because of the nature of national security, especially the secrecy involved, we are sometimes less than certain about whether these restrictions are warranted. In short, do the threats to national security justify the threats to (and actual curtailments of) our freedoms? This basic dilemma has plagued our country from the very beginning, and is still with us today.

Did a "national security" interest during World War II, for example, justify the forced relocation of American citizens of Japanese descent from the West Coast? (See *Korematsu* v. *United States,* 323 U.S. 214, 1944, where the Supreme Court upheld this procedure.) Moreover, were the actions taken to protect the country from Communists and the "communist threats" of the 1940s and 1950s justifiable on national security grounds? Certainly there were restrictions on civil liberties imposed by such measures as the Alien Registration and Sedition Act (the Smith Act) of 1940, the Internal Security Act of 1950 and the extensive governmental loyalty programs. More recently, do the needs of national security warrant actions taken by the government with respect to surveillance of demonstrators, the secrecy of government documents, or the use of "extraordinary police powers" in emergency situations? Was, for example, the "Ellsberg break-in," so much discussed during the Senate Watergate hearings, justified on national security grounds? Here again, these actions invariably impose restraints on our civil and political liberties.

Actions of the government in the name of national security usually come during periods of tensions, e.g., in anticipation of, during, or just after war; or in the wake of violent demonstrations and riots. Under such conditions, greater stress is usually placed on national security than on freedoms. Patriotism, loyalty and conformity become expected norms of behavior; dissent, questioning and nonconformity are denounced as unpatriotic, disloyal, or at the very least suspect.

In any event, at one time or another governments (national, state and local) in the United States have taken actions with the stated objective of protecting national security. Quite often, however, some of these actions conflict with what many consider their constitutional rights and liberties. In our governmental system, the courts play a major role in reconciling these conflicting interests. This chapter focuses on how courts, especially the Supreme Court, have responded to the conflict between freedom and national security.

SEDITION AND ESPIONAGE

The Bill of Rights was less than a decade old when war hysteria (activated by France) prompted the Federalist-dominated Congress to enact several measures in

1798 to protect the government from internal subversion. One of these—the Sedition Act—contained restrictions which cut deeply into the free speech and press guarantees of the First Amendment. Aimed at stifling criticism of the Administration's foreign policies, the most suppressive provision of the act made it illegal for anyone to "write, print or publish ... any false, scandalous and malicious writing ... against the government of the United States, or either house of the Congress ... , or the President ... , with intent to defame ... , or to bring them ... into contempt or disrepute or to excite against them ... the hatred of the good people of the United States. ... ." In short, the act allowed legal punishment for nothing more than political criticism of governmental officials. Federalist-dominated courts, however, generally precluded constitutional challenges to the act by those charged with violating it. Consequently, the Supreme Court was never presented with the issue since the act, passed as a temporary measure, expired in 1801 after being in force a little less than three years.

Some of President Lincoln's actions during the Civil War produced severe tensions between the exercise of federal warpower and liberties guaranteed by the Bill of Rights. However, Congress did not enact policy again in this area until World War I, at which time it enacted two measures. The Espionage Act of 1917 made it a crime for any person to attempt to obstruct military recruiting, to attempt to cause acts of insubordination in the armed forces, and to make false statements and reports calculated to interfere with the successful prosecution of the war. The act also authorized the Postmaster General to exclude from the mails treasonable and seditious matter.

In 1918, Congress passed the Sedition Act as a comprehensive amendment to the Espionage Act. This new law was much more suppressive than the 1917 Espionage Act, and its language was similar in tone to the 1798 Sedition Act. The most stringent provision of the 1918 law made it a crime to ". . . utter, print or publish disloyal, profane, scurrilous, or abusive language about the form of government, the Constitution, soldiers and sailors, [the] flag, or uniform of the armed forces . . ." with intent to bring scorn, contempt and disrepute upon them. The provision also made it illegal for one "by word or act [to] support or favor the cause of the . . . [enemy] in the present war, or by word or act [to] oppose the cause of the United States."

Unlike the first Congressional enactments in this area, the constitutionality of these statutes was passed upon by the Supreme Court. The validity of the Espionage Act was considered in *Schenck* v. *United States* (249 U.S. 47, 1919). Schenck was convicted for printing and circulating leaflets allegedly calculated to obstruct recruiting and to cause insubordination in the military forces. One side of the leaflet in question proclaimed that the Conscription Act violated the Thirteenth Amendment in that "a conscript is little more than a convict." It also intimated that the war was a monstrous wrong against humanity perpetrated by Wall Street interests. On the other side of the leaflet, an article entitled "Assert Your Rights," reference was made to arguments in support of the draft as coming from "cunning politicians" and "a mercenary capitalist press." It further encouraged people to speak out in opposition to the draft for "silent consent [helps] to support an infamous conspiracy."

In appealing the conviction, Schenck argued that the statute infringed his freedom of speech and press guarantees of the First Amendment. However, Justice Oliver Wendell Holmes, speaking for a unanimous Court, rejected this contention. It was here that Holmes put forth the now familiar clear-and-present-danger test. Said Holmes: "The question in every case is whether the words used are used in such circumstances and are of such a nature as to create a clear and present danger that they will bring about the substantive evils that Congress has a right to prevent." Applying this test, Holmes rejected the notion that freedom of speech and freedom of the press were absolutes; rather, he contended that judges must consider the circumstances in which such expressions are made. "The most stringent protection of free speech," said Holmes, "would not protect a man in falsely shouting fire in a theater and causing a panic." He concluded by noting that "[w]hen a nation is at war, many things that might be said in time of peace are such a hindrance to its effort that their utterance will not be endured so long as men fight, and no Court could regard them as protected by any constitutional right."

The clear-and-present-danger test, although portending protection for all but the most dangerous views calculated to produce substantive evils immediately, did not achieve that purpose in subsequent prosecutions under both the Espionage and Sedition Acts. For example, in *Frohwerk* v. *United States* (249 U.S. 204, 1919)[2] the Court upheld an Espionage Act conviction where the accused had published, in a German-language newspaper, articles examining the constitutionality of the war and the draft. Obviously, the danger from such publication was not imminent, but Justice Holmes begged the question when he contended: ". . . it is impossible to say that it might not have been found that the circulation of the paper was in quarters where a little breath would be enough to kindle a flame and that the fact was known and relied upon by those who sent the paper out."

The constitutionality of the Sedition Act was sustained in *Abrams* v. *United States* (250 U.S. 616, 1919). The case was an appeal of a conviction for publishing two leaflets in which abusive language, the indictment charged, "intended to bring the form of government of the United States into contempt." In condemning the government's sending an expeditionary force to Russia, one leaflet referred to the "President's cowardly silence about the intervention in Russia, [as revealing] the hypocrisy of the plutocratic gang in Washington." The leaflet went on to charge "that German militarism combined with allied capitalism . . . to crush the Russian revolution" and that capitalism is the "only . . . enemy of the workers of the world." The other leaflet, entitled "Workers—Wake Up!," called for a general strike and reminded Russian-emigrant factory workers that they were producing ammunition that was being used not only to murder Germans but also to kill Russians fighting for freedom.

The Supreme Court virtually ignored the clear-and-present-danger test in affirming the conviction. In rejecting the appellant's contention that the leaflets were within the protection of the First Amendment, Justice John Clark's opinion for the Court emphasized that the purpose of the pamphlets was "not an attempt

---

[2] See also *Debs* v. *United States* (249 U.S. 211, 1919), and *Pierce* v. *United States* (252 U.S. 239, 1920).

to bring about a change of administration by candid discussion." Rather, Clark contended, the pamphlets were designed to "excite, at the supreme crisis of the war, disaffection, sedition, riots, and . . . revolution" in an attempt to defeat the government's war plans. Consequently, the argument that the pamphlets had only the limited purpose of preventing injury to the Russian cause was not a sufficient defense. "Men," argued Clark, "must be held to have intended and to be accountable for the effects which their acts were likely to produce."

Justices Holmes and Brandeis dissented. Holmes's dissent has since become a classic statement in defense of freedom of speech. To him, the Court should have used the clear-and-present-danger test. "[N]obody can suppose that the surreptitious publishing of a silly leaflet by an unknown man, without more," said Holmes, "would present any immediate danger that its opinions would hinder the success of government arms or have any appreciable tendency to do so."

He concluded:

> Persecution for the expression of opinions seems to me perfectly logical. If you have no doubt of your premises or your power and want a certain result with all your heart you naturally express your wishes in law and sweep away all opposition. To allow opposition by speech seems to indicate that you think the speech impotent, as when a man says that he has squared the circle, or that you do not care whole-heartedly for the result, or that you doubt either your power or your premises. But when men have realized that time has upset many fighting faiths, they may come to believe even more than they believe the very foundations of their own conduct that the ultimate good desired is better reached by free trade in ideas—that the best test of truth is the power of the thought to get itself accepted in the competition of the market, and that truth is the only ground upon which their wishes safely can be carried out. . . . [I] think that we should be eternally vigilant against attempts to check the expression of opinions that we loathe and believe to be fraught with death unless they so imminently threaten immediate interference with the lawful and pressing purposes of the law that an immediate check is required to save the country.

But Holmes's views were not to carry the day. The Court majority continued to ignore the clear-and-present-danger test and affirmed several convictions where nothing more than discussion of the merits of the war was involved.

In 1940, Congress enacted the Alien Registration Act, now popularly known as the Smith Act. Concerned with the increasing possibility of United States involvement in World War II, the act was viewed as an essential wartime measure designed to prevent espionage and sedition. One of the first prosecutions under the act involved a group of Trotskyites who were convicted of conspiring to advocate insubordination in the armed forces and the overthrow of the government by force and violence. The convictions were affirmed by the Court of Appeals and the Supreme Court refused to hear the case (*Dunne* v. *United States*, 138 F.2d 137; 320 U.S. 790, 1943). In another early prosecution under the act several pro-Nazis were indicted for conspiracy to violate Section 1 of the act by distributing leaflets that urged insubordination in the armed forces. The trial judge died during the trial and the indictment was later ordered dismissed when the government failed to undertake a new trial (*United States* v. *McWilliams*, 163 F.2d 695, 1947).

The most significant and controversial litigation, however, was to come in the postwar era against native Communists under the advocacy, conspiracy, and membership clauses of Section 2. Specifically, these provisions made it illegal for any person to: (1) knowingly or willfully advocate . . . or teach the overthrow or destruction of any government in the United States by force and violence; (2) print, publish, and disseminate written matter advocating such overthrow; (3) participate in the organization of any group dedicated to such purposes; and (4) acquire and hold membership in such a group with knowledge of its purposes.

In the years immediately following World War II relations between the United States and the Soviet Union deteriorated to the point of a "cold-war" impasse. Suspicion mounted that the international Communist conspiracy was being actively supported by native Communists and these suspicions were stirred into a kind of widespread public hysteria as some Republican politicians charged that Communists were occupying positions in government and had infiltrated the military-industrial complex. Stung by Republican charges of official insensitivity to and toleration of Communists in such vital places, the Democratic party realized that being tagged with a "soft on Communism" label could be very damaging in the forthcoming general elections. Hence, in 1948 the Justice Department moved to enforce the Smith Act against the American Communist party when 11 of its leaders were charged in an indictment with: (1) willfully and knowingly conspiring to organize the Communist party, a group of persons who teach and advocate the overthrow of the government by force and violence; and (2) willfully and knowingly advocating and teaching the duty and necessity of overthrowing the government by force and violence.

After a marathon trial lasting nine months, the Communist leaders were found guilty as charged. Subsequently, their convictions were affirmed by both the Court of Appeals for the Second Circuit and the Supreme Court in *Dennis* v. *United States*. Both courts found that the act, on its face and as applied, did not cut too deeply into constitutional guarantees. In fact, Chief Justice Fred Vinson, writing the leading opinion for the Supreme Court, adopted as correct and appropriate the test applied in the Court of Appeals by Judge Learned Hand. To Judge Hand, the crucial question was "whether the gravity of the evil, discounted by its improbability, justifies such invasion of free speech as is necessary to avoid the danger." The Chief Justice reasoned that since the government's very existence was at stake, the clear-and-present-danger test did not mean that the government could not act until the *putsch* was about to be executed. Knowledge of the existence of a group aiming at overthrow "as speedily as circumstances would permit" was deemed sufficient to justify restrictive governmental action. In concluding, Vinson flatly rejected the Communist assertion that the criterion which the Constitution requires the government to apply is the "success or probability of success" of their advocacy.

Justices Frankfurter and Jackson wrote concurring opinions in which they focused on the application of the clear-and-present-danger test in such cases.

Frankfurter, reiterating his position in earlier decisions, rejected the test as "a sonorous formula which is in fact only a euphemistic disguise for an unresolved conflict" incapable of resolving the conflicting interests in the case. For him, a "candid and informed weighing of competing interests within the confines of the judicial process" provides a more meaningful approach to the conflict resolution.

Unlike Frankfurter, Justice Jackson did not make an outright condemnation of the clear-and-present-danger test. It was certainly applicable to the kinds of cases for which it was originally devised—hotheaded speech on a street corner, or circulation of a few incendiary pamphlets, or parading by some zealots behind a red flag, or refusal of a handful of school children to salute [the American] flag." But, he contended, the test was never intended to be applied to this kind of case. To adhere to the test, he concluded, would in effect "hold [the] Government captive in a judge-made verbal trap."

The dissents of Black and Douglas condemned the statute as unconstitutional on its face because it permitted previous restraint on freedom of speech and freedom of the press. In addition, they both complained that the clear-and-present-danger test had not been met by the majority. As Douglas observed: "How it can be said that there is a clear and present danger that this advocacy will succeed is . . . a mystery."

Having successfully enforced the act against the Communist party's highest leaders, the Government moved against many lower-level leaders. Public opinion in support of such action had been molded by the "exposés" of Senator Joseph McCarthy, the deadlocked Korean War, and continued uneasy relations with the Soviet Union. In the final years of the Truman Administration and the first years of the Eisenhower presidency almost 100 convictions under Sections 2 and 3 of the act were obtained and the Supreme Court refused to review them. In 1955, however, the Court granted certiorari in the cases of 14 second-string Communists from California and, in its decision two years later (*Yates* v. *United States*, 354 U.S. 298, 1957), modified its *Dennis* holding. Contending that the government's reliance on *Dennis* was misplaced, Justice John Marshall Harlan emphasized in his opinion for the Court that *Dennis* had not obliterated the distinction between mere advocacy of the abstract doctrine of forcible overthrow of the government and action-inciting advocacy calculated to achieve forcible overthrow. Having failed to make such a distinction, he argued, the evidence presented in *Yates* (primarily the same upon which the *Dennis* convictions rested) was insufficient to prove "advocacy of action." Harlan also rejected the district court's conclusion that the act punished per se "mere doctrinal justification of forcible overthrow," engaged in with an intent to bring the overthrow about. On the contrary, he contended that although such advocacy may be "uttered with the hope that it may ultimately lead to violent revolution, [it] is too remote from concrete action to be regarded as the kind of indoctrination preparatory to action which was condemned in *Dennis*."

To be sure, the Court did not return to the pre-*Dennis* clear- and-present-danger rule. However, *Yates* established more stringent evidentiary requirements. Showing that defendants had advocated and taught the doctrines set forth in the various Communist classics was held to be insufficient. It was necessary to show that such advocacy was one of an incitement to action with a specific intent to bring about that action.

The more stringent evidentiary requirements made further convictions under the advocacy and conspiracy clauses of the act extremely difficult, if not impossible. As a matter of fact, the indictments against nine of the *Yates* defendants, whose cases were remanded by the Court for new trials, were dismissed after the government admitted that it was unable to satisfy those requirements. In addition, the *Yates* ruling served as a basis for reversal of a number of convictions by the courts of appeals and the government dropped other prosecutions.

The Court's retreat from *Dennis* must be considered in the context of swiftly changing foreign and domestic conditions. In the first place, aggression of the North Korean Communists had been sucessfully checked with the conclusion of peace negotiations in 1953. Furthermore, the public hysteria over internal subversion by native Communists had subsided with the McCarthy censure action in the United States Senate in 1954 and his subsequent death. In addition, Stalin's death in 1953 was followed by a slight thaw in the cold war and a move toward peaceful coexistence in American-Soviet relations. Add to these factors the changes in Supreme Court personnel after 1953, particularly the addition of Warren and Brennan, and the move away from *Dennis* to the more libertarian construction of the Smith Act in *Yates* is more readily understood.

Several prosecutions under the membership clause of the Smith Act had been initiated prior to the government's setback in *Yates*. After some seven years of litigation, the Supreme Court sustained the constitutionality of the clause in *Scales* v. *United States* (367 U.S. 203, 1961). Justice John Marshall Harlan's opinion for the 5–4 majority rejected the petitioner's contention that the membership clause had been repealed by Section 4(f) of the Internal Security Act of 1950 which stipulates that "neither the holding of office nor membership in any Communist organization shall constitute per se a violation of . . . this section or of any other criminal statute." Harlan contended that there was a constitutional difference between the membership to which Section 4(f) applied and the membership made illegal by the Smith Act. The latter was "knowing" and "active" membership—the "active" quality being correctly applied in the lower court's construction of the clause. This distinction not only saved the provision from the alleged repeal but also overcame the argument that the clause was unconstitutionally broad because of its condemnation of mere passive and nominal membership. Thus, Scales' conviction was valid because the trial court had appropriately construed the statute as condemning only "active" membership, applicable to those who had knowledge of or who personally harbored, a specific intent to bring about the forcible overthrow of the government.

In dissent, Justice Douglas complained that the majority's action legalized "guilt by association." He contended that there was no evidence of overt acts but only beliefs and ideas, and no matter how revolting they are, the First Amendment protects them. He also contended, as did the other dissenters, that the majority had "practically rewritten the statute" to save it.

In another membership clause decision announced with *Scales* (*Noto* v. *United*

States, 367 U.S. 290, 1961), the Court reversed the conviction on the grounds of insufficient evidence. Justice Harlan held that the government's evidence did not satisfy the statutory requirement of proof of "present illegal party advocacy." The only fact the evidence showed, he concluded, was that the Communist party to which Noto belonged was merely engaged in "abstract teaching of Communist theory."

Increasing intensity in the opposition to United States' involvement in the Vietnam War again raised questions pertaining to the limits of freedom of expression in challenging governmental war policies. To supplement existing laws against obstruction of the draft, Congress, in 1965, passed a statute making destruction of draft cards a federal crime. The statute's aim was to put an end to the well publicized "draft-card burning" ceremonies as an expression of opposition to the war. Several persons have been convicted under the statute and the Supreme Court affirmed the convictions and upheld the constitutionality of the statute in *United States* v. *O'Brien, supra.*

In a related action against Vietnam War protestors, several persons (including famed pediatrician Dr. Benjamin Spock and Yale University Chaplain William Sloan Coffin) were indicted and convicted for violating a provision of the Selective Service Act (50 U.S.C. 462a, 1958 ed.) by conspiring to counsel and aid persons in resisting the draft for service in the Vietnam War. The convictions were reversed by the Court of Appeals for the First Circuit. Dr. Spock and another defendant were ordered acquitted because of insufficient evidence of conspiracy on their part, while the cases of Chaplain Coffin and another defendant were remanded for possible new trials because of trial court error. The court made it clear, however, that while the kind of expression used by the defendants was intricately tied in with general anti-war advocacy which is protected by the First Amendment, conspiracy to counsel and aid young men to resist the draft does not have such protection (*U.S.* v. *Spock,* 416 F. 2d 165, 1st Cir., 1969).

Legislation against sedition and subversion has not been limited to Congressional action; a number of states have enacted and enforced laws directed at expressions inimical to the general welfare and security of the government. Variously titled as "criminal anarchy" or "criminal syndicalism" statutes, such laws were originally enacted to deal with late nineteenth- and early twentieth-century anarchists. But they served as convenient tools against various brands of revolutionaries during the "Red scare" period of the 1920s and 1930s. The New York statute enacted in 1902 was typical of legislation on the subject. It defined criminal anarchy as the doctrine which held that organized government should be overthrown by force and violence—by assassination of governmental executives or by other unlawful means—and the statute made it a crime for any person to advocate the doctrine in writing or in speech.[3] The statute was upheld in *Gitlow* v. *New York* against the

---

[3] The California Criminal Syndicalism Act, which contained limitations on expression similar to those in the New York law discussed here, was upheld in *Whitney* v. *California* (274 U.S. 357, 1927). In that case, Justice Louis Brandeis' concurring opinion was devoted to a further clarification of the clear-and-present-danger test. In brief, he contended that "[t]o justify suppression of free speech there must be reasonable grounds to fear that serious evil will

challenge that it abridged the constitutional guarantees of freedom of speech and freedom of the press.[4]

The Supreme Court's position in support of the constitutionality of criminal syndicalism statutes changed in *Brandenburg* v. *Ohio*, where the Court struck down a statute similar to the one it upheld in *Gitlow*. The Ohio criminal syndicalism law punished persons who "advocate or teach the duty, necessity, or propriety of crime, sabotage, violence, or unlawful methods of terrorism as a means of accomplishing industrial or political reform." In *Brandenburg,* the leader of a Ku Klux Klan group convicted under this statute contended that the act was unconstitutional under the First and Fourteenth Amendments. The Supreme Court, in a per curiam decision, agreed with this position, stating that "constitutional guarantees of free speech and free press do not permit a State to forbid or proscribe advocacy of the use of force or of law violation except where such advocacy is directed to inciting or producing imminent lawless action and is likely to incite or produce such action." Since the Ohio statute "by its own words and as applied purports to punish mere advocacy," the Court said it "falls within the condemnation of the First and Fourteenth Amendments."

The role of the states in dealing with internal security and subversion is far from clear. Indeed, after World War II, when there was considerable federal activity directed at subversion generally and Communist activities specifically, the Court showed concern about possible conflicting state regulatory activity in this area. In *Pennsylvania* v. *Nelson* (350 U.S. 497, 1956), for example, a majority of six Justices agreed that a state sedition law must be set aside because Congress had preempted the field in protecting the country from seditious conduct. Chief Justice Earl Warren contended that the "pervasiveness" of federal legislation was indicative of the Congressional intention to have sole occupancy in the field. State laws have to be limited to sedition against the state. Justices Harold Burton, Sherman Minton, and Stanley Reed dissented, arguing that in the absence of an expressed exclusivity by Congress, states shared concurrent power in the area. In any event the *Nelson* decision, coupled with the strictures of *Brandenburg,* narrows the role of the states in dealing with problems of internal security and subversion.

INCULCATING LOYALTY ?

Following World War II, both the federal and the state governments instituted procedures designed to protect their operations from internal subversion. Generally,

---

result if free speech is practiced. . . ." Moreover, he maintained, "no danger flowing from speech can be deemed clear and present, unless the incidence of the evil apprehended is so imminent that it may befall before there is opportunity for full discussion." On the other hand, he concluded, "[i]f there be time to explore through discussion the falsehood and fallacies, to avert evil by the processes of education, the remedy . . . is more speech, not enforced silence."

[4] For a discussion of the Court's "legislative reasonableness" test applied in *Gitlow*, see Chap. 3.

the procedures had two objectives: (1) securing loyal employees, and (2) detecting and dismissing disloyal employees.

The first postwar federal loyalty program was instituted in 1947 by an Executive Order issued by the Truman Administration. The order required the Civil Service Commission to conduct loyalty investigations of almost all employees before they were permitted to enter the competitive service of the Executive branch. A pre-entry loyalty check of a noncompetitive appointee was to be conducted by the specific agency making the appointment. The order also created loyalty boards in the various agencies of the Executive branch and required them to conduct hearings on charges of disloyalty brought against any employee of the agency. Several levels of review were available for a person challenging the determination of his agency board, with the ultimate administrative review assigned to the Loyalty Review Board created by the executive order.

Many charged that the order and the procedures instituted to enforce it cut deeply into constitutional guarantees. For one thing, gossip and rumor could be the basis for an investigation in which the employee often was not afforded confrontation and cross-examination privileges. Furthermore, the order collided with First Amendment associational guarantees by authorizing the Attorney General to compile a list of subversive organizations and by directing investigators to consider a person's membership in, or sympathy with, such groups in determining his loyalty. In a subsequent Executive Order issued by President Truman, it became possible to dismiss an employee when a hearing resulted in inconclusive findings but a reasonable doubt as to loyalty existed. This new standard led to the reopening of a number of earlier cases decided under the stricter standard and the ultimate dismissal of a number of persons who had previously been given clearance.

The standard for discharge on loyalty grounds became more sweeping under the program inaugurated by President Eisenhower in 1953. In fact, the standard of "disloyalty" was replaced by the standard of "security risk." Under it, discharge was possible after a hearing in which it was found merely that a person's employment "may not be consistent with the interests of national security." An employee could be labelled a "security risk" and dismissed for: (1) sexual immorality and perversion; (2) drug addiction; (3) excessive intoxication; (4) criminal, infamous, dishonest, or notoriously disgraceful conduct; (5) conspiring to commit or committing, acts of treason, sabotage, sedition, or espionage; (6) membership in, or affiliation and sympathetic association with, subversive groups. Furthermore, investigations were not restricted to current behavior; earlier cases in which clearance had been granted could be reopened and tested against the new standard.

The Court considered the constitutionality of the Truman program in two 1951 cases. In *Bailey* v. *Richardson* (182 F.2d 46, 1950; 341 U.S. 918, 1951) the Court of Appeals for the District of Columbia sustained a removal for disloyalty, but it held that under the doctrine enunciated in *United States* v. *Lovett* (328 U.S. 303,

1946),[5] the loyalty board order barring an employee from the federal service for three years constituted a bill of attainder. The validity of the removal was based on the principle that since there is no constitutional right to federal employment, the due process and First Amendment claims are without merit. An equally divided Supreme Court (Justice Clark did not participate) affirmed the decision without opinion.

At issue in the second case—*Joint Anti-Fascist Refugee Committee* v. *McGrath* (341 U.S. 123, 1951)—was the Attorney General's procedure in compiling the list of subversive organizations. In a 5–3 decision (Justice Tom Clark did not participate), the Supreme Court reversed a lower court ruling which had denied relief to several groups in attempts to remove their names from the Attorney General's list. That each of the majority justices (Burton, Frankfurter, Jackson, Douglas, and Black) wrote an opinion is indicative of the difficulty in reaching agreement in this area. Only Justice Douglas agreed with Justice Burton, who announced the judgment in this case. They took the position that the Attorney General's action in designating the complaining groups was arbitrary and without authority under the Executive Order. Other opinions by majority justices stressed the denial of due process because the Attorney General had blacklisted the groups without notice and hearing. For Justice Black, the Executive Order itself was unconstitutional because the First Amendment bars punishing organizations and their members merely because of beliefs. He also contended that "officially prepared and proclaimed blacklists" constitute a bill of attainder.

In the years following the *Bailey* and *Joint Anti-Fascist* rulings, the Warren Court ruled on a number of "loyalty dismissals" but carefully avoided constitutional issues. Instead, reversals were based on such procedural and statutory grounds as the lack of authorization for discharge under the terms of the loyalty order held in *Peters* v. *Hobby* (349 U.S. 331, 1955); the lack of statutory authority for dismissals in "nonsensitive" positions in *Cole* v. *Young* (351 U.S. 536, 1956); or the failure to follow established administrative procedures noted in *Service* v. *Dulles* (354 U.S. 363, 1957).

Several Congressional enactments have included provisions designed to protect national security from disloyal individuals operating in the private sector. Aware of Communist infiltration into the labor movement, Congress included a provision in the Taft-Hartley Act of 1947 designed to stimulate a kind of "self-policing" by labor unions. Specifically, Section 9(h) of the act denied any labor union access to the facilities of the National Labor Relations Board unless each of its officers had executed and filed with the board an affidavit swearing: (1) that he is not a member of, or affiliated with, the Communist party; and (2) that he does not believe in, is not a member of, or does not support any organization that believes in or teaches the doctrine of forcible overthrow of the government of the United States. The

[5] The Court held as an unconstitutional bill of attainder a rider appended to an appropriations act which prohibited payment of the salaries of three designated federal officials who had incurred the wrath of the House Committee on Un-American Activities.

Court upheld the constitutionality of the provision in *American Communications Association* v. *Douds* (339 U.S. 94, 1950). Chief Justice Fred Vinson, announcing the Court's judgment and writing the principal opinion, accepted the statute as a valid exercise of the commerce power. He admitted that the statute imposed some restriction on political freedom but contended that the legislative action designed to prevent disruptive political strikes justified the relatively small restrictions placed on First Amendment freedoms. In dissent, Justice Hugo Black expressed his oft-proclaimed view that governments can impose penalties for personal conduct but not for beliefs or for the conduct of others with whom one associates. He felt it most unfortunate that the majority had, in effect, legalized "guilt by association."

In practice, Section 9(h) of the Taft-Hartley Act—the affidavit provision—upheld in *Douds* proved ineffective. Consequently, it was repealed by the Labor Management Reporting and Disclosure Act of 1959 and replaced by a provision (Section 504) which made it a crime for a member of the Communist party to serve as an officer or as an employee (excluding clerical and custodial positions) of any labor organization. This new statute, however, did not fare as well in the courts as did its predecessor. In *United States* v. *Brown* (381 U.S. 437, 1965) the Supreme Court held that it was an unconstitutional bill of attainder. Chief Justice Earl Warren, writing the opinion for the 5—4 majority, noted that the statute does not—as it should—set forth a general rule of conduct detailing "specified acts" and "specified characteristics," the commission or possession of which would make a person ineligible for union office and employment. Nor does it "leave to the courts and juries the job of deciding what persons have committed the specified acts or possess the specified characteristics." Instead, the Chief Justice contended, Congress was guilty of usurping the judicial function by "designating in no uncertain terms the persons who possess the feared characteristics" (members of the Communist party) who are thus prohibited from holding "union office without incurring criminal liability." In short, he concluded, Congress "cannot specify the people upon whom the sanction it prescribes is to be levied."

Justice Byron White disagreed, in an opinion supported by Justices Tom Clark, John Marshall Harlan, and Potter Stewart. He argued that tested against the traditional definition of a bill of attainder, the statute in no way imposes "legislative punishment of particular individuals." Criticizing the majority for its "too narrow view of the legislative process," White contended that Congress had done no more than adopt a fairer and more effective method of forestalling political strikes. Certainly, he noted, there were ample findings to support the conclusion of Congress "that members of the Communist party were likely to call political strikes." Hence, he concluded that the statute did not have a punitive purpose; rather, it was "reasonably related to a permissible legislative objective."

In another action designed to prevent disruption of industrial production for national defense purposes, Congress included a provision in the Subversive Activities Control Act of 1950 which made it illegal for a member of a Communist-action group which is under final order to register[6] "to engage in any

---

[6] See The Communist Party Registration Controversy discussed in the next section of this chapter.

employment in any defense facility." However, the Supreme Court declared the provision unconstitutional in *United States* v. *Robel* (389 U.S. 258, 1967). In his opinion for the 7–2 majority, Chief Justice Earl Warren emphasized that while Congress has the power to enact legislation "to keep from sensitive positions in defense facilities those who would use their positions to disrupt production," it may not enact legislation (as involved here) which is so sweeping that it condemns not only association which may be constitutionally proscribed but also association which is protected by the First Amendment as well. Justice Byron White's dissent questioned the majority's balancing of the interests in favor of a right "not mentioned in the Constitution." Chiding the majority for concluding that the danger presented by Robel was insufficient to put him to the choice of membership in the Communist party or employment in a defense facility, he indicated a preference for the judgment of Congress and the Executive branch in weighing those competing interests.

Uncovering and removing disloyal employees has been a major concern of the several states also. The basic ingredients of these loyalty programs have been the oath-taking requirement and/or the filing of a non-Communist disclaimer affidavit. The courts until recently have generally found such requirements constitutionally acceptable on the grounds that one does not have a constitutional right to state employment and that states, exercising their authority to determine the fitness and competence of their employees, may require of employees some type of affirmation or disclaimer that they have not or do not advocate forcible overthrow of the government nor belong to organizations engaged in such advocacy. Justice Tom Clark emphasized this principle in *Garner* v. *Board of Public Works* (341 U.S. 716, 1951) in which the Court upheld the Los Angeles loyalty program covering municipal employees. Approving the disclaimer affidavit, upon which every employee was required to indicate his past (limited to the preceding five years) or present affiliation with the Communist party or the Communist Political Association, Justice Clark contended:

> Past conduct may well relate to present fitness; past loyalty may have a reasonable relationship to present and future trust. Both are commonly inquired into in determining fitness for both high and low positions in private industry and are not less relevant in public employment.

The oath requirement in which an employee had to indicate that he had not advocated or taught the doctrine of forcible overthrow of the government during the preceding five-year period was sustained against ex post facto and bill of attainder claims. Justice Clark noted simply that the ordinance requiring the oath did not impose "punishment for past conduct lawful at the time it was engaged in." He further noted that the activity proscribed by the oath had been denied employees by a Charter provision enacted two years prior to the "preceding five-year period" covered by the oath. He also brushed aside the bill of attainder attack with the statement that "we are unable to conclude that punishment is imposed by a general regulation which merely provides standards or qualifications and eligibility for employment."

Supporters of loyalty oaths thought it essential to shield juvenile innocence and young adult idealism from the "cunning proselytizing" of Communists and subversives who had somehow managed to infiltrate the sensitive setting of the public schoolroom. The Court's early approach to oaths for public school teachers is illustrated in *Adler* v. *Board of Education* (342 U.S. 485, 1952). At issue was New York's Feinberg Law which required the State Board of Regents to publish, after notice and hearing, a list of subversive organizations which advocate the forcible overthrow of the government. Membership in an organization included on this list was *prima facie* evidence of disqualification. An earlier statutory provision denied employment in the civil service and public school system to any person who advocated the forcible overthrow of the government or who was affiliated with any organization engaged in such advocacy.

The Court upheld the law and, in an opinion by Justice Sherman Minton, reasserted the doctrines that one does not have a constitutional right to public employment and that disclosure of associational ties with subversive groups may be compelled of employees in determining their fitness and competence. Justice Minton underscored the justification for such an inquiry of those seeking employment in the public schools when he noted:

> A teacher works in a sensitive area in a schoolroom. There he shapes the attitude of young minds towards the society in which they live. In this the state has a vital concern. It must preserve the integrity of the schools.

In both the *Garner* and *Adler* cases, *supra,* the statutes were upheld because they carefully distinguished between "knowing membership" and "innocent membership," without knowledge of the organization's illegal purposes. By excluding the latter from punishment, the laws did not suffer the infirmity of "overbreadth." In striking down Oklahoma's loyalty-oath statute in *Wieman* v. *Updegraff* (344 U.S. 183, 1952) the Court made it clear that the Constitution requires such a distinction. As Justice Tom Clark noted in the opinion for the Court, the state courts had construed the statute so that "the fact of membership alone disqualifies," and as such the "indiscriminate classification of innocent with knowing activity must fall as an assertion of arbitrary power."

A practice employed in some states was to disqualify from public employment any person who, asserting the Fifth Amendment guarantee against compulsory self-incrimination, refused to answer questions put to him by investigating committees concerning Communist and subversive activities. In *Slochower* v. *Board of Higher Education of the City of New York* (350 U.S. 551, 1956) the Supreme Court condemned this practice as applied to a college professor because of the automatic assumption of one's guilt merely for asserting a valid constitutional privilege. The net effect was to punish a person for invoking a constitutional right. The Court extended this precedent to strike down actions denying lawyers admission to the bar for refusing to answer questions concerning their Communist affiliations and activities (*Schware* v. *New Mexico Board of Bar Examiners*, 353 U.S. 232, 1957; *Konigsberg* v. *State Bar of California*, 353 U.S. 252, 1957).[7]

The Court undercut the impact of its *Slochower*, *Schware*, and *Konigsberg* rulings in *Belian* v. *Board of Education* (357 U.S. 399, 1958) and *Lerner* v. *Casey* (357 U.S. 468, 1958). In these cases employees had been dismissed after invoking the Fifth Amendment in refusing to answer questions concerning Communist party affiliations and activities. In *Belian*, the Court felt that the Board's action in discharging a teacher for "incompetence"[8] rather than for disloyalty was not in conflict with the *Slochower* line of cases. Likewise, the Court held that Lerner's discharge as a New York subway employee on "reliability" grounds was sufficiently distinguishable from *Slochower* so as not to offend due process.

The last Warren Court position on state loyalty oaths for public employees is illustrated in *Elfbrandt* v. *Russell* (384 U.S. 11, 1966), *Keyishian* v. *Board of Regents of New York* (385 U.S. 589, 1967), and *Whitehall* v. *Elkins* (389 U.S. 54, 1967). At issue in *Elfbrandt* was the constitutionality of the Arizona loyalty oath requiring an affirmation of allegiance and support of the federal and the Arizona constitutions and laws. The oath was supplemented by a statute which made criminal the knowing membership in the Communist party or in any other organization which has as one of its purposes the violent overthrow of the government. The Court held that the oath and the accompanying statute abridged the freedom of association protected by the First and Fourteenth Amendments. Justice William O. Douglas's opinion for the majority found both the oath and the statute constitutionally defective for failure to exclude from penalty association by one who does not subscribe to an organization's unlawful ends. In *Keyishian*, the Court reversed *Adler* v. *Board of Education* and struck down New York's Feinberg Law and other provisions of the education law implementing the loyalty program. Justice William J. Brennan's opinion emphasized the need for precision and specificity in regulations touching First Amendment freedoms. He contended that New York's scheme was interwoven in a maze of vagueness and "wholly lacking in terms susceptible of objective measurement." Likewise, in *Whitehall* v. *Elkins*, the Court found the statutory basis of the Maryland oath suffering from a similar infirmity of vagueness. Justice Douglas, in delivering the opinion for the majority, called the case a "classic example of the need for 'narrowly drawn' legislation . . . in this sensitive and important First Amendment area."

---

[7] The Court reaffirmed its displeasure with disclaimer oaths as a bar admission requirement more than a decade later when, by a 5-4 vote, it held that Arizona's Communist disclosure provision was unconstitutional in *Baird* v. *State Bar* (401 U.S. 1, 1971). But on the same day, by another 5-4 vote in *Law Students Civil Rights Research Council, Inc.* v. *Wadmond* (401 U.S. 154, 1971) (with Justice Potter Stewart switching positions) the Court found New York's test, which requires an applicant to affirm his belief in the United States form of government and his loyalty thereto, sufficiently particularized as to be "fully cognizant of constitutional guarantees."

[8] Belian had refused to answer questions about her past Communist activities even before invoking the Fifth Amendment at a subsequent HUAC meeting.

In 1972, however, the Burger Court did not feel that the Massachusetts loyalty oath was inflicted with such vagueness. In *Cole* v. *Richardson* (405 U.S. 676, 1972), a research sociologist at Boston State Hospital refused to subscribe to the loyalty oath required by state law. The Massachusetts statute required public employees to swear or affirm to "uphold and defend" the federal and state constitutions and to "oppose the overthrow of the government of the United States of America or of this Commonwealth by force, violence or by any illegal or unconstitutional method." Shortly after refusing to subscribe to this oath, Mrs. Richardson was fired from her research position. A federal district court found that the "oppose the overthrow" clause in the oath was "fatally vague and unspecific" and declared it unconstitutional. The Supreme Court, in a 4-3 holding, reversed. Chief Justice Burger, in the majority opinion supported by Justices Stewart, White, and Blackmun, said that the district court had erroneously given a literal interpretation to the "oppose the overthrow" clause. He contended that "such a literal approach to that clause is inconsistent with the Court's approach to the 'support' oaths." "Just as the connotatively active word 'support' has been interpreted to mean simply a commitment to abide by our constitutional system," said Burger, "the second clause of this oath is merely oriented to the negative implication of this notion; it is a commitment not to use illegal and constitutionally unprotected force to change the constitutional system." Burger concluded that the "purpose of the oath is clear on its face" and that it could not be assumed that there was a legislative intention in using such terms as "oppose" and "overthrow" "to impose obligations of specific, positive action on oath-takers." Hence, he held that the oath's provisions could not be considered unconstitutionally vague.

Justices Douglas, Brennan, and Marshall dissented. Douglas, reemphasizing his longstanding distaste for "test oaths [as] notorious tools of tyranny [that] are . . . unspeakably odious to a free people," maintained that the "oppose the overthrow" provision of the oath was clearly unconstitutional by the Court's earlier rulings. To him, "advocacy of basic fundamental changes in Government, which might popularly be described as 'overthrow' is within the protection of the First Amendment even when it is restrictively construed."

In his separate dissent, Justice Thurgood Marshall, joined by Justice Brennan, took a glance backward at the pervasiveness of governmental loyalty oaths in the post-World War II era. He suggested that because the American people have been literally "inundated" with oaths as a prerequisite for obtaining a wide variety of privileges and services, they are taken perfunctorily as so many are unaware of or insensitive to the "difficult constitutional issues" that are posed by these instruments for insuring loyalty. He cautioned that an uncritical acceptance of such oaths could well lead to their transformation into "an instrument of thought control and a means of enforcing complete political conformity."

In an unusual show of agreement, the Warren Court holdovers and the four Nixon appointees all agreed that Indiana's political party loyalty oath was unconstitutional in *Communist Party of Indiana* v. *Whitcomb* (414 U.S. 441, 1974). They disagreed, however, on the critical constitutional issue involved. In Justice Brennan's opinion for the Court, supported by the other four Warren Court holdovers, the oath was held to violate the constitutional guarantees of freedom of speech, press, and association. The critical defect of the statute for them was that its provisions were not limited to "action-inciting" advocacy. But Justice Lewis Powell's concurring opinion supported by the other three Nixon appointees, focused on the narrow position that the law was discriminatory because it placed on the Communist Party "burdens not imposed on the established [Democratic and Republican] parties." In the course of his opinion Justice Powell hinted that such a loyalty oath properly drawn could meet constitutional muster. Hence, the unanimous decision in this case does not settle the loyalty oath issue conclusively as might appear at first glance.

THE COMMUNIST PARTY REGISTRATION CONTROVERSY

Congress employed the "exposure" technique designed to bring Communist groups out into the open by setting forth an elaborate registration scheme in the Internal Security Act of 1950. Declaring that the Communist conspiracy represented a threat to national security, the act required "communist-action" and "communist-front" organizations to register with the Attorney General. A Subversive Activities Control Board was created and charged with the duty of conducting hearings to determine the status of organizations to which the Government sought to apply the act. Under the act, a finding against an organization results in an order to register in the category designated, which requires a disclosure of officers, finances, etc. The act of registration produces a number of disabilities for the organization and its members, e.g., restriction on organizational mailing privileges and denial of passports.

After a protracted hearing, the Board found the act applicable to the Communist Party, U.S.A., and an order was entered in April, 1953, requiring the Party to register as a "communist-action" group. That order was set aside by the Supreme Court in 1956 because the Board's finding included some tainted evidence by several Government witnesses. A subsequent hearing produced a similar finding and an order to register. In *Communist Party* v. *Subversive Activities Control Board* (367 U.S. 1, 1961) the Supreme Court affirmed the order and sustained the constitutionality of the registration provisions. Justice Felix Frankfurter's voluminous opinion boiled down to a balancing of competing interests. The Government's interest in protecting against the threat from such groups far outweighed the First Amendment claims. In this connection, the case was very distinguishable from the NAACP membership cases where the alleged public interest in disclosure was too insubstantial to warrant such an intrusion into First Amendment rights. Frankfurter was careful to avoid the Fifth Amendment self-incrimination issue, insisting that the claim was prematurely raised since it had not been invoked by party officers as individuals. The issue would be appropriately litigable in proceedings stemming from a failure to register under a final order.

When faced with a final order to register shortly thereafter, Party leaders refused to comply, asserting the self-incrimination claim. The Party was subsequently prosecuted, convicted, and fined $120,000 for failure to register. The Court of Appeals for the District of Columbia reversed the conviction in *Communist Party of the United States* v. *United States* (331 F.2d 807, 1963), holding that the trial court had erred in refusing to consider the self-incrimination issue. In his opinion for the court, Chief Judge David Bazelon emphasized that "the act of registering [under the act] is necessarily incriminating" although no other information except the registrant's name is given. He contended that a letter sent to the Attorney General (signed with the party seal) refusing to comply for fear of self-incrimination was a sufficient assertion of the claim. Hence, since no one was available to complete the forms by reason of a valid claim of the self-incrimination guarantee, the government had the burden of showing that a volunteer was available to provide the information. Judge Bazelon was careful to deny any organizational assertion of the privilege or assertion of it by an individual for the organization or its members. The Supreme Court refused to review the case, allowing the Court of Appeals holding to stand.

Having failed in its efforts to require the Communist party to register, the government proceeded to enforce the provisions of the act requiring individual members of a "communist-action" group to register upon default of the organization. In *Albertson* v. *Subversive Activities Control Board* (382 U.S. 70, 1965) the Supreme Court reversed a Court of Appeals decision which had affirmed Board orders for individual registration. Justice William J. Brennan, in his opinion for the Court, contended that the lower court had erred in holding that the self-incrimination claim was prematurely raised. The effect of the holding below, he continued, was to force the petitioners to a choice of registration without a decision on the merits of their self-incrimination claim or of refusing to register and risk "mounting penalties while awaiting the government's pleasure" of initiating prosecution for failure to register. He concluded that putting them to such a choice amounts to a denial of the Fifth Amendment protection against compulsory self-incrimination because the admission of membership in the Communist party could result in prosecution under the membership clause of the Smith Act, *supra*.

OUTLAWING THE COMMUNIST PARTY

On March 4, 1954, Congressman Martin Dies,[9] speaking in the House of Representatives in support of a bill he had introduced to outlaw the American Communist party, declared:

> We have been investigating communism for 18 years. The time has come now to do something very definite and conclusive about it. The present laws are inadequate, as shown by the fact that under these laws we have only prosecuted a handful of Communists. Under my measure, I promise you, if my experience of 7 years as head of [HUAC] means anything, that it will once and for all end the issue so far as the United States is concerned.

[9] Dies was chairman of the Un-American Activities Committee from its creation in 1938 until 1945.

Over the next several months this bill was considered with a variety of other anti-Communist measures proposed by both major parties. After considerable debate and the intervention of the Republican Administration, the Communist Control Act eventually emerged and was passed on August 24, 1954.

The act set forth a finding of Congress that the Communist party of the United States is "in fact an instrumentality of a conspiracy" directed by a hostile foreign power and that because of its dedication to the forcible overthrow of the government, its existence presents "a clear, present and continuing danger" to national security. Consequently, the act declares that the Party "should be outlawed." The key provision of the act withholds from the Communist party all "of the rights, privileges, and immunities attendant upon legal bodies created under the jurisdiction of the laws of the United States or any political subdivisions thereof." However, a degree of legal existence is preserved for the Party under a provision that states that the Party and its members are still subject to the requirements of the Internal Security Act of 1950. In any event, the major consequence of the Communist Control Act is the elimination of Communist party candidates from election ballots for public office.

Several other provisions of the act are directed at Communists in the labor movement. A category of "Communist-infiltrated" organizations is established as an addition to the "Communist-action" and "Communist-front" organizations to which the registration and penalty provisions of the Internal Security Act of 1950 apply. Upon a finding by the Subversive Activities Control Board that a labor union is a "Communist-infiltrated" organization, it loses privileges accorded labor unions under federal labor legislation. In addition, those who remain members of the "tainted" unions are prohibited employment in facilities engaged in production for national defense.

The Supreme Court has never been asked to consider the constitutionality of the act's outlawry provision. However, its decisions in such matters as registration under the Internal Security Act, Communists as officials of labor unions and as employees in defense facilities, and the right of Communists to travel abroad[10] would seem to indicate a partial rejection of Congress' ultimate intent.

LEGISLATIVE INVESTIGATIONS

The manner in which Congress has allowed some of its committees to use the investigatory power as a means of dealing with the Communist threat has been a subject of continuous controversy since the end of World War II. Undoubtedly convinced that exposure of Communist and fellow travelers served a useful purpose in protecting national security, investigators went virtually unchecked by Congress in their quest to uncover Communists and to expose their operations. By far the most celebrated and controversial uses of the investigative power for that purpose were by the House Un-American Activities Committee and the Senate Permanent Sub-Committee on Investigations under the domination of Senator Joseph

[10]These matters are discussed elsewhere in this chapter.

McCarthy. While there were complaints that the various inquiries of these committees were not in pursuance of a valid legislative purpose but were instead undertaken for personal aggrandizement, the most critical charges were directed at the committees' operational methods. The general atmosphere created was that of a "trial," but one in which the witness did not enjoy the safeguards of a trial. Charges were made against witnesses by using hearsay evidence, allowing the witnesses no opportunity to confront their accusers. Probers badgered witnesses and treated them with rank discourtesy. Not infrequently there were one-member hearings, after which that member proceeded to formulate the committee's report on an issue.

Constitutional questions raised by the methods of the House Committee on Un-American Activities were first considered by the Supreme Court in *Watkins* v. *United States* (354 U.S. 178, 1957). The case involved a contempt conviction of a witness before the House Committee on Un-American Activities for refusal to answer questions about his associates in his past Communist party activities. The witness rested his refusal on First Amendment grounds stressing that the Committee had no authority to ask the questions since they were not relevant to its legislative concerns. He further contended that the Committee lacked power "to undertake the public exposure of persons because of their past activities." In a 6–1 decision (Justices Burton and Whittaker did not participate), the Court reversed the conviction on due process grounds. Chief Justice Earl Warren's opinion stressed the vagueness of the Committee's authorizing resolution and the failure of the sub-committee chairman to provide sufficient clarifying information relative to the subject of the investigation. Since the Committee must "limit its inquiries to statutory pertinency," the witness was given no basis for determining that pertinency in trying to decide whether he should answer the questions. Although the decision was grounded in the "void for vagueness" principle, the Chief Justice further emphasized the applicability of limiting principles of the Bill of Rights to legislative investigations. He contended that not only are the guarantees against compulsory self-incrimination and unreasonable searches and seizures applicable, but Congressional investigating committees are limited by the First Amendment freedoms as well. Justice Tom Clark's dissent was largely a plea for judicial restraint in dealing with powers of Congress. To him, the majority action represented a "mischievous curbing of the informing function of the Congress," and it erroneously sustained the witness's claim of a "right to silence" under conditions which the Constitution does not guarantee.

The Court applied similar restrictions to state legislative investigations in *Sweezy* v. *New Hampshire* (354 U.S. 234, 1957), a case decided on the same day as *Watkins*. Like Watkins, Sweezy was convicted of contempt for refusal to answer questions of a legislative committee (a one-man committee comprised of the state Attorney General) concerning his activities in the Wallace Progressive party. Also like Watkins, Sweezy contended that the inquiry infringed First Amendment freedoms. While condemning the vagueness of the authorizing resolution and the unfettered discretion given to the Attorney General as the central vices in the case, Chief Justice Warren's opinion was even more emphatic regarding First Amendment restrictions on legislative investigations. He contended that political freedom of the individual is a fundamental principle of a democratic society and that the rights to engage in political expression and association are basic premises undergirding the American constitutional system that are enshrined in the First Amendment and are applicable to the states through the Fourteenth Amendment.

Two years later in *Barenblatt* v. *United States*, the Court made a significant retreat from its *Watkins* and *Sweezy* position. In a 5–4 decision it sustained a contempt conviction of a witness who invoked the First Amendment in refusing to answer questions put to him by the House Committee on Un-American Activities. Undoubtedly reacting to Congressional criticism of its rulings in Communist cases and to threats to curb its jurisdiction, the Court majority now considered the HUAC authorizing resolution sufficiently clear and definitive when supplemented by the clarifying statements of the probers. Justice John Marshall Harlan contended for the majority that the vagueness condemned in *Watkins* had resulted from the failure of the Committee to make sufficient clarifying and illuminating statements regarding the purpose of the inquiry. Such was not the case in *Barenblatt*. The chairman had specified the subject of the inquiry with sufficient clarity. Setting forth a comprehensive statement of the "balancing-of-interests" test and over the vigorous dissent of Justice Hugo Black, Harlan dismissed Barenblatt's First Amendment claims by asserting that the Government's national security interests override the competing interests of the individual.

In a companion case, *Uphaus* v. *Wyman* (360 U.S. 72, 1959), the Court applied the principles of *Barenblatt* to reject an attack on the legislative investigating procedures of New Hampshire that had been condemned two years earlier in *Sweezy*. After applying the *Barenblatt* principles to uphold contempt convictions in *Wilkinson* v. *United States* (365 U.S. 399) and *Braden* v. *United States* (365 U.S. 431), in 1961, the Court returned to the stricter standards laid down in *Watkins* and reversed a number of contempt convictions between 1961 and 1965 (see *Deutch* v. *United States*, 367 U.S. 456, 1961; *Russell* v. *United States*, 369 U.S. 749; and *Yellin* v. *United States*, 374 U.S. 109, 1963).

Furthermore, in 1963 the Court indicated that legislative investigating committees were not going to find it easy to use the "balancing" test to justify intrusions into constitutionally protected rights. In *Gibson* v. *Florida Legislative Investigating Committee* (372 U.S. 539), legislative investigators were rebuffed in their demand for membership information from an official of the Miami branch of the NAACP. With the Court's decision in *NAACP* v. *Alabama, supra*, precluding a demand for the organization's membership list, the committee sought to compel the Reverend Mr. Gibson, as branch president, to refer to the membership list in his possession and answer questions relative to the membership status of particular persons. The committee's stated purpose was to determine if Communists had infiltrated groups like the NAACP. In reversing Gibson's contempt conviction that resulted from his refusal to bring his records and answer questions therefrom, the Court emphasized the state's burden to "convincingly show a substantial relation between the information sought and a subject of overriding and compelling state interest." Justice Arthur Goldberg's opinion for the Court noted that the record did not disclose a "substantial connection between the Miami branch of the NAACP and

Communist activities" which was essential to demonstrate the "overriding and compelling state interest" needed to justify this intrusion into associational rights.

By 1969 the House shifted in investigative emphasis from Communists to domestic dissidents and various New Left revolutionaries. HUAC was disbanded and its successor in the internal security field was given the title of House Committee on Internal Security (HCIS). The move away from the preoccupation (of more than two decades) with investigating domestic Communist activity to a broader range of groups threatening internal security is reflected in the charter of the new committee. For example, it is authorized to investigate "the extent, character, objectives, and activities within the U.S. of organizations or groups, their members, agents, and affiliates, which incite or employ acts of force, violence, terrorism, or any unlawful means, to obstruct or oppose the lawful authority of the Government of the U.S. in the execution of any law or policy affecting the internal security of the U.S. . . ." While critics of the Committee have gone through an annual ritual of attempting to starve it out of existence by urging Congress not to appropriate operating funds, it survived through the 1974 fiscal year. But in 1975, the House abolished the HCIS and transferred its functions to the Judiciary Committee.

NATIONAL SECURITY AND TRAVEL ABROAD

Federal law requires that in order to travel abroad a person must be issued a valid passport by the Secretary of State. Few questions relative to the scope of the Secretary's passport power arose prior to the end of World War II. Curtailment of foreign travel during the two world wars was considered essential to national security. But when the Government adopted, as a Cold War strategem, the policy of refusing passports to native Communists and their sympathizers because their travel abroad would be detrimental to national interests, serious constitutional questions were raised. To be sure, when travel restrictions are applied to persons merely because of their associations and beliefs, basic First Amendment freedoms are placed under serious stress.

The Supreme Court first considered the passport problem in *Kent* v. *Dulles* (356 U.S. 116, 1957). In that case passports were denied because of a refusal to file an affidavit concerning Communist party membership. In a 5–4 decision the Court held that the Secretary of State did not have the statutory authority to deny the passports for failure to file the required affidavit. Justice William O. Douglas, in his opinion for the Court, contended that the right to travel was embraced in the liberty protected by the Fifth Amendment. Furthermore, Douglas contended that since the Secretary's action was not based on a grant of legislative authority, the important First Amendment belief and associational issues need not be considered. The four dissenters—Justices Clark, Harlan, Burton, and Whittaker—contended that the necessary statutory authority existed.

That the High Court did not look with favor upon the indiscriminate restrictions on travel allowed under a provision of the Internal Security Act of 1950, is illustrated in *Aptheker* v. *Secretary of State* (378 U.S. 500, 1964). The provision, which denied passports to members of "Communist-action" and "front" organizations, was considered too sweeping to be consistent with constitutionally protected freedoms. In declaring the provision unconstitutional, Justice Arthur Goldberg pointed out for the majority that the restrictions applied regardless of the purpose of the proposed travel and the "security-sensitivity of the areas in which [a member of such an organization] wishes to travel." The dissenters—Justices Clark, Harlan, and White—once again contended that in a proper balancing of competing interests, "the degree of restraint upon travel is outweighed by the dangers to our very existence."

The Court made good on its "security-sensitivity of areas" exception one year later in *Zemel* v. *Rusk* (381 U.S. 1, 1956). In affirming a State Department refusal to issue passports for travel to Cuba, Chief Justice Earl Warren contended for the Court that area restrictions are supported by legislative authority and that the "liberty" to travel established in *Kent* v. *Dulles, supra*, is not absolute but may be subject to reasonable restrictions in the interest of national security. The First Amendment claims were rejected also as the Chief Justice held that "[t]he right to speak and publish does not carry with it the unrestrained right to gather information." He concluded that the restrictions here were not based upon associations or beliefs but "upon foreign policy considerations affecting all citizens." Justice William O. Douglas' dissent stressed the view that the restriction had been made for the wrong reason. For example, he noted that "a theater of war may be too dangerous for travel," but the "so-called danger" involved here was Cuban communism. Since there are numbers of such regimes and considerable Communist thought in the world, he contended that Americans must mingle with them if those phenomena are to be known and understood.

The State Department has applied the *Zemel* rule to refuse travel to students, professors, chess players, and others to specified Communist countries. Some persons have insisted on traveling to the restricted areas despite the possibility of criminal sanctions. In 1963, a group of 58 students defied the Cuban travel ban by initiating their trips from Prague and Paris. Having been advised that traveling to Cuba without a passport validated for that purpose was a violation of travel control law and regulations, several persons were indicted for conspiring to induce American citizens to travel to a restricted area without a valid passport. In affirming the federal district court dismissal of the charge in *United States* v. *Laub* (385 U.S. 475, 1967), the Supreme Court held that the statutory provision under which criminal charges were brought was not intended by Congress to enforce the State Department's area restrictions policy. The statute was merely directed at departure from, and entry into, the United States. In addition, the Court noted that great weight must be given to the State Department's consistent position over a long period of time that there was no statutory authority for criminal prosecution for travel to restricted areas.

In a decision on December 20, 1967, the Court of Appeals for the District of Columbia appeared to modify *Zemel* significantly by holding that the State Department could not enforce its restricted-area travel policy by denying passports to persons who might visit such places. The case developed from a denial of a passport to Professor Staughton Lynd for travel to England. His passport had been revoked earlier for defying the ban on travel to North Vietnam. The court maintained that the State Department did not possess the statutory authority to control a person's travel; it could only prescribe the areas where passports could be taken. Hence, the government's only weapon to prohibit travel to restricted areas is the extraction of a promise from the traveller that he will not take the passport into a restricted area. The court emphasized that the passport must be issued although the traveller indicates his intention to disregard the ban and enter the restricted area without his passport. In short, the Secretary of State can "control the lawful travel of the passport" but is without "authority to control the travel of the person." The State Department decided against an appeal of the decision, but it has endorsed a bill which would make it criminal to travel to countries declared "off limits" for national security reasons.

COVERT GOVERNMENT SURVEILLANCE

Two intelligence techniques that have come to surface and have generated considerable emotional debate in recent years are warrantless electronic surveillance and deployment of government-sponsored informants.[11] These techniques were apparently used by the Nixon administration in security investigations. The Senate Watergate hearings, as well as earlier hearings conducted by a subcommittee of the Senate Judiciary Committee,[12] are replete with vignettes and bizarre events involving intelligence operations and information gathering.

The Supreme Court, in *Katz* v. *United States* and *Berger* v. *New York* (*infra*, Chap. 5), held for the first time that electronic surveillance constituted a search and seizure within the terms of the Fourth Amendment. Prior to these decisions, federal courts had long excluded wiretap evidence based on statutory rather than constitutional grounds. In a sense *Katz* and *Berger* overcame the presumption that electronic surveillance would be unconstitutional only if there were physical trespass. The rulings recognized that technological refinements made physical trespass for surveillance a thing of the past. However, the question of the extent to which *Katz* and *Berger* would apply to electronic surveillance when done in the name of national security remained open. This question became especially salient since in 1968 Congress passed the Omnibus Crime Control and Safe Streets Act which repealed, in effect, the underlying statutory grounds as applied to national security. In 1972, the Supreme Court faced this question in *United States* v. *United States District Court* (407 U.S. 297). There, a district court ordered the government to disclose to a defendant, charged with bombing a CIA office in Michigan,

---

[11] This discussion relies heavily on the thorough study of "The National Security Interest and Civil Liberties" in 85 *Harvard Law Review*, 1130–1326 at 1244–1284. Those interested in a detailed critical analysis of the two intelligence techniques discussed here as well as other aspects of national security are encouraged to see this excellent Note.

[12] See footnote 15, *infra*.

conversations overheard by warrantless electronic surveillance. The government sought to have the order vacated, but its request was denied by a Court of Appeals. Justice Powell's majority opinion, affirming the Court of Appeals decision, held that "the customary Fourth Amendment requirement of judicial approval prior to initiation of a search or surveillance" applied to cases involving domestic aspects of national security. Powell specifically rejected government contentions that "special circumstances applicable to domestic security surveillances" called for exceptions to the Fourth Amendment warrant requirement to prevent "obstruct [ing] the President in the discharge of his constitutional duty to protect domestic security." "Official surveillance, whether its purpose be criminal investigation or on-going intelligence gathering," he asserted, "risks infringement of constitutionally protected privacy of speech." "Security surveillances," he continued, "are especially sensitive because of the inherent vagueness of the domestic security concept, the necessarily broad and continuing nature of intelligence gathering, and the temptation to utilize such surveillances to oversee political dissent." In this final analysis, Powell declared that the President's authority in protecting domestic security is subject to the commands of the Fourth Amendment. He was careful, however, to indicate that the Court was "express [ing] no opinion as to the issues which may be involved with respect to activities of foreign powers or their agents." Justices Douglas and White concurred separately while Justice Rehnquist did not participate in the case. Subsequently, the case was discussed by participants in the Watergate hearings relative to the Presidential authority to support the surreptitious entry into the office of Daniel Ellsberg's psychiatrist. On that issue, the decision's impact remained unclear.

Government Informers

The use of government informers in national security surveillance is not a new phenomenon. During the 1940s and 1950s, for example, Communist and communist-affiliated groups were heavily infiltrated by informers. More recently, the focus of informers and intelligence activity has shifted to civil rights and anti-war groups. Because much support for the civil rights and anti-war causes emanates from college and university campuses, government informers were particularly active on campuses. Informers were also active in black communities during and after the large-city demonstrations of the 1960s. Some idea of the scope of the use of informers was provided by the Media Papers, FBI documents stolen in 1971 in Media, Pennsylvania. The papers disclosed FBI attempts to infiltrate a 1969 conference of war resisters at Haverford College and the 1970 national convention of the Association of Black Students. In addition, they indicated FBI efforts at recruiting new informers to establish "constant surveillance in black communities and New Left organizations."[13] In Philadelphia's black community, for example, the offices of such organizations as CORE, SCLC, and the Black Coalition were selected for surveillance by such informers.

The Media Papers did indeed underscore the extent to which the government

[13] See The *New York Times*, April 8, 1971, p. 22. col. 1.

was making use of undercover informers. Even so, the Supreme Court thus far has not found the Fourth Amendment "search and seizures" provision applicable to such activity. In *Hoffa* v. *United States* (385 U.S. 293, 1966), for example, the Court held that testimony by an informer of conversations of a defendant was not a "search" and hence was admissible evidence since the defendant had consented to the presence of the informer. The fact that the informer did not reveal his true purpose to the defendant did not vitiate this consent. Indeed, as Justice Stewart's opinion for the Court explained, a citizen's belief that "a person to whom he voluntarily confides his wrongdoing will not reveal it" is not protected by the Fourth Amendment. "The risk of being . . . betrayed by an informer," said Stewart, "is the kind of risk we necessarily assume whenever we speak." Despite widespread criticism, *Hoffa* remains essentially intact.[14]

The revelation of the United States Army's involvement in massive surveillance of civilians attracted as much or perhaps more attention than did the FBI's government informer system and portends even more serious challenges to individual liberties. Apparently, the military intelligence gathering system mushroomed in the wake of the civil disorders of the late 1960s when the Army was called on to assist in quelling them. It was U.S. Senator Sam Ervin—more recently known as chairman of the Senate Watergate Committee—whose Subcommittee on Constitutional Rights of the Senate Committee on the Judiciary unveiled much of the operations of the military intelligence system. Testimony before the Ervin subcommittee by several former military intelligence agents revealed various methods of undercover infiltration of college campuses, anti-war demonstrations, and welfare and civil rights gatherings. Such practices as encouraging agents to adopt the counterculture dress and life-style, to look and act militant, to use student identification cards from other colleges (and claim to be just visiting the school in question), and to become freelance photographers were described as frequent and commonplace. Moreover, former Army Intelligence agents testified that undercover activities centered on many persons—ranging from Dr. Martin Luther King, Jr., and folksingers Arlo Guthrie and Joan Baez, to retired Army generals. The former agents also reported that the Army, through a dummy corporation using an Alexandria, Virginia, Post Office Box, subscribed to publications ranging from the *New York Times* and the *National Observer* to the *Berkeley Barb*.[15]

The question of the constitutionality of such military surveillance activity was presented to the Supreme Court in 1972 in *Laird* v. *Tatum* (408 U.S. 1). However,

---

[14] See, for example, the 1971 case of *United States* v. *White* (considered in Chap. 5, *infra*), where the Court ruled that no prior warrants were necessary for the use of government informers who carry transmitters which record or broadcast conversations with subjects of investigations. Justice White's opinion of the Court echoed the *Hoffa* case doctrine that a person assumes the risk of "being betrayed by an informer" and concluded that the method of an informer's reporting—whether by memory, tape-recording, or simultaneous transmission—of the conversation did not sufficiently distinguish *White* from *Hoffa*.

[15] See *Hearings on Data Banks, Computers and the Bill of Rights Before the Subcomm. on Constitutional Rights of the Senate Comm. on the Judiciary*, 92d Cong., First Sess., pt. I (1971).

in a 5–4 decision (with Justice Byron White joining the four Nixon appointees), the Court stayed away from the constitutional issue by holding that the "mere existence" of investigative and data-gathering activity by the government presented no justifiable issue under the First Amendment. The Court's conclusion was based on the fact that there was neither a showing of objective harm nor a threat of a specific future harm. Brushing aside claims of the respondents that "their rights were being invaded by the Army's alleged 'surveillance of lawful civilian political activity,' " Chief Justice Burger, speaking for the majority, said that the activity was justified so that the Army would be ready to respond effectively with a minimum of force "when called upon to assist local authorities." Burger noted that much of the information gathered was obtained from news reports but that some information was received from "Army Intelligence Agents who attended meetings that were open to the public" and from "civilian law enforcement agencies." Acknowledging that prior cases indicated "that constitutional violations may arise from the deterrent, or 'chilling,' effect of governmental regulations that fall short of a direct prohibition against the exercise of First Amendment rights," the Chief Justice sought to forge a distinction. In the Court's earlier cases, he argued, "the challenged exercise of governmental power was regulatory, proscriptive, or compulsory in nature and the complainant was either presently or prospectively subject to the regulations, proscriptions or compulsions that he was challenging." But in this case, he concluded, the respondents merely "disagree with the judgments made by the Executive Branch with respect to the type and amount of information the Army needs."

Justices Douglas, Brennan, Stewart, and Marshall dissented. The sharpest dissent was filed by Douglas, who argued that the Army had no Congressional or constitutional authorization for its surveillance activities. "One can search the Constitution in vain," Douglas said, "for any such authority." Moreover, he contended that the "controversy is not a remote, imaginary conflict." The surveillance was "massive and comprehensive," not casual, and the Army's reports were "widely circulated and were exchanged with reports of the FBI, state and municipal police departments, and the CIA," and the data-collecting sources and methods consisted of "staking-out teams of agents, creating command posts inside meetings, posing as press photographers, posing as TV newsmen, posing as students, shadowing public figures." Such surveillance, he concluded, "is at war with the principles of the First Amendment" and he cautioned against submitting to it.

Secrecy, Security, Confidentiality

As mentioned elsewhere, turbulent times increase the conflicts between the interest in national security and the interest in freedom. Such was the situation surrounding the release and publication of the Pentagon Papers. For example, when in 1971 the *New York Times*, the *Washington Post*, and other leading newspapers came into possession of and published secret papers on the "History of United States Decision-Making Process on Viet Nam Policy," anti-war protest groups received an unexpected weapon that enabled them to expand further an already increasing popular clamor to end the war. But President Nixon and his supporters were equally determined to continue the conflict until "peace with honor" could be achieved. With release of the Papers coming at this time, the Vietnam War loomed larger as an issue in the upcoming 1972 Presidential campaign and the increasing sharpness of debate thereon generally served to heighten and illuminate the division and tension in the country over the war.

It was in this kind of setting that the Pentagon Papers case arose. In fact the *New York Times* found the Papers to be such a rich source of information and news for its readers that it began to publish verbatim significant parts of the documents. The government's immediate response was to initiate judicial action to restrain further publication on the ground that publishing the Pentagon Papers could (or would) seriously endanger certain national security interests. Because of the desirability of immediate resolution of such an important question, lower courts accelerated their actions and the controversy reached the Supreme Court in short order. Only two days after the *Times* first began publishing the Papers in mid-June 1971, the government filed an action in a federal district court for a preliminary injunction against further publication. The motion was denied four days later. The next week the Court of Appeals for the Second Circuit reversed the district court and remanded the case for further hearings. Simultaneously, the government sought to enjoin the *Washington Post* from publishing the same documents. But lower federal courts in the District of Columbia refused to grant injunctive relief. The *New York Times'* petition for certiorari was granted by the Supreme Court and it agreed to hear the case only three days after the Court of Appeals had reversed the district court. At the same time, the government's petition for certiorari in the *Washington Post* case was granted and the companion cases were argued and decided in late June, 1971.

In a per curiam 6–3 decision, the Supreme Court agreed with both district court decisions and held that the government had not met its "heavy burden of showing justification for the enforcement of such a [prior] restraint" on the publication of the Pentagon Papers. All nine Justices filed opinions in the case. Justices Douglas, Black, and Brennan concurred basically on the same First Amendment theory.[16] As Brennan explained, "the First Amendment tolerates absolutely no prior judicial restraints of the press predicated upon surmise or conjecture that untoward consequences may result." Justice Marshall also concurred, focusing on the power of the Court to proscribe "behavior that Congress has specifically declined to prohibit." Marshall said that "it is clear that Congress has specifically rejected passing legislation that would have clearly given the President the power he seeks here and [that would have] made the current activity of the newspapers unlawful." He concluded that it is not a function of the Court "to sling itself into every breach perceived by some Government official nor . . . to take upon itself the burden of enacting law . . . that Congress has refused to pass." Stewart and White also concurred.

Chief Justice Burger and Justices Harlan and Blackmun dissented. Justice Harlan,

---

[16] See Chap. 3, *supra,* for a general discussion of prior restraint cases.

whose opinion was joined by the other dissenters, was distressed over the speed with which the Court decided the cases. Harlan said that "a sufficient basis for affirming the Court of Appeals . . . in the *Times* litigation" existed since the court's order was based on its conclusion "that because of the time elements the Government had not been given an adequate opportunity to present its case to the District Court." As to the *Washington Post* case, Harlan said that "the scope of the judicial function in passing upon the activities of the Executive Branch . . . in the field of foreign affairs is very narrowly restricted" and, consequently, the Court should have remanded the case for further consideration of national security issues. Both Chief Justice Burger and Justice Blackmun, in separate dissents, echoed Harlan's concern over the "unseemly haste" in which the cases were decided.

Another situation involving the Pentagon Papers arose in *Gravel* v. *United States* (408 U.S. 606, 1972). There, the Court held that although the Speech or Debate Clause (in Article I, Section 6 of the Constitution) protected members of Congress and their aides (so long as the conduct involved would be "immune legislative conduct" if performed by the member of Congress himself), it did not provide immunity for testifying before a grand jury about plans to privately publish the Pentagon Papers. Here, U.S. Senator Mike Gravel of Alaska had read parts of the Pentagon Papers to a subcommittee hearing and placed all of the study in the public record. Subsequent press reports indicated that he had arranged for private publication of the Pentagon Papers. Subsequently, an aide to Senator Gravel was subpoenaed to appear before a federal grand jury investigating possible law violations stemming from the release and publication of the Pentagon Papers. Gravel, as an intervenor, sought to quash the subpoena, arguing that the Speech or Debate Clause protected his aide from appearing before the grand jury. A federal district court denied the motion to quash, holding that "the private republication of the documents was not privileged by the Speech or Debate Clause." The Court of Appeals for the First Circuit modified the district court's holding by indicating that "neither Senator nor aide could be questioned about [the plans for private republication] because of a common law privilege."

In reversing the Court of Appeals, Justice Byron White's opinion for the 6–3 majority clarified the extent of the protections provided to members of Congress and their aides by the Speech or Debate Clause. He argued that the privilege is invocable by the member of Congress or an aide to the member on the member's behalf but "in all events the privilege available to the aide is confined to those services that would be immune legislative conduct if performed [by members of Congress themselves]." "While the Speech or Debate Clause recognizes speech, voting and other legislative acts as exempt from liability that might otherwise attach," continued White, "it does not privilege either Senator or aide to violate an otherwise valid criminal law in preparing for or implementing legislative acts." White concluded that a valid grand jury inquiry could continue and that Senator Gravel's aide could be compelled to testify "so long as legislative acts of the Senator are not impugned."

Justices Douglas, Brennan, and Marshall dissented. Douglas said he "would construe the Speech and Debate Clause to insulate Senator Gravel and his aides from inquiry concerning the Pentagon Papers, and Beacon Press (the private publishing firm) from inquiry concerning publication of them, for that publication was but another way of informing the public of what had gone on in the privacy of the Executive Branch concerning the conception and pursuit of the so-called 'war' in Vietnam." Brennan, whose dissent was joined by Douglas and Marshall, was very critical of the decision's restrictive sweep on the speech and debate privilege of members of Congress. He felt that ensconced therein were dangers to the legislative process that "are vital to the workings of our democratic system." Brennan also took exception to White's "narrow view of the legislative function" and said that if Senator Gravel was incorrect in his contention "that his hearing on the Pentagon Papers had a direct bearing on the work of his Subcommittee on Buildings and Grounds," Congress should "call him to task," not the Court. "What is at stake," he continued, "is the right of an elected representative to inform, and the public to be informed, about matters relating directly to the workings of our Government."

Another highly debated issue to come before the Court in 1972 was the extent to which reporters could preserve the confidentiality of their news sources. Beginning in the 1960s a number of dissident, militant groups not only *vocally* expressed their opposition to policies of the government, and to the political system generally, but *demonstrated* their opposition through illegal, obstructive actions. Under such circumstances, these organizations aroused both the concern of the government—for surveillance and security purposes; and of enterprising newsmen—for newsgathering and reporting purposes. And whereas these groups attempt to erect an iron curtain between themselves and the government, they have on occasion granted newsmen access to their meetings provided confidentiality is assured.

But when a news story in the morning paper gives law enforcement officials reason to believe that internal security (prevention of civil disorders) or criminal activity (use of drugs) may be involved, can reporters be compelled to reveal their sources pursuant to certain governmental investigations or grand jury inquiries? This was the question presented to the Court in *Branzburg* v. *Hayes, In re Pappas*, and *United States* v. *Caldwell*, decided together in 1972. In all three cases, newsmen had attempted to avoid testifying before grand juries. In *Branzburg*, a Kentucky reporter who had written several major articles on drug traffic sought to avoid being required to name the persons he saw possessing marijuana and hashish. In *Pappas*, a Massachusetts television newsman sought to have quashed a grand jury summons requiring him to report on activities that he observed while in a Black Panther Party headquarters. And in *Caldwell*, the government appealed a Court of Appeals decision that held that a *New York Times* reporter was not to be held in contempt for refusing to appear before a Federal grand jury to discuss certain interviews he had with Black Panther Party members. In another 5–4 decision in which the four Nixon appointees were joined by Justice White, the Supreme Court held that newsmen, like other citizens, had no privilege to refuse to appear before a grand jury and to answer questions as to their information or sources. In his majority opinion, Justice White rejected the claims made by the newsmen that there must be demonstrated a compelling need for the information in their possession because of its relevance to a crime and because it is unavailable from other sources to override their First Amendment guarantees to protect their sources and information from compelled disclosure. "The heart of the claim," said White, "is that the burden on news gathering resulting from compelling reporters to disclose confidential information outweighs any public interest in obtaining the information." White proceeded to discuss generally testimonial privilege for newsmen, saying that none existed at common law and that none exists by federal statute. He declined to establish such a privilege in these cases. "On the records now before us," said White, "we perceive no basis for holding that the public interest in law enforcement in ensuring effective grand jury proceedings is insufficient to override the consequential, but uncertain, burden on news gathering which is said to result from insisting that reporters, like other citizens, respond to relevant questions put to them in the course of a valid grand jury investigation or criminal trial." Moreover, White was unimpressed by evidence indicating that news sources would disappear if newsmen were compelled by subpoena to testify before grand juries. "Estimates of the inhibiting effect of such subpoenas on the willingness of informants to make disclosures to newsmen," thought White, "are widely divergent and to a great extent speculative." White was careful to conclude his opinion by noting that "[o]fficial harassment of the press undertaken not for purposes of law enforcement but to disrupt a reporter's relationship with his news sources would have no justification." (Apparently, to White, *official harassment* "for purposes of law enforcement" is permissible!) Justice Powell, who concurred in White's majority opinion, filed a separate concurrence that attempted to clarify the end of White's opinion. Powell said that if a "newsman is called upon to give information bearing only a remote and tenuous relationship to the subject of the investigation, or if he has some other reason to believe that his testimony implicates confidential source relationships without a legitimate need of law enforcement, he will have access to the Court on a motion to quash and an appropriate protective order may be entered."

The inadequacies in the remedy proposed by Powell were apparent to Justice Stewart, whose sharp dissenting opinion was joined by Justices Brennan and Marshall. Stewart asserted that "[t]he Court's crabbed view of the First Amendment reflects a disturbing insensitivity to the critical role of an independent press in our society...." Furthermore, the Court's action "invites state and federal authorities to undermine the historic independence of the press by attempting to annex the journalistic profession as an investigative arm of government...." Stewart then outlined a three-part test to apply when reporters are called to testify before grand juries. It provides "that the government must: (1) show that there is probable cause to believe that the newsman has information which is clearly relevant to a specific probable violation of law; (2) demonstrate that the information can not be obtained by alternate means less destructive of First Amendment rights; and (3) demonstrate a compelling and overriding interest in the information." Justice Douglas, in a separate dissent, stated that in his opinion newsmen had an absolute right not to appear and testify before a grand jury. Douglas also felt that the Court's decision would "impede the wide open and robust dissemination of ideas and counterthought which a free press both fosters and protects and which is essential to the success of intelligent self-government."

The *Branzburg* decision has prompted new and renewed attempts by legislators to frame so-called shield laws that would provide reporters with much of the protection that the Supreme Court's decision took away. The debate over such proposals in the states and in the Congress is very vigorous, perhaps mainly because the First Amendment states unequivocally that "Congress shall make no law ... abridging the freedom of speech, or of the press."

The cases that follow illustrate some of the significant issues reviewed in this commentary.

DENNIS v. UNITED STATES
341 U.S. 494; 95 L. Ed. 1137; 71 S. Ct. 857 (1951)

MR. CHIEF JUSTICE VINSON *announced the judgment of the Court and an opinion in which* MR. JUSTICE REED, MR. JUSTICE BURTON, *and* MR. JUSTICE MINTON *join.*

Petitioners were indicted in July 1948, for violation of the conspiracy provisions of the Smith Act 54 Stat 670, 671, ch 439, 18 USC (1946 ed) section 11, during the period of April, 1945, to July, 1948. . . . [T]he case was set for trial on January 17, 1949 [and a] verdict of guilty as to all the petitioners was returned by the jury on October 14, 1949. The Court of Appeals affirmed the convicitons. . . . We granted certiorari . . . limited to the following two questions: (1) Whether either section 2 or section 3 of the Smith Act, inherently or as construed and applied in the instant case, violates the First Amendment and other provisions of the Bill of Rights; (2) whether either section 2 or section 3 of the Act, inherently or as construed and applied in the instant case, violates the First and Fifth Amendment because of indefiniteness.

Sections 2 and 3 of the Smith Act 54 Stat 670, 671, ch 439, 18 USC (1946 ed) sections 10, 11 (see present 18 USC section 2385), provide as follows:

Sec. 2.

(a) It shall be unlawful for any person—

(1) to knowingly or willfully advocate, abet, advise, or teach the duty, necessity, desirability, or propriety of overthrowing or destroying any government in the United States by force or violence, or by the assassination of any officer of such government;

(2) with the intent to cause the overthrow or destruction of any government in the United States, to print, publish, edit, issue, circulate, sell, distribute, or publicly display any written or printed matter advocating, advising, or teaching the duty, necessity, desirability, or propriety of overthrowing or destroying any government in the United States by force or violence;

(3) to organize or help to organize any society, group, or assembly of persons who teach, advocate, or encourage the overthrow or destruction of any government in the United States by force or violence; or to be or become a member of, or affiliate with, any such society, group, or assembly of persons, knowing the purposes thereof.

(b) For the purposes of this section, the term "government in the United States" means the Government of the United States, the government of any State, Territory, or possession of the United States, the government of the District of Columbia, or the government of any political subdivision of any of them.

Sec. 3. It shall be unlawful for any person to attempt to commit, or to conspire to commit, any of the acts prohibited by the provisions of . . . this title.

The indictment charged the petitioners with willfully and knowingly conspiring (1) to organize as the Communist Party of the United States of America a society, group and assembly of persons who teach and advocate the overthrow and destruction of the Government of the United States by force and violence, and (2) knowingly and willfully to advocate and teach the duty and necessity of overthrowing and destroying the Government of the United States by force and violence. The indictment further alleged that section 2 of the Smith Act proscribes these acts and that any conspiracy to take such actions is a violation of section 3 of the Act.

. . . Our limited grant of the writ of certiorari has removed from our consideration any question as to the sufficiency of the evidence to support the jury's determination that petitioners are guilty of the offense charged. Whether on this record petitioners did in fact advocate the overthrow of the Government by force and violence is not before us, and we must base any discussion of this point upon the conclusions stated in the opinion of the Court of Appeals, which treated the issue in great detail. That court held that the record in this case amply supports the necessary finding of the jury that petitioners, the leaders of the Communist Party in this country, were unwilling to work within our framework of democracy, but intended to initiate a violent revolution whenever the propitious occasion appeared.

. . .

It will be helpful in clarifying the issues to treat next the contention that the trial judge improperly interpreted the statute by charging that the statute required an unlawful intent before the jury could convict. More specifically, he charged that the jury could not find the petitioners guilty under the indictment unless they found that petitioners had the intent "to overthrow the government by force and violence as speedily as circumstances permit."

. . . The structure and purpose of the statute demand the inclusion of intent as an element of the crime. Congress was concerned with those who advocate and organize for the overthrow of the Government. Certainly those who recruit and combine for the purpose of advocating overthrow intend to bring about that overthrow. We hold that the statute requires as an essential element of the crime proof of the intent of those who are charged with its violation to overthrow the Government by force and violence.

. . .

The obvious purpose of the statute is to protect existing Government, not from change by peaceable, lawful and constitutional means, but from change by violence, revolution and terrorism. That it is within the *power* of the Congress to protect the Government of the United States from armed rebellion is a proposition which requires little discussion. Whatever theoretical merit there may be to the argument that there is a "right" to rebellion against dictatorial governments is without force where the existing structure of the government provides for peaceful and orderly change. We reject any principle of governmental helplessness in the face of preparation for revolution, which principle, carried to its logical conclusion, must lead to anarchy. No one could conceive that it is not within the power of Congress to prohibit acts intended to overthrow the Government by force and violence. The question with which we are concerned here is not whether Congress has such *power*, but whether the *means* which it has employed conflict with the First and Fifth Amendments to the Constitution.

One of the bases for the contention that the means which Congress has employed are invalid takes the form of an attack on the face of the statute on the grounds that by its terms it prohibits academic discussion of the merits of Marxism-Leninism, that it stifles ideas and is contrary to all concepts of a free speech and a free press. Although we do not agree that the language itself has that significance, we must bear in mind that it is the duty of the federal courts to interpret federal legislation in a manner not inconsistent with the demands of the Constitution. . . .

The very language of the Smith Act negates the interpretation which petitioners would have us impose on that Act. It is directed at advocacy, not discussion. Thus, the trial judge properly charged the jury that they could not convict if they found that petitioners did "no more than pursue peaceful studies and discussions or teaching and advocacy in the realm of ideas." He further charged that it was not unlawful "to conduct in an American college and university a course explaining the philosophical theories set forth in the books which have been placed in evidence." Such a charge is in strict accord with the statutory language, and illustrates the meaning to be placed on those words. Congress did not intend to eradicate the free discussion of political theories, to destroy the traditional rights of Americans to discuss and evaluate ideas without fear of governmental sanction. Rather Congress was concerned with the very kind of activity in which the evidence showed these petitioners engaged.

But although the statute is not directed at the hypothetical cases which petitioners have conjured, its application in this case has resulted in convictions for the teaching and advocacy of the overthrow of the Government by force and violence, which, even though coupled with the intent to accomplish that overthrow, contains an element of speech. For this reason, we must pay special heed to the demands of the First Amendment marking out the boundaries of speech.

We pointed out in *Douds* . . . that the basis of the First Amendment is the hypothesis that speech can rebut speech, propaganda will answer propaganda, free debate of ideas will result in the wisest governmental policies. It is for this reason that this Court has recognized the inherent value of free discourse. An analysis of the leading cases in this Court which have involved direct limitations on speech, however, will demonstrate that both the majority of the Court and the dissenters in particular cases have recognized that this is not an unlimited, unqualified right, but that the societal value of speech must, on occasion, be subordinated to other values and considerations.

No important case involving free speech was decided by this Court prior to *Schenck* v. *United States* . . . (1919). Indeed, the summary treatment accorded an argument based upon an individual's claim that the First Amendment protect certain utterances indicates that the Court at earlier dates placed no unique emphasis upon that right. It was not until the classic dictum of Justice Holmes in the Schenck case that speech per se received that emphasis in a majority opinion. . . . Writing for a unanimous Court, Justice Holmes stated that the "question in every case is whether the words used are used in such circumstances and are of such a nature as to create a clear and present danger that they may bring about the substantive evils that Congress has a right to prevent.". . .

[Here Vinson examines the application of clear and present danger between *Schenck* and *Gitlow*.]

. . .

The rule we deduce from these cases is that where an offense is specified by a statute in nonspeech or nonpress terms, a conviction relying upon speech or press as evidence of violation may be sustained only when the speech or publication created a "clear and present danger" of attempting or accomplishing the prohibited crime, e.g., interference with enlistment. The dissents, we repeat, in emphasizing the value of speech, were addressed to the argument of the sufficiency of the evidence.

The next important case before the Court in which free speech was the crux of the conflict was *Gitlow* v. *New York,* 268 U.S. 652. . . . There New York had made it a crime to "advocate . . . the necessity or propriety of overthrowing . . . the government by force. . . . ." The evidence of violation of the statute was that the defendant had published a Manifesto attacking the Government and capitalism. The convictions were sustained, Justices Holmes and Brandeis dissenting. The majority refused to apply the "clear and present danger" test to the specific utterance. Its reasoning was as follows:

The "clear and present danger" test was applied to the utterance itself in *Schenck* because the question was merely one of sufficiency of evidence under an admittedly constitutional statute. *Gitlow,* however, presented a different question. There a legislature had found that a certain kind of speech was, itself, harmful and unlawful. The constitutionality of such a state statute had to be adjudged by this Court just as it determined the constitutionality of any state statute, namely, whether the statute was "reasonable." Since it was entirely reasonable for a state to attempt to protect itself from violent overthrow, the statute was perforce reasonable. The only question remaining in the case became whether there was evidence to support the conviction, a question which gave the majority no difficulty. Justices Holmes and Brandeis refused to accept this approach, but insisted that wherever speech was the evidence of the violation, it was necessary to show that the speech created the "clear and present danger" of the substantive evil which the legislature had the right to prevent. Justices Holmes and Brandeis, then, made no distinction between a federal statute which made certain acts unlawful, the evidence to support the conviction being speech, and a statute which made speech itself the crime. This approach was emphasized in *Whitney* v. *California,* 274 U.S. 357. . . .

Although no case subsequent to *Whitney* and *Gitlow* has expressly overruled the majority opinions in those cases, there is little doubt that subsequent opinions have inclined toward the Holmes-Brandeis rationale. . . .

In this case we are squarely presented with the application of the "clear and present danger" test, and must decide what that phrase imports. We first note that many of the cases in which this Court has reversed convictions by use of this or similar tests have been based on the fact that the interest which the State was attempting to protect was itself too insubstantial to warrant restriction to speech. . . . Overthrow of the Government by force and violence is certainly a substantial enough interest for the Government to limit speech. Indeed, this is the ultimate value of any society, for if a society cannot protect its very structure from armed internal attack, it must follow that no subordinate value can be protected. If, then, this interest may be protected, the literal problem which is presented is what has been meant by the use of the phrase "clear and present danger" of the utterances bringing about the evil within the power of Congress to punish.

Obviously, the words cannot mean that before the Government may act, it must wait until the *putsch* is about to be executed, the plans have been laid and the signal is awaited. If Government is aware that a group aiming at its overthrow is attempting to indoctrinate its members and to commit them to a course whereby they will strike when the leaders feel the circumstances permit, action by the Government is required. The argument that there is no need for Government to concern itself, for Government is strong, it possesses ample powers to put down a rebellion, it may defeat the revolution with ease needs no answer. For that is not the question. Certainly an attempt to overthrow the Government by force even though doomed from the outset because of inadequate numbers or power of the revolutionists, is a sufficient evil for Congress to prevent. The damage which such attempts create both physically and politically to a nation makes it impossible to measure the validity in terms of the probability of success, or the immediacy of a successful attempt. In the instant case the trial judge charged the jury that they could not convict unless they found that petitioners intended to overthrow the Government "as speedily as circumstances would permit." This does not mean, and could not properly mean, that they would not strike until there was certainty of success. What was meant was that the revolutionists would strike when they thought the time was ripe. We must therefore reject the contention that success or probability of success is the criterion.

The situation with which Justices Holmes and Brandeis were concerned in *Gitlow* was a comparatively isolated event, bearing little relation in their minds to any substantial threat to the safety of the community. . . . They were not confronted with any situation comparable to the instant one—the development of an apparatus designed and dedicated to the overthrow of the Government, in the context of world crisis after crisis.

Chief Judge Learned Hand, writing for the majority below, interpreted the phrase as follows: "In each case [courts] must ask whether the gravity of the 'evil,' discounted by its improbability, justifies such invasion of free speech as is necessary to avoid the danger." 183 F.2d at 212. We adopt this statement of the rule. . . . [I] t is as succinct and inclusive as any other we might devise at this time. It takes into consideration those factors which we deem relevant, and relates their significances. More we cannot expect from words.

Likewise, we are in accord with the court below, which affirmed the trial court's finding that the requisite danger existed. The mere fact that from the period 1945 to 1948 petitioners' activities did not result in an attempt to overthrow the Government by force and violence is of course no answer to the fact that there was a group that was ready to make the attempt. The formation by petitioners of such a highly organized conspiracy, with rigidly disciplined members subject to call when the leaders, these petitioners, felt that the time had come for action, coupled with the inflammable nature of world conditions, similar uprisings in other countries, and the touch-and-go nature of our relations with countries with whom petitioners were in the very least ideologically attuned, convince us that their convictions were justified on this score. And this analysis disposes of the contention that a conspiracy to advocate as distinguished from the advocacy itself, cannot be constitutionally restrained, because it comprises only the preparation. It is the existence of the conspiracy which creates the danger. . . . If the ingredients of the reaction are present, we cannot bind the Government to wait until the catalyst is added.

Although we have concluded that the finding that there was a sufficient danger to warrant the application of the statute was justified on the merits, there remains the problem of whether the trial judge's treatment of the issue was correct. He charged the jury, in relevant part, as follows:

> In further construction and interpretation of the statute I charge you that it is not the abstract doctrine of overthrowing or destroying organized government by unlawful means which is denounced by this law, but the teaching and advocacy of action for the accomplishment of that purpose, by language reasonably and ordinarily calculated to incite persons to such action. Accordingly, you cannot find the defendants or any of them guilty of the crime charged unless you are satisfied beyond a reasonable doubt that they conspired to organize a society, group and assembly of persons who teach and advocate the overthrow or destruction of the Government of the United States by force and violence and to advocate and teach the duty and necessity of overthrowing or destroying the government of the United States by force and violence, with the intent that such teaching and advocacy be of a rule or principle of

action and by language reasonably and ordinarily calculated to incite persons to such action, all with the intent to cause the overthrow or destruction of the Government of the United States by force and violence as speedily as circumstances would permit.

. . .

If you are satisifed that the evidence establishes beyond a reasonable doubt that the defendants, or any of them, are guilty of a violation of the statute, as I have interpreted it to you, I find as a matter of law that there is sufficient danger of a substantive evil that the Congress has a right to prevent to justify the application of the statute under the First Amendment of the Constitution. . . .

It is thus clear that he reserved the question of the existence of the danger for his own determination, and the question becomes whether the issue is of such a nature that it should have been submitted to the jury.

. . . The argument that the action of the trial court is erroneous, in declaring as a matter of law that such violation shows sufficient danger to justify the punishment despite the First Amendment, rests on the theory that a jury must decide a question of the application of the First Amendment. We do not agree.

When facts are found that establish the violation of a statute, the protection against conviction afforded by the First Amendment is a matter of law. The doctrine that there must be a clear and present danger of a substantive evil that Congress has a right to prevent is a judicial rule to be applied as a matter of law by the courts. The guilt is established by proof of facts. Whether the First Amendment protects the activity which constitutes the violation of the statute must depend upon a judicial determination of the scope of the First Amendment applied to the circumstances of the case. . . .

The question in this case is whether the statute which the legislature has enacted may be constitutionally applied. In other words, the Court must examine judicially the application of the statute to the particular situation to ascertain if the Constitution prohibits the conviction. We hold that the statute may be applied where there is a "clear and present danger" of the substantive evil which the legislature had the right to prevent. Bearing, as it does, the marks of a "question of law," the issue is properly one for the judge to decide.

There remains to be discussed the question of vagueness whether the statute as we have interpreted it is too vague, not sufficiently advising those who would speak of the limitations upon their activity. It is urged that such vagueness contravenes the First and Fifth Amendments. This argument is particularly nonpersuasive when presented by petitioners, who, the jury found, intended to overthrow the Government as speedily as circumstances would permit. . . .

We agree that the standard as defined is not a neat, mathematical formulary. Like all verbalizations it is subject to criticism on the score of indefiniteness. But petitioners themselves contend that the verbalization, "clear and present danger," is the proper standard. We see no difference from the standpoint of vagueness, whether the standard of "clear and present danger" is one contained in *haec verba* within the statute, or whether it is the judicial measure of constitutional applicability. We have shown the indeterminate standard the phrase necessarily connotes. We do not think we have rendered that standard any more indefinite by our attempt to sum up the factors which are included within its scope. . . . Where there is doubt as to the intent of the defendants, the nature of their activities, or their power to bring about the evil, this Court will review the convictions with the scrupulous care demanded by our Constitution. But we are not convinced that because there may be borderline cases at some time in the future, these convictions should be reversed because of the argument that these petitioners could not know that their activities were constitutionally proscribed by the statute.

. . .

We hold that sections 2 (a) (1), (2) (a) (3) and 3 of the Smith Act, do not inherently, or as construed or applied in the instant case, violate the First Amendment and other provisions of the Bill of Rights, or the First and Fifth Amendments because of indefiniteness. Petitioners intended to overthrow the Government of the United States as speedily as the circumstances would permit. Their conspiracy to organize the Communist Party and to teach and advocate the overthrow of the Government of the United States by force and violence created a "clear and present danger" of an attempt to overthrow the Government by force and violence. They were properly and constitutionally convicted for violation of the Smith Act. The judgments of conviction are.

Affirmed.

MR. JUSTICE CLARK *took no part in the consideration or decision of this case.*

MR. JUSTICE FRANKFURTER, *concurring in affirmance of the judgment.*

. . .

The demands of free speech in a democratic society as well as the interest in national security are better served by candid and informed weighing of the competing interests, within the confines of the judicial process, than by announcing dogmas too inflexible for the non-Euclidian problems to be solved.

But how are competing interests to be assessed? Since they are not subject to quantitative ascertainment, the issue necessarily resolves itself into asking, who is to make the adjustment —who is to balance the relevant factors and ascertain which interest is in the circumstances to prevail? Full responsibility for the choice cannot be given to the courts. Courts are not representative bodies. They are not designed to be a good

reflex of a democratic society. Their judgment is best informed, and therefore most dependable, within narrow limits. Their essential quality is detachment, founded on independence. History teaches that the independence of the judiciary is jeopardized when courts become embroiled in the passions of the day and assume primary responsibility in choosing between competing political, economic and social pressures.

Primary responsibility for adjusting the interests which compete in the situation before us of necessity belongs to the Congress. The nature of the power to be exercised by this Court has been delineated in decisions not charged with the emotional appeal of situations such as that now before us. We are to set aside the judgment of those whose duty it is to legislate only if there is no reasonable basis for it. . . . [W]e must scrupulously observe the narrow limits of judicial authority even though self-restraint is alone set over us. Above all we must remember that this Court's power of judicial review is not "an exercise of the powers of a super-legislature."

. . .

. . . Unless we are to compromise judicial impartiality and subject these defendants to the risk of an ad hoc judgment influenced by the impregnating atmosphere of the times, the constitutionality of their conviction must be determined by principles established in cases decided in more tranquil periods. If those decisions are to be used as a guide and not as an argument, it is important to view them as a whole and to distrust the easy generalizations to which some of them lend themselves.

[Frankfurter here reviews how the Court has recognized and resolved conflict between speech and competing interests in various types of cases.]

. . .

I must leave to others the ungrateful task of trying to reconcile all these decisions. In some instances we have too readily permitted juries to infer deception from error, or intention from argumentative or critical statements. . . . In other instances we weighted the interest in free speech so heavily that we permitted essential conflicting values to be destroyed. . . . Viewed as a whole, however, the decisions express an attitude toward the judicial function and a standard of values which for me are decisive of the case before us.

First.—Free-speech cases are not an exception to the principle that we are not legislators, that direct policy-making is not our province. How best to reconcile competing interests is the business of legislatures, and the balance they strike is a judgment not to be displaced by ours, but to be respected unless outside the pale of fair judgment.

On occasion we have strained to interpret legislation in order to limit its effect on interests protected by the First Amendment. . . . In some instances we have denied to States the deference to which I think they are entitled. . . .

But in no case has a majority of this Court held that a legislative judgment, even as to freedom of utterance, may be overturned merely because the Court would have made a different choice between the competing interests had the initial legislative judgment been for it to make.

. . .

Second.—A survey of the relevant decisions indicates that the results which we have reached are on the whole those that would ensue from careful weighing of conflicting interests. The complex issues presented by regulation of speech in public places, by picketing, and by legislation prohibiting advocacy of crime have been resolved by scrutiny of many factors besides the imminence and gravity of the evil threatened. The matter has been well summarized by a reflective student of the Court's work.

The truth is that the clear-and-present-danger test is an oversimplified judgment unless it takes account also of a number of other factors: the relative seriousness of the danger in comparison with the value of the occasion for speech or political activity; the availability of more moderate controls than those which the state has imposed; and perhaps the specific intent with which the speech or activity is launched. No matter how rapidly we utter the phrase "clear and present danger," or how closely we hyphenate the words, they are not a substitute for the weighing of values. They tend to convey a delusion of certitude when what is most certain is the complexity of the strands in the web of freedoms which the judge must disentangle. Freund, On Understanding the Supreme Court, 27, 28.   •

. . .

Third.—Not every type of speech occupies the same position on the scale of values. There is no substantial public interest in permitting certain kinds of utterances: "the lewd and obscene, the profane, the libelous, and the insulting or 'fighting' words—those which by their very utterance inflict injury or tend to incite an immediate breach of the peace." *Chaplinsky* v. *New Hampshire*, 315 U.S. 568. . . . We have frequently indicated that the interest in protecting speech depends on the circumstances of the occasion. . . . It is pertinent to the decision before us to consider where on the scale of values we have in the past placed the type of speech now claiming constitutional immunity.

The defendants have been convicted of conspiring to organize a party of persons who advocate the overthrow of the Government by force and violence. . . .

. . . Even though advocacy of overthrow deserves little protection, we should hesitate to prohibit it if we thereby inhibit the interchange of rational ideas so essential to representative government and free society.

But there is underlying validity in the distinction between advocacy and the interchange of ideas, and we do not discard a useful tool because it may be misused. That such a distinction could be used unreasonably by those in power against hostile or unorthodox views does not negate the fact that it may be used reasonably against an organization wielding the power of the centrally controlled international Communist movement. The object of the conspiracy before us is clear enough that the chance of error in saying that the defendants conspired to advocate rather than to express ideas is slight. Mr. Justice Douglas quite properly points out that the conspiracy before us is not a conspiracy to overthrow the Government. But it would be equally wrong to treat it as a seminar in political theory.

These general considerations underlie decision of the case before us.

On the one hand is the interest in security. The Communist Party was not designed by these defendants as an ordinary political party. For the circumstances of its organization, its aims and methods, and the relation of the defendants to its organization and aims we are concluded by the jury's verdict. The jury found that the Party rejects the basic premise of our political system. . . .

. . . But in determining whether application of the statute to the defendants is within the constitutional powers of Congress, we are not limited to the facts found by the jury. We must view such a question in the light of whatever is relevant to a legislative judgment. We may take judicial notice that the Communist doctrines which these defendants have conspired to advocate are in the ascendency in powerful nations who cannot be acquitted of unfriendliness to the institutions of this country. We may take account of evidence brought forward at this trial and elsewhere, much of which has long been common knowledge. In sum, it would amply justify a legislature in concluding that recruitment of additional members for the Party would create a substantial danger to national security.

On the other hand is the interest in free

. . .

speech. The right to exert all governmental powers in aid of maintaining our institutions and resisting their physical overthrow does not include intolerance of opinions and speech that cannot do harm although opposed and perhaps alien to dominant, traditional opinion. The treatment of its minorities, especially their legal position, is among the most searching tests of the level of civilization attained by a society. It is better for those who have almost unlimited power of government in their hands to err on the side of freedom. We have enjoyed so much freedom for so long that we are perhaps in danger of forgetting how much blood it cost to establish the Bill of Rights.

. . . Suppressing advocates of overthrow inevitably will also silence critics who do not advocate overthrow but fear that their criticism may be so construed. No matter how clear we may be that the defendants now before us are preparing to overthrow our Government at the propitious moment, it is self-delusion to think that we can punish them for their advocacy without adding to the risks run by loyal citizens who honestly believe in some of the reforms these defendants advance. It is a sobering fact that in sustaining the conviction before us we can hardly escape restriction on the interchange of ideas.

. . .

It is not for us to decide how we would adjust the clash of interests which this case presents were the primary responsibility for reconciling it ours. Congress has determined that the danger created by advocacy of overthrow justifies the ensuing restriction on freedom of speech. The determination was made after due deliberation, and the seriousness of the congressional purpose is attested by the volume of legislation passed to effectuate the same ends.

Can we then say that the judgment Congress exercised was denied it by the Constitution? Can we establish a constitutional doctrine which forbids the elected representatives of the people to make this choice? Can we hold that the First Amendment deprives Congress of what it deemed necessary for the Government's protection?

To make validity of legislation depend on judicial reading of events still in the womb of time—a forecast, that is, of the outcome of forces at best appreciated only with knowledge of the topmost secrets of nations—is to charge the judiciary with duties beyond its equipment.

. . .

MR. JUSTICE JACKSON, *concurring.*

The Communist Party . . . does not seek its strength primarily in numbers. Its aim is a relatively small party whose strength is in selected, dedicated, indoctrinated, and rigidly disciplined members. From established policy it tolerates no deviation and no debate. It seeks members that are, or may be, secreted in strategic posts in transportation, communications, industry, government, and especially in labor unions where it can compel employers to accept and retain its members. It also seeks to infiltrate and control organizations of professional and other groups. Through these placements in positions of power it seeks a leverage over society that will make up in power of coercion what it lacks in power of persuasion.

The Communists have no scruples against sabotage, terrorism, assassination, or mob disorder; but violence is not with them, as with the anarchists, an end in itself. The Communist Party advocates force only when prudent and profitable. Their strategy of stealth precludes premature or uncoordinated outbursts of violence, except, of course, when the blame will be placed on shoulders other than their own. They resort to violence as to truth, not as a principle but as an expedient. Force or violence, as they would resort to it, may never be necessary, because infiltration and deception may be enough.

Force would be utilized by the Communist Party not to destroy government but for its capture.

. . .

The foregoing is enough to indicate that, either by accident or design, the Communist strategem outwits the anti-anarchist pattern of statute aimed against "overthrow by force and violence" if qualified by the doctrine that only "clear and present danger" of accomplishing that result will sustain the prosecution.

The "clear-and-present-danger" test was an innovation by Mr. Justice Holmes in the Schenck Case, reiterated and refined by him and Mr. Justice Brandeis in later cases, all arising before the era of World War II revealed the subtlety and efficacy of modernized revolutionary techniques used by totalitarian parties. In those cases, they were faced with convictions under so-called criminal syndicalism statutes aimed at anarchists but which, loosely construed, had been applied to punish socialism, pacifism, and left-wing ideologies, the charges often resting on far-fetched inferences which, if true, would establish only technical or trivial violations. They proposed "clear and present danger" as a test for the sufficiency of evidence in particular cases.

I would save it, unmodified, for application as a "rule of reason" in the kind of case for which it was devised. When the issue is criminality of a hot-headed speech on a street corner, or circulation of a few incendiary pamphlets, or parading by some zealots behind a red flag, or refusal of a handful of school children to salute our flag, it is not beyond the capacity of the judicial process to gather, comprehend, and weigh the necessary materials for decision whether it is a clear and present danger of substantive evil or a harmless letting off of steam. It is not a prophecy, for the danger in such cases has matured by the time of trial or it was never present. The test applies and has meaning where a conviction is sought to be based on a speech or writing which does not directly or explicitly advocate a crime but to which such tendency is sought to be attributed by construction or by implication from external circumstances. The formula in such cases favors freedoms that are vital to our society, and, even if sometimes applied too generously, the consequences cannot be grave. But its recent expansion has extended, in particular to Communists, unprecedented immunities. Unless we are to hold our Government captive in a judge-made verbal trap, we must approach the problem of a well-organized nation-wide conspiracy, such as I have described, as realistically as our predecessors faced the trivialities that were being prosecuted until they were checked with a rule of reason.

I think reason is lacking for applying that test to this case.

If we must decide that this Act and its application are constitutional only if we are convinced that petitioners' conduct creates a "clear and present danger" of violent overthrow, we must appraise imponderables, including international and national phenomena which baffle the best informed foreign offices and our most experienced politicians. We would have to foresee and predict the effectiveness of Communist propaganda, opportunities for infiltration, whether, and when, a time will come that they consider propitious for action, and whether and how fast our existing government will deteriorate. And we would have to speculate as to whether an approaching Communist coup would not be anticipated by a nationalistic fascist movement. No doctrine can be sound whose application requires us to make a prophecy of that sort in the guise of a legal decision. The judicial process simply is not adequate to a trial of such far-flung issues. The answers given would reflect our own political predilections and nothing more.

The authors of the clear-and-present-danger test never applied it to a case like this, nor would I. If applied as it is proposed here, it means that the Communist plotting is protected during its period of incubation; its preliminary stages of organization and preparation are immune from

the law; the Government can move only after imminent action is manifest, when it would, of course, be too late.

...

What really is under review here is a conviction of conspiracy, after a trial for conspiracy, on an indictment charging conspiracy, brought under a statute outlawing conspiracy. With due respect to my colleagues, they seem to me to discuss anything under the sun except the law of conspiracy. One of the dissenting opinions even appears to chide me for "invoking the law of conspiracy." As that is the case before us, it may be more amazing that its reversal can be proposed without even considering the law of conspiracy.

...

I do not suggest that Congress could punish conspiracy to advocate something, the doing of which it may not punish. Advocacy or exposition of the doctrine of communal property ownership, or any political philosophy unassociated with advocacy of its imposition by force or seizure of government by unlawful means would not be reached through conspiracy prosecution. But it is not forbidden to punish its teaching or advocacy, and the end being punishable, there is no doubt of the power to punish conspiracy for the purpose.

...

While I think there was power in Congress to enact this statute and that, as applied in this case, it cannot be held unconstitutional, I add that I have little faith in the long-range effectiveness of this conviction to stop the rise of the Communist movement. Communism will not go to jail with these Communists. No decision by this Court can forestall revolution whenever the existing government fails to command the respect and loyalty of the people and sufficient distress and discontent is allowed to grow up among the masses. Many failures by fallen governments attest that no government can long prevent revolution by outlawry. Corruption, ineptitude, inflation, oppressive taxation, militarization, injustice, and loss of leadership capable of intellectual initiative in domestic or foreign affairs are allies on which the Communists count to bring opportunity knocking to their door. Sometimes I think they may be mistaken. But the Communists are not building just for today—the rest of us might profit by their example.

MR. JUSTICE BLACK dissenting.

. . .

At the outset I want to emphasize what the crime involved in this case is, and what it is not. These petitioners were not charged with an attempt to overthrow the Government. They were not charged with overt acts of any kind designed to overthrow the Government. They were not even charged with saying anything or writing anything designed to overthrow the Government. The charge was that they agreed to assemble and to talk and publish certain ideas at a later date. The indictment is that they conspired to organize the Communist Party and to use speech or newspapers and other publications in the future to teach and advocate the forcible overthrow of the Government. No matter how it is worded, this is a virulent form of prior censorship of speech and press, which I believe the First Amendment forbids. I would hold section 3 of the Smith Act authorizing this prior restraint unconstitutional on its face and as applied.

. . .

So long as this Court exercises the power of judicial review of legislation, I cannot agree that the First Amendment permits us to sustain laws suppressing freedom of speech and press on the basis of Congress' or our own notions of mere "reasonableness." Such a doctrine waters down the First Amendment so that it amounts to little

more than an admonition to Congress. The Amendment as so construed is not likely to protect any but those "safe" or orthodox views which rarely need its protection. . . .

Public opinion being what it now is, few will protest the conviction of these Communist petitioners. There is hope, however, that in calmer times, when present pressures, passions and fears subside, this or some later Court will restore the First Amendment liberties to the high preferred place where they belong in a free society.

MR. JUSTICE DOUGLAS, dissenting.

If this were a case where those who claimed protection under the First Amendment were teaching the techniques of sabotage, the assassination of the President, the filching of documents from public files, the planting of bombs, the art of street warfare, and the like, I would have no doubt. The freedom to speak is not absolute; the teaching of methods of terror and other seditious conduct should be beyond the pale along with obscenity and immorality. This case was argued as if those were the facts. The argument imported much seditious conduct into the record. That is easy and it has popular appeal, for the activities of Communists in plotting and scheming against the free world are common knowledge. But the fact is that no such evidence was introduced at the trial. There is a statute which makes a seditious conspiracy unlawful. Petitioners, however, were not charged with a "conspiracy to overthrow" the Government. They were charged with a conspiracy to form a party and groups and assemblies of people who teach and advocate the overthrow of our Government by force or violence and with a conspiracy to advocate and teach its overthrow by force and violence. It may well be that indoctrination in the techniques of terror to destroy the Government would be indictable under either statute. But the teaching which is condemned here is of a different character.

So far as the present record is concerned, what petitioners did was to organize people to teach and themselves teach the Marxist-Leninist doctrine contained chiefly in four books: Foundations of Leninism by Stalin (1924), The Communist Manifesto by Marx and Engels (1848), State and Revolution by Lenin (1917), History of the Communist Party of the Soviet Union (B) (1939).

Those books are to Soviet Communism what Mein Kampf was to Nazism. If they are understood, the ugliness of Communism is revealed, its deceit and cunning are exposed, the nature of its activities becomes apparent, and the chances of its success less likely. That is not, of course, the reason why petitioners chose these books for their classrooms. They are fervent Communists to whom these volumes are gospel. They preached the creed with the hope that some day it would be acted upon.

The opinion of the Court does not outlaw these texts nor condemn them to the fire, as the Communists do literature offensive to their creed. But if the books themselves are not outlawed, if they can lawfully remain on library shelves, by what reasoning does their use in a classroom become a crime? It would not be a crime under the Act to introduce these books to a class, though that would be teaching what the creed of violent overthrow of government is. The Act, as construed, requires the element of intent—that those who teach the creed believe in it. The crime then depends not on what is taught but on who the teacher is. That is to make freedom of speech turn not on *what is said,* but on the intent with which it is said. Once we start down that road we enter territory dangerous to the liberties of every citizen.

. . .

Free speech has occupied an exalted position because of the high service it has given our society. Its protection is essential to the very existence of a democracy. The airing of ideas releases pressures which otherwise might become destructive. When ideas compete in the market for acceptance, full and free discussion exposes the false and they gain few adherents. Full and free discussion even of ideas we hate encourages the testing of our own prejudices and preconceptions. Full and free discussion keeps a society from becoming stagnant and unprepared for the stresses and strains that work to tear all civilizations apart.

Full and free discussion has indeed been the first article of our faith. We have founded our political system on it. It has been the safeguard of every religious, political, philosophical, economic, and racial group amongst us. We have counted on it to keep us from embracing what is cheap and false; we have trusted the common sense of our people to choose the doctrine true to our genius and to reject the rest. This has been the one single outstanding tenet that has made our institutions the symbol of freedom and equality. We have deemed it more costly to liberty to suppress a despised minority than to let them vent their spleen. We have above all else feared the political censor. We have wanted a land where our people can be exposed to all the diverse creeds and cultures of the world.

There comes a time when even speech loses its constitutional immunity. Speech innocuous one year may at another time fan such destructive flames that it must be halted in the interests of the safety of the Republic. That is the meaning of the clear and present danger test. When conditions are so critical that there will be no time to avoid the evil that the speech threatens, it is time to call a halt. Otherwise, free speech which is the strength of the Nation will be the cause of its destruction.

Yet free speech is the rule, not the exception. The restraint to be constitutional must be based on more than fear, on more than passionate opposition against the speech, on more than a revolted dislike for its contents. There must be some immediate injury to society that is likely if speech is allowed.

The nature of Communism as a force on the world scene would, of course, be relevant to the issue of clear and present danger of petitioners' advocacy within the United States. But the primary consideration is the strength and tactical position of petitioners and their converts in this country. On that there is no evidence in the record. If we are to take judicial notice of the threat of Communists within the nation, it should not be difficult to conclude that *as a political party* they are of little consequence. Communists in this country have never made a respectable or serious showing in any election. I would doubt that there is a village, let alone a city or country or state, which the Communists could carry. Communism in the world scene is no bogey-man; but Communists as a political faction or party in this country plainly is. Communism has been so thoroughly exposed in this country that it has been crippled as a political force. Free speech has destroyed it as an effective political party. It is inconceivable that those who went up and down this country preaching the doctrine of revolution which petitioners espouse would have any success. In days of trouble and confusion when bread lines were long, when the unemployed walked the streets, when people were starving, the advocates of a shortcut by revolution might have a chance to gain adherents. But today there are no such conditions. The country is not in despair; the people know Soviet Communism; the doctrine of Soviet revolution is exposed in all of its ugliness and the American people want none of it.

How it can be said that there is a clear and present danger that this advocacy will succeed is, therefore, a mystery. Some nations less resilient than the United States, where illiteracy is high and where democratic traditions are only budding, might have to take drastic steps and jail these men for merely speaking their creed. But in America they are miserable merchants of unwanted ideas; their wares remain unsold. The fact that their ideas are abhorrent does not make them powerful.

The political impotence of the Communists in this country does not, of course, dispose of the problem. Their numbers; their positions in industry and government; the extent to which they have in fact infiltrated the police, the armed services, transportation, stevedoring, power plants, munitions works, and other critical places—these facts all bear on the likelihood that their advocacy of the Soviet theory of revolution will endanger the Republic. But the record is silent on these facts. If we are to proceed on the basis of judicial notice, it is impossible for me to say that the Communists in this country are so potent or so strategically deployed that they must be suppressed for their speech. I could not so hold unless I were willing to conclude that the activities in recent years of committees of Congress, of the Attorney General, of labor unions, of state legislatures, and of Loyalty Boards were so futile as to leave the country on the edge of grave peril. To believe that petitioners and their following are placed in such critical positions as to endanger the Nation is to believe the incredible. It is safe to say that the followers of the creed of Soviet Communism are known to the F.B.I.; that in case of war with Russia they will be picked up overnight as were all prospective saboteurs at the commencement of World War II; that the invisible army of petitioners is the best known, the most beset, and the least thriving of any fifth column in history. Only those held by fear and panic could think otherwise.

. . .

The First Amendment provides that "Congress shall make no law . . . abridging the freedom of speech." The Constitution provides no exception. This does not mean, however, that the Nation need hold its hand until it is in such weakened condition that there is not time to protect itself from incitement to revolution. Seditious conduct can always be punished. But the command of the First Amendment is so clear that we should not allow Congress to call a halt to free speech except in the extreme case of peril from the speech itself. The First Amendment makes confidence in the common sense of our people and in their maturity of judgment the great postulate of our democracy. Its philosophy is that violence is rarely, if ever, stopped by denying civil liberties to those advocating resort to force. The First Amendment reflects the philosophy of Jefferson "that it is time enough for the rightful purposes of civil government for its officers to interfere when principles break out into overt acts against peace and good order." The political censor has no place in our public debates. Unless and until extreme and necessitous circumstances are shown, our aim should be to keep speech unfettered and to allow the processes of law to be invoked only when the provocateurs among us move from speech to action.

Vishinsky wrote in 1948 in The Law of the Soviet State, "In our state, naturally there can be no place for freedom of speech, press, and so on for the foes of socialism."

Our concern should be that we accept no such standard for the United States. Our faith should be that our people will never give support to these advocates of revolution, so long as we remain loyal to the purposes for which our Nation was founded.

BRANDENBURG v. OHIO
395 U.S. 444; 23 L. Ed. 2d 430; 89 S. Ct. 1827 (1969)

Per Curiam.

The appellant, a leader of a Ku Klux Klan group, was convicted under the Ohio Criminal Syndicalism statute of "advocat[ing] ... the duty, necessity, or propriety of crime, sabotage, violence, or unlawful methods of terrorism as a means of accomplishing industrial or political reform" and of "voluntarily assembl[ing] with any society, group or assemblage of persons formed to teach or advocate the doctrines of criminal syndicalism." He was fined $1,000 and sentenced to one to 10 years' imprisonment. The appellant challenged the constitutionality of the ... statute under the First and Fourteenth Amendments to the United States Constitution, but the intermediate appellate court of Ohio affirmed his conviction without opinion. The Supreme Court of Ohio dismissed his appeal, *sua sponte,* "for the reason that no substantial constitutional question exists herein." ... We reverse.

The record shows that a man, identified at trial as the appellant, telephoned an announcer-reporter on the staff of a Cincinnati television station and invited him to come to a Ku Klux Klan "rally" to be held at a farm in Hamilton County. With the cooperation of the organizers, the reporter and a cameraman attended the meeting and filmed the events. Portions of the films were later broadcast on the local station and on a national network.

The prosecution's case rested on the films and on testimony identifying the appellant as the person who communicated with the reporter and who spoke at the rally. The State also introduced into evidence several articles appearing in the film, including a pistol, a rifle, a shotgun, ammunition, a Bible, and red hood worn by the speaker in the films.

One film showed 12 hooded figures, some of whom carried firearms. They were gathered around a large wooden cross, which they burned. No one was present other than the participants and the newsmen who made the film. Most of the words uttered during the scene were incomprehensible when the film was projected, but scattered phrases could be understood that were derogatory of Negroes and, in one instance, of Jews.[1] Another scene on the same film showed the appellant, in Klan regalia, making a speech. The speech, in full, was as follows:

This is an organizers' meeting. We have had quite a few members here today which are— we have hundreds, hundreds of members throughout the State of Ohio. I can quote from a newspaper clipping from the Columbus Ohio Dispatch, five weeks ago Sunday morning. The Klan has more members in the State of Ohio than does any other organization. We're not a revengent organization, but if our President, our Congress, our Supreme Court, continues to suppress the white, Caucasian race, it's possible that there might have to be some revengence taken.

We are marching on Congress July the Fourth, four hundred thousand strong. From there we are dividing into two groups, one group to march on St. Augustine, Florida, the other group to march into Mississippi. Thank you.

The second film showed six hooded figures one of whom, later identified as the appellant, repeated a speech very similar to that recorded on the first film. The reference to the possibility

[1] The significant phrases that could be understood were:
"How far is the nigger going to—yeah"
"This is what we are going to do to the niggers"
"A dirty nigger"
"Send the Jews back to Israel"
"Let's give them back to the dark garden"
"Save America"
"Let's go back to constitutional betterment"
"Bury the niggers"
"We intend to do our part"
"Give us our state rights"
"Freedom for the whites"
"Nigger will have to fight for every inch he gets from now on."

of "revengence" was omitted, and one sentence was added: "Personally, I believe the nigger should be returned to Africa, the Jew returned to Israel." Though some of the figures in the films carried weapons, the speaker did not.

The Ohio Criminal Syndicalism Statute was enacted in 1919. . . . In 1927, this Court sustained the constitutionality of California's Criminal Syndicalism Act, the text of which is quite similar to that of the laws of Ohio. *Whitney* v. *California,* 274 U.S. 357 (1927). The Court upheld the statute on the ground that, without more, "advocating" violent means to effect political and economic change involves such danger to the security of the State that the State may outlaw it. But *Whitney* has been throughly discredited by later decisions. See *Dennis* v. *United States,* 341 U.S. 494, at 507 (1951). These later decisions have fashioned the principle that the constitutional guarantees of free speech and free press do not permit a State to forbid or proscribe advocacy of the use of force or of law violation except where such advocacy is directed to inciting or producing imminent lawless action and is likely to incite or produce such action. As we said in *Noto* v. *United States,* 367 U.S. 290, 297–298 (1961), "the mere abstract teaching . . . of the moral propriety or even moral necessity for a resort to force and violence, is not the same as preparing a group for violent action and steeling it to such action." A statute which fails to draw this distinction impermissibly intrudes upon the freedoms guaranteed by the First and Fourteenth Amendments. It sweeps within its condemnation speech which our Constitution has immunized from governmental control. . . .

Measured by this test, Ohio's Criminal Syndicalism Act cannot be sustained. The Act punishes persons who "advocate or teach the duty, necessity, or propriety" of violence "as a means of accomplishing industrial or political reform"; or who publish or circulate or display any book or paper containing such advocacy; or who "justify" the commission of violent acts "with intent to exemplify, spread or advocate the propriety of the doctrines of criminal syndicalism"; or who"... voluntarily assemble" with a group formed "to teach or advocate the doctrines of criminal syndicalism." Neither the indictment nor the trial judge's instructions to the jury in any way refined the statute's bald definition of the crime in terms of mere advocacy not distinguished from incitement to imminent lawless action.

Accordingly, we are here confronted with a statute which, by its own words and as applied, purports to punish mere advocacy and to forbid, on pain of criminal punishment, assembly with others merely to advocate the described type of action. Such a statute falls within the condemnation of the First and Fourteenth Amendments. The contrary teaching of *Whitney* v. *California; supra,* cannot be supported, and that decision is therefore overruled.

Reversed.

MR. JUSTICE DOUGLAS, *concurring.*

While I join the opinion of the Court, I desire to enter a *caveat.*

The "clear and present danger" test was adumbrated by Mr. Justice Holmes in a case arising during World War I.... The case was *Schenck* v. *United States,* 249 U.S. 47, where the defendant was charged with attempts to cause insubordination in the military and obstruction of enlistment. The pamphlets that were distributed urged resistance to the draft, denounced conscription, and impugned the motives of those backing the war effort. The First Amendment was tendered as a defense. Mr. Justice Holmes in rejecting that defense said:

The question in every case is whether the words used are used in such circumstances and are of such a nature as to create a clear and present danger that they will bring about the substantive evils that Congress has a right to prevent. It is a question of proximity and degree.

Frohwerk v. *United States,* 249 U.S. 204, also authored by Mr. Justice Holmes, involved prosecution and punishment for publication of articles very critical of the war effort in World War I. *Schenck* was referred to as a conviction for obstructing security "by words of persuasion." And the conviction in *Frohwerk* was sustained because "the circulation of the paper was in quarters where a little breath would be enough to kindle a flame."

Debs v. *United States,* 249 U.S. 211, was the third of the trilogy of the 1918 Term. Debs was convicted of speaking in opposition to the war where his "opposition was so expressed that its natural and intended effect would be to obstruct recruiting."...

In the 1919 Term, the Court applied the Schenck doctrine to affirm the convictions of other dissidents in World War I. *Abrams* v. *United States,* 250 U.S. 616, was one instance. Mr. Justice Holmes, with whom Mr. Justice Brandeis concurred, dissented....

Another instance was *Schaefer* v. *United States,* 251 U.S. 466, in which Mr. Justice Brandeis, joined by Mr. Justice Holmes, dissented. A third was *Pierce* v. *United States,* 252 U.S. 239, in which Mr. Justice Brandeis, joined by Mr. Justice Holmes, dissented.

Those then were the *World War I* cases that put the gloss of "clear and present danger" on the First Amendment. Whether the war power— the greatest leveler of them all—is adequate to sustain that doctrine is debatable. The dissents in *Abrams, Schaefer,* and *Pierce* show how easily "clear and present danger" is manipulated to crush what Brandeis called "the fundamental right of free men to strive for better conditions through new legislation and new institutions" by argument and discourse (*Pierce* v. *United States, supra,* at 273) even in time of war. Though I doubt if the "clear and present danger" test is congenial to the First Amendment in time of a declared war, I am certain it is not reconcilable with the First Amendment in days of peace.

The Court quite properly overrules *Whitney* v.

California which involved advocacy for ideas which the majority of the Court deemed unsound and dangerous.

Mr. Justice Holmes, though never formally abandoning the "clear and present danger" test, moved closer to the First Amendment ideal when he said in dissent in *Gitlow:*

> Every idea is an incitement. If offers itself for belief and if believed it is acted on unless some other belief outweighs it or some failure of energy stifles the movement at its birth. The only difference between the expression of an opinion and an incitement in the narrower sense is the speaker's enthusiasm for the result. Eloquence may set fire to reason. But whatever may be thought of the redundant discourse before us it had no chance of starting a present conflagration. If in the long run the beliefs expressed in proletarian dictatorship are destined to be accepted by the dominant forces of the community, the only meaning of free speech is that they should be given their chance and have their way.

We have never been faithful to the philosophy of that dissent.

The Court in *Herndon* v. *Lowry,* 301 U.S. 242, overturned a conviction for exercising First Amendment rights to incite insurrection because of lack of evidence of incitement. In *Bridges* v. *California,* 314 U.S. 252, 261–263, we approved the "clear and present danger" test in an elaborate dictum that tightened it and confined it to a narrow category. But in *Dennis* v. *United States,* 341 U.S. 494, we opened wide the door, distorting the "clear and present danger" test beyond recognition.

In that case the prosecution dubbed an agreement to teach the Marxist creed—a "conspiracy." The case was submitted to a jury on a charge that the jury could not convict unless they found the defendants "intended to overthrow the government 'as speedily as circumstances would permit.' " The Court sustained convictions under that charge, construing it to mean a determination of "whether the gravity of the 'evil, discounted by its improbability, justifies such invasion of free speech as is necessary to avoid the danger.' "

Out of the "clear and present danger" test came other offspring. Advocacy and teaching of forcible overthrow of government as an abstract principle is immune from prosecution. *Yates* v. *United States,* 354 U.S. 298, 318. But an "active" member, who has a guilty knowledge and intent of the aim to overthrow the Government by violence, *Noto* v. *United States,* 367 U.S. 290, may be prosecuted. *Scales* v. *United States,* 367 U.S. 203. And the power to investigate, backed by the powerful sanction of contempt, includes the power to determine which of the two categories fits the particular witness. *Barenblatt* v. *United States,* 360 U.S. 109. And so the investigator roams at will through all of the beliefs of the witness, ransacking his conscience and his innermost thoughts.

Judge Learned Hand who wrote for the Court of Appeals in affirming the judgment in *Dennis,* coined the "not improbable" test which this Court adopted and which Judge Hand preferred over the "clear and present danger" test. Indeed, in his book, The Bill of Rights, p. 59 (1958), in referring to Holmes' creation of the "clear and present danger" test, he said, "I cannot help thinking that for once Homer nodded."

My own view is quite different. I see no place in the regime of the First Amendment for any "clear and present danger" test whether strict and tight as some would make it or freewheeling as the Court in *Dennis* rephrased it.

When one reads the opinions closely and sees when and how the "clear and present danger" test has been applied, great misgivings are aroused. First, the threats were often loud but always puny and made serious only by judges so wedded to the *status quo* that critical analysis made them nervous. Second, the test was so twisted and perverted in *Dennis* as to make the trial of those teachers of Marxism an all-out political trial which was part and parcel of the

Cold War that has eroded substantial parts of the First Amendment.

Action is often a method of expression and within the protection of the First Amendment.

Suppose one tears up his own copy of the Constitution in eloquent protest to a decision of this Court. May he be indicted?

Suppose one rips his own Bible to shreds to celebrate his departure from one "faith" and his embrace of atheism. May he be indicted?

Last Term the Court held in *United States* v. *O'Brien,* 391 U.S. 367, that a registrant under Selective Service who burned his draft card in protest to the war in Vietnam could be prosecuted. The First Amendment was tendered as a defense and rejected. . . .

But O'Brien was not prosecuted for not having his draft card available when asked for it by a federal agent. He was indicted, tried and convicted for burning the card. And this Court's affirmance of that conviction was not, with all respect, consistent with the First Amendment.

The act of praying often involves body posture and movement as well as utterances. It is nonetheless protected by the Free Exercise Clause. Picketing, as we have said on numerous occasions, is "free speech plus." . . . That means that it can be regulated when it comes to the "plus" or "action" side of the protest. It can be regulated as to the number of pickets and the place and hours because traffic and other community problems would otherwise suffer.

But none of these considerations are implicated in the symbolic protest to the Vietnam war in the burning of a draft card.

One's beliefs have long been thought to be sanctuaries which government could not invade. *Barenblatt* is one example of the ease with which that sanctuary can be violated. The lines drawn by the Court between the criminal act of being an "active" Communist and the innocent act of being a nominal or inactive Communist mark the difference only between deep and abiding belief and casual or uncertain belief. But I think that all matters of belief are beyond the reach of subpoenas or the probings of investigators. That is why the invasions of privacy made by investigating committees was notoriously unconstitutional. That is the deepseated fault in the infamous loyalty-security hearings which, since 1947 when Truman launched them, have processed 20,000,000 men and women. Those hearings were primarily concerned with one's thoughts, ideas, beliefs, and convictions. They were the most blatant violations of the First Amendment we have ever known.

The line between what is permissible and not subject to control and what may be made impermissible and subject to regulation is the line between ideas and overt acts.

The example usually given by those who punish speech is the case of one who falsely shouts fire in a crowded theatre.

This is, however, a classic case where speech is brigaded with action. They are indeed inseparable and a prosecution can be launched for the overt acts actually caused. Apart from rare instances of that kind, speech is, I think, immune from prosecution. Certainly there is no constitutional line between advocacy of abstract ideas as in *Yates* and advocacy of political action as in *Scales.* The quality of advocacy turns on the depth of the conviction; and government has no power to invade that sanctuary of belief and conscience.

BARENBLATT v. UNITED STATES
360 U.S. 109; 3 L. Ed. 2d 1115; 79 S.Ct. 1081 (1959)

MR. JUSTICE HARLAN *delivered the opinion of the Court.*

Once more the Court is required to resolve the conflicting constitutional claims of congressional power and of an individual's right to resist its exercise.... In the present case congressional efforts to learn the extent of a nationwide, indeed world wide, problem have brought one of its investigating committees into the field of education. Of course, broadly viewed, inquiries cannot be made into the teaching that is pursued in any of our educational institutions. When academic teaching-freedom and its corollary learning-freedom, so essential to the well-being of the Nation, are claimed, this Court will always be on the alert against intrusion by Congress into this constitutionally protected domain. But this does not mean that the Congress is precluded from interrogating a witness merely because he is a teacher. An educational institution is not a constitutional sanctuary from inquiry into matters that may otherwise be within the constitutional legislative domain merely for the reason that inquiry is made of someone within its walls. ...

We here review petitioner's conviction . . . for contempt of Congress, arising from his refusal to answer certain questions put to him by a Subcommittee of the House Committee on Un-American Activities during the course of an inquiry concerning alleged Communist infiltration into the field of education. ...

The case is before us for the second time. Petitioner's conviction was originally affirmed in 1957 by a unanimous panel of the Court of Appeals, 100 App DC 13, 240 F.2d 875. This Court granted certiorari, vacated the judgment of the Court of Appeals, and remanded the case to that court for further consideration in light of *Watkins* v. *United States,* 354 U.S. 178 which had reversed a contempt of Congress conviction, and which was decided after the Court of Appeals' decision here had issued. Thereafter the Court of Appeals, sitting en banc, reaffirmed the conviction by a divided court. ...

Pursuant to a subpoena, and accompanied by counsel, petitioner on June 28, 1954, appeared as a witness before this congressional Subcommittee. After answering a few preliminary questions and testifying that he had been a graduate student and teaching fellow at the University of Michigan from 1947 to 1950 and an instructor in psychology at Vassar College from 1950 to shortly before his appearance before the Subcommittee, petitioner objected generally to the right of the Subcommittee to inquire into his "political" and "religious" beliefs or any "other personal and private affairs" or "associational activities," upon grounds set forth in a previously prepared memorandum which he was allowed to file with the Subcommittee. Thereafter petitioner specifically declined to answer each of the following five questions:

> "Are you now a member of the Communist Party?" [Count One.]
> "Have you ever been a member of the Communist Party?" [Count Two.]
> ..."Did you know Francis Crowley as a member of the Communist Party?" [Count Three.]
> "Were you ever a member of the Haldane Club of the Communist Party while at the University of Michigan?" [Count Four.]

"Were you a member while a student of the University of Michigan Council of Arts, Sciences, and Professions?" [Count Five.]

In each instance the grounds of refusal were those set forth in the prepared statement. Petitioner expressly disclaimed reliance upon "the Fifth Amendment."....

Petitioner's various contentions resolve themselves into three propositions: First, the compelling of testimony by the Subcommittee was neither legislatively authorized nor constitutionally permissible because of the vagueness of Rule XI of the House of Representatives, Eighty-Third Congress, the charter of authority of the parent Committee. Second, petitioner was not adequately appraised of the pertinency of the Subcommittee's questions to the subject matter of the inquiry. Third, the questions petitioner refused to answer infringed rights protected by the First Amendment.

Subcommittee's Authority to Compel Testimony

At the outset it should be noted that Rule XI authorized this Subcommittee to compel testimony within the framework of the investigative authority conferred on the Un-American Activities Committee. Petitioner contends that *Watkins* v. *United States* nevertheless held the grant of this power in all circumstances ineffective because of the vagueness of Rule XI in delineating the Committee jurisdiction to which its exercise was to be appurtenant. . . .

The *Watkins Case* cannot properly be read as standing for such a proposition. A principal contention in *Watkins* was that the refusals to answer were justified because the requirement of 2 USC section 192 that the questions asked be "pertinent to the question under inquiry" had not been satisfied. This Court reversed the conviction solely on that ground, holding that *Watkins* had not been adequately apprised of the subject matter of the Subcommittee's investi-

gation or the pertinency thereto of the questions he refused to answer. . . .

Petitioner also contends, independently of *Watkins*, that the vagueness of Rule XI deprived the Subcommittee of the right to compel testimony in this investigation into Communist activity. We cannot agree with this contention, which in its furthest reach would mean that the House Un-American Activities Committee under its existing authority has no right to compel testimony in any circumstances. Granting the vagueness of the Rule, we may not read it in isolation from its long history in the House of Representatives. . . .

In light of this long and illuminating history it can hardly be seriously argued that the investigation of Communist activities generally, and the attendant use of compulsory process, was beyond the purview of the Committee's intended authority under Rule XI. . . .

Pertinency Claim

Undeniably a conviction for contempt under 2 USC section 192 cannot stand unless the questions asked are pertinent to the subject matter of the investigation. But the factors which led us to rest decision on this ground in *Watkins* were very different from those involved here.

In *Watkins* the petitioner had made specific objection to the Subcommittee's questions on the ground of pertinency; the question under inquiry had not been disclosed in any illuminating manner; and the questions asked the petitioner were not only amorphous on their face, but in some instances clearly foreign to the alleged subject matter of the investigation—"Communism in labor."

In contrast, petitioner in the case before us raised no objections on the ground of pertinency at the time any of the questions were put to him. It is true that the memorandum which petitioner brought with him to the Subcommittee hearing contained the statement, "to ask me whether I am or have been a member of the Communist

Party may have dire consequences. I might wish to . . . challenge the pertinency of the question to the investigation.". . . These statements cannot, however, be accepted as the equivalent of a pertinency objection. At best they constituted but a contemplated objection to questions still unasked, and buried as they were in the context of petitioner's general challenge to the power of the Subcommittee they can hardly be considered adequate, within the meaning of what was said in *Watkins* to trigger what would have been the Subcommittee's reciprocal obligation had it been faced with a pertinency objection.

We need not, however, rest decision on petitioner's failure to object on this score, for here "pertinency" was made to appear "with undisputable clarity.". . . In light of his prepared memorandum of constitutional objections there can be no doubt that this petitioner was well aware of the Subcommittee's authority and purpose to question him as it did. . . . The subject matter of the inquiry had been identified at the commencement of the investigation as Communist infiltration into the field of education. . . .

Petitioner's contentions on this aspect of the case cannot be sustained.

Constitutional Contentions

The precise constitutional issue confronting us is whether the Subcommittee's inquiry into petitioner's past or present membership in the Communist Party transgressed the provisions of the First Amendment. . . .

. . . Undeniably, the First Amendment in some circumstances protects an individual from being compelled to disclose his associational relationships. However, the protections of the First Amendment, unlike a proper claim of the privilege against self-incrimination under the Fifth Amendment, do not afford a witness the right to resist inquiry in all circumstances. Where First Amendment rights are asserted to bar governmental interrogation, resolution of the issue always involves a balancing by the courts of the competing private and public interests at stake in the particular circumstances shown. . . .

The first question is whether this investigation was related to a valid legislative purpose, for Congress may not constitutionally require an individual to disclose his political relationships or other private affairs except in relation to such a purpose.

That Congress has wide power to legislate in the field of Communist activity in this Country, and to conduct appropriate investigations in aid thereof, is hardly debatable. The existence of such power has never been questioned by this Court, and it is sufficient to say, without particularization, that Congress has enacted or considered in this field a wide range of legislative measures, not a few of which have stemmed from recommendations of the very Committee whose actions have been drawn in question here. In the last analysis this power rests on the right of self-preservation, "the ultimate value of any society.". . .

On these premises, this Court in its constitutional adjudications has consistently refused to view the Communist Party as an ordinary political party, and has upheld federal legislation aimed at the Communist problem which in a different context would certainly have raised constitutional issues of the gravest character. . . . To suggest that because the Communist Party may also sponsor peaceable political reforms the constitutional issues before us should now be judged as if that Party were just an ordinary political party from the standpoint of national security, is to ask this Court to blind itself to world affairs which have determined the whole course of our national policy since the close of World War II. . . .

We think that investigatory power in this domain is not to be denied Congress solely because the field of education is involved. . . .

Nor can we accept the further contention that this investigation should not be deemed to have been in furtherance of a legislative purpose because the true objective of the Committee and of the Congress was purely "exposure." So long as Congress acts in pursuance of its constitutional power, the Judiciary lacks authority to intervene on the basis of the motives which spurred the exercise of that power. . . .

Finally, the record is barren of other factors which in themselves might sometimes lead to the conclusion that the individual interests at stake were not subordinate to those of the state. There is no indication in this record that the Subcommittee was attempting to pillory witnesses. Nor did petitioner's appearance as a witness follow from indiscriminate dragnet procedures, lacking in probable cause for belief that he possessed information which might be helpful to the Subcommittee. . . .

We conclude that the balance between the individual and the governmental interests here at stake must be struck in favor of the latter, and that therefore the provisions of the First Amendment have not been offended. . . .

Affirmed.

MR. JUSTICE BLACK, *with whom* THE CHIEF JUSTICE *and* MR. JUSTICE DOUGLAS *concur, dissenting.* . . .

It goes without saying that a law to be valid must be clear enough to make its commands understandable. For obvious reasons, the standard of certainty required in criminal statutes is more exacting than in non-criminal statutes. This is simply because it would be unthinkable to convict a man for violating a law he could not understand. This Court has recognized that the stricter standard is as much required in criminal contempt cases as in all other criminal cases, and has emphasized that the "vice of vagueness" is especially pernicious where legislative power over an area involving speech, press, petition and assembly is involved. . . . For a statute broad enough to support infringement of speech, writings, thoughts and public assemblies, against

the unequivocal command of the First Amendment necessarily leaves all persons to guess just what the law really means to cover, and fear of a wrong guess inevitably leads people to forego the very rights the Constitution sought to protect above all others. . . .

Measured by the foregoing standards, Rule XI cannot support any conviction for refusal to testify. . . .

. . . On the Court's own test, the issue is whether Barenblatt can know with sufficient certainty, at the time of his interrogation, that there is so compelling a need for his replies that infringement of his rights of free association is justified. The record does not disclose where Barenblatt can find what that need is. . . .

But even if Barenblatt could evaluate the importance to the Government of the information sought, Rule XI would still be too broad to support his conviction. For we are dealing here with governmental procedures which the Court itself admits reach to the very fringes of congressional power. In such cases more is required of legislatures than a vague delegation to be filled in later by mute acquiescence. If Congress wants ideas investigated, if it even wants them investigated in the field of education, it must be prepared to say so expressly and unequivocally. And it is not enough that a court through exhaustive research can establish, even conclusively, that Congress wished to allow the investigation. I can find no such unequivocal statement here.

For all these reasons, I would hold that Rule XI is too broad to be meaningful and cannot support petitioner's conviction. . . .

I do not agree that laws directly abridging First Amendment freedoms can be justified by a congressional or judicial balancing process. There are . . . cases suggesting that a law which primarily regulates conduct but which might also indirectly affect speech can be upheld if the effect on speech is minor in relation to the need for control of the conduct. With these cases I agree. . . . [But such cases cannot] be read as allowing legislative bodies to pass laws abridging freedom of speech, press and association merely because of hostility to views peacefully expressed in a place where the speaker had a right to be. Rule XI, on its face and as here applied, since it attempts inquiry into beliefs, not action—ideas and associations, not conduct—does just that.

To apply the Court's balancing test under such circumstances is to read the First Amendment to say "Congress shall pass no law abridging freedom of speech, press, assembly and petition, unless Congress and the Supreme Court reach the joint conclusion that on balance the interest of the Government in stifling these freedoms is greater than the interest of the people in having them exercised." This is clearly akin to the notion that neither the First Amendment nor any other provision of the Bill of Rights should be enforced unless the Court believes it is *reasonable* to do so. . . . Unless we . . . accept the notion that the Bill of Rights means what it says and that this Court must enforce that meaning, I am of the opinion that our great charter of liberty will be more honored in the breach than in the observance.

But even assuming what I cannot assume, that some balancing is proper in this case, I feel that the Court after stating the test ignores it completely. At most it balances the right of the Government to preserve itself, against Barenblatt's right to refrain from revealing Communist affiliations. Such a balance, however, mistakes the factors to be weighed. In the first place, it completely leaves out the real interest in Barenblatt's silence, the interest of the people as a whole in being able to join organizations, advocate causes and make political "mistakes" without later being subjected to governmental penalties for having dared to think for themselves. It is this right, the right to err politically, which keeps us strong as a Nation. For no number of laws against communism can have as much effect as the personal conviction which comes from having heard its arguments and rejected them, or from having once accepted its tenets and later recognized their worthlessness. Instead, the obloquy which results from investigations such as this not only stifles "mistakes" but prevents all but the most courageous from hazarding any views which might at some later time become disfavored. This result, whose importance cannot be overestimated, is doubly crucial when it affects the universities, on which we must largely rely for the experimentation and development of new ideas essential to our country's welfare. It is these interests of society, rather than Barenblatt's own right to silence, which I think the Court should put on the balance against the demands of the Government, if any balancing process is to be tolerated. . . . Moreover, I cannot agree with the Court's notion that First Amendment freedoms must be abridged in order to "preserve" our country. That notion rests on the unarticulated premise that this Nation's security hangs upon its power to punish people because of what they think, speak or write about, or because of those with whom they associate for political purposes. The Government, in its brief, virtually admits this position when it speaks of the "communication of unlawful ideas." I challenge this premise, and deny that ideas can be proscribed under our Constitution. . . . The First Amendment means to me . . . that the only constitutional way our Government can preserve itself is to leave its people the fullest possible freedom to praise, criticize or discuss, as they see fit, all governmental policies and to suggest, if they desire, that even its most fundamental postulates are bad and should be changed; "Therein lies the security of the Republic, the very foundation of constitutional government." On that premise this land was created, and on that premise it has grown to greatness. Our Constitution assumes that the common sense of the people and their attachment to our country will enable them, after free discussion, to withstand ideas that are wrong. To say that our patriotism must be protected against false ideas by means other than these is, I think, to make a baseless charge. . . .

The Court implies, however, that the ordinary rules and requirements of the Constitution do not apply because the Committee is merely after Communists and they do not constitute a political party but only a criminal gang. . . .

. . . [N]o matter how often or how quickly we repeat the claim that the Communist Party is not a political party, we cannot outlaw it, as a group, without endangering the liberty of all of us. The reason is not hard to find, for mixed among those aims of communism which are illegal are perfectly normal political and social goals. And muddled with its revolutionary tenets is a drive to achieve power through the ballot, if it can be done. These things necessarily make it a political party whatever other, illegal, aims it may have. . . .

The fact is that once we allow any group which has some political aims or ideas to be driven from the ballot and from the battle for men's minds because some of its members are bad and some of its tenets are illegal, no group is safe. Today we deal with Communists or suspected Communists. In 1920, instead, the New York Assembly suspended duly elected legislators on the ground that, being Socialists, they were disloyal to the country's principles. In the 1830s the Masons were hunted as outlaws and subversives, and abolitionists were considered revolutionaries of the most dangerous kind in both North and South. Earlier still, at the time of the universally unlamented alien and sedition laws, Thomas Jefferson's party was attacked and its members were derisively called "Jacobins." Fisher Ames described the party as a "French faction" guilty of "subversion" and "officered, regimented and formed to subordination." Its members, he claimed, intended to "take arms against the laws as soon as they dare." History should teach us then, that in times of high emotional excitement minority parties and groups which advocate extremely unpopular social or governmental innovations will always be typed as criminal gangs and attempts will always be made to drive them out. . . .

Finally, I think Barenblatt's conviction violates the Constitution because the chief aim, purpose and practice of the House Un-American Activities Committee, as disclosed by its many reports, is to try witnesses and punish them because they are or have been Communists or because they refuse to admit or deny Communist affiliations. The punishment imposed is generally punishment by humiliation and public shame. . . .

I do not question the Committee's patriotism and sincerity in doing all this. I merely feel that it cannot be done by Congress under our Constitution. For, even assuming that the Federal Government can compel witnesses to testify as to Communist affiliations in order to subject them to ridicule and social and economic retaliation, I cannot agree that this is a legislative function. Such publicity is clearly punishment, and the Constitution allows only one way in which people can be convicted and punished. As we said in [*U.S.* v.] *Lovett,* "Those who wrote our Constitution well knew the danger inherent in special legislative acts which take away the life, liberty or property of particular named persons because the legislature thinks them guilty of conduct which deserves punishment. *They intended to safeguard the people of this country from punishment without trial by duly constituted courts.*" 328 U.S. at 317. (Italics added.) Thus if communism is to be made a crime, and Communists are to be subjected to "pains and penalties," I would still hold this conviction bad, for the crime of communism, like all others, can be punished only by court and jury after a trial with all judicial safeguards. . . .

Ultimately all the questions in this case really boil down to one—whether we as a people will try fearfully and futilely to preserve democracy by adopting totalitarian methods, or whether in accordance with our traditions and our Constitution we will have the confidence and courage to be free.

I would reverse this conviction.

NEW YORK TIMES CO. v. UNITED STATES
403 U.S. 713; 29 L. Ed. 2d 822; 91 S. Ct. 2140 (1971)

Per Curiam.

We granted certiorari in these cases in which the United States seeks to enjoin the New York Times and the Washington Post from publishing the contents of a classified study entitled "History of U.S. Decision-Making Process on Viet Nam Policy." *Post*, pp. 942, 943.

"Any system of prior restraints of expression comes to this Court bearing a heavy presumption against its constitutional validity." *Bantam Books, Inc.* v. *Sullivan*, 372 U.S. 58, 70 (1963); see also *Near* v. *Minnesota*, 283 U.S. 697 (1931). The Government "thus carries a heavy burden of showing justification for the imposition of such a restraint." *Organization for a Better Austin* v. *Keefe* (1971). The District Court for the Southern District of New York in the *New York Times* case and the District Court for the District of Columbia and the Court of Appeals for the District of Columbia Circuit in the *Washington Post* case held that the Government had not met that burden. We agree.

The judgment of the Court of Appeals for the District of Columbia Circuit is therefore affirmed. The order of the Court of Appeals for the Second Circuit is reversed and the case is remanded with directions to enter a judgment affirming the judgment of the District Court for the Southern District of New York. . . .

MR. JUSTICE BLACK, *with whom* MR. JUSTICE DOUGLAS *joins, concurring.*

I adhere to the view that the Government's case against the Washington Post should have been dismissed and that the injunction against the New York Times should have been vacated without oral argument when the cases were first presented to this Court. I believe that every moment's continuance of the injunctions against these newspapers amounts to a flagrant, indefensible, and continuing violation of the First Amendment. . . . In my view it is unfortunate that some of my Brethren are apparently willing to hold that the publication of news may sometimes be enjoined. Such a holding would make a shambles of the First Amendment. . . .

In the First Amendment the Founding Fathers gave the free press the protection it must have to fulfill its essential role in our democracy. The press was to serve the governed, not the governors. The Government's power to censor the press was abolished so that the press would remain forever free to censure the Government. The press was protected so that it could bare the secrets of government and inform the people. Only a free and unrestrained press can effectively expose deception in government. And paramount among the responsibilities of a free press is the duty to prevent any part of the government from deceiving the people and sending them off to distant lands to die of foreign fevers and foreign shot and shell. In my view, far from deserving condemnation for their courageous reporting, The New York Times, The Washington Post, and other newspapers should be commended for serving the purpose that the Founding Fathers saw so clearly. In revealing the workings of government that led to the Vietnam war, the newspapers nobly did precisely that which the Founders hoped and trusted they would do.

The Government's case here is based on

premises entirely different from those that guided the Framers of the First Amendment. . . . The Government argues in its brief that in spite of the First Amendment, "[t]he authority of the Executive Department to protect the nation against publication of information whose disclosure would endanger the national security stems from two interrelated Sources: the constitutional power of the President over the conduct of foreign affairs and his authority as Commander-in-Chief."

In other words, we are asked to hold that despite the First Amendment's emphatic command, the Executive Branch, the Congress, and the Judiciary can make laws enjoining publication of current news and abridging freedom of the press in the name of "national security." The Government does not even attempt to rely on any act of Congress. Instead it makes the bold and dangerously far-reaching contention that the courts should take it upon themselves to "make" a law abridging freedom of the press in the name of equity, presidential power and national security, even when the representatives of the people in Congress have adhered to the command of the First Amendment and refused to make such a law. . . . To find that the President has "inherent power" to halt the publication of news by resort to the courts would wipe out the First Amendment and destroy the fundamental liberty and security of the very people the Government hopes to make "secure." . . .

MR. JUSTICE DOUGLAS, *with whom* MR. JUSTICE BLACK *joins, concurring.*

. . .

The dominant purpose of the First Amendment was to prohibit the widespread practice of governmental suppression of embarrassing information. It is common knowledge that the First Amendment was adopted against the widespread use of the common law of seditious libel to punish the dissemination of material that is embarrassing to the powers-that-be. See T. Emerson, The System of Freedom of Expression, c. V

(1970); Z. Chafee, Free Speech in the United States, c. XIII (1941). The present cases will, I think, go down in history as the most dramatic illustration of that principle. A debate of large proportions goes on in the Nation over our posture in Vietnam. That debate antedated the disclosure of the contents of the present documents. The latter are highly relevant to the debate in progress.

Secrecy in government is fundamentally anti-democratic, perpetuating bureaucratic errors. Open debate and discussion of public issues are vital to our national health. On public questions there should be "uninhibited, robust, and wide-open" debate. . . .

MR. JUSTICE BRENNAN, *concurring.*

I write separately in these cases only to emphasize what should be apparent: that our judgments in the present cases may not be taken to indicate the propriety in the future, of issuing temporary stays and restraining orders to block the publication of material sought to be suppressed by the Government. So far as I can determine, never before has the United States sought to enjoin a newspaper from publishing information in its possession. . . .

The error that has pervaded these cases from the outset was the granting of any injunctive relief whatsoever, interim or otherwise. The entire thrust of the Government's claim throughout these cases has been that publication of the material sought to be enjoined "could," or "might," or "may" prejudice the national interest in various ways. But the First Amendment tolerates absolutely no prior judicial restraints of the press predicated upon surmise or conjecture that untoward consequences may result. Our cases it is true, have indicated that there is a single, extremely narrow class of cases in which the First Amendment's ban on prior judicial restraint may be overridden. Our cases have thus far indicated that such cases may arise only when the Nation "is at war," *Schenck* v. *United States* (1919), during which times "[n]o one would question but that a government might prevent actual obstruction to its recruiting service or the publication of the sailing dates of transports or the number and location of troops." *Near* v. *Minnesota* (1931). Even if the present world situation were assumed to be tantamount to a time of war, or if the power of presently available armaments would justify even in peacetime the suppression of information that would set in motion a nuclear holocaust, in neither of these actions has the Government presented or even alleged that publication of items from or based upon the material at issue would cause the happening of an event of that nature. "The chief purpose of [the First Amendement's] guaranty [is] to prevent previous restraints upon publication." *Near* v. *Minnesota*. Thus, only governmental allegation and proof that publication must inevitably, directly, and immediately cause the occurrence of an event kindred to imperiling the safety of a transport already at sea can support even the issuance of an interim restraining order. In no event may mere conclusions be sufficient: for if the Executive Branch seeks judicial aid in preventing publication, it must inevitably submit the basis upon which that aid is sought to scrutiny by the judiciary. And therefore, every restraint issued in this case, whatever its form, has violated the First Amendment—and not less so because that restraint was justified as necessary to afford the courts an opportunity to examine the claim more thoroughly. Unless and until the Government has clearly made out its case, the First Amendment commands that no injunction may issue.

MR. JUSTICE STEWART, *with whom* MR. JUSTICE WHITE *joins, concurring.*

In the governmental structure created by our Constitution, the Executive is endowed with enormous power in the two related areas of national defense and international relations. This power, largely unchecked by the Legislative and Judicial branches, has been pressed to the very hilt since the advent of the nuclear missile age. For better or worse, the simple fact is that a President of the United States possesses vastly greater constitutional independence in these two vital areas of power than does, say, a prime minister of a country with a parliamentary form of government.

In the absence of the governmental checks and balances present in other areas of our national life, the only effective restraint upon executive policy and power in the areas of national defense and international affairs may lie in an enlightened citizenry—in an informed and critical public opinion which alone can here protect the values of democratic government. For this reason, it is perhaps here that a press that is alert, aware, and free most vitally serves the basic purpose of the First Amendment. For without an informed and free press there cannot be an enlightened people.

Yet it is elementary that the successful conduct of international diplomacy and the maintenance of an effective national defense require both confidentiality and secrecy. Other nations can hardly deal with this Nation in an atmosphere of mutual trust unless they can be assured that their confidences will be kept. And within our own executive departments, the development of considered and intelligent international policies would be impossible if those charged with their formulation could not communicate with each other freely, frankly, and in confidence. In the area of basic national defense the frequent need for absolute secrecy is, of course, self-evident.

I think there can be but one answer to this dilemma, if dilemma it be. The responsibility must be where the power is. If the Constitution gives the Executive a large degree of unshared power in the conduct of foreign affairs and the maintenance of our national defense, then under the Constitution the Executive must have the largely unshared duty to determine and preserve the degree of internal security necessary to exercise that power successfully. . . .

This is not to say that Congress and the courts

have no role to play. Undoubtedly Congress has the power to enact specific and appropriate criminal laws to protect government property and preserve government secrets. Congress has passed such laws, and several of them are of very colorable relevance to the apparent circumstances of these cases. And if a criminal prosecution is instituted, it will be the responsibility of the courts to decide the applicability of the criminal law under which the charge is brought. Moreover, if Congress should pass a specific law authorizing civil proceedings in this field, the courts would likewise have the duty to decide the constitutionality of such a law as well as its applicability to the facts proved.

But in the cases before us we are asked neither to construe specific regulations nor to apply specific laws. We are asked, instead, to perform a function that the Constitution gave to the Executive, not the Judiciary. We are asked, quite simply, to prevent the publication by two newspapers of material that the Executive Branch insists should not, in the national interest, be published. I am convinced that the Executive is correct with respect to some of the documents involved. But I cannot say that disclosure of any of them will surely result in direct, immediate, and irreparable damage to our Nation or its people. That being so, there can under the First Amendment be but one judicial resolution of the issues before us. I join the judgments of the Court.

MR. JUSTICE WHITE, *with whom* MR. JUSTICE STEWART *joins, concurring.*

I concur in today's judgments, but only because of the concededly extraordinary protection against prior restraints enjoyed by the press under our constitutional system. I do not say that in no circumstances would the First Amendment permit an injunction against publishing information about government plans or operations. Nor, after examining the materials the Government characterizes as the most sensitive and destructive, can I deny that revelation of these documents will do substantial damage to public interests. Indeed, I am confident that their disclosure will have that result. But I nevertheless agree that the United States has not satisfied the very heavy burden that it must meet to warrant an injunction against publication in these cases, at least in the absence of express and appropriately limited congressional authorization for prior restraints in circumstances such as these.

The Government's position is simply stated: The responsibility of the Executive for the conduct of the foreign affairs and for the security of the Nation is so basic that the President is entitled to an injunction against publication of a newspaper story whenever he can convince a court that the information to be revealed threatens "grave and irreparable" injury to the public interest; and the injunction should issue whether or not the material to be published would be lawful under relevant criminal statutes enacted by Congress, and regardless of the circumstances by which the newspaper came into possession of the information.

At least in the absence of legislation by Congress, based on its own investigations and findings, I am quite unable to agree that the inherent powers of the Executive and the courts reach so far as to authorize remedies having such sweeping potential for inhibiting publications by the press. . . .

It is not easy to reject the proposition urged by the United States and to deny relief on its good-faith claims in these cases that publication will work serious damage to the country. But that discomfiture is considerably dispelled by the infrequency of prior-restraint cases. Normally, publication will occur and the damage be done before the Government has either opportunity or grounds for suppression. So here, publication has already begun and a substantial part of the threatened damage has already occurred. . . .

What is more, terminating the ban on publication of the relatively few sensitive documents the Government now seeks to suppress does not mean that the law either requires or invites newspapers or others to publish them or that they will be immune from criminal action if they do. Prior restraints require an unusually heavy justification under the First Amendment; but failure by the Government to justify prior restraints does not measure its constitutional entitlement to a conviction for criminal publication. That the Government mistakenly chose to proceed by injunction does not mean that it could not successfully proceed in another way.

When the Espionage Act was under consideration in 1917, Congress eliminated from the bill a provision that would have given the President broad powers in time of war to proscribe, under threat of criminal penalty, the publication of various categories of information related to the national defense. Congress at that time was unwilling to clothe the President with such far-reaching powers to monitor the press, and those opposed to this part of the legislation assumed that a necessary concomitant of such power was the power to "filter out the news to the people through some man." However, these same members of Congress appeared to have little doubt that newspapers would be subject to criminal prosecution if they insisted on publishing information of the type Congress had itself determined should not be revealed. . . .

The Criminal Code contains numerous provisions potentially relevant to these cases. Section 797 makes it a crime to publish certain photographs or drawings of military installations. Section 798, also in precise language, proscribes knowing and willful publication of any classified information concerning the cryptographic systems or communication intelligence activities of the United States as well as any information obtained from communication intelligence operations. If any of the material here at issue is of this nature, the newspapers are presumably now on full notice of the position of the United States and must face the consequences if they publish. I would have no difficulty in sustaining convictions under these sections on facts that would not justify the intervention of equity and the imposition of a prior restraint.

The same would be true under those sections of the Criminal Code casting a wider net to protect the national defense. Section 793(e) makes it a criminal act for any unauthorized possessor of a document "relating to the national defense" either (1) willfully to communicate or cause to be communicated that document to any person not entitled to receive it or (2) willfully to retain the document and fail to deliver it to an officer of the United States entitled to receive it. The subsection was added in 1950 because pre-existing law provided no penalty for the unauthorized possessor unless demand for the documents was made. . . . Of course, in the cases before us, the unpublished documents have been demanded by the United States and their import has been made known at least to counsel for the newspapers involved. In *Gorin* v. *United States* (1941), the words "national defense" as used in a predecessor of § 793 were held by a unanimous Court to have "a well understood connotation"—a "generic concept of broad connotations, referring to the military and naval establishments and the related activities of national preparedness"—and to be "sufficiently definite to apprise the public of prohibited activities" and to be consonant with due process. 312 U.S., at 28. Also, as construed by the Court in *Gorin*, information "connected with the national defense" is obviously not limited to that threatening "grave and irreparable" injury to the United States.

It is thus clear that Congress has addressed itself to the problems of protecting the security of the country and the national defense from unauthorized disclosure of potentially damaging information. Cf. *Youngstown Sheet & Tube Co.* v. *Sawyer* (1952). It has not, however, authorized the injunctive remedy against threatened publication. It has apparently been satisfied to rely on criminal sanctions and their deterrent effect on the responsible as well as the irresponsible press. I am not, of course, saying that either of these newspapers has yet committed a crime or that either would commit a crime if it published all the material now in its possession.

That matter must await resolution in the context of a criminal proceeding if one is instituted by the United States. In that event, the issue of guilt or innocence would be determined by procedures and standards quite different from those that have purported to govern these injunctive proceedings.

MR. JUSTICE MARSHALL, *concurring.*

The Government contends that the only issue in these cases is whether in a suit by the United States, "the First Amendment bars a court from prohibiting a newspaper from publishing material whose disclosure would pose a 'grave and immediate danger to the security of the United States.' " With all due respect, I believe the ultimate issue in these cases is even more basic than the one posed by the Solicitor General. The issue is whether this Court or the Congress has the power to make law.

In these cases there is no problem concerning the President's power to classify information as "secret" or "top secret." Congress has specifically recognized Presidential authority, which has been formally exercised in Exec. Order 10501 (1953), to classify documents and information. Nor is there any issue here regarding the President's power as Chief Executive and Commander in Chief to protect national security by disciplining employees who disclose information and by taking precautions to prevent leaks.

The problem here is whether in these particular cases the Executive Branch has authority to invoke the equity jurisdiction of the courts to protect what it believes to be the national interest. The Government argues that in addition to the inherent power of any government to protect itself, the President's power to conduct foreign affairs and his position as Commander in Chief give him authority to impose censorship on the press to protect his ability to deal effectively with foreign nations and to conduct the military affairs of the country. Of course, it is beyond cavil that the President has broad powers by virtue of his primary responsibility for the conduct of our foreign affairs and his position as Commander in Chief. And in some situations it may be that under whatever inherent powers the Government may have, as well as the implicit authority derived from the President's mandate to conduct foreign affairs and to act as Commander in Chief, there is a basis for the invocation of the equity jurisdiction of this Court as an aid to prevent the publication of material damaging to "national security," however that term may be defined.

It would, however, be utterly inconsistent with the concept of separation of powers for this Court to use its power of contempt to prevent behavior that Congress has specifically declined to prohibit. There would be a similar damage to the basic concept of these co-equal branches of Government if when the Executive Branch has adequate authority granted by Congress to protect "national security" it can choose instead to invoke the contempt power of a court to enjoin the threatened conduct. The Constitution provides that Congress shall make laws, the President execute laws, and courts interpret laws. *Youngstown Sheet & Tube Co.* v. *Sawyer* (1952). It did not provide for government by injunction in which the courts and the Executive Branch can "make law" without regard to the action of Congress. It may be more convenient for the Executive Branch if it need only convince a judge to prohibit conduct rather than ask the Congress to pass a law, and it may be more convenient to enforce a contempt order than to seek a criminal conviction in a jury trial. Moreover, it may be considered politically wise to get a court to share the responsibility for arresting those who the Executive Branch has probable cause to believe are violating the law. But convenience and political considerations of the moment do not justify a basic departure from the principles of our system of government. . . .

. . . [However] it is clear that Congress has specifically rejected passing legislation that would have clearly given the President the power he seeks here and made the current activity of the newspapers unlawful. When Congress specifically declines to make conduct unlawful it is not for this Court to redecide those issues to overrule Congress. See *Youngstown Sheet & Tube Co.* v. *Sawyer,* 343 U.S. 579 (1952).

On at least two occasions Congress has refused to enact legislation that would have made the conduct engaged in here unlawful and given the President the power that he seeks in this case. . . .

Either the Government has the power under statutory grant to use traditional criminal law to protect the country or, if there is no basis for arguing that Congress has made the activity a crime, it is plain that Congress has specifically refused to grant the authority the Government seeks from this Court. In either case this Court does not have authority to grant the requested relief. It is not for this Court to fling itself into every breach perceived by some Government official nor is it for this Court to take on itself the burden of enacting law, especially a law that Congress has refused to pass.

MR. CHIEF JUSTICE BURGER, *dissenting.*

So clear are the constitutional limitations on prior restraint against expression, that from the time of *Near* v. *Minnesota* (1931), until recently in *Organization for a Better Austin* v. *Keefe* (1971), we have had little occasion to be concerned with cases involving prior restraints against news reporting on matters of public interest. There is, therefore, little variation among the members of the Court in terms of resistance to prior restraints against publication. Adherence to this basic constitutional principle, however, does not make these cases simple. In these cases, the imperative of a free and unfettered press comes into collision with another imperative, the effective functioning of a complex modern government and specifically the effective exercise of certain constitutional powers of the Executive. Only those who view the First Amendment as an absolute in all circumstances—a view I respect, but reject—can find such cases as these to be simple or easy.

These cases are not simple for another and more immediate reason. We do not know the facts of the cases. No district Judge knew all the facts. No Court of Appeals judge knew all the facts. No member of this Court knows all the facts.

Why are we in this posture, in which only those judges to whom the First Amendment is absolute and permits of no restraint in any circumstances or for any reason, are really in a position to act?

I suggest we are in this posture because these cases have been conducted in unseemly haste. . . . The prompt setting of these cases reflects our universal abhorrence of prior restraint. But prompt judicial action does not mean unjudicial haste.

Here, moreover, the frenetic haste is due in large part to the manner in which the Times proceeded from the date it obtained the purloined documents. It seems reasonably clear now that the haste precluded reasonable and deliberate judicial treatment of these cases and was not warranted. The precipitate action of this Court aborting trials not yet completed is not the kind of judicial conduct that ought to attend the disposition of a great issue.

The newspapers make a derivative claim under the First Amendment; they denominate this right as the public "right to know"; by implication, the Times asserts a sole trusteeship of that right by virtue of its journalistic "scoop." The right is asserted as an absolute. Of course, the First Amendment right itself is not an absolute, as Justice Holmes so long ago pointed out in his aphorism concerning the right to shout "fire" in a crowded theatre if there was no fire. There are other exceptions, some of which Chief Justice Hughes mentioned by way of example in *Near* v. *Minnesota.* There are no doubt other exceptions no one has had occasion to describe or discuss. Conceivably such exceptions may be lurking in these cases and would have been flushed had they been properly considered in the trial courts, free from unwarranted deadlines and frenetic pressures. An issue of this importance should be tried and heard in a judicial atmosphere conducive to thoughtful, reflective deliberation, especially when haste, in terms of hours, is unwarranted in light of the long period the Times, by its own choice, deferred publication.

It is not disputed that the Times has had unauthorized possession of the documents for three to four months, during which it has had its expert anaylsts studying them, presumably digesting them and preparing the material for publication. During all of this time, the Times presumably in its capacity as trustee of the public's "right to know," has held up publication for purposes it considered proper and thus public knowledge was delayed. No doubt this was for a good reason; the analysis of 7,000 pages of complex material drawn from a vastly greater volume of material would inevitably take time and the writing of good stories takes time. But why should the United States Government, from whom this information was illegally acquired by someone, along with all the counsel, trial judges, and appellate judges be placed under needless pressure? After these months of deferral, the alleged "right to know" has somehow and suddenly become a right that must be vindicated instanter.

Would it have been unreasonable since the newspaper could anticipate the Government's objections to release of secret material, to give the Government an opportunity to review the entire collection and determine whether agreement could be reached on publication? Stolen or not, if security was not in fact jeopardized, much of the material could no doubt have been declassified, since it spans a period ending in 1968. With such an approach—one that great newspapers have in the past practiced and stated editorially to be the duty of an honorable press—the newspapers and Government might well have narrowed the area of disagreement as to what was not publishable, leaving the remainder to be resolved in orderly litigation, if necessary. To me it is hardly believable that a newspaper long regarded as a great institution in

American life would fail to perform one of the basic and simple duties of every citizen with respect to the discovery or possession of stolen property or secret government documents. That duty, I had thought—perhaps naively—was to report forthwith, to responsible public officers. This duty rests on taxi drivers, Justices, and the *New York Times.* The course followed by the Times, whether so calculated or not, removed any possibility of orderly litigation of the issues. If the action of the judges up to now has been correct, that result is sheer happenstance.

Our grant of the writ of certiorari before final judgment in the *Times* case aborted the trial in the District Court before it had made a complete record pursuant to the mandate of the Court of Appeals for the Second Circuit.

The consequence of all this melancholy series of events is that we literally do not know what we are acting on. As I see it, we have been forced to deal with litigation concerning rights of great magnitude without an adequate record, and surely without time for adequate treatment either in the prior proceedings or in this Court. It is interesting to note that counsel on both sides, in oral argument before this Court, were frequently unable to respond to questions on factual points. Not surprisingly they pointed out that they had been working literally "around the clock" and simply were unable to review the documents that give rise to these cases and were not familiar with them. This court is in no better posture. . . .

I would affirm the Court of Appeals for the Second Circuit and allow the District Court to complete the trial aborted by our grant of certiorari, meanwhile preserving the status quo in the *Post* case. I would direct that the District Court on remand give priority to the *Times* case to the exclusion of all other business of that court but I would not set arbitrary deadlines. . . .

We all crave speedier judicial processes but when judges are pressured as in these cases the result is a parody of the judicial function.

MR. JUSTICE HARLAN, *with whom* THE CHIEF JUSTICE *and* MR. JUSTICE BLACKMUN *join, dissenting.*

These cases forcefully call to mind the wise admonition of Mr. Justice Holmes, dissenting in *Northern Securities Co.* v. *United States* (1904):

> Great cases like hard cases make bad law. For great cases are called great, not by reason of their real importance in shaping the law of the future, but because of some accident of immediate overwhelming interest which appeals to the feelings and distorts the judgment. These immediate interests exercise a kind of hydraulic pressure which makes what previously was clear seem doubtful, and before which even well settled principles of law will bend.

With all respect, I consider that the Court has been almost irresponsibly feverish in dealing with these cases.

Both the Court of Appeals for the Second Circuit and the Court of Appeals for the District of Columbia Circuit rendered judgment on June 23. The New York Times' petition for certiorari, its motion for accelerated consideration thereof, and its application for interim relief were filed in this Court on June 24 at about 11 a.m. The application of the United States for interim relief in the *Post* case was also filed here on June 24 at about 7:15 p.m. This Court's order setting a hearing before us on June 26 at 11 a.m., a course which I joined only to avoid the possibility of even more peremptory action by the Court, was issued less than 24 hours before. The record in the *Post* case was filed with the Clerk shortly before 1 p.m. on June 25; the record in the *Times* case did not arrive until 7 or 8 o'clock that same night. The briefs of the parties were received less than two hours before argument on June 26.

This frenzied train of events took place in the name of the presumption against prior restraints created by the First Amendment. Due regard for the extraordinarily important and difficult questions involved in these litigations should have led the Court to shun such a precipitate timetable. In order to decide the merits of these cases properly, some or all of the following questions should have been faced:

1. Whether the Attorney General is authorized to bring these suits in the name of the United States. Compare *In re Debs* with *Youngstown Sheet & Tube Co.* v. *Sawyer* (1952). This question involves as well the construction and validity of a singularly opaque statute—the Espionage Act, 18 U.S.C. 793 (e).

2. Whether the First Amendment permits the federal courts to enjoin publication of stories which would present a serious threat to national security. See *Near* v. *Minnesota* (1931) (dictum).

3. Whether the threat to publish highly secret documents is of itself a sufficient implication of national security to justify an injunction on the theory that regardless of the contents of the documents harm enough results simply from the demonstration of such a breach of secrecy.

4. Whether the unauthorized disclosure of any of these particular documents would seriously impair the national security.

5. What weight should be given to the opinion of high officers in the Executive Branch of the Government with respect to questions 3 and 4.

6. Whether the newspapers are entitled to retain and use the documents notwithstanding the seemingly uncontested facts that the documents, or the originals of which they are duplicates, were purloined from the Government's possession and that the newspapers received them with knowledge that they had been feloniously acquired.

7. Whether the threatened harm to the national security or the Government's possessory interest in the documents justifies the issuance of an injunction against publication in light of—

a. The strong First Amendment policy against prior restraints on publication;

b. The doctrine against enjoining conduct in

violation of criminal statutes; and

c. The extent to which the materials at issue have apparently already been otherwise disseminated.

These are difficult questions of fact, of law, and of judgment; the potential consequences of erroneous decision are enormous. The time which has been available to us, to the lower courts, and to the parties has been wholly inadequate for giving these cases the kind of consideration they deserve. It is a reflection on the stability of the judicial process that these great issues—as important as any that have arisen during my time on the Court—should have been decided under the pressures engendered by the torrent of publicity that has attended these litigations from their inception.

Forced as I am to reach the merits of these cases, I dissent from the opinion and judgments of the Court. Within the severe limitations imposed by the time constraints under which I have been required to operate, I can only state my reasons in telescoped form, even though in different circumstances I would have felt constrained to deal with the cases in the fuller sweep indicated above.

It is a sufficient basis for affirming the Court of Appeals for the Second Circuit in the *Times* litigation to observe that its order must rest on the conclusion that because of the time elements the Government had not been given an adequate opportunity to present its case to the District Court. At the least this conclusion was not an abuse of discretion.

In the *Post* litigation the Government had more time to prepare; this was apparently the basis for the refusal of the Court of Appeals for the District of Columbia Circuit on rehearing to conform its judgment to that of the Second Circuit. But I think there is another and more fundamental reason why this judgment cannot stand—a reason which also furnishes an additional ground for not reinstating the judgment of the District Court in the *Times* litigation, set aside by the Court of Appeals. It is plain to me

that the scope of the judicial function in passing upon the activities of the Executive Branch of the Government in the field of foreign affairs is very narrowly restricted. This view is, I think, dictated by the concept of separation of powers upon which our constitutional system rests.

In a speech on the floor of the House of Representatives, Chief Justice John Marshall, then a member of that body, stated:

> The President is the sole organ of the nation in its external relations, and its sole representative with foreign nations. 10 Annals of Cong. 613 (1800).

From that time, shortly after the founding of the Nation, to this, there has been no substantial challenge to this description of the scope of executive power. See *United States* v. *Curtiss-Wright Corp.* (1936).

From this constitutional primacy in the field of foreign affairs, it seems to me that certain conclusions necessarily follow. Some of these were stated concisely by President Washington, declining the request of the House of Representatives for the papers leading up to the negotiation of the Jay Treaty:

> The nature of foreign negotiations requires caution, and their success must often depend on secrecy; and even when brought to a conclusion a full disclosure of all the measures, demands, or eventual concessions which may have been proposed or contemplated would be extremely impolite; for this might have a pernicious influence on future negotiations, or produce immediate inconveniences perhaps danger and mischief, in relation to other powers. J. Richardson, Messages and Papers of the Presidents, 194-195 (1896).

The power to evaluate the "pernicious influence" of premature disclosure is not, however, lodged in the Executive alone. I agree that, in performance of its duty to protect the values of the First Amendment against political pressures, the judiciary must review the initial Executive determination to the point of satisfying itself that the subject matter of the dispute does lie within the proper compass of the President's foreign relations power. Constitutional considerations forbid "a complete abandonment of judicial control." Moreover, the judiciary may properly insist that the determination that disclosure of the subject matter would irreparably impair the national security be made by the head of the Executive Department concerned—here the Secretary of State or the Secretary of Defense—after actual personal consideration by that officer. This safeguard is required in the analogous area of executive claims of privilege for secrets of state.

But in my judgment the judiciary may not properly go beyond these two inquiries and redetermine for itself the probable impact of disclosure on the national security.

> The very nature of executive decisions as to foreign policy is political, not judicial. Such decisions are wholly confided by our Constitution to the political departments of the government, Executive and Legislative. They are delicate, complex, and involve large elements of prophecy. They are and should be undertaken only by those directly responsible to the people whose welfare they advance or imperil. They are decisions of a kind for which the Judiciary has neither aptitude, facilities nor responsibility and which has long been held to belong in the domain of political power not subject to judicial intrusion or inquiry. *Chicago & Southern Air Lines* v. *Waterman Steamship Corp.* (1948) (Jackson, J.).

Even if there is some room for the judiciary to override the executive determination, it is plain that the scope of review must be exceedingly narrow. I can see no indication in the opinions of either the District Court or the Court of Appeals in the *Post* litigation that the conclusions of the Executive were given even the deference owing to an administrative agency, much less that owing to a co-equal branch of the Government operating within the field of its constitutional prerogative.

Accordingly, I would vacate the judgment of the Court of Appeals for the District of Columbia Circuit on this ground and remand the case for further proceedings in the District Court. Before the commencement of such further proceedings, due opportunity should be afforded the Government for procuring from the Secretary of State or the Secretary of Defense or both an expression of their views on the issue of national security. The ensuing review by the District Court should be in accordance with the views expressed in this opinion. And for the reasons stated above I would affirm the judgment of the Court of Appeals for the Second Circuit.

Pending further hearings in each case conducted under the appropriate ground rules, I would continue the restraints on publication. I cannot believe that the doctrine prohibiting prior restraints reaches to the point of preventing courts from maintaining the *status quo* long enough to act responsibly in matters of such national importance as those involved here.

MR. JUSTICE BLACKMUN, *dissenting.*

I join Mr. Justice Harlan in his dissent. I also am in substantial accord with much that Mr. Justice White says, by way of admonition, in the latter part of his opinion. . . .

Two federal district courts, two United States courts of appeals, and this Court—within a period of less than three weeks from inception until today—have been pressed into hurried decision of profound constitutional issues on inadequately developed and largely assumed facts without the careful deliberation that, one would hope, should characterize the American judicial process. There has been much writing about the law and little knowledge and less digestion of the facts. In the

New York case the judges, both trial and appellate, had not yet examined the basic material when the case was brought here. In the District of Columbia case, little more was done, and what was accomplished in this respect was only on required remand, with the Washington Post, on the excuse that it was trying to protect its source of information, initially refusing to reveal what material it actually possessed, and with the District Court forced to make assumptions as to that possession.

With such respect as may be due to the contrary view, this, in my opinion, is not the way to try a lawsuit of this magnitude and asserted importance. It is not the way for federal courts to adjudicate, and to be required to adjudicate, issues that allegedly concern the Nation's vital welfare. The country would be none the worse off were the cases tried quickly, to be sure, but in the customary and properly deliberative manner. The most recent of the material, it is said, dates no later than 1968, already about three years ago, and the Times itself took three months to formulate its plan of procedure and, thus, deprived its public for that period.

The First Amendment, after all, is only one part of an entire Constitution. Article II of the great document vests in the Executive Branch primary power over the conduct of foreign affairs and places in that branch the responsibility for the Nation's safety. Each provision of the Constitution is important, and I cannot subscribe to a doctrine of unlimited absolutism for the First Amendment at the cost of downgrading other provisions. First Amendment absolutism has never commanded a majority of this Court. See, for example, *Near* v. *Minnesota* (1931), and *Schenck* v. *United States* (1919). What is needed here is a weighing, upon properly developed standards, of the broad right of the press to print and of the very narrow right of the Government to prevent. The parties here are in disagreement as to what those standards should be. But even the newspapers concede that there

are situations where restraint is in order and is constitutional. . . .

I therefore would remand these cases to be developed expeditiously, of course, but on a schedule permitting the orderly presentation of evidence from both sides, with the use of discovery, if necessary, as authorized by the rules, and with the preparation of briefs, oral argument, and court opinions of a quality better than has been seen to this point. In making this last statement, I criticize no lawyer or judge. I know from past personal experience the agony of time pressure in the preparation of litigation. But these cases and the issues involved and the courts, including this one, deserve better than has been produced thus far. . . .

The Court, however, decides the cases today the other way. I therefore add one final comment.

I strongly urge, and sincerely hope, that these two newspapers will be fully aware of their ultimate responsibilities to the United States of America. Judge Wilkey, dissenting in the District of Columbia case, after a review of only the affidavits before his court (the basic papers had not then been made available by either party), concluded that there were a number of examples of documents that, if in the possession of the Post, and if published, "could clearly result in great harm to the nation," and he defined "harm" to mean "the death of soldiers, the destruction of alliances, the greatly increased difficulty of negotiation with our enemies, the inability of our diplomats to negotiate. . . ." I, for one, have now been able to give at least some cursory study not only to the affidavits, but to the material itself. I regret to say that from this examination I fear that Judge Wilkey's statements have possible foundation. I therefore share his concern. I hope that damage has not already been done. If, however, damage has been done, and if, with the Court's action today, these newspapers proceed to publish the critical documents and there results therefrom "the death of soldiers, the destruction of alliances, the greatly increased difficulty of negotiation with our enemies, the inability of our diplomats to negotiate," to which list I might add the factors of prolongation of the war and of further delay in the freeing of United States prisoners, then the Nation's people will know where the responsibility for these sad consequences rests.

BRANZBURG v. HAYS

408 U.S. 665; 33 L. Ed. 2d 626; 92 S.Ct. 2646 (1972)

Opinion of the Court by MR. JUSTICE WHITE, *announced by* THE CHIEF JUSTICE.

The issue in these cases* is whether requiring newsmen to appear and testify before State or federal grand juries abridges the freedom of speech and press guaranteed by the First Amendment. We hold that it does not.

. . . *Branzburg* . . . brings before us two judgments of the Kentucky Court of Appeals, both involving the petitioner . . . , a staff reporter for the Courier-Journal . . . [Louisville].

On November 15, 1969, the Courier-Journal carried a story under petitioner's by-line describing in detail his observations of two young residents of Jefferson County synthesizing hashish from marihuana, an activity which, they asserted, earned them about $5,000 in three weeks. The article included a photograph of a pair of hands working above a laboratory table on which was a substance identified by the caption as hashish. The article stated that petitioner had promised not to reveal the identity of the two hashish makers. Petitioner was shortly subpoenaed by the Jefferson County grand jury; he appeared, but refused to identify the individuals he had seen possessing marihuana or the persons he had seen making hashish from marihuana. A state trial court judge ordered

*The other companion cases are *United States v. Caldwell* and *In re Pappas.*

petitioner to answer these questions and rejected his contention that the Kentucky reporters' privilege statute, . . . the First Amendment of the United States Constitution, or sections 1, 2, and 8 of the Kentucky Constitution authorized his refusal to answer. Petitioner then sought prohibition and mandamus in the Kentucky Court of Appeals on the same grounds, but the Court of Appeals denied the petition. . . .

The second case involving petitioner Branzburg arose out of his later story published on January 10, 1971, which described in detail the use of drugs in Frankfort, Franklin County, Kentucky. The article reported that in order to provide a comprehensive survey of the "drug scene" in Frankfort, petitioner had "spent two weeks interviewing several dozen drug users in the capital city" and had seen some of them smoking marihuana. A number of conversations with and observations of several unnamed drug users were recounted. Subpoenaed to appear before a Franklin County grand jury "to testify in the matter of violation of statutes concerning use and sale of drugs," petitioner Branzburg moved to quash the summons, the motion was denied although an order was issued protecting Branzburg from revealing "confidential associations, sources or information" but requiring that he "answer any questions which concern or pertain to any criminal act, the commission of which was actually observed by him." . . . [The Kentucky Court of Appeals affirmed]. . . .

In the Matter of Paul Pappas ... originated when petitioner Pappas, a television newsman-photographer working out of the Providence, Rhode Island, office of a New Bedford, Massachusetts, television station, was called to New Bedford on July 30, 1970, to report on civil disorders there which involved fires and other turmoil. He intended to cover a Black Panther news conference at that group's headquarters in a boarded-up store. Petitioner found the streets around the store barricaded, but he ultimately gained entrance to the area and recorded and photographed a prepared statement read by one of the Black Panther leaders at about 3:00 p.m. He then asked for and received permission to re-enter the area. Returning at about 9:00 p.m. that evening, he was allowed to enter and remain inside Panther headquarters. As a condition of entry, Pappas agreed not to disclose anything he saw or heard inside the store except an anticipated police raid which Pappas, "on his own," was free to photograph and report as he wished. Pappas stayed inside the headquarters for about three hours, but there was no police raid, and petitioner wrote no story and did not otherwise reveal what had transpired in the store while he was there. Two months later, petitioner was summoned before the Bristol County Grand Jury and appeared, answered questions as to his name, address, employment, and what he had seen and heard outside Panther headquarters, but refused to answer any questions about what had taken place inside headquarters while he was there, claiming that the First Amendment afforded him a privilege to protect confidential informants and their information. A second summons was then served upon him, again directing him to appear before the Grand Jury and "to give such evidence as he knows relating to any matters which may be inquired of on behalf of the commonwealth before ... the Grand Jury." His motion to quash on First Amendment and other grounds was denied by the trial judge who, noting the absence of a statutory newsman's privilege in Massachusetts, ruled that petitioner had no constitutional privilege to refuse to divulge to the Grand Jury what he had seen and heard, including the identity of persons he had observed. ... [T]he Supreme Judicial Court of Massachusetts ... reaffirmed prior Massachusetts holdings that testimonial privileges were "exceptional" and "limited," stating that "[t]he principle that the public 'has a right to every man's evidence' " had usually been preferred, in the Commonwealth, to countervailing interests. ... The Court ... "adhere[d] to the view that there exists no constitutional newsman's privilege, either qualified or absolute, to refuse to appear and testify before a court or grand jury." Any adverse effect upon the free dissemination of news by virtue of petitioner's being called to testify was deemed to be only "indirect, theoretical, and uncertain." ... The denial of the motion to quash was affirmed and we granted a writ of certiorari to petitioner Pappas. ...

United States v. *Caldwell* ... arose from subpoenas issued by a federal grand jury in the Northern District of California to respondent Earl Caldwell, a reporter for the New York Times assigned to cover the Black Panther Party and other black militant groups. A subpoena ... was served on respondent on February 2, 1970, ordering him to appear before the grand jury to testify and to bring with him notes and tape recordings of interviews given him for publication by officers and spokesmen of the Black Panther Party concerning the aims, purposes, and activities of that organization. Respondent objected to the scope of this subpoena, and an agreement between his counsel and the government attorneys resulted in a continuance. A second subpoena was served on March 16, which omitted the documentary requirement and simply ordered Caldwell "to appear ... to testify before the Grand Jury." Respondent and his employer, the New York Times, moved to quash on the ground that the unlimited breadth of the subpoenas and the fact that Caldwell would have to appear in secret before the grand jury would destroy his working relationship with the Black

Panther Party and "suppress vital First Amendment freedoms ... by driving a wedge of distrust and silence between the news media and the militants."... Respondent argued that "so drastic an incursion upon First Amendment freedoms" should not be permitted "in the absence of a compelling governmental interest—not shown here—in requiring Mr. Caldwell's appearance before the grand jury." ...

On April 6, the District Court denied the motion to quash ... on the ground that "*every person* within the jurisdiction of the government" is bound to testify upon being properly summoned.... Nevertheless, the court accepted respondent's First Amendment arguments to the extent of issuing a protective order providing that although respondent must divulge whatever information had been given to him for publication, he "shall not be required to reveal confidential associations, sources or information received, developed or maintained by him as a professional journalist in the course of his efforts to gather news for dissemination to the public through the press or other news media." The court held that the First Amendment afforded respondent a privilege to refuse disclosure of such confidential information until there had been "a showing by the Government of a compelling and overriding national interest in requiring Mr. Caldwell's testimony which cannot be served by any alternative means." ...

Subsequently, the term of the grand jury expired, a new grand jury was convened, and a new subpoena ... was issued and served on May 22, 1970. A new motion to quash by respondent and memorandum in opposition by the Government were filed, and by stipulation of the parties, the motion was submitted on the prior record. The court denied the motion to quash.... Respondent refused to appear before the grand jury, and the court issued an order to show cause why he should not be held in contempt. Upon his further refusal to go before the grand jury, respondent was ordered committed for contempt until such time as he

complied with the court's order or until the expiration of the term of the grand jury.

Respondent Caldwell appealed the contempt order, and the Court of Appeals reversed.... Absent compelling reasons for requiring his testimony, he was held privileged to withhold it. The court also held, for similar First Amendment reasons, that absent some special showing of necessity by the Government, attendance by Caldwell at a secret meeting of the grand jury was something he was privileged to refuse because of the potential impact of such an appearance on the flow of news to the public. We granted the United States petition for certiorari....

I

Petitioners Branzburg and Pappas and respondent Caldwell press First Amendment claims that may be simply put: that to gather news it is often necessary to agree either not to identify the source of information published or to publish only part of the facts revealed, or both; that if the reporter is nevertheless forced to reveal these confidences to a grand jury, the source so identified and other confidential sources of other reporters will be measurably deterred from furnishing publishable information, all to the detriment of the free flow of information protected by the First Amendment.... The heart of the claim is that the burden on news gathering resulting from compelling reporters to disclose confidential information outweighs any public interest in obtaining the information....

The sole issue before us is the obligation of reporters to respond to grand jury subpoenas as other citizens do and to answer questions relevant to an investigation into the commission of crime. Citizens generally are not constitutionally immune from grand jury subpoenas; and neither the First Amendment nor other constitutional provision protects the average citizen from disclosing to a grand jury information that he has received in confidence. The claim is, however, that reporters are exempt from these obligations. . . . This asserted burden on news gathering is said to make compelled testimony from newsmen constitutionally suspect and to require a privileged position for them.

It is clear that the First Amendment does not invalidate every incidental burdening of the press that may result from the enforcement of civil or ciminal statutes of general applicability. Under prior cases, otherwise valid laws serving substantial public interests may be enforced against the press as against others, despite the possible burden that may be imposed. . . .

Despite the fact that news gathering may be hampered, the press is regularly excluded from grand jury proceedings, our own conferences, the meetings of other official bodies gathered in executive session, and the meetings of private organizations. Newsmen have no constitutional right of access to the scenes of crime or disaster when the general public is excluded, and they may be prohibited from attending or publishing information about trials if such restrictions are necessary to assure a defendant a fair trial before an impartial tribunal. . . .

It is thus not surprising that the great weight of authority is that newsmen are not exempt from the normal duty of appearing before a grand jury and answering questions relevant to a criminal investigation. At common law, courts consistently refused to recognize the existence of any privilege authorizing a newsman to refuse to reveal confidential information to a grand jury. . . .

The prevailing constitutional view of the newsman's privilege is very much rooted in the ancient role of the grand jury which has the dual function of determining if there is probable cause to believe that a crime has been committed and of protecting citizens against unfounded criminal prosecutions. Grand jury proceedings are constitutionally mandated for the institution of federal criminal prosecutions for capital or other serious crimes, and "its constitutional prerogatives are rooted in long centuries of Anglo-American history." . . . Because its task is to inquire into the existence of possible criminal conduct and to return only well-founded indictments, its investigative powers are necessarily broad. . . . Hence the grand jury's authority to subpoena witnesses is not only historic, . . . but essential to its task. . . .

A number of States have provided newsmen a statutory privilege of varying breadth, but the majority have not done so, and none has been provided by federal statute. Until now the only testimonial privilege for unofficial witnesses that is rooted in the Federal Constitution is the Fifth Amendment privilege against compelled self-incrimination. We are asked to create another by interpreting the First Amendment to grant newsmen a testimonial privilege that other citizens do not enjoy. This we decline to do. Fair and effective law enforcement aimed at providing security for the person and property of the individual is a fundamental function of government, and the grand jury plays an important, constitutionally mandated role in this process. On the records now before us, we perceive no basis for holding that the public interest in law enforcement and in ensuring effective grand jury proceedings is insufficient to override the consequential, but uncertain, burden on news gathering which is said to result from insisting that reporters, like other citizens, respond to relevant questions put to them in the course of a valid grand jury investigation or criminal trial.

This conclusion itself involves no restraint on what newspapers may publish or on the type or quality of information reporters may seek to acquire, nor does it threaten the vast bulk of confidential relationships between reporters and their sources. . . . Only where news sources themselves are implicated in crime or possess information relevant to the grand jury's task need they or the reporter be concerned about grand jury subpoenas. . . .

Thus, we cannot seriously entertain the notion that the First Amendment protects a newsman's agreement to conceal the criminal conduct of his source, or evidence thereof, on the theory that it is better to write about crime than to do something about it. Insofar as any reporter in these cases undertook not to reveal or testify about the crime he witnessed, his claim of privilege under the First Amendment presents no substantial question. The crimes of news sources are no less reprehensible and threatening to the public interest when witnessed by a reporter than when they are not.

There remain those situations where a source is not engaged in criminal conduct but has information suggesting illegal conduct by others. Newsmen frequently receive information from such sources pursuant to a tacit or express agreement to withhold the source's name and suppress any information that the source wishes not published. Such informants presumably desire anonymity in order to avoid being entangled as a witness in a criminal trial or grand jury investigation. They may fear that disclosure will threaten their job security or personal safety or that it will simply result in dishonor or embarrassment.

The argument that the flow of news will be diminished by compelling reporters to aid the grand jury in a criminal investigation is not irrational, nor are the records before us silent on the matter. But we remain unclear how often and to what extent informers are actually deterred from furnishing information when newsmen are forced to testify before a grand jury. The available data indicates that some newsmen rely a great deal on confidential sources and that some informants are particularly sensitive to the threat of exposure and may be silenced if it is held by this Court that, ordinarily, newsmen must testify pursuant to subpoenas, but the evidence fails to demonstrate that there would be a significant constriction of the flow of news to the public if this Court reaffirms the prior common law and constitutional rule regarding the testimonial obligations of newsmen. . . .

Accepting the fact . . . that an undetermined number of informants not themselves implicated in crime will nevertheless, for whatever reason, refuse to talk to newsmen if they fear identification by a reporter in an official investigation, we cannot accept the argument that the public interest in possible future news about crime from undisclosed, unverified sources must take precedence over the public interest in pursuing and in thus deterring the commission of such crimes in the future. . . .

Of course, the press has the right to abide by its agreement not to publish all the information it has, but the right to withhold news is not equivalent to a First Amendment exemption from the ordinary duty of all other citizens to furnish relevant information to a grand jury performing an important public function. Private restraints on the flow of information are not so favored by the First Amendment that they override all other public interests. . . .

Neither are we now convinced that a virtually impenetrable constitutional shield, beyond legislative or judicial control, should be forged to protect a private system of informers operated by the press to report on criminal conduct, a system that would be unaccountable to the public, would pose a threat to the citizen's justifiable expectations of privacy, and would equally protect well-intentioned informants and those who for pay or otherwise betray their trust to their employer or associates. The public through its elected and appointed law enforcement officers regularly utilizes informers, and in proper circumstances may assert a privilege against disclosing the identity of these informers. . . . Such informers enjoy no constitutional protection. Their testimony is available to the public when desired by grand juries or at criminal trials; their identity cannot be concealed from the defendant when it is critical to his case. . . .

The argument for such a constitutional privilege rests heavily on those cases holding that the infringement of protected First Amendment rights must be no broader than necessary to achieve a permissible governmental purpose. . . .

We do not deal, however, with a governmental institution that has abused its proper function, as a legislative committee does when it "expose[s] for the sake of exposure." . . . Nothing in the record indicates that these grand juries were "prob[ing] at will and without relation to existing need." . . . Also, there is no attempt here by the grand juries to invade protected First Amendment rights by forcing wholesale disclosure of names and organizational affiliations for a purpose which is not germane to the determination of whether crime has been committed. . . .

The privilege claimed here is conditional, not absolute; given the suggested preliminary showings and compelling need, the reporter would be required to testify. Presumably, such a rule would reduce the instances in which reporters could be required to appear, but predicting in advance when and in what circumstances they could be compelled to do so would be difficult. Such a rule would also have implications for the issuance of compulsory process to reporters at civil and criminal trials and at legislative hearings. If newsmen's confidential sources are as sensitive as they are claimed to be, the prospect of being unmasked whenever a judge determines the situation justifies it is hardly a satisfactory solution to the problem. For them, it would appear that only an absolute privilege would suffice.

We are unwilling to embark the judiciary on a long and difficult journey to such an uncertain destination. The administration of a constitutional newsman's privilege would present practical and conceptual difficulties of a high order. Sooner or later, it would be necessary to define those categories of newsmen who qualified for the privilege, a questionable procedure in light of the traditional doctrine that liberty of the press is the right of the lonely pamphleteer who uses carbon paper or a mimeograph just as much as of the large metropolitan publisher who utilizes the latest photocomposition methods. . . .

Thus, in the end, by considering whether enforcement of a particular law served a "com-pelling" governmental interest, the courts would be inextricably involved in distinguishing between the value of enforcing different criminal laws. By requiring testimony from a reporter in investigations involving some crimes but not in others, they would be making a value judgment which a legislature had declined to make, since in each case the criminal law involved would represent a considered legislative judgment, not constitutionally suspect, of what conduct is liable to criminal prosecution. . . .

At the federal level, Congress has freedom to determine whether a statutory newsman's privilege is necessary and desirable and to fashion standards and rules as narrow or broad as deemed necessary to address the evil discerned and, equally important, to re-fashion those rules as experience from time to time may dictate. There is also merit in leaving state legislatures free, within First Amendment limits, to fashion their own standards in light of the conditions and problems with respect to the relations between law enforcement officials and press in their own areas. . . .

Finally, as we have earlier indicated, news gathering is not without its First Amendment protections, and grand jury investigations if instituted or conducted other than in good faith, would pose wholly different issues for resolution under the First Amendment. Official harassment of the press undertaken not for purposes of law enforcement but to disrupt a reporter's relationship with his news sources would have no justification. Grand juries are subject to judicial control and subpoenas to motions to quash. We do not expect courts will forget that grand juries must operate within the limits of the First Amendment as well as the Fifth.

III

We turn, therefore, to the disposition of the cases before us. From what we have said, it necessarily follows that the decision in *United*

States v. *Caldwell* . . . must be reversed. If there is no First Amendment privilege to refuse to answer the relevant and material questions asked during a good-faith grand jury investigation, then it is *a fortiori* true that there is no privilege to refuse to appear before such a grand jury until the Government demonstrates some "compelling need" for a newsman's testimony. . . .

The [Branzburg] decisions . . . must be affirmed. Here, petitioner refused to answer questions that directly related to criminal conduct which he had observed and written about. . . . [I]f what petitioner wrote was true, he had direct information to provide the grand jury concerning the commission of serious crimes.

The only question presented at the present time in *In the Matter of Paul Pappas*, . . . is whether petitioner Pappas must appear before the grand jury to testify pursuant to subpoena. . . . We affirm the decision of the Massachusetts Supreme Judicial Court and hold that petitioner must appear before the grand jury to answer the questions put to him, subject, of course, to the supervision of the presiding judge as to "the propriety, purposes, and scope of the grand jury inquiry and the pertinence of the probable testimony. " . . .

[The separate concurring opinion of Justice Lewis Powell and the dissenting opinion of Justice William O. Douglas are not reprinted here.]

MR. JUSTICE STEWART, *with whom* MR. JUSTICE BRENNAN *and* MR. JUSTICE MARSHALL *join, dissenting.*

The Court's crabbed view of the First Amendment reflects a disturbing insensitivity to the critical role of an independent press in our society. . . . The Court . . . invites state and federal authorities to undermine the historic independence of the press by attempting to annex the journalistic profession as an investigative arm of government. . . .

I

The reporter's constitutional right to a confidential relationship with his source stems from the broad societal interest in a full and free flow of information to the public. It is this basic concern that underlies the Constitution's protection of a free press. . . .

Enlightened choice by an informed citizenry is the basic ideal upon which an open society is premised, and a free press is thus indispensable to a free society. Not only does the press enhance personal self-fulfillment by providing the people with the widest possible range of fact and opinion, but it also is an incontestable precondition of self-government. The press "has been a mighty catalyst in awakening interest in governmental affairs, exposing corruption among public officers and employees and generally informing the citizenry of public events and occurrences. . . ."

A

. . .

A corollary of the right to publish must be the right to gather news. The full flow of information to the public protected by the free press guarantee would be severely curtailed if no protection whatever were afforded to the process by which news is assembled and disseminated. We have, therefore, recognized that there is a right to publish without prior governmental approval, *Near* v. *Minnesota*, 283 U.S. 697; *New York Times* v. *United States,* 403 U.S. 713, a right to distribute information, see, e.g., *Lovell* v. *Griffin*, 303 U.S. 444, . . . and a right to receive printed matter, *Lamont* v. *Postmaster General*, 381 U.S. 301.

No less important to the news dissemination process is the gathering of information. News must not be unnecessarily cut off at its source, for without freedom to acquire information the right to publish would be impermissibly compromised. . . .

B

The right to gather news implies, in turn, a right to a confidential relationship between a reporter and his source. This proposition follows as a matter of simple logic once three factual predicates are recognized: (1) newsmen require informants to gather news; (2) confidentiality—the promise or understanding that names or certain aspects of communications will be kept off-the-record—is essential to the creation and maintenance of a news-gathering relationship with informants; and (3) the existence of an unbridled subpoena power—the absence of a constitutional right protecting, in *any* way, a confidential relationship from compulsory process—will either deter sources from divulging information or deter reporters from gathering and publishing information. . . .

After today's decision, the potential informant can never be sure that his identity or off-the-record communications will not subsequently be revealed through the compelled testimony of a newsman. A public spirited person inside government, who is not implicated in any crime, will now be fearful of revealing corruption or other governmental wrong-doing, because he will now know he can subsequently be identified by use of compulsory process. The potential source, must, therefore, choose between risking exposure by giving information or avoiding the risk by remaining silent.

The reporter must speculate about whether contact with a controversial source or publication of controversial material will lead to a subpoena. In the event of a subpoena, under today's decision, the newsman will know that he must choose between being punished for contempt if he refuses to testify, or violating his profession's ethics and impairing his resourcefulness as a reporter if he discloses confidential information. . . .

Again, the common sense understanding that such deterrence will occur is buttressed by concrete evidence. The existence of deterrent effects through fear and self-censorship was impressively developed in the District Court in *Caldwell*. Individual reporters and commentators have noted such effects. Surveys have verified that an unbridled subpoena power will substantially impair the flow of news to the public, especially in sensitive areas involving governmental officials, financial affairs, political figures, dissidents, or minority groups that require in-depth, investigative reporting. And the Justice Department has recognized that "compulsory process in some circumstances may have a limiting effect on the exercise of First Amendment rights. " . . .

Thus, we cannot escape the conclusion that when neither the reporter nor his source can rely on the shield of confidentiality against unrestrained use of the grand jury's subpoena power, valuable information will not be published and the public dialogue will inevitably be impoverished.

II

Posed against the First Amendment's protection of the newsman's confidential relationships in these cases is society's interest in the use of the grand jury to administer justice fairly and effectively. . .

[T]he longstanding rule making every person's evidence available to the grand jury is not absolute. The rule has been limited by the Fifth Amendment, the Fourth Amendment, and the evidentiary privileges of the common law. . . . [T]he Court [has] noted that "some confidential matters are shielded from considerations of policy, and perhaps in [some] cases for *special reasons* a witness may be excused from telling all he knows." And in *United States* v. *Bryan*, 339 U.S. 323, the Court observed that any exemption from the duty to testify before the grand jury "presupposes a very real interest to be protected." *Id.* at 331-332.

Such an interest must surely be the First Amendment protection of a confidential relationship that I have discussed above in Part I. As noted there, this protection does not exist for the purely private interest of the newsman or his informant, nor even, at bottom, for the First Amendment interests of either partner in the news-gathering relationship. Rather it functions to insure nothing less than democratic decision-making through the free flow of information to the public, and it serves, thereby, to honor the "profound national commitment to the principle that debate on public issues should be uninhibited, robust, and wide-open. " . . .

In striking the proper balance between the public interest of the efficient administration of justice and the First Amendment guarantee of the fullest flow of information . . . because of their "delicate and vulnerable" nature . . . and their transcendent importance for the just functioning of our society, First Amendment rights require special safeguards. . . .

Governmental officials must . . . demonstrate that the information sought is *clearly* relevant to a *precisely* defined subject of governmental inquiry. They must demonstrate that it is reasonable to think the witness in question has that information. And they must show that there is not any means of obtaining the information less destructive of First Amendment liberties. . . .

I believe the safeguards developed in our decisions involving governmental investigations must apply to the grand jury inquiries in these cases. Surely the function of the grand jury to aid in the enforcement of the law is no more important than the function of the legislature, and its committees, to make the law. . . .

Accordingly, when a reporter is asked to appear before a grand jury and reveal confidences, I would hold that the government must (1) show that there is probable cause to believe that the newsman has information which is clearly relevant to a specific probable violation of law; (2) demonstrate that the information sought cannot be obtained by alternative means less destructive of First Amendment rights; and (3) demonstrate a compelling and overriding interest in the information. . . .

The crux of the Court's rejection of any newsman's privilege is its observation that only "where news sources themselves are implicated in crime or possess information relevant to the grand jury's task need they or the reporter be concerned about grand jury subpoenas." But this is a most misleading construct. For it is obviously not true that the only persons about whom reporters will be forced to testify will be those "confidential informants involved in actual criminal conduct" and those having "information suggesting illegal conduct by others. " . . . [G]iven the grand jury's extraordinarily broad investigative powers and weak standards of relevance and materiality that apply during such inquiries, reporters, if they have no testimonial privilege, will be called to give information about informants who have neither committed crimes nor have information about crime. It is to avoid deterrence of such sources and thus to prevent needless injury to First Amendment values that I think the government must be required to show probable cause that the newsman has information which is clearly relevant to a specific probable violation of criminal law. . . .

Both the "probable cause" and "alternative means" requirements would thus serve the vital function of mediating between the public interest in the administration of justice and the constitutional protection of the full flow of information. These requirements would avoid a direct conflict between these competing concerns, and they would generally provide adequate protection for newsmen. . . .

The error in the Court's absolute rejection of First Amendment interests in these cases seems to me to be most profound. For in the name of advancing the administration of justice, the Court's decision, I think, will only impair the achievement of that goal. People entrusted with law enforcement responsibility, no less than private citizens, need general information relating to controversial social problems. Obviously, press reports have great value to government, even when the newsman cannot be compelled to testify before a grand jury. The sad paradox of the Court's position is that when a grand jury may exercise an unbridled subpoena power, and sources involved in sensitive matters become fearful of disclosing information, the newsman will not only cease to be a useful grand jury witness; he will cease to investigate and publish information about issues of public import. I cannot subscribe to such an anomalous result, for, in my view, the interests protected by the First Amendment are not antagonistic to the administration of justice. Rather, they can, in the long run, only be complementary, and for that reason must be given great "breathing space." . . .

Accordingly, I would affirm the judgment of the Court of Appeals in . . .*Caldwell.* In the other two cases before us, *Branzburg* . . . and . . . *In the Matter of Paul Pappas,* I would vacate the judgments and remand the cases for further proceedings not inconsistent with the views I have expressed in this opinion.

SELECTED REFERENCES

Barber, Kathleen, "Legal Status of the American Communist Party," 15 *Journal of Public Law* 94 (1966).

Chafee, Zechariah, *Free Speech in the United States* (Cambridge, Mass.: Harvard University Press, 1948).

Cook, Thomas I., *Democratic Rights versus Communist Activity* (Garden City, N.Y.: Doubleday & Co., Inc., 1954).

Gellhorn, Walter, *Individual Freedom and Governmental Restraint* (Baton Rouge, La.: L. S. U. Press, 1956.)

Goodman, Walter, *The Committee: The Extraordinary Career of the House Committee on Un-American Activities* (New York: Farrar, Straus & Giroux, Inc., 1968).

Guttmann, Allen and Benjamin Ziegler, eds., *Communism, the Courts and the Constitution* (Boston: D. C. Heath, 1964).

Latham, Earl, *The Communist Controversy in Washington from the New Deal to McCarthy* (Cambridge, Mass.: Harvard University Press, 1966).

Levy, Leonard W., *Legacy of Suppression: Freedom of Speech and Press in Early American History* (Cambridge, Mass.: Harvard University Press, 1960).

McCloskey, Robert G., "Free Speech, Sedition and the Constitution," 45 *American Political Science Review* 662 (1951).

Note, "The National Security Interest and Civil Liberties," 85 *Harvard Law Review* 1130 (1972). (Includes extensive reference notes to materials on major problems of national security.)

5 The Rights of the Accused

Mapp v. *Ohio*   *Coolidge* v. *New Hampshire*   *Adams* v. *Williams*   *United States* v. *White*
Malloy v. *Hogan*   *Kastigar* v. *United States*   *Gideon* v. *Wainwright*   *Miranda* v. *Arizona*
Harris v. *New York*   *In re Gault*   *Apodaca* v. *Oregon*   *Furman* v. *Georgia*

The Warren Court, particularly after 1961, wrought radical changes in the constitutional rules applying to "cops and robbers." Prior to these revolutionary changes, state criminal procedures were based largely on state constitutional and statutory provisions. Specific guarantees of the federal Bill of Rights were not applicable; Chief Justice Marshall's early decision in *Barron* v. *Baltimore* supported this position. Although eroded after 1925, *Barron* still was considered good law, particularly where the rights of the accused were concerned. Time and again the Court brushed aside arguments that the Fourteenth Amendment was intended to reverse *Barron* and to incorporate the Bill of Rights. Even the Court's acceptance of the "selective incorporation" theory announced in *Palko* v. *Connecticut, supra*, did not result in any immediate change in the application of Bill of Rights guarantees to state criminal procedures. For more than two decades after *Palko*, the Court held to the position that the states were not restricted by specific procedures of the Bill of Rights in their criminal procedures. But beginning in 1961 the Court made a dramatic change in its position—so dramatic in fact that it may be characterized as revolutionary.

By 1969, however, a number of forces combined to slow down, and in some instances, signal a reversal of this trend. Richard Nixon, as the new President, had played on the law-and-order theme during his successful campaign for the Presidency. One of the things he saw as crucial to reversal of the alarming rise of serious crimes in the country was Supreme Court decisions that supported the "peace forces" and would remove the "barbed wire of legalism" protecting the "criminal forces." Chief Justice Earl Warren's declaration in the spring of 1968 of his intention to retire, the controversy surrounding President Johnson's attempt to elevate Associate Justice Abe Fortas to fill that impending vacancy, and the subsequent resignation of Justice Fortas from the Court all combined to present the new President two seats on the Court for him to fill immediately upon taking office. In his new Chief Justice Warren E. Burger and the new Associate Justice Harry A. Blackmun, the President found the kind of "strict constructionist" jurists he felt were needed on the Court to redirect the trend of decisions in the criminal law area. Nixon did not have to wait long for additional support to further this objective when in rapid succession in 1971 Justice Hugo Black died and Justice John M. Harlan II retired because of poor health. These seats were filled by Lewis F. Powell and William Rehnquist, two lawyers with strong credentials consistent with President Nixon's "law and order" views. The commentary that follows examines several dimensions of the Warren Court "criminal law explosion" as well as several initial Burger Court actions in some of those areas.

THE SEARCH AND SEIZURE PROBLEM

Despite the noble profession of justice expressed in the Fourth Amendment that "the right of the people to be secure in their persons, houses, papers, and effects, against unreasonable searches and seizures, shall not be violated . . . ," most persons whose liberty was in conflict with state governmental authority were not the beneficiaries of this guarantee. For the states, as primary enforcers of criminal law under our federal system, were not bound by the Fourth Amendment. State actions were governed by similar provisions in state bills of rights, and the enforcement of those guarantees was at best wavering, uncertain, and uneven. By contrast, for those whose liberty was in conflict with federal authority, the Fourth Amendment had real meaning. As far back as 1886, in *Boyd* v. *United States* (116 U.S. 616), the Court tied the Fourth Amendment to the Fifth Amendment's self-incrimination provision holding that an unreasonable search and seizure is the same as a compulsion of a person to be a witness against himself. Subsequently, the Court ruled in *Weeks* v.*United States* (232 U.S. 383, 1914) that evidence obtained in violation of the Amendment is inadmissible in criminal prosecutions.

Some states voluntarily adopted the *Weeks* rule, but most did not, and when in *Wolf* v. *Colorado* (338 U.S. 25, 1949) the Court was urged to make the rule obligatory on the states, it refused to do so. Though the Court agreed that the Fourth Amendment guarantee against unreasonable searches and seizures was enforceable against the states through the Fourteenth Amendment, the Court nevertheless concluded that the exclusionary rule announced in *Weeks* was not an "essential ingredient" of that guarantee. The Court emphasized that the exclusionary rule was merely a rule of evidence imposed on federal courts, and state courts were free to admit or exclude illegally seized evidence as thier laws might require.

Subsequent cases involving the Fourth Amendment revealed the impracticality of the *Wolf* rule. In *Rochin* v. *California* (342 U.S. 165, 1952), for example, the Court bypassed the rule in reversing a state narcotics conviction. The evidence admitted in the case had been obtained after forcible entry without a warrant and the subsequent pumping of the stomach of the accused. Clearly here was a case where the evidence was tainted, but the *Wolf* precedent would allow its admission. However, Justice Felix Frankfurter solved the dilemma by simply holding that due process was offended because the conduct used by the police to obtain the evidence "shocks the conscience."

But in *Irvine* v. *California* (347 U.S. 128, 1954) the Court still clung to *Wolf*. Here, evidence used in supporting a conviction for illegal bookmaking was obtained by taking advantage of Irvine's periodic absences from his residence. A key made by a locksmith enabled the police to enter Irvine's house and plant a concealed microphone that allowed them to monitor his conversations from a neighboring garage. On two subsequent occasions the police reentered the residence to relocate the microphone for better results. Testimony as to what the officers heard was admitted at the trial. Justice Robert H. Jackson delivered the opinion for the five-man majority affirming the conviction. Though Justice Jackson recognized the unsavory methods employed in obtaining the evidence and suggested that there was evidence of trespassing and probably burglary, he nevertheless held that under the *Wolf* rule the evidence was admissible. His defense of the rule was essentially this: to exclude the evidence would result in the guilty person's escaping punishment and his subsequent release would further endanger society, while the exclusion does nothing to punish the wrongdoing official. Justice Frankfurter dissented and said he would have followed the *Rochin* rule because of the "additional aggravating conduct" of the police. Justice William O. Douglas' dissent echoed his familiar theme that the Court should never have departed from the exclusionary rule when it decided *Wolf*, while Justice Hugo Black thought the action infringed the self-incrimination guarantee. Justice Tom Clark, although concurring, expressed serious doubts about the admissibility of evidence allowed under *Wolf* and stated that had he been on the Court in 1949 he would have supported the application of the *Weeks* rule to the states.

Two subsequent actions portended the demise of the *Wolf* rule. First, Chief Justice Earl Warren's strong dissent in *Briethaupt* v. *Abram* (352 U.S. 432, 1957) indicated that at least four justices were ready to overrule *Wolf*. The Court majority in *Briethaupt* upheld a conviction based on evidence obtained by taking a blood sample from the accused (while he was unconscious in a hospital) to prove intoxication. In a second action in 1960, the Court struck down the "silver platter" doctrine in *Elkins* v. *United States* (364 U.S. 206). That doctrine had permitted evidence illegally obtained by state officers to be admitted in federal prosecutions so long as there was no complicity.

In 1961 the *Wolf* rule was finally laid to rest in *Mapp* v. *Ohio*. *Mapp* commenced a period of revolutionary holdings in criminal due process by the Warren Court. Here the Court reversed a conviction for posession of obscene literature in which the evidence against the accused was obtained by forcible police entry without a search warrant. In his opinion for the five-man majority, Justice Tom Clark stressed the need to observe the command of the Fourth Amendment. He noted that the Court had held in *Wolf* that the right to privacy embodied in that Amendment was enforceable against the states and that it should no longer be permitted "to remain an empty promise." He concluded that "nothing can destroy a government more quickly than its failure to observe its laws, or worse, its disregard of the charter of its own existence."

Justice John Marshall Harlan's dissent was essentially a plea for judicial restraint and observance of precedents. He cautioned the majority that "the preservation of a proper balance between state and federal responsibility in the administration of criminal justice demands patience on the part of those who might like to see things move faster among the states [in this area]."

In its first application of the *Mapp* rule, the Court appeared to make a mild retreat. In *Ker* v. *California* (374 U.S. 23, 1963), the Court affirmed a conviction where the evidence was obtained without a search warrant and entry was gained by using the building manager's passkey. Justice Clark's opinion for the majority distinguished between state's evidence and evidence held inadmissible because it violates a federal statute. Noting that the evidence would have been inadmissible in a federal prosecution because a federal statute would bar it, he emphasized that such a prohibition had no application to a state prosecution "where admissibility is governed by constitutional standards." He concluded that the "demands of our federal system" compel such a distinction and that the states should not be "precluded from developing workable rules governing arrests, searches, and seizures to meet the practical demands of effective criminal investigation and law enforcement" so long as such rules do not offend federal constitutional standards.

But if *Ker* implied any "soft" application of *Mapp*, it was quickly dispelled one year later in *Aguillar* v. *Texas* (378 U.S. 108, 1964). Here the Court reversed a narcotics conviction and in doing so made it clear that the *Mapp* rule must be obeyed and that no shabby subterfuges would be tolerated. In speaking for the Court, Justice Arthur Goldberg said that an inquiry as to the constitutionality of a search warrant should begin with the rule that "the informed and deliberate determinations of magistrates empowered to issue warrants . . . are to be preferred over the hurried action of officers . . . who may happen to make the arrests." The "informant's 'suspicion,' 'belief,' or 'mere conclusion'" are not enough, insisted Goldberg. Probable cause to support issuance of a warrant must "be found from facts or circumstances presented under oath or affirmation."

The Court explicated further these principles in *Spinelli* v. *United States* (393 U.S. 410, 1969), when it reversed a federal criminal conviction for interstate travel in aid of bookmaking. Mr. Justice Harlan II's opinion for the Court emphasized that the affidavit in support of the application for a search warrant was inadequate because it did not meet the "two-pronged test" of *Aguillar*—(1) enumeration of the "underlying circumstances" essential to the issuing officer's assessment of the validity of information supplied by informants; and (2) sufficiency of data supplied by the affiant-officers to establish credibility of their informant and the reliability of his information. In holding that probable cause had not been sufficiently established for issuance of the warrant, Harlan maintained that the Court was not retreating from its established propositions which hold that:

(1) only the probability, and not a prima facie showing, of criminal activity is the standard of probable cause;

(2) affidavits of probable cause are tested by much less rigorous standards than those governing admissibility of evidence at trial;

(3) in determining probable cause, issuing magistrates are not proscribed from the use of their common sense; and

(4) reviewing courts should accord great deference to determinations of probable cause by issuing magistrates.

This rule was reaffirmed in *Coolidge* v. *New Hampsire* in 1971 and, at the same time, the Court examined extensively the warrantless search issue.[1] The case involved a conviction for murder where critical evidence was obtained from the search and seizure of the defendant's automobile. The warrant authorizing this action was issued by the state attorney general (acting as a justice of the peace) who had immediately assumed command of the investigation when the murder was reported. The state had attempted to support this procedure on the basis of *Ker* v. *California, supra*. But Justice Potter Stewart, speaking for the Court, made it clear that this procedure was *not* "one of those workable rules governing arrests, searches, and seizures [referred to in *Ker*] to meet the practical demands of effective criminal investigation and law enforcement." Furthermore, the state's attempt to distinguish between the standard of reasonableness required of Federal officials under the Fourth Amendment and that governing state officers under the Fourteenth Amendment was unpersuasive. Justice Potter Stewart emphasized that the issuing officer was not the "neutral and detached magistrate" that the Constitution requires. For "prosecutors and policemen" he argued, "simply cannot be asked to maintain the requisite neutrality with regard to their own investigations—the 'competitive enterprises' which must rightly engage their single-minded attention." Consequently, he concluded, a search conducted under such a defective warrant could not stand. Furthermore, it did not fall within one of the exceptions to the warrant requirement enunciated by the Court over the years, e.g., (1) a search incident to a lawful arrest; (2) where the evidence seized was in "plain view" of the police; and (3) where it would be impractical to secure a warrant for search of an automobile when it is an instrument of a crime.

One of the most expansive applications of the *Mapp* rule was made in *Camara* v. *City and County of San Francisco* (387 U.S. 523, 1967). There, the Court held that administrative searches by municipal health and safety inspectors are limited by the safeguards of the Fourth Amendment. Justice Byron White's opinion for the majority emphasized the basic purpose of the Amendment—to safeguard the privacy and the security of individuals against arbitrary invasions by governmental officials. While the governmental interest in enforcing housing codes may be substantial, it is not so overriding as to preclude conformity with the warrant

---

[1] See below p. 255, ff.

requirement of the Amendment. (Cf. *Wyman* v. *James*, 400 U.S. 309, 1971.) He made it clear, however, that the ruling was not intended to foreclose a prompt inspection, even without a warrant, when an emergency dictates it.

Should *Mapp* be applied prospectively to cases arising after that decision or retrospectively to cases decided under the *Wolf* rule where such persons had long since exhausted judicial remedies and were serving sentences? This question was answered almost four years after *Mapp* in *Linkletter* v. *Walker* (381 U.S. 618, 1965). Speaking for the majority, Justice Tom Clark noted that the Constitution is silent on the question and thus the Court was free to make its own determination based on the purpose of the decision. In making that determination, Clark examined several factors, including the purpose of the new rule, reliance placed on the old *Wolf* rule, and the impact and effect on the administration of justice resulting from a retrospective application. This examination led him and the Court to conclude that *Mapp* should be applied prospectively.

In a case decided near the end of the Court's 1970 term, Chief Justice Warren E. Burger's dissent forecast a possible contraction of the *Mapp* exclusionary rule with the gradual depletion of the Warren Court "activist" bloc. In *Bivens* v. *Six Unknown Agents* (403 U.S. 388, 1971), the Court, while reaffirming the suppression doctrine, construed the Fourth Amendment to permit actions for damages upon proof of injury resulting from the actions of federal officers in violation of the Fourth Amendment. As Justice William J. Brennan pointed out, "where federally protected rights have been invaded, it has been the rule from the beginning that courts will be alert to adjust their remedies so as to grant the necessary relief."

In his dissent, Chief Justice Burger objected to this act of "judicial legislation," but he was even more troubled by the "high price" the exclusionary rule "extracts from society." He could not accept the "deterrent" benefit as an appropriate balance against "the release of countless guilty criminals" for there was no "empirical evidence" to support the rationale that suppression of evidence does in fact deter police abridgement of Fourth Amendment guarantees. Furthermore, the Chief Justice argued, the judiciary's mechanistic application of the exclusionary rule cuts deeper into society's interests because it allows no distinctions between "deliberate and flagrant . . . violations of the Fourth Amendment" and those "inadvertent errors of judgment" that often result from the "pressure of police work" but do not result in "grave injustices." Putting it even more bluntly, Burger asserted that "[f]reeing either a tiger or a mouse in a schoolroom is an illegal act, but no rational person would suggest that these two acts should be punished in the same way." In short, the response should be in proportion to the "gravity of the need." Consequently, in the light of such shortcomings, he proposed that Congress take the lead in developing "reasonable and effective substitutes" for the exclusionary rule. He thought this approach would better serve the public interest than an outright reversal of *Weeks* and *Mapp*, for even he recognized the danger inherent in such a quick step. As he put it:

> Obviously the public interest would be poorly served if law enforcement officials were suddenly to gain the impression, however erroneous, that all constitutional

restraints on police had somehow been removed—that an open season on "criminals" had been declared. I am concerned lest some such mistaken impression might be fostered by a flat overruling of the Suppression Doctrine cases. For years we have relied upon it as the exclusive remedy for unlawful official conduct; in a sense we are in a situation akin to the narcotics addict whose dependence on drugs precludes any drastic or immediate withdrawal of the supposed prop, regardless of how futile its continued use may be.

Three years later in *United States* v. *Calandra* (414 U.S. 338, 1974), the contraction of the exclusionary rule forecasted in the Burger dissent in *Bivens* reached fruition. The case involved the use of illegally seized records from which questions were put to a witness in a federal grand jury investigation. A federal district court granted the motion to suppress the records and the Court of Appeals for the Sixth Circuit, citing *Weeks,* affirmed. Chief Justice Burger and the three other Nixon appointees (Blackmun, Powell, and Rehnquist) were joined by Warren Court holdover Justices Stewart and White in reversal. Distinguishing the grand jury process from a criminal trial, Justice Powell, in his majority opinion, did not want the grand jury process to be hampered by "technical procedural and evidentiary rules" that apply to criminal trials. Powell tightened the reins on the exclusionary rule when he asserted that it was not "a personal constitutional right," but a "judicially-created remedy" to deter illegal searches by law enforcement officials. Furthermore, he felt that the fears of the dissenters that the decision provides a powerful incentive to disregard the strictures of the Fourth Amendment in order to obtain indictments pale in the face of the inadmissibility of illegally seized evidence at trial.

But such justifications did not satisfy Justices Brennan, Douglas, and Marshall. In focusing on the "deterrent" purpose, Brennan contended that the majority had submerged the central purpose of the exclusionary rule. It was designed, he argued, to assure the people "that the government would not profit from its [own] lawless behavior."

Another dimension of the search and seizure problem that is repeatedly raised during the course of day-to-day law enforcement activities concerns the constitutionally permissible limits of searches incident to a lawful arrest. Beginning with the Court's holding in *Carroll* v. *United States* (267 U.S. 132, 1925), that "[w]hen a man is legally arrested for an offense, whatever is found upon his person or in his control which it is unlawful for him to have and which may be used to prove the offense may be seized and held as evidence in the prosecution," the Court has accepted cases periodically that were vehicles for further explication of the doctrine. At times it adopted an expanded view of the doctrine and approved fairly extensive warrantless searches incident to arrests. This is well illustrated by such decisions as *Harris* v. *United States* (331 U.S. 145, 1947), where the Court validated an extensive search of a four-room apartment supported only by the arrest warrant, and *United States* v. *Rabinowitz* (339 U.S. 56, 1950), where a one and one-half hour search of an office, including desks, safes and file cabinets was approved as incident to the arrest.

On the other hand, the Court has at times adopted a more limited view of the doctrine. In the 1931 and 1932 cases of *Go-Bart Importing Co.* v. *United States* (282 U.S. 344) and *United States* v. *Lefkowitz* (285 U.S. 452), for example, the Court held defective the less extensive searches of offices in which the arrest warrants were executed because the arresting officers "had an abundance of information and time to swear out a valid [search] warrant [and] failed to do so." Likewise in *Trupiano* v. *United States* (334 U.S. 699, 1948), the Court in reaffirming this position, asserted that "[i]t is a cardinal rule that in seizing goods and articles, law enforcement agents must secure and use search warrants wherever reasonably practicable" for "[a] search or seizure without a warrant as an incident to a lawful arrest has always been considered to be a strictly limited right."

The Court reiterated these principles in *Chimel* v. *California* (395 U.S. 752 1969), and took the occasion to lay to rest the principles of *Harris* and *Rabinowitz* which had often been relied on to approve extensive warrantless searches incident to arrests. In his opinion for the Court, Justice Potter Stewart stressed that such searches, to be consistent with the Fourth Amendment, must be limited to the arrestee's "person and the area from within which he might have obtained either a weapon" or something that could have been used as evidence against him.

In dissent, Justice Byron White complained about the constantly shifting constitutional standards in this area over the last 50 years. But with the exception of "one brief interlude," he argued that the rule enunciated in *Harris, supra,* had clearly been accepted as the law for more than two decades and as such should be followed. He struck a familiar law and order theme when he opined that the majority holding has the practical effect of rendering fruitless many searches for which probable cause exists because they may not be conducted immediately.

In early 1974, with Warren Court holdovers Justices Stewart and White joining the four Nixon appointees (Burger, Blackmun, Powell, and Rehnquist), the Court indicated its developing "law and order" stance and signaled a partial retreat from the stricter standards of Chimel. In *United States* v. *Robinson* (414 U.S. 218), and a companion case, *Gustafson* v. *Florida* (414 U.S. 260), the Court held that a full search of the person in a lawful custodial arrest was a permissible exception to the warrant requirement of the Fourth Amendment. Both cases involved arrests for motor vehicle violations and in each case the subsequent search of the offender uncovered possession of narcotics. The evidence so obtained was admitted at subsequent trials where convicitions resulted. In affirming both convictions, Justice William Rehnquist for the majority in *Robinson* and a plurality in *Gustafson*, expanded the permissible limits of the "stop and frisk" doctrine of *Terry* v. *Ohio, infra,* when he held that a search incident to a valid arrest under the circumstances of these cases was not limited to frisking the outer garments for weapons. Nor did Rehnquist consider it unreasonable to conduct such a search although the arresting officer did not suspect that the offender was armed or that it was possible for him to destroy evidence of the crime for which the arrest was made. For him, affirmative authority to search having resulted from the lawful arrests was sufficient to meet the reasonableness requirement of the Fourth Amendment.

Dissenting in both cases, Justices Douglas, Brennan, and Marshall chided the majority for its "clear and marked departure from [the Court's] long tradition of case-by-case adjudication of the reasonableness of searches and seizures under the Fourth Amendment." Justice Marshall made it clear in his opinion for the three that the conduct of law enforcement officials in this area must be subjected to "the more detached, neutral scrutiny" of the judiciary to assure that the commands of the Fourth Amendment remain "meaningful" guarantees to the citizen. The actions in these cases led Marshall to speculate that the majority's approach could result in serious discriminatory treatment of citizens. For example, he wondered if the result of the case would have been the same had the person arrested been a businessman whose wallet was seized instead of a student whose cigaret package was seized. He concluded that the search went far beyond what was "reasonably necessary" to insure the officer's safety, prevent escape from custody, and preserve any evidence of the crime for which the arrest was effected.

The Court attempted to clarify the law in another controversial area of warrantless search doctrine when, near the end of its 1967 term, it upheld "stop and frisk" procedures in *Terry* v. *Ohio* (392 U.S. 1, 1968), and in *Sibron* v. *New York* (392 U.S. 40). Generally these laws permit policemen to stop and frisk suspicious persons without meeting the "probable cause" standard of the Fourth Amendment. Speaking for the 8-1 majority in *Terry,* Chief Justice Earl Warren made it clear that the Court was not retreating from the warrant requirement of the Fourth Amendment but was merely applying a more practical standard, which exempts from the probable cause requirement a limited search for weapons if the search is otherwise reasonable. He emphasized that the sole justification of a search of this nature "is the protection of the police officer and others nearby and it must therefore be confined in scope to an intrusion reasonably designed to discover [hidden weapons] " which may be used in assaulting the officer. The Chief Justice concluded that the reasonableness of each search will have to be decided according to its circumstances.

Justice Douglas was the lone dissenter. He said it was illogical to let police search without probable cause when they acted without a warrant, while they had to show probable cause if they applied to a magistrate for a warrant. "To give the police greater power than a magistrate is to take a long step down the totalitarian path. Perhaps such a step is desirable to cope with modern forms of lawlessness. But if it is taken, it should be the deliberate choice of the people through a constitutional amendment."

The "stop and frisk" decision represented a significant reversal in the trend of Warren Court decisions which tended to protect those suspected of crime from the hands of overzealous police. Consequently, the outspoken "law and order" critics of the Court were pleased by the decision. But by the same token the decision aroused the apprehensions and disapproval of minority groups and other civil liberties spokesmen.

In its first consideration of the stop and frisk issue, the Burger Court indicated an expansive construction to *Terry.* In *Adams* v. *Williams,* with the four Nixon appointees joining Justices Potter Stewart and Byron White to form the majority, the Court construed *Terry* to permit an officer to stop a person who he has reason to believe is involved in criminal conduct, although probable cause to effect an arrest may not be evident. As Justice William Rehnquist, who wrote the Court's opinion put it, "[t]he Fourth Amendment does not require a policeman who lacks the precise level of information necessary for probable cause to arrest to simply shrug his shoulders and allow a crime to occur or a criminal to escape." Furthermore, Rehnquist continued, an informant's tip, if supported by sufficient "indicia of reliability" justifies the stop and subsequent frisk. Consequently, the argument that *Terry* requires that probable cause for a "stop and frisk" can only be based on an officer's personal observation is rejected as a defectively narrow reading of that decision.

Each of the three dissenting Justices—Douglas, Brennan, and Marshall—wrote separate opinions in which they decried the majority's expansive application of *Terry*. Douglas stressed that extending the "stop and frisk" practice to "possessory offenses" represented a serious intrusion on Fourth Amendment guarantees and could only be tolerated where direct observation of the police and other "well authenticated information shows 'that criminal activity may be afoot.' " For Justice Brennan, the state had not shown sufficient cause to justify the stop, while Justice Marshall argued that the majority had gone considerably beyond the intent of *Terry* which held that officers were only permitted to undertake warrantless searches for weapons. And such action, he maintained, seriously erodes the guarantees of the Fourth Amendment. He warned that the majority's action could lead to the harrassment of innocent persons by "police officers who have only the slightest suspicion of improper conduct."

The federal government's response to the rash of "skyjacking" activity in the early 1970s focused on another dimension of the warrantless search. Involved was the pre-boarding screening operation which required every passenger to be scanned by a magnetometer and to submit to a search of carry-on baggage. Occasionally, a passenger was subjected to a more extensive search if his observable characteristics (physical and behavioral) fit the "profile" of a potential hijacker. For some, subjection to this kind of governmental intrusion represented an outrageous assault on Fourth Amendment guarantees. The most notable protest was that of U.S. Senator Vance Hartke (D., Ind.), who initially refused to submit to the security check, but later relented to avoid possible sanctions against airlines for breach of the security regulations. While affirming a conviction for illegal possession of narcotics in *United States* v. *Slocum* (464 F.2d. 1180, 1972), the Court of Appeals for the Third Circuit reviewed and sustained the constitutionality of the anti-skyjacking program. Chief Judge Collins J. Seitz balanced the interests involved and concluded that the "limited" search was "justified by a reasonable governmental interest in protecting national air commerce" and, as such, did not abridge the Fourth Amendment prohibition against unreasonable searches and seizures.

Technological advances of the twentieth century have added another dimension to the problem of protecting privacy. Major difficulties center around wiretapping and recording conversations through concealed electronic devices. Privacy can easily be invaded by employing such methods and the consequences are often as damaging as those resulting from forced entry and seizure. Nevertheless, the Supreme Court recognized a constitutional difference in *Olmstead* v. *United States* (227 U.S. 438,

1928). In that case, it affirmed a conviction for conspiracy to violate the National Prohibition Act where evidence was obtained by wiretapping. Chief Justice William H. Taft's opinion for the five-man majority emphasized the historical purpose of the Fourth Amendment as being the protection of one's house, person, papers, and effects from forced governmental search and seizure. He maintained that "the language of the Amendment cannot be extended and expanded to include telephone wires, reaching the whole world from the defendant's house or office." Taft concluded that "[t]he intervening wires are not part of his house or office, any more than are the highways along which they are stretched."

The dissenters were greatly disturbed at the possibilities for dilution of the privacy guarantee that the decision portended. Justice Oliver Wendell Holmes found this method of obtaining evidence "dirty business" and warned that "the government ought not use evidence obtainable, and only obtainable by a criminal act," for it is "a less evil that some criminals should escape than that the Government should play an ignoble part." Justice Louis Brandeis' more comprehensive dissent condemned the majority's narrow application of the Fourth Amendment. He expressed considerable concern about government intrusion into privacy in the future when he noted:

> The progress of science in furnishing the Government with means of espionage is not likely to stop with wiretapping. Ways may some day be developed by which the Government, without removing papers from secret drawers, can reproduce them in court, and by which it will be enabled to expose to a jury the most intimate occurrences at home. Advances in the psychic and related sciences may bring means of exploring unexpressed beliefs, thoughts and emotions. . . . Can it be that the Constitution affords no protection against such invasions of individual security?

Six years later Congress acted to plug the privacy gap left by *Olmstead*. The Federal Communications Act of 1934 included a provision (Section 605) prohibiting the intercepting and divulging of tele-communications. The provision's effectiveness in federal prosecutions was assured in *Nardonne* v. *United States* (302 U.S. 397, 1937) where the Court held inadmissible evidence obtained by federal officials through wiretapping. But an attempt to extend this prohibition to state criminal prosecutions was rejected in *Schwartz* v. *Texas* (344 U.S. 199, 1952). Undoubtedly, the Court's distinction was based on the *Wolf* rule governing the admissibility of evidence in state courts. However, an attempt to use *Schwartz* as a means of evading *Nardonne* was rejected in *Benanti* v. *United States* (355 U.S. 96, 1957), when the Court held inadmissible in federal prosecutions evidence obtained by state officers under state-approved wiretapping systems.

When the *Wolf* rule was struck down in *Mapp* the major support for *Schwartz* was undermined, and in *Lee* v. *Florida* (392 U.S. 378, 1968), the Court announced that "*Schwartz* . . . cannot survive the demise of *Wolf*. . . ." Justice Potter Stewart's opinion for the Court stressed that the wiretapping law is applicable to the states by its unequivocal prohibition of the interception and divulging of telephone messages.

Stewart concluded that the statutory prohibition supported by the *Mapp* exclusionary rule renders inadmissible, in state prosecutions, evidence obtained by wiretapping. Justices Black and Harlan wrote separate dissenting opinions in which they contended that the statute should not be interpreted as prescribing a rule of evidence. Black charged that the majority, impatient with Congress "in this day of rapid creation of new judicial rules," was rewriting the statute through judicial decree. He warned that the inevitable result of such new rules was "to make conviction of criminals more difficult."

Congress' failure to heed Justice Brandeis' warning in his *Olmstead* dissent when it passed the Federal Communications Act, left law enforcement officers free to employ a variety of electronic eavesdropping devices to invade the privacy of the unsuspecting. Thus the Court, following the narrow *Olmstead* construction of the Fourth Amendment, affirmed a number of convictions in which evidence obtained by various eavesdropping devices was admitted. In *Goldman* v. *United States* (316 U.S. 129, 1942), use of a detectaphone to monitor conversations in an adjoining office was not considered an unreasonable search and seizure. Likewise, the Court held that the Fourth Amendment was not breached in *On Lee* v. *United States* (343 U.S. 747, 1952). Here On Lee made incriminating statements to a former employee who just "happened" to drop by for a "friendly chat" but who had concealed on his person a radio transmitter that enabled a narcotics agent to monitor the "friendly chat." The agent's testimony as to what he heard was admitted as evidence in the successful prosecution. In addition, the Court allowed convictions to stand where evidence was obtained by electronic devices devoid of unlawful physical invasion of privacy or where "undercover agents" were privy to conversations with the consent of the "suspect." (Cf. *Lopez* v. *United States,* 373 U.S. 427, 1963; *Hoffa* v. *United States,* 385 U.S. 293, 1966; *Osborn* v. *United States,* 385 U.S. 323, 1966; and *United States* v. *White, infra.*)

The Court has made it clear, however, that overzealous methods to invade privacy are inconsistent with the Fourth Amendment. In *Silverman* v. *United States* (363 U.S. 505, 1961), the Court condemned as an unreasonable invasion of privacy the transformation of the entire heating system into a conductor of sound.[2] Likewise, New York's permissive eavesdrop statute[3] was invalidated in *Berger* v. *New York* (388 U.S. 41, 1967), because of its failure to conform with essential safeguards for searches and seizures required by the Fourth and Fourteenth Amendments. Justice Tom Clark's opinion for the majority emphasized that the use of electronic devices to capture conversations was a " 'search' within the meaning

---

[2] See also *Wong Sun* v. *United States* (371 U.S. 471, 1963) where the Court for the first time specifically held that the Fourth Amendment excludes verbal evidence which "derives . . . immediately from an unlawful entry and unauthorized arrest."

[3] The New York statute authorizes the issuance of a general warrant for eavesdropping upon affirmance by a law enforcement official who merely states his belief that evidence of a crime may thereby be obtained; describes the person whose communications are to be intercepted and the purpose of the interception; and identifies the telephone number or telegraph line involved.

of the [Fourth] Amendment." Consequently, he argued, the statute cannot stand because it lacks the particularity required by the Fourth Amendment as to the specific crime committed or being committed, the conversations sought, or the place to be searched. He concluded that the statute was a "broadside authorization . . . resulting in trespassory intrusion" of privacy rather than one "carefully circumscribed" so as to prevent unauthorized invasions thereof.

Justice William O. Douglas wrote a brief concurring opinion setting forth the view that "at long last" the Court had overruled "*sub silentio, Olmstead* . . . and its offspring. . . ."

Justice Hugo Black complained in dissent that the Court had forged requirements that make the enactment of an acceptable eavesdropping statute "completely impossible . . . because of [its] hostility to eavesdropping as 'ignoble' and 'dirty business.' " He reemphasized his view expressed in *Wolf* and *Mapp* that the Fourth Amendment does not, in and of itself, contain an exclusionary requirement and, hence, does not forbid the use of the evidence obtained under the New York statute. His basic disagreement with the majority, therefore, was one of interpretation. To him, the framers of the Bill of Rights did not include "words" in enumerating the things secured against unreasonable searches and seizures by the Fourth Amendment. But the Court's decision, he argued, is one of "judicial substitution"—adding the term "words" to the Fourth Amendment.

The Fourth Amendment is also a barrier to the electronic eavesdropping activities of federal officials such as those involved in *Katz* v. *United States* (389 U.S. 347). *Katz* involved a conviction for the interstate transmission of betting information by telephone where evidence against the accused was obtained by electronic listening and recording devices affixed to a public telephone booth from which he placed his calls. The Court reversed the conviction and held that the methods employed by the government constituted a search and seizure within the meaning of the Fourth Amendment. In his opinion for the Court, Justice Potter Stewart made it clear that one does not shed his right to privacy because he makes his calls from a public telephone booth. When a person enters such a booth, said Stewart, closes the door behind him and pays his toll to make a call, he is "entitled to assume that the words he utters into the mouthpiece will not be broadcast to the world." Justice Stewart concluded that "[t]o read the Constitution more narrowly is to ignore the vital role that the public telephone has come to play in private communication."

Justice Hugo Black, the lone dissenter, objected because he did not believe that electronic eavesdropping constitutes a search or seizure within the meaning of the Fourth Amendment. Reiterating his strict constructionist view of Bill of Rights guarantees, Black contended that the Court did not possess the power to "update" the Amendment to achieve a result which many now consider desirable.

Many members of Congress felt even more strongly than Justice Black about *Katz* and the other Court decisions which limit the use of wiretapping and bugging in criminal investigations. This Congressional attitude reflected a growing public concern about "crime in the streets" and the need for greater police authority to combat it. Hence, Congress included in the Omnibus Crime Control and Safe

Streets Act of 1968 a provision permitting limited use of wiretapping and bugging in the investigation of a variety of federal crimes.[4] A warrant must be obtained from a federal judge granting permission for such surveillance, but in cases of "emergency" investigations of organized crime and national security matters, a law enforcement officer may proceed to employ his listening devices for 48 hours without a warrant. In instituting the process, the Court made it clear in *United States* v. *Giordano* (416 U.S. 505, 1974), that under the statute only the Attorney General or his statutory designee may authorize an application for a wiretapping warrant. Failure to adhere to this statutory requirement resulted in the suppression of the intercepted evidence and the reversal of several narcotics convictions. In addition, the statute authorizes the use of wiretaps and oral intercepts by state officials under warrants issued by state courts in the investigation of "any crime dangerous to life, limb, or property and punishable by imprisonment for more than one year."

The *Katz* ruling was denatured further when the Burger Court ruled in *United States* v. *White* that the warrant requirement of the Fourth Amendment does not apply to "bugged" informers. Justice Byron White's plurality opinion (supported by Burger, Blackmun, and Stewart) stressed the risk of disclosure whenever a person's conversations are heard by others. Hence, he argued, the nature of the device employed to capture the conversation did not make a constitutional difference. In short, the "bugging" device was treated in the same manner as the informant's memory. (Cf. *Hoffa* v. *United States, supra.*) What's more, White insisted that constitutional barriers should not be erected to prevent gathering accurate probative evidence, for "[a] n electronic recording will many times produce a more reliable rendition of what a defendant has said than will the unaided memory of a police agent."

Characterizing electronic surveillance as "the greatest leveler of human privacy ever known," Justice William O. Douglas filed a sharp dissent. For him how this and other forms of eavesdropping could be considered reasonable within the meaning of the Fourth Amendment was a "mystery." Condemning the Court's resuscitation of earlier bugging decisions that had largely been eroded by the likes of *Berger* and *Katz,* he warned of the decision's "chilling" effect on people speaking their minds and expressing their views on important matters.

In *Alderman* v. *United States* (394 U.S. 165, 1969), the Supreme Court dealt a crushing blow to the federal government's electronic surveillance activities by holding that the accused must be allowed to examine the records of any illegal eavesdropping of his private conversations and other conversations that took place on his premises. This was necessary, the Court explained, in order for the accused to ascertain if the evidence against him was derived from the illegal bugging. Furthermore, by rejecting the argument that the accused should only have access to

---

[4] Included are: violations of the Atomic Energy Act, sabotage, treason, rioting, unlawful payments or loans to labor organizations, murder, kidnapping, robbery, sports bribes, wagering offenses, Presidential assassination, extortion, embezzlement from pension and welfare funds, racketeering offenses, theft from interstate shipment, and interstate transportation of stolen property.

such records after a camera examination by the trial judge as to relevancy, the Court presented the government a choice: either risk some disclosures that may have an adverse effect on national security and other investigations, or drop some prosecutions.

The Federal Government's electronic surveillance activities were dealt another blow in 1972 when a unanimous Court, including three of the Nixon appointees, refused to approve an evasion of the warrant requirement of the 1968 Omnibus Crime Act based on national security claims. In *United States* v. *United States District Court for the Eastern District of Michigan, S. D.,* Chapter 4, *supra,* the Government sought to justify the warrantless wiretaps under a section of the statute which disclaims any attempt on the part of Congress to limit the President's power "to protect against the overthrow of the Government." But the Court rejected this position as contrary to the intent of Congress. In his opinion, Justice Lewis Powell asserted that the statutory provision upon which the Government relied was not an affirmative grant of power to conduct warrantless searches, but only a disclaimer of Congressional intent to define the President's power in national security matters.

SELF-INCRIMINATION

The Fifth Amendment provides in part that "no person . . . shall be compelled in any criminal case to be a witness against himself. . . ." Over the years the Supreme Court has given an expansive interpretation to this guarantee as applied to federal action. For example, it has permitted persons to invoke the claim in grand jury proceedings and Congressional committee hearings. (*Counselman* v. *Hitchcock,* 142 U.S. 546, 1892; *Emspak* v. *United States,* 349 U.S. 190, 1955.)

The most revolutionary change in the judicial attitude relative to this federal constitutional guarantee has been in its application to state proceedings. Beginning with *Twining* v. *New Jersey* (211 U.S. 78, 1908), the Supreme Court held for more than half a century that state proceedings were not governed by its provisions. At issue in that case was a state procedure that permitted the trial jury to consider the failure of the defendant to take the witness stand and deny evidence presented against him. In rejecting the appellant's self-incrimination claim, the Court held that the protection against compulsory self-incrimination was not one of the privileges and immunities protected by the Fourteenth Amendment from state infringement. Rather, the crucial question was whether the self-incrimination privilege was "an immutable principle of justice which is the inalienable possession of every citizen of a free government."

While the Court held steadfastly to this position in the decades following *Twining* and reaffirmed it in *Adamson* v. *California, supra* (where a similar criminal procedure raised the same issue), it did reverse a number of state convictions on due process grounds in which the alleged compulsory self-incrimination took the form of coerced confessions. (*Brown* v. *Mississippi,* 297 U.S. 278, 1936; *Chambers* v. *Florida,* 309 U.S. 227, 1940; *Spano* v. *New York,* 360 U.S. 315, 1959.) The early coerced confession cases generally involved some physical abuse on the part of the law enforcement official to break down the will of the accused, but the general pattern since *Brown* v. *Mississippi* and *Chambers* v. *Florida* has been to induce the confession by employing mental and psychological ploys and trickery. Thus in *Spano* v. *New York*, the Court reversed a state conviction for murder, which was based upon a confession obtained after eight hours of continuous questioning by a team of officers, followed by a plea from a rookie policeman—a childhood friend of the suspect—who used this relationship to get the suspect's sympathy by falsely stating that his job would be lost (at a time when his wife was expecting their fourth child) if the defendant did not cooperate and confess. The interrogators persisted in their quest for a confession despite the suspect's repeated refusals to answer questions on the advice of his lawyer who had personally surrendered his client to the police. Chief Justice Earl Warren's opinion emphasized the need for the police to "obey the law while enforcing the law." He concluded that the confession lacked the "voluntariness" required by due process because the "petitioner's will was overborne by official pressure, fatigue and sympathy falsely aroused."

The Court has continued to reject confessions extracted by coercive methods, but a growing minority of Justices expressed dissatisfaction with the majority's test for determining the "involuntariness" of confessions in *Haynes* v. *Washington* (373 U.S. 503, 1963). A bare majority of the Court reversed Haynes' conviction for robbery because the confession upon which it was based was obtained after 16 hours of incommunicado interrogation (during which the accused was not allowed to call his family) in a general "atmosphere of substantial coercion and inducement created by statements and actions of state authorities." Justice Tom Clark, speaking for the four dissenters, contended that the majority had departed from earlier precedents in confession cases and had enlarged the requirements under which state courts had previously determined the voluntariness of confessions.

The long line of coerced confession cases gradually eroded the *Twining-Adamson* doctrine. The Court's action in *Mapp* made the *Weeks* rule applicable to the states; its 1963 decision in *Gideon* made the Sixth Amendment's guarantee of assistance of counsel obligatory on the states. It was a logical development to the application of the self-incrimination provision of the Fifth Amendment to the states which was announced in *Malloy* v. *Hogan*. It is not surprising, then, that Justice Harlan, in dissent, characterized the majority's approach as amounting to "nothing more or less than 'incorporation' [of the guarantees of the first eight amendments into the Fourteenth] in snatches." In delivering the majority opinion in *Malloy*, Justice William J. Brennan took note of the shift to the federal standard in many post-*Twining* and *Adamson* state cases and contended that such a "shift reflects recognition that the American system of criminal prosecution is accusatorial, not inquisitorial, and that the Fifth Amendment privilege is its essential mainstay." He concluded that "the Fourteenth Amendment secures against state invasion the same privilege [to remain silent] that the Fifth Amendment guarantees against federal infringement. . . ."

On the same day the Court announced the *Malloy* ruling, it decided the related issue of whether one jurisdiction in our federal system (a state) may compel a witness to answer questions after a grant of immunity from prosecution under its laws, while simultaneously leaving him open to prosecution in another jurisdiction (the federal government) on the basis of testimony thus disclosed. In *Murphy* v. *Waterfront Commission of New York Harbor* (378 U.S. 52, 1964), the Court foreclosed this possibility and declared that "in light of the history, policies and purposes of the privilege against self-incrimination . . . , [the privilege] protects a state witness against incrimination under federal as well as state law and a federal witness against incrimination under state law as well as federal law."

In *Griffin* v. *California* (380 U.S. 609, 1965), the Court cited *Malloy* as authority to strike down the "comment" rule (on failure of defendant to testify at his trial) which had been approved almost 60 years earlier in *Twining* and reaffirmed in *Adamson*. In his opinion for the majority, Justice William O. Douglas made it clear that whether authorized by statute or not, the comment rule is a relic of the "inquisitorial system of criminal justice" which, in effect, is a court-imposed penalty for exercising a constitutional right. As such, he concluded, the procedure violates the Fifth and Fourteenth Amendments.

The Court was not so generous when asked to discard another precedent on the authority of *Malloy* and its earlier decision in *Mapp* v. *Ohio*. In *Schmerber* v. *California* (384 U.S. 755, 1966), the Court was asked to reverse a conviction where evidence of intoxication was obtained from a blood sample taken from the injured petitioner (at the direction of the police and over his objection) while in the emergency room of a hospital. In rejecting the petitioner's claim that the action abridged the privilege against self-incrimination, Justice William J. Brennan's opinion for the majority stressed the testimonial and communicative nature of evidence to which the privilege extended. He concluded that the withdrawal of blood under the circumstances did not involve the type of compulsion condemned by the Constitution.

Aside from eliminating the comment rule in criminal trials, *Malloy's* most significant impact has been in the area of investigations by various state bodies. In *Spevack* v. *Klein* (385 U.S. 11, 1967), for example, the Court held that an attorney may not be disbarred for invoking the self-incrimination privilege in refusing to produce demanded records and to testify in a judicial inquiry. In an opinion joined by three other members of the Court, Justice William O. Douglas contended that there is "no room in the privilege against self-incrimination for classifications of people" and that the protection extends to lawyers just as to other individuals. He concluded that the guarantee "should not be watered down by imposing the dishonor of disbarment and the deprivation of livelihood as a price for asserting it." Similarly, in *Garrity* v. *New Jersey* (385 U.S. 493, 1967), decided the same day, the Court extended the guarantee to protect police officers who had refused to answer questions during an investigation by the state attorney general on alleged traffic ticket-fixing. The officers were advised that they could assert their self-incrimination protection, but in doing so they would be subject to removal from office. Put to such a choice, they chose to answer questions, some of which formed the basis for a subsequent prosecution for conspiracy to obstruct the enforcement of traffic laws. In the opinion supporting the Court's reversal of these convictions, Justice Goldberg maintained that the crucial question presented was not whether a governmental employee had a constitutional right to his job, but whether the government can obtain incriminating evidence from him by threatening to discharge him. In rejecting the exercise of such authority, Goldberg concluded that the choice given the officers between self-incrimination or loss of employment was a form of compulsion prohibited by the Fourteenth Amendment.

Invoking the privilege against compulsory self-incrimination has at times stymied federal and state investigations that were considered crucial to certain public interests and needs. Recalcitrant witnesses found this to be a particularly useful device for withholding testimony in the early 1950s during extensive Congressional investigations of subversive activity. To circumvent this constitutional roadblock, Congress and state legislatures have enacted immunity statutes. In practice, these laws are designed to compel the witnesses to talk in exchange for personal immunity from prosecution for any criminal activity that flows from his disclosures.

While recognizing the important values underlying the privilege, the courts have accepted some accommodation between the commands of the constitutional guarantee and the needs of government in the performance of its functions essential to the maintenance of an orderly society. Federal immunity statutes have been approved in *Brown* v. *Walker* (161 U.S. 591, 1896), *Ullman* v. *United States* (350 U.S. 442, 1956), and *Kastigar* v. *United States*. In the former, the 5-4 majority, taking a narrow view of the guarantee, held that it should be construed as only protecting a person against a criminal prosecution which might flow from his testimony. But the provision, they argued, was not intended to shield him from public opprobrium.

Such a balancing of private rights against governmental interests for the public good was reaffirmed in the *Ullman* case. There, Justice Frankfurter asserted for the 5-4 majority that the exchange was a constitutionally permissible one since the immunity effectively removes the danger that the privilege was designed to prevent. The statutes at issue in both the *Brown* and *Ullman* cases were construed as affording "transactional" immunity (absolute immunity against future prosecution concerning any *transaction* which a person's testimony discloses). But in the *Kastigar* case, the Court upheld the 1970 immunity statute (a partial Congressional response to the crisis in law and order), construing it as affording only "use and derivate use" immunity. The majority, speaking through Justice Lewis Powell, contended that "transactional" immunity affords broader protection than that guaranteed by the Fifth Amendment and hence Congress could discard it. The "use and derivative use" standard (the testimony nor evidence derived therefrom cannot be used in a subsequent criminal proceeding against the witness) was considered permissible since it afforded protection commensurate with the privilege against self-incrimination. The same principle was applied to state immunity grants in *Zicarelli* v. *New Jersey State Commission of Investigation* (406 U.S. 205, 1972) decided on the same day.

The dissenting Justices in each of the three cases maintained that as a general proposition, the immunity statutes greatly diminished the constitutional guarantee and for some of them—Stephen Field in *Brown*, Hugo Black and William O. Douglas in *Ullman*, and Douglas in *Kastigar*—the Fifth Amendment affords absolute protection against compulsion to testify. But given the rejection of the absolutist position, Justices Douglas and Thurgood Marshall in *Kastigar* could settle for no less than a continuation of "transactional" immunity so the witness would be assured that "he is not testifying about matters for which he may later be prosecuted." What bothered them most was the admission of Justice Powell that a person accorded immunity could be subsequently prosecuted if the prosecution proves that the evidence it proposes to use "is derived from a legitimate source wholly independent of the compelled testimony."

THE RIGHT TO COUNSEL

One of the basic tenets of American jurisprudence is that a person charged with a criminal offense should have his "day" in court. Hence, the framers of the Bill of Rights included in the Sixth Amendment a provision that guarantees to the accused "in all criminal prosecutions," the right to assistance of counsel for his defense. Pursuant to that provision Congressional action and judicial decisions secured the right in federal prosecutions. But as a result of the doctrine enunciated in *Barron* v. *Baltimore, supra,* the states were left free to determine their own rules on counsel.

Almost a century after *Barron* was decided, the due process clause of the Fourteenth Amendment began to be invoked as a limitation on the states with respect to the counsel guarantee. In 1932, the Court decided *Powell* v. *Alabama* (287 U.S. 45), the first of the celebrated *Scottsboro* cases. Seven ignorant and illiterate Negro boys had been charged for the rape of two white girls, a capital crime in Alabama. During the arraignment, at which they pleaded not guilty, the presiding judge did not inquire as to whether they wished or were able to employ counsel, or if they had relatives or friends with whom they might wish to communicate for purposes of obtaining assistance. Instead, he appointed all members of the local bar to serve as counsel for "the purpose of arraignment." When the trial of the first case began six days later, no counsel appeared for the defendants, nor was there any indication that any member of the local bar had made any preparation for the trial of the case. At this time, however, an attorney from Tennessee (the home of the defendants) appeared "at the request of persons interested in the case" to lend what assistance he could to local counsel appointed by the court. After an attempt to place the full responsibility for representation on the "volunteer" from Tennessee failed, one member of the local bar accepted the assignment reluctantly and the case proceeded to trial.

The subsequent convictions were affirmed by the state supreme court, but the United States Supreme Court reversed on the grounds that the rather casual and callous manner in which counsel was provided offended the due process clause of the Fourteenth Amendment. Justice George Sutherland's opinion for the seven-man majority emphasized assistance of counsel as a fundamental ingredient of a fair trial. He contended that the right to be heard would be of little consequence, even for the educated and intelligent, "if it did not comprehend the right to be heard by counsel." In reaching its decision, the Court took judicial notice of the youthfulness of the defendants, their illiteracy, the public hostility, the incommunicado imprisonment while awaiting trial, and, above all, the capital nature of the crime with which they were charged. Subsequently, Justice Sutherland's opinion was construed to be limited to the circumstances of the case.

Nevertheless, much of Sutherland's discussion of counsel tended to support the position advanced by some that assistance of counsel in any criminal trial was an essential requirement of due process. Ten years later in *Betts* v. *Brady* (316 U.S. 455, 1942) the issue was before the Court again. In affirming a conviction in a non-capital case in which the defendant was denied court-appointed counsel, the Court made it clear that "[t]he due process clause of the Fourteenth Amendment does not [automatically] incorporate . . . the specific guarantees found in the Sixth Amendment." It did recognize, however, that "the denial by a state of rights or privileges embodied in that and other . . . amendments may, in certain circumstances," constitute in a given case a deprivation of "due process of law in violation of the Fourteenth Amendment." Reduced to its simplest terms, what the Court said was that assistance of counsel was not essential to a fair trial in some cases, but that it was in others if "special circumstances" existed. Hence, this rule became the standard for a case-by-case determination of the essentiality of the counsel guarantee.

Twenty-one years later, however, the Court abandoned the "special circumstances" rule in *Gideon* v. *Wainwright*. Justice Black's opinion for the Court made it clear that in its current view of the due process clause of the Fourteenth Amendment the counsel guarantee of the Sixth Amendment is obligatory on the states. Black indicated that the Court, in reality, was merely returning to the principles enunciated in *Powell* v. *Alabama*.

The decision had an immediate impact on the administration of criminal justice. On the same day it decided *Gideon*, the Court held in *Douglas* v. *California* (372 U.S. 353, 1963) that the right to counsel extends to the first appeal from a criminal conviction where appeal is granted as a matter of right under state law. Justice Douglas contended for the six-man majority that "where the merits of the one and only appeal which an indigent has of right are decided without benefit of counsel, . . . an unconstitutional line has been drawn between rich and poor." He concluded that if counsel is denied at this stage, "[t]he indigent, where the record is unclear or the errors are hidden, has only the right to a meaningless ritual, while the rich man has a meaningful appeal."[5] During its next term the Court approved, without opinion, the retrospective application of the Gideon rule in *Pickelsimer* v. *Wainwright* (375 U.S. 2, 1963).

Almost immediately lower courts were confronted with the question of whether the counsel guarantee extends to nonfelonious criminal prosecutions. (Cf. *In*

[5] But in *Ross* v. *Moffit* (417 U.S. 356, 1974), decided more than a decade later, the Court refused to extend this guarantee to *discretionary appeals* to the highest state court and to the federal courts.

Application of Stevenson, 458 P.2d 414; *Blake* v. *Municipal Court* 51 Cal. Rptr. 771; and *James* v. *Headley*, 5th Cir, 410 F. 2d 325.) The Supreme Court considered the issue fully in *Argersinger* v. *Hamlin* (407 U.S. 25, 1972). In reversing a concealed weapons conviction of an indigent defendant (who was not provided counsel) where a 90-day jail sentence was imposed, the Court emphasized that the Constitution proscribes imprisonment for any offense—petty, misdemeanor, or felony—unless the defendant is represented by counsel at his trial. Speaking for the Court, Justice William O. Douglas contended that in many instances the legal and constitutional issues and questions in a petty or misdemeanor case are just as complex as they are in a more serious felony. Consequently, he concluded, if fair trials are to be guaranteed defendants in such "minor" prosecutions, assistance of counsel must be guaranteed. But Douglas tempered the requirement somewhat by indicating that this counsel rule applies in cases where imprisonment *may* be imposed. Hence, this would not place on the state the very heavy burden of providing counsel in the general "run of misdemeanors" where incarceration is not among the penalties that can be imposed.

THE COUNSEL AND SELF-INCRIMINATION RULES IN PRE-TRIAL INTERROGATION

One of the questons left unanswered in *Gideon* was whether or not a suspect is entitled to counsel during police interrogation. The answer came one year later in *Escobedo* v. *Illinois* (378 U.S. 478, 1964). There, the Court reversed a murder conviction based upon statements made during interrogation because police denied the repeated requests of the suspect's counsel to consult with his client. Justice Arthur Goldberg's opinion for the majority stressed the need for counsel when the police action shifts from the investigatory to the accusatory stage, i.e., when the focus is directed on the accused and the purpose of interrogation is to elicit a confession. Goldberg pointed out that at that stage legal aid and advice are most critical and the accused is entitled to consult with counsel. The case also points up an inextricable relationship between the protection against compulsory self-incrimination and the right to assistance of counsel.

Much of the criticism directed at the Court for its *Escobedo* ruling was misplaced since the limited question decided was merely the right of a suspect to consult with retained counsel. Left unanswered, however, were several crucial questions which go to the heart of police operations in solving crimes. The two with the greatest potential impact pertained to: (1) police responsibility for informing the suspect of his constitutional rights; and (2) whether or not a suspect can make an intelligent waiver of those rights without the advice of counsel. The Court answered both questions two years later in *Miranda* v. *Arizona* and in doing so reversed four convictions. Condemning the custodial interrogation methods used in each case, Chief Justice Earl Warren's majority opinion made it clear that the prosecution may not use statements against the accused elicited during custodial interrogation "unless it demonstrates the use of effective safeguards to secure" his constitutional rights. Hence, prior to any questioning, the accused must be: (1) warned of his right to remain silent and that any statement he makes may be used as evidence against him; and (2) informed of his right to the presence of counsel. If he desires counsel and is indigent, the government must make provision for it. Warren recognized that there may be cases where the accused may wish to proceed without counsel, but he cautioned that such waiver must be "made voluntarily, knowingly, and intelligently," and that proof of such waiver is the burden of the prosecution.

Undoubtedly, the Court was not oblivious to the sweeping impact such rulings could have upon the administration of state criminal law.[6] Consequently, it held in *Johnson* v. *New Jersey* (384 U.S. 719, 1966), decided one week later, that both *Escobedo* and *Miranda* would be limited to a prospective application. In fact, the Court ruled that the new standards announced in *Escobedo* and *Miranda* would apply only to cases *begun after* the announcement of these two cases. Thus, the Court was even more restrictive here than in its earlier prospective application of *Mapp* and *Griffin* where the new standards applied to cases *still pending* on direct appeal.

A significant contraction of the warning guarantees required by *Miranda* is evident from the Court's decision in *Harris* v. *New York*. With the two Nixon appointees (Chief Justice Warren Burger and Associate Justice Harry Blackmun) joining three dissenters in *Miranda* (Harlan II, Stewart, and White) to form a 5-4 majority, the Court held that the prosecution is not precluded from the use of statements that admittedly do not meet the *Miranda* test, as an impeachment tool in attacking the credibility of an accused's trial testimony. The Chief Justice construed *Miranda* as proscribing use of the "warningless" statements only in the prosecution's "case in chief," but not for all purposes. Burger made it clear that this ruling would stymie any effort to use "the shield" provided by *Miranda* as a "license [for] perjury free from the risks of confrontation with prior inconsistent utterances."

In dissent, Justice William J. Brennan, joined by Justices Douglas and Marshall (Justice Black dissented without opinion), argued that the historic values of the privilege against compulsory self-incrimination are jeopardized by a construction of *Miranda* that makes an exception for the admissibility of tainted statements as an impeachment tool. He found the words of a dissenting opinion in a 1966 New York Court of Appeals' case (*People* v. *Kulis*, 18 N.Y. 2d 318) appropriate in emphasizing his concern: "An incriminating statement is as incriminating when used to impeach credibility as it is when used as direct proof of guilt and no constitutional distinction can legitimately be drawn." What this case does, he concluded, is to make possible police evasions of the *Miranda* imperatives and to

[6] A provision of the Omnibus Crime Control and Safe Streets Act of 1968 makes the *Miranda* rules inapplicable to federal cases, thus allowing admission in evidence of voluntary confessions, even if the suspect was not warned of his constitutional rights. The Act also set aside the *Mallory* rule (*Mallory* v. *United States*, 352 U.S. 449, 1957) under which delayed arraignment could render a voluntary confession inadmissible in a federal trial. The new procedure permits police to hold a suspect up to six hours before arraignment without rendering defective a confession obtained during that prearraignment period.

permit the prosecution to spring the defective statements on a defendant who "has the temerity to testify in his own defense."

The Burger Court's chipping away at the *Miranda* rule continued during the 1973 term in *Michigan* v. *Tucker* (417 U.S. 433, 1974). There the court reversed a federal district court and the Court of Appeals for the Sixth Circuit where habeas corpus relief had been granted a prisoner who, during questioning before the *Miranda* rule was enunciated, was not advised of his right to appointed counsel if he could establish indigence. Since the trial and subsequent conviction took place after *Miranda*, the Court agreed that *Miranda* was applicable under its ruling in *Johnson* v. *New Jersey, supra. Tucker* had convinced the lower courts that the privilege against compulsory self-incrimination requires, except in very limited circumstances, exclusion of all evidence elicited without the *Miranda* warnings at a subsequent trial.

In his opinion for the Court, Justice William Rehnquist took the position that the Constitution requires a fair trial, but not a perfect one. Hence, some errors which occur in police investigation may not so infect the proceedings as to require reversal. To him, the record did not reveal police conduct sufficient to breach the protection against compulsory self-incrimination. Citing *Harris* v. *New York, supra,* he concluded that "failure to give interrorgated suspects full *Miranda* warnings does not entitle the suspect to insist that statements made by him be excluded in every conceivable context."

Only Justice Douglas dissented. His major complaint was the Court's departure from its *Miranda* holding. Furthermore, he charged that the Court had been involved in an exercise of balancing interests when Rehnquist contended that the Court "must consider society's interests in the effective prosecution of criminals in light of the protection our pre-*Miranda* standards afford criminal defendants." Such a characterization of the issues in this case, he concluded, "offends his sense of justice."

Does the right to assistance of counsel extend to the preliminary hearing? In *Coleman* v. *Alabama* (399 U.S. 1, 1970), the Court held that this is a "critical stage" of the criminal proceeding and, as such, counsel is constitutionally required. Justice William J. Brennan's plurality opinion underscored the significance of this hearing to an accused: (1) cross-examination of witnesses could expose flaws in the prosecution's case; (2) examination of witnesses could set the stage for impeachment during cross-examination at trial; (3) bail may be obtained and psychiatric examinations may be expedited; and (4) preservation of testimony favorable to him.[7]

To Chief Justice Burger, assistance of counsel at this stage of the criminal proceeding was good public policy but he rejected the notion that the Constitution requires it because, he argued, a preliminary hearing is not "a criminal prosecution" within the meaning of the Sixth Amendment. Hence, it should be made available to the accused by rule or statute.

[7] The Court denied a retrospective application, however, in *Adams* v. *Illinois* (405 U.S. 278, 1972).

Is the traditional "line-up" procedure employed in identifying suspects a "critical stage" in the criminal proceeding at which constitutional imperatives must be observed? In *United States* v. *Wade* (388 U.S. 218, 1967), the Court rejected a self-incrimination challenge to this identification ritual, but at the same time held that the accused *is entitled* to the presence of counsel at this post-indictment "critical stage" and that counsel for the accused *must be notified* of the impending "line-up."[8] On the same day, the Court held this requirement applicable to state criminal proceedings in *Gilbert* v. *California* (388 U.S. 263).

Five years later in *Kirby* v. *Illinois* (406 U.S. 682, 1972), the four Nixon appointees (Burger, Blackmun, Powell, and Rehnquist) joined Justice Potter Stewart in greatly narrowing the application of the Wade-Gilbert rule. For them, the "critical stage" had not yet been reached at a police station line-up held prior to indictment or formal charge. Speaking for all of the majority except Justice Powell, Justice Stewart argued that longstanding judicial precedent clearly established that the "right to counsel attaches only at or after the time that adversary judicial proceedings have been initiated against an accused." He concluded that only when "a defendant finds himself faced with the prosecutorial forces of organized society and is immersed in the intricacies of substantive and procedural criminal law is the "critical stage" reached where the command of the Sixth Amendment must be observed.

Justice William J. Brennan, whose dissenting opinion was supported by Justices William O. Douglas and Thurgood Marshall, took issue with the majority for brushing aside the Court's assertion in *Wade* that "the Sixth Amendment guarantee encompasses counsel's assistance whenever necessary to assure a meaningful 'defence.' " Brennan thought that there were inherent in the confrontation at a "line-up" the same kinds of "hazards to a fair trial" that are inherent in such a confrontation that occurs during the formal criminal trial. Hence, he concluded, the guiding hand of counsel is constitutionally required at the former stage, no less so than is clear at the latter.

To what extent are the various constitutional safeguards guaranteed adults accused of crime available to juveniles? The Court considered this crucial question in *In re Gault* in 1967. In reversing a juvenile court decision which had committed a youngster to an industrial school for the remainder of his minority (six years), the Court held that in such proceedings the due process clause of the Fourteenth Amendment requires that: (1) adequate notice of the hearing be given; (2) the child must be informed of his right to counsel (including assigned counsel); and (3) the privileges against self-incrimination and confrontation must be extended to him. Justice Abe Fortas' opinion for the five-man majority was careful to limit the holding to the actual "proceedings" process. He concluded that the unique values of the juvenile system would be in no way impaired by this "constitutional domestication."

In *McKeiver* v. *Pennsylvania* and *In re Burrus* (403 U.S. 528, 1971), however,

---

[8] The Omnibus Crime Control Act of 1968 negates the counsel guarantee announced in *Wade* by permitting the admission of testimony in federal prosecutions of those identifying a suspect even if the suspect had no lawyer when identified in a police lineup.

the Court did not agree that such "constitutional domestication" includes the right to trial by jury in juvenile court delinquency proceedings. Noting that "fundamental fairness" is the essential ingredient of due process in such proceedings, Justice Harry Blackmun's plurality opinion emphasized that there are other instruments of the juvenile process that can best serve its purposes and that states should not be impeded in searching for improvements by the imposition of jury trials. Such trials, he concluded, are not indispensable to a "fair and equitable" proceeding. He cautioned that injection of the jury trial in juvenile matters as a matter of right could well burden juvenile courts with many of the evils characteristic of modern criminal courts, e.g., lengthy delays and possibly the damaging public proceeding.

Justice Douglas, in dissent, focused on the results coming from such proceedings. He contended that where the state uses the juvenile proceeding as a forum for prosecution of a criminal act out of which is issued a confinement order for a period of time or where such a possibility is a stark reality, then the procedural protections afforded adults must be available to juveniles. After all, he continued, the Court made it clear in *Gault* that the guarantees protected by the Bill of Rights and the Fourteenth Amendment are not the exclusive preserve of adults.

OTHER FAIR TRIAL ISSUES

During the "criminal law explosion" of the 1960s, the Supreme Court handed down a number of decisions on the scope of the fair trial guarantees proclaimed in the Sixth Amendment. In several trials, guarantees which had previously been construed as limiting only the federal government, were made binding on the states. The historic right to a trial by jury in criminal cases was made obligatory on the states in *Duncan* v. *Louisiana, supra.* To be sure, all states guarantee jury trials in cases involving *serious* offenses, but there are wide variations among them as to what constitutes a *serious* offense. The *Duncan* case involved a conviction for simple battery which, under Louisiana law, carries a maximum penalty of a two-year jail term and/or a fine of not more than $300. The defendant was sentenced to only 60 days in jail and was fined $150. However, because the trial court had denied his request for a jury trial, the Supreme Court held that the statutory penalty was heavy enough to classify the offense as "serious." Under such circumstances, the Court concluded, the Fourteenth Amendment entitles the accused to the jury trial guarantee proclaimed in the Sixth Amendment.

A new dimension to the impartial jury issue was considered by the Court in *Witherspoon* v. *Illinois* (391 U.S. 510, 1968). In earlier cases the Court had held: (1) that persons may not be systematically excluded from juries because of race (*Norris* v. *Alabama*, 294 U.S. 587, 1935); (2) that states may fix different and higher qualification for jurors for special types of criminal cases (*Fay* v. *New York*, 332 U.S. 261, 1947); and (3) that states may exempt women from jury duty (*Hoyt* v. *Florida*, 368 U.S. 57, 1961); overruled in *Taylor* v. *Louisiana*, 43 L.W. 4167 , 1975). The *Witherspoon* case involved an appeal of a convicted murderer who was awaiting execution. He challenged the long-established practice of excusing all prospective jurors who indicate that they have conscientious scruples against capital punishment. The Supreme Court held that such a procedure results in the selection of a "prosecution prone" jury that is more likely than the average jury to make a finding of guilt and to impose the death penalty. In an opinion for the 6-3 majority, Justice Potter Stewart contended that "a state may not entrust the determination of whether a man should live or die to a tribunal organized to return a verdict of death." But Stewart carefully limited the holding to the imposition of the death penalty and not to the actual determination of guilt.

Justice Hugo Black wrote a vigorous dissent in which he charged that the decision would result in the selection of juries with a bias against capital punishment. On the larger issue of the role of the Court in reviewing state criminal procedures, Black accused the majority of "making law" and of weakening law enforcement "at a time of serious crime in our nation."

But the Court refused to set aside another state policy regulating trial jury procedures in *Johnson* v. *Louisiana* (406 U.S. 536) and *Apodaca* v. *Oregon* in 1972. In 5–4 decisions, Louisiana and Oregon statutes that permit nonunanimous verdicts in noncapital criminal prosecutions were upheld in the face of due process and equal protection challenges.[9] Speaking for the majority in *Johnson* and a plurality in *Apodaca*, Justice Byron White maintained that the Court had never held that jury unanimity was a requisite of due process. To him, the proof-beyond-a-reasonable-doubt principle is not violated merely because a small minority of jurors (three in *Johnson* and two in *Apodaca*) may not be convinced of the guilt of the accused. While greater certainty may be inferred from the unanimous verdict, White emphasized that the state satisfies acceptable standards of proof by convincing nine of 12 jurors to convict. Certainly, he concluded, "want of jury unanimity is not to be equated with the existence of a reasonable doubt."

Because *Johnson* was tried before *Duncan* v. *Louisiana*, *supra*, where the jury trial guarantee of the Sixth Amendment was made applicable to the states, the unanimity requisite of that guarantee was not as issue. However, it was raised and rejected in *Apodaca* as Justice White contended that the "reasonable doubt" standard, which the petitioner argued could only be met by a unanimous verdict, was not a requisite of the Amendment's guarantee. To be sure, he concluded, the "reasonable doubt" standard developed separately as an essential ingredient of due process.

Each of the dissenters (Douglas, Brennan, Stewart, and Marshall) wrote opinions. Justice Douglas complained that it was absurd for the majority to construe the Constitution to permit nonunanimous decisions in state prosecutions, while still construing the Sixth Amendment as requiring unanimous verdicts in federal prosecutions. Noting that a cornerstone of our jurisprudence is that if we err it should be on the side of the guilty going free rather than sending the innocent to jail, he emphasized that the "proof beyond a reasonable doubt principle" provides

---

[9] In *Colegrove* v. *Battin* (413 U.S. 149, 1973), the Court approved the use of six-member juries for civil cases under the Seventh Amendment. Justice Brennan argued that preservation of the common law jury trial in civil cases and not jury characteristics was the central concern of the framers.

"concrete substance for the presumption of innocence." And, he concluded, the unanimous jury verdict undergirds that principle.

For Justice William J. Brennan, whose opinion was supported by Justice Thurgood Marshall, the disastrous consequence of the majority's holding was its potential for obliteration of minority views. As he put it, "consideration of minority views may become nothing more than a matter of grace" where a verdict may be reached by a 9-3 or 10-2 vote. Hence, he contended that unanimity was absolutely essential, given a realistic appraisal of the jury selection and deliberation processes, if views of jurors in the minority are to have a fair consideration.

Justice Potter Stewart came down hard on the potential negation of the views of identifiable minority groups. He felt the concern the Court had shown over the years for the protection of minorities against systematic exclusion from the jury process was markedly undermined by this decision. To be sure, he concluded, the requirement of a unanimous verdict is essential in minimizing "the potential bigotry of those who might convict on inadequate evidence, or acquit when evidence of guilt is clear." Such possibility of racial bigotry among jurors was blunted somewhat, however, when several months later the Court held in *Ham* v. *South Carolina* (409 U.S. 524, 1973), that the Fourteenth Amendment requires the trial judge, upon timely request of the defendant, on voir dire examination to inquire into the possible racial prejudice of potential jurors.

An unusual twist to the racial composition of juries issue was presented to the Court in *Peters* v. *Kiff* (407 U.S. 493, 1972). There a white petitioner sought federal habeas corpus relief on the grounds that there was systematic exclusion of blacks from both the grand jury that indicted him and the petit jury that convicted him. In affirming the districts court's denial of relief, the Court of Appeals of the Fifth Curcuit held that discrimination had not been suffered because the petitioner was not a member of the excluded racial group and hence lacked standing to bring the action. In a 6-3 decision, the Supreme Court disagreed. In his plurality opinion, Justice Thurgood Marshall contended that systematic exclusion from juries injures not only defendants of the excluded class, but others as well. They are injured, he asserted, because the exclusion negates the community cross-sectional quality of representation. He concluded that exclusion of an identifiable racial group "deprives the jury of a perspective on human events that may have been unsuspected in any case.". . .

The Court considered the right to a speedy trial in *Klopfer* v. *North Carolina* (386 U.S. 213, 1967). In reversing a state court action approving a statutory *nolle prosequi* procedure (which permits the prosecutor to reopen the case at his pleasure), the Supreme Court held that the Fourteenth Amendment makes obligatory on the states the Sixth Amendment's guarantee of a speedy trial. Chief Justice Warren's opinion noted that the state procedure condoned a form of oppression by making it impossible for the accused to exonerate himself until the prosecutor chooses to restore his case to the court docket.

The standards for determining when a defendant has been denied a speedy trial were set forth in *Barker* v. *Wingo* (407 U.S. 514, 1972). There, the petitioner's trial was delayed for more than five years (the state was granted 16 continuances) after his arrest while the prosecution sought to convict first a coindictee as a part of its strategy to use his testimony against the petitioner. All but three of the motions for continuance were uncontested, but the petitioner's motions to dismiss the indictment during the hearings for the twelfth, fifteenth, and sixteenth continuances were denied.

At the subsequent trial the crucial testimony leading to the petitioner's conviction was given by the coindictee. In rejecting both a fixed-time period in which the accused must be brought to trial and the demand-waiver rule (a vague concept where the right to a speedy trial is assumed to be waived unless the defendant asserts a "timely" demand) as "inflexible approaches" to the problem, Justice Lewis Powell's opinion for the Court emphasized the necessity of evaluating speedy trial cases on an *ad hoc* basis. Among the factors which courts should consider in weighing claims alleging denial of the right, Powell identified the following:

(1) length of delay;
(2) reasons for the delay;
(3) the defendant's assertion of his right; and
(4) prejudice to the defendant.

In the end, however, Justice Powell noted that application of these factors to specific cases would not automatically provide the answer, but courts must consider any number of other relevant factors in a proper balancing of interests. But in the case at hand, he concluded that the trial court had not erred because the record disclosed that the defendant's repeated acquiescence in the prosecution's continuance requests was properly construed as a waiver of the speedy-trial guarantee.

What is the remedy when courts find that the speedy-trial guarantee has been impaired? The answer was suggested in *Barker* when Justice Powell argued that while dismissal of the indictment may be an "unsatisfactorily severe remedy," it is the only possible one. One year later in *Strunk* v. *United States* (412 U.S. 434, 1973), the Court applied this principle to reverse a court of appeals ruling that had ordered a reduction in sentence as an appropriate remedy where the speedy-trial guarantee had been infringed. Chief Justice Burger indicated that "severe remedies are not necessarily unique in the application of constitutional standards."

The Sixth Amendment right of confrontation and cross-examination was made applicable to state criminal proceedings in *Pointer* v. *Texas* (380 U.S. 400, 1965). The Court reversed a conviction because the testimony of a witness in a preliminary hearing—where the defendant was without counsel and no cross-examination was allowed—was admitted as evidence at the trial. The Court cited both *Malloy* and *Gideon* and held that the right of the accused to confront the witnesses against him is a fundamental right essential to a fair trial. Justice Hugo Black's opinion for the Court emphasized that the right of cross-examination is, without doubt, included in the confrontation guarantee.

In another Sixth Amendment action, the Court held in *Washington* v. *Texas* (388 U.S. 14, 1967), that the right of the accused "to have the compulsory process for obtaining witnesses in his favor" is binding on the states through the due process clause of the Fourteenth Amendment. At issue was a statutory procedure which prohibited persons charged or convicted as co-participants in the same crime from testifying for one another, but which allowed the prosecution to use them to testify against one another. Chief Justice Warren, who spoke for the majority, emphasized the right of the accused not only to confront and challenge the testimony of prosecution witnesses but also to present his own witnesses to establish his defense. Contending that the defendant has just as much right as the prosecution to present his version of the facts to the jury, Warren concluded:

> The right of an accused to have compulsory process for obtaining witnesses in his favor stands on no lesser footing than the other Sixth Amendment rights that we have previously held applicable to the states. . . .

One of the most controversial issues to reach the Court during the 1960s involved the conflicting constitutional claims of the accused to a fair trial free from prejudicial publicity and of a "free press" to gather and report news about a criminal case. In balancing these interests, the Court emphasized that the maintenance of an atmosphere free from inflamed public opinion is essential to the selection of an unbiased jury. Thus in *Irwin* v. *Dowd* (366 U.S. 717, 1961) the Court, for the first time, reversed a state conviction solely on the ground of prejudicial pre-trial publicity. Justice Tom Clark's opinion for the Court cited the "pattern of deep and bitter prejudice" permeating the community which was reflected in the "voir dire examination of the majority of the jurors finally" selected to hear the case. He further noted that eight of the 12 jurors had expressed the belief that the petitioner was guilty. Consequently, he concluded that the sincere assurances of fairness and impartiality proclaimed by jurors could be given little weight in meeting the constitutional requirement of impartiality, particularly where one's life was at stake.

Five years later, in *Sheppard* v. *Maxwell* (384 U.S. 333, 1966) the Court reversed a state murder conviction because of prejudicial publicity both before and during the trial. Referring to the "Roman holiday" atmosphere created by "circulation conscious editors catering to the insatiable interest of the American public in the bizarre," Justice Tom Clark contended that the public had been so inflamed and prejudiced as to make impossible a fair trial before an impartial jury. He condemned the trial court for permitting the trial to take place in a "carnival atmosphere" and for its failure to take necessary precautions for insulation of the jury.[10]

---

[10] In 1968, the American Bar Association made significant modifications in its Cannons of Professional Ethics. Recommended by a committee headed by Massachusetts Supreme Court Judge Paul C. Reardon, the major thrust of the new rules is directed at the conduct and responsibilities of prosecutors, defense attorneys, judges, court employees, and law enforcement officials in the discharge of their duties in criminal proceedings. Attorneys, for example, are forbidden to release or authorize release of information in connection with pending or imminent criminal litigation with which they are associated if there is a reasonable likelihood that such dissemination will interfere with a fair trial. This restriction applies to such matters as comment on prior criminal record, the existence or contents of a confession or statement of the accused, results of any tests or the refusal to submit to tests, the identity of prospective witnesses, and the possible nature of the plea. The restrictions recommended to govern the

The use of television has presented the Court with another dimension of the free press-fair trial issue. In *Rideau* v. *Louisiana* (373 U.S. 723, 1963), the Court reversed a murder conviction where the defendant's confession was presented on "live" television and then rerun by video-tape on two other occasions. Noting that the station's viewing range covered the entire area from which jurors were drawn, the Court held that refusal of the defendant's request for a change of venue was a denial of due process.

Televising of the actual trial was at issue in *Estes* v. *Texas* (381 U.S. 532, 1965). The case presented an appeal of the conviction of Texas financier Billie Sol Estes for swindling. Under Texas law, the question of televising court proceedings was left to the discretion of the trial judge. A motion to prohibit televising the trial was rejected (the hearing on the motion was itself televised) and it proceeded under limited video coverage. In a 5–4 decision, the Court reversed the conviction and emphasized the right of the accused to have his day in court free from the distractions inherent in telecasting. Justice Tom Clark, speaking for the majority, said that "the chief function of our judicial machinery is to ascertain the truth" and that the use of television injects an irrelevant factor toward that end. Furthermore, he noted that television has an infectious impact on the participants in a trial. The jury, "nerve center of the fact-finding process," is subjected to considerable distraction. The testimony of witnesses will often be impaired. If the trial is being conducted before an elective judge, the political capital to be gained from such exposure may impair his effectiveness. And finally, the defendant may suffer from "a form of mental harrassment resembling a police lineup or the third degree."

In the major dissent, Justice Potter Stewart thought the introduction of television into the courtroom an unwise policy but that on the specific record of the "limited use of the medium," the defendant's constitutional rights were not impaired. Stewart expressed great concern about the "intimation" in the majority and concurring opinions that "there are limits upon the public's right to know what goes on in the courts" and the implicit limitations upon First Amendment guarantees.

THE PROTECTION AGAINST
CRUEL AND UNUSUAL PUNISHMENT

In the celebrated "electric chair" case (*Louisiana ex rel. Francis* v. *Resweber*,

---

conduct of court employees and law enforcement officers are similar in nature and the new rules simply recommend that "judges should refrain from any conduct or the making of any statements that may tend to interfere with the right of the people or of the defendant to a fair trial." Appropriate judicial and law enforcement officials are urged to adopt regulations with appropriate sanctions to make the standards applicable to their employees. A limited use of the contempt power is recommended to enforce compliance in addition to the professional sanctions which the Bar may apply to its members.

329 U.S. 459, 1947) the Court assumed that the Eighth Amendment's prohibition against cruel and unusual punishment was applicable to the states under the Fourteenth Amendment. Nevertheless, it rejected the petitioner's claim that to subject him to the electric chair for a second time, after mechanical failure had prevented his execution the first time, constituted cruel and unusual punishment. Justice Stanley Reed's opinion emphasized that the cruelty against which the constitutional prohibition is directed is "cruelty inherent in the method of punishment, not the necessary suffering involved in any method employed to extinguish life humanely."

A decade later in *Trop* v. *Dulles* (356 U.S. 86, 1958), the Court invoked the cruel and unusual punishment provision to invalidate a section of the Immigration and Nationality Act of 1940 which permitted the taking away of citizenship as punishment for wartime desertion from the military. In the prevailing opinion, Chief Justice Earl Warren stressed the serious consequences of denationalization. He contended that such punishment is the "total destruction of the individual's status in organized society" and "[h]is very existence is at the sufferance of the country in which he happens to find himself."

In a subsequent action, the Warren Court extended the cruel and unusual punishment prohibition to invalidate a state statute making drug addiction a crime. In *Robinson* v. *California* (370 U.S. 660, 1962), the Court held that the statute allowed the infliction of a cruel and unusual punishment because it "makes the 'status' of narcotics addiction a criminal offense, for which the offender may be prosecuted 'at any time before he reforms'." Several lower courts have construed this decision and its assumptions and have invalidated convictions for public drunkenness of chronic alcoholics. In *Driver* v. *Hinnant* (356 F.2d 761, 1966), for example, the Court of Appeals for the Fourth Circuit reversed such a conviction and concluded that "the chronic alcoholic has not drunk voluntarily," rather, "his . . . excess now derives from disease."

The Supreme Court refused to accept this logic in *Powell* v. *Texas* (392 U.S. 514, 1968). In a 5–4 decision, the Court held that jailing a chronic alcoholic for public drunkenness did not constitute cruel and unusual punishment. While no opinion gained majority support, Justice Thurgood Marshall's plurality opinion warned of the danger of undermining the common law doctrine of criminal responsibility with an extension of the *Robinson* holding to cases like *Powell.* Carefully distinguishing the two cases, Marshall noted that in *Robinson,* the Court condemned the state action because it inflicted punishment for mere status of addiction, whereas in *Powell* the state had properly "imposed upon the appellant a criminal sanction for public behavior which may create substantial health and safety hazards both for the appellant and for members of the general public, and which offends the moral and esthetic sensibilities of a large segment of the population."

Marshall was further troubled by the argument that the chronic alcoholic suffers from a compulsion to drink over which he has no control. He noted that if the appellant could not be convicted for public drunkenness, then it would be difficult to see how a person could be convicted for murder, "if that [person], while exhibiting normal behavior in all other respects, suffers from a compulsion to kill. . . ." He concluded that existing medical knowledge is inconclusive as to whether chronic alcoholics "suffer from such an irresistible compulsion to drink and to get drunk in public that they are utterly unable to control their performance of either or both of these acts. . . ." In the end, he argued that in the almost complete absence of rehabilitation and treatment facilities, it would be difficult to contend that "the criminal process [as applied here] is utterly lacking in social value." What Marshall really seems to be suggesting is that in most instances a derelict might be better off in jail for a fixed term.

Justice Abe Fortas' dissent accepted the contention that alcoholism is a disease that removes a person's will to stay sober. He argued that the *Robinson* drug addiction holding is controlling, since to jail a person for being drunk in public is to punish him for a condition that he cannot change. Hence, the state action constitutes cruel and unusual punishment.

As noted in the "electric chair" case of 1947, the Court did not rule directly on the constitutionality of the death penalty. Twenty-five years later, however, the issue was squarely before it in *Furman* v. *Georgia* and two companion cases.[11] The 5–4 ruling holding the death penalty unconstitutional as prescribed by the laws of Georgia and Texas produced a clear division between the holdover Warren Court justices of the majority (Douglas, Brennan, Stewart, White, and Marshall) and the four Nixon appointees constituting the minority (Burger, Blackmun, Powell, and Rehnquist). Consequently, it appears that at least on this issue, President Nixon's appointments had returned partially the "law and order" dividends he had sought.

In its brief per curiam opinion, the Court held that the imposition and implementation of the death penalty in *the circumstances of the three cases* constitutes cruel and unusual punishment in violation of the Eighth and Fourteenth Amendments. However, there was little agreement among the majority beyond that statement of principle and each wrote a concurring opinion without support from any of his brethren. Three of the majority justices (Douglas, Stewart, and White) found the statutes defective because they failed to mandatorily impose the death penalty for specific crimes, allowing juries to exercise considerable discretion in each case. This led them to express concern about the discriminatory application of the penalty possible under such statutory schemes. Statistics were cited which revealed the substantial differential treatment between whites and nonwhites, "the poor who lack 'political clout' " and the more socially prominent. And as Justice Douglas proclaimed, the "statutes are pregnant with discrimination" and are thus incompatible "with the idea of equal protection of the laws . . . implicit in the ban on 'cruel and unusual punishments.' " Justice Potter Stewart set forth the argument that the death penalty in these cases is "cruel" because the juries in their discretion go "excessively . . . beyond, not in degree, but in kind, the punishments that the state legislatures [had] determined to be necessary." It is "unusual," he continued, because of its infrequent imposition as punishments for murder and rape. Because

[11] *Jackson* v. *Georgia* and *Branch* v. *Texas* (408 U.S. 239, 1972).

of this infrequent imposition, Justice Byron White could not see any effective contribution of the death penalty as a deterrent to crime. Hence, he characterized it as a "pointless and needless extinction of life with only marginal contributions to any discernible social or public purposes."

While Douglas, Stewart, and White were careful to limit their holding to the death penalty as imposed under the laws of Georgia and Texas, Justices Brennan and Marshall indicated a desire to declare it unconstitutional *per se*. Brennan argued that imposition of the death penalty as a punishment for crimes is cruel and unusual punishment because "it does not comport with human dignity," and Justice Thurgood Marshall felt that such a mode of punishment was "no longer consistent with our 'self-respect.' " Furthermore, Marshall maintained abolition of the death penalty is "a major milestone in the long road up from barbarism."

Each of the dissenters wrote opinions and, unlike the majority Justices, they joined in each other's opinion. Essentially, theirs was a plea for judicial restraint and deference to legislatures in prescribing penalties deemed necessary as punishments for crime. As Chief Justice Burger noted, a thorough analysis of the intent of the framers of the Eighth Amendment does not support the conclusion that the death penalty was one of the cruel and unusual punishments banned by the Amendment, nor has the Court in its long history read the intent differently. Hence, he concluded, the legislative judgment must be respected since the evidence of offense to society is not so great as to warrant abandoning it.

The dissenters emphasized that only two members of the majority had held that the death penalty *per se* is cruel and unusual punishment. Hence, the ruling did not prevent legislatures from prescribing capital punishment for specified crimes. Undoubtedly, President Nixon got this same message and, in his recommendations on crime and law enforcement transmitted to Congress in March of 1973 and again in his State of the Union address in January, 1974, he urged the adoption of the mandatory death penalty for specified federal crimes. The enactment of his recommendations and the modification of state statutes to conform with the ruling in *Furman* undoubtedly will produce litigation that will present to the Court the "gut" issue of the constitutionality of the death penalty *per se*.

The cases that follow focus on some of the most significant issues reviewed in this commentary.

MAPP v. OHIO
367 U.S. 643; 6 L. Ed. 2d 1081; 81 S. Ct. 1684 (1961)

MR. JUSTICE CLARK *delivered the opinion of the Court.*

Appellant stands convicted of knowingly hav-

ing had in her possession and under her control certain lewd and lascivious books, pictures, and photographs in violation of . . . Ohio's Revised Code. . . .

On May 23, 1957, three Cleveland police officers arrived at appellant's residence in that city pursuant to information that "a person [was] hiding out in the home, who was wanted for questioning in connection with a recent bombing, and that there was a large amount of policy paraphernalia being hidden in the home." Miss Mapp and her daughter by a former marriage lived on the top floor of the two-family dwelling. Upon their arrival at that house, the officers knocked on the door and demanded entrance but appellant, after telephoning her attorney, refused to admit them without a search warrant. They advised their headquarters of the situation and undertook a surveillance of the house.

The officers again sought entrance some three hours later when four or more additional officers arrived on the scene. When Miss Mapp did not come to the door immediately, at least one of the several doors to the house was forcibly opened and the policemen gained admittance. Meanwhile Miss Mapp's attorney arrived, but the officers, having secured their own entry, and continuing in their defiance of the law, would permit him neither to see Miss Mapp nor to enter the house. It appears that Miss Mapp was halfway down the stairs from the upper floor to the front door when the officers, in this highhanded manner, broke into the hall. A paper, claimed to be a warrant, was held up by one of the officers. She grabbed the "warrant" and placed it in her bosom. A struggle ensued in which the officers recovered the piece of paper and as a result of which they handcuffed appellant because she had been "belligerent" in resisting their official rescue of the "warrant" from her person. Running roughshod over appellant, a policeman "grabbed" her, "twisted [her] hand," and she "yelled [and] pleaded with him" because "it was hurting." Appellant, in handcuffs, was then forcibly taken upstairs to her bedroom where the officers searched a dresser, a chest of drawers, a closet and some suitcases. They also looked into a photo album and through personal papers

belonging to the appellant. The search spread to the rest of the second floor including the child's bedroom, the living room, the kitchen and a dinette. The basement of the building and a trunk found therein were also searched. The obscene materials for possession of which she was ultimately convicted were discovered in the course of that widespread search.

At the trial no search warrant was produced by the prosecution, nor was the failure to produce one explained or accounted for. At best, [said the State Supreme Court] "There is, in the record, considerable doubt as to whether there ever was any warrant for the search of defendant's home." . . . The Ohio Supreme Court believed a "reasonable argument" could be made that the conviction should be reversed "because the 'methods' employed to obtain the [evidence] . . . were such as to 'offend "a sense of justice," ' " but the court found determinative the fact that the evidence had not been taken "from defendant's person by the use of brutal or offensive physical force against defendant." . . . [Hence, it found that the conviction was valid.]

The State says that even if the search were made without authority, or otherwise unreasonably, it is not prevented from using the unconstitutionally seized evidence at trial, citing *Wolf* v. *Colorado* . . . in which this Court did indeed hold "that in a prosecution in a State court for a State crime the Fourteenth Amendment does not forbid the admission of evidence obtained by an unreasonable search and seizure." . . .

Seventy-five years ago in *Boyd* v. *United States,* 116 U.S. 616 (1886) . . . , considering the Fourth and Fifth Amendments as running "almost into each other" on the facts before it, this Court held that the doctrines of those Amendments "apply to all invasions on the part of the government and its employees of the sanctity of a man's home and the privacies of life. It is not the breaking of his doors, and the rummaging of his drawers, that constitutes the essence of the offense; but it is the invasion of his indefeasible right of personal security, personal liberty and private liberty. . . . Breaking into a house and opening boxes and drawers are circumstances of aggravation; but any forcible and compulsory extortion of a man's own testimony or of his private papers to be used as evidence to convict him of crime or to forfeit his goods, is within the condemnation . . . [of those Amendments] ."

. . . The Court in the *Weeks* case clearly stated that use of the seized evidence involved "a denial of the constitutional rights of the accused." . . . Thus, in the year 1914, in the *Weeks* case, this Court "for the first time" held that "in a federal prosecution the Fourth Amendment barred the use of evidence secured through an illegal search and seizure." (*Wolf* v. *Colorado*. . . .) This Court has ever since required of federal law officers a strict adherence to that command which this Court has held to be a clear, specific, and constitutionally required—even if judicially implied—deterrent safeguard without insistence upon which the Fourth Amendment would have been reduced to "a form of words." . . . It meant, quite simply, that conviction by means of unlawful seizures and enforced confessions . . . should find no sanction in the judgments of the courts. . . ."

There are in the cases of this Court some passing references to the *Weeks* rule as being one of evidence. But the plain and unequivocal language of *Weeks*—and its later paraphrase in *Wolf*—to the effect that the *Weeks* rule is of constitutional origin, remains entirely undisturbed. . . .

In 1949, thirty-five years after *Weeks* was announced, this Court, in *Wolf* v. *Colorado* . . . , again for the first time, discussed the effect of the Fourth Amendment upon the States through the operation of the Due Process Clause of the Fourteenth Amendment. It said:

> [W]e have no hesitation in saying that were a State affirmatively to sanction such police incursion into privacy it would run counter to the guaranty of the Fourteenth Amendment.

Nevertheless, after declaring that the "security of one's privacy against arbitrary intrusion by the police" is "implicit in the 'concept of ordered liberty' and as such enforceable against the States through the Due Process Clause," cf. *Palko* v. *Connecticut,* 302 U.S. 319 (1937) . . . , and announcing that it "stoutly adhere[d]" to the *Weeks* decision, the Court decided that the *Weeks* exclusionary rule would not then be imposed upon the States as "an essential ingredient of the right." . . . The Court's reasons for not considering essential to the right of privacy, as a curb imposed upon the States by the Due Process Clause, that which decades before had been posited as part and parcel of the Fourth Amendment's limitation upon federal encroachment of individual privacy, were bottomed on factual considerations.

While they are not basically relevant to a decision that the exclusionary rule is an essential ingredient of the Fourth Amendment as the right it embodies is vouchsafed against the States by the Due Process Clause, we will consider the current validity of the factual grounds upon which *Wolf* was based.

The Court in *Wolf* first stated that "[t]he contrariety of views of the States" on the adoption of the exclusionary rule of *Weeks* was "particularly impressive" . . . ; and, in this connection, that it could not "brush aside the experience of States which deem the incidence of such conduct by the police too slight to call for a deterrent remedy . . . by overriding the [States'] relevant rules of evidence." . . . While in 1949, prior to the *Wolf* case, almost two-thirds of the States were opposed to the use of the exclusionary rule, now, despite the *Wolf* case, more than half of those since passing upon it, by their own legislative or judicial decision, have wholly or partly adopted or adhered to the *Weeks* rule. See *Elkins* v. *United States,* 364 U.S. 206 (1960). . . . Significantly, among those now following the rule is California which, according to its highest court, was "compelled to reach that conclusion because other remedies have completely failed to secure compliance with the constitutional provisions. . . ." The experience of California that such other remedies have been worthless and futile is buttressed by the experience of other States. The obvious futility of relegating the Fourth Amendment to the protection of other remedies has, moreover, been recognized by this Court since *Wolf*. . . .

Likewise, time has set its face against what *Wolf* called the "weighty testimony" of *People* v. *Defore,* 242 N.Y. 13, 150 N.E. 585 (1926). There Justice (then Judge) Cardozo, rejecting adoption of the *Weeks* exclusionary rule in New York, had said that "the Federal rule as it stands is either too strict or too lax." . . . However, the force of that reasoning has been largely vitiated by later decisions of this Court. These include the recent discarding of the "silver platter" doctrine which allowed federal judicial use of evidence seized in violation of the Constitution by state agents, *Elkins* v. *United States,* 364 U.S. 206, 111; the relaxation of the formerly strict requirements as to standing to challenge the use of evidence thus seized, so that now the procedure of exclusion, "ultimately referable to constitutional safeguards," is available to anyone even "legitimately on [the] premises" unlawfully searched, *Jones* v. *United States,* 362 U.S. 257, 111 (1960); and, finally, the formulation of a method to prevent state use of evidence unconstitutionally seized by federal agents, *Rea* v. *United States,* 350 U.S. 214, 111 (1956). Because there can be no fixed formula, we are admittedly met with "recurring questions of the reasonableness of searches." But less is not to be expected when dealing with a Constitution, and, at any rate, "reasonableness is in the first instance for the [trial court] . . . to determine." *United States* v. *Rabinowitz,* 339 U.S. 56, . . . (1950).

It, therefore, plainly appears that the factual considerations supporting the failure of the *Wolf* Court to include the *Weeks* exclusionary rule when it recognized the enforceability of the right to privacy against the States in 1949, while not basically relevant to the constitutional consideration, could not, in any analysis, now be deemed controlling.

. . . Only last Term, after again carefully re-examining the *Wolf* doctrine in *Elkins* v. *United States . . .* , the Court pointed out that "the controlling principles" as to search and seizure and the problem of admissibility "seemed clear" . . . until the announcement in *Wolf* "that the Due Process Clause of the Fourteenth Amendment does not itself require state courts to adopt the exclusionary rule" of the *Weeks* case. . . . At the same time the Court pointed out, "the underlying constitutional doctrine which *Wolf* established . . . that the Federal Constitution . . . prohibits unreasonable searches and seizures by state officers" had undermined the "foundation upon which the admissibility of state-seized evidence in a federal trial originally rested. . . ." *Ibid.* The Court concluded that it was therefore obliged to hold, although it chose the narrower ground on which to do so, that all evidence obtained by an unconstitutional search and seizure was inadmissible in a federal court regardless of its source. Today we once again examine *Wolf's* constitutional documentation of the right to privacy free from unreasonable state intrusion, and, after its dozen years on our books, are led by it to close the only courtroom door remaining open to evidence secured by official lawlessness in flagrant abuse of that basic right, reserved to all persons as a specific guarantee against that very same unlawful conduct. We hold that all evidence obtained by searches and seizures in violation of the Constitution is, by the same authority, inadmissible in a state court.

Since the Fourth Amendment's right of privacy has been declared enforceable against the States through the Due Process Clause of the Fourteenth, it is enforceable against them by the same sanction of exclusion as is used against the Federal Government. . . .

Indeed, we are aware of no restraint, similar to that rejected today, conditioning the enforcement of any other basic constitutional right. The right to privacy, no less important than any other right carefully and particularly reserved to the people, would stand in marked contrast to all other rights declared as "basic to a free society." *Wolf* v. *Colorado,* . . . (338 U.S., at 27). This Court has not hesitated to enforce as strictly against the States as it does against the Federal Government the right of free speech and of a free press, the rights to notice and to a fair public trial, including, as it does, the right not to be convicted by use of a coerced confession, however logically relevant it be, . . . and without regard to its reliability. *Rogers* v. *Richmond*, 365 U.S. 534, . . . (1961). And nothing could be more certain than that when a coerced confession is involved, "the relevant rules of evidence" are overridden without regard to "the incidence of such conduct by the police," slight or frequent. Why should not the same rule apply to what is tantamount to coerced testimony by way of unconstitutional seizure of goods, papers, effects, documents, etc.? . . .

Moreover, our holding that the exclusionary rule is an essential part of both the Fourth and Fourteenth Amendments is not only the logical dictate of prior cases, but it also makes very good sense. There is no war between the Constitution and common sense. Presently, a federal prosecutor may make no use of evidence illegally seized, but a State's attorney across the street may, although he supposedly is operating under the enforceable prohibitions of the same Amendment. Thus the State, by admitting evidence unlawfully seized, serves to encourage disobedience to the Federal Constitution which it is bound to uphold. . . .

There are those who say, as did Justice (then Judge) Cardozo, that under our constitutional exclusionary doctrine "the criminal is to go free because the constable has blundered." *People* v. *Defore*, 242 N.Y. at 21. . . . In some cases this will undoubtedly be the result. But, as was said in *Elkins*, "there is another consideration—the imperative of judicial integrity." . . . The criminal

goes free, if he must, but it is the law that sets him free. Nothing can destroy a government more quickly than its failure to observe its laws, or worse, its disregard of the charter of its own existence. . . .

The ignoble shortcut to conviction left open to the State tends to destroy the entire system of constitutional restraints on which the liberties of the people rest. Having once recognized that the right to privacy embodied in the Fourth Amendment is enforceable against the States, and that the right to be secure against rude invasions of privacy by state officers is, therefore, constitutional in origin, we can no longer permit that right to remain an empty promise. Because it is enforceable in the same manner and to like effect as other basic rights secured by the Due Process Clause, we can no longer permit it to be revocable at the whim of any police officer who, in the name of law enforcement itself, chooses to suspend its enjoyment. Our decision, founded on reason and truth, gives to the individual no more than that which the Constitution guarantees him, to the police officer no less than that to which honest law enforcement is entitled, and, to the courts, that judicial integrity so necessary in the true administration of justice.

The judgment of the Supreme Court of Ohio is reversed and the cause remanded for further proceedings not inconsistent with this opinion.

Reversed and remanded.

MR. JUSTICE BLACK, *concurring.*

I am still not persuaded that the Fourth Amendment, standing alone, would be enough to bar the introduction into evidence against an accused of papers and effects seized from him in violation of its commands. For the Fourth Amendment does not itself contain any provision expressly precluding the use of such evidence, and I am extremely doubtful that such a provision could properly be inferred from nothing more than the basic command against unreasonable searches and seizures. Reflection on the problem, however, in the light of cases coming before the Court since *Wolf*, has led me to conclude that when the Fourth Amendment's ban against unreasonable searches and seizures is considered together with the Fifth Amendment's ban against compelled self-incrimination, a constitutional basis emerges which not only justifies but actually requires the exclusionary rule.

The close interrelationship between the Fourth and Fifth Amendments, as they apply to this problem, has long been recognized and, indeed, was expressly made the ground for this Court's holding in *Boyd* v. *United States*. There the Court fully discussed this relationship and declared itself "unable to perceive that the seizure of a man's private books and papers to be used in evidence against him is substantially different from compelling him to be a witness against himself." It was upon this ground that Mr. Justice Rutledge largely relied in his dissenting opinion in the *Wolf* case. And, although I rejected the argument at that time, its force has, for me at least, become compelling with the more thorough understanding of the problem brought on by recent cases. In the final analysis, it seems to me that the *Boyd* doctrine, though perhaps not required by the express language of the Constitution strictly construed, is amply justified from an historical standpoint, soundly based in reason, and entirely consistent with what I regard to be the proper approach to interpretation of our Bill of Rights. . . .

. . . As I understand the Court's opinion in this case, we again reject the confusing "shock-the-conscience" standard of the *Wolf* and *Rochin* cases and, instead, set aside this state conviction in reliance upon the precise, intelligible and more predictable constitutional doctrine enunciated in the *Boyd* case. I fully agree with Mr. Justice Bradley's opinion that the two Amendments upon which the *Boyd* doctrine rests are of vital importance in our constitutional scheme of liberty and that both are entitled to a liberal rather than a niggardly interpretation. The courts

of the country are entitled to know with as much certainty as possible what scope they cover. The Court's opinion, in my judgment, dissipates the doubt and uncertainty in this field of constitutional law and I am persuaded, for this and other reasons stated, to depart from my prior views, to accept the *Boyd* doctrine as controlling in this state case and to join the Court's judgment and opinion which are in accordance with that constitutional doctrine.

MR. JUSTICE DOUGLAS, *concurring.*

When we allow States to give constitutional sanction to the "shabby business" of unlawful entry into a home (to use an expression of Mr. Justice Murphy, *Wolf* v. *People of State of Colorado*), . . . we did indeed rob the Fourth Amendment of much meaningful force. . . .

Without judicial action making the exclusionary rule applicable to the States, *Wolf* v. *People of State of Colorado* in practical effect reduced the guarantee against unreasonable searches and seizures to "a dead letter," as Mr. Justice Rutledge said in his dissent. . . .

. . . Once evidence, inadmissible in a federal court, is admissible in a state court a "double standard" exists which, as the Court points out, leads to "working arrangements" that undercut federal policy and reduce some aspects of law enforcement to shabby business. The rule that supports that practice does not have the force of reason behind it.

MR. JUSTICE HARLAN, *whom* MR. JUSTICE FRANKFURTER *and* MR. JUSTICE WHIITAKER *join, dissenting.*

In overruling the *Wolf* case the Court, in my opinion, has forgotten the sense of judicial restraint which, with due regard for *stare decisis*, is one element that should enter into deciding whether a past decision on this Court should be overruled. Apart from that I also believe that the *Wolf* rule represents sounder Constitutional doctrine than the new rule which now replaces it.

From the Court's statement of the case one would gather that the central, if not controlling, issue on this appeal is whether illegally state-seized evidence is Constitutionally admissible in a state prosecution, an issue which would of course face us with the need for re-examining *Wolf*. However, such is not the situation. For, although the question was indeed raised here and below among appellant's subordinate points, the new and pivotal issue brought to the Court by this appeal is whether Sec. 2905.34 of the Ohio Revised Code making criminal the *mere* knowing possession or control of obscene material, and under which appellant has been convicted, is consistent with the rights of free thought and expression assured against state action by the Fourteenth Amendment. That was the principal issue which was decided by the Ohio Supreme Court, which was tendered by appellant's Jurisdictional Statement, and which was briefed and argued in this Court.

In this posture of things, I think it fair to say that five members of this Court have simply "reached out" to overrule *Wolf*. With all respect for the views of the majority, and recognizing that *stare decisis* carries different weight in Constitutional adjudication than it does in non-constitutional decision, I can perceive no justification for regarding this case as an appropriate occasion for re-examining *Wolf*.

The action of the Court finds no support in the rule that decision of Constitutional issues should be avoided wherever possible. For in overruling *Wolf*, the Court, instead of passing upon the validity of Ohio's Sec. 2905.34, has simply chosen between two Constitutional questions. Moreover, I submit that it has chosen the more difficult and less appropriate of the two questions. The Ohio statute which, as construed by the State Supreme Court, punishes knowing possession or control of obscene material, irrespective of the purposes of such possession or control (with exceptions not here applicable) and irrespective of whether the accused had any reasonable opportunity to rid himself of the material after discovering that it was obscene, surely presents a constitutional question which is both simpler and less far-reaching than the question which the Court decides today. It seems to me that justice might well have been done in this case without overturning a decision on which the administration of criminal law in many of the States has long justifiably relied. . . .

I am bound to say that what has been done is not likely to promote respect either for the Court's adjudicatory process or for the stability of its decisions. . . .

I would not impose upon the States this federal exclusionary remedy. The reasons given by the majority for now suddenly turning its back on *Wolf* seem to me notably unconvincing.

First, it is said that "the factual grounds upon which *Wolf* was based" have since changed, in that more States now follow the *Weeks* exclusionary rule than was so at the time *Wolf* was decided. While that is true, a recent survey indicated that at present one half of the States still adhere to the common-law nonexclusionary rule, and one, Maryland, retains the rule as to felonies. . . . But in any case surely all this is beside the point, as the majority itself indeed seems to recognize. Our concern here, as it was in *Wolf*, is not with the desirability of that rule but only with the question whether the States are Constitutionally free to follow it or not as they may themselves determine, and the relevance of the disparity of views among the States on this point lies simply in the fact that the judgment involved is a debatable one. Moreover, the very fact on which the majority relies, instead of lending support to what is now being done, points away from the need of replacing voluntary state action with federal compulsion.

The preservation of a proper balance between state and federal responsibility in the administration of criminal justice demands patience on the part of those who might like to see things move faster among the States in this respect. Problems of criminal law enforcement vary widely from State to State. One State, in considering the totality of its legal picture, may conclude that the need for embracing the *Weeks* rule is pressing because other remedies are unavailable or inadequate to secure compliance with the substantive Constitutional principle involved. Another, though equally solicitous of Constitutional rights, may choose to pursue one purpose at a time, allowing all evidence relevant to guilt to be brought into a criminal trial, and dealing with Constitutional infractions by other means. Still another may consider the exclusionary rule too rough and ready a remedy, in that it reaches only unconstitutional intrusions which eventuate in criminal prosecution of the victims. Further, a State after experimenting with the *Weeks* rule for a time may, because of unsatisfactory experience with it, decide to revert to a nonexclusionary rule. And so on.... For us the question remains, as it has always been, one of state power, not one of passing judgment on the wisdom of one state course or another. In my view this Court should continue to forbear from fettering the States with an adamant rule which may embarrass them in coping with their own peculiar problems in criminal law enforcement.

Further, we are told that imposition of the *Weeks* rule on the States makes "very good sense," in that it will promote recognition by state and federal officials of their "mutual obligation to respect the same fundamental criteria" in their approach to law enforcement, and will avoid "needless conflict between state and federal courts." Indeed the majority now finds an incongruity in *Wolf's* discriminating perception between the demands of "ordered liberty" as respects the basic right of "privacy" and the means of securing it among the States. That perception, resting both on a sensitive regard for our federal system and a sound recognition of this Court's remoteness from particular state problems, is for me the strength of that decision.

An approach which regards the issue as one of achieving procedural symmetry or of serving administrative convenience surely disfigures the boundaries of this Court's functions in relation to the state and federal courts. Our role in promulgating the *Weeks* rule and its extensions ... was quite a different one than it is here. There, in implementing the Fourth Amendment, we occupied the position of a tribunal having the ultimate responsibility for developing the standards and procedures of judicial administration within the judicial system over which it presides. Here we review State procedures whose measure is to be taken not against the specific substantive commands of the Fourth Amendment but under the flexible contours of the Due Process Clause. I do not believe that the Fourteenth Amendment empowers this Court to mould state remedies effectuating the right to freedom from "arbitrary intrusion by the police" to suit its own notions of how things should be done. ...

In conclusion, it should be noted that the majority opinion in this is in fact an opinion only for the *judgment* overruling *Wolf*, and not for the basic rationale by which four members of the majority have reached that result. For my Brother Black is unwilling to subscribe to their view that the *Weeks* exclusionary rule derives from the Fourth Amendment itself, ... but joins the majority opinion on the premise that its end result can be achieved by bringing the Fifth Amendment to the aid of the Fourth. ... On that score I need only say that whatever the validity of the "Fourth-Fifth Amendment" correlation which the *Boyd* case ... found, ... we have only very recently again reiterated the long-established doctrine of this Court that the Fifth Amendment privilege against self-incrimination is not applicable to the States. ...

I regret that I find so unwise in principle and so inexpedient in policy a decision motivated by the high purpose of increasing respect for constitutional rights. But in the last analysis I think this Court can increase respect for the Constitution only if it rigidly respects the limitations which the Constitution places upon it, and respects as well the principles inherent in its own processes. In the present case I think we exceed both, and that our voice becomes only a voice of power, not of reason.

COOLIDGE v. NEW HAMPSHIRE
403 U.S. 443; 29 L. Ed. 2d 564; 91 S. Ct. 2022 (1971)

MR. JUSTICE STEWART *delivered the opinion of the Court.* *

We are called upon in this case to decide issues under the Fourth and Fourteenth Amendments arising in the context of a state criminal trial for the commission of a particularly brutal murder. . . .

Pamela Mason, a 14-year-old girl, left her home in Manchester, New Hampshire on the evening of January 13, 1964, during a heavy snowstorm, apparently in response to a man's telephone call for a babysitter. Eight days later, after a thaw, her body was found by the site of a major north-south highway several miles away. She had been murdered. The event created great alarm in the area, and the police immediately began a massive investigation.

On January 28, having learned from a neighbor that the petitioner Edward Coolidge, had been away from home on the evening of the girl's disappearance, the police went to his house to question him. They asked him, among other things, if he owned any guns, and he produced three, two shotguns and a rifle. They also asked whether he would take a lie detector test concerning his account of his activities on the night of the disappearance. He agreed to do so on the following Sunday, his day off. The police later described his attitude on the occasion of this visit as fully "cooperative." His wife was in the house throughout the interview.

On the following Sunday, a policeman called Coolidge early in the morning and asked him to come down to the police station for the trip to Concord, New Hampshire, where the lie detector test was to be administered. That evening, two plain clothes policemen arrived at the Coolidge house, where Mrs. Coolidge was waiting with her mother-in-law for her husband's return. These two policemen were not the two who had visited the house earlier in the week, and they apparently did not know that Coolidge had displayed three guns for inspection during the earlier visit. The plainclothesmen told Mrs. Coolidge that her husband was in "serious trouble" and probably would not be home that night. They asked Coolidge's mother to leave, and proceeded to question Mrs. Coolidge. During the course of the interview they obtained from her four guns belonging to Coolidge, and some clothes that Mrs. Coolidge thought her husband might have been wearing on the evening of Pamela Mason's disappearance.

Coolidge was held in jail on an unrelated charge that night, but he was released the next day.[1] During the ensuing two and a half weeks, the State accumulated a quantity of evidence to support the theory that it was he who had killed Pamela Mason. On February 19, the results of the investigation were presented at a meeting between the police officers working on the case and the State Attorney General, who had personally taken charge of all police activities relating to the murder, and was later to serve as chief prosecutor at the trial. At this meeting, it was decided that there was enough evidence to

---

*Parts II A, II B, and II C of this opinion are joined only by MR. JUSTICE DOUGLAS, MR. JUSTICE BRENNAN, and MR. JUSTICE MARSHALL.

[1] During the lie detector test, Coolidge had confessed to a theft of money from his employer. . . .

justify the arrest of Coolidge on the murder charge and a search of his house and two cars. At the conclusion of the meeting, the Manchester police chief made formal application, under oath, for the arrest and search warrants. The complaint supporting the warrant for a search of Coolidge's Pontiac automobile, the only warrant which concerns us here, stated that the affiant "has probable cause to suspect and believe, and does suspect and believe, and herewith offers satisfactory evidence, that there are certain objects and things used in the Commission of said offense, now kept, and concealed in or upon a certain vehicle, to wit: 1951 Pontiac two-door sedan. * * *'" The warrants were then signed and issued by the Attorney General himself, acting as a justice of the peace. . . .

The police arrested Coolidge in his house on the day the warrant was issued. Mrs. Coolidge asked whether she might remain in the house with her small child, but was told that she must stay elsewhere, apparently in part because the police believed that she would be harassed by reporters if she were accessible to them. When she asked whether she might take her car, she was told that both cars had been "impounded," and that the police would provide transporation for her. Some time later, the police called a towing company, and about two and a half hours after Coolidge had been taken into custody the cars were towed to the police station. It appears that at the time of the arrest the cars were parked in the Coolidge driveway, and that although dark had fallen they were plainly visible both from the street and from inside the house where Coolidge was actually arrested. The 1951 Pontiac was searched and vacuumed on February 21, two days after it was seized, again a year later, in January 1965, and a third time in April, 1965.

At Coolidge's subsequent jury trial on the charge of murder, vacuum sweepings, including particles of gun powder, taken from the Pontiac were introduced in evidence against him, as part of an attempt by the State to show by micro-

scopic analysis that it was highly probable that Pamela Mason had been in Coolidge's car. Also introduced in evidence was one of the guns taken by the police on their Sunday evening visit to the Coolidge house—a .22 calibre Mossberg rifle, which the prosecution claimed was the murder weapon. Conflicting ballistics testimony was offered on the question whether the bullets found in Pamela Mason's body had been fired from this rifle. Finally, the prosecution introduced vacuum sweepings of the clothes taken from the Coolidge house that same Sunday evening, and attempted to show through microscopic analysis that there was a high probability that the clothes had been in contact with Pamela Mason's body. Pretrial motions to suppress all this evidence were referred by the trial judge to the New Hampshire Supreme Court, which ruled the evidence admissible. The jury found Coolidge guilty and he was sentenced to life imprisonment. The New Hampshire Supreme Court affirmed . . . and we granted certiorari to consider the constitutional questions raised by the admission of this evidence. . . .

I

The petitioner's first claim is that the warrant authorizing the seizure and subsequent search of his 1951 Pontiac automobile was invalid because not issued by a "neutral and detached magistrate." Since we agree with the petitioner that the warrant was invalid for this reason, we need not consider his further argument that the allegations under oath supporting the issuance of the warrant were so conclusory as to violate relevant constitutional standards. . . .

In this case, the determination of probable cause was made by the chief "government enforcement agent" of the State—the Attorney General—who was actively in charge of the investigation and later was to be chief prosecutor at the trial. To be sure, the determination was formalized here by a writing bearing the title "Search Warrant".... [T]he State argues that the Attorney General, who was unquestionably authorized as a justice of the peace to issue warrants under then existing state law, did in fact act as a "neutral and detached magistrate." Further, the State claims that *any* magistrate, confronted with the showing of probable cause made by the Manchester chief of police, would have issued the warrant in question. To the first proposition it is enough to answer that there could hardly be a more appropriate setting than this for a *per se* rule of disqualification rather than a case-by-case evaluation of all the circumstances. Without disrespect to the state law enforcement agent here involved, the whole point of the basic rule so well expressed by Mr. Justice Jackson [in *Johnson* v. *U.S.*, 333 U.S. 10–14] is that prosecutors and policemen simply cannot be asked to maintain the requisite neutrality with regard to their own investigations— the "competitive enterprises" which must rightly engage their single-minded attention....

We find no escape from the conclusion that the seizure and search of the Pontiac automobile cannot constitutionally rest upon the warrant issued by the state official who was the chief investigator and prosecutor in this case. Since he was not the neutral and detached magistrate required by the Constitution, the search stands on no firmer ground than if there had been no warrant at all. If the seizure and search are to be justified, they must, therefore, be justified on some other theory.

II

The State proposes three distinct theories to bring the facts of this case within one or another of the exceptions to the warrant requirement. In considering them, we must not lose sight of the Fourth Amendment's fundamental guarantee....

A

The State's first theory is that the seizure and subsequent search of Coolidge's Pontiac on February 19 were "incident" to a valid arrest. We assume that the arrest of Coolidge inside his house was valid, so that the first condition of a warrantless "search incident" is met. And since the events in issue took place in 1964, we assess the State's argument in terms of the law as it existed before *Chimel* v. *California*, 395 U.S. 752, which substantially restricted the "search incident" exception to the warrant requirement, but did so only prospectively. But even under pre-*Chimel* law the State's position is untenable.

The leading case in the area before *Chimel* was *United States* v. *Rabinowitz*, 339 U.S. 56, which was taken to stand "for the proposition, *inter alia*, that a warrantless search 'incident to a lawful arrest' may generally extend to the area that is considered to be in the 'possession' or under the 'control' of the person arrested." In this case, Coolidge was arrested inside his house; his car was outside in the driveway. The car was not touched until Coolidge had been removed from the scene. It was then seized and taken to the station, but it was not actually searched until the next day....

Even assuming, *arguendo*, that the police might have searched the Pontiac in the driveway when they arrested Coolidge in the house, *Preston* v. *United States*, 376 U.S. 364, makes plain that they could not legally seize the car, remove it, and search it at their leisure without a warrant. In circumstances virtually identical to those here, Mr. Justice Black's opinion for a unanimous Court held that "[o]nce an accused is under arrest and in custody, then a search [of his car] made at another place, without a warrant, is simply not incident to the arrest." *Id.*, at 367. Search incident doctrine, in short, has no applicability to this case.

B

The second theory put forward by the State to justify a warrantless seizure and search of the Pontiac car is that under *Carroll* v. *United States*, 267 U.S. 132, the police may make a warrantless search of an automobile whenever they have probable cause to do so, and, under our decision last Term in *Chambers* v. *Maroney*, 399 U.S. 42, whenever the police may make a legal contemporaneous search under *Carroll*, they may also seize the car, take it to the police station, and search it there. But even granting that the police had probable cause to search the car, the application of the *Carroll* case to these facts would extend it far beyond its original rationale. . . .

The underlying rationale of *Carroll* and of all the cases which have followed it is that there is

a necessary difference between a search of a store, dwelling house, or other structure in respect of which a proper official warrant readily may be obtained and a search of a ship, motor boat, wagon, or automobile for contraband goods, where it is not practicable to secure a warrant, because the vehicle can be quickly moved out of the locality or jurisdiction in which the warrant must be sought. 267 U.S., at 153. . . .

In this case, the police had known for some time of the probable role of the Pontiac car in the crime. Coolidge was aware that he was a suspect in the Mason murder, but he had been extremely cooperative throughout the investigation, and there was no indication that he meant to flee. He had already had ample opportunity to destroy any evidence he thought incriminating. There is no suggestion that, on the night in question, the car was being used for any illegal purpose, and it was regularly parked in the driveway of his house. The opportunity for search was thus hardly "fleeting." The objects

which the police are assumed to have had probable cause to search for in the car were neither stolen nor contraband nor dangerous. . . .

C

The State's third theory in support of the warrantless seizure and search of the Pontiac car is that the car itself was an "instrumentality of the crime," and as such might be seized by the police on Coolidge's property because it was in plain view. Supposing the seizure to be thus lawful, the case of *Cooper* v. *California,* 386 U.S. 58, is said to support a subsequent warrantless search at the station house, with or without probable cause. Of course, the distinction between an "instrumentality of crime" and "mere evidence" was done away with by *Warden* v. *Hayden*, 387 U.S. 294, and we may assume that the police had probable cause to seize the automobile. But, for the reasons that follow, we hold that the "plain view" exception to the warrant requirement is inapplicable to this case. . . .

What the "plain view" cases have in common is that the police officer in each of them had a prior justification for an intrusion in the course of which he came inadvertently across a piece of evidence incriminating the accused. The doctrine serves to supplement the prior justification— whether it be a warrant for another object, hot pursuit, search incident to lawful arrest, or some other legitimate reason for being present unconnected with a search directed against the accused —and permits the warrantless seizure. Of course, the extension of the original justification is legitimate only where it is immediately apparent to the police that they have evidence before them; the "plain view" doctrine may not be used to extend a general exploratory search from one object to another until something incriminating at last emerges. . . .

In the light of what has been said, it is apparent that the "plain view" exception cannot justify the police seizure of the Pontiac car in this case. The police had ample opportunity to obtain a valid warrant; they knew the automobile's exact description and location well in advance; they intended to seize it when they came upon Coolidge's property. And this is not a case involving contraband or stolen goods or objects dangerous in themselves.

The seizure was therefore unconstitutional, and so was the subsequent search at the station house. Since evidence obtained in the course of the search was admitted at Coolidge's trial, the judgment must be reversed and the case remanded to the New Hampshire Supreme Court.

D

...

Much the most important part of the conflict that has been so notable in this Court's attempts over a hundred years to develop a coherent body of Fourth Amendment law has been caused by disagreement over the importance of requiring law enforcement officers to secure warrants. Some have argued that a determination by a magistrate of probable cause as a precondition of any search or seizure is so essential that the Fourth Amendment is violated whenever the police might reasonably have obtained a warrant but failed to do so. Others have argued with equal force that a test of reasonableness, applied after the fact of search or seizure when the police attempt to introduce the fruits in evidence, affords ample safeguard for the rights in question, so that "[t]he relevant test is not whether it is reasonable to procure a search warrant, but whether the search was reasonable."

Both sides to the controversy appear to recognize a distinction between search and seizures that take place on a man's property—his home or office—and those carried out elsewhere. It is accepted, at least as a matter of principle, that a search or seizure carried out on a suspect's premises without a warrant is *per se* unrea-

sonable, unless the police can show that it falls within one of a carefully defined set of exceptions based on the presence of "exigent circumstances." As to other kinds of intrusions, however, there has been disagreement about the basic rules to be applied, as our cases concerning automobile searches, electronic surveillance, street searches and administrative searches make clear.

With respect to searches and seizures carried out on a suspect's premises, the conflict has been over the question of what qualifies as an "exigent circumstance.". . .

The most common situation in which Fourth Amendment issues have arisen has been that in which the police enter the suspect's premises, arrest him, and then carry out a warrantless search and seizure of evidence. Where there is a warrant for the suspect's arrest, the evidence seized may later be challenged either on the ground that the warrant was improperly issued because there was not probable cause, or on the ground that the police search and seizure went beyond that which they could carry out as an incident to the execution of the arrest warrant. Where the police act without an arrest warrant, the suspect may argue that an arrest warrant was necessary, that there was no probable cause to arrest, or that even if the arrest was valid, the search and seizure went beyond permissible limits. . . . This Court has chosen on a number of occasions to assume the validity of an arrest and decide the case before it on the issue of the scope of permissible warrantless search. The more common inquiry has therefore been: "Assuming a valid police entry for purposes of arrest, what searches and seizures may the police carry out without prior authorization by a magistrate?"

Two very broad and sharply contrasting answers to this question have been assayed by this Court in the past. The answer of *Trupiano* v. *United States, supra*, was that *no* searches and seizures could be legitimated by the mere fact of valid entry for purposes of arrest, so long as there was no showing of special difficulties in obtaining a warrant for search and seizure. The contrasting answer in *Harris* v. *United States*, 331 U.S. 145, and *United States* v. *Rabinowitz*, *supra*, was that a valid entry for purposes of arrest served to legitimate warrantless searches and seizures throughout the premises where the arrest occurred, however spacious those premises might be.

The approach taken in *Harris* and *Rabinowitz* was open to the criticism that it made it so easy for the police to arrange to search a man's premises without a warrant that the Constitution's protection of a man's "effects" became a dead letter. The approach taken in *Trupiano*, on the other hand, was open to the criticism that it was absurd to permit the police to make an entry in the dead of night for purposes of seizing the "person" by main force, and then refuse them permission to seize objects lying around in plain sight. It is arguable that if the very substantial intrusion implied in the entry and arrest are "reasonable" in Fourth Amendment terms, then the less intrusive search incident to arrest must also be reasonable.

This argument against the *Trupiano* approach is of little force so long as it is assumed that the police must, in the absence of one of a number of defined exceptions based on "exigent circumstances," obtain an arrest warrant before entering a man's house to seize his person. If the Fourth Amendment requires a warrant to enter and seize the person, then it makes sense as well to require a warrant to seize other items that may be on the premises. The situation is different, however, if the police are under no circumstances required to obtain an arrest warrant before entering to arrest a person they have probable cause to believe has committed a felony. If no warrant is ever required to legitimate the extremely serious intrusion of a midnight entry to seize the person, then it can be argued plausibly that a warrant should never be required to legitimate a very sweeping search incident to such an entry and arrest. If the arrest without a warrant is *per se* reasonable under the Fourth Amendment, then it

is difficult to perceive why a search incident in the style of *Harris* and *Rabinowitz* is not *per se* reasonable as well.

It is clear, then, that the notion that the warrantless entry of a man's house in order to arrest him on probable cause is *per se* legitimate is in fundamental conflict with the basic principle of Fourth Amendment law that searches and seizures inside a man's house without a warrant are *per se* unreasonable in the absence of some one of a number of well defined "exigent circumstances." This conflict came to the fore in *Chimel* v. *California, supra*. The Court there applied the basic rule that the "search incident to arrest" is an exception to the warrant requirement and that its scope must therefore be strictly defined in terms of the justifying "exigent circumstances." The exigency in question arises from the dangers of harm to the arresting officer and of destruction of evidence within the reach of the arrestee. Neither exigency can conceivably justify the far-ranging searches authorized under *Harris* and *Rabinowitz*. The answer of the dissenting opinion of Mr. Justice White in *Chimel*, supported by no decision of this Court, was that a warrantless entry for the purpose of arrest on probable cause is legitimate and reasonable no matter what the circumstances. From this it was said to follow that the full-scale search incident to arrest was also reasonable since it was a lesser intrusion.

The same conflict arises in this case. Since the police knew of the presence of the automobile and planned all along to seize it, there was no "exigent circumstance" to justify their failure to obtain a warrant. The application of the basic rule of Fourth Amendment law therefore requires that the fruits of the warrantless seizure be suppressed. . . .

The fundamental objection . . . to the line of argument adopted by Mr. Justice White in his dissent in this case and in *Chimel* v. *California, supra*, is that it proves too much. If we were to agree with Mr. Justice White that the police may, whenever they have probable cause, make a warrantless entry for the purpose of making an arrest, and that seizures and searches of automobiles are likewise *per se* reasonable given probable cause, then by the same logic *any* search or seizure could be carried out without a warrant, and we would simply have read the Fourth Amendment out of the Constitution....

... The rule that "searches conducted outside the judicial process, without prior approval by judge or magistrate, are *per se* unreasonable under the Fourth Amendment—subject only to a few specifically established and well-delineated exceptions," is not so frail that its continuing vitality depends on the fate of a supposed doctrine of warrantless arrest. The warrant requirement has been a valued part of our constitutional law for decades, and it has determined the result in scores and scores of cases in courts all over this country. It is not an inconvenience to be somehow "weighed" against the claims of police efficiency. It is, or should be, an important working part of our machinery of government, operating as a matter of course to check the "well-intentioned but mistakenly overzealous, executive officers" who are a part of any system of law enforcement. If it is to be a true guide to constitutional police action, rather than just a pious phrase, then "[t]he exceptions cannot be enthroned into the rule."...

> *The judgment is reversed and the case is remanded to the Supreme Court of New Hampshire for further proceedings not inconsistent with this opinion. It is so ordered.*

MR. JUSTICE WHITE, *with whom* THE CHIEF JUSTICE *joins, concurring and dissenting.*

I would affirm the judgment. In my view, Coolidge's Pontiac was lawfully seized as evidence of the crime in plain sight and thereafter was lawfully searched under *Cooper* v. *California.* . . .

... [I]t is apparent that seizure of evidence without warrant is not itself an invasion either of personal privacy or of property rights beyond that already authorized by law. Only the possessory interest of a defendant in his effects is implicated. And in these various circumstances, at least where the discovery of evidence is "inadvertent," the Court would permit the seizure because, it is said, "the minor peril to Fourth Amendment protections" is overridden by the "major gain in effective law enforcement" inherent in avoiding the "needless inconvenience" of procuring a warrant. I take this to mean that both the possessory interest of the defendant and the importance of having a magistrate confirm that what the officer saw with his own eyes is in fact contraband or evidence of crime are not substantial constitutional considerations. Officers in these circumstances need neither guard nor ignore the evidence while a warrant is sought. Immediate seizure is justified and reasonable under the Fourth Amendment.

The Court would interpose in some or all of these situations, however, a condition that the discovery of the disputed evidence be "inadvertent." If it is "anticipated," that is, if "the police know in advance the location of the evidence and intend to seize it," the seizure is invalid.

I have great difficulty with this approach. Let us suppose officers secure a warrant to search a house for a rifle. While staying well within the range of a rifle search, they discover two photographs of the murder victim both in plain sight in the bedroom. Assume also that the discovery of the one photograph was inadvertent but finding the other was anticipated. The Court would permit the seizure of only one of the photographs. But in terms of the "minor" peril to Fourth Amendment values there is surely no difference between these two photographs: the interference with possession is the same in each case and the officers' appraisal of the photograph they expected to see is no less reliable than their judgment about the other. And in both situations the acutal inconvenience and danger to evidence remains identical if the officers must depart and secure a warrant. The Court, however, states that the State will suffer no constitutionally cognizable inconvenience from invalidating anticipated seizures since it had probable cause to search for the items seized and could have included them in a warrant.

This seems a punitive and extravagant application of the exclusionary rule. If the police have probable cause to search for a photograph as well as a rifle and they proceed to seek a warrant, they could have no possible motive for deliberately including the rifle but omitting the photograph. Quite the contrary is true. Only oversight or careless mistake would explain the omission in the warrant application if the police were convinced they had probable cause to search for the photograph. Of course, they may misjudge the facts and not realize they have probable cause for the picture, or the magistrate may find against them and not issue a warrant for it. In either event the officers may validly seize the photograph for which they had no probable cause to search but the other photograph is excluded from evidence when the Court subsequently determines that the officers, after all, had probable cause to search for it. . . .

By invalidating otherwise valid, plain sight seizures where officers have probable cause and presumably, although the Court does not say so, opportunity to secure a warrant, the Court seems to turn in the direction of the *Trupiano* rule, rejected in *Rabinowitz* and not revived in *Chimel*. But it seems unsure of its own rule.

It is careful to note that Coolidge's car is not contraband, stolen or in itself dangerous. Apparently, contraband, stolen or dangerous materials may be seized when discovered in the course of an otherwise authorized search even if the discovery is fully anticipated and a warrant could have been obtained. The distinction the Court draws between contraband and mere evidence of crime is reminiscent of the confusing and un-

workable approach that I thought *Warden* v. *Hayden, supra,* had firmly put aside.

Neither does the Court in so many words limit *Chimel*; on the contrary, it indicates that warrantless *Chimel*-type searches will not be disturbed, even if the police "anticipate that they will find specific evidence during the course of such a search." The Court also concedes that, when an arresting officer "comes within plain view of a piece of evidence, not concealed, although outside of the area under the immediate control of the arrestee, the officer may seize it, so long as the plain view was obtained in the course of an appropriately limited search of the arrestee." Yet today's decision is a limitation on *Chimel*, for in the latter example, the Court would permit seizure only if the plain view was inadvertently obtained. . . .

II

In the case before us, the officers had probable cause both to arrest Coolidge and to seize his car. In order to effect his arrest, they went to his home—perhaps the most obvious place in which to look for him. They also may have hoped to find his car at home and, in fact, when they arrived on the property to make the arrest, they did find [it] there. Thus, even assuming that the Fourth Amendment protects against warrantless seizures outside the house, the fact remains that the officers had legally entered Coolidge's property to effect an arrest and that they seized the car only after they observed it in plain view before them. The Court, however, would invalidate this seizure on the premise that officers should not be permitted to seize effects in plain sight when they have anticipated they will see them.

Even accepting this premise of the Court, seizure of the car was not invalid. The majority makes an assumption that, when the police went to Coolidge's house to arrest him, they anticipated that they would also find the 1951 Pontiac there. In my own reading of the record, however, I have found no evidence to support this assumption. For all the record shows, the police, although they may have hoped to find the Pontiac at Coolidge's home, did not know its exact location when they went to make the arrest, and their observation of it in Coolidge's driveway was truly inadvertent. Of course, they did have probable cause to seize the car, and, if they had had a valid warrant as well, they would have been justified in looking for it in Coolidge's driveway—a likely place for it to be. But if the fact of probable cause bars this seizure, it also bars seizures not only of cars found at a house, but also of cars parked in a parking lot, hidden in some secluded spot, or delivered to the police by a third party at the police station. This would simply be a rule that the existence of probable cause bars all warrantless seizures.

It is evident on the facts of this case that Coolidge's Pontiac was subject to seizure if proper procedures were employed. It is also apparent that the Pontiac was in plain view of the officers who had legally entered Coolidge's property to effect his arrest. I am satisfied that it was properly seized whether or not the officers expected that it would be found where it was. . . .

ADAMS v. WILLIAMS
407 U.S. 143; 32 L. Ed. 2d 612; 92 S. Ct. 1921 (1972)

MR. JUSTICE REHNQUIST *delivered the opinion of the Court.*

Respondent Robert Williams was convicted in a Connecticut state court of illegal possession of a handgun found during a "stop and frisk," as well as possession of heroin that was found during a full search incident to his weapons arrest. After respondent's conviction was affirmed by the Supreme Court of Connecticut, this Court denied certiorari. Williams' petition for federal habeas corpus relief was denied by the District Court and by a divided panel of the Second Circuit, but on rehearing *en banc* the Court of Appeals granted relief. That court held that evidence introduced at Williams' trial had been obtained by an unlawful search of his person and car, and thus the state court judgments of conviction should be set aside. Since we conclude that the policeman's actions here conformed to the standards this Court laid down in *Terry* v. *Ohio* we reverse.

Police Sgt. John Connolly was alone early in the morning on car patrol duty in a high crime area of Bridgeport, Connecticut. At approximately 2:15 A.M. a person known to Sgt. Connolly approached his cruiser and informed him that an individual seated in a nearby vehicle was carrying narcotics and had a gun at his waist.

After calling for assistance on his car radio, Sgt. Connolly approached the vehicle to investigate the informant's report. Connolly tapped on the car window and asked the occupant, Robert Williams to open the door. When Williams rolled down the window instead, the sergeant reached into the car and removed a fully loaded revolver from Williams' waistband. The gun had not been visible to Connolly from outside the car, but it was in precisely the place indicated by the informant. Williams was then arrested by Connolly for unlawful possession of the pistol. A search incident to that arrest was conducted after other officers arrived. They found substantial quantities of heroin on Williams' person and in the car, and they found a machete and a second revolver hidden in the automobile.

Respondent contends that the initial seizure of his pistol, upon which rested the later search and seizure of other weapons and narcotics, was not justified by the informant's tip to Sgt. Connolly. He claims that absent a more reliable informant, or some corroboration of the tip, the policeman's actions were unreasonable under the standards set forth in *Terry* v. *Ohio*.

In *Terry* this Court recognized that "a police officer may in appropriate circumstances and in an appropriate manner approach a person for purposes of investigating possibly criminal behavior even though there is no probable cause to make an arrest." 392 U.S., at 22. The Fourth Amendment does not require a policeman who lacks the precise level of information necessary for probable cause to arrest to simply shrug his shoulders and allow a crime to occur or a criminal to escape. On the contrary, *Terry* recognizes that it may be the essence of good police work to adopt an intermediate response. A brief stop of a suspicious individual, in order to determine his identity or to maintain the status quo momentarily while obtaining more information, may be most reasonable in light of the facts known to the officer at the time.

The Court recognized in *Terry* that the policeman making a reasonable investigatory stop should not be denied the opportunity to protect himself from attack by a hostile suspect. "When an officer is justified in believing that the individual whose suspicious behavior he is investigating at close range is armed and presently dangerous to the officer or to others," he may conduct a limited protective search for concealed weapons. The purpose of this limited search is not to discover evidence of crime, but to allow the officer to pursue his investigation without fear of violence, and thus the frisk for weapons might be equally necessary and reasonable whether or not carrying a concealed weapon violated any applicable state law. So long as the officer is entitled to make a forcible stop and has reason to believe that the suspect is armed and dangerous, he may conduct a weapons search limited in scope to this protective purpose.

Applying these principles to the present case we believe that Sgt. Connolly acted justifiably in responding to his informant's tip. The informant was known to him personally and had provided him with information in the past. This is a stronger case than obtains in the case of an anonymous telephone tip. The informant here came forward personally to give information that was immediately verifiable at the scene. Indeed, under Connecticut law, the informant herself might have been subject to immediate arrest for making a false complaint had Sgt. Connolly's investigation proven the tip incorrect. Thus, while the Court's decisions indicate that this informant's unverified tip may have been insufficient for a narcotics arrest or search warrant, see, e.g., *Spinelli* v. *United States*, 393 U.S. 410 (1969); *Aguilar* v. *Texas*, 378 U.S. 108 (1964), the information carried enough indicia of reliability to justify the officer's forcible stop of Williams.

In reaching this conclusion, we reject respondent's argument that reasonable cause for a stop and frisk can only be based on the officer's personal observation, rather than on information supplied by another person. Informants' tips, like all other clues and evidence coming to a policeman on the scene, may vary greatly in their value and reliability. One simple rule will not cover every situation. Some tips, completely lacking in indicia of reliability, would either warrant no police response or require further investigation before a forcible stop of a suspect would be authorized. But in some situations—for example, when the victim of a street crime seeks immediate police aid and gives a description of his assailant, or when a credible informant warns of a specific impending crime—the subtleties of the hearsay rule should not thwart an appropriate police response.

While properly investigating the activity of a person who was reported to be carrying narcotics and a concealed weapon and who was sitting alone in a car in a high crime area at 2:15 in the morning, Sgt. Connolly had ample reason to fear for his safety. When Williams rolled down his window, rather than complying with the policeman's request to step out of the car so that his movements could more easily be seen, the revolver allegedly at Williams' waist became an even greater threat. Under these circumstances the policeman's action in reaching to the spot where the gun was thought to be hidden constituted a limited intrusion designed to insure his safety, and we conclude that it was reasonable. The loaded gun seized as a result of this intrusion was therefore admissible at Williams' trial.

Once Sgt. Connolly had found the gun precisely where the informant had predicted, probable cause existed to arrest Williams for unlawful possession of the weapon. Probable cause to arrest depends "upon whether, at the moment the arrest was made . . . the facts and circumstances within [the arresting officers'] knowledge and of which they had reasonably trustworthy information were sufficient to warrant a prudent man in believing that the [suspect] had committed or was committing an offense." *Beck v. Ohio*, 379 U.S. 89 (1964). In the present case the policeman found Williams in possession of a gun in precisely the place predicted by the informant. This tended to corroborate the reliability of the informant's further report of narcotics, and together with the surrounding circumstances certainly suggested no lawful explanation for possession of the gun. Probable cause does not require the same type of specific evidence of each element of the offense as would be needed to support a conviction. Rather, the court will evaluate generally the circumstances at the time of the arrest to decide if the officer had probable cause for his action. Under the circumstances surrounding Williams' possession of the gun seized by Sgt. Connolly, the arrest on weapons charge was supported by probable cause, and the search of his person and of the car

incident to that arrest was lawful. The fruits of the search were therefore properly admitted at Williams' trial, and the Court of Appeals erred in reaching a contrary conclusion.

Reversed.

MR. JUSTICE MARSHALL, *with whom* MR. JUSTICE DOUGLAS *joins, dissenting.*

Four years have passed since we decided *Terry v. Ohio* and its companion cases. They were the first cases in which this Court explicitly recognized the concept of "stop and frisk" and squarely held that police officers may, under appropriate circumstances, stop and frisk persons suspected of criminal activity even though there is less than probable cause for an arrest. This case marks our first opportunity to give some flesh to the bones of *Terry* et al. Unfortunately, the flesh provided by today's decision cannot possibly be made to fit on *Terry's* skeletal framework.

. . . In *Terry* we said that "We do not retreat from our holdings that the police must, whenever practicable, obtain advance judicial approval of searches and seizures through the warrant procedure." Yet, we upheld the stop and frisk in *Terry* because we recognized that the realities of on-the-street law enforcement require an officer to act at times on the basis of strong evidence, short of probable cause, that criminal activity is taking place and that the criminal is armed and dangerous. Hence, *Terry* stands only for the proposition that police officers have a "narrowly drawn authority to . . . search for weapons" without a warrant.

In today's decision the Court ignores the fact that *Terry* begrudgingly accepted the necessity for creating an exception from the warrant requirement of the Fourth Amendment and treats this case as if warrantless searches were the rule rather than the "narrowly drawn" exception. This decision betrays the careful balance that *Terry* sought to strike between a citizen's right to privacy and his government's responsibility for effective law enforcement and expands the concept of warrantless searches far beyond anything heretofore recognized as legitimate. I dissent. . . .

The Court erroneously attempts to describe the search for the gun as a protective search incident to a reasonable investigatory stop. But, as in *Terry, Sibron* and *Peters*, there is no occasion in this case to determine whether or not police officers have a right to seize and to restrain a citizen in order to interrogate him. The facts are clear that the officer intended to make the search as soon as he approached the respondent. He asked no questions; he made no investigation; he simply searched. There was nothing apart from the information supplied by the informant to cause the officer to search. Our inquiry must focus, therefore, as it did in *Terry* on whether the officer had sufficient facts from which he could reasonably infer that respondent was not only engaging in illegal activity, but also that he was armed and dangerous. The focus falls on the informant.

The only information that the informant had previously given the officer involved homosexual conduct in the local railroad station. The following colloquy took place between respondent's counsel and the officer at the hearing on respondent's motion to suppress the evidence that had been seized from him.

Q. Now, with respect to the information that was given you about homosexuals in the Bridgeport Police Station [*sic*], did that lead to an arrest? *A.* No.

Q. An arrest was not made? *A.* No. There was no substantiating evidence.

Q. There was no substantiating evidence? *A.* No.

Q. And what do you mean by that? *A.* I didn't have occasion to witness these individuals committing any crime of any nature.

Q. In other words, after this person gave you the information, you checked for corroboration before you made an arrest. Is that right? *A.* Well, I checked to determine the possibility of homosexual activity.

Q. And since an arrest was made, I take it you didn't find any substantiating information. *A.* I'm sorry counselor, you say since an arrest was made.

Q. Was not made. Since an arrest was not made, I presume you didn't find any substantiating information. *A.* No.

Q. So that, you don't recall any other specific information given you about the commission of crimes by this informant? *A.* No.

Q. And you still thought this person was reliable. *A.* Yes.

Were we asked to determine whether the information supplied by the informant was sufficient to provide probable cause for an arrest and search, rather than a stop and frisk, there can be no doubt that we would hold that it was insufficient. This Court has squarely held that a search and seizure cannot be justified on the basis of conclusory allegations of an unnamed informant who is allegedly credible. In the recent case of *Spinelli* v. *United States*, 393 U.S. 410 (1969), Mr. Justice Harlan made it plain beyond any doubt that where police rely on an informant to make a search and seizure, they must know that the informant is generally trustworthy and that he has obtained his information in a reliable way. Since the testimony of the arresting officer in the instant case patently fails to demonstrate that the informant was known to be trustworthy and since it is also clear that the officer had no idea of the source of the informant's "knowledge," a search and seizure would have been illegal.

Assuming *arguendo* that this case truly involves not an arrest and a search incident thereto, but a stop and frisk, we must decide whether or not the information possessed by the officer justified this interference with respondent's liberty. *Terry*, our only case to actually uphold a stop and frisk, is not directly on point, because the police officer in that case acted on the basis of his own personal observations. No informant was involved. But the rationale of *Terry* is still controlling, and it requires that we condemn the conduct of the police officer in encountering the respondent.

Terry did not hold that whenever a policeman has a hunch that a citizen is engaging in criminal activity, he may engage in a stop and frisk. It held that if police officers want to stop and frisk, they must have specific facts from which they can reasonably infer that an individual is engaged in criminal activity and is armed and dangerous. It was central to our decision in *Terry* that the police officer acted on the basis of his own personal observations and that he carefully scrutinized the conduct of his suspects before interfering with them in any way. . . .

If the Court does not ignore the care with which we examined the knowledge possessed by the officer in *Terry* when he acted, then I cannot see how the actions of the officer in this case can be upheld. The Court explains what the officer knew about respondent before accosting him. But what is more significant is what he did not know. With respect to the scene generally, the officer had no idea how long respondent had been in the car, how long the car had been parked, or to whom the car belonged. With respect to the gun, the officer did not know if or when the informant had ever seen the gun, or whether the gun was carried legally, as Connecticut law permitted, or illegally. And with respect to the narcotics, the officer did not know what kind of narcotics respondent allegedly had, whether they were legally or illegally possessed, what the basis of the informant's knowledge was, or even whether the informant was capable of distinguishing narcotics from other substances.

Unable to answer any of these questions, the officer nevertheless determined that it was necessary to intrude on respondent's liberty. I believe that his determination was totally unreasonable. As I read *Terry*, an officer may act on the basis of *reliable* information short of probable cause to make a stop, and ultimately a frisk, if necessary;

but, the officer may not use unreliable, unsubstantiated, conclusory hearsay to justify an invasion of liberty. *Terry* never meant to approve the kind of knee-jerk police reaction that we have before us in this case.

Even assuming that the officer had some legitimate reason for relying on the informant, *Terry* requires, before any stop and frisk is made, that the reliable information in the officer's possession demonstrate that the suspect is both armed and *dangerous* [Emphasis in original]. The fact remains that Connecticut specifically authorizes persons to carry guns so long as they have a permit. Thus, there was no reason for the officer to infer from anything that the informant said that the respondent was dangerous. His frisk was, therefore, illegal under *Terry*.

Even if I could agree with the Court that the stop and frisk in this case was proper, I could not go further and sustain the arrest, and the subsequent searches. It takes probable cause to justify an arrest and search and seizure incident thereto. Probable cause means that the "facts and circumstances before the officer are such as to warrant a man of prudence and caution in believing that the offense has been committed." "[G]ood faith is not enough to constitute probable cause." . . .

This case marks a departure from the mainstream of our Fourth Amendment cases. . . . In *Johnson* v. *United States*, 333 U.S. 10 (1948), for example, the arresting officer had an informant's tip and actually smelled opium coming from a room. This Court still found the arrest unlawful. And in *Spinelli* v. *United States*, we found that there was no probable cause even where an informant's information was corroborated by personal observation. If there was no probable cause in those cases, I find it impossible to understand how there can be probable cause in this case.

Mr. Justice Douglas was the sole dissenter in *Terry*. He warned of the "powerful hydraulic pressures throughout our history that bear heavily on the Court to water down constitutional guarantees. . . ." While I took the position then that we were not watering down rights, but were hesitantly and cautiously striking a necessary balance between the rights of American citizens to be free from government intrusion into their privacy and their government's urgent need for a narrow exception to the warrant requirement of the Fourth Amendment, today's decision demonstrates just how prescient Mr. Justice Douglas was.

It seems that the delicate balance that *Terry* struck was simply too delicate, too susceptible to the "hydraulic pressures" of the day. As a result of today's decision, the balance struck in *Terry* is now heavily weighted in favor of the government. And the Fourth Amendment, which was included in the Bill of Rights to prevent the kind of arbitrary and oppressive police action involved herein, is dealt a serious blow. Today's decision invokes the spectre of a society in which innocent citizens may be stopped, searched and arrested at the whim of police officers who have only the slightest suspicion of improper conduct.

UNITED STATES v. WHITE

401 U.S. 745; 28 L. Ed. 2d 453; 91 S. Ct. 1122 (1971)

MR. JUSTICE WHITE *announced the judgment of the Court and an opinion in which* THE CHIEF JUSTICE, MR. JUSTICE STEWART, *and* MR. JUSTICE BLACKMUN *join.*

In 1966, respondent James A. White was tried and convicted under two consolidated indictments charging various illegal transactions in narcotics . . . . He was fined and sentenced as a second offender to 25-year concurrent sentences. The issue before us is whether the Fourth Amendment bars from evidence the testimony of governmental agents who related certain conversations which had occurred between defendant White and a government informant, Harvey Jackson, and which the agents overheard by monitoring the frequency of a radio transmitter carried by Jackson and concealed on his person. On four occasions the conversations took place in Jackson's home; each of these conversations was overheard by an agent concealed in a kitchen closet with Jackson's consent and by a second agent outside the house using a radio receiver. Four other conversations—one in respondent's home, one in a restaurant, and two in Jackson's car—were overheard by the use of radio equipment. The prosecution was unable to locate and produce Jackson at the trial and the trial court overruled objections to the testimony of the agents who conducted the electronic surveillance. The jury returned a guilty verdict and defendant appealed.

The Court of Appeals read *Katz* v. *United States*, 389 U.S. 347 . . . , as overruling *On Lee* v. *United States,* 343 U.S. 747 . . . and interpreting the Fourth Amendment to forbid the introduction of the agents' testimony in the circumstances of this case. Accordingly, the court reversed but without adverting to the fact that the transactions at issue here had occurred before *Katz* was decided in this Court. In our view, the Court of Appeals misinterpreted both the *Katz* case and the Fourth Amendment and in any event erred in applying the *Katz* case to events that occurred before that decision was rendered by this Court.

Until *Katz* v. *United States,* neither wiretapping nor electronic eavesdropping violated a defendant's Fourth Amendment rights "unless there has been an official search and seizure of his person, or such a seizure of his papers or his tangible material effects, or an actual physical invasion of his house 'or curtilage' for the purpose of making a seizure." *Olmstead* v. *United States*, 277 U.S. 438. . . .

Katz v. *United States*, however, finally swept away doctrines that electronic eavesdropping is permissible under the Fourth Amendment unless physical invasion of a constitutionally protected area produced the challenged evidence. . . .

The Court of Appeals understood *Katz* to render inadmissible against White the agents' testimony concerning conversations that Jackson broadcast to them. We cannot agree. *Katz* involved no revelation to the Government by a party to conversations with the defendant nor did the Court indicate in any way that a defendant has a justifiable and constitutionally protected expectation that a person with whom he is conversing will not then or later reveal the conversation to the police.

Hoffa v. *United States*, 385 U.S. 293 . . . , which was left undisturbed by *Katz*, held that however strongly a defendant may trust an apparent colleague, his expectations in this respect are not protected by the Fourth Amendment when it turns out that the colleague is a government agent regularly communicating with the authorities. In these circumstances, "no interest legitimately protected by the Fourth Amendment is involved," for that amendment affords no protection to "a wrongdoer's misplaced belief that a person to whom he voluntarily confides his wrongdoing will not reveal it." . . . No warrant to "search and seize" is required in such circumstances, nor is it when the Government sends to defendant's home a secret agent who conceals his identity and makes a purchase of narcotics from the accused, *Lewis* v. *United States*, 385 U.S. 206 . . . or when the same agent, unbeknown to the defendant, carries electronic equipment to record the defendant's words and the evidence so gathered is later offered in evidence. *Lopez* v. *United States*, 373 U.S. 427. . . .

Conceding that *Hoffa, Lewis,* and *Lopez*

remained unaffected by *Katz*, the Court of Appeals nevertheless read both *Katz* and the Fourth Amendment to require a different result if the agent not only records his conversations with the defendant but instantaneously transmits them electronically to other agents equipped with radio receivers. Where this occurs, the Court of Appeals held, the Fourth Amendment is violated and the testimony of the listening agents must be excluded from evidence.

To reach this result it was necessary for the Court of Appeals to hold that *On Lee* v. *United States* was no longer good law. In that case, which involved facts very similar to the case before us, the Court first rejected claims of a Fourth Amendment violation because the informer had not trespassed when he entered the defendant's premises and conversed with him. To this extent the Court's rationale cannot survive *Katz*. . . . But the Court announced a second and independent ground for its decision; for it went on to say that overruling *Olmstead* and *Goldman* would be of no aid to *On Lee* since he "was talking confidentially and indiscreetly with one he trusted, and he was overheard. . . . It would be a dubious service to the genuine liberties protected by the Fourth Amendment to make them bedfellows with spurious liberties improvised by farfetched analogies which would liken eavesdropping on a conversation, with the connivance of one of the parties, to an unreasonable search or seizure. We find no violation of the Fourth Amendment here." . . . We see no indication in *Katz* that the Court meant to disturb that understanding of the Fourth Amendment or to disturb the result reached in the *On Lee* case, nor are we now inclined to overturn this view of the Fourth Amendment.

Concededly a police agent who conceals his police connections may write down for official use his conversations with a defendant and testify concerning them, without a warrant authorizing his encounters with the defendant and without otherwise violating the latter's Fourth Amendment rights . . . . For constitutional purposes, no different result is required if the agent instead of immediately reporting and transcribing his conversations with defendant, either (1) simultaneously records them with electronic equipment which he is carrying on his person, . . . (2) or carries radio equipment which simultaneously transmits the conversations either to recording equipment located elsewhere or to other agents monitoring the transmitting frequency. . . . If the conduct and revelations of an agent operating without electronic equipment do not invade the defendant's constitutionally justifiable expectations of privacy, neither does a simultaneous recording of the same conversations made by the agent or by others from transmissions received from the agent to whom the defendant is talking and whose trustworthiness the defendant necessarily risks.

Our problem is not what the privacy expectations of particular defendants in particular situations may be or the extent to which they may in fact have relied on the discretion of their companions. Very probably, individual defendants neither know nor suspect that their colleagues have gone or will go to the police or are carrying recorders or transmitters. Otherwise, conversation would cease and our problem with these encounters would be non-existent or far different from those now before us. Our problem, in terms of the principles announced in *Katz*, is what expectations of privacy are constitutionally "justifiable"—what expectations the Fourth Amendment will protect in the absence of a warrant. So far, the law permits the frustration of actual expectations of privacy by permitting authorities to use the testimony of those associates who for one reason or another have determined to turn to the police, as well as by authorizing the use of informants in the manner exemplified by *Hoffa* and *Lewis*. If the law gives no protection to the wrongdoer whose trusted accomplice is or becomes a police agent, neither should it protect him when that same agent has recorded or transmitted the conversations which are later offered in evidence to prove the State's case. . . .

Inescapably, one contemplating illegal activities must realize and risk that his companions may be reporting to the police. If he sufficiently doubts their trustworthiness, the association will very probably end or never materialize. But if he has no doubts, or allays them, or risks what doubt he has, the risk is his. . . . Given the possibility or probability that one of his colleagues is cooperating with the police, it is only speculation to assert that the defendant's utterances would be substantially different or his sense of security any less if he also thought it possible that the suspected colleague is wired for sound. At least there is no persuasive evidence that the difference in this respect between the electronically equipped and the unequipped agent is substantial enough to require discrete constitutional recognition, particularly under the Fourth Amendment which is ruled by fluid concepts of "reasonableness."

Nor should we be too ready to erect constitutional barriers to relevant and probative evidence which is also accurate and reliable. An electronic recording will many times produce a more reliable rendition of what a defendant has said than will the unaided memory of a police agent. It may also be that with the recording in existence it is less likely that the informant will change his mind, less chance that threat or injury will suppress unfavorable evidence and less chance that cross-examination will confound the testimony. Considerations like these obviously do not favor the defendant, but we are not prepared to hold that a defendant who has no constitutional right to exclude the informer's unaided testimony nevertheless has a Fourth Amendment privilege against a more accurate version of the events in question. . . .

The Court of Appeals was in error for another reason. In *Desist* v. *United States*, 394 U.S. 244, we held that our decision in *Katz* v. *United States* applied only to those electronic surveillances that occurred subsequent to the date of that decision. Here the events in question took place in late 1965 and early 1966, long prior to

Katz. . . . The court should have judged this case by the pre-*Katz* law and under that law, as *On Lee* clearly holds, the electronic surveillance here involved did not violate White's rights to be free from unreasonable searches and seizures.

*The judgment of
the Court of Appeals is reversed.*

MR. JUSTICE BLACK, *while adhering to his views expressed in* Linkletter *v.* Walker . . . *concurs in the judgment of the Court for the reasons set forth in his dissent in* Katz *v.* United States. . . .

[MR. JUSTICE BRENNAN'S *concurring opinion is not reprinted here.*]

MR. JUSTICE DOUGLAS, *dissenting.*

The issue in this case is clouded and concealed by the very discussion of it in legalistic terms. What the ancients knew as "eavesdropping," we now call "electronic surveillance"; but to equate the two is to treat man's first gunpowder on the same level as the nuclear bomb. Electronic surveillance is the greatest leveler of human privacy ever known. How most forms of it can be held "reasonable" within the meaning of the Fourth Amendment is a mystery. To be sure, the Constitution and Bill of Rights are not to be read as covering only the technology known in the eighteenth century. Otherwise its concept of "commerce" would be hopeless when it comes to the management of modern affairs. At the same time the concepts of privacy which the Founders enshrined in the Fourth Amendment vanish completely when we slavishly allow an all-powerful government, proclaiming law and order, efficiency, and other benign purposes, to penetrate all the walls and doors which men need to shield them from the pressures of a turbulent life around them and give them the health and strength to carry on.

That is why a "strict construction" of the Fourth Amendment is necessary if every man's liberty and privacy are to be constitutionally honored.

When Franklin D. Roosevelt on May 21, 1940, authorized wiretapping in cases of "fifth column" activities and sabotage and limited it "insofar as possible to aliens," he said that "under ordinary and normal circumstances wiretapping by Government agents should not be carried on for the excellent reason that it is almost bound to lead to abuse of civil rights." . . .

Today no one perhaps notices because only a small, obscure criminal is the victim. But every person is the victim, for the technology we exalt today is everyman's master. Any doubter should read Arthur R. Miller's The Assault On Privacy (1971). After describing the monitoring of conversations and their storage in data banks, Professor Miller goes on to describe "human monitoring" which he calls the "ultimate step in mechanical snooping"–a device for spotting unorthodox or aberrational behavior across a wide spectrum. "Given the advancing state of both the remote sensing art and the capacity of computers to handle an uninterrupted and synoptic data flow, there seem to be no physical barriers left to shield us from intrusion."

When one reads what is going on in this area today, our judicial treatment of the subject seems as remote from reality as the well-known Baron Parke was remote from the social problems of his day. . . .

As a result of *Berger* and of *Katz*, both wiretapping and electronic surveillance through a "bug" or other device are now covered by the Fourth Amendment. . . .

The threads of thought running through our recent decisions are that these extensive intrusions into privacy made by electronic surveillance make self-restraint by law enforcement officials an inadequate protection, that the requirement of warrants under the Fourth Amendment is essential to a free society.

Monitoring, if prevalent, certainly kills free

discourse and spontaneous utterances. Free discourse—a First Amendment value—may be frivolous or serious, humble or defiant, reactionary or revolutionary, profane or in good taste; but it is not free if there is surveillance. Free discourse liberates the spirit, though it may produce only froth. The individual must keep some facts concerning his thoughts within a small zone of people. At the same time he must be free to pour out his woes or inspirations or dreams to others. He remains the sole judge as to what must be said and what must remain unspoken. This is the essence of the idea of privacy implicit in the First and Fifth Amendments as well as in the Fourth....

Now that the discredited decisions in *On Lee* and *Lopez* are resuscitated and revived, must everyone live in fear that every word he speaks may be transmitted or recorded and later repeated to the entire world? I can imagine nothing that has a more chilling effect on people speaking their minds and expressing their views on important matters. The advocates of that regime should spend some time in totalitarian countries and learn first-hand the kind of regime they are creating here....

[The dissenting opinions of JUSTICES HARLAN *and* MARSHALL *are not reprinted here.]*

MALLOY v. HOGAN
378 U.S. 1; 12 L. Ed. 2d 653; 84 S. Ct. 1489 (1964)

MR. JUSTICE BRENNAN *delivered the opinion of the Court.*

In this case we are asked to reconsider prior decisions holding that the privilege against self-incrimination is not safeguarded against state action by the Fourteenth Amendment....

The petitioner was arrested during a gambling raid in 1959 by Hartford, Connecticut, police. He pleaded guilty to the crime of pool-selling, a misdemeanor, and was sentenced to one year in jail and fined $500. The sentence was ordered to be suspended after 90 days, at which time he was to be placed on probation for two years. About 16 months after his guilty plea, petitioner was ordered to testify before a referee appointed by the Superior Court of Hartford County to conduct an inquiry into alleged gambling and other criminal activities in the county. The petitioner was asked a number of questions related to events surrounding his arrest and conviction. He refused to answer any question

"on the grounds it may tend to incriminate me." The Superior Court adjudged him in contempt, and committed him to prison until he was willing to answer the questions. Petitioner's application for a writ of habeas corpus was denied by the Superior Court, and the Connecticut Supreme Court of Errors affirmed.... The latter court held that the Fifth Amendment's privilege against self-incrimination was not available to a witness in a state proceeding, that the Fourteenth Amendment extended no privilege to him, and that the petitioner had not properly invoked the privilege available under the Connecticut Constitution. We granted certiorari.... We reverse. We hold that the Fourteenth Amendment guaranteed the petitioner the protection of the Fifth Amendment's privilege against self-incrimination, and that under the applicable federal standard, the Connecticut Supreme Court of Errors erred in holding that the privilege was not properly invoked.

. . .

We hold today that the Fifth Amendment's exception from compulsory self-incrimination is also protected by the Fourteenth Amendment against abridgment by the States. Decisions of the Court since *Twining* and *Adamson* have departed from the contrary view expressed in those cases. We discuss first the decisions which forbid the use of coerced confessions in state criminal prosecutions.

Brown v. *Mississippi*, 297 U.S. 278, . . . was the first case in which the Court held that the Due Process Clause prohibited the States from using the accused's coerced confessions against him. The Court in *Brown* felt impelled, in light of *Twining*, to say that its conclusion did not involve the privilege against self-incrimination. "Compulsion by torture to extort a confession is a different matter." 297 U.S. 285. . . . But this distinction was soon abandoned, and today the admissibility of a confession in a state criminal prosecution is tested by the same standard applied in federal prosecutions since 1897, when, in *Bram* v. *United States,* 168 U.S. 532 . . . the Court held that "In criminal trials, in the courts of the United States, wherever a question arises whether a confession is incompetent because not voluntary, the issue is controlled by that portion of the Fifth Amendment to the Constitution of the United States commanding that no person 'shall be compelled in any criminal case to be a witness against himself.' " . . . Under this test, the constitutional inquiry is not whether the conduct of state officers in obtaining the confession was shocking, but whether the confession is "free and voluntary. . . ." In other words the person must not have been compelled to incriminate himself. We have held inadmissible even a confession secured by so mild a whip as the refusal under certain circumstances, to allow a suspect to call his wife until he confessed. *Haynes* v. *Washington*, 373 U.S. 503.

The marked shift to the federal standard in state cases began with *Lisenba* v. *California*, 314 U.S. 219, . . . where the Court spoke of the accused's "free choice to admit, to deny, or to refuse to answer." . . . The shift reflects recognition that the American system of criminal prosecution is accusatorial, not inquisitorial, and that the Fifth Amendment privilege is its essential mainstay. . . . Governments, state and federal, are thus constitutionally compelled to establish guilt by evidence independently and freely secured, and may not by coercion prove a charge against an accused out of his own mouth. Since the Fourteenth Amendment prohibits the States from inducing a person to confess through "sympathy falsely aroused," . . . or other like inducement far short of "compulsion by torture," . . . it follows *a fortiori* that it also forbids the States to resort to imprisonment, as here, to compel him to answer questions that might incriminate him. The Fourteenth Amendment secures against state invasion the same privilege that the Fifth Amendment guarantees against federal infringement—the right of a person to remain silent unless he chooses to speak in the unfettered exercise of his will, and to suffer no penalty, as held in *Twining*, for such silence.

. . .

The respondent Sheriff concedes in his brief that under our decisions, particularly those involving coerced confessions, "the accusatorial system has become a fundamental part of the fabric of our society and, hence, is enforceable against the States." The State urges, however, that the availability of the federal privilege to a witness in a state inquiry is to be determined according to a less stringent standard than is applicable in a federal proceeding. We disagree. We have held that the guarantees of the First Amendment, . . . the prohibition of unreasonable searches and seizures of the Fourth Amendment, . . . and the right to counsel guaranteed by the Sixth Amendment, . . . are all to be enforced against the States under the Fourteenth Amendment according to the same standards that protect those personal rights against federal encroachment. In the coerced confession cases, involving the policies of the privilege itself, there has been no suggestion that a confession might be considered coerced if used in a federal but not a state tribunal. The Court thus has rejected the notion that the Fourteenth Amendment applies to the states only a "watered-down, subjective version of the individual guarantees of the Bill of Rights." ... What is accorded is a privilege of refusing to incriminate one's self, and the feared prosecution may be by either federal or state authorities. ... It would be incongruous to have different standards determine the validity of a claim of privilege based on the same feared prosecution, depending on whether the claim was asserted in a state or federal court. Therefore, the same standards must determine whether an accused's silence in either a federal or state proceeding is justified.

We turn to the petitioner's claim that the State of Connecticut denied him the protection of his federal privilege. It must be considered irrelevant that the petitioner was a witness in a statutory inquiry and not a defendant in a criminal prosecution, for it has long been settled that the privilege protects witnesses in similar federal inquiries. ... We recently elaborated the content of the federal standard in *Hoffman* v. *United States,* 341 U.S. 479:

> The privilege afforded not only extends to answers that would in themselves support a conviction ... but likewise embraces those which would furnish a link in the chain of evidence needed to prosecute ... if the witness, upon interposing his claim, were required to prove the hazard ... he would be compelled to surrender the very protection which the privilege is designed to guarantee. To sustain the privilege, it need only be evident from the implications of the questions, in the setting in which it is asked, that a responsive answer to the question or an explanation of why it cannot be answered might be dangerous because injurious disclosure could result. 341 U.S. at 486–487, 71 S. Ct. at 818.

We also said that, in applying that test, the judge must be

"perfectly clear, from a careful consideration of all the circumstances in the case, that the witness is mistaken, and that the answer[s] *cannot possibly* have such tendency" to incriminate. 341 U.S. at 488. . . .

The State of Connecticut argues that the Connecticut courts properly applied the federal standards to the facts of this case. We disagree.

The investigation in the course of which petitioner was questioned began when the Superior Court of Hartford County appointed the Honorable Ernest A. Inglis, formerly Chief Justice of Connecticut, to conduct an inquiry into whether there was reasonable cause to believe the crimes, including gambling, were being committed in Hartford County. Petitioner appeared on January 16 and 25, 1961, and in both instances he was asked substantially the same questions about the circumstances surrounding his arrest and conviction for pool-selling in late 1959. The questions which petitioner refused to answer may be summarized as follows: (1) for whom did he work on September 11, 1959; (2) who selected and paid his counsel in connection with his arrest on that date and subsequent conviction; (3) who selected and paid his bondsman; (4) who paid his fine; (5) what was the name of the tenant in the apartment in which he was arrested; and (6) did he know John Bergoti. The Connecticut Supreme Court of Errors ruled that the answers to these questions could not tend to incriminate him because the defenses of double jeopardy and the running of the one-year statute of limitations on misdemeanors would defeat any prosecution growing out of his answers to the first five questions. As for the sixth question, the court held that petitioner's failure to explain how a revelation of his relationship with Bergoti would incriminate him vitiated his claim to the protection of the privilege afforded by state law.

The conclusions of the Court of Errors, tested by the federal standard, fail to take sufficient account of the setting in which the questions were asked. The interrogation was part of a wide-ranging inquiry into crime, including gambling, in Hartford. It was admitted on behalf of the State at oral argument—and indeed it is obvious from the questions themselves—that the State desired to elicit from the petitioner the identity of the person who ran the pool-selling operation in connection with which he had been arrested in 1959. It was apparent that petitioner might apprehend that if this person were still engaged in unlawful activity, disclosure of his name might furnish a link in a chain of evidence sufficient to connect the petitioner with a more recent crime for which he might still be prosecuted.

. . .

Reversed.

While MR. JUSTICE DOUGLAS *joins the opinion of the Court, he also adheres to his concurrence in* Gideon v. Wainwright, *372 U.S. 335, 345.*

MR. JUSTICE HARLAN, *whom* MR. JUSTICE CLARK *joins, dissenting.*

Connecticut has adjudged this petitioner in contempt for refusing to answer questions in a state inquiry. The courts of the State, whose laws embody a privilege against self-incrimination, refused to recognize the petitioner's claim of privilege, finding that the questions asked him were not incriminatory. This Court now holds the contempt adjudication unconstitutional because, it is decided: (1) the Fourteenth Amendment makes the Fifth Amendment privilege against self-incrimination applicable to the States; (2) the federal standards justifying a claim of this privilege likewise applies to the States; and (3) judged by that standard the petitioner's claim of privilege should have been upheld.

Believing that the reasoning behind the Court's decision carries extremely mischievous, if not dangerous consequences for our federal

system in the realm of criminal law enforcement, I must dissent. . . .

I can only read the Court's opinion as accepting in fact what it rejects in theory: the application to the States, via the Fourteenth Amendment, of the forms of federal criminal procedure embodied within the first eight Amendments to the Constitution. While it is true that the Court deals today with only one aspect of state criminal procedure, and rejects the wholesale "incorporation" of such federal constitutional requirements, the logical gap between the Court's premises and its novel constitutional conclusion can, I submit, be bridged only by the additional premise that the Due Process Clause of the Fourteenth Amendment is a shorthand directive to this Court to pick and choose among the provisions of the first eight amendments and apply those chosen, freighted with their entire accompanying body of federal doctrine, to law enforcement in the States.

I accept and agree with the proposition that continuing reexamination of the constitutional conception of the Fourteenth Amendment "due process" of law is required, and that development of the community's sense of justice may in time lead to expansion of the protection which due process affords. In particular in this case, I agree that principles of justice to which due process gives expression, as reflected in decisions of this Court, prohibit a State, as the Fifth Amendment prohibits the Federal Government, from imprisoning a person *solely* because he refuses to give evidence which may incriminate him under the laws of the State. I do not understand, however, how this process of reexamination, which must refer always to the guiding standard of due process of law, including, of course, reference to the particular guarantees of the Bill of Rights, can be short-circuited by the simple device of incorporating into due process, without critical examination, the whole body of law which surrounds a specific prohibition directed against the Federal Government. The consequence of such an approach to due process as it pertains to the States is inevitably disregard of all relevant differences which may exist between state and federal criminal law and its enforcement. The ultimate result is compelled uniformity, which is inconsistent with the purpose of our federal system and which is achieved either by encroachment on the States' sovereign powers or by dilution in federal law enforcement of the specific protections found in the Bill of Rights.

· · ·

The Court's approach in the present case is in fact nothing more or less than "incorporation" in snatches. If, however, the Due Process Clause *is* something more than a reference to the Bill of Rights and protects only those rights which derive from fundamental principles, as the majority purports to believe, it is just as contrary to precedent and just as illogical to incorporate the provision of the Bill of Rights one at a time as it is to incorporate them all at once.

The Court's undiscriminating approach to the Due Process Clause carries serious implications for the sound working of our federal system in the field of criminal law.

The Court concludes, almost without discussion, that "the same standards must determine whether an accused's silence in either a federal or state proceeding is justified." . . . About all that the Court offers in explanation of this conclusion is the observation that it would be "incongruous" if different standards governed the assertion of a privilege to remain silent in state and federal tribunals. Such "incongruity," however, is at the heart of our federal system. The powers and responsibilities of the state and federal governments are not congruent; under our Constitution, they are not intended to be. Why should it be thought, as an *a priori* matter, that limitations on the investigative power of the States are in all respects identical with limitations on the investigative power of the Federal Government? This certainly does not follow from the fact that we deal here with constitutional requirements; for the provisions of the Constitution which are construed are different.

As the Court pointed out in *Abbate* v. *United States,* 359 U.S. 187, . . . "the States under our federal system have the principal responsibility for defining and prosecuting crimes." The Court endangers this allocation of responsibility for the prevention of crime when it applies to the States' doctrines developed in the context of federal law enforcement, without any attention to the special problems which the States as a group or particular States may face. If the power of the States to deal with local crime is unduly restricted, the likely consequence is a shift of responsibility in this area to the Federal Government, with its vastly greater resources. Such a shift, if it occurs, may in the end serve to weaken the very liberties which the Fourteenth Amendment safeguards by bringing us close to the monolithic society which our federalism rejects. Equally dangerous to our liberties is the alternative of watering down protections against the Federal Government embodied in the Bill of Rights so as not unduly to restrict the powers of the States. . . .

Rather than insisting, almost by rote, that the Connecticut court, in considering the petitioner's claim of privilege, was required to apply the "federal standard," the Court should have fulfilled its responsibility under the Due Process Clause by inquiring whether the proceedings below met the demands of fundamental fairness which due process embodies. Such an approach may not satisfy those who see in the Fourteenth Amendment a set of easily applied "absolutes" which can afford a haven from unsettling doubt. It is, however, truer to the spirit which requires this Court constantly to re-examine fundamental principles and at the same time enjoins it from reading its own preferences into the Constitution.

· · ·

MR. JUSTICE WHITE *wrote a brief dissent in which* MR. JUSTICE STEWART *concurred.*

KASTIGAR v. UNITED STATES

406 U.S. 441; 32 L. Ed. 2d 212; 92 S. Ct. 1653 (1972)

MR. JUSTICE POWELL *delivered the opinion of the Court.*

This case presents the question whether the United States Government may compel testimony from an unwilling witness, who invokes the Fifth Amendment privilege against compulsory self-incrimination, by conferring on the witness immunity from use of the compelled testimony in subsequent criminal proceedings, as well as immunity from use of evidence derived from the testimony.

Petitioners were subpoenaed to appear before a United States grand jury in the Central District of California on February 4, 1971. The Government believed that petitioners were likely to assert their Fifth Amendment privilege. Prior to the scheduled appearances, the Government applied to the District Court for an order directing petitioners to answer questions and produce evidence before the grand jury under a grant of immunity conferred pursuant to 18 U.S.C. §§ 6002, 6003. Petitioners opposed issuance of the order, contending primarily that the scope of the immunity provided by the statute was not coextensive with the scope of the privilege against self-incrimination, and therefore was not sufficient to supplant the privilege and compel their testimony. The District Court rejected this contention, and ordered petitioners to appear before the grand jury and answer its questions under the grant of immunity.

Petitioners appeared but refused to answer questions, asserting their privilege against compulsory self-incrimination. They were brought before the District Court, and each persisted in his refusal to answer the grand jury's ques-

tions. . . . The court found both in contempt, and committed them to the custody of the Attorney General until either they answered the grand jury's questions or the term of the grand jury expired. The Court of Appeals for the Ninth Circuit affirmed. This Court granted certiorari to resolve the important question whether testimony may be compelled by granting immunity from the use of the compelled testimony and evidence derived therefrom ("use and derivative use" immunity), or whether it is necessary to grant immunity from prosecution for offenses to which compelled testimony relates ("transactional" immunity).

The power of government to compel persons to testify in court or before grand juries and other governmental agencies is firmly established in Anglo-American jurisprudence. . . . While it is not clear when grand juries first resorted to compulsory process to secure the attendance and testimony of witnesses, the general common law principle that "the public has a right to every man's evidence" was considered an "indubitable certainty" which "cannot be denied" by 1742. The power to compel testimony, and the corresponding duty to testify, are recognized in the Sixth Amendment requirements that an accused be confronted with the witnesses against him, and have compulsory process for obtaining witnesses in his favor. . . .

But the power to compel testimony is not absolute. There are a number of exemptions from the testimonial duty, the most important of which is the Fifth Amendment privilege against compulsory self-incrimination. The privilege reflects a complex of our fundamental values and aspirations, and marks an important advance in the development of our liberty. It can be asserted in any proceeding, civil or criminal, administrative or judicial, investigatory or adjudicatory; and it protects against any disclosures which the witness reasonably believes could be used in a criminal prosecution or could lead to other evidence that might be so used. This Court has been zealous to safeguard the values which underlie the privilege.

Immunity statutes, which have historical roots deep in Anglo-American jurisprudence, are not incompatible with these values. Rather they seek a rational accommodation between the imperatives of the privilege and the legitimate demands of government to compel citizens to testify. The existence of these statutes reflects the importance of testimony, and the fact that many offenses are of such a character that the only persons capable of giving useful testimony are those implicated in the crime. . . .

Petitioners contend first that the Fifth Amendment's privilege against compulsory self-incrimination . . . deprives Congress of power to enact laws which compel self-incrimination, even if complete immunity from prosecution is granted prior to the compulsion of the incriminatory testimony. In other words, petitioners assert that no immunity statute, however drawn, can afford a lawful basis for compelling incriminatory testimony. They ask us to reconsider and overrule *Brown* v. *Walker*, 161 U.S. 591 (1896), and *Ullmann* v. *United States*, 350 U.S. 442 (1956), decisions which uphold the constitutionality of immunity statutes.

We find no merit to this contention and reaffirm the decisions in *Brown* and *Ullman*.

Petitioners' second contention is that the scope of immunity provided by the federal witness immunity statute, 18 U.S.C. § 6002, is not coextensive with the scope of the Fifth Amendment privilege against compulsory self-incrimination, and therefore is not sufficient to supplant the privilege and compel testimony over a claim of the privilege. The statute provides that when a witness is compelled by district court order to testify over a claim of the privilege:

> the witness may not refuse to comply with the order on the basis of his privilege against self-incrimination; but no testimony or other information compelled under the order (or any information directly or indirectly derived from such testimony or other information) may be used against the witness in any criminal case, except a prosecution for perjury, giving a false statement, or otherwise failing to comply with the order.

The constitutional inquiry, rooted in logic and history, as well as in the decisions of this Court, is whether the immunity granted under this statute is coextensive with the scope of the privilege. If so, petitioners' refusals to answer based on the privilege were unjustified, and the judgments of contempt were proper, for the grant of immunity has removed the dangers against which the privilege protests. If, on the other hand, the immunity granted is not as comprehensive as the protection afforded by the privilege, petitioners were justified in refusing to answer, and the judgments of contempt must be vacated.

Petitioners draw a distinction between statutes which provide transactional immunity and those which provide, as does the statute before us, immunity from use and derivative use. They contend that a statute must at a minimum grant full transactional immunity in order to be coextensive with the scope of the privilege. . . . The statute [here under consideration], does not "afford . . . absolute immunity against future prosecution" . . . .

The statute's explicit proscription of the use in any criminal case of "testimony or other information compelled under the order (or any information directly or indirectly derived from such testimony or other information)" is consonant with Fifth Amendment standards. We hold that such immunity from use and derivative use is coextensive with the scope of the privilege against self-incrimination, and therefore is sufficient to compel testimony over a claim of the privilege. While a grant of immunity must afford protection commensurate with that afforded by the privilege, it need not be broader. Transactional immunity, which accords full immunity from prosecution for the offense to which the compelled testimony relates, affords the witness considerably broader protection than does the Fifth Amendment privilege. The privilege has never been construed to mean that one who invokes it cannot subsequently be prosecuted. Its sole concern is to afford protection against being "forced to give testimony leading to the infliction of 'penalties affixed to . . . criminal acts.' " Immunity from the use of compelled testimony and evidence derived directly and indirectly therefrom affords this protection. It prohibits the prosecutorial authorities from using the compelled testimony in *any* respect, and it therefore insures that the testimony cannot lead to the infliction of criminal penalties on the witness. . . .

In *Murphy* v. *Waterfront Comm'n*, 378 U.S. 52 (1964), the Court carefully considered immunity from use of compelled testimony and evidence derived therefrom. . . .

The issue before the Court . . . was whether New Jersey and New York could compel the witnesses, whom these States had immunized from prosecution under their laws, to give testimony which might then be used to convict them of a federal crime. Since New Jersey and New York had not purported to confer immunity from federal prosecution, the Court was faced with the question what limitations the Fifth Amendment privilege imposed on the prosecutorial powers of the Federal Government, a nonimmunizing sovereign. After undertaking an examination of the policies and purposes of the privilege, the Court overturned the rule that one jurisdiction within our federal structure may compel a witness to give testimony which could be used to convict him of a crime in another jurisdiction. The Court held that the privilege protects state witnesses against incrimination under federal as well as state law, and federal witnesses against incrimination under state as well as federal law. Applying this principle to the state immunity legislation before it, the Court held the constitutional rule to be that:

a state witness may not be compelled to give testimony which may be incriminating under federal law unless the compelled testimony and its fruits cannot be used in any manner by federal officials in connection with a criminal prosecution against him. We conclude, moreover, that in order to implement this constitutional rule and accommodate the interests of the State and Federal Government in investigating and prosecuting crime, the Federal Government must be prohibited from making any such use of compelled testimony and its fruits.

The Court emphasized that this rule left the state witness and the Federal Government, against which the witness had immunity only from the *use* of the compelled testimony and evidence derived therefrom, "in substantially the same position as if the witness had claimed his privilege in the absence of a state grant of immunity."

It is true that in *Murphy* the Court was not presented with the precise question presented by this case, whether a jurisdiction seeking to compel testimony may do so by granting only use and derivative use immunity, for New Jersey and New York had granted petitioners transactional immunity. The Court heretofore has not squarely confronted this question. . . . But both the reasoning of the Court in *Murphy* and the result reached compel the conclusion that use and derivative use immunity is constitutionally sufficient to compel testimony over a claim of the privilege. Since the privilege is fully applicable and its scope is the same whether invoked in a state or in a federal jurisdiction, the *Murphy* conclusion that a prohibition on use and derivative use secures a witness' Fifth Amendment privilege against infringement by the Federal Government demonstrates that immunity from use and derivative use is coextensive with the scope of the privilege. As the *Murphy* Court noted, immunity from use and derivative use "leaves the witness and the Federal Government in substantially the same position as if the witness had claimed his privilege" in the absence of a grant of immunity. The *Murphy* Court was concerned solely with the danger of incrimination under federal law, and held that immunity from use and derivative use was sufficient to displace the danger. This protection, coextensive, with the privilege, is the degree of protection which the Constitution requires, and is all that the Constitution requires even against the jurisdiction compelling testimony by granting immunity.

Although an analysis of prior decisions and the purpose of the Fifth Amendment privilege indicates that use and derivative use immunity is coextensive with the privilege, we must consider additional arguments advanced by petitioners against the sufficiency of such immunity. We start from the premise, repeatedly affirmed by this Court, that an appropriately broad immunity grant is compatible with the Constitution.

Petitioners argue that use and derivative use immunity will not adequately protect a witness from various possible incriminating uses of the compelled testimony: for example, the prosecutor or other law enforcement officials may obtain leads, names of witnesses, or other information not otherwise available which might result in a prosecution. It will be difficult and perhaps impossible, the argument goes, to identify, by testimony or cross-examination, the subtle ways in which the compelled testimony may disadvantage a witness, especially in the jurisdiction granting the immunity.

This argument presupposes that the statute's prohibition will prove impossible to enforce. The statute provides a sweeping proscription of any use, direct or indirect, of the compelled testimony and any information derived therefrom:

> no testimony or other information compelled under the order (or any information directly or indirectly derived from such testimony or other information) may be used against the witness in any criminal case.... 18 U.S.C. § 6002.

This total prohibition on use provides a comprehensive safeguard, barring the use of compelled testimony as an "investigatory lead," and also barring the use of any evidence obtained by focusing investigation on a witness as a result of his compelled disclosures.

A person accorded this immunity ... and subsequently prosecuted, is not dependent for the preservation of his rights upon the integrity and good faith of the prosecuting authorities. As stated in *Murphy*:

> Once a defendant demonstrates that he has testified, under a state grant of immunity, to matters related to the federal prosecution, the federal authorities have the burden of showing that their evidence is not tainted by establishing that they had an independent, legitimate source for the disputed evidence. 378 U.S., at 79 n. 18.

This burden of proof, which we reaffirm as appropriate, is not limited to a negation of taint; rather, it imposes on the prosecution the affirmative duty to prove that the evidence it proposes to use is derived from a legitimate source wholly independent of the compelled testimony.

This is very substantial protection, commensurate with that resulting from invoking the privilege itself. ... The statute, like the Fifth Amendment, grants neither pardon nor amnesty. Both the statute and the Fifth Amendment allow the government to prosecute using evidence from legitimate independent sources. ...

We conclude that the immunity provided by 18 U.S.C. § 6002 leaves the witness and the prosecutorial authorities in substantially the same position as if the witness had claimed the Fifth Amendment privilege. The immunity therefore is coextensive with the privilege and suffices to supplant it. The judgment of the Court of Appeals for the Ninth Circuit accordingly is

Affirmed.

MR. JUSTICE BRENNAN *and* MR. JUSTICE REHNQUIST *took no part in the consideration or decision of this case.*

MR. JUSTICE DOUGLAS *dissenting.*

My views on the question of the scope of immunity that is necessary to force a witness to give up his guarantee against self-incrimination contained in the Fifth Amendment are so well known, see *Ullmann* v. *United States,* 350 U.S. 422, 440 (dissenting), and *Piccirillo* v. *New York,* 400 U.S. 548, 549 (dissenting), that I need not write at length. . . .

If, as some have thought, the Bill of Rights contained only "counsels of moderation" from which courts and legislatures could deviate according to their conscience or discretion, then today's contraction of the Self-Incrimination Clause of the Fifth Amendment would be understandable. But that has not been true, starting with Chief Justice Marshall's opinion in *United States* v. *Burr,* 25 F. Cas. p. 38 (No. 14, 692e), where he ruled that the reach of the Fifth Amendment was so broad as to make the privilege applicable when there was a mere possibility of a criminal charge being made.

The Court said in *Hale* v. *Henkel,* 201 U.S. 43, 67 that "if the criminality has already been taken away, the Amendment ceases to apply." In other words, the immunity granted is adequate if it operates as a complete pardon for the offense. That is the true measure of the Self-Incrimination Clause. As Mr. Justice Brennan has stated: ". . . use immunity literally misses half the point of the privilege, for it permits the compulsion without removing the criminality." *Piccirillo* v. *New York, supra,* 400 U.S. at 567 (dissenting).

As Mr. Justice Brennan has also said:

Transactional immunity . . . provides the individual with an assurance that he is not testifying about matters for which he may later be prosecuted. No question arises of tracing the use or non-use of information gleaned from the witness' compelled testimony. The sole question presented to a court is whether the subsequent prosecution is related to the substance of the compelled testimony. Both witness and government know precisely where they stand. Respect for law is furthered when the individual knows his position and is not left suspicious that a later prosecution was actually the fruit of his compelled testimony. 400 U.S., at 568-569.

When we allow the prosecution to offer only "use" immunity we allow it to grant far less than it has taken away. For while the precise testimony that is compelled may not be used, leads from that testimony may be pursued and used to convict the witness. My view is that the Framers put it beyond the power of Congress to *compel* anyone to confess his crimes. The Self-Incrimination Clause creates . . . "the federally protected right of silence," making it unconstitutional to use a law "to pry open one's lips and make him a witness against himself." That is indeed one of the chief procedural guarantees in our accusatorial system. Government acts in an ignoble way when it stoops to the end which we authorize today. . . .

MR. JUSTICE MARSHALL'S *dissenting opinion is not reprinted here.*

GIDEON v. WAINWRIGHT
372 U.S. 335; 9 L. Ed. 2d 799; 83 S. Ct. 792 (1963)

MR. JUSTICE BLACK *delivered the opinion of the Court.*

Petitioner was charged in a Florida state court with having broken and entered a poolroom with intent to commit a misdemeanor. This offense is a felony under Florida law. Appearing in court without funds and without a lawyer, petitioner asked the court to appoint counsel for him, whereupon the following colloquy took place:

> *The Court:* Mr. Gideon, I am sorry, but I cannot appoint Counsel to represent you in this case. Under the laws of the State of Florida, the only time the Court can appoint Counsel to represent a Defendant is when that person is charged with a capital offense. I am sorry, but I will have to deny your request to appoint Counsel to defend you in this case.
> *The Defendant:* The United States Supreme Court says I am entitled to be represented by Counsel.

Put to trial before a jury, Gideon conducted his defense about as well as could be expected from a layman. He made an opening statement to the jury, cross-examined the State's witnesses, presented witnesses in his own defense, declined to testify himself, and made a short argument "emphasizing his innocence to the charge contained in the Information filed in this case." The jury returned a verdict of guilty, and petitioner was sentenced to serve five years in the state prison. Later, petitioner filed in the Florida Supreme Court this habeas corpus petition attacking his conviction and sentence on the ground that the trial court's refusal to appoint counsel for him denied him rights "guaranteed by the Constitution and the Bill of Rights by the United States Government." ... [T]he State Supreme Court, "upon consideration thereof" but without an opinion, denied all relief. ...

The facts upon which Betts claimed that he had been unconstitutionally denied the right to have counsel appointed to assist him are strikingly like the facts upon which Gideon here bases his federal constitutional claim. Betts was indicted for robbery in a Maryland state court. In arraignment, he told the trial judge of his lack of funds to hire a lawyer and asked the court to appoint one for him. Betts was advised that it was not the practice in that county to appoint counsel for indigent defendants except in murder and rape cases. He then pleaded not guilty, had witnesses summoned, cross-examined the State's witnesses, examined his own, and chose not to testify himself. He was found guilty by the judge, sitting without a jury, and sentenced to eight years in prison. Like Gideon, Betts sought release by habeas corpus, alleging that he had been denied the right to assistance of counsel in violation of the Fourteenth Amendment. Betts was denied any relief, and on review this Court affirmed. It was held that a refusal to appoint counsel for an indigent defendant charged with a felony did not necessarily violate the "due process" clause of the Fourteenth Amendment, which for reasons given the Court deemed to be the only applicable federal constitutional provision. The Court said:

> Asserting denial [of due process] is to be tested by an appraisal of the totality of facts in a given case. That which may, in one

setting, constitute a denial of fundamental fairness, shocking to the universal sense of justice, may, in other circumstances, and in the light of other considerations, fall short of such denial. (316 U. S., at 462).

Treating due process as "a concept less rigid and more fluid than those envisaged in other specific and particular provisions of the Bill of Rights," the Court held that refusal to appoint counsel under the particular facts and circumstances in the *Betts* case was not so "offensive to the common and fundamental ideas of fairness" as to amount to a denial of due process. Since the facts and circumstances of the two cases are so nearly indistinguishable, we think the *Betts* v. *Brady* holding if left standing would require us to reject Gideon's claim that the Constitution guarantees him the assistance of counsel. Upon full reconsideration we conclude that *Betts* v. *Brady* should be overruled.

The Sixth Amendment provides, "In all criminal prosecutions, the accused shall enjoy the right . . . to have the Assistance of Counsel for his defense." We have construed this to mean that in federal courts counsel must be provided for defendants unable to employ counsel unless the right is competently and intelligently waived. (*Johnson* v. *Zerbst*, 304 U.S. 458, 1958). Betts argued that this right is extended to indigent defendants in state courts by the Fourteenth Amendment. In response the Court stated that, while the Sixth Amendment laid down "no rule for the conduct of the states, the question recurs whether the constraint laid by the amendment upon the national courts expresses a rule so fundamental and essential to a fair trial, and so, to due process of law, that it is made obligatory upon the states by the Fourteenth Amendment." (316 U.S., at 465.) In order to decide whether the Sixth Amendment's guarantee of counsel is of this fundamental nature, the Court in *Betts* set out and considered "relevant data on the subject . . . afforded by constitutional and statutory provisions subsisting in the colonies and the states prior to the inclusion of the Bill of Rights in the national Constitution, and in the constitutional, legislative, and judicial history of the states to the present." (316 U.S., 471.) It was for this reason the *Betts* Court refused to accept the contention that the Sixth Amendment's guarantee of counsel for indigent federal defendants was extended to, or, in the words of that court, "made obligatory upon the states by the Fourteenth Amendment." Plainly, had the Court concluded that appointment of counsel for an indigent criminal defendant was "a fundamental right, essential to a fair trial," it would have held that the Fourteenth Amendment requires appointment of counsel in a state court, just as the Sixth Amendment requires in a federal court.

We think the Court in *Betts* had ample precedent for acknowledging that those guarantees of the Bill of Rights which are fundamental safeguards of liberty immune from federal abridgement are equally protected against state invasion by the "due process" clause of the Fourteenth Amendment. This same principle was recognized, explained, and applied in *Powell* v. *Alabama,* 287 U.S. 45 (1932), a case upholding the right of counsel, where the Court held that despite sweeping language to the contrary in *Hurtado* v. *California,* 110 U.S. 516 (1884), the Fourteenth Amendment "embraced" those "fundamental principles of liberty and justice which lie at the base of all our civil and political institutions," even though they had been "specifically dealt with in another part of the federal Constitution." (287 U.S., at 67.) In many cases other than *Powell* and *Betts*, this Court has looked to the fundamental nature of the original Bill of Rights guarantees to decide whether the Fourteenth Amendment makes them obligatory on the states. Explicitly recognized to be of this "fundamental nature" and therefore made immune from state invasion by the Fourteenth, or some part of it, are the First Amendment's freedoms of speech, press, religion, assembly, association, and petition for redress of grievances. For the same reason, though not always in precisely the same terminology, the Court has made obligatory on the states the Fifth Amendment's command that private property shall not be taken for public use without just compensation, the Fourth Amendment's prohibition of unreasonable searches and seizures, and the Eighth's ban on cruel and unusual punishment. On the other hand, this Court in *Palko* v. *Connecticut*, 302 U.S. 319 (1937), refused to hold that the Fourteenth Amendment made the double jeopardy provision of the Fifth Amendment obligatory on the states. In so far as refusing, however, the court, speaking through Mr. Justice Cardozo, was careful to emphasize that "immunities that are valid against the federal government by force of the specific pledges of particular amendments have been found to be implicit in the concept of ordered liberty, and thus, through the Fourteenth Amendment, become valid as against the states" and that guarantees "in their origin . . . effective against the federal government alone" had by prior cases "been taken over from the earlier articles of the Federal Bill of Rights and brought within the Fourteenth Amendment by a process of absorption." (302 U.S., at 324-325, 326.)

We accept *Betts* v. *Brady's* assumption, based as it was on our prior cases, that a provision of the Bill of Rights which is "fundamental and essential to a fair trial" is made obligatory upon the states by the Fourteenth Amendment. We think the Court in *Betts* was wrong, however, in concluding that the Sixth Amendment's guarantee of counsel is not one of these fundamental rights. Ten years before *Betts* v. *Brady*, this Court, after full consideration of all historical data examined in *Betts*, had unequivocally declared that "the right to the aid of counsel is of this fundamental character." *Powell* v. *Alabama*, 287 U.S. 45, 68 (1932). While the Court at the close of its *Powell* opinion did by its language, as it frequently does, limit its holding to the particular facts and circumstances of that case, its conclusions about the fundamental

nature of the right to counsel are unmistakable. Several years later, in 1936, the Court reemphasized what it had said about the fundamental nature of the right to counsel in this language:

> We concluded that certain fundamental rights, safeguarded by the first eight amendments against federal action, were also safeguarded against state action by the due process clause of the Fourteenth Amendment, and among them the fundamental right of the accused to the aid of counsel in a criminal prosecution. *Grossjean* v. *American Press Co.*, 297 U. S. 233, 243-244 (1936).

And again in 1938 this Court said:

> [The assistance of counsel] is one of the safeguards of the Sixth Amendment deemed necessary to insure fundamental human rights of life and liberty. . . . The Sixth Amendment stands as a constant admonition that if the constitutional safeguards it provides be lost, justice will not "still be done." *Johnson* v. *Zerbst*, 304 U. S. 458, 462 (1938). . . .

In the light of these and many other prior decisions of this Court, it is not surprising that the *Betts* Court, when faced with the contention that "one charged with crime, who is unable to obtain counsel, must be furnished counsel by the state," conceded that "expressions in the opinions of this court lend color to the argument . . ." 316 U.S., at 462-463. The fact is that in deciding as it did—that "appointment of counsel is not a fundamental right, essential to a fair trial"—the Court in *Betts* v. *Brady* made an abrupt break with its own well-considered precedents. In returning to these old precedents, sounder we believe than the new, we but restore constitutional principles established to achieve a fair system of justice. Not only these precedents but also reason and reflection require us to recognize that in our adversary system of criminal justice, any person haled into court, who is too poor to hire a lawyer, cannot be assured a fair trial unless counsel is provided for him. This seems to us to be an obvious truth. Governments, both state and federal, quite properly spend vast sums of money to establish machinery to try defendants accused of crime. Lawyers to prosecute are everywhere deemed essential to protect the public's interest in an orderly society. Similarly, there are few defendants charged with crime, few, indeed, who fail to hire the best lawyers they can get to prepare and present their defenses. That government hires lawyers to prosecute and defendants who have the money hire lawyers to defend are the strongest indications of a widespread belief that lawyers in criminal courts are necessities, not luxuries. The right of one charged with crime to counsel may not be deemed fundamental and essential to fair trials in some countries, but it is in ours. From the very beginning, our state and national constitutions and laws have laid great emphasis on procedural and substantive safeguards designed to assure fair trials before impartial tribunals in which every defendant stands equal before the law. This noble ideal cannot be realized if the poor man charged with crime has to face his accusers without a lawyer to assist him. A defendant's need for a lawyer is nowhere better stated than in the moving words of Mr. Justice Sutherland in *Powell* v. *Alabama*:

The right to be heard would be, in many cases, of little avail if it did not comprehend the right to be heard by counsel. Even the intelligent and educated layman has small and sometimes no skill in the science of law. If charged with crime, he is incapable, generally, of determining for himself whether the indictment is good or bad. He is unfamiliar with the rules of evidence. Left without the aid of counsel he may be put on trial without a proper charge, and convicted upon incompetent evidence, or evidence irrelevant to the issue or otherwise inadmissible. He lacks both the skill and knowledge adequately to prepare his defense, even though he have a perfect one. He requires the guiding hand of counsel

at every step in the proceedings against him. Without it, though he be not guilty, he faces the danger of conviction because he does not know how to establish his innocence. 287 U.S., at 68–69.

The Court in *Betts* v. *Brady* departed from the sound wisdom upon which the Court's holding in *Powell* v. *Alabama* rested. Florida, supported by two other states, asked that *Betts* v. *Brady* be left intact. Twenty-two states, as friends of the Court, argue that *Betts* was "an anachronism when handed down" and that it should now be overruled. We agree.

The Judgment is reversed and the cause is remanded to the Supreme Court of Florida for further action not inconsistent with this opinion.

MR. JUSTICE CLARK, *concurring*.

I must conclude ... that the Constitution makes no distinction between capital and noncapital cases. The Fourteenth Amendment requires due process of law for the deprival of "liberty" just as for deprival of "life," and there cannot constitutionally be a difference in the sanction involved. How can the Fourteenth Amendment tolerate a procedure which it condemns in capital cases on the ground that deprival of liberty may be less onerous than deprival of life—a value judgment not universally accepted—or that only the latter deprival is irrevocable? I can find no acceptable rationalization for such a result, and I therefore concur in the judgment of the Court.

MR. JUSTICE HARLAN, *concurring*.

I agree that *Betts* v. *Brady* should be overruled, but consider it entitled to a more respectful burial than has been accorded, at least on the part of those of us who were not on the Court when that case was decided.

I cannot subscribe to the view that *Betts* v. *Brady* represented "an abrupt break with its own well-considered precedents." . . . The principles declared in *Powell* and *Betts* . . . had a troubled journey throughout the years that have followed first the one case and then the other. Even by the time of the *Betts* decision, dictum in at least one of the Court's opinions had indicated that there was an absolute right to the services of counsel in the trial of state capital cases. "Such dicta continued to appear in subsequent decisions" and any lingering doubts were finally eliminated by the holding of *Hamilton* v. *Alabama, 368 U.S. 52.*

In noncapital cases, the "special circumstances" rule has continued to exist in form while its substance has been substantially and steadily eroded. . . . The Court has come to recognize, in other words, that the mere existence of a serious criminal charge constituted in itself special circumstances requiring the services of counsel at trial. In truth the *Betts* v. *Brady* rule is no longer a reality.

This evolution, however, appears not to have been fully recognized by many state courts, in this instance charged with the front-line responsibility for the enforcement of constitutional rights. . . . To continue a rule which is honored by this Court only with lip service is not a healthy thing and in the long run will do disservice to the federal system.

The special circumstances rule has been formally abandoned in capital cases, and the time has now come when it should be abandoned in noncapital cases, at least as to offenses which, as the one involved here, carry the possibility of a substantial prison sentence. (Whether the rule should extend to all criminal cases need not be decided.) This indeed does no more than to make explicit something that has long since been foreshadowed in our decisions.

In agreeing with the Court that the right to counsel in a case such as this should now be expressly recognized as a fundamental right embraced in the Fourteenth Amendment, I wish to make a further observation. When we hold a right or immunity, valid against the Federal Government, to be "implicit in the concept of ordered liberty" and thus valid against the States, I do not read our past decisions to suggest that by so holding, we automatically carry over an entire body of federal law and apply it in full sweep to the States. Any such concept would disregard the frequently wide disparity between the legitimate interests of the States and of the Federal Government, the divergent problems that they face, and the significantly different consequences of their actions. . . . In what is done today I do not understand the Court to depart from the principles laid down in *Palko* v. *Connecticut* . . . or to embrace the concept that the Fourteenth Amendment "incorporates" the Sixth Amendment as such.

On these premises I join in the judgment of the Court.

MIRANDA v. ARIZONA
384 U.S. 436; 16 L. Ed. 2d 694; 86 S. Ct. 1602 (1966)*

MR. CHIEF JUSTICE WARREN *delivered the opinion of the Court.*

The cases before us raise questions which go to the roots of our concepts of American criminal jurisprudence: the restraints society must observe consistent with the Federal Constitution in prosecuting individuals for crime. More specifically, we deal with the admissibility of statements obtained from an individual who is subjected to custodial police interrogation and the necessity for procedures which assure that the individual is accorded his privilege under the Fifth Amendment to the Constitution not to be compelled to incriminate himself.

We dealt with certain phases of this problem recently in *Escobedo* v. *State of Illinois*. . . .

. . . We granted certiorari in these cases . . . in order further to explore some facets of the problems, thus exposed, of applying the privilege against self-incrimination to in-custody interrogation, and to give concrete constitutional guidelines for law enforcement agencies and courts to follow.

We start here, as we did in *Escobedo,* with the premise that our holding is not an innovation in our jurisprudence, but is an application of principles long recognized and applied in other settings. We have undertaken a thorough re-examination of the *Escobedo* decision and the principles it announced, and we re-affirm it.

. . .

*This opinion applies to the companion cases of *Vignera* v. *New York, Westover* v. *United States,* and *California* v. *Stewart* (Eds.).

Our holding will be spelled out with some specificity in the pages which follow but briefly stated it is this: the prosecution may not use statements, whether exculpatory or inculpatory, stemming from custodial interrogation of the defendant unless it demonstrates the use of procedural safeguards effective to secure the privilege against self-incrimination. By custodial interrogation, we mean questioning initiated by law enforcement officers after a person has been taken into custody or otherwise deprived of his freedom of action in any significant way. As for the procedural safeguards to be employed, unless other fully effective means are devised to inform accused persons of their right of silence and to assure a continuous opportunity to exercise it, the following measures are required. Prior to any questioning, the person must be warned that he has a right to remain silent, that any statement he does make may be used as evidence against him, and that he has a right to the presence of any attorney, either retained or appointed. The defendant may waive effectuation of these rights, provided the waiver is made voluntarily, knowingly and intelligently. If, however, he indicates in any manner and at any stage of the process that he wishes to consult with an attorney before speaking there can be no questioning. Likewise, if the individual is alone and indicates in any manner that he does not wish to be interrogated, the police may not question him. The mere fact that he may have answered some questions or volunteered some statements on his own does not deprive him of the right to refrain from answering any further inquiries until he has consulted with an attorney and thereafter consents to be questioned.

The constitutional issue we decided in each of these cases is the admissibility of statements obtained from a defendant questioned while in custody and deprived of his freedom of action. In each, the defendant was questioned by police officers, detectives, or a prosecuting attorney in a room in which he was cut off from the outside world. In none of these cases was the defendant given a full and effective warning of his rights at the outset of the interrogation process. In all the cases, the questioning elicited oral admissions, and in three of them, signed statements as well which were admitted at their trials. They all thus share salient features—incommunicado interrogation of individuals in a police-dominated atmosphere, resulting in self-incriminating statements without full warning of constitutional rights.

An understanding of the nature and setting of this in-custody interrogation is essential to our decisions today. The difficulty in depicting what transpires at such interrogations stems from the fact that in this country they have largely taken place incommunicado. From extensive factual studies undertaken in the early 1930s, including the famous Wickersham Report to Congress by a Presidential Commission, it is clear that police violence and the "third degree" flourished at that time. In a series of cases decided by this Court long after these studies, the police resorted to physical brutality—beating, hanging, whipping— and to sustained and protracted questioning incommunicado in order to extort confessions. The 1961 Commission on Civil Rights found much evidence to indicate that "some policemen still resort to physical force to obtain confessions.". . . The use of physical brutality and violence is not, unfortunately, relegated to the past or to any part of the country. . . .

The examples given above are undoubtedly the exception now, but they are sufficiently widespread to be the object of concern. Unless a proper limitation upon custodial interrogation is achieved—there can be no assurance that practices of this nature will be eradicated in the foreseeable future. . . .

[Here the Chief Justice reviewed some of the current literature which sets forth modern techniques of in-custody interrogation.]

The question in these cases is whether the privilege is fully applicable during a period of custodial interrogation. . . . We are satisfied that all the principles embodied in the privilege apply to informal compulsion exerted by law-enforcement officers during in-custody questioning. An individual swept from familiar surroundings into police custody, surrounded by antagonistic forces, and subjected to the techniques of persuasion described above cannot be otherwise than under compulsion to speak. As a practical matter, the compulsion to speak in the isolated setting of the police station may well be greater than in courts or other official investigations, where there are often impartial observers to guard against intimidation or trickery. . . .

Today, then, there can be no doubt that the Fifth Amendment privilege is available outside of criminal court proceedings and serves to protect persons in all settings in which their freedom of action is curtailed from being compelled to incriminate themselves. . . . In order to combat [inherently compelling] pressures and to permit a full opportunity to exercise the privilege against self-incrimination, the accused must be adequately and effectively apprised of his rights and the exercise of those rights must be fully honored. . . .

At the outset, if a person in custody is to be subjected to interrogation he must first be informed in clear and unequivocal terms that he has the right to remain silent. For those unaware of the privilege the warning is needed simply to make them aware of it—the threshold requirement for an intelligent decision as to its exercise. More important, such a warning is an absolute prerequisite in overcoming the inherent pressures of the interrogation atmosphere. It is not just the subnormal or woefully ignorant who succumb to an interrogator's imprecations, whether implied or expressly stated, that the interrogation will continue until a confession is obtained or that silence in the face of accusation is itself damning and will bode ill when presented to a jury. Further, the warning will show the individual that his interrogators are prepared to recognize his privilege should he choose to exercise it. . . .

The warning of the right to remain silent must be accompanied by the explanation that anything said can and will be used against the individual in court. This warning is needed in order to make him aware not only of the privilege, but also of the consequences of foregoing it. It is only through an awareness of these consequences that there can be any assurance of real understanding and intelligent exercise of the privilege. Moreover, this warning may serve to make the individual more acutely aware that he is faced with a phase of the adversary system— that he is not in the presence of persons acting solely in his interest.

The circumstances surrounding in-custody interrogation can operate very quickly to overbear the will of one merely made aware of his privilege by his interrogators. Therefore, the right to have counsel present at the interrogation is indispensable to the protection of the Fifth Amendment privilege under the system we delineate today. Our aim is to assure that the individual's right to choose between silence and speech remains unfettered throughout the interrogation process. A once-stated warning, delivered by those who will conduct the interrogation cannot itself suffice to that end among those who most require knowledge of their rights. A mere warning given by the interrogators is not alone sufficient to accomplish that end. Prosecutors themselves claim that the admonishment of the right to remain silent without more "will benefit only the recidivist and the professional." Brief for the National District Attorneys Association as *amicus curiae*, p. 14. Even preliminary advice given to the accused by his own attorney can be swiftly overcome by the secret interrogation process. . . . Thus, the need for counsel to protect the Fifth Amendment privilege comprehends not merely a right to consult prior to questioning, but also to have counsel present during any questioning if the defendant so desires.

The presence of counsel at the interrogation may serve several significant subsidiary functions as well. If the accused decides to talk to his interrogators, the assistance of counsel can mitigate the dangers of untrustworthiness. With a lawyer present the likelihood that the police will practice coercion is reduced, and if coercion is nevertheless exercised the lawyer can testify to it in court. The presence of a lawyer can also help to guarantee that the accused gives a fully accurate statement to the police and that the statement is rightly reported by the prosecution at trial. . . .

An individual need not make a pre-interrogation request for a lawyer. While such request affirmatively secures his right to have one, his failure to ask for a lawyer does not constitute a waiver. No effective waiver of the right to counsel during interrogation can be recognized unless specifically made after the warnings we here delineate have been given. The accused who does not know his rights and therefore does not make a request may be the person who most needs counsel. . . .

Accordingly we hold that an individual held for interrogation must be clearly informed that he has the right to consult with a lawyer and to have the lawyer with him during interrogation under the system for protecting the privilege we delineate today. As with the warnings of the right to remain silent and that anything stated can be used in evidence against him, this warning is an absolute prerequisite to interrogation. . . .

If an individual indicates that he wishes the assistance of counsel before any interrogation occurs, the authorities cannot rationally ignore or deny his request on the basis that the individual does not have or cannot afford a retained attorney. The financial ability of the individual has no relationship to the scope of the rights involved here. The privilege against self-incrimination secured by the Constitution applies to all individuals. The need for counsel in order to protect the privilege exists for the indigent as well as the affluent. In fact, were we to limit these constitutional rights to those who can retain an attorney, our decision today would be of little significance. . . . While authorities are not required to relieve the accused of his poverty, they have the obligation not to take advantage of indigence in the administration of justice. . . .

In order fully to apprise a person interrogated of the extent of his rights under this system then, it is necessary to warn him not only that he has the right to consult with an attorney, but also that if he is indigent a lawyer will be appointed to represent him. . . .

Once warnings have been given, the subsequent procedure is clear. If the individual indicates in any manner, at any time prior to or during questioning, that he wishes to remain silent, the interrogation must cease. At this point he has shown that he intends to exercise his Fifth Amendment privileges; any statement taken after the person invokes his privilege cannot be other than the product of compulsion, subtle or otherwise. Without the right to cut off questioning, the setting of in-custody interrogation operates on the individual to overcome free choice in producing a statement after the privilege has been once invoked. If the individual states that he wants an attorney, the interrogation must cease until an attorney is present. At that time, the individual must have an opportunity to confer with the attorney and to have him present during any subsequent questioning. If the individual cannot obtain an attorney and he indicates that he wants one before speaking to police, they must respect his decision to remain silent.

This does not mean, as some have suggested, that each police station must have a "station house lawyer" present at all times to advise prisoners. It does mean, however, that if police propose to interrogate a person they must make known to him that he is entitled to a lawyer and that if he cannot afford one, a lawyer will be provided for him prior to any interrogation. . . .

If the interrogation continues without the presence of an attorney and a statement is taken, a heavy burden rests on the Government to demonstrate that the defendant knowingly and intelligently waived his privilege against self-incrimination and his right to retained or appointed counsel. . . .

In dealing with statements obtained through interrogation, we do not purport to find all confessions inadmissible. Confessions remain a proper element in law enforcement. Any statement given freely and voluntarily without any compelling influences is, of course, admissible in evidence. The fundamental import of the privilege while an individual is in custody is not whether he is allowed to talk to the police without the benefit of warning and counsel, but whether he can be interrogated. There is no requirement that police stop a person who enters a police station and states that he wishes to confess to a crime, or a person who calls the police to offer a confession or any other statement he desires to make. Volunteered statements of any kind are not barred by the Fifth Amendment and their admissibility is not affected by our holding today.

To summarize, we hold that when an individual is taken into custody or otherwise deprived of his freedom by the authorities and is subjected to questioning, the privilege against self-incrimination is jeopardized. Procedural safeguards must be employed to protect the privilege, and unless other fully effective means are adopted to notify the person of his right of silence and to assure that the exercise of the right will be scrupulously honored, the following measures are required. He must be warned prior to any questioning that he has the right to remain silent, that anything he says can be used against him in a court of law, that he has the right to the presence of an attorney, and that if he cannot afford an attorney one will be appointed for him prior to any questioning if he so desires. Opportunity to exercise these rights must be afforded to him throughout the interrogation. After such warnings have been given, and such opportunity afforded him, the individual may knowingly and intelligently waive these rights and agree to answer questions or make a statement. But unless and until such warnings and waiver are demonstrated by the prosecution at trial, no evidence obtained as a result of interrogation can be used against him.

[Here Chief Justice Warren examines the argument that society's need for interrogation outweighs the privileges.]

. . .

Because of the nature of the problem and because of its recurrent significance in numerous cases, we have to this point discussed the relationship of the Fifth Amendment privilege to police interrogation without specific concentration on the facts of the cases before us. We turn now to these facts to consider the application to these cases of the constitutional principles discussed above. In each instance, we have concluded that statements were obtained from the defendant under circumstances that did not meet constitutional standards for protection of the privilege.

No. 759. Miranda v. Arizona.

On March 13, 1963, petitioner, Ernesto Miranda, was arrested at his home and taken in custody to a Phoenix police station. He was there identified by the complaining witness. The police then took him to Interrogation Room No. 2 of the detective bureau. There he was questioned by two police officers. The officers admitted at trial that Miranda was not advised that he had a right to have an attorney present. Two hours later, the officers emerged from the interrogation room with a written confession signed by Miranda. . . .

At his trial before a jury, the written confession was admitted into evidence over the objection of defense counsel. . . . Miranda was found guilty of kidnapping and rape. . . . On appeal, the Supreme Court of Arizona. . . affirmed the conviction. . . .

We reverse. From the testimony of the officers and by the admission of respondent, it is

clear that Miranda was not in any way apprised of his right to consult with an attorney and to have one present during the interrogation, nor was his right not to be compelled to incriminate himself effectively protected in any other manner. Without these warnings the statements were inadmissible. The mere fact that he signed a statement which contained a typed-in clause stating that he had full knowledge of his legal rights does not approach the knowing and intelligent waiver required to relinquish constitutional rights. . . .

No. 760. Vignera v. New York.

Petitioner, Michael Vignera was picked up by New York police on October 14, 1960, in connection with the robbery three days earlier of a Brooklyn dress shop. . . . [A] detective questioned Vignera with respect to the robbery. Vignera orally admitted the robbery to the detective. The detective was asked on cross-examination at trial by defense counsel whether Vignera was warned of his right to counsel before being interrogated. The prosecution objected to the question and the trial judge sustained the objection. Thus, the defense was precluded from making any showing that warnings had not been given. . . . At Vignera's trial on a charge of first degree robbery, [a] detective testified as to the oral confession. . . . At the conclusion of the testimony, the trial judge charged the jury in part as follows:

> The law doesn't say that the confession is void or invalidated because the police officer didn't advise the defendant as to his rights. Did you hear what I said? I am telling you what the law of the State of New York is.

Vignera was found guilty of first degree robbery. . . . The conviction was affirmed without opinion by the Appellate Division, Second Department . . . and by the Court of Appeals, also without opinion. . . .

We reverse. . . . Vignera . . . was not effectively apprised of his Fifth Amendment privilege or of his right to have counsel present and his statements are inadmissible.

No. 761. Westover v. United States.

At approximately 9:45 p.m. on March 20, 1963, petitioner . . . was arrested by local police in Kansas City as a suspect in two Kansas City robberies. A report was also received from the FBI that he was wanted on a felony charge in California. The local authorities took him to a police station and placed him in a line-up on the local charges, and at about 11:45 p.m. he was booked. Kansas City police interrogated Westover on the night of his arrest. He denied any knowledge of criminal activities. The next day local officers interrogated him again throughout the morning. Shortly before noon they informed the FBI that they were through interrogating Westover and that the FBI could proceed to interrogate him. There is nothing in the record to indicate that Westover was ever given any warning as to his rights by local police. . . .

After two or two and one-half hours, Westover signed separate confessions to each of these two robberies which had been prepared by one of the agents during this interrogation. . . .

Westover was tried by a jury in federal court and convicted of the California robberies. His statements were introduced at trial. . . . On appeal, the conviction was affirmed by the Court of Appeals for the Ninth Circuit. . . .

We reverse. On the facts of this case we cannot find that Westover knowingly and intelligently waived his right to remain silent and his right to consult with proper counsel prior to the time he made the statement. . . .

No. 584. California v. Stewart.

. . . At the time of Stewart's arrest, police also arrested Stewart's wife and three other persons who were visiting him. These four were jailed along with Stewart and were interrogated. Stewart was taken to the University Station of the Los Angeles Police Department where he was placed in a cell. During the next five days, police interrogated Stewart on nine different occasions. Except during the first interrogation session,

when he was confronted with an accusing witness, Stewart was isolated with his interrogators.

During the ninth interrogation session, Stewart admitted that he had robbed the deceased and stated that he had not meant to hurt her. Police then brought Stewart before a magistrate for the first time. Since there was no evidence to connect them with any crime, the police then released the other four persons arrested with him.

Nothing in the record specifically indicates whether Stewart was or was not advised of his right to remain silent or his right to counsel. . . .

. . . At his trial, transcripts of the first interrogation and the confession at the last interrogation were introduced in evidence. The jury found Stewart guilty of robbery and first degree murder and fixed the penalty as death. On appeal, the Supreme Court of California reversed. . . . It held that under this Court's decision in *Escobedo*, Stewart should have been advised of his right to remain silent and of his right to counsel and that it would not presume in the face of a silent record that the police advised Stewart of his rights.

We affirm. In dealing with custodial interrogation, we will not presume that a defendant has been effectively apprised of his rights and that his privilege against self-incrimination has been adequately safeguarded on a record that does not show that any warnings have been given or that any effective alternative has been employed. . . .

Therefore, in accordance with the foregoing, the judgments [below] . . . are reversed. It is so ordered.

MR. JUSTICE CLARK'S *opinion dissenting in Nos. 759, 760, and 761, and concurring in the result in No. 584 is not reprinted here.*

MR. JUSTICE HARLAN, *whom* MR. JUSTICE STEWART *and* MR. JUSTICE WHITE *join, dissenting.*

I believe the decision of the Court represents poor constitutional law and entails harmful consequences for the country at large. How serious these consequences may prove to be only time can tell. But the basic flaws in the Court's justification seem to me readily apparent now once all sides of the problem are considered.

. . .

While the fine points of this scheme [the majority's requirement of warnings in interrogation] are far less clear than the Court admits, the tenor is quite apparent. The new rules are not designed to guard against police brutality or other unmistakably banned forms of coercion. Those who use third-degree tactics and deny them in court are equally able and destined to lie as skillfully about warnings and waivers. Rather, the thrust of the new rules is to negate all pressures, to reinforce the nervous or ignorant suspect, and ultimately to discourage any confession at all. The aim in short is toward "voluntariness" in a utopian sense, or to view it from a different angle, voluntariness with a vengeance.

To incorporate this notion into the Constitution requires a strained reading of history and precedent and a disregard of the very pragmatic concerns that alone may on occasion justify such strains. I believe that reasoned examination will show that the Due Process Clauses provide an adequate tool for coping with confessions and that, even if the Fifth Amendment privilege against self-incrimination be invoked, its precedents taken as a whole do not sustain the present rules. Viewed as a choice based on pure policy, these new rules prove to be a highly debatable if not one-sided appraisal of the competing interests imposed over widespread objection, at the very time when judicial restraint is most called for by the circumstances. . . .

The Court's new rules aim to offset . . . minor pressures and disadvantages intrinsic to any kind of police interrogation. . . . The rules work for reliability in confessions almost only in the Pickwickian sense that they can prevent some from being given at all. . . .

What the Court largely ignores is that its rules impair, if they will not eventually serve wholly to frustrate, an instrument of law enforcement that has long and quite reasonably been thought worth the price paid for it. There can be little doubt that the Court's new code would markedly decrease the number of confessions. To warn the suspect that he may remain silent and remind him that his confession may be used in court are minor obstructions. To require also an express waiver by the suspect and an end to questioning whenever he demurs must heavily handicap questioning. And to suggest or provide counsel for the suspect simply invites the end of the interrogation. . . .

How much harm this decision will inflict on law enforcement cannot fairly be predicted with accuracy. Evidence on the role of confessions is notoriously incomplete. . . . We do know that some crimes cannot be solved without confessions, that ample expert testimony attests to their importance in crime control, and that the Court is taking a real risk with society's welfare in imposing its new regime on the country. The social costs of crime are too great to call the new rules anything but a hazardous experimentation.

While passing over the costs and risks of its experiment, the Court portrayed the evils of normal police questioning in terms which I think are exaggerated. Albeit stringently confined by the due process standards interrogation is no doubt often inconvenient and unpleasant for the suspect. However, it is no less so for a man to be arrested and jailed, to have his house searched, or to stand trial in court, yet all this may properly happen to the most innocent given probable cause, a warrant, or an indictment. Society has always paid a stiff price for law and order, and peaceful interrogation is not one of the dark moments of the law.

. . .

In closing this necessarily truncated discussion of policy considerations attending the new confession rules, some reference must be made to their ironic untimeliness. There is now in progress in this country a massive reexamination of criminal law enforcement procedures on a scale never before witnessed. . . .

It is no secret that concern has been expressed lest long-range and lasting reforms be frustrated by this Court's too rapid departure from existing constitutional standards. Despite the Court's disclaimer, the practical effect of the decision made today must inevitably be to handicap seriously sound efforts at reform. . . .

. . . I would adhere to the due process test and reject the new requirements inaugurated by the Court. On this premise my disposition of each of these cases can be stated briefly.

In two of the three cases coming from state courts, *Miranda* v. *Arizona* (No. 759) and *Vignera* v. *New York* (No. 760), the confessions were held admissible and no other errors worth comment are alleged by petitioners. I would affirm in these two cases. The other state case is *California* v. *Stewart* (No. 584) where the state supreme court held the confession inadmissible and reversed the conviction. In that case I would dismiss the writ of certiorari on the ground that no final judgment is before us. . . . If the merits of the decision in *Stewart* be reached, then I believe it should be reversed and the case remanded so the state supreme court may pass on the other claims available to respondent.

In the federal case, *Westover* v. *United States* (No. 761) . . . [i]t is urged that the confession was . . . inadmissible because not voluntary even measured by due process standards and because federal-state cooperation brought the *McNabb-Mallory* rule into play under *Anderson* v. *United States*, 318 U.S. 350. . . . However, the facts alleged fall well short of coercion in my view, and I believe the involvement of federal agents in petitioner's arrest and detention by the State too slight to invoke *Anderson*. . . . I would therefore affirm Westover's conviction.

In conclusion: Nothing in the letter or the spirit of the Constitution or in the precedents squares with the heavy handed and one-sided action that is so precipitously taken by the Court in the name of fulfilling its constitutional responsibilities. The foray which the Court takes today brings to mind the wise and farsighted words of Mr. Justice Jackson in *Douglas* v. *City of Jeanette,* 319 U.S. 157 . . . (separate opinion): "This Court is forever adding new stories to the temples of constitutional law, and the temples have a way of collapsing when one story too many is added. " . . .

The dissenting opinion of MR. JUSTICE WHITE, *with whom* MR. JUSTICE HARLAN *and* MR. JUSTICE STEWART *joined is omitted.*

HARRIS v. NEW YORK
401 U.S. 222; 28 L. Ed. 2d 1; 91 S. Ct. 643 (1971)

MR. CHIEF JUSTICE BURGER *delivered the opinion of the Court.*

We granted the writ in this case to consider petitioner's claim that a statement made by him to police under circumstances rendering it inadmissible to establish the prosecution's case in chief under *Miranda* v. *Arizona* . . . may not be used to impeach his credibility.

The State of New York charged petitioner . . . with twice selling heroin to an undercover police officer. At a subsequent jury trial the officer was the State's chief witness, and he testified as to details of the two sales. . . .

Petitioner took the stand in his own defense. He admitted knowing the undercover police officer but denied a sale on January 4, 1966. He admitted making a sale of contents of a glassine bag to the officer on January 6 but claimed it was baking powder and part of a scheme to defraud the purchaser.

On cross-examination petitioner was asked seriatim whether he had made specified statements to the police immediately following his arrest on January 7—statements that partially contradicted petitioner's direct testimony at trial. In response to the cross-examination, petitioner testified that he could not remember virtually any of the questions or answers recited by the prosecutor. At the request of petitioner's counsel the written statement from which the prosecutor had read questions and answers in his impeaching process was placed in the record for possible use on appeal; the statement was not shown to the jury.

The trial judge instructed the jury that the statements attributed to petitioner by the prosecution could be considered only in passing on petitioner's credibility and not as evidence of guilt. In closing summations both counsel argued the substance of the impeaching statements. The jury then found petitioner guilty.... The New York Court of Appeals affirmed....

At trial the prosecution made no effort in its case in chief to use the statements allegedly made by petitioner, conceding that they were inadmissible under *Miranda* v. *Arizona*. ... The transcript of the interrogation used in the impeachment, but not given to the jury, shows that no warning of a right to appointed counsel was given before questions were put to petitioner when he was taken into custody. Petitioner makes no claim that the statements made to the police were coerced or involuntary.

Some comments in the *Miranda* opinion can indeed be read as indicating a bar to use of an uncounseled statement for any purpose, but discussion of that issue was not at all necessary to the Court's holding and cannot be regarded as controlling. *Miranda* barred the prosecution from making its case with statements of an accused made while in custody prior to having or effectively waiving counsel. It does not follow from *Miranda* that evidence inadmissible against an accused in the prosecution's case in chief is barred for all purposes, provided of course that the trustworthiness of the evidence satisfies legal standards.

In *Walder* v. *United States*, 347 U.S. 62, the Court permitted physical evidence, inadmissible in the case in chief, to be used for impeachment purposes.

"It is one thing to say that the Government cannot make an affirmative use of evidence unlawfully obtained. It is quite another to say that the defendant can turn the illegal method by which evidence in the Government's possession was obtained to his own advantage, and provide himself with a shield against contradiction of his untruths. Such an extension of the *Weeks* doctrine would be a perversion of the Fourth Amendment. . . ."

It is true that Walder was impeached as to collateral matters included in his direct examination, whereas petitioner here was impeached as to testimony bearing more directly on the crimes charged. We are not persuaded that there is a difference in principle that warrants a result different from that reached by the Court in *Walder*. Petitioner's testimony in his own behalf concerning the events of January 7 contrasted sharply with what he told the police shortly after his arrest. The impeachment process here undoubtedly provided valuable aid to the jury in assessing petitioner's credibility, and the benefits of this process should not be lost, in our view, because of the speculative possibility that impermissible police conduct will be encouraged thereby. Assuming that the exclusionary rule has a deterrent effect on proscribed police conduct, sufficient deterrence flows when the evidence in question is made unavailable to the prosecution in its case in chief.

Every criminal defendant is privileged to testify in his own defense, or to refuse to do so. But that privilege cannot be construed to include the right to commit perjury.... Having voluntarily taken the stand, petitioner was under an obligation to speak truthfully and accurately, and the prosecution here did no more than utilize the traditional truth-testing devices of the adversary process. . . .

The shield provided by *Miranda* cannot be perverted into a license to use perjury by way of a defense, free from the risk of confrontation with prior inconsistent utterances. We hold, therefore, that petitioner's credibility was appropriately impeached by use of his earlier conflicting statements.

Affirmed.

MR. JUSTICE BLACK *[dissented without opinion]*.

MR. JUSTICE BRENNAN, *with whom* MR. JUSTICE DOUGLAS *and* MR. JUSTICE MARSHALL *join, dissenting.*

It is conceded that the question-and-answer statement used to impeach petitioner's direct testimony was, under *Miranda* v. *Arizona* . . . constitutionally inadmissible as part of the State's direct case against petitioner. I think that the Constitution also denied the State the use of the statement on cross-examination to impeach the credibility of petitioner's testimony given in his own defense. The decision in *Walder* v. *United States* [*supra*] is not, as the Court today holds, dispositive to the contrary. Rather, that case supports my conclusion.

The State's case against Harris depended upon the jury's belief of the testimony of the undercover agent that petitioner "sold" the officer heroin on January 4 and again on January 6. Petitioner took the stand and flatly denied having sold anything to the officer on January 4. He countered the officer's testimony as to the January 6 sale with testimony that he had sold the officer two glassine bags containing what appeared to be heroin, but that actually the bags contained only baking powder intended to deceive the officer in order to obtain $12. The statement contradicted petitioner's direct testimony as to the events of both days. The statement's version of the events on January 4 was that the officer had used petitioner as a middleman to buy some heroin from a third person with money furnished by the officer. The version of the events on January 6 was that petitioner had again acted for the officer in buying two bags of heroin from a third person for which petitioner received $12 and a part of the heroin. Thus, it is clear that the statement was used to impeach petitioner's direct testimony not on collateral matters but on matters directly related to the crimes for which he was on trial.

Walder v. *United States* was not a case where tainted evidence was used to impeach an accused's direct testimony on matters directly related to the case against him. In *Walder* the evidence was used to impeach the accused's testimony on matters *collateral* to the crime charged. Walder had been indicted in 1950 for purchasing and possessing heroin. When his motion to suppress use of the narcotics as illegally seized was granted, the Government dismissed the prosecution. Two years later Walder was indicted for another narcotics violation completely unrelated to the 1950 one. Testifying in his own defense, he said on direct examination that he had never in his life possessed narcotics. On cross-examination he denied that law enforcement officers had seized narcotics from his home two years earlier. The Government was then permitted to introduce the testimony of one of the officers involved in the 1950 seizure, that when he had raided Walder's home at that time he had seized narcotics there.

The Court held that on facts where "the defendant went beyond a mere denial of complicity in the crimes of which he was charged and made the sweeping claim that he had never dealt in or possessed any narcotics," . . . the exclusionary rule of *Weeks* v. *United States* . . . would not extend to bar the Government from rebutting this testimony with evidence, although tainted, that petitioner had in fact possessed narcotics two years before. The Court was careful, however, to distinguish the situation of an accused whose testimony, as in the instant case, was a "denial of complicity in the crimes of which he was charged," that is, where illegally obtained evidence was used to impeach the accused's direct testimony on matters directly related to the case against him. . . .

From this recital of facts it is clear that the evidence used for impeachment in *Walder* was related to the earlier 1950 prosecution and had no direct bearing on "the elements of the case" being tried in 1952. The evidence tended solely to impeach the credibility of the defendant's direct testimony that he had never in his life possessed heroin. But that evidence was completely unrelated to the indictment on trial and did not in any way interfere with his freedom to deny all elements of that case against him. In contrast, here, the evidence used for impeachment, a statement concerning the details of the very sales alleged in the indictment, was directly related to the case against petitioner. . . .

[T]he Fifth Amendment's privilege against self-incrimination . . . is fulfilled only when an accused is guaranteed the right "to remain silent unless he chooses to speak in the *unfettered* exercise of his own will." The choice of whether to testify in one's own defense must therefore be "unfettered," since that choice is an exercise of the constitutional privilege [which] forbids the prosecution to use a tainted statement to impeach the accused who takes the stand. The prosecution's use of the tainted statement "cuts down on the privilege by making its assertion costly." Thus, the accused is denied an "unfettered" choice when the decision whether to take the stand is burdened by the risk that an illegally obtained prior statement may be introduced to impeach his direct testimony denying complicity in the crime charged against him. We settled this proposition in *Miranda* where we said: "The

privilege against self-incrimination protects the individual from being compelled to incriminate himself in any manner. . . . [S]tatements merely intended to be exculpatory by the defendant are often used to impeach his testimony at trial. . . . These statements are incriminating in any meaningful sense of the word and may not be used without the full warnings and effective waiver required for any other statement." . . .

This language completely disposes of any distinction between statements used on direct as opposed to cross-examination. "An incriminating statement is as incriminating when used to impeach credibility as it is when used as direct proof of guilt and no constitutional distinction can legitimately be drawn."

The objective of deterring improper police conduct is only part of the larger objective of safeguarding the integrity of our adversary system. . . . [T]he constitutional foundation underlying the privilege [against self-incrimination] is the respect a government . . . must accord to the dignity and integrity of its citizens." These values are plainly jeopardized if an exception against admission of tainted statements is made for those used for impeachment purposes. Moreover, it is monstrous that courts should aid or abet the lawbreaking police officer. . . . Thus, even to the extent that *Miranda* was aimed at deterring police practices in disregard of the Constitution, I fear that today's holding will seriously undermine the achievement of that objective. The Court today tells the police that they may freely interrogate an accused incommunicado and without counsel and know that although any statement they obtain in violation of *Miranda* cannot be used on the State's direct case, it may be introduced if the defendant has the temerity to testify in his own defense. This goes far toward undoing much of the progress made in conforming police methods to the Constitution. I dissent.

IN RE GAULT
387 U.S. 1; 18 L. Ed. 2d 527; 87 S. Ct. 1428 (1967)

MR. JUSTICE FORTAS *delivered the opinion of the Court.*

This is an appeal under 28 U.S.C. Sec. 1257(2) from a judgment of the Supreme Court of Arizona affirming the dismissal of a petition for a writ of habeas corpus. . . . The petition sought the release of Gerald Francis Gault, petitioners' 15-year-old son, who had been committed as a juvenile delinquent to the State Industrial School by the Juvenile Court of Gila County, Arizona. The Supreme Court of Arizona affirmed dismissal of the writ. . . . The court agreed that the constitutional guarantee of due process of law is applicable in such proceedings. It held that Arizona's Juvenile Code is to be read as "impliedly" implementing the "due process concept." . . . It concluded that the proceedings ending in commitment of Gerald Gault did not offend those requirements. We do not agree, and we reverse. We begin with a statement of the facts.

On Monday, June 8, 1964, at about 10 A.M., Gerald Francis Gault and a friend, Ronald Lewis, were taken into custody by the Sheriff of Gila County. Gerald was then still subject to a six months' probation order. . . . The police action on June 8 was taken as the result of a verbal complaint by a neighbor of the boys, Mrs. Cook, about a telephone call made to her in which the caller or callers made lewd or indecent remarks. It will suffice for the purposes of this opinion to say that the remarks or questions put to her were of the irritatingly offensive, adolescent, sex variety.

At the time Gerald was picked up, his mother and father were both at work. No notice that Gerald was being taken into custody was left at the home. No other steps were taken to advise them that their son had, in effect, been arrested. Gerald was taken to the Children's Detention Home. . . . The deputy probation officer, Flagg, who was also superintendent of the Detention Home told Mrs. Gault "why Jerry was there" and said that a hearing would be held in Juvenile Court at 3 o'clock the following day, June 9.

Officer Flagg filed a petition with the Court on the hearing day, June 9, 1964. It was not served on the Gaults. Indeed, none of them saw this petition until the habeas corpus hearing on August 17, 1964. The petition was certainly formal. It made no reference to any factual basis for the judicial action which it initiated. It recited only that "said minor is under the age of 18 years and in need of the protection of this Honorable Court [and that] said minor is a delinquent minor." It prayed for a hearing and an order regarding "the care and custody of said minor." . . .

On June 9, Gerald, his mother, his older brother, and Probation Officers Flagg and Henderson appeared before the Juvenile Judge in chambers. Gerald's father was not there. He was at work out of the city. Mrs. Cook, the complainant, was not there. No one was sworn at this hearing. No transcript or recording was made. No memorandum or record of the substance of the proceedings was prepared. Our information about the proceedings and the subsequent hearing on June 15, derives entirely from the testimony of the Juvenile Court Judge, Mr. and Mrs. Gault, and Officer Flagg at the habeas corpus proceedings conducted two months later. From this, it appears that at the July 9 hearing

Gerald was questioned by the judge about the telephone call. There was conflict as to what he said. His mother recalled that Gerald said he only dialed Mrs. Cook's number and then handed the telephone to his friend, Ronald. Officer Flagg recalled that Gerald had admitted making the lewd remarks. Judge McGhee testified that Gerald "admitted making one of these [lewd] statements." At the conclusion of the hearing, the judge said he would "think about it." Gerald was taken back to the Detention Home. . . . On June 11 or 12, after having been detained since June 8, Gerald was released and driven home.* There is no explanation in the record as to why he was kept in the Detention Home or why he was released. At 5 P.M. on the day of Gerald's release, Mrs. Gault received a note signed by Officer Flagg. It was on plain paper, not letterhead. Its entire text is as follows:

"Mr. Gault:

Judge McGhee has set Monday June 15, 1964 at 11:00 A.M. as the date and time for further hearings on Gerald's delinquency.

/s/Flagg"

At the appointed time on Monday, June 15, Gerald, his father and mother, Ronald Lewis and his father, and Officers Flagg and Henderson were present before Judge McGhee. Witnesses at the habeas corpus proceedings differed in their recollections of Gerald's testimony at the June 15 hearing. Mr. and Mrs. Gault recalled that Gerald again testified that he had only dialed the number and that the other boy had made the remarks. Officer Flagg agreed that at this hearing Gerald did not admit making the lewd remarks. But Judge McGhee recalled that "there was some admission again of some of the lewd statements.

*There is a conflict between the recollection of Mrs. Gault and that of Officer Flagg. Mrs. Gault testified that Gerald was released on Friday, June 12, Officer Flagg that it had been on Thursday, June 11. This was from memory; he had no record, and the note was undated.

He—he didn't admit any of the more serious lewd statements." Again, the complainant, Mrs. Cook, was not present. Mrs. Gault asked that Mrs. Cook be present "so she could see which boy had done the talking, the dirty talking over the phone." The Juvenile Judge said "she didn't have to be present at that hearing." The judge did not speak to Mrs. Cook or communicate with her at any time. Probation Officer Flagg had talked to her once—over the telephone on June 9.

At this June 15 hearing a "referral report" made by the probation officers was filed with the court, although not disclosed to Gerald or his parents. This listed the charge as "Lewd Phone Calls." At the conclusion of the hearing, the judge committed Gerald as a juvenile delinquent to the State Industrial School "for the period of his minority (that is, until 21), unless sooner discharged by the process of law." . . .

No appeal is permitted by Arizona law in juvenile cases. On August 3, 1964, a petition for a writ of habeas corpus was filed with the Supreme Court of Arizona and referred by it to the Superior Court for hearing.

At the habeas corpus hearing on August 17, Judge McGhee was vigorously cross-examined as to the basis for his actions. He testified that he had taken into account the fact that Gerald was on probation. He was asked "under what section of . . . the code you found the boy delinquent?" . . .

. . . In substance, he concluded that Gerald came within [the state statute] which specifies that a "delinquent child" includes one "who has violated a law of the state or an ordinance or regulation of a political subdivision thereof." . . . The judge also testified that he acted under [the statutory provision] which includes in the definition of a "delinquent child" one who, as the judge phrased it, is "habitually involved in immoral matters." . . .

The Superior Court dismissed the writ, and appellants sought review in the Arizona Supreme Court. . . .

The Supreme Court handed down an elaborate and wide-ranging opinion affirming dismissal of the writ. . . . [Appellants] urge that we hold the Juvenile Code of Arizona invalid on its face or as applied in this case because, contrary to the Due Process Clause of the Fourteenth Amendment, the juvenile is taken from the custody of his parents and committed to a state institution pursuant to proceedings in which the Juvenile Court has virtually unlimited discretion, and in which the following basic rights are denied:

1. Notice of the charges;
2. Right to counsel;
3. Right to confrontation and cross-examination;
4. Privilege against self-incrimination;
5. Right to a transcript of the proceedings; and
6. Right to appellate review.

. . .

This Court has not heretofore decided the precise question. In *Kent* v. *United States,* 383 U.S. 541, 86 S.Ct. 1045, 16 L.Ed. 2d 84 (1966), we considered the requirements for a valid waiver of the "exclusive" jurisdiction of the Juvenile Court of the District of Columbia so that a juvenile could be tried in the adult criminal court of the District. . . . [We] emphasized the necessity that "the basic requirements of due process and fairness" be satisfied in such proceedings. *Hale* v. *State of Ohio,* 332 U.S. 596, 68 S.Ct. 302, 92 L.Ed. 224 (1948), involved the admissibility, in a state criminal court of general jurisdiction, of a confession of a 15-year-old boy. The Court held that the Fourteenth Amendment applied to prohibit the use of the coerced confession. Mr. Justice Douglas said, "Neither man nor child can be allowed to stand condemned by methods which flout constitutional requirements of due process of law." . . . Accordingly, while these cases relate only to restricted aspects of the subject, they unmistakably indicate that, whatever may be their precise

impact, neither the Fourteenth Amendment nor the Bill of Rights is for adults alone.

. . .

From the inception of the juvenile court system, wide differences have been tolerated—indeed insisted upon—between the procedural rights accorded to adults and those of juveniles. In practically all jurisdictions, there are rights granted to adults which are withheld from juveniles. In addition to the specific problems involved in the present case, for example, it has been held that the juvenile is not entitled to bail, to indictment by grand jury, to a public trial or to trial by jury. It is frequent practice that rules governing the arrest and interrogation of adults by the police are not observed in the case of juveniles.

. . .

The right of the State, as *parens patriae*, to deny to the child procedural rights available to his elders was elaborated by the assertion that a child, unlike an adult, has a right "not to liberty but to custody." He can be made to attorn to his parents, to go to school, etc. If his parents default in effectively performing their custodial functions—that is, if the child is "delinquent"—the state may intervene. In doing so, it does not deprive the child of any rights, because he has none. It merely provides the "custody" to which the child is entitled. On this basis, proceedings involving juveniles were described as "civil" not "criminal" and therefore not subject to the requirements which restrict the state when it seeks to deprive a person of his liberty.

. . . Juvenile court history has . . . demonstrated that unbridled discretion, however benevolently motivated, is frequently a poor substitute for principle and procedure. . . . The absence of substantive standards has not necessarily meant that children receive careful, compassionate, individualized treatment. The absence of procedural rules based upon constitutional principle has not always produced fair, efficient, and effective procedures. Departures from established principles of due process have frequently resulted not in enlightened procedure, but in arbitrariness.

. . .

. . . [I]t is urged that the juvenile benefits from informal proceedings in the court. The early conception of the juvenile court proceeding was one in which a fatherly judge touched the heart and conscience of the erring youth by talking over his problems, by paternal advice and admonition, and in which, in extreme situations, benevolent and wise institutions of the State provided guidance and help "to save him from a downward career." Then, as now, goodwill and compassion were admirably prevalent. But recent studies have, with surprising unanimity, entered sharp dissent as to the validity of this gentle conception. They suggest that the appearance as well as the actuality of fairness, the partiality and orderliness—in short, the essentials of due process may be a more impressive and more therapeutic attitude so far as the juvenile is concerned. . . . While due process requirements will, in some instances, introduce a degree of order and regularity to juvenile court proceedings to determine delinquency, and in contested cases will introduce some elements of the adversary system, nothing will require that the conception of the kindly juvenile judge be replaced by its opposite, nor do we here rule upon the question whether ordinary due process requirements must be observed with respect to hearings to determine the disposition of the delinquent child.

Ultimately, however, we confront the reality of that portion of the juvenile court process with which we deal in this case. A boy is charged with misconduct. The boy is committed to an institution where he may be restrained of liberty for years. It is of no constitutional consequence—and of limited practical meaning—that the institution to which he is committed is called an Industrial School. The fact of the matter is that, however euphemistic the title, a "receiving home" or an "industrial school" for juveniles is an institution of confinement in which the child is incarcerated for a greater or lesser time. His world becomes "a building with white-washed walls, regimented routine and institutional laws. . . ." Instead of mother and father and sisters and brothers and friends and classmates, his world is peopled by guards, custodians, state employees, and "delinquents" confined with him for anything from waywardness to rape and homicide.

In view of this, it would be extraordinary if our Constitution did not require the procedural regularity and the exercise of care implied in the phrase "due process." Under our Constitution, the condition of a boy does not justify a kangaroo court. The traditional ideas of juvenile court procedure, indeed, contemplated that time would be available and care would be used to establish precisely what the juvenile did and why he did it—was it a prank of adolescence or a brutal act threatening serious consequences to himself or society unless corrected? Under traditional notions, one would assume that in a case like that of Gerald Gault, where the juvenile appears to have a home, a working mother and father, and an older brother, the Juvenile Judge would have made a careful inquiry and judgment as to the possibility that the boy could be disciplined and dealt with at home, despite his previous transgressions. Indeed, so far as appears in the record before us, except for some conversation with Gerald about his school work and his "wanting to go to . . . Grand Canyon with his father," the points to which the judge directed his attention were little different from those that would be involved in determining any charge of violation of a penal statute. The essential difference between Gerald's case and a normal criminal case is that safeguards available to adults were discarded in Gerald's case. The summary procedure as well as the long commitment were possible because Gerald was 15 years of age instead of over 18.

If Gerald had been over 18, he would not have been subject to Juvenile Court proceedings. For the particular offense immediately involved, the maximum punishment would have been a fine of $5 to $50, or imprisonment in jail for not more than two months. Instead, he was committed to custody for a maximum of six years. If he had been over 18 and had committed an offense to which such a sentence might apply, he would have been entitled to substantial rights under the Constitution of the United States as well as under Arizona's laws and constitution. The United States Constitution would guarantee him rights and protections with respect to arrest, search, [sic] and seizure, and pretrial interrogation. It would assure him of specific notice of the charges and adequate time to decide his course of action and to prepare his defense. He would be entitled to clear advice that he could be represented by counsel, and, at least if a felony were involved, the State would be required to provide counsel if his parents were unable to afford it. If the court acted on the basis of his confession, careful procedures would be required to assure its voluntariness. If the case went to trial, confrontation and opportunity for cross examination would be guaranteed. So wide a gulf between the State's treatment of the adult and of the child requires a bridge sturdier than mere verbiage, and reasons more persuasive than cliché can provide. . . .

We now turn to the specific issues which are presented to us in the present case.

Notice of Charges

. . .

We cannot agree with the court's conclusion that adequate notice was given in this case. Notice, to comply with due process requirements, must be given sufficiently in advance of scheduled court proceedings so that reasonable opportunity to prepare will be afforded, and it must "set forth the alleged misconduct with particularity." . . . The "initial hearing" in the present case was a hearing on the merits. Notice at that time is not timely; and even if there were a conceivable purpose served by the deferral proposed by the court below, it would have to yield to the requirements that the child and his parents or guardian be notified, in writing, of the specific charge or factual allegations to be considered at the hearing, and that such written notice be given at the earliest practicable time, and in any event sufficiently in advance of the hearing to permit preparation. Due process of law requires notice of the sort we have described—that is, notice which would be deemed constitutionally adequate in a civil or criminal proceeding. . . . .

Right To Counsel

Appellants charge that the Juvenile Court proceedings were fatally defective because the court did not advise Gerald or his parents of their right to counsel, and proceeded with the hearing, the adjudication of delinquency and the order of commitment in the absence of counsel. . . . The Supreme Court of Arizona pointed out that "[t]here is disagreement [among the various jurisdictions] as to whether the court must advise the infant that he has a right to counsel." . . . It referred to a provision of the Juvenile Code which it characterized as requiring "that the probation officer shall look after the interests of neglected, delinquent and dependent children," including representing their interests in court. The court argued that "The parent and the probation officer may be relied upon to protect the infant's interests." . . . It said that juvenile courts have the discretion, but not the duty, to allow such representation. . . . We do not agree. Probation officers, in the Arizona scheme, are also arresting officers. They initiate proceedings and file petitions which they verify . . . alleging the delinquency of the child; and they test-ify . . . against the child. And here the probation officer was also superintendent of the Detention Home. The probation officer cannot act as counsel for the child. His role in the adjudicatory hearing, by statute and in fact, is as arresting officer and witness against the child. Nor can the judge represent the child. . . . A proceeding where the issue is whether the child will be found to be "delinquent" and subjected to the loss of his liberty for years is comparable in seriousness to a felony prosecution. The juvenile needs the assistance of counsel to cope with problems of law, to make skilled inquiry into the facts, to insist upon regularity of the proceedings, and to ascertain whether he has a defense and to prepare and submit it. The child "requires the guiding hand of counsel at every step in the proceedings against him."

. . .

Confrontation, Self-incrimination, Cross-Examination

Appellants urge that the writ of habeas corpus should have been granted because of the denial of the rights of confrontation and cross-examina-tion in the Juvenile Court hearings, and because the privilege against self-incrimination was not observed. . . .

Our first question, then, is whether Gerald's admission was improperly obtained and relied on as the basis of decision, in conflict with the Federal Constitution. For this purpose, it is necessary briefly to recall the relevant facts.

Mrs. Cook, the complainant, and the recipient of the alleged telephone call, was not called as a witness. Gerald's mother asked the Juvenile Court Judge why Mrs. Cook was not present and the judge replied that "she didn't have to be present." So far as appears, Mrs. Cook was spoken to only once, by Officer Flagg, and this was by telephone. . . . Gerald had been ques-tioned by the probation officer after having been

taken into custody. The exact circumstances of this questioning do not appear in the record. Gerald was also questioned by the Juvenile Court Judge at each of the two hearings. The judge testified in the habeas corpus proceeding that Gerald admitted making "some of the lewd statements . . . [but not] any of the more serious lewd statements." . . .

We shall assume that Gerald made admissions of the sort described by the Juvenile Court Judge. . . . Neither Gerald nor his parents was advised that he did not have to testify or make a statement, or that an incriminating state-ment might result in his commitment as a "delinquent." . . .

. . . Specifically, the question is whether, in such a proceeding, an admission by the juvenile may be used against him in the absence of clear and unequivocal evidence that the admission was made with knowledge that he was not obligated to speak and would not be penalized for re-maining silent. In light of *Miranda* v. *Ari-zona,* . . . we must also consider whether, if the privilege against self-incrimination is available, it can effectively be waived unless counsel is present or the right to counsel has been waived.

. . .

It would indeed be surprising if the privilege against self-incrimination were available to hard-ened criminals but not to children. The language of the Fifth Amendment . . . is unequivocal and without exception. And the scope of the privi-lege is comprehensive.

. . .

Against the application to juveniles of the right to silence, it is argued that juvenile pro-ceedings are "civil" and not "criminal," and therefore the privilege should not apply. It is true that the statement of the privilege in the Fifth Amendment . . . is that no person "shall be com-pelled in any *criminal* case to be a witness against himself." However, it is also clear that the availability of the privilege does not turn upon the type of proceeding in which its protection is invoked, but upon the nature of the statement or admission and the exposure which it invites. . . .

It would be entirely unrealistic to carve out of the Fifth Amendment all statements by juveniles on the ground that these cannot lead to "criminal" involvement. . . . [J]uvenile proceedings to determine "delinquency," which may lead to commitment to a state institution, must be regarded as "criminal" for purposes of the privilege against self-incrimination. To hold otherwise would be to disregard substance because of the feeble enticement of the "civil" label-of-convenience which has been attached to juvenile proceedings. Instead, in over half of the States, there is not even assurance that the juvenile will be kept in separate institutions, apart from adult "criminals." . . . For this purpose, at least, commitment is a deprivation of liberty. It is incarceration against one's will, whether it is called "criminal" or "civil."

. . .

We conclude that the constitutional privilege against self-incrimination is applicable in the case of juveniles as it is with respect to adults. We appreciate that special problems may arise with respect to waiver of the privilege by or on behalf of children, and that there may well be some differences in techniques—but not in principle—depending upon the age of the child and the presence and competence of parents. The participation of counsel will, of course, assist the police, juvenile courts and appellate courts in administering the privilege. If counsel is not present for some permissible reason when an admission is obtained, the greatest care must be taken to assure that the admission was voluntary, in the sense not only that it has not been coerced or suggested, but also that it is not the product of ignorance of rights or of adolescent fantasy, fright or despair.

. . .

. . . We now hold that, absent a valid confession, a determination of delinquency and an order of commitment to a state institution cannot be sustained in the absence of sworn testimony subjected to the opportunity for cross-examination in accordance with our law and constitutional requirements.

. . .

Judgment reversed and cause remanded with directions.

MR. JUSTICE BLACK *and* MR. JUSTICE WHITE *wrote separate concurring opinions which are not reprinted here.*

MR. JUSTICE STEWART, *dissenting.*

The Court today uses an obscure Arizona case as a vehicle to impose upon thousands of juvenile courts throughout the Nation restrictions that the Constitution made applicable to adversary criminal trials. I believe the Court's decision is wholly unsound as a matter of constitutional law, and sadly unwise as a matter of judicial policy. Whether treating with a delinquent child, a neglected child, a defective child, or a dependent child, a juvenile proceeding's whole purpose and mission is the very opposite of the mission and purpose of a prosecution in a criminal court. The object of the one is the correction of a condition. The object of the other is conviction and punishment for a criminal act.

. . .

The inflexible restrictions that the Constitution so wisely made applicable to adversary criminal trials have no inevitable place in the proceedings of those public social agencies known as juvenile or family courts. And to impose the Court's long catalog of requirements upon the country is to invite a long step backwards into the Nineteenth Century. In that era there were no juvenile proceedings, and a child was tried in a conventional criminal court with all the trappings of a conventional trial. So it was that a 12-year-old boy named James Guild was tried in New Jersey for killing Catherine Beakes. A jury found him guilty of murder, and he was sentenced to death by hanging. The sentence was executed. It was all very constitutional.

A state in all its dealings must, of course, accord every person due process of law. And due process may require that some of the restrictions which the Constitution has placed upon criminal trials must be imposed upon juvenile proceedings. For example, I suppose that all would agree that a brutally coerced confession could not constitutionally be considered in a juvenile court hearing. But it surely does not follow that the testimonial privilege against self-incrimination is applicable in all juvenile proceedings. Similarly, due process clearly requires timely notice of the purpose and scope of any proceedings affecting the relationship of parent and child.... But it certainly does not follow that notice of a juvenile hearing must be framed with all the technical niceties of a criminal indictment. . . .

In any event, there is no reason to deal with issues such as these in the present case. The Supreme Court of Arizona found that the parents of Gerald Gault "knew of their right to counsel, to subpoena and cross examine witnesses against Gerald and the possible consequences of a finding of delinquency." . . . It further found that "Mrs. Gault knew the exact nature of the charge against Gerald from the day he was taken to the detention home." . . . And . . . no issue of compulsory self-incrimination is presented by this case.

I would dismiss the appeal.

APODACA v. OREGON
406 U.S. 404; 32 L.Ed.2d 184; 92 S.Ct. 1628 (1972)

MR. JUSTICE WHITE *announced the judgment of the Court in an opinion in which* THE CHIEF JUSTICE, MR. JUSTICE BLACKMUN, *and* MR. JUSTICE REHNQUIST *joined.*

Robert Apodaca, Henry Morgan Cooper, Jr., and James Arnold Madden were convicted respectively of assault with a deadly weapon, burglary in a dwelling, and grand larceny before separate Oregon juries, all of which returned less than unanimous verdicts. The vote in the cases of Apodaca and Madden was 11-1, while the vote in the case of Cooper was 10-2, the minimum requisite vote under Oregon law for sustaining a conviction. After their convictions had been affirmed by the Oregon Court of Appeals and review had been denied by the Supreme Court of Oregon, all three sought review in this Court upon a claim that conviction of crime by less than unanimous jury violates the right to trial by jury in criminal cases specified by the Sixth Amendment and made applicable to the States by the Fourteenth. We granted certiorari to consider this claim which we now find to be without merit.

In *Williams* v. *Florida*, 399 U.S. 78 (1970), we had occasion to consider a related issue: whether the Sixth Amendment's right to trial by jury requires that all juries consist of 12 men. After considering the history of the 12-man requirement and the functions it performs in contemporary society, we concluded that it was not of constitutional stature. We reach the same conclusion today with regard to the requirement of unanimity.

Like the requirement that juries consist of 12

men, the requirement of unanimity arose during the Middle Ages and had become an accepted feature of the common-law jury by the 18th century. But, as we observed in *Williams*, "the relevant constitutional history casts considerable doubt on the easy assumption ... that if a given feature existed in a jury at common law in 1789, then it was necessarily preserved in the Constitution." The most salient fact in the scanty history of the Sixth Amendment ... is that, as it was introduced by James Madison in the House of Representatives, the proposed Amendment provided for trial

> by an impartial jury of the freeholders of the vicinage, with the requisite of unanimity for conviction, of the right of challenge, and other accustomed requisites. ... 1 Annuals of Cong. 435 (1789).

Although it passed the House with little alteration, this proposal ran into considerable opposition in the Senate. ... [T]he Amendment that ultimately emerged from the committee and then from Congress and the States provided only for trial

> by an impartial jury of the State and district wherein the crime shall have been committed, which district shall have been previously ascertained by law. ...

... [O]ne can draw conflicting inferences from this legislative history. One possible inference is that Congress eliminated references to unanimity and to other "accustomed requisites" of the jury because those requisites were thought already to be implicit in the very concept of jury. A contrary explanation ... is that the deletion was intended to have some substantive effect. Surely one fact that is absolutely clear from this history is that, after a proposal had been made to specify precisely which of the common-law requisites of the jury were to be preserved by the Constitution, the Framers explicitly rejected the proposal and instead left such specification to

the future. ... [W]e must accordingly consider what is meant by the concept "jury" and determine whether a feature commonly associated with it is constitutionally required. ...

Our inquiry must focus upon the function served by the jury in contemporary society. ... [T]he purpose of trial by jury is to prevent oppression by the Government by providing a "safeguard against the corrupt or overzealous prosecutor and against the compliant, biased, or eccentric judge." *Duncan* v. *Louisiana*, 391 U.S. at 156. "Given this purpose, the essential feature of a jury obviously lies in the interposition between the accused and his accuser of the commonsense judgment of a group of laymen. ... " *Williams* v. *Florida*, 399 U.S. at 100. A requirement of unanimity, however, does not materially contribute to the exercise of this commonsense judgment. ... [A] jury will come to such a judgment as long as it consists of a group of laymen representative of a cross section of the community who have the duty and the opportunity to deliberate, free from outside attempts at intimidation, on the question of a defendant's guilt. In terms of this function we perceive no difference between juries required to act unanimously and those permitted to convict or acquit by votes of 10 to two or 11 to one. Requiring unanimity would obviously produce hung juries in some situations where nonunanimous juries will convict or acquit.* But in either case, the interest of the defendant in having the judgment of his peers interposed between himself and the officers of the State who prosecute and judge him is equally well served.

Petitioners nevertheless argue that unanimity serves other purposes constitutionally essential to the continued operation of the jury system. Their principal contention is that a Sixth Amend-

*The most complete statistical study of jury behavior has come to the conclusion that when juries are required to be unanimous, "the probability that an acquittal minority will hang the jury is about as great as that a guilty minority will hang it." H. Kalven & H. Zeisel, The American Jury 461 (1966).

ment "jury trial" made mandatory on the States by virtue of the Due Process Clause of the Fourteenth Amendment, *Duncan* v. *Louisiana, supra,* should be held to require a unanimous jury verdict in order to give substance to the reasonable doubt standard otherwise mandated by the Due Process Clause.

We are quite sure, however, that the Sixth Amendment itself has never been held to require proof beyond a reasonable doubt in criminal cases. The reasonable doubt standard developed separately from both the jury trial and the unanimous verdict. . . . [T]he rule requiring proof of crime beyond a reasonable doubt did not crystallize in this country until after the Constitution was adopted. And in that case, which held such a burden of proof to be constitutionally required, the Court purported to draw no support from the Sixth Amendment.

Petitioners' argument that the Sixth Amendment requires jury unanimity in order to give effect to the reasonable doubt standard thus founders on the fact that the Sixth Amendment does not require proof beyond a reasonable doubt at all. The reasonable doubt argument is rooted, in effect, in due process and has been rejected in *Johnson* v. *Louisiana* [decided today].

Petitioners also cite quite accurately a long line of decisions of this Court upholding the principle that the Fourteenth Amendment requires jury panels to reflect a cross section of the community. See, *e.g., Whitus* v. *Georgia,* 385 U.S. 545 (1967); *Smith* v. *Texas,* 311 U.S. 128 (1940); *Norris* v. *Alabama,* 294 U.S. 587 (1935); *Strauder* v. *West Virginia,* 100 U.S. 303 (1880). They then contend that unanimity is a necessary precondition for effective application of the cross section requirement, because a rule permitting less than unanimous verdicts will make it possible for convictions to occur without the acquiescence of minority elements within the community.

There are two flaws in this argument. One is petitioners' assumption that every distinct voice in the community has a right to be represented on every jury and a right to prevent conviction of a defendant in any case. All that the Constitution forbids, however, is systematic exclusion of identifiable segments of the community from jury panels and from the juries ultimately drawn from those panels; a defendant may not, for example, challenge the makeup of a jury merely because no members of his race are on the jury, but must prove that his race has been systematically excluded. See *Swain* v. *Alabama,* 380 U.S. 202, 208-209 (1965); *Cassell* v. *Texas,* 339 U.S. 282, 286-287 (1950). No group, in short, has the right to block convictions; it has only the right to participate in the overall legal processes by which criminal guilt and innocence are determined.

We also cannot accept petitioners' second assumption—that minority groups, even when they are represented on a jury, will not adequately represent the viewpoint of those groups simply because they may be outvoted in the final result. They will be present during all deliberations, and their views will be heard. We cannot assume that the majority of the jury will refuse to weigh the evidence and reach a decision upon rational grounds, just as it must now do in order to obtain unanimous verdicts, or that a majority will deprive a man of his liberty on the basis of prejudice when a minority is presenting a reasonable argument in favor of acquittal. We simply find no proof for the notion that a majority will disregard its instructions and cast its votes for guilt or innocence based on prejudice rather than the evidence.

We accordingly affirm the judment of the Court of Appeals of Oregon.

It is so ordered.
Judgment affirmed.

MR. JUSTICE DOUGLAS, *with whom* MR. JUSTICE BRENNAN *and* MR. JUSTICE MARSHALL *concur, dissenting.*

[This opinion also applies to the companion case—*Johnson* v. *Louisiana.*]

The Constitution does not mention unanimous juries. Neither does it mention the presumption of innocence nor does it say that guilt must be proven beyond a reasonable doubt in all criminal cases. Yet it is almost inconceivable that anyone would have questioned whether proof beyond a reasonable doubt was in fact the constitutional standard. And, indeed, when such a case finally arose we had little difficulty disposing of the issue. *In re Winship*, 397 U.S. 358, 364.

The Court, speaking through Mr. Justice Brennan, stated that the

> use of the reasonable-doubt standard is indispensable to command the respect and confidence of the community in applications of the criminal law. It is critical that the moral force of the criminal law not be diluted by a standard of proof that leaves people in doubt whether innocent men are being condemned. It is also important in our free society that every individual going about his ordinary affairs have confidence that his government cannot adjudge him guilty of a criminal offense without convincing a proper fact-finder of his guilt with utmost certainty.
>
> Lest there remain any doubt about the constitutional stature of the reasonable-doubt standard, we explicitly hold that the Due Process Clause protects the accused against conviction except upon proof beyond a reasonable doubt of every fact necessary to constitute the crime with which he is charged. *Ibid.*

I had similarly assumed that there was no dispute that the Federal Constitution required a unanimous jury in all criminal cases. After all, it has long been explicit constitutional doctrine that the Seventh Amendment civil jury must be unanimous. See *American Publishing Co.* v. *Fisher*, 166 U.S. 464, where the Court said that "unanimity was one of the peculiar and essential features of trial by jury at the common law. No

authorities are needed to sustain this proposition." Like proof beyond a reasonable doubt, the issue of unanimous juries in criminal cases simply never arose. Yet in cases dealing with juries it had always been assumed that a unanimous jury was required. See *Maxwell* v. *Dow*, 176 U.S. 581, 586; *Patton* v. *United States*, 281 U.S. 276, 288; *Andres* v. *United States*, 333 U.S. 740, 748. Today the bases of those cases are discarded and two centuries of American history are shunted aside.

The result of today's decision is anomalous: though unanimous jury decisions are not required in state trials, they are constitutionally required in federal prosecutions. How can that be possible when both decisions stem from the Sixth Amendment?

We held unanimously in 1948 that the Bill of Rights requires a unanimous jury verdict:

> Unanimity in jury verdicts is required where the Sixth and Seventh Amendments apply. In criminal cases this requirement of unanimity extends to all issues—character or degree of the crime, guilt and punishment—which are left to the jury. A verdict embodies in a single finding the conclusions by the jury upon all the questions submitted to it. *Andres* v. *United States*, 333 U.S. 740.

After today's decision, a man's property may only be taken away by a unanimous jury vote, yet he can be stripped of his liberty by a lesser standard. How can that result be squared with the law of the land as expressed in the settled and traditional requirements of procedural due process?

Rule 31(a) of the Federal Rules of Criminal Procedure states, "The verdict shall be unanimous." That Rule was made by this Court with the concurrence of Congress pursuant to 18 U.S.C. section 3771. After today a unanimous verdict will be required in a federal prosecution but not in the state prosecution. Yet the sources of the right in each case are the Sixth and Fourteenth Amendments. I fail to see how with reason we can maintain those inconsistent dual positions. . . .

I would construe the Sixth Amendment, when applicable to the States, precisely as I would when applied to the Federal Government.

The plurality approves a procedure which diminishes the reliability of jury. First, it eliminates the circumstances in which a minority of jurors (a) could have rationally persuaded the entire jury to acquit, or (b) while unable to persuade the majority to acquit, nonetheless could have convinced them to convict only on a lesser-included offense. Second, it permits prosecutors in Oregon and Louisiana to enjoy a conviction-acquittal ratio substantially greater than that ordinarily returned by unanimous juries.

The diminution of verdict reliability flows from the fact that nonunanimous juries need not debate and deliberate as fully as must unanimous juries. As soon as the requisite majority is attained, further consideration is not required either by Oregon or by Louisiana even though the dissident jurors might, if given the chance, be able to convince the majority. Such persuasion does in fact occasionally occur in States where the unanimous requirement applies: "In roughly one case in ten, the minority eventually succeeds in reversing an initial majority, and these may be cases of special importance." One explanation for this phenomenon is that because jurors are often not permitted to take notes and because they have imperfect memories, the forensic process of forcing jurors to defend their conflicting recollections and conclusions flushes out many nuances which otherwise would go overlooked. This collective effort to piece together the puzzle of historical truth, however, is cut short as soon as the requisite majority is reached. . . . Indeed, if a necessary majority is immediately obtained, then no deliberation at all is required. . . . (There is a suggestion that this may have happened in the 10–2 verdict rendered in only 41 minutes in Apodaca's case.) To be sure, in jurisdictions other than these two States, initial majorities

normally prevail in the end, but about a tenth of the time the rough and tumble of the juryroom operates to reverse completely their preliminary perception of guilt or innocence. The Court now extracts from the juryroom this automatic check against hasty fact-finding by relieving jurors of the duty to hear out fully the dissenters.

It is said that there is no evidence that majority jurors will refuse to listen to dissenters whose votes are unneeded for conviction. Yet human experience teaches that polite and academic conversation is no substitute for the earnest and robust argument necessary to reach unanimity. As mentioned earlier, in Apodaca's case, whatever courtesy dialogue transpired could not have lasted more than 41 minutes. I fail to understand why the Court should lift from the States the burden of justifying so radical a departure from an accepted and applauded tradition and instead demand that these defendants document with empirical evidence what has always been thought to be too obvious for further study.

. . . [I]n *Williams* v. *Florida*, 300 U.S. 78, we held that a State could provide a jury less than 12 in number in criminal trial. We said "What few experiments have occurred—usually in the civil area—indicate that there is no 'discernible difference between the results reached by the two different-sized juries. In short, neither currently available evidence nor theory suggests that the 12-man jury is necessarily more advantageous to the defendant than a jury composed of fewer members."

That rationale of *Williams* can have no application here. *Williams* requires that the change be neither more nor less advantageous to either the State or the defendant. It is said that such a showing is satisfied here since a 3:9 (Louisiana) or 2:10 (Oregon) verdict will result in acquittal. Yet experience shows that the less than unanimous jury overwhelmingly favors the States.

Moreover, even where an initial majority wins the dissent over to its side, the ultimate result in unanimous jury States may nonetheless reflect the reservations of uncertain jurors. I refer to many compromise verdicts on lesser-included offenses and lesser sentences. Thus, even though a minority may not be forceful enough to carry the day, their doubts may nonetheless cause a majority to exercise caution. Obviously, however, in Oregon and Louisiana, dissident jurors will not have the opportunity through full deliberation to temper the opposing faction's degree of certainty of guilt.

The new rule also has an impact on cases in which a unanimous jury would have neither voted to acquit nor to convict, but would have deadlocked. In unanimous jury States, this occurs about 5.6 percent of the time. Of these deadlocked juries, Kalven and Zeisel say that 56 percent contain either one, two, or three dissenters. In these latter cases, the majorities favor the prosecution 44 percent (of the 56 percent) but the defendant only 12 percent (of the 56 percent). Thus, by eliminating these deadlocks, Louisiana wins 44 cases for every 12 that it loses, obtaining in this band of outcomes a substantially more favorable conviction ratio (3.67) than the unanimous jury ratio of slightly less than two guilty verdicts for every acquittal. . . . By eliminating the one and two dissenting juror cases, Oregon does even better, gaining 4.25 convictions for every acquittal. While the statutes on their face deceptively appear to be neutral, the use of the nonunanimous jury stacks the truth-determining process against the accused. Thus, we take one step more away from the accusatorial system that has been our proud boast.

It is my belief that a unanimous jury is necessary if the great barricade known as proof beyond a reasonable doubt is to be maintained. This is not to equate proof beyond a reasonable doubt with the requirement of a unanimous jury. That would be analytically fallacious since a deadlocked jury does not bar, as double jeopardy, retrial for the same offense. . . .

Suppose a jury begins with the substantial minority but then in the process of deliberation a sufficient number changes to reach the required 9:3 or 10:2 for a verdict. Is not there still a lingering doubt about that verdict? Is it not clear that the safeguard of unanimity operates in this context to make it far more likely that guilt is established beyond a reasonable doubt?

The late Learned Hand said that "as a litigant I should dread a lawsuit beyond almost anything else short of sickness and death." At the criminal level that dread multiplies. Any person faced with the awesome power of government is in great jeopardy, even though innocent. Facts are always elusive and often two-faced. What may appear to one to imply guilt may carry no such overtones to another. Every criminal prosecution crosses treacherous ground, for guilt is common to all men. Yet the guilt of one may be irrelevant to the charge on which he is tried or indicate that if there is to be a penalty, it should be of an extremely light character.

The risk of loss of his liberty and the certainty that if found guilty he will be "stigmatized by the conviction" were factors we emphasized in *Winship* in sustaining the requirement that no man should be condemned where there is reasonable doubt about his guilt.

We therefore have always held that in criminal cases we would err on the side of letting the guilty go free rather than sending the innocent to jail. We have required proof beyond a reasonable doubt as "concrete substance for the presumption of innocence.". . .

The requirements of a unanimous jury verdict in criminal cases and proof beyond a reasonable doubt are so embedded in our constitutional law and touch so directly all the citizens and are such important barricades of liberty that if they are to be changed they should be introduced by constitutional amendment.

Today the Court approves a nine to three verdict. Would the Court relax the standard of reasonable doubt still further by resorting to eight to four verdicts or even a majority rule? Moreover, in light of today's holdings and that of *Williams* v. *Florida,* in the future would it invalidate three to two or even two to one convictions? . . .

The vast restructuring of American law which is entailed in today's decisions is for political not for judicial action. Until the Constitution is rewritten, we have the present one to support and construe. It has served us well. We lifetime appointees, who sit here only by happenstance, are the last who should sit as a Committee of Revision on rights as basic as those involved in the present cases.

Proof beyond a reasonable doubt and unanimity of criminal verdicts and the presumption of innocence are basic features of the accusatorial system. What we do today is not in that tradition but more in the tradition of the inquisition. Until amendments are adopted setting new standards, I would let no man be fined or imprisoned in derogation of what up to today was indisputably the law of the land.

FURMAN v. GEORGIA; JACKSON v. GEORGIA; BRANCH v. TEXAS
408 U.S. 238; 33 L.Ed. 2d 346; 92 S. Ct. 2726 (1973)

PER CURIAM

[Furman] was convicted of murder in Georgia and was sentenced to death. . . . [Jackson] was convicted of rape in Georgia and was sentenced to death. . . . [Branch] was convicted of rape in Texas and was sentenced to death. . . . Certiorari was granted limited to the following question: "Does the imposition and carrying out of the death penalty in [these cases] constitute cruel and unusual punishment in violation of the Eighth and Fourteenth Amendments?" . . . The Court holds that the imposition and carrying out of the death penalty in these cases constitutes cruel and unusual punishment in violation of the Eighth and Fourteenth Amendments. The judgment in each case is therefore reversed insofar as it leaves undisturbed the death sentence imposed, and the cases are remanded for further proceedings. . . .

MR. JUSTICE DOUGLAS, MR. JUSTICE BRENNAN, MR. JUSTICE STEWART, MR. JUSTICE WHITE, *and* MR. JUSTICE MARSHALL *have filed separate opinions in support of the judgments.*

THE CHIEF JUSTICE, MR. JUSTICE BLACKMUN, MR. JUSTICE POWELL, *and* MR. JUSTICE REHNQUIST *have filed separate dissenting opinions.*

MR. JUSTICE DOUGLAS, *concurring.*

. . .

It has been assumed in our decisions that punishment by death is not cruel, unless the manner of execution can be said to be inhuman and barbarous. . . . It is also said in our opinions that the proscription of cruel and unusual punishments "is not fastened to the obsolete, but may acquire meaning as public opinion becomes enlightened by a humane justice." . . .

The generalities of a law inflicting capital punishment is one thing. What may be said of the validity of a law on the books and what may be done with the law in its application do or may lead to quite different conclusions.

It would seem to be incontestable that the death penalty inflicted on one defendant is "unusual" if it discriminates against him by reason of his race, religion, wealth, social position, or class, or if it is imposed under a procedure that gives room for the play of such prejudices.

There is evidence that the provision of the English Bill of Rights of 1689 from which the language of the Eighth Amendment was taken was concerned primarily with selective or irregular application of harsh penalties and that its aim was to forbid arbitrary and discriminatory penalties of a severe nature. . . .

The words "cruel and unusual" certainly include penalties that are barbaric. But the words, at least when read in light of the English proscription against selective and irregular use of penalties, suggest that it is "cruel and unusual" to apply the death penalty—or any other penalty—selectively to minorities whose numbers are few, who are outcasts of society, and who are unpopular, but whom society is willing to see suffer though it would not countenance general application of the same penalty across the boards. . . .

There is increasing recognition of the fact that the basic theme of equal protection is implicit in "cruel and unusual" punishments. "A penalty . . . should be considered 'unusually' imposed if it is administered arbitrarily or discriminatorily." . . . The President's Commission on Law Enforcement and Administration of Justice recently concluded:

Finally there is evidence that the imposition of the death sentence and the exercise of dispensing power by the courts and the executive follow discriminatory patterns. The death sentence is disproportionately imposed and carried out on the poor, the Negro, and the members of unpopular groups.

A study of capital cases in Texas from 1924 to 1968 reached the following conclusions:

Application of the death penalty is unequal: most of those executed were poor, young, and ignorant.

Seventy-five of the 460 cases involved codefendants, who, under Texas law, were given separate trials. In several instances, where a white and a Negro were codefendants, the white was sentenced to life imprisonment or a term of years, and the Negro was given the death penalty.

Another ethnic disparity is found in the type of sentence imposed for rape. The Negro convicted of rape is far more likely to get the death penalty than a term sentence, whereas whites and Latins are far more likely to get a term sentence than the death penalty. . . .

Former Attorney General Ramsey Clark has said, "It is the poor, the sick, the ignorant, the powerless and the hated who are executed." One searches our chronicles in vain for the execution of any member of the affluent strata of this society. The Leopolds and Leobs are given prison terms, not sentenced to death.

Jackson, a Black, convicted of the rape of a white woman, was 21 years old. A court-appointed psychiatrist said that Jackson was of average education and average intelligence, that he was not an imbecile or schizophrenic or psychotic, that his traits were the product of environmental influences, and that he was competent to stand trial. . . . Jackson was a convict who had escaped from a work gang in the area, a result of a three-year sentence for auto theft. He was at large for three days and during that time had committed several other offenses—burglary, auto theft, and assault and battery.

Furman, a Black, killed a householder while seeking to enter the home at night. Furman shot the deceased through a closed door. He was 26 years old and had finished the sixth grade in school. Pending trial he was committed to the Georgia Central State Hospital for a psychiatric examination on his plea of insanity tendered by court-appointed counsel. The superintendent reported that a unanimous staff diagnostic conference on the same data had concluded: "that this patient should retain his present diagnosis of Mental Deficiency, Mild to Moderate, with

Psychotic Episodes associated with Convulsive Disorder." The physicians agreed that "at present the patient is not psychotic, but he is not capable of cooperating with his counsel in the preparation of his defense"; and the staff believed "that he is in need of further psychiatric hospitalization and treatment."

Later he reported that the staff diagnosis was Mental Deficiency, Mild to Moderate, with Psychotic Episodes associated with Convulsive Disorder. He concluded, however, that Furman was "not psychotic at present, knows right from wrong and is able to cooperate with his counsel in preparing his defense."

Branch, a Black, entered the rural home of a 65-year-old widow, a White, while she slept and raped her, holding his arm against her throat. Thereupon he demanded money and for 30 minutes or more the widow searched for money, finding little. As he left, Jackson said if the widow told anyone what happened, he would return and kill her. The record is barren of any medical or psychiatric evidence showing injury to her as a result of Branch's attack.

He had previously been convicted of felony theft and found to be a borderline mentally deficient and well below the average IQ of Texan prison inmates. He had the equivalent of five and a half years of grade school education. He had a "dull intelligence" and was in the lower fourth percentile of his class.

We cannot say from facts disclosed in these records that these defendants were sentenced to death because they were Black. Yet our task is not restricted to an effort to divine what motives impelled these death penalties. Rather we deal with a system of law and of justice that leaves to the uncontrolled discretion of judges or juries the determination whether defendants committing these crimes should die or be imprisoned. Under these laws no standards govern the selection of the penalty. People live or die, dependent on the whim of one man or of 12. . . .

In a Nation committed to Equal Protection of the Laws there is no permissible "caste" aspect of law enforcement. Yet we know that the discretion of judges and juries in imposing the death penalty enables the penalty to be selectively applied, feeding prejudices against the accused if he is poor and despised, poor and lacking political clout, or if he is a member of a suspect or unpopular minority, and saving those who by social position may be in a more protected position. . . .

The high service rendered by the "cruel and unusual" punishment clause of the Eighth Amendment is to require legislatures to write penal laws that are evenhanded, nonselective, and nonarbitrary, and to require judges to see to it that general laws are not applied sparsely, selectively, and spottily to unpopular groups. . . .

Any law which is nondiscriminatory on its face may be applied in such a way as to violate the Equal Protection Clause of the Fourteenth Amendment. . . . Such conceivably might be the fate of a mandatory death penalty, where equal or lesser sentences were imposed on the elite, a harsher one on the minorities or members of the lower castes. Whether a mandatory death penalty would otherwise be constitutional is a question I do not reach.

I concur in the judgments of the Court.

MR. JUSTICE WHITE *concurring.*

. . . In joining the Court's judgment . . . I do not at all intimate that the death penalty is unconstitutional *per se* or that there is no system of capital punishment that would comport with the Eighth Amendment. That question . . . is not presented by these cases and need not be decided.

The narrower question to which I address myself concerns the constitutionality of capital punishment statutes under which (1) the legislature authorizes the imposition of the death penalty for murder or rape; (2) the legislature does not itself mandate the penalty in any particular class or kind of case (that is, legislative will is not frustrated if the penalty is never imposed) but delegates to judges or juries the decisions as to those cases, if any, in which the penalty will be utilized; and (3) judges and juries have ordered the death penalty with such infrequency that the odds are now very much against imposition and execution of the penalty with respect to any convicted murderer or rapist. It is in this context that we must consider whether the execution of these petitioners violate the Eighth Amendment.

I begin with what I consider a near truism: that the death penalty could so seldom be imposed that it would cease to be a credible deterrent or measurably to contribute to any other end of punishment in the criminal justice system. . . .

[W]hen imposition of the penalty reaches a certain degree of infrequency, it would be very doubtful that any existing general need for retribution would be measurably satisfied. Nor could it be said with confidence that society's need for specific deterrence justifies death for so few when for so many in like circumstances life imprisonment or shorter prison terms are judged sufficient, or that community values are measurably reinforced by authorizing a penalty so rarely invoked.

Most important, a major goal of the criminal law—to deter others by punishing the convicted criminal—would not be substantially served where the penalty is so seldom invoked that it ceases to be the credible threat essential to influence the conduct of others. . . . [C]ommon sense and experience tell us that seldom-enforced laws become ineffective measures for controlling human conduct and that the death penalty, unless imposed with sufficient frequency, will make little contribution to deterring those crimes for which it may be exacted.

The imposition and execution of the death penalty are obviously cruel in the dictionary sense. But the penalty has not been considered cruel and unusual punishment in the constitutional sense because it was thought justified by the social ends it was deemed to serve. At the moment that it ceases realistically to further these purposes, however, the emerging question is whether its imposition in such circumstances would violate the Eighth Amendment. It is my view that it would, for its imposition would then be the pointless and needless extinction of life with only marginal contributions to any discernible social or public purposes. A penalty with such negligible returns to the State would be patently excessive and cruel and unusual punishment violative of the Eighth Amendment.

It is also my judgment that this point has been reached with respect to capital punishment as it is presently administered under the statutes involved in these cases. Concededly, it is difficult to prove as a general proposition that capital punishment, however administered, more effectively serves the ends of the criminal laws than does imprisonment. But however that may be, I cannot avoid the conclusion that as the statutes before us are now administered, the penalty is so infrequently imposed that the threat of execution is too attenuated to be of substantial service to criminal justice. . . .

I concur in the judgments of the Court.

MR. JUSTICE MARSHALL, *concurring.*

. . .

The criminal acts with which we are confronted are ugly, vicious, reprehensible acts. Their sheer brutality cannot and should not be minimized. But, we are not called upon to condone the penalized conduct; we are asked only to examine the penalty imposed on each of the petitioners and to determine whether or not it violates the Eighth Amendment. The question then is not whether we condone rape or murder, for surely we do not; it is whether capital punishment is "a punishment no longer consistent with our self-respect" and, therefore, violative of the Eighth Amendment. . . .

Candor compels me to confess that I am not oblivious to the fact that this is truly a case of life and death. Hanging in the balance are not only the lives of these three petitioners, but those of the almost 600 other condemned men and women in this country currently awaiting execution. While this fact cannot affect our ultimate decision, it necessitates that the decision be free from any possibility of error. . . .

[Here follows a lengthy discussion of the development of the cruel-and-unusual-punishment prohibition in English and American law and an evaluation of six purposes conceivably served by capital punishment.]

There is but one conclusion that can be drawn from all of this— i.e., the death penalty is an excessive and unnecessary punishment which violates the Eighth Amendment. The statistical evidence is not convincing beyond all doubt, but, it is persuasive. . . . The point has now been reached at which deference to the legislatures is tantamount to abdication of our judicial roles as factfinders, judges, and ultimate arbiters of the Constitution. We know that at some point the presumption of constitutionality accorded legislative acts gives way to a realistic assessment of those acts. This point comes when there is sufficient evidence available so that judges can determine not whether the legislature acted wisely, but whether it had any rational basis whatsoever for acting. We have this evidence before us now. There is no rational basis for concluding that capital punishment is not excessive. It therefore violates the Eighth Amendment.

In addition, even if capital punishment is not excessive, it nonetheless violates the Eighth Amendment because it is morally unacceptable to the people of the United States at this time in their history.

In judging whether or not a given penalty is morally acceptable, most courts have said that the punishment is valid unless "it shocks the conscience and sense of justice of the people." . . . Defenses of capital punishment are always mounted on deterrent or other similar theories. This should not be surprising. It is the people of this country who have urged in the past that prisons rehabilitate as well as isolate offenders, and it is the people who have injected a sense of

purpose into our penology. I cannot believe that at this stage in our history, the American people would ever knowingly support purposeless vengeance. Thus, I believe that the great mass of citizens would conclude on the basis of the material already considered that the death penalty is immoral and therefore unconstitutional. . . .

At a time in our history when the streets of the Nation's cities inspire fear and despair, rather than pride and hope, it is difficult to maintain objectivity and concern for our fellow citizens. But, the measure of a country's greatness is its ability to retain compassion in time of crisis. No nation in the recorded history of man has a greater tradition of revering justice and fair treatment for all its citizens in times of turmoil, confusion, and tension than ours. This is a country which stands tallest in troubled times, a country that clings to fundamental principles, cherishes its constitutional heritage, and rejects simple solutions that compromise the values which lie at the roots of our democratic system.

In striking down capital punishment, this Court does not malign our system of government. On the contrary, it pays homage to it. Only in a free society could right triumph in difficult times, and could civilization record its magnificent advancement. In recognizing the humanity of our fellow beings, we pay ourselves the highest tribute. We achieve "a major milestone in the long road up from barbarism" and join the approximately 70 other jurisdictions in the world which celebrate their regard for civilization and humanity by shunning capital punishment.

I concur in the judgments of the Court.

MR. CHIEF JUSTICE BURGER, *with whom* MR. JUSTICE BLACKMUN, MR. JUSTICE POWELL *and* MR. JUSTICE REHNQUIST *join, dissenting.*

If we were possessed of legislative power, I would either join with Mr. Justice Brennan and Mr. Justice Marshall or, at the very least, restrict the use of capital punishment to a small category of the most heinous crimes. Our constitutional inquiry, however, must be divorced from personal feelings as to the morality and efficacy of the death penalty and be confined to the meaning and applicability of the uncertain language of the Eighth Amendment. There is no novelty in being called upon to interpret a constitutional provision that is less than self-defining, but of all our fundamental guarantees, the ban on "cruel and unusual punishments" is one of the most difficult to translate into judicially manageable terms. The widely divergent views of the Amendment expressed in today's opinions reveal the haze that surrounds this constitutional command. Yet it is essential to our role as a court that we not seize upon the enigmatic character of the guarantee as an invitation to enact our personal predilections into law. . . .

I do not suggest that the presence of the word "unusual" in the Eighth Amendment is merely vestigial, having no relevance to the constitutionality of any punishment that might be devised. But where, as here, we consider a punishment well known to history, and clearly authorized by legislative enactment, it disregards the history of the Eighth Amendment and all the judicial comment that has followed to rely on the term "unusual" as affecting the outcome of these cases. Instead, I view these cases as turning on the single question whether capital punishment is "cruel" in the constitutional sense. The term "unusual" cannot be read as limiting the ban on "cruel" punishments or as somehow expanding the meaning of the term "cruel." For this reason I am unpersuaded by the facile argument that since capital punishment has always been cruel in the everyday sense of the word, and has become unusual due to decreased use, it is, therefore, now "cruel and unusual." . . .

In the 181 years since the enactment of the Eighth Amendment, not a single decision of this Court has cast the slightest shadow of a doubt on the constitutionality of capital punishment. In rejecting Eighth Amendment attacks on particu-

lar modes of execution, the Court has more than once implicitly denied that capital punishment is impermissibly "cruel" in the constitutional sense. . . . It is only 14 years since Mr. Chief Justice Warren, speaking for four members of the Court, stated without equivocation.

. . . Whatever the arguments may be against capital punishment, both on moral grounds and in terms of accomplishing the purposes of punishment—and they are forceful—the death penalty has been employed throughout our history, and, in a day when it is still widely accepted, it cannot be said to violate the constitutional concept of cruelty. *Trop* v. *Dulles,* 356 U.S., at 99 . . . .

Before recognizing such an instant evolution in the law, it seems fair to ask what factors have changed that capital punishment should now be "cruel" in the constitutional sense as it has not been in the past. It is apparent that there has been no change of constitutional significance in the nature of the punishment itself. Twentieth-century modes of execution surely involve no greater physical suffering than the means employed at the time of the Eighth Amendment's adoption. And although a man awaiting execution must inevitably experience extraordinary mental anguish, no one suggests that this anguish is materially different from that experienced by condemned men in 1791, even though protracted appellate review processes have greatly increased the waiting time on "death row." To be sure, the ordeal of the condemned man may be thought cruel in the sense that all suffering is thought cruel. But if the Constitution proscribed every punishment producing severe emotional stress, then capital punishment would clearly have been impermissible in 1791. . . .

There are no obvious indications that capital punishment offends the conscience of society to such a degree that our traditional deference to the legislative judgment must be abandoned. It is not a punishment such as burning at the stake that everyone would ineffably find to be repugnant to all civilized standards. Nor is it a punishment so roundly condemned that only a few aberrant legislatures have retained it on the statute books. Capital punishment is authorized by statute in 40 States, the District of Columbia and in the federal courts for the commission of certain crimes. On four occasions in the last 11 years Congress has added to the list of federal crimes punishable by death. In looking for reliable indicia of contemporary attitude, none more trustworthy has been advanced. . . .

Today the Court has not ruled that capital punishment is *per se* violative of the Eighth Amendment; nor has it ruled that the punishment is barred for any particular class or classes of crimes. . . . The actual scope of the Court's ruling . . . is not entirely clear. This much, however, seems apparent: if the legislatures are to continue to authorize capital punishment for some crimes, juries and judges can no longer be permitted to make the sentencing determination in the same manner they have in the past. This approach—not urged in oral arguments or briefs—misconceives the nature of the constitutional command against "cruel and unusual punishments," disregards controlling case law, and demands a rigidity in capital cases which, if possible of achievement, cannot be regarded as a welcome change. Indeed the contrary seems to be the case. . . .

The critical factor in the concurring opinions of both Mr. Justice Stewart and Mr. Justice White is the infrequency with which the penalty is imposed. This factor is taken not as evidence of society's abhorrence of capital punishment . . . but as the earmark of a deteriorated system of sentencing. It is concluded that petitioners' sentences must be set aside, not because the punishment is impermissibly cruel, but because juries and judges have failed to exercise their sentencing discretion in acceptable fashion.

To be sure, there is a recitation cast in Eighth Amendment terms: petitioners' sentences are "cruel" because they exceed that which the legislatures have deemed necessary for all cases; petitioners' sentences are "unusual" because they exceed that which is imposed in most cases. This application of the words of the Eighth Amendment suggests that capital punishment can be made to satisfy Eighth Amendment values if its rate of imposition is somehow multiplied; it seemingly follows that the flexible sentencing system created by the legislatures, and carried out by juries and judges, has yielded more mercy than the Eighth Amendment can stand. . . .

This novel formulation of Eighth Amendment principles . . . does not lie at the heart of these concurring opinions. The decisive grievance of the opinions . . . is that the present system of discretionary sentencing in capital cases has failed to produce evenhanded justice; the problem is not that two few have been sentenced to die, but that the selection process has followed no rational pattern. This claim of arbitrariness is not only lacking in empirical support, but it manifestly fails to establish that the death penalty is a "cruel and unusual" punishment. . . . The approach of these concurring opinions has no antecedent in the Eighth Amendment cases. It is essentially and exclusively a procedural due process argument. . . .

Real change could clearly be brought about if legislatures provided mandatory death sentences in such a way as to deny juries the opportunity to bring in a verdict on a lesser charge; under such a system, the death sentence could only be avoided by a verdict of acquittal. If this is the only alternative that the legislatures can safely pursue under today's ruling, I would have preferred that the Court opt for total abolition.

It seems remarkable to me that with our basic trust in lay jurors as the keystone in our system of criminal justice, it should not be suggested that we take the most sensitive and important of all decisions away from them. I could more easily be persuaded that mandatory sentences of death, without the intervening and ameliorating impact of lay jurors, are so arbitrary and doctrinaire that they violate the Constitution. The very infrequency of death penalties imposed by jurors attests their cautious and discriminating reservation of that penalty for the most extreme cases. I had thought that nothing was clearer in history . . . than the American abhorrence of "the common-law rule imposing a mandatory death sentence on all convicted murderers." . . . I do not see how this history can be ignored and how it can be suggested that the Eighth Amendment demands the elimination of the most sensitive feature of the sentencing system. . . .

Since there is no majority of the Court on the ultimate issue presented in these cases, the future of capital punishment in this country has been left in an uncertain limbo. Rather than providing a final unambiguous answer on the basic constitutional question, the collective impact of the majority's ruling is to demand an undetermined measure of change from the various state legislatures and the Congress. While I cannot endorse the process of decision making that has yielded today's result and the restraints which that result imposes on legislative action, I am not altogether displeased that legislative bodies have been given the opportunity, and indeed unavoidable responsibility, to make a thorough re-evaluation of the entire subject of capital punishment. If today's opinions demonstrate nothing else, they starkly show that this is an area where legislatures can act far more effectively than courts. . . .

The highest judicial duty is to recognize the limits on judicial power and to permit the democratic processes to deal with matters falling outside of those limits. The "hydraulic pressures" that Holmes spoke of [in the Northern Securities case] as being generated by cases of great import have propelled the Court to go beyond the limits of judicial power, while fortunately leaving some room for legislative judgment.

SELECTED REFERENCES

Bishop, A. N., "Rights and Responsibilities of the Defendant Pleading Guilty," 49 *Journal of Urban Law*, (Aug., 1971).

Creamer, J. S., *The Law of Arrest, Search, and Seizure* (Philadelphia: W. B. Saunders Co., 1968).

Dunaj, S. M., "Will the Trumpet of Gideon be Heard in All the Halls of Justice?" 25 *University of Miami Law Review* 450 (1971).

Gillers, Stephen, *Getting Justice: The Rights of the People* (New York: Basic Books, 1971).

Graham, Fred, *The Self-Inflicted Wound* (New York: Macmillan, 1970).

Medalie, Richard J., *From Escobedo to Miranda: The Anatomy of a Supreme Court Decision* (Washington: Lerner Law Book Co., 1966).

Mettsner, Michael, "Litigating Against the Death Penalty: The Strategy Behind Furman," 82 *Yale Law Journal* 1111 (1973).

Murphy, Walter, *Wiretapping on Trial: A Case Study in the Judicial Process* (New York: Random House, Inc., 1965).

Note, "Fourth Amendment, Electronic Eavesdropping, and the Invasion of Privacy," 17 *South Dakota Law Review* 238 (1972).

Note, "Implications of *Wyman* v. *James:* The Burger Court, the Fourth Amendment and the Privacy of the Home," 48 *Denver Law Journal* 87 (1971).

Note, "Jury Unanimity: Historical Accident or Safeguard of the Accused?" 25 *University of Florida Law Review* 388 (1973).

Stephens, O. H., "Burger Court: New Dimensions in Criminal Justice," 60 *Georgetown Law Journal* 249 (1971).

Uviller, H. R., "*Barker* v. *Wingo:* Speedy Trial Gets A Fast Shuffle," 72 *Columbia Law Review* 1376 (1972).

Zarr, Melvyn, *The Bill of Rights and the Police* (New York: Oceana Publications, 1970).

6 Discrimination and the Rights Revolution

Plessy v. *Ferguson*   *Brown* v. *Board of Education of Topeka, Kansas I and II*
Milliken v. *Bradley*   *Jones* v. *Mayer*   *South Carolina* v. *Katzenbach*   *Kirkpatrick* v. *Preisler*
Griggs v. *Duke Power Co.*   *Wyman* v. *James*   *James* v. *Valtierra*
San Antonio Independent School District v. *Rodriquez*   *Frontiero* v. *Richardson*
Roe v. *Wade*

The continuous struggle of black Americans for justice and equality has opened up many new dimensions in our constitutional law. But perhaps one of the more important contributions of that struggle has been in the awakening of other minorities, and white Americans as well, to the racism and injustice that exist in the United States. Blacks have long been treated unfairly because of race and color, but so have others. Chicanos and Latinos, for example, have also endured injustices with respect to education, employment, and political participation. And the difficulties of blacks and browns have been compounded by the fact that many in these groups also belong to another group that has been long forgotten—the poor. Although it is true that in raw numbers there are more white poor than black poor, on a proportionate basis blacks have shouldered a much heavier burden of the evils of poverty. According to the 1970 census, almost one-third of the blacks in the United States live in poverty.

Women have also suffered from "minority" deprivations. Because of sex, they too have encountered inequities in education, employment, and in their legal status. And today women, just as blacks, browns, and the poor, are "on the march."

These groups are engaged in attacks on racism, sexism, and poverty. And where better to carry their fight than to the courts where numbers, prestige, status, and wealth, presumably have less bearing on decisional outcomes. This chapter attempts to describe the response of the Supreme Court to the concerns of these groups. While much of the discussion focuses on efforts of blacks to attain racial justice, it also considers court actions affecting the rights of other minority groups. This development should allow us to place in sharper perspective the problems and possibilities involved in attempts to redress minority grievances through the judiciary.

SEEDS OF LEGAL RACISM

After the Civil War and for almost a half century, the judicial role in promoting racial justice was anything but positive. The Civil War and Reconstruction, to be sure, brought about enactments of the Thirteenth, Fourteenth, and Fifteenth Amendments. However, decisions of the Supreme Court, such as that in the *Civil Rights Cases* (109 U.S. 3, 1883) effectively thwarted, or at least put into mothballs, the efforts to make the provisions of the Civil War Amendments more than empty guarantees. This, along with other decisions by the Court, created a climate conducive to fostering rather than eliminating racial segregation. Consequently, and as the situation in the South returned to "normalcy"—white southerners again fully in control—state legislatures were able to design fairly comprehensive systems of racial segregation in both the public and private sectors of society.

The Court gave approval and impetus to segregation practices when in *Plessy* v. *Ferguson* it upheld as a valid exercise of state police power a Louisiana statute requiring racial segregation of passengers on trains. The Court construed the statute's racial separation provisions as nondiscriminatory. Segregation of the races was not the discrimination proscribed by the equal protection clause. However, the first Justice John Marshall Harlan, the lone dissenter, took issue with his fellow justices. Harlan maintained that "the Constitution is color-blind" and does not permit authorities to consider race in their actions.

Nevertheless by its decision in *Plessy*, the Court gave support to those who fostered racial segregation and injustice, not only in the area of transportation but in other areas such as education and places of public accommodation. But just as *Plessy* supported and legitimated widespread racial injustice, the famous School Desegregation Cases of 1954 (*Brown* v. *Board of Education of Topeka*) reversed that trend and spurred the drive for racial justice in American life. Let us trace judicial activity in various problem areas.

PUBLIC EDUCATION

The field of public education probably affords the best illustration of the separate-but-equal doctrine in practice and the evolution of the present judicial attitude on the equal protection clause of the Fourteenth Amendment. Just three years after the *Plessy* decision, the Court had before it *Cumming* v. *Board of Education* (175 U.S. 528, 1899), a case which illustrates the practical economic problems of operating a biracial school system. Challenged was the action of a county school board in Georgia discontinuing the black high school because of financial difficulties while maintaining the high school for whites. Black taxpayers had sought unsuccessfully to restrain the expenditure of public funds for support of the white high school so long as a high school was not available for their children. The Supreme Court sustained the state court's denial of this relief and Justice Harlan, the dissenter in *Plessy*, contended that the relief sought was not a proper remedy. He argued that the record showed that the school was suspended temporarily for economic reasons and did not reveal any desire on the part of the school board to act in a racially discriminatory manner. Thus, the Court avoided the constitutional issue of segregation.

The issue was again avoided nine years later in *Berea College* v. *Kentucky* (211 U.S. 45, 1908), where the Court upheld as a valid regulation of corporate charters a Kentucky law requiring both public and private educational institutions to keep blacks and whites separate in their operations. Similarly, the constitutional issue was avoided in *Gong Lum* v. *Rice* (275 U.S. 78, 1927), when the Court upheld Mississippi's power to exclude Orientals from white public schools. Thus, in avoiding the school segregation issue the Court, in effect, sanctioned its constitutional foundation.

A change in judicial attitude on segregated education first appeared in a decision of the Maryland Court of Appeals. In *Pearson* v. *Murray* (182 Atl. 590, 1936), a qualified black applicant was denied admission to the University of Maryland School of Law solely on account of race. Instead, the applicant was offered an out-of-state scholarship which covered expenses for his legal education elsewhere. While refusing to rule on the issue of segregated education, the state court did examine the standard of equality afforded and found the policy deficient. Adhering to the doctrine of the "present" nature of constitutional rights, the court held that establishment of a separate school for blacks to begin operations at some future date was not an adequate remedy; rather, immediate equality could only be furnished by admission to the white law school.

This was essentially the position adopted by the United States Supreme Court two years later in *Missouri ex rel. Gaines* v. *Canada* (305 U.S. 337, 1938). Like Maryland, Missouri provided blacks an opportunity to obtain legal education via the "out-of-state scholarship arrangement." However, the Supreme Court held that admission to the white law school was the only appropriate remedy consistent with the constitutional standard of equality. The Court also gave notice that it would no longer ignore the "equal" part of the separate-but-equal formula. Chief Justice Charles Evans Hughes, who delivered the Court's opinion stressed equality of treatment in rejecting the "scholarship arrangement." He contended:

> The basic consideration is not as to what sort of opportunities other states provide, but as to what opportunities Missouri itself furnishes to white students and denies to [N]egroes wholly upon the ground of color. The admissibility of laws separating the races in the enjoyment of privileges afforded by the State rests wholly upon the equality of the privileges which the laws give to the separated groups within the State. The question here is not a duty of the state to supply legal training, or of the equality of the training which it does supply, but

of its duty when it provides such training to furnish it to the residents of the State upon the basis of an equality of right. . . .

The Court reaffirmed the *Gaines* doctrine ten years later in *Sipuel* v. *Board of Regents of the University of Oklahoma* (322 U.S. 631, 1948).

Missouri and five southern states responded to the *Gaines* ruling by establishing separate law schools for blacks.[1] This action inevitably led to litigation focusing on comparable facilities of separate schools in determining the standard of equality required by the equal protection clause. The first case in which the Supreme Court was presented the "comparable facilities" issue was *Sweatt* v. *Painter* (339 U.S. 629, 1950). Involved were the law schools for whites and blacks in Texas. The Court found that the educational opportunities at the black law school were not equal to those afforded white students at the University of Texas. Though the Court stopped short of overturning the separate-but-equal doctrine, per se, as urged by petitioner, it was apparent that the doctrine was being eroded. In fact the language of Chief Justice Fred Vinson's opinion appeared to forecast its doom when he noted that there were "qualities which are incapable of objective measurement" and that the law school "cannot be effective in isolation from the individuals and institutions with which the law interacts."

Further evidence of this erosion came in *McLaurin* v. *Oklahoma* (339 U.S. 637, 1950), announced on the same day with *Sweatt*. In *McLaurin*, a black graduate student was admitted to the University of Oklahoma but was segregated from white students through special seating arrangements in the classroom, library, and cafeteria. The Court held that these practices conflicted with the equal protection clause since that clause requires that black students be accorded the same treatment as other students. The Court said that the segregated practices to which McLaurin was subjected impaired his "ability to study, to engage in discussion and exchange views with other students, and, in general, to learn his profession."

Immediately following the *Sweatt* and *McLaurin* decisions, the legal attack on segregated education shifted from the graduate and professional schools to the elementary and secondary school level. The first action brought in December, 1950 challenged the constitutionality of South Carolina's school segregation laws. Similar challenges were made in Kansas, Virginia, Delaware, and the District of Columbia during the following year. The constitutional issue of racially segregated educational facilities was argued in each case, but the lower courts held steadfastly to the separate-but-equal doctrine.

In the Supreme Court the four actions against state laws were consolidated for purposes of argument and decision in *Brown* v. *Board of Education of Topeka, Kansas, infra*; they raised the same issue under the equal protection clause of the Fourteenth Amendment. The District of Columbia case, *Bolling* v. *Sharpe* (347 U.S. 497, 1954), raised the same question, but was decided under the due process clause of the Fifth Amendment because the equal protection clause of the Fourteenth Amendment is not applicable to the District's policies. Speaking for a unanimous

---

[1] Texas, Louisiana, Florida, North Carolina, and South Carolina.

Court on May 17, 1954, Chief Justice Earl Warren declared the separate-but-equal doctrine unconstitutional in public education, thus overruling the *Plessy* precedent. The Court went to the core of the problem and considered not only tangible inequalities, but also the nature and consequences of segregation. Warren found sufficient evidence that segregation inculcates a sense of inferiority in black children and impairs their ability to learn. Consequently, such segregation with the sanction of law denies the black children the equal protection of the laws.

The Court, probably anticipating the impact of the decision, announced its judgment but delayed its decree. After examination of additional briefs and further argument on the question of the appropriate remedy during the 1954 Fall Term, the implementation decree was announced on May 31, 1955 (*Brown* v. *Board of Education*, 349 U.S. 294, 1955). The Court rejected the "immediacy" argument of the victorious appellants and leaned more toward the "gradualism" urged by the appellees. The cases were remanded to the federal district courts with instructions to order local school districts to proceed with desegregation of public schools "with all deliberate speed."

In practice, district courts showed considerable leniency in passing on local desegregation plans. They tolerated procedural maneuvers and often granted delays which were hardly consistent with the intent of the Court's "deliberate speed" formula. At times delays resulted from actions by state legislatures and state officials that made it difficult if not impossible for local school boards to follow court mandates. These boards were also under heavy local pressures to resist, evade, or at least delay final desegregation orders. In addition, there were threats of violence. But in *Cooper* v. *Aaron* (358 U.S. 1, 1958) the Supreme Court made it clear that it would not tolerate postponement of court orders (and hence enjoyment of constitutional rights) in the face of threatened or actual violence. Meeting in a rare special session (necessitated by the need to resolve the issue of postponing a desegregation order before the beginning of the school term), the Court rejected the rationale supporting the postponement of the Little Rock desegregation plan and condemned the actions of state officials designed to scuttle enforcement of the district court order. Holding that "the constitutional rights of the [black children] are not to be sacrificed or yielded to the violence and disorder which have followed upon the actions of the Governor and Legislature . . . ," the Court concluded that "the constitutional rights of children not to be discriminated against in school admission on grounds of race or color can neither be nullified openly and directly by state [officials] nor nullified indirectly by them through evasive schemes for segregation whether attempted 'ingeniously or ingenuously.' "

While the Court had used strong language in *Cooper* to condemn the obstruction to desegregation attempted by state officials, it showed considerable leniency and deference to lower courts when presented with plans designed to keep the number of blacks attending schools with whites at a minimum. For example, shortly after its decision in *Cooper* the Court upheld the Alabama pupil-placement laws in *Shuttleworth* v. *Birmingham Board of Education* (358 U.S. 101, 1958). Essentially, this was an arrangement adopted by several states to delay and/or minimize the impact of the *Brown* decision. Under the guise of using such nonracial factors as scholastic aptitude and achievement, health, moral character and residence in assignment of pupils to schools, local school authorities could control the number of blacks attending white schools. A three-judge federal district court upheld the Alabama law, noting that its purpose was to admit pupils to schools on the basis of individual merit irrespective of race. The court presumed that the law would be administered to accomplish that purpose only. The Supreme Court's affirmance was on "these limited grounds" and without opinion.

An extreme state response to the *Brown* decision was the provision for closing public schools when faced with a final desegregation decree. This was part of Virginia's "massive resistance" program fashioned by Governor J. Lindsay Almond. This "weapon" was used by Prince Edward County, (Prince Edward County was one of the school districts involved in the *Brown* case), when authorities faced with a final desegregation order, closed schools in 1959. During the ensuing five-year period, while the issue was kicked up and down the judicial ladder, white children attended private segregated schools largely supported by a state financed grant-in-aid tuition program. Black children, however, had no formal schooling at all, the black community having rejected a segregated program similar to that provided for whites. The Supreme Court finally resolved the issue and rejected this evasive approach in *Griffin* v. *School Board of Prince Edward County* (377 U.S. 218, 1964). Not only did the Court find the Virginia law defective because of its discriminatory purpose and effect, but it took the unusual step of empowering the federal district court to order the taxing authority to exercise its power in providing funds "to reopen, operate and maintain" the public school system on a nondiscriminatory basis.

Toward the end of the first decade of controversy over school desegration in the South, the problem of de facto school segregation in the North emerged. It rapidly developed into an emotion-packed issue, focusing attention on the traditional neighborhood school policy, housing patterns, and the myriad problems of urban ghettoes.

Those attacking de facto segregation argued that *Brown* imposed a duty on school authorities to eliminate such conditions, though the segregation had developed spontaneously and without any positive official action. In effect, they contended that there was a constitutional duty to take positive action to "integrate" segregated schools and bring about a better racial balance.

Proponents of the neighborhood school policy countered with the argument that the command of *Brown* was essentially a negative obligation, i.e., school authorities could not operate public schools in a racially discriminatory manner. Essentially, they argued that *Brown* was directed at segregation resulting from positive action of public authorities, but it did not condemn school segregation resulting from changing residential patterns where only private action is involved.

These conflicting interpretations of the *Brown* decision were argued in state courts and in lower federal courts. As frequently happens, judges of state and federal courts differ in their interpretation of decisions of the Supreme Court. Here, they differed on whether *Brown* places a constitutional duty on school authorities to take positive action to eliminate de facto segregation not of their own making. In this regard, the New York Court of Appeals applied the "positive action" theory more liberally than most courts by holding in *Balaban* v. *Rubin* (250 N.Y.S. 2d 281, 1964), that school boards may consider race among other relevant factors in achieving a particular balance of population groups within an attendance zone.

A leading federal case on the issue is *Bell* v. *School City of Gary, Indiana* (324 F.2d 209, 7th Cir., 1963); cf. *Barksdale* v. *Springfield School Committee*, (237 F. Supp. 543, 348 F. 2d 261, 1965). There, the Court of Appeals for the Seventh Circuit affirmed a district court judgment dismissing a complaint against the Gary school board alleging the operation of segregated schools contrary to the *Brown* rule. In his opinion of a unanimous court, Circuit Judge F. Ryan Duffy upheld the neighborhood school policy, accepting the school board's contention that "there is no affirmative U.S. Constitutional duty to change innocently arrived at school attendance districts by the mere fact that shifts in population either increase or decrease the percentage of either Negro or white pupils." Judge Duffy's opinion did not curtail the board's authority to take action on its own to eliminate de facto segregation. But his acceptance of the district court's holding (that a school system developed on the neighborhood policy without any intention or purpose of racial segregation does not have to be abandoned because the resulting effect is to have a racial imbalance) certainly strengthens the position of school board members advocating the status quo.

However, in *Hobson* v. *Hansen* (269 F. Supp. 401, 1967) Circuit Judge J. Skelly Wright (sitting in the District Court for the District of Columbia pursuant to 23 U.S.C. sec. 291 [c]) delivered a most scathing attack on de facto segregation. In his opinion, Judge Wright made an expansive and bold application of *Brown.* Upon a finding of racial and economic discrimination in the operation of the District of Columbia school system, he issued an injunction prohibiting the use of the ability-grouping "track system" and optional attendance zones. He further ordered the busing of black children from overcrowded schools to the underpopulated schools in white neighborhoods and a substantial integration of the faculty of each school. When the district school board (controlled by blacks) would not authorize Superintendent Hansen to appeal, he resigned, threatening to make the appeal as a private citizen.

The Supreme Court refused to review the *Balaban* and *Bell* cases, so at that time, the law on de facto segregation was essentially this: the *Brown* rule *does not require* school authorities to take action to eliminate de facto segregation, *nor does it prohibit* official action that uses *race* among other factors to achieve a desired balance among racial groups in a school district.[2]

Overall the slow pace of school desegregation was very disappointing to those who viewed *Brown* as a major step toward full equality for blacks. Not only was a start toward desegregation in some districts delayed for years by legal maneuvering, but the grade-a-year plan allowed up to a dozen years to effect complete desegregation. The Supreme Court indicated its growing impatience with the manner in which the "deliberate speed" formula was being abused when, in rejecting a plan

---

[2] For further discussion of de facto segregation in public schools, see pp. 365-366 *infra.*

for gradual desegregation of recreational facilities in *Watson* v. *Memphis* (373 U.S. 526, 1963), Justice Arthur Goldberg asserted:

> It is far from clear that the mandate of the second Brown decision requiring that desegregation proceed with "all deliberate speed" would today be fully satisfied by types of plans or programs for desegregation of public educational facilities which eight years ago might have been deemed sufficient.

The Court showed further impatience with the pace of desegregation in *Rogers* v. *Paul* (382 U.S. 198, 1965). Here, it ordered immediate admission of blacks to a Fort Smith, Arkansas high school where the grade-a-year plan adopted in 1957 was three years short of complete implementation.

Growing discontent with the progress of school desegregation moved the issue into the political arena as Congress was considering an omnibus civil rights bill in 1963. When Congress eventually enacted the measure (Civil Rights Act of 1964) it contained a title on public school desegregation. That title denies federal financial aid to any program administered in a racially discriminatory manner. Pursuant to this provision, the U.S. Office of Education late in 1964 made eligibility for federal aid contingent on compliance with a court-ordered desegregation plan or in the absence thereof, compliance with guidelines for school desegregation issued by the Department of Health, Education and Welfare, popularly known as the *H.E.W. Guidelines.*

The new policy had an immediate impact since the withholding of federal financial aid would have serious fiscal consequences for many school districts where no effort at all or at most a token effort had been made to desegregate their schools. Faced with the possibility of a loss of substantial funds, especially in view of the passage of the Elementary and Secondary Education Act of 1965, most districts grudgingly moved to comply with the *Guidelines.*[3]

Indeed, the most authoritative statement on the constitutionality of the *H.E.W. Guidelines* was given by Circuit Judge John Minor Wisdom of the Court of Appeals for the Fifth Circuit in *United States* v. *Jefferson County Board of Education* (372 F.2d 836, 1966). In reversing district court holdings involving seven school districts in Alabama and Louisiana, Judge Wisdom held that the standards for desegregation prescribed by the *Guidelines* are within the rationale of the *Brown* ruling and the Congressional objectives of the Civil Rights Act of 1964. In what must be

[3] These first *Guidelines,* issued in April 1965, set the fall of 1967 as the target date for desegregation of all public school systems. A revision of the *Guidelines* in March 1968 moved the target date to the opening of the 1968-1969 school year, or, at the latest, the opening of the 1969-1970 year.

Without rejecting the policy of "compliance now" or abandonging the 1969-1970 target, the Nixon Administration adopted a flexible policy under which delays in implementing desegregation plans would be granted if warranted by "bona fide educational and administrative problems." On such grounds, the Court of Appeals for the Fifth Circuit granted the Administration's request for a three-month delay in implementing the plans of 33 recalcitrant districts in Mississippi as the 1969-1970 school year began. But the Supreme Court overturned these actions (see p. 362).

considered the most far-reaching statement on the obligation of school boards, Judge Wisdom asserted that "the law imposes an absolute duty to integrate, in the sense that a disproportionate concentration of Negroes in certain schools cannot be ignored [for] racial mixing of students is a high priority goal." Upon petition for a rehearing, the Court of Appeals (en banc) adopted Judge Wisdom's opinion, attaching some clarifying statements and alterations to the decree (*United States* v. *Jefferson County Board of Education*, 380 F.2d 385, 1967). The Supreme Court refused to review this judgment in *Caddo Parish School Board* v. *United States* (386 U.S. 1001, 1967).

After avoiding for 13 years the issue of whether *Brown* required school boards to take affirmative action to integrate schools,[4] on May 27, 1968 the Supreme Court decided three cases in which it intimated that in order to meet the command of *Brown*, school officials may have to take positive action to integrate. In *Green* v. *County School Board of New Kent County, Virginia,* (391 U.S. 430), the Court examined the "freedom-of-choice" desegregation plan (which allows a pupil to choose his own school) and found its operational results unacceptable in meeting the *Brown* requirement "of a racially nondiscriminatory school system." Justice Brennan's opinion for the Court emphasized that the burden on a school board today is to come forth with realistically workable plans for a speedier and more effective conversion to a unitary, nonracial school system. Brennan noted that not a single white student had chosen to attend the black school and that 85 percent of black school children still attended the all-black school. He said that an acceptable system must not have "a 'white' school and a 'negro' school, but just schools." The other two cases—*Monroe* v. *Board of Commissioners* (391 U.S. 450) and *Raney* v. *Board of Education* (391 U.S. 443)—raised the same issue, although the plan under attack in *Monroe* was a variation of the "freedom-of-choice" plan known as "free transfer."

The Court was careful to limit its ruling to the specific plans involved in *Green* and did not declare such plans unconstitutional on their face. Nonetheless, in *Alexander* v. *Holmes County Board of Education* (396 U.S. 19, 1969), the Court dashed any hope that "freedom-of-choice" or any other plan could be used constitutionally to delay further the implementation of *Brown.* In a unanimous per curiam opinion, the "new" Burger Court blunted actions of the Nixon Administration by overturning a decision of the Court of Appeals for the Fifth Circuit that had sanctioned a delay in desegregation of 33 Mississippi school districts. The Court declared the standard of "all deliberate speed [no] longer constitutionally permissible" and ordered desegregation "at once."

In responding to that mandate, a number of school districts, with the approval of lower federal courts, devised plans for total desegregation that required

---

[4] The Court had refused to hear lower court actions which held that *Brown* only prohibits segregation and does not require integration. Cf. *Bell* v. *School City of Gary, Indiana, supra,* and *Downs* v. *Board of Education* (336 F. 2d 988, 10th Cir., 1964). However, it did uphold a ruling in the Court of Appeals for the Fifth Circuit sustaining the constitutionality of the *H.E.W. Guidelines* where Circuit Judge John Minor Wisdom declared that *Brown* imposes an absolute duty to integrate where there is a disproportionate concentration of blacks in certain schools. See *United States* v. *Jefferson County Board of Education, supra.*

considerable movement of pupils by school bus. Despite its use as an emotional political issue in the 1968 Presidential campaign and its subsequent condemnation by President Nixon, "busing" was approved by the Burger Court as an acceptable tool which could be employed in effecting constitutionally acceptable desegregation plans. In *Swann* v. *Charlotte-Mecklenburg Board of Education* (402 U.S. 1, 1971), Chief Justice Burger, speaking for a unanimous Court, made it clear that where there was a long history of school segregation and school authorities had defaulted in their constitutional duty to produce an acceptable desegregation plan, lower federal courts possessed considerable discretion in fashioning equitable remedial relief. Consequently, the District Court's plan that included limited use of mathematical ratios of black and white pupils, the pairing and grouping of noncontiguous school zones, and a system of bus transportation to implement the racial ratio scheme was constitutionally acceptable as a means of dismantling the dual system. Regarding the sensitive issue of bussing children out of their neighborhoods (in this case from largely white suburbs to the largely black inner city and vice versa) to a more distant school, the Chief Justice's language was somewhat conciliatory. He noted, for example:

> Absent a constitutional violation there would be no basis for judicially ordering assignment of students on a racial basis. All things being equal, with no history of discrimination, it might well be desirable to assign pupils to schools nearest their homes. But all things are not equal in a system that has been deliberately constructed and maintained to enforce racial segregation. The remedy for such segregation may be administratively awkward, inconvenient and even bizarre in some situations and may impose burdens on some; but all awkwardness and inconvenience cannot be avoided in the interim period when remedial adjustments are being made to eliminate the dual school systems.

Since in Charlotte-Mecklenburg *all things were not equal*, the Chief Justice held that the busing component of the district court's order was constitutionally appropriate. He took judicial notice of the fact that the district had employed a bus transportation system for years and that the distances travelled and the amount of time required in the instant plan compared favorably with Charlotte's previous transportation plan.

In another busing decision (*North Carolina State Board of Education* v. *Swann*, 402 U.S. 43, 1971), the Court affirmed a lower court decision that had ruled unconstitutional a North Carolina anti-bussing law. The statute provided that "[n]o student shall be assigned or compelled to attend any school on account of race, creed, color or national origin" and specifically prohibited "involuntary bussing of students" and expenditure of public funds for busing. Chief Justice Burger, speaking for a unanimous Court, held that "if a state imposed limitation on a school authority's discretion operates to inhibit or obstruct the operation of a unitary school system or impede the disestablishing of a dual system, it must fall; state policy must give way when it operates to hinder vindication of federal constitutional guarantees."

However, the Court's line of unanimous school desegregation opinions was broken in a 1972 decision involving schools in a Virginia county. In *Wright* v. *Emporia* (407 U.S. 451) a 5-4 majority held that the city of Emporia could not set up a separate school system in a context where such separation might adversely affect a desegregation order for dismantling a dual school system on a county-wide basis. Here the city of Emporia, which had been a part of Greenville County, Virginia school system, attempted to establish its own system after a district court had found the county system to be in violation of *Brown*. "Only when it became clear," said Justice Stewart for the majority, "that segregation in the county system was finally to be abolished did Emporia attempt to take its children out of the county system." Stewart thus agreed with the district court's conclusion "that if Emporia were allowed to establish an independent system, Negroes remaining in the county schools would be deprived of what *Brown II* promised them: a school system in which all vestiges of enforced racial segregation have been eliminated."

But Chief Justice Burger, joined by the other three Nixon appointees, Justices Blackmun, Powell, and Rehnquist, issued a sharp dissent. Burger criticized the majority for implying that severance of Emporia from the county system would bring about something less than unitary schools. The Chief Justice said that residence alone would determine school assignment and "would in no sense depend on race." In general, Burger's dissent concerned the limits of judicial power and the discretion that must be left to local authorities. "A local school board plan," said Burger, "that will eliminate dual schools, stop discrimination, and improve the quality of education ought not to be cast aside because a judge can evolve some other plan that accomplishes the same result or what he considers a preferable result. . . . Such an approach gives controlling weight to sociological theories," opined the Chief Justice, but "not constitutional doctrine."

Burger clarified further his position on this issue in his concurring opinion in *United States* v. *Scotland Neck City Board of Education* (407 U.S. 493, 1972), decided the same day as *Wright*. In *Scotland Neck*, Justice Stewart, speaking for the same five members of the Court who comprised the majority in *Wright*, enjoined implementation of a state law authorizing creation of a new school district in Scotland Neck, North Carolina, a city (like Emporia, Virginia) that "was part of a larger school district then in the process of dismantling a dual school system." Stewart noted that the statute "was enacted with the effect of creating a refuge for white students" of the larger school system and "interferes with the desegregation" of this larger system. This time, Chief Justice Burger, again joined by Justices Blackmun, Powell, and Rehnquist, concurred. Burger distinguished the facts in *Scotland Neck* from those in *Wright*. In *Scotland Neck*, said Burger, "operation of a separate school system . . . would preclude meaningful desegregation" for almost one-third of the students involved and "the effect of the withdrawal would thus be dramatically different from the effect which could be anticipated in Emporia." He also cited the differences in the motivations involved in the two cases. "The Scotland Neck severance," said the Chief Justice, "was substantially motivated by the desire to create a predominantly white system" while "the record shows that Emporia's decision was not based on the projected racial composition of the proposed new system."

What could prove to be the Burger Court's most important and far-reaching school desegregation decision came in *Keyes* v. *School District No. 1* (413 U.S. 921), a 1973 case involving public education in Denver, Colorado. Here, for the first time, the Court made a definitive statement on northern style de facto segregation and put northern school districts on notice that where "intentional segregation" occurred in particular units, those units must be desegregated. In remanding the case to the district court to determine whether a policy of intentional segregation in a substantial portion of a school district is indicative that other parts of the district were likewise affected by a "segregative intent," Justice William J. Brennan, who spoke for the Court, emphasized that the school board had the unmistakable burden of proving that its policies and practices with respect to school site location, school size, school renovations and additions, student attendance zones, student assignment and transfer options, mobile classroom units, transportation of students, assignment of faculty and staff, and so forth, considered together and premised on the board's so-called neighborhood school concept were not designed to create or maintain a policy of racial segregation in the inner-city schools.

In a concurring opinion, Justice William O. Douglas took judicial notice of the painful but certain progress in school desegregation in the South and the lack of such effort in many nonsouthern cities with large minority populations. Echoing the charges of many apologists of southern school systems, he noted that many northern school systems were now as fully segregated as those of the South before the implementation of *Brown*. He charged that this northern system was being condoned under the "*de facto-de jure* distinction nurtured by lower courts and accepted complacently by many of the same voices which denounced the evils of segregated schools in the South." Consequently, he thought it was high time to discard the *de facto-de jure* formula and "formulate constitutional principles of national rather than merely regional application."

In dissent, Justice William Rehnquist complained of the Court's "confusing enunciation of evidentiary rules" so that the trial court would more likely on remand reach the kind of decision he felt the majority desired. In addition, he was greatly troubled by the Court's new standard of equating the district-wide consequences of segregation in individual attendance zones, where legal segregation had never been required, with those districts that legally required segregated schools. In short, he did not feel that the finding of purposeful segregation in one attendance zone in Denver could be the basis for imputing a segregatory intent to the entire system.

It is too early to assess fully the impact of *Keyes*. But one thing is already fairly clear—as the traditional neighborhood school policy is altered to produce greater racial balance in big city school districts of the North, there will be an acceleration of "white flight" to suburbia. Hence, big city public school systems, like the one in Denver, Colorado could become increasingly black and resegregated. However the remedy proposed by Federal District Judge Robert Mehrige in *Bradley* v. *School Board of the City of Richmond* (338 F. Supp. 67, 1972), struck at the heart of such patterns. Noting that the undesirable racial balance in Richmond and the two adjoining suburban districts involved stemmed partly from invidious state action,

Judge Mehrige ordered consolidation of the three districts and extensive "two-way busing" of pupils to achieve the degree of integration he felt had been commanded by *Brown*. But the Court of Appeals for the Fourth Circuit thought that Judge Mehrige's remedy was "neither necessary [n] or justified" since state-imposed segregation in each of the districts "had been completely removed." 462 F. 2d 1058, 1972. The appeals court's decision was left standing when the Supreme Court (with Justice Lewis Powell, as a former member of the Richmond school board, disqualifying himself) split 4-4 on appeal.

Shortly thereafter, however, the Court accepted for review the case of *Milliken* v. *Bradley*, where another federal district court utilized the inter-district busing remedy to dismantle racially segregated schools in Detroit and its surrounding suburbs. This time all nine justices heard the case and by a 5-4 margin (with Justice Potter Stewart joining the four Nixon appointees) overturned the lower court order. Chief Justice Warren Burger's opinion for the majority rejected inter-district busing as a remedy to meet the command of Brown except in those cases where both districts were found to operate racially segregated schools. In Burger's view such a busing remedy could only be employed where discriminatory acts in one district produced discrimination in the other or where there was collusive action in the gerrymandering of the districts involved.

Justice Thurgood Marshall, who was Chief Counsel for the petitioners in *Brown*, expressed his outrage at the majority position in a sharp dissent. Characterizing the ruling as an "emasculation of our constitutional guarantee of equal protection of the laws," Marshall complained that the decision had the effect of saying to black children in inner city schools of large metropolitan areas that you have no remedy to enforce your constitutional rights declared in *Brown*. For him, however, there was a remedy and there were precedents to support it. He noted that public education was a state function and that school districts had been created for administrative purposes. Hence, such district lines are not sacrosanct because they had been considered flexible for a variety of purposes and they should not stand as barriers to the relief sought. He concluded that the state's duty "to achieve the greatest possible degree of desegregation" could not be accomplished unless the surrounding suburban districts are involved in the desegregation remedy.

An equally controversial issue—affirmative action admissions programs in higher education—was sidestepped by the Court during the same term. In *DeFunis* v. *Odegaard* (416 U.S. 312, 1974), the petitioner, a white student who was denied admission to the University of Washington's law school, charged that the school's admissions policies fostered "reverse discrimination" and hence abridged the equal protection clause of the Fourteenth Amendment. The University admitted that the petitioner's grades and Law School Aptitude Test scores were higher than those of some 36 black, Latino, and other minority students who were admitted. However, the University justified its policy by indicating its use of a broad range of factors, in addition to raw grades and test scores, to arrive at admissions decisions. It further defended its administrative discretion as supportive of its affirmative action program to expand opportunities for legal education to members of those groups whose access to the legal profession in the past had been negligible. However, a state trial court agreed with DeFunis and ordered his admission in 1971. The Washington Supreme Court reversed that ruling, but DeFunis was allowed to remain in school as the case was appealed to the U.S. Supreme Court.

With completion of his studies assured just a few weeks later, five justices of the Court (the four Nixon appointees and Justice Stewart) saw no need to decide the issue. The case was not instituted as a class action and was now moot. The majority did concede, however, that with such admissions policies in widespread use the issue would undoubtedly confront the Court again in the near future.

Among the minority, Justice William O. Douglas was most critical of the Court for avoiding the issue. He was sure that the issue would come back again with "relative speed." On the merits, Douglas intimated that as currently constituted and applied the Washington policies infringed equal protection. To him, any policy that was not administered in a "racially neutral way" is constitutionally defective, no matter what the social ends. On the other hand, however, he did not think that universities should be limited to "mechanical criteria" in determining admissions. It would be perfectly proper to consider such factors as past deprivations resulting from racially discriminatory policies. But if such consideration is based on race instead of "individual merits," equal protection is abridged. For, as Douglas concluded, the equal protection clause "commands the elimination of racial barriers, not their creation in order to satisfy our theory as to how society ought to be organized."

While the constitutional issue was left unsettled, the impact of this "non-decision" could well be the immediate alteration of affirmative action admissions policies to cut back on the intake of minority students in higher education generally. And indeed with the widespread interest generated on the affirmative action issue by this case, as evidenced by the large number of *amici curiae* briefs filed, affirmative action programs in other areas (particularly employment) may well be decelerated or even phased out.

An interesting dimension of the racial discrimination problem in the public schools focusing on an Oriental problem was considered by the Supreme Court in *Lau* v. *Nichols* (414 U.S. 563, 1974). Involved was a charge by non-English-speaking Chinese pupils that the San Francisco Board of Education, in failing to provide them English language instruction, violated the provision of the 1964 Civil Rights Act which prohibits discrimination on the basis of national origin, etc., in "any program or activity receiving federal financial assistance." The Supreme Court agreed that the charge of discrimination was proved and reversed the lower federal court decisions unanimously. Justice William O. Douglas, whose opinion was supported by Justices Brennan, Marshall, Powell, and Rehnquist, argued that not only had the San Francisco Board of Education failed to comply with its own state code to provide bilingual instruction, but it had violated section 601 of the 1964 Civil Rights Act as well. Such a denial, he concluded, denies the non-English speaking minority "a meaningful opportunity to participate in the educational program." Douglas saw no need to reach the Equal Protection clause argument.

While school desegregation was proceeding with obviously more "deliberation" than "speed" in the decade following *Brown*, a vigorous campaign began against segregation practices of eating places, hotels, theaters, and other places providing accommodations for the public. The tactics employed were markedly different from those used in the school segregation controversy—sit-ins and massive demonstrations were substituted for court challenges. Of course, these tactics themselves became the subject of litigation as discussed in Chapter 3. The objective was to prod the conscience of the various communities and the nation generally into a reexamination of racial segregation as a moral proposition. Beginning in 1960, demonstrations spread throughout the South and thousands of demonstrators, mostly college and high school students, were arrested and jailed. Though numerous appeals were taken to the Supreme Court, the Court was able to dispose of the cases without tackling the tough constitutional issue of segregated accommodations. Cf. *Garner* v. *Louisiana* (368 U.S. 157, 1961). Apparently, most of the justices were not yet ready to reexamine the *Civil Rights Cases* (109 U.S. 3, 1883), where the Court limited the command of the equal protection clause to state action only, excluding the discriminatory actions of private individuals who provide various accommodations for the public.

In a few scattered instances segregation practices were abandoned as a result of demonstrations, but in the end it took the public accommodations title of the 1964 Civil Rights Act to ban this form of private discrimination. This legislation was challenged immediately after it was signed by President Johnson. But a federal district court in Georgia sustained the constitutionality of the act and denied attempts to enjoin its enforcement as applied to a restaurant and a motel. In Alabama, however, a federal district court held the public accommodations title unconstitutional as applied to a local eating establishment. Upon appeal of both rulings, the Supreme Court held the legislation to be a valid exercise of the commerce power (*Heart of Atlanta Motel* v. *United States* and *Katzenbach* v. *McClung*, 379 U.S. 294, 1964).

Having waged a successful campaign against segregated public accommodations, civil rights groups marshalled forces for a concerted effort against discrimination in the housing market. State action promoting racially segregated housing had long ago been declared an infringement of the equal protection clause of the Fourteenth Amendment. In 1917, the Supreme Court invalidated an ordinance of Louisville, Kentucky which established separate residential districts for blacks and whites (*Buchanan* v. *Warley*, 245 U.S. 60), and in 1948, the Court dealt restrictive covenant arrangements a crushing blow by holding them unenforceable in state courts (*Shelley* v. *Kraemer*, 324 U.S. 1; see also *Barrows* v. *Jackson*, 346 U.S. 249, 1952). However, segregated housing patterns continued to develop primarily as a result of private action initiated and sustained by policies of the real estate industry.

The technique employed by groups challenging housing discrimination was essentially that of massive demonstrations and pressure on state and local legislative bodies for "open occupancy" legislation. Where these efforts were successful, the courts have upheld such legislation as a valid exercise of state power to achieve a nondiscriminatory housing market. However, a challenge to the California fair housing law went beyond the courts to the people in the 1964 general election. Using the popular initiative and referendum, opponents of open housing pushed through an amendment to the state constitution nullifying the state fair housing law and rendering the legislature powerless to enact such legislation in the future. In the referendum, the people of California overwhelmingly approved as state policy "private" discrimination in the housing market. But after examining the amendment in terms of its "immediate objective," the state supreme court declared adoption of the amendment to be an unconstitutional state involvement in promoting private discrimination contrary to the equal protection of the laws. The U.S. Supreme Court affirmed this judgment in *Reitman* v. *Mulkey* (387 U.S. 369, 1967), on the same equal protection grounds and in doing so rejected the proposition that constitutional rights may be submitted to a popular referendum. In 1969 the Supreme Court in *Hunter* v. *Erickson* (393 U.S. 385) held unconstitutional as a denial of equal protection an amendment to the city charter of Akron, Ohio. Even though adopted in a popular referendum by majority vote, the amendment, in effect, placed "special burdens" on racial minorities by preventing the city council from enacting fair housing ordinances unless approved in a referendum by a majority of the city's voters. "The sovereignty of the people," said the Court, "is itself subject to those constitutional limitations which have been duly adopted and remain unrepealed."

Despite the spread of fair housing laws at the state and local level, the Johnson Administration pushed for a national law to ban discrimination in the sale and rental of housing. For three successive years (1966–1968) President Lyndon Johnson included such a proposal in civil rights bills submitted to Congress. The proposal got nowhere in 1966 and 1967; in 1968 it was floundering with only a remote possibility of passage. However, the assassination of the Reverend Martin Luther King, Jr., on April 4, 1968 and the widespread urban violence that followed, spurred immediate Congressional approval of a fair housing law. And in signing the measure President Johnson hailed "fair housing for all human beings who live in this country as now a part of the American way of life."

The law bans discrimination in the sale and rental of 80 percent of the nation's housing. Excluded from its provisions are owner-occupied dwellings of four units or less and privately-owned single family homes where sale and rental transactions do not involve the services of a real estate broker. The nondiscriminatory provisions also extend to financing and brokerage services. The Department of Housing and Urban Development is charged with seeking voluntary compliance, but enforcement is possible through civil actions by individuals and by the Attorney General, who is authorized to file suits against the offender(s) where a pattern or general practice of discrimination is found.

Just two months after the enactment of the 1968 law, the Supreme Court resurrected an amorphous federal statute that had been passed to enforce the Thirteenth Amendment and construed it to apply to private discrimination in the housing market. In *Jones* v. *Mayer* the Court held that the provision of the Civil Rights Act of 1866 which guarantees to black citizens the same right "enjoyed by white[s] . . . to inherit, purchase, lease, sell, hold, and convey real and personal property" prohibits racial discrimination in the sale of housing by a private developer. Justice Potter Stewart, who wrote the Court's opinion, said that the statute's language was "plain and unambiguous" in its declaration of property rights available to *all* citizens and "on its face . . . appears to prohibit *all* discrimination against Negroes in sale or rental of property." Furthermore, Justice Stewart had no doubt about the authority of Congress to act. He noted that the act was grounded in the Thirteenth Amendment which proclaims in absolute terms that "neither slavery nor involuntary servitude . . . shall exist within the United States. . . ." Stewart concluded that while this amendment "by its own unaided force and effect abolished slavery and established universal freedom," the enabling section empowered Congress to enact "all laws necessary and proper to abolish all badges and incidents of slavery."

The Court emphasized that its action in no way "diminished the significance of the [1968 fair housing law]" since there were vast differences between the two measures. Justice Stewart noted, for example, that the 1866 act was "a general statute applicable only to racial discrimination in the rental and sale of property" with remedial relief available only through private action while, on the other hand, the 1968 statute was a comprehensive housing measure (applicable to a number of discriminatory practices and exempting specific types of units) "enforceable by a complete arsenal of federal authority."

Justices Harlan and White dissented and, in an opinion written by Harlan, felt that the decision was "most ill-considered and ill-advised." Harlan thought that since the political branches had recently produced fair housing legislation geared to the current dynamics of society there was no need to grant the relief sought under the old statute. However, the heart of Harlan's dissent was that neither the language of the 1866 act nor its legislative history can support the conclusion reached by the majority that the statute was intended to extend to private action.

In a related development, the Supreme Court interpreted the public accommodations section of the Civil Rights Act of 1964 to cover a privately owned recreational facility that catered to interstate travelers (*Daniel* v. *Paul*, 395 U.S. 298, 1969). Justice William J. Brennan, who spoke for the Court, brushed aside attempts of defendant Paul, owner of the Lake Nixon Club (located about 12 miles from Little Rock, Arkansas), to evade the strictures of the act by selling membership cards and advertising his establishment as a "private club." Brennan found that the operations of the club generally, and its snack bar in particular, were so affected by interstate commerce that the entire facility was a place of public accommodation within the meaning of the 1964 act.

Three years later, in *Moose Lodge No. 107* v. *Irvis* (407 U.S. 163, 1972), however, the Court construed the "state action" concept narrowly in upholding the right of a private club to refuse service to blacks. Speaking for the 6–3 majority,

Justice William Rehnquist contended that the state's action in granting a liquor license to a private club whose policy excluded service to blacks did not in and of itself constitute the kind of state involvement proscribed by the equal protection clause of the Fourteenth Amendment. "To hold otherwise," he concluded, "would utterly emasculate the distinction between private as distinguished from State conduct as set forth in the *Civil Rights Cases* and adhered to in subsequent decisions."

In dissent Justice William O. Douglas once again stressed a more expansive "state action" concept as he had done so often in the public accommodations sit-in cases. To him, the Pennsylvania regulatory scheme operates in such a fashion as to support the Lodge's racial exclusion policy by requiring that "[e]very club license shall adhere to all provisions of its Constitution and By-laws." And the Moose Constitution clearly limits membership to the "Caucasian or White race."

The Burger Court's restrained view of "state involvement" was also evidenced in *Palmer* v. *Thompson* (403 U.S. 217, 1971). By a 5–4 decision the Court refused to force the city of Jackson, Mississippi, to reopen its public swimming pools. The pools had been closed after lower federal courts ruled that Jackson must desegregate its recreational facilities, including swimming pools. Although the city desegregated other facilities (e.g., public parks and golf courses), it decided to close the municipal pools. Blacks in Jackson sued to compel reopening of the pools by the city. But this time, the lower court rejected their plea, holding that the equal protection clause had not been violated since the pools were closed for economic rather than racial reasons. But it was one of the Warren Court holdovers, Justice Hugo Black, who wrote the majority opinion affirming the lower court's position. To the petitioner's argument that the pool closings were unconstitutional because they were "motivated by a desire to avoid desegregation," Black declared that "no case in this Court has held that a legislative act may violate equal protection solely because of the motivations of the men who voted for it." Black said that the facts "show no state action affecting blacks differently from whites" and he refused to "stretch" the Thirteenth Amendment to apply it to this case.

The four dissenting justices (White, Douglas, Marshall, and Brennan) took sharp exception to such reasoning. Justice White, for example, argued that "a State may not have an official stance against desegregating public facilities and implement it by closing those facilities in response to a desegregation order." White continued: "The fact is that closing the pools is an expression of official policy that Negroes are unfit to associate with whites. Closing pools to prevent interracial swimming is little different from laws or customs forbidding Negroes and whites from eating together or from cohabiting or inter-marrying." And Justice Douglas maintained "that though a State may discontinue any of its municipal services . . . it may not do so for the purpose of perpetuating or installing *apartheid* or because it finds life in a multiracial community difficult or unpleasant." (Emphasis added.)

But the Burger Court took a different position on an arrangement designed to help "private segregated academies" meet their recreational needs. In *Gilmore* v. *City of Montgomery, Alabama* (417 U.S. 356, 1974), the Court nullified a city action granting to such an academy exclusive possession and control of a city-owned facility for their athletic contests and recreational activities. Justice Harry Blackmun's opinion emphasized that this arrangement (coming at a time when the city was under a court order to desegregate its recreation facilities) had the effect of creating enclaves of segregation "by depriving blacks of equal access to them." The Court, however, avoided a more difficult question of whether such private academies can be enjoined from utilizing public facilities altogether.

VOTING RIGHTS AND REAPPORTIONMENT

Despite the voting rights guarantee of the Fifteenth Amendment, systematic exclusion of black Americans from the electoral process was commonplace for almost a century after the amendment's adoption. This condition was in large measure a consequence of our federal system. States not only exercise power to determine who can vote in state and local contests, but in practice, one's participation in federal elections is essentially in the hands of state officials as well.

Putting aside earlier practices of threats and physical intimidation, states devised several legal schemes to circumvent the Fifteenth Amendment and thwart its objective. While such legal barriers were successful in generally disfranchising Southern blacks, they were gradually eliminated as the Supreme Court found them constitutionally deficient.

One of the early schemes was the so-called grandfather-clause literacy provision. Its basic design was to employ a literacy test for voting and exclude from its application all persons whose ancestors had voted on or before January 1, 1866. Obviously few, if any, blacks could inherit this permanent enfranchisement, while many whites could. In *Guinn* v. *United States* (238 U.S. 347, 1915), the Supreme Court struck down this Oklahoma scheme as an infringement of the Fifteenth Amendment.

The traditional one-party system in the South facilitated one of the most effective legal barriers to black suffrage. With the Republican Party largely dormant, the real contests for public office were in the Democratic Party primary elections. Hence, the black man's vote could be rendered ineffective by denying his participation in Democratic Party primaries. A decision of the Supreme Court in *Newberry* v. *United States* (256 U.S. 232, 1921), in which the majority held that as far as federal elections were concerned the primary was "in no real sense" a part thereof, undoubtedly influenced the Texas legislature as it took action to perfect the white primary. After two unsuccessful attempts to exclude blacks from Democratic primaries by state law (*Nixon* v. *Herndon,* 273 U.S. 536, 1927 and *Nixon* v. *Condon,* 286 U.S. 73, 1932), the action of the state Democratic Party convention to exclude blacks from its primaries avoided constitutional infirmity. In *Grovey* v. *Townsend* (295 U.S. 45, 1935), the Court ruled that this party action did not infringe the Fourteenth Amendment since no state action was involved. The Court concluded that the Democratic Party was simply acting as a private voluntary group.

By 1941, a change in judicial attitude on the status of primary elections was indicated in *United States* v. *Classic* (313 U.S. 299). Involved was a federal prosecution of a Louisiana election official for ballot fraud in a Congressional primary election. The district court had rejected federal regulation of such contests largely on the authority of the *Newberry* decision. But in reversing this holding, the Supreme Court held that the right to vote in such primary elections is secured by the federal Constitution and that Congress has the authority to regulate primaries "when they are a step in the exercise by the people of their choice of representatives in Congress."

The *Classic* decision clearly forecast the downfall of the white primary by rejecting the "private" status theory of primary elections. In fact that downfall came only three years later in *Smith* v. *Allwright* (321 U.S. 649, 1944), when the Court had before it another challenge to the Texas white primary system. The Court thus eliminated this impediment to Negro suffrage by directly reversing *Grovey* v. *Townsend*. Political parties and party primaries were regulated by massive state legislation and party action was for all practical purposes "state action." Hence, party action, which discriminated against blacks, was really state action contrary to the command of the Fifteenth Amendment.

Several schemes designed to resurrect the white primary proved to be little more than delaying nuisances. The South Carolina effort to make the party a truly private club by repealing some 150 statutory provisions governing primary elections was rejected by the lower federal courts and the Supreme Court denied certiorari (*Rice* v. *Elmore*, 333 U.S. 875, 1948). A Texas county's evasive scheme took the form of a pre-primary election from which black voters were excluded. The winner filed in the regular Democratic primary and was usually elected without opposition. In *Terry* v. *Adams* (345 U.S. 461, 1953), the Supreme Court rejected the "private" status claim of the "Jaybird" group and held that its primary was an integral part of the election process that must conform with the command of the Fifteenth Amendment.

Despite the death of the white primary, blacks attempting to vote in many southern areas continued to meet stiff resistance from both official and nonofficial sources. Cumbersome registration procedures and "understanding" tests administered by hostile registration officials in an atmosphere of fear, threatened economic intimidation, and deeply-rooted apathy succeeded in keeping all but a few blacks off voter registration rolls. The larger the potential black vote, the more determined was the resistance. For example, when the large black registration in Tuskegee, Alabama (county seat of Macon County) presaged a possible takeover of city government by black officials, the state legislature enacted a statute gerrymandering nearly all resident blacks out of the city. In declaring the act unconstitutional in *Gomillion* v. *Lightfoot* (364 U.S. 339, 1960), the Supreme Court rejected Alabama's "political-question" argument. It held that while in form the act was merely a redefinition of municipal boundaries, "the inescapable human effect of [that] essay in geometry and geography" was to deprive blacks of their voting rights secured by the Fifteenth Amendment.

Black leaders and civil-rights activists correctly recognized that judicial declarations alone would not secure the ballot for blacks. Hence, they marshalled forces to a concerted effort to break the remaining resistance to black suffrage by concentrating on Presidential and Congressional action to implement the Fifteenth Amendment. Their efforts resulted in the Civil Rights Acts of 1957, 1960, 1964, and 1965.

Although the acts of 1957 and 1960[5] were generally viewed by blacks and civil-rights groups as rather mild palliatives for a serious defect in our democratic political system, the fact that Congress had finally taken some action to enforce to Fifteenth Amendment was considered a significant step in the southern blacks' quest for political equality. The chief defect of these acts was the continued reliance on the courts. Litigation could be dragged on for a long period of time in the courtrooms of local federal judges who might reasonably be expected to be sympathetic to maintenance of the status quo.

The 1964 Civil Rights Act, while primarily directed at discrimination in public accommodations and other areas, dealt a crippling blow to the literacy and "understanding" tests which had been effective in thwarting black voter registration. In *Lassiter* v. *Northampton County Board of Elections* (360 U.S. 45, 1959), the Supreme Court had warned that although literacy tests were constitutional, they could not be employed as instruments of racial discrimination. But evidence gathered by the Civil Rights Commission indicated that this warning had been largely ignored by southern registrars. Consequently, the act provided that registration officials had to apply their standards equally and administer their tests in writing, keeping the test papers for possible review.

After the 1964 elections, there was considerable evidence that the black man's right to vote had still not been secured in many areas of the South. The registration machinery was still in the hands of state and local officials, most of whom were opposed to black voting rights. Consequently, at President Johnson's urging and following massive demonstrations in the South, Congress passed a comprehensive voting rights act in 1965. The major improvement over the earlier laws was the provision for federal machinery for voter registration. In addition, the act suspended the use of literacy, understanding, and other tests in states and voting districts where less than 50 percent of the voting-age residents were registered in 1964 or actually voted in the 1964 Presidential election. Criminal sanctions could be applied also to anyone attempting to harm, threaten, or prevent persons from voting or civil-rights workers from assisting potential voters. Finally, the act directed the Justice Department to institute injunctive action against the enforcement of the poll tax requirement in the five states retaining it.

One of the discrimination devices suspended by the act—the "understanding" test—had been struck down in the case of *Louisiana* v. *United States* (380 U.S. 145, 1965) by the time the President signed the measure. In that case the Supreme

---

[5] The 1957 act created a Civil Rights Commission and charged it (among other duties) to gather evidence of denials of the right to vote. More significantly, blacks were relieved of the burden of filing their own lawsuits as the Attorney General was empowered to seek injunctions against those conspiring to deny the right to vote. The 1960 Act continued to place reliance on the courts. Upon application of the Attorney General and after a finding of a persistent pattern of discrimination, federal district judges were empowered to appoint referees to register qualified persons to vote in both federal and state elections.

Court upheld a district court ruling invalidating the Louisiana constitutional and statutory provisions which required every applicant for voting to "be able to understand" and "give a reasonable interpretation" of any provision of the state or federal constitution. Justice Hugo Black's opinion for the Court emphasized the discriminatory manner in which the test had been applied:

> The applicant facing a registrar in Louisiana . . . [is] compelled to leave his voting fate to that official's uncontrolled power to determine whether the applicant's understanding of the Federal or State Constitution is satisfactory. As the evidence showed, colored people, even some with the most advanced education and scholarship, were declared by voting registrars with less education to have an unsatisfactory understanding of . . . [those constitutions]. This is not a test but a trap, sufficient to stop even the most brilliant man on his way to the voting booth.

As expected, officials in Louisiana, Alabama, and Mississippi immediately challenged the act's constitutionality. The challenges came in the form of state court injunctions forbidding local election officials to enter on voting rolls the names of persons registered by federal examiners. Instead of instituting actions under Section 12(d) of the act to dissolve these injunctions, the Attorney General filed a motion to bring action in the original jurisdiction of the Supreme Court against the three states. In the meantime, South Carolina brought an injunctive action in the original jurisdiction of the Court against enforcement of the act by the Attorney General. After a consideration of the complex jurisdictional questions posed by these simultaneous actions, the Supreme Court accepted the South Carolina suit—*South Carolina* v. *Katzenbach*—as an appropriate vehicle for testing the constitutionality of the act's basic provisions. The Court upheld the act primarily on the authority of Congress to enact legislation pursuant to the Fifteenth Amendment. Chief Justice Earl Warren's opinion for the Court emphasized the massive findings of state defiance of the command of the Amendment, and the Congressional conclusion that sterner and more elaborate measures were needed to protect the right to vote. Quoting from Chief Justice John Marshall in *Gibbons* v. *Ogden* (9 Wheat. 1, 1824), Warren concluded that the power of Congress to enforce the Fifteenth Amendment, "like all others vested in [it], is complete in itself, may be exercised to its utmost extent, and acknowledges no limitations, other than are prescribed in the Constitution."

Soon after the *South Carolina* decision, the Court struck down the poll tax in *Harper* v. *Virginia Board of Elections* (383 U.S. 663, 1966). The Court based the holding entirely on the equal protection clause of the Fourteenth Amendment. Justice William O. Douglas, speaking for the Court, maintained that "voter qualifications have no relation to wealth nor to paying or not paying" a tax. He concluded that "wealth, like race, creed, or color, is not germane to one's ability to participate intelligently in the electoral process."

The 1964 Voting Rights Act also contains a provision designed to aid Spanish-speaking voters. It provides that no person who has obtained at least a sixth-grade education from an accredited school in the United States or its territories, in which the predominant classroom language was other than English, shall be denied the right to vote because of his inability to read or write English. The provision had particular relevance for New York City, with its large Puerto Rican population, where literacy in English was required as a condition for voting. In *Katzenbach* v. *Morgan* (384 U.S. 641, 1966), the Supreme Court reversed a ruling of the District Court for the District of Columbia and upheld the provision's constitutionality as a valid exercise of Congressional power to enforce the equal protection clause of the Fourteenth Amendment. Justice Brennan's opinion for the Court emphasized that the New York literacy test was not in question under the Fourteenth Amendment. The crucial question, however, was the power of Congress under the Amendment to suspend operation of the test. Referring to the "necessary and proper" clause, he concluded that the provision was appropriate legislation to enforce the equal protection clause.

Simultaneous with the voting rights revolution was the drive to reapportion state legislatures. Here was a controversy involving the failure of rural-oriented state legislatures to honor reapportionment provisions of their state constitutions. This situation had caused those areas that had increased in population—cities and suburbs—to become increasingly underrepresented in state legislatures, while those areas that had stood still or had in fact lost population (rural) became increasingly overrepresented. For some time the Supreme Court had refused to enter the controversy, relying mainly on the "political question" doctrine (*Colegrove* v. *Green*, 328 U.S. 549, 1946). And though *Gomillion* v. *Lightfoot*, discussed above, raised the political issue anew, the Court was able to circumvent it by saying that unlike *Colegrove* where the state (Illinois) had failed to act, here (in *Gomillion*) the state (Alabama) had taken "affirmative action" to deprive blacks of their right to vote.

But in 1962, just two years after *Gomillion*, the Court found in *Baker* v. *Carr* (396 U.S. 186, 1962), that the "political question" doctrine was not a barrier to considering reapportionment since that doctrine, upon close reexamination, had not even commanded a majority in *Colegrove*. In any event, the Court held in *Baker* that reapportionment was a justiciable question subject to judicial remedies. And the judicial remedy was not long forthcoming. On June 15, 1964 in *Reynolds* v. *Sims* (377 U.S. 533), the Court stated that the "one man, one vote" formula was the constitutional rule to be followed in reapportionment of both houses of state legislatures. Subsequent Court decisions have generally applied this rule to other aspects of the electoral process. (See, for example, *Avery* v. *Midland County*, 390 U.S. 474, 1968; but compare and contrast *Sailors* v. *Board of Education of Kent County*, 387 U.S. 203; and *Abate* v. *Mundt*, 403 U.S. 182, 1971.)

The Court, in effect, fashioned its *Reynolds* decision largely on the basis of two earlier cases, *Gray* v. *Sanders* (372 U.S. 368, 1963), and *Wesberry* v. *Sanders* (376 U.S. 1, 1964). In *Wesberry*, for example, the Court said that "while it may not be possible to draw congressional districts with mathematical precision, . . . [the Constitution requires] as nearly as is practicable one man's vote in a congressional election is to be worth as much as another's." The Court had occasion in a 1969 case (*Kirkpatrick* v. *Preisler*) to elucidate on *Wesberry'* "as nearly as practicable" standard. Here the Court rejected "Missouri's argument that there is a fixed numerical or percentage population variance small enough to be considered de minimis and to satisfy without question the 'as nearly as practicable' standard." That standard, said the Court, "requires that the State make a good-faith effort to achieve precise mathematical equality."

Overall, the impact of the Court's reapportionment decisions has been mixed. While reapportionment has helped to increase urban (and black) representation, it has also resulted in increased suburban representation and influence, especially at the state level. Moreover, the effect of reapportionment on policy outputs of state legislatures has by no means lived up to expectations of those forces bent on dealing with pressing urban and social problems. (See Selected References.)

In more recent cases the Supreme Court has been faced with situations in which state legislatures allegedly restructured electoral districts so as to reduce or minimize black representation. (*Whitcomb* v. *Chavis*, 403 U.S. 124, 1971; but compare *Connor* v. *Johnson*, 402 U.S. 690, 1971.) In *Whitcomb*, for example, the Court upheld a state legislature's power to restructure its electoral districts against claims that its objective and result was to dilute black representation. In 1965 the Indiana legislature enacted statutes establishing Marion County, which embraces Indianapolis with its large concentration of black residents, as a multi-member district from which eight senators and 15 representatives were to be elected at-large to the state legislature. A federal district court agreed with black challengers that the multi-member district scheme operated to minimize and cancel out the voting strength of blacks and consequently deprived them of equal protection of the laws. In its reasoning the lower court noted that there was an identifiable racial minority in the Indianapolis ghetto with specific legislative interests that were significantly different from the interests of those residing elsewhere. Such areas of substantive law as housing regulations, welfare and health care, law enforcement, urban renewal and anti-discrimination statutes were cited as examples of the divergent interests of ghetto residents and nonresidents. This finding, coupled with such factors as the strong party control of nominations, the responsibility of legislators to the party and county at large, and the absence of any particular legislators who were accountable to ghetto residents led to the court's finding of invidious discrimination.

The Supreme Court, however, was not so persuaded and reversed the lower court in a 6–3 decision. In his opinion for the Court, Justice Byron White emphasized that while there may be flaws in the multi-member scheme, such districts are not "inherently invidious and violative of the Fourteenth Amendment." More specifically, he noted that there was no showing that the multi-member districts in Marion County and in other areas of Indiana were "conceived or operated as purposeful devices to further racial or economic discrimination."

Absent evidence that blacks "had less opportunity than did other Marion County residents to participate in the political processes and to elect legislators of their choice," White argued that "the failure of the ghetto to have legislative seats in proportion to its population emerges more as a function of losing elections than of built-in bias against poor Negroes." Indeed, he continued, "[t]he voting power of ghetto residents may have been 'cancelled out' as the District Court held, but this seems a mere euphemism for political defeat at the polls." White specifically disagreed with the lower court's view that ghetto votes could not be adequately or equally represented unless some of the county's legislative seats were reserved for ghetto residents serving the interests of the ghetto majority. "The mere fact," said White, "that one interest group or another concerned with the outcome of Marion County elections has found itself outvoted and without legislative seats of its own provides no basis for invoking constitutional remedies where, as here, there is no indication that this segment of the population is being denied access to the political system." Moreover, he concluded, to uphold the position of one racial group would make it difficult to reject claims of any other groups (e.g., Republicans, Democrats, Labor) who find themselves similarly disadvantaged.

Justice Douglas, joined by Justices Brennan and Marshall, dissented, strongly supporting the "outstanding job" the district court had done. Douglas maintained that "the test for multi-member districts is whether there are invidious effects," and that in this case he thought there were. Douglas concluded that the effect of the multi-member district in Marion County was to "purposely wash blacks out of the system and once this is done the system has a constitutional defect."

But actions in other areas point to an "opening up" of the electoral process. In 1972, for example, the Court struck down lengthy residency requirements for voting in state elections as violative of the equal protection clause (*Dunn* v. *Blumstein*, 405 U.S. 330). Here the Court declared invalid Tennessee requirements that made one year of residency in the state and three months of residency in the county prerequisites for voting.

Similarly, the Voting Rights Act Amendments of 1970 included a provision prohibiting "durational" residence requirements for voting in Presidential elections. Specifically, states were precluded from closing voter registration more than 30 days prior to such elections. In adopting this policy, Congress specifically found that lengthy residency requirements do "not bear a reasonable relationship to any compelling state interest in the conduct of presidential elections." In addition, the 1970 Amendments barred the use of literacy tests in all elections for a five-year period and lowered the voting age to 18 for national and state-local elections. The Supreme Court, in *Oregon* v. *Mitchell* (400 U.S. 112, 1970) upheld the constitutionality of each of these amendments except the lowered voting age as applied to state and local elections. The Court reasoned that Congress did not possess the power to fasten such a requirement on the states and their local units. But the Twenty-Sixth Amendment to the Constitution, ratified in 1971, lowering the voting age to 18 for all elections, accomplished this objective.

THE MISCEGENATION ISSUE

In our federal system the regulation of domestic relations is reserved to the states. Laws in this area commonly prescribe such matters as the age of marital consent, the issuance of licenses, the marriage ceremony, grounds for divorce, and custody of children. Under this authority some states, in bolstering their segregation policies, enacted antimiscegenation statutes—laws prohibiting marriages between blacks and whites. But over the years the Supreme Court steadfastly declined to review state court decisions that upheld the validity of these antimiscegenation laws. However, the Court indicated a change in its attitude on the subject in its disposition of *McLaughlin* v. *Florida* (379 U.S. 184, 1964). At issue was the validity of a conviction under a Florida statute which provided:

> Any [N]egro man and white woman, or any white man and [N]egro woman, who are not married to each other, who shall habitually live in and occupy in the nighttime the same room shall be punished by imprisonment not exceeding twelve months, or by fine not exceeding five hundred dollars.

A unanimous Court found that the statute unconstitutionally infringed the equal protection clause of the Fourteenth Amendment. Justice Byron White pointed to the statute's discriminatory treatment of the interracial couple since "no other couple other than a Negro and white person [could] be convicted under the statute." Such a racial classification embodied in a criminal statute, White contended, is " 'constitutionally suspect' " and is " 'in most circumstances irrelevant' to any constitutionally acceptable legislative purpose." But he made it clear that the Court was not reaching the interracial marriage issue.

Three years later, however, the issue was squarely before the Court in *Loving* v. *Virginia* (388 U.S. 1, 1967). In that case the Virginia law prohibiting interracial marriages was struck down as an unconstitutional infringement of the equal protection and due process clauses of the Fourteenth Amendment. Chief Justice Earl Warren's opinion for a unanimous Court condemned the white supremacy basis of the statute and noted that the Court has consistently repudiated legislation with ancestral distinctions "as being odious to a free people whose institutions are founded upon the doctrine of equality!"

EMPLOYMENT

Discriminatory employment practices are prohibited under Title VII of the Civil Rights Act of 1964. In *Griggs* v. *Duke Power Co.*, the Supreme Court unanimously held that the act bars the use of employment practices that operate to exclude blacks if the practices are unrelated to job performance. In that case, black employees of the Duke Power Company contested requirements that conditioned employment in, or transfer to, jobs within the company upon having completed high school or passing a standardized intelligence test. The practical effect of these requirements was to preclude blacks from employment in or promotion to jobs in the highest paying departments of the company. Chief Justice Burger, speaking for the Court, said that the act "proscribes not only overt discrimination but also practices that are fair in form, but discriminatory in operation." "The touchstone," noted Burger, "is business necessity. If an employment practice which operates to exclude Negroes cannot be shown to be related to job performance, the practice is prohibited." Here, Burger continued, "neither the high school completion requirement nor the general intelligence test is shown to bear a demonstrable relationship to successful performance of the jobs for which it was used." To Duke Power's contention that the requirements were made without the intention of discrimination against blacks, Burger said that "good intent or absence of discriminatory intent does not redeem employment procedures or testing mechanisms that operate as 'built-in headwinds' for minority groups and are unrelated to measuring job capability."

The Equal Employment Opportunity Act of 1972 in part amends the Civil Rights Act of 1964 and expands that act's coverage of employment of minority group members and employees of the federal government. In addition, it improves the enforcement procedures of the 1964 act through a section that permits initiation of civil actions in the federal courts if alleged unlawful employment practices are not satisfactorily resolved through administrative action within 30 days after a charge is filed. Judicial remedies made available in the 1972 act include injunctive proceedings against those engaged in the unlawful employment practices and judicial authority to order "such affirmative action as may be appropriate," including reinstatement on the job with back pay. Another section of the act specifically requires that all personnel actions affecting federal government employees "be made free from any discrimination based on race, color, religion, sex, or national origin" and provides for Civil Service Commission enforcement. An Equal Employment Opportunity Coordinating Council is also established by the statute. The Council is given "the responsibility for developing and implementing agreements, policies and practices designed to maximize effort, promote efficiency, and eliminate conflict, competition, duplication and inconsistency among . . . - agencies and branches of the Federal Government responsible for the implementation and enforcement of equal employment opportunity legislation, orders and policies."

CIVIL RIGHTS AND THE POOR

Poor people in American experience deprivation and discrimination solely because of their low socioeconomic status. In the most affluent nation on earth they barely subsist. Their everyday life is burdened by inadequate food and clothing, delapidated housing, high unemployment, grossly inferior schools, and high crime rates. It is as if they lived in another country, another world, and most of them do! In actual numbers, whites form the majority of poor people in this country. Nonetheless, because blacks and other minority groups constitute a disproportionate number of those in poverty, the drive to eliminate poverty and live a decent life may be viewed as one of the new dimensions of the overall civil-rights struggle. Consequently, the nation's poor have also resorted to the judiciary (in addition to other political institutions) in attempting to achieve their objectives. This section reviews the stance of the Supreme Court with respect to problems affecting the rights of the poor.

In a series of recent cases, the Court has been faced with questions concerning the requirements and conditions under which welfare benefits are administered to the poor. In *King* v. *Smith* (392 U.S. 309, 1968), for example, the Court held invalid an Alabama regulation that denied federally-provided benefits (Aid to Families with Dependent Children—AFDC) "to the children of a mother who 'cohabits' in or outside her home with any single or married able-bodied man." Chief Justice Warren's majority opinion striking down the regulation first cited the AFDC program's definition of a "dependent child": "an age-qualified [under eighteen or under twenty-one and a student] needy child ... who has been deprived of parental support or care by reason of the death, continued absence from the home, or physical or mental incapability of a parent, and who is living with any one of several listed relatives." Here, Mrs. Smith's children lost benefits in 1966 because "a Mr. Williams came to her home on weekends and had sexual relations with her." By viewing a "substitute father" as "a nonabsent parent within the federal statute," said Warren, Alabama "denies aid to an otherwise eligible needy child on the basis that his substitute parent is not absent from the home." Warren examined two justifications Alabama gave for its interpretation of the "nonabsent" language. Alabama first said that its regulation "discourages illicit sexual relationships and illegitimate births." Further, the state contended that the regulation "puts families in which there is an informal 'marital' relationship on a par with those in which there is an ordinary marital relationship, because families of the latter sort are not eligible for AFDC assistance."

As to the first argument, Warren said that "Congress has determined that immorality and illegitimacy should be dealt with through rehabilitative measures rather than measures that punish dependent children, and that protection of such children is the paramount goal of AFDC." "It is simply inconceivable," continued Warren, "that Alabama is free to discourage immorality and illegitimacy by the device of absolute disqualification of needy children." Warren said Alabama's second argument "fails to take account of the circumstance that children of fathers living in the home are in a very different position from children of mothers who cohabit with men not their fathers: the child's father has a legal duty to support him, while the unrelated substitute father, at least in Alabama, does not." Warren concluded that "Congress intended the term 'parent' in [the AFDC statute] to include only those persons with a legal duty of support."

A different type of state regulation was at issue in *Shapiro* v. *Thompson* (394 U.S. 618, 1969). Several states and the District of Columbia required that welfare recipients reside within their jurisdiction for one year before granting benefits. These rules, which allegedly tended to discourage the poor from moving to such jurisdictions, were held in *Shapiro* to create classifications that constituted invidious discrimination violative of the equal protection clause of the Fourteenth Amendment. In his majority opinion, Justice William J. Brennan noted that the "waiting period device is well suited to discourage the influx of poor families in need of assistance." "An indigent who desires to migrate, resettle, find a new job, start a new life," said Brennan, "will doubtless hesitate if he knows that he must risk making the move without the possibility of falling back on state welfare assistance during his first year of residence, when his need may be most acute." For Brennan, such purposeful action to inhibit migration by the poor is "irrational and unconstitutional" under traditional equal protection tests.

One of the most oft-cited justifications supporting the residency classification policy is that it is essential to protect the state's welfare resources from claims of indigents who move to a state only to get larger benefits. But to Brennan, "a State may no more try to fence out those indigents who seek higher benefits than it may try to fence out indigents generally." He further noted that "the fundamental right of interstate movement" was affected by the classification and that therefore "its constitutionality must be judged by the stricter standard of whether it promotes a *compelling* state interest." "Under this standard," he concluded, "the waiting period requirement clearly violates the Equal Protection Clause."

Justice John M. Harlan, in dissent, was extremely critical of the majority's use of the "compelling interest" equal protection doctrine. He was especially upset because the majority could make a statutory classification subject to the compelling interest test "if the result of the classification may be to affect a fundamental right, regardless of the basis of the classification." Harlan felt that such a doctrine was "unfortunate because it creates an exception which threatens to swallow the standard equal protection rule," and it was "unnecessary" because "the right affected is one assured by the Federal Constitution" and "any infringement can be dealt with under the Due Process Clause."

Overall, the *Shapiro* holding, especially when examined in light of *Dunn* v. *Blumstein* (405 U.S. 336, 1972) (prohibiting lengthy residency requirements for voting in state and local elections) has considerable importance for the poor. At least two of the onerous burdens encountered when the poor move from one state to another—lack of welfare benefits when they are most acutely needed and exclusion from voting—are eliminated by these decisions.

In *Goldberg* v. *Kelly* (397 U.S. 254, 1970), the Court held that procedural due process requires a state to afford a welfare recipient an opportunity for an evidentiary hearing *prior* to the termination of public assistance payments. Speaking for the majority, Justice Brennan noted that while some governmental benefits may be terminated administratively without affording the recipient a pre-termination evidentiary hearing, welfare benefits were outside this category. Indeed, said Brennan:

> For qualified recipients, welfare provides the means to obtain essential food, clothing, housing and medical care. Thus, the crucial factor in this context—a factor not present in the case of the blacklisted governmental contractor, the discharged government employee, the taxpayer denied a tax exemption, or virtually anyone else whose government entitlements are ended—is that the termination of aid pending resolution of a controversy over eligibility may deprive an *eligible* recipient of the very means by which to live while he waits. Since he lacks independent resources, his situation becomes immediately desperate.

To meet the requisites of due process in this context, concluded Brennan, a recipient must "have timely and adequate notice detailing the reasons for a proposed termination and an effective opportunity to defend by confronting any adverse witnesses and by presenting his own arguments and evidence orally."

Chief Justice Warren Burger and Justices Hugo Black and Potter Stewart dissented. Their position was best articulated by Justice Black, who suggested that the new procedure would "lead to constitutionally imposed, time-consuming delays of a full adversary process of administrative and judicial review." Black was also concerned about persons receiving aid without being eligible. He said that officials probably erroneously added names to the welfare lists "in order to alleviate immediate suffering, and undoubtedly some people are drawing relief who are not entitled under the law to do so." "In other words," he continued, "although some recipients might be on the lists for payment wholly because of deliberate fraud on their part, the Court holds that the government is helpless and must continue, until after an evidentiary hearing, to pay money that it does not owe, never has owed, and never could owe."

Although *Goldberg* precludes the unilateral cut-off of benefits by the state, other regulations imposed by states in the administration of welfare programs indicate still additional problems faced by the poor. For example, in *Dandrige* v. *Williams* (397 U.S. 471, 1970), decided only two weeks after *Goldberg*, the Court upheld a Maryland regulation under which most families received AFDC benefits in accordance with their standard of need (determined by family size), but which imposed a ceiling of $250 per month on the grant "regardless of the size of the family and its actual need." In his majority opinion, Justice Potter Stewart said that the Court "need not explore all the reasons that the State advances in justification of the regulation." "It is enough," he asserted, "that a solid foundation for the regulation can be found in the State's legitimate interest in encouraging employment and in avoiding discrimination between welfare families and the families of the working poor." Stewart noted that "the Equal Protection Clause does not require a State to choose between attacking every aspect of a problem or not attacking the problem at all." The Maryland rule, continued Stewart, is "rationally based and free from invidious discrimination."

Justices Douglas, Brennan, and Marshall dissented. They believed that the Maryland regulation was inconsistent with the Social Security Act that created the AFDC program. Justice Marshall was particularly concerned about "the Court's emasculation of the Equal Protection Clause as a constitutional principle applicable to the area of social welfare administration." He argued, that the appellees here were "needy dependent children and families who are discriminated against by the State." "The basis of that discrimination—the classification of individuals into large and small families," continued Marshall, "is too arbitrary and too unconnected to the asserted rationale, the impact on those discriminated against—the denial of even a subsistence existence—too great, and the supposed interests served too contrived and attenuated to meet the requirements of the Constitution."

A year later, in *Wyman* v. *James* (400 U.S. 309, 1971), the Court upheld a New York regulation that required—as a condition to continuance of public assistance—periodic caseworker visitations to homes of AFDC recipients. Here Mrs. James, who began receiving AFDC assistance shortly after her son's birth in 1967, refused such a visit by a caseworker in her home, and, as a consequence, lost AFDC benefits. Justice Harold Blackmun, speaking for the Court, concluded that "the home visitation as structured by the New York statutes and regulations is a reasonable administrative tool [which] serves a valid and proper administrative purpose for the dispensation of the AFDC program." Hence, he asserted, "it is not an unwarranted invasion of personal privacy and violates no right guaranteed by the Fourth Amendment" because such visits do "not descend to the level of unreasonableness." Blackmun distinguished several other cases that turned on Fourth Amendment issues, including one case (*See* v. *City of Seattle* 387 U.S. 541, 1967), in which a commercial warehouse owner refused to let a fire department representative enter his warehouse as a part of a "routine, periodic city-wide" inspection. The Court in *See* held that such administrative entry can be prevented unless it is carried out pursuant to a warrant.

This distinction did not impress Justice Thurgood Marshall who, joined by Justices Douglas and Brennan, issued a sharp dissent. He did not understand "why a commercial warehouse deserves more protection than this poor woman's home." He also attacked the two explanations set forth to justify the home visit rule. The first, "to protect dependent children from 'abuse' and 'exploitation,' " is concededly to prevent "heinous crimes," said Marshall, "but [such interests] are not confined to indigent households." Marshall wondered whether "the majority [would] sanction, in the absence of probable cause, compulsory visits to all American homes for the purpose of discovering child abuse." The second justification was based on the contention that home visits were necessary to determine if the family was eligible for AFDC benefits. Marshall noted that "federal [AFDC] regulations do not require the home visit." Concluding, Marshall declared that he finds "no little irony in the fact that the burden of today's departure from principled adjudication is placed upon the lowly poor."

In *Jefferson* v. *Hackney* (406 U.S. 535, 1972) the Court upheld a Texas scheme (necessitated by a state constitutional ceiling on welfare assistance grants) under which AFDC benefits were reduced by greater proportions than other welfare assistance programs. The Texas system provided for 100 percent implementation of the old-age assistance benefit, 95 percent of aid to the blind and to the disabled, but only 75 percent to AFDC recipients. The appellants claimed a violation of equal protection "because the proportion of AFDC recipients who are Black or Mexican-American is higher than the proportion of the aged, blind or disabled welfare recipients who fall within these minority groups." (While less than 40 percent of those on old-age assistance were blacks or Mexican-Americans, 87 percent of those on AFDC were in these minority groups.) Justice William Rehnquist's majority opinion rejected the equal protection argument, stating that the Court "cannot say that Texas' decision to provide somewhat lower welfare benefits for AFDC recipients is invidious or irrational." Rehnquist described the allegations of racial discrimination as "unproven" and cited the district Court's finding that "payment by Texas of a lesser percentage of unmet needs to the recipients of AFDC than to the recipients of other welfare programs is not the result of racial or ethnic prejudice."

In computing benefits, Texas employs a percentage reduction procedure which results in lower benefits that would tend to penalize those who earn outside income. Some other states use alternative computation procedures that, using the same factual base, result in higher benefits to the recipient. Acknowledging that "the two systems of accounting for outside income yield somewhat different results," and demonstrating that the Texas method results in lower actual benefits paid out, Rehnquist, nevertheless, contended that "if Texas were to switch to the alternative system of recognizing outside income, it would be forced to lower its percentage reduction factor, in order to keep down its welfare budget." "Lowering the percentage," he said, "would result in less money for those who need the welfare benefits the most—those with no outside income—and the State has been unwilling to do this."

Justices Douglas, Brennan, and Marshall dissented, indicating that in their view the Texas AFDC computation scheme was violative of the Social Security Act. Douglas, for example, said the majority "ignores the explicit congressional policy in favor of work incentives and upholds a system which provides penalties and disincentives for those who seek employment." Marshall not only presented strong statutory arguments against the majority's position on reduction computations but also indicated that "the disparity [in the percentage reductions] between the various social welfare programs is not permissible under the federal statutory framework."

Several other decisions of the Supreme Court have considerable importance for the poor. In *James* v. *Valtierra*, in 1971, for example, the Court upheld a California statute that "provided that no low-rent [federally-financed] housing project should be developed, constructed or acquired in any manner by a state public body until the project was approved by a majority of those voting at a community election." A federal district court agreed with plaintiffs who contended the statute denied them equal protection of the laws and enjoined its enforcement. But in appeal the Supreme Court reversed. In his opinion for the majority, Justice Black rejected the plaintiff's argument "that the mandatory nature of the . . . referendum constitutes unconstitutional discrimination because it hampers persons desiring public housing from achieving their objective when no such roadblock faces other groups seeking to influence other public decisions to their advantage." To him, it was clear that the referendum procedure "ensures that all the people of a community will have a voice in a decision which may lead to large expenditures of local governmental funds for increased public services and to lower tax revenues." The California referendum statute, he concluded, is a "procedure for democratic decision-making" that does not violate the equal protection clause.

Justice Marshall, joined by Justices Brennan and Blackmun, dissented. Marshall said that the California statute "on its face constitutes invidious discrimination which the Equal Protection Clause of the Fourteenth Amendment plainly prohibits." He contended further that "singling out the poor to bear a burden not placed on any other class of citizens tramples the values that the Fourteenth Amendment was designed to protect."

In *San Antonio Independent School District* v. *Rodriguez,* a 1973 decision, the Supreme Court rejected challenges to the property tax that provides a significant part of public school finance in 49 of the 50 states. Here, Rodriguez contended that the Texas system of supplementing state aid to school districts by means of an ad valorem tax on property within the jurisdiction of the individual school district violated the equal protection clause. Rodriguez, whose children attended schools in a district with lower per pupil expenditures but higher property tax rates than in other area districts, argued that substantial differences in per pupil expenditures among the districts resulted from the differences in the value of the property taxed within each district. Justice Lewis Powell, speaking for a 5–4 majority of the Court, said that the financing system, although not perfect, "abundantly satisfies" the constitutional standard for equal protection since the system "rationally furthers a legitimate state purpose or interest." Powell said that the traditional equal protection standard applied since "the Texas system does not operate to the peculiar disadvantage of any suspect class" and since education, although an important state service, is not a "fundamental" right because it is not "explicitly or implicitly guaranteed by the Constitution."

Concurring, Justice Potter Stewart characterized the property tax system as "chaotic and unjust" but not in violation of the Constitution. Stewart said that "the Texas system does not rest 'on grounds wholly irrelevant to the achievement of the state's objective' " and that it "impinges upon no substantive constitutional rights or liberties."

Justices Brennan, White, Douglas, and Marshall dissented. White was in sharp disagreement with Powell's narrow construction of equal protection. "The Equal Protection Clause," explained White, "permits discriminations between classes but requires that the classification bear some rational relationship to a permissible object sought to be attained by the statute." White said that the Texas scheme did not pass this "rational relationship" test. In separate dissents, Brennan and Marshall sought to demonstrate that education is a fundamental right. Marshall filed by far the sharpest dissenting opinion. He called the Court's holding "a retreat from our historic commitment to equality of educational opportunity" and an "unsupportable acquiescence in a system which deprives children in their earliest years of the chance to reach their full potential as citizens." Marshall emphasized the disparities in per pupil expenditures and tax rates between the districts involved and noted the "invidious characteristics of the group wealth classification present" in the case.

In *Boddie* v. *Connecticut* (401 U.S. 371, 1971) the Court held that states cannot deny access to their courts to persons seeking divorces solely because of inability to pay court costs. The case involved indigent welfare recipients who desired divorces but who were unable to pay the necessary filing and other court fees (about $60 in all) in order to obtain a hearing. They claimed that the due process and equal protection clauses required Connecticut to grant them access to courts. In accepting Boddie's due process contention, Justice John Harlan's opinion for the Court emphasized the state's authority over the marriage status. "Given the basic position of the marriage relationship in this society's hierarchy of values and the concomitant state monopolization of the means for legally dissolving [it]," he asserted, "due process does prohibit the State from denying, solely because of inability to pay, access to its courts to individuals who seek judicial dissolution of their marriages." Harlan's opinion in *Boddie*, however, is self-limiting, since two important factors must be present in cases attempting to use the result as a binding precedent: (1) the presence of a fundamental or basic interest and (2) "state monopolization" over resolution of the dispute.

Several of the other opinions in *Boddie*, however, were not so limited. Justice Douglas, for example, concurred, saying that the decision should have rested on the broader base of equal protection. "An invidious discrimination based on poverty," said Douglas, "is adequate for this case." Justice Brennan, in another concurring opinion, said that "[t]he right to be heard in some way at some time extends to all proceedings entertained by courts." "The possible distinctions suggested by the Court today," cautioned Brennan, "will not withstand analysis." Brennan was concerned over the "state monopolization" language used by Harlan in the majority opinion.

But the Burger Court moved away from this "access" trend in civil matters with two 5–4 decisions in 1973. In each instance, the four Nixon appointees were joined by Justice Byron White of the Warren Court. First, in *United States* v. *Kras* (409 U.S. 434, 1973), the inability of an unemployed indigent to pay the $50 filing fee in a bankruptcy petition was at issue. A federal district court had agreed with the petitioner's argument that denying him the opportunity to file for bankruptcy because of his inability to pay the filing fee violated the due process and equal protection guarantees of the Fifth Amendment. Relying on the *Boddie* decision, the district court concluded that "a discharge in bankruptcy was a 'fundamental interest' that could be denied only when a 'compelling government interest was demonstrated.' " But a five-member majority of the Supreme Court rejected this reliance upon *Boddie* as misplaced. Speaking for them, Justice Harold Blackmun maintained that bankruptcy should not be regarded as a fundamental right that demands the showing of a "compelling governmental interest" to justify significant regulation. Furthermore, he contended, this subject does not touch upon "the suspect criteria of race, nationality or alienage." Hence, he argued, "rational justification" was the appropriate standard and Congress had met it. For example, while the court action sought in *Boddie* was the only way to dissolve the marriage, the statute involved in *Kras* permits "negotiated agreements" and very low installment payments. In short, the indigent bankrupt is offered effective alternatives. In the end, he held, any extension of the *Boddie* principle to bankruptcy proceedings should start with the Congress.

The dissenting justices (Douglas, Stewart, Brennan, and Marshall) were sharply critical of the majority for in effect holding, as Justice Stewart remarked, "that some of the poor are too poor even to go bankrupt." Because they believed that access to the courts to determine the claim of a legal right is fundamental, any denial of that access because of inability to pay filing fees, constituted for them the kind of invidious discrimination between rich and poor contrary to equal protection.

The second case, *Ortwein* v. *Schwab* (410 U.S. 656) involved an action by welfare recipients to have a court review of Oregon administrative action reducing their benefits without payment of the required $25 filing fee. The Supreme Court affirmed the Oregon courts' denial of relief. In its per curiam opinion, the Court cited *Kras* rather than *Boddie* as the governing precedent, noting that the interest alleged by the welfare recipients (to have administrative action reducing their benefits judicially reviewed), was far less significant than that asserted by the indigent divorce seekers in *Boddie*.

The same four dissenters restated their argument advanced in *Kras*. As Justice William O. Douglas noted, the majority's action simply "broadens and fortifies the 'private preserve' for the affluent . . . [by upholding] a scheme of judicial review whereby justice remains a luxury for the wealthy." Furthermore, Douglas noted, *Kras* should not be considered applicable to this case because relief through "nonjudicial accommodation" was not available. Even more crucial was the fact that the majority's ruling permits a state to deny "initial access to the courts for review of an adverse administrative determination."

The Supreme Court did not exhibit this kind of deference to state procedures permitting pre-judgment garnishment of wages (in Wisconsin and about 20 other states) and pre-judgment seizure of goods under writs of replevin (in Pennsylvania and Florida) without any prior hearing. In 1969, in *Sniadach* v. *Family Finance Corporation* (395 U.S. 337, 1969), the Court indicated that wages were "a specialized type of property" and that the consequences of wage garnishment (e.g., hardship on wage earners with families to support) were quite severe. Justice Douglas's brief majority opinion stated that "[w]here the taking of one's property is so obvious, it needs no extended argument to conclude that absent notice and a prior hearing this pre-judgment garnishment procedure violates the fundamental principles of due process."

Three years later, in *Fuentes* v. *Shevin* (407 U.S. 67, 1972), the Court in a 4–3 decision ruled that due process requires that an opportunity for a hearing be provided before the State can authorize its agents to seize property in the possession of a debtor upon the application of his creditor. Justice Stewart's majority opinion noted that "essential reason for the hearing requirement is to prevent unfair and mistaken deprivations of property." "Due process," said Stewart, "is afforded only by the kinds of 'notice' and 'hearing' that are aimed at establishing the validity, or at least the probable validity, of the underlying claim against the alleged debtor *before* he can be deprived of his property." Chief Justice Burger and Justices White and Blackmun did not believe that the Constitution guarantees such a right to a defaulting buyer-debtor. In Justice White's dissenting opinion, supported by Burger and Blackmun, the creditor's property interest is considered just "as deserving as that of the debtor." White argued that under the Court's historic view of what procedures due process requires "under any given set of circumstances," the creditors had the right under state laws to take possession of the property *pending final hearing*. White chided the majority that it should best leave such legislative matters to the experts employed by legislative bodies. Certainly, he did not think the procedures struck down were "some barbaric hangover from bygone days."

Overall, Supreme Court decisions affecting rights of the poor have been mixed.

During the decade of the Sixties with the Warren Court "activism" in full sway, significant gains were made as a "strict scrutiny" approach to equal protection issues was emphasized in addition to traditional due process scrutiny. Legislative and administrative actions were immediately suspect if they provided for classification schemes based on such factors as race and wealth, particularly where "fundamental interests" were at stake. The "rationality of a legitimate governmental objective" justification no longer sufficed. Instead, where "fundamental rights" were at stake, the government was required to demonstrate a "compelling interest" to support a particular classification scheme. Hence, welfare recipients benefitted from this approach in *Shapiro* v. *Thompson, Goldberg* v. *Kelly,* and *Boddie* v. *Connecticut;* the indigent voter in *Harper* v. *Virginia Board of Elections;* and the indigent renter in *Lindsey* v. *Normet* (405 U.S. 56, 1972). In addition, due process requirements were construed to provide poor wage earners access to the courts to protect their property rights in *Sniadach* v. *Family Finance Corp.* and *Fuentes* v. *Shevin.*

Some of these gains, however, have been blunted by several Burger Court decisions (e.g., *James* v. *Valtierra, Wyman* v. *James, United States* v. *Kras, Jefferson* v. *Hackney,* and *San Antonio Independent School District* v. *Rodriguez.*) It is clear that so far the reconstituted Court has indicated a reluctance to expand further the new equal protection doctrine of the Warren era and accept additional concerns of the poor as "fundamental rights." Such behavior of the Court toward the poor, just as toward blacks, seems to reflect that the change in membership of the Burger Court has brought with it some fundamental changes in judicial philosophy with respect to the role of courts in fashioning socioeconomic policies. The Burger Court, unlike the Warren Court, does not appear disposed to support those who are unrepresented or underrepresented (e.g., blacks, Chicanos, and the poor) in the political process. That the Court majority no longer reflects this concern is clearly illustrated in the directness and sharpness of the dissenting opinions of Justice Thurgood Marshall in *Dandridge,* in *Wyman,* in *Jefferson,* in *James,* and in *Rodriguez.*

Whether the several Court decisions won by poor litigants have made any meaningful difference must be investigated. In short, have the actions of the judicial branch really improved the general lot of poor Americans?

EQUAL RIGHTS FOR WOMEN

The poor are not the only group involved in the struggle for equality. Women, who finally secured the right to vote in 1920 by virtue of the Nineteenth Amendment are, more than 50 years later, still clamoring for full constitutional rights by way of another amendment, popularly called the Equal Rights Amendment. While this battle is being fought on many fronts, our chief concern here is with court decisions, primarily those of the Supreme Court, involving the rights of women.

Early decisions of the Supreme Court indicated that there were reasonable justifications to conclude that women could be treated differently from men, especially in such matters as job opportunities and conditions of employment. [See for example, *Bradwell* v. *Illinois* (83 U.S. 130, 1872), especially the concurring opinion of Mr. Justice Bradley at 141-142; and *Muller* v. *Oregon* (208 U.S. 412, 1908).] And most importantly, the Court held that such differential treatment did not abridge the Federal Constitution. Moreover, the theories advanced in these earlier decisions were reflected in a Supreme Court decision as late as 1948, In *Goesaert* v. *Cleary* (335 U.S. 464, 1948), for example, the Court rejected an equal protection challenge and upheld a Michigan law that denied issuance of a bartender's license to any woman except one who was "the wife or daughter of the male owner" of a licensed liquor establishment. Speaking for the majority, Justice Frankfurter maintained that the statutory classification scheme was "not without a basis in reason." The legislature, he contended, had a reasonable basis for believing serious moral and social problems could result from women tending bars. Consequently, legislatures are not without power to "devise preventive measures." Justifying the "wife-daughter" exemption, Frankfurter concluded that "the legislature need not go to the full length of the prohibition if it believes that as to a defined group of females other factors are operating which either eliminate or reduce the moral and social problems otherwise calling for prohibition." But Justice Rutledge, joined by Justices Douglas and Murphy, dissented. While noting that the equal protection clause does not require a legislature to devise classification schemes with mathematical precision, Rutledge argued, however, that it "does require lawmakers to refrain from invidious distinctions of the sort drawn by the statute challenged in this case." Indeed, he continued, the "inevitable result of the classification (some, not *all*, women are prevented from becoming bartenders) belies the assumption that the statute was motivated by a legislative solicitude for the moral and physical well-being of women, who, but for the law, would be employed as barmaids."

However, as the California Supreme Court put it in 1971, *Goesaert* was decided "well before the recent and major growth of public concern about and opposition to sex discrimination." (*Sail'er Inn, Inc.* v. *Kirby*, 485 P. 2d 529 at 539, fn. 15.) In fact, it would be difficult for any court today to maintain theories underlying *Goesaert* and earlier cases such as *Muller* v. *Oregon* (208 U.S. 412). This move away from those theories may be gleaned from the "equal protection position" of the Court in *Shapiro* v. *Thompson* (1969), a position which might well place sex within the group of "suspect" classifications. In any event, spurred by the egalitarian mood of the 1960s, litigation involving women's rights is on the increase. As a matter of fact, in the *Sail'er Inn* case referred to above, the California Supreme Court struck down a statute, similar to the one involved in the 1948 *Goesaert* case, as violative of the California constitution, the 1964 Civil Rights Act, and the Fourteenth Amendment. The statute forbade women to work as bartenders. If such statutes applied to racial or ethnic minorities, said the court, they would "readily be recognized as invidious and impermissible." Consequently, the court concluded that sexual classifications should be "properly treated as suspect, particularly when . . . made with respect to employment."

Increasingly since 1970, lower federal courts have decided a wide range of sex discrimination cases. For example, in *Seidenberg* v. *McSorleys' Old Ale House, Inc.* (317 F. Supp. 593, S.D.N.Y., 1970) a federal district court held that a bar's refusal to serve women constituted "state action" in violation of the Equal Protection Clause. Also, in *LaFleur* v. *Cleveland Board of Education* (465 F. 2d 1184, 6th Cir., 1972) a Court of Appeals held that a school board rule requiring pregnant teachers to take unpaid leaves of absence beginning five months before the expected birth of a child and extending at least three months after the child's birth was "arbitrary and unreasonable." The *LaFleur* court said that "pregnant women teachers have been singled out for unconstitutionally unequal restrictions upon their employment" because of their sex. On the other hand, however, a federal district court in Connecticut upheld a teaching contract clause requiring pregnant teachers to apply for and take leaves of absence to begin not less than four months prior to the expected date of birth of the child. (*Green* v. *Waterford Board of Education*, 349 F. Supp. 687, D. Conn. 1972.) The *Green* court indicated that the traditional standard of equal protection review—"whether the classification at issue is without any reasonable basis"—was to be applied in the case and concluded that the maternity leave section of the contract was "not so lacking in rational basis as to constitute a denial of equal protection."

In early 1974, the Supreme Court settled the confused state of the law on maternity leaves when it affirmed the Court of Appeals ruling in the *LaFleur* case. (*Cleveland Board of Education* v. *LaFleur*, 414 U.S. 632). Justice Potter Stewart, who delivered the opinion for the Court, held that the arbitrary cutoff dates embraced in maternity leave regulations are violative of due process "since they create a conclusive presumption that every teacher who is four or five months pregnant is physically incapable of continuing her duties." Such a rule, he continued, ignores the differences among individuals in their capacities to perform their duties during pregnancy. He concluded that the mandatory maternity leave rules enforced by the board had "no rational relationship to the valid state interest of preserving continuity of instruction."

Chief Justice Burger and Justice William Rehnquist dissented because they felt that the board's regulation was well within permissible limits of legislative classification statutes. They concluded that "if legislative bodies are to be permitted to draw a general line anywhere short of the delivery room," they could "find no judicial standard of measurement" that would invalidate those involved in this case.

In addition, the Court has decided several other cases upholding women's rights. In a per curiam decision in *Phillips* v. *Martin Marietta Corporation* (400 U.S. 542, 1971), for example, the Court held that an employer who hired men with pre-school-age children cannot refuse to hire women with such children. Also in *Reed* v. *Reed* (404 U.S. 71, 1972) the Court declared violative of the equal protection clause a provision of the Idaho Probate Code which provides that in determining the administrator of estates from among persons in the same class "males must be preferred to females." Speaking for the majority in *Reed*, Chief Justice Burger said that "to give a mandatory preference to members of either sex over members of the other, merely to accomplish the elimination of hearings on the merits, is to make the very kind of arbitrary legislative choice forbidden by the

Equal Protection Clause." Still further, in a 1973 decision, the Court indicated that military service regulations cannot treat dependents of female members of the armed forces differently from the way they treat dependents of male members. (*Frontiero* v. *Richardson*.) And most important, a plurality of the justices in *Frontiero* concluded that sex was a "suspect" classification and should be treated accordingly. In another 1973 decision, the Court restricted reference to sex in employment want-ads, holding that such restrictions did not violate the First Amendment guarantee of freedom of the press. (*Pittsburgh Press* v. *Pittsburgh Human Relations Commission*, 41 LW 5055).

Indications of the increasing support activity to bolster women's rights are also reflected on other fronts. Both Title VII of the Civil Rights Act of 1964 and the Equal Employment Opportunity Act of 1972, for example, make employment discrimination because of sex (as well as race, color, religion, or national origin) "an unlawful employment practice." And, of course, there is much activity and controversy concerning the proposed Twenty-Seventh Amendment, popularly called the Equal Rights Amendment. That amendment simply states that "equality of rights under the law shall not be denied or abridged by the United States or by any other state on account of sex." Under the amendment, Congress is authorized to pass appropriate legislation to enforce its provisions. Opponents of the proposed amendment suggest that an amendment is unnecessary in view of existing federal law and the possibility of establishing even higher standards. (See, for example, Paul Freund, "The Equal Rights Amendment is Not the Way," 6 *Harvard Civil Rights/Civil Liberties Law Review*, 234, 1971). On the other hand, proponents of the amendment contend that neither existing protections nor incremental expansions of these protections is adequate. (See, for example, Norman Dorsen and Susan Deller Ross, "The Necessity of a Constitutional Amendment," *ibid.*, at 216.) In any event, the struggle over ratification of the Equal Rights Amendment is far from over. But regardless of its fate, the battle for equal rights for women seems destined to continue for some time to come.

THE RIGHT OF PRIVACY

The right of privacy is yet another right illumined by the "rights revolution" and recent events indicate that we may expect many battles over the scope and nature of this newly enshrined constitutional right. But the issue of "privacy," as Alan Westin documents in his *Privacy and Freedom* (New York: Atherton, 1967) has been with us for some time. Technological advances and other pressures on privacy have given rise to a recognition in our public law of the importance of safeguarding the right of privacy as over against competing interests. It was not until 1965 however, in *Griswold* v. *Connecticut* (381 U.S. 479), that the Supreme Court took a major step toward enshrining a right of privacy into the constitutional citadel.

In *Griswold* the Court by a 7–2 vote held a Connecticut law that forbade dissemination of birth control information was violative of the right of marital privacy. Justice Douglas, who spoke for the majority, said that the Connecticut law interfered with "a right of privacy older than the Bill of Rights." Douglas spoke of "zones of privacy" and admitted that privacy as a specific right is not protected by the Constitution. However, he thought it was within a "penumbra" of certain fundamental guarantees such as those enunciated in the First, Third, Fourth, and Fifth Amendments. In his formulation Douglas also cited the Ninth Amendment which indicated that the delineation of certain rights in the Bill of Rights did not mean that there are not other rights "retained by the people."

Justice Black issued a sharp dissent. He attacked the majority for creating a constitutional right of privacy when there was nothing in the constitution to warrant such a development. Moreover, Black differed with the manner by which the Court had developed its own notion of the right of privacy and had incorporated it into the meaning of the due process clause of the Fourteenth Amendment. Black had long warned the Court that the due process clause was meant to include *only* the provisions of the first eight amendments as limitations on the states and *no more*. To do otherwise, Black said, allows the Court to write its own notions of due process rather than those intended by the framers of the Fourteenth Amendment.

The 1973 celebrated "Abortion Cases" gave the Court a most visible opportunity to review the issue of whether there is a constitutional right of privacy. And the Court used the opportunity to reaffirm its *Griswold* position, namely, that there is a constitutional right of privacy that limits the states in their actions. Justice Blackmun, who spoke for the Court in a 7–2 decision in *Roe* v. *Wade*, admitted that "the Constitution does not explicitly mention any right of privacy." However, he indicated that "in a line of decisions . . . going back perhaps as far as . . . 1891, the Court has recognized that a right of personal privacy, or a guarantee of certain areas or zones of privacy does exist under the Constitution." Justices White and Rehnquist dissented. Their dissents, as well as how Justice Blackmun balanced this constitutional right of privacy as over against competing state interests, is discussed in *Roe* v. *Wade*. (See pp. 462-468 infra.)

Watergate and related events have kept matters relating to the right of privacy in the spotlight. A critical question raised here is the extent to which government iself encroaches upon privacy. Some discussion of this question is found in Chapter 4 of this volume, "Freedom and Security: Problems Old and New." Particularly relevant is a discussion of "Covert Government Surveillance" (p. 194) of persons by modern electronic means and by use of paid government informers. Moreover, there appears to be continuing revelations regarding the extent to which government and private agencies gather and use information that invades the right of privacy. This latter problem has been and is the concern of Presidential Commissions, congressional committees, and others. But one thing is already clear: neither the inquiries of commissions and committees nor their reports and recommendations will end the controversy over the right of privacy.

The cases that follow focus on some of the most significant issues examined in this essay.

PLESSY v. FERGUSON
163 U. S. 537; 41 L. Ed. 256; 16 S. Ct. 1138 (1896)

MR. JUSTICE BROWN *delivered the opinion of the Court.*

This case turns upon the constitutionality of an act of the general assembly of the state of Louisiana, passed in 1890, providing for separate railway carriages for the white and colored races. . . .

The 1st section of the statute enacts "that all railway companies carrying passengers in their coaches in this state shall provide equal but separate accommodations for the white and colored races, by providing two or more passenger coaches for each passenger train, or by dividing the passenger coaches by a partition so as to secure separate accommodations: *Provided,* That this section shall not be construed to apply to street railroads. No person or persons shall be permitted to occupy any coaches other than the ones assigned to them, on account of the race they belong to."

By the 2d section it was enacted "that the officers of such passenger trains shall have power and are hereby required to assign each passenger to the coach or compartment used for the race to which such passenger belongs; any passenger insisting on going into a coach or compartment to which by race he does not belong, shall be liable to a fine of $25 or in lieu thereof to imprisonment for a period of not more than twenty days in the parish prison."

. . .

The information filed in the criminal district court charged in substance that Plessy, being a passenger between two stations within the state of Louisiana, was assigned by officers of the company to the coach used for the race to which he belonged, but he insisted upon going into a coach used by the race to which he did not belong. Neither in the information nor plea was his particular race or color averred.

The petition for the writ of prohibition averred that petitioner was seven eighths Caucasian and one eighth African blood; that the mixture of colored blood was not discernible in him, and that he was entitled to every right, privilege, and immunity secured to citizens of the United States of the white race; and that, upon such theory, he took possession of a vacant seat in a coach where passengers of the white race were accommodated, and was ordered by the conductor to vacate said coach and take a seat in another assigned to persons of the colored race, and having refused to comply with such demand he was forcibly ejected with the aid of a police officer, and imprisoned in the parish jail to answer a charge of having violated the above act.

The constitutionality of this act is attacked upon the ground that it conflicts both with the Thirteenth Amendment of the Constitution, abolishing slavery, and the Fourteenth Amendment, which prohibits certain restrictive legislation on the part of the states.

1. That it does not conflict with the Thirteenth Amendment, which abolished slavery and involuntary servitude, except as a punishment for crime, is too clear for argument.

. . .

A statute which implies merely a legal distinction between the white and colored races—a distinction which is founded in the color of the two races, and which must always exist so long as white men are distinguished from the other race by color—has no tendency to destroy the legal equality of the two races, or re-establish a state of involuntary servitude. Indeed, we do not understand that the Thirteenth Amendment is strenuously relied upon by the plaintiff in error in this connection.

2. By the Fourteenth Amendment, all persons born or naturalized in the United States, and subject to the jurisdiction thereof, are made citizens of the United States and of the state wherein they reside; and the states are forbidden from making or enforcing any law which shall abridge the privileges or immunities of citizens of the United States, or shall deprive any person of life, liberty, or property without due process of law, or deny to any person within their jurisdiction the equal protection of the laws.

. . .

The object of the amendment was undoubtedly to enforce the absolute equality of the two races before the law, but in the nature of things it could not have been intended to abolish distinctions based upon color, or to enforce social, as distinguished from political, equality, or a commingling of the two races upons terms unsatisfactory to either. Laws permitting and even requiring their separation in places where they are liable to be brought into contact do not necessarily imply the inferiority of either race to the other, and have been generally, if not universally, recognized as within the competency of the state legislatures in the exercise of their police power. The most common instance of this is connected with the establishment of separate schools for white and colored children, which have been held to be a valid exercise of the legislative power even by courts of states where the political rights of the colored race have been longest and most earnestly enforced.

One of the earliest of these cases is that of *Roberts* v. *Boston*, 5 Cush. 198, in which the supreme judicial court of Massachusetts held that the general school committee of Boston had power to make provision for the instruction of colored children in separate schools established exclusively for them, and to prohibit their attendance upon the other schools. . . . It was held that the powers of the committee extended to the "establishment of separate schools for children of different ages, sexes, and colors. . . .- Similar laws have been enacted by Congress under its general power of legislation over the District of Columbia . . . as well as by the legislatures of many of the states, and have been generally, if not uniformly, sustained by the courts. . . .

Laws forbidding the intermarriage of the two races may be said in a technical sense to interfere with the freedom of contract, and yet have been universally recognized as within the police power of the state, *State* v. *Gibson*, 36 Ind. 389 (10 Am. Rep. 42).

The distinction between laws interfering with the political equality of the negro and those requiring the separation of the two races in schools, theaters, and railway carriages, has been frequently drawn by this court. Thus, in *Strauder* v. *West Virginia*, 100 U.S. 303: it was held that a law of West Virginia limiting to white male persons, twenty-one years of age and citizens of the state, the right to sit upon juries, was a discrimination which implied a legal inferiority in civil society, which lessened the security of the right of the colored race, and was a step towards reducing them to a condition of servility. . . .

Much nearer, and, indeed almost directly in point, is the case of the *Louisville, N.O. & T.R.Co.* v. *Mississippi*, 133 U.S. 587 wherein the railway company was indicted for a violation of a statute of Mississippi, enacting that all railroads carrying passengers should provide equal, but separate, accommodations for the white and colored races, by providing two or more passenger cars for each passenger train, or by dividing the passenger cars by a partition, so as to secure separate accommodations. The case was presented in a different aspect from the one under consideration, inasmuch as it was an indictment against the railway company for failing to provide the separate accommodations, but the question considered was the constitutionality of the law. In that case, the supreme court of Mississippi, 66 Miss. 662, had held that the statute applied solely to commerce within the state, and, that being the construction of the state statute by its highest court, was accepted as conclusive. "If it be a matter," said the court, "respecting commerce wholly within a state, and not interfering with commerce between the states, then, obviously, there is no violation of the commerce clause of the Federal Constitution. . . . . No question arises under this section as to the power of the state to separate in different compartments interstate passengers, or to affect in any manner, the privileges and rights of such passengers. All that we can consider is, whether the state has the power to require that railroad trains within her limits shall have separate accommodations for the two races; that affecting only commerce within the state is no invasion of the powers given to Congress by the commerce clause."

. . .

. . . [I]t is . . . suggested by the learned counsel for the plaintiff in error that the same argument that will justify the state legislature in requiring railways to provide separate accommodations for the two races will also authorize them to require separate cars to be provided for people whose hair is of a certain color, or who are aliens, or who belong to certain nationalities, or to enact laws requiring colored people to walk upon one side of the street, and white people upon the other, or requiring white men's houses to be painted white, and colored men's black, or their vehicles or business signs to be of different colors, upon the theory that one side of the street is as good as the other, or that a house or vehicle of one color is as good as one of another color. The reply to all this is that every exercise of the police power must be reasonable, and extend only to such laws as are enacted in good faith for the promotion of the public good, and not for the annoyance or oppression of a particular class. . . .

So far, then, as a conflict with the Fourteenth Amendment is concerned, the case reduces itself to the question whether the statute of Louisiana is a reasonable regulation, and with respect to this there must necessarily be a large discretion on the part of the legislature. In determining the question of reasonableness it is at liberty to act with reference to the established usages, customs, and traditions of the people, and with a view to the promotion of their comfort, and the preservation of the public peace and good order. Gauged by this standard, we cannot say that a law which authorizes or even requires the separation of the two races in public conveyances is unreasonable or more obnoxious to the Fourteenth Amendment than the acts of Congress requiring separate schools for colored children in the District of Columbia, the constitutionality of which does not seem to have been questioned, or the corresponding acts of state legislatures.

We consider the underlying fallacy of the plaintiff's argument to consist in the assumption that the enforced separation of the two races stamps the colored race with a badge of inferiority. If this be so, it is not by reason of anything found in the act, but solely because the colored race chooses to put that construction upon it. The argument necessarily assumes that if, as has been more than once the case, and is not unlikely to be so again, the colored race should become the dominant power in the state legislature, and should enact a law in precisely similar terms, it would thereby relegate the white race to an inferior position. We imagine that the white race, at least, would not acquiesce in this assumption. The argument also assumes that social prejudices may be overcome by legislation, and that equal rights cannot be secured to the negro except by an enforced commingling of the two races. We cannot accept this proposition. If the two races are to meet on terms of social equality, it must be the result of natural affinities, a mutual appreciation of each other's merits and a voluntary consent of individuals. . . . Legislation is powerless to eradicate racial instincts or to abolish distinctions based upon physical differences, and the attempt to do so can only result in accentuating the difficulties of the present situation. If the civil and political rights of both races be equal, one cannot be inferior to the other civilly or politically. If one race be inferior to the other socially, the Constitution of the United States cannot put them upon the same plane.

It is true that the question of the proportion of colored blood necessary to constitute a colored person, as distinguished from a white person, is one upon which there is a difference of opinion in the different states, some holding that any visible admixture of black stamps the person as belonging to the colored race (*State* v. *Chavers,* 5 Jones, L. 11); others that it depends upon the predominance of blood (*Gray* v. *State,* 4 Ohio 354; *Monroe* v. *Collins,* 17 Ohio St. 665); and still others that the predominance of white blood must only be in the proportion of three fourths. *People* v. *Dean*, 14 Mich. 406; *Jones* v. *Com.* 80 Va. 544. But these are questions to be determined under the laws of each state and are not properly put in issue in this case. Under the allegation of his petition it may undoubtedly become a question of importance whether, under the laws of Louisiana, the petitioner belongs to the white or colored race.

The judgment of the court
below is therefore affirmed.

MR. JUSTICE BREWER *did not hear the argument or participate in the decision of this case.*

MR. JUSTICE HARLAN *dissenting.*

. . .

. . . [W]e have before us a state enactment that compels, under penalties, the separation of the two races in railroad passenger coaches, and makes it a crime for a citizen of either race to enter a coach that has been assigned to citizens of the other race.

Thus the state regulates the use of a public highway by citizens of the United States solely upon the basis of race.

However apparent the injustice of such legislation may be, we have only to consider whether it is consistent with the Constitution of the United States.

. . .

In respect of civil rights, common to all citizens, the Constitution of the United States does not, I think, permit any public authority to know the race of those entitled to be protected in the enjoyment of such rights. Every true man has pride of race, and under appropriate circumstances, when the rights of others, his equals before the law, are not to be affected, it is his privilege to express such pride and to take such action based upon it as to him seems proper. But I deny that any legislative body or judicial tribunal may have regard to the race of citizens when the civil rights of those citizens are involved. Indeed such legislation as that here in questions is inconsistent, not only with that equality of rights which pertains to citizenship, national and state, but with the personal liberty enjoyed by every one within the United States.

. . .

. . . [The Thirteenth, Fourteenth and Fifteenth Amendments] removed the race line from our governmental systems. They had, as this court has said, a common purpose, namely, to secure "to a race recently emancipated, a race that through many generations have been held in slavery, all the civil rights that the superior race enjoys." They declared, in legal effect, this court has further said, "that the law in the states shall be the same for the black as for the white: that all persons, whether colored or white, shall stand equal before the laws of the states, and, in regard to the colored race, for whose protection the amendment was primarily designed, that no discrimination shall be made against them by law because of their color." We also said: "The words of the amendment, it is true, are prohibitory, but they contain a necessary implication of a positive immunity, or right, most valuable to the colored race—the right to exemption from unfriendly legislation against them distinctively as colored——exemption from legal discriminations, implying inferiority in civil society, lessening the security of their enjoyment of the rights which others enjoy, and discriminations which are steps towards reducing them to the condition of a subject race." . . .

It was said in argument that the statute of Louisiana does not discriminate against either race, but prescribes a rule applicable alike to white and colored citizens. But this argument does not meet the difficulty. Everyone knows that the statute in question had its origin in the purpose, not so much to exclude white persons from railroad cars occupied by blacks, as to exclude colored people from coaches occupied or assigned to white persons. Railroad corporations of Louisiana did not make discrimination among whites in the matter of accommodation for travelers. The thing to accomplish was, under the guise of giving equal accommodation for whites and blacks to compel the latter to keep to themselves while traveling in railroad passenger coaches. No one would be so wanting in candor to assert the contrary. The fundamental objection, therefore, to the statute is that it interferes with the personal freedom of citizens. "Personal liberty," it has been well said, "consists in the power of locomotion, of changing situation, or removing one's person to whatsoever place one's own inclination may direct, without imprisonment or restraint, unless by due course of law." 1 Bl. Com. 134. If a white man and a black man choose to occupy the same public conveyance on a public highway, it is their right to do so, and no government, proceeding alone on grounds of race, can prevent it without infringing the personal liberty of each.

It is one thing for railroad carriers to furnish, or to be required by law to furnish, equal accommodations for all whom they are under a legal duty to carry. It is quite another thing for government to forbid citizens of the white and black races from traveling in the same public conveyance, and to punish officers of railroad companies for permitting persons of the two races to occupy the same passenger coach. If a state can prescribe as a rule of civil conduct, that whites and blacks shall not travel as passengers in the same railroad coach, why may it not so regulate the use of the streets of its cities and towns as to compel white citizens to keep on one side of the street and black citizens to keep on the other? Why may it not, upon like grounds, punish whites and blacks who ride together in street cars or in open vehicles on a public road or street? Why may it not require sheriffs to assign whites to one side of the court-room and blacks to the other? And why may it not also prohibit the commingling of the two races in the galleries of legislative halls or in public assemblages convened for the political questions of the day? Further, if this statute of Louisiana is consistent with the personal liberty of citizens, why may not the state require the separation in railroad coaches of native and naturalized citizens of the United States, or of Protestants and Roman Catholics?

The answer given at the argument to these questions was that regulations of the kind they suggest would be unreasonable, and could not, therefore, stand before the law. Is it meant that the determination of questions of legislative power depends upon the inquiry whether the statute whose validity is questioned is, in the judgment of the courts, a reasonable one, taking all the circumstances into consideration? A statute may be unreasonable merely because a sound public policy forbade its enactment. But I do not understand that the courts have anything to do with the policy or expediency of legislation. A statute may be valid, and yet upon grounds of public policy may well be characterized as unreasonable. Mr. Sedgwick correctly states the rule when he says that the legislative intention being clearly ascertained, "the courts have no other duty to perform than to execute the legislative will, without any regard to their views as to the wisdom or justice of the particular enactment." Sedgw. Stat. & Const. L. 324. . . .

The white race deems itself to be the dominant race in this country. And so it is, in prestige, in achievements, in education, in wealth, and in power. So, I doubt not that it will continue to be for all time, if it remains true to its great heritage and holds fast to the principles of constitutional liberty. But in view of the Constitution, in the eye of the law, there is in this country no superior, dominant, ruling class of citizens. There is no caste here. Our Constitution is color-blind, and neither knows nor tolerates classes among citizens. In respect of civil rights, all citizens are equal before the law. The humblest is the peer of the most powerful. The law regards man as man, and takes no account of his surroundings or of his color when his civil rights as guaranteed by the supreme law of the land are involved. It is therefore to be regretted that this high tribunal, the final expositor of the fundamental law of the land, has reached the conclusion that it is competent for a state to regulate the enjoyment by citizens of their civil rights solely upon the basis of race.

In my opinion, the judgment this day rendered will, in time, prove to be quite as pernicious as the decision made by this tribunal in the *Dred Scott Case*. . . . The recent amendments of the Constitution, it was supposed, had eradicated these principles (announced in that decision) from our institutions. But it seems that we have yet, in some of the states, a dominant race, a superior class of citizens, which assumes to regulate the enjoyment of civil rights, common to all citizens, upon the basis of race. The present decision, it may well be apprehended, will not stimulate aggressions, more or less brutal and irritating, upon the admitted rights of colored citizens, but will encourage the belief that it is possible, by means of state enactments, to defeat the beneficent purposes which the people of the United States had in view when they adopted the recent amendments of the Constitution. . . . Sixty millions of whites are in no danger from the presence here of eight millions of blacks. The destinies of the two races in this country are indissolubly linked together, and the interests of both require that the common government of all shall not permit the seeds of race hate to be planted under the sanction of law. What can more certainly arouse race hate, what more certainly create and perpetuate a feeling of distrust between these races, than state enactments which in fact proceed on the ground that colored citizens are so inferior and degraded that they cannot be allowed to sit in public coaches occupied by white citizens? That, as all will admit, is the real meaning of such legislation as was enacted in Louisiana.

The sure guaranty of the peace and security of each race is the clear, distinct, unconditional recognition by our governments, national and state, of every right that inheres in civil freedom, and of the equality before the law of all citizens of the United States without regard to race. State enactments, regulating the enjoyment of civil rights, upon the basis of race, are cunningly devised to defeat legitimate results of the war, under the pretense of recognizing equality of rights, can have no other result than to render permanent peace impossible and to keep alive a conflict of races, the continuance of which must do harm to all concerned.

. . .

The arbitrary separation of citizens, on the basis of race, while they are on a public highway, is a badge of servitude wholly inconsistent with the civil freedom and the equality before the law established by the Constitution. It cannot be justified upon any legal grounds.

If evils will result from the commingling of the two races upon public highways established for the benefit of all, they will be infinitely less than those that will surely come from state legislation regulating the enjoyment of civil rights upon the basis of race. We boast of the freedom enjoyed by our people above all other peoples. But it is difficult to reconcile that boast with a state of the law which, practically, puts the brand of servitude and degradation upon a large class of our fellow citizens, our equals before the law. The thin disguise of "equal" accommodations for passengers in railroad coaches will not mislead anyone, or atone for the wrong this day done.

. . .

I am of opinion that the statute of Louisiana is inconsistent with the personal liberty of citizens, white and black, in that state, and hostile to both the spirit and letter of the Constitution of the United States. If laws of like character should be enacted in the several states of the Union, the effect would be in the highest degree mischievous. Slavery as an institution tolerated by law would, it is true, have disappeared from our country, but there would remain a power in the states, by sinister legislation, to interfere with the full enjoyment of the blessings of freedom; to regulate civil rights, common to all citizens, upon the basis of race; and to place in a condition of legal inferiority a large body of American citizens, now constituting a part of the political community, called the people of the United States, for whom and by whom, through representatives, our government is administered. Such a system is inconsistent with the guarantee given by the Constitution to each state of a republican form of government, and may be stricken down by congressional action, or by the courts in the discharge of their solemn duty to maintain the supreme law of the land anything in the Constitution or laws of any state to the contrary notwithstanding.

For the reasons stated, I am constrained to withhold my assent from the opinion and judgment of the majority.

BROWN v. *BOARD OF EDUCATION OF TOPEKA, KANSAS I*
347 U. S. 483; 98 L. Ed. 873; 74 S. Ct. 686 (1954)

CHIEF JUSTICE WARREN *delivered the opinion of the Court.*

These cases came to us from the States of Kansas, South Carolina, Virginia, and Delaware. They are premised on different facts and different local conditions, but a common legal question justifies their consideration together in this consolidated opinion.

In each of the cases, minors of the Negro race, through their legal representatives, seek aid of the courts in obtaining admission to the public schools of their community on a non-segregated basis. . . . In each of the cases other than the Delaware case, a three-judge federal district court denied relief to the plaintiffs on the so-called "separate but equal" doctrine, announced by the Court in *Plessy* v. *Ferguson.* . . . In the Delaware case, the Supreme Court of Delaware adhered to that doctrine, but ordered that the plaintiffs be admitted to the white schools because of their superiority to the Negro schools.

The plaintiffs contend that segregated public schools are not "equal" and cannot be made "equal," and that hence they are deprived of the equal protection of the laws. Because of the obvious importance of the question presented, the Court took jurisdiction. Argument was heard in the 1952 Term, and reargument was heard this Term on certain questions propounded by the Court.

Reargument was largely devoted to the circumstances surrounding the adoption of the Fourteenth Amendment in 1868. It covered exhaustively consideration of the Amendment in Congress, ratification by the states, then existing practices in racial segregation, and the views of proponents and opponents of the Amendment. This discussion and our own investigation convince us that, although these sources cast some light, it is not enough to resolve the problem with which we are faced. At best, they are inconclusive. The most avid proponents of the post-War Amendments undoubtedly intended them to remove all legal distinctions among "all persons born or naturalized in the United States." Their opponents, just as certainly were antagonistic to both the letter and spirit of the Amendments and wished them to have the most limited effect. What others in Congress and the state legislatures had in mind cannot be determined with any degree of certainty.

An additional reason for the inconclusive nature of the Amendment's history, with respect to segregated schools, is the status of public education at that time. In the South, the movement toward free common schools, supported by general taxation, had not yet taken hold. Education for white children was largely in the hands of private groups. Education for Negroes was almost nonexistent, and practically all of the race was illiterate. In fact, any education of Negroes was forbidden by law in some states. Today, in contrast, many Negroes have achieved outstanding success in the arts and sciences as well as in the business and professional world. It is true that public education had already advanced further in the North, but the effect of the Amendment on Northern States was generally ignored in the Congressional debates. Even in the North, the conditions of public education did not approximate those existing today. The curriculum was usually rudimentary; ungraded schools were common in rural areas; the school term was but three months a year in many states; and compulsory school attendance was virtually unknown. As a consequence, it is not surprising that there should be so little in the history of the Fourteenth Amendment relating to its intended effect on public education.

In the first cases in this Court construing the Fourteenth Amendment, decided shortly after its adoption, the Court interpreted it as proscribing all state-imposed discriminations against the Negro race. The doctrine of "separate but equal" did not make its appearance in the Court until 1896 in the case of *Plessy* v. *Ferguson*, . . . involving not education but transportation. American courts have since labored with the doctrine for over half a century. In this Court, there have been six cases involving the "separate but equal" doctrine in the field of public education. In *Cumming* v. *Board of Education of Richmond County* and *Gong Lum* v. *Rice,* the validity of the doctrine itself was not challenged. In more recent cases, all on the graduate school level, inequality was found in that specific benefits enjoyed by white students were denied to Negro students of the same educational qualifications *(State of Missouri ex. rel. Gaines* v. *Canada, Sipuel* v. *Board of Regents of University of Oklahoma, Sweatt* v. *Painter,* and *McLaurin* v. *Oklahoma State Regents).* In none of these cases was it necessary to re-examine the doctrine to grant relief to the Negro plaintiff. And in *Sweatt* v. *Painter,* . . . the Court expressly reserved decision on the question whether *Plessy* v. *Ferguson* should be held inapplicable to public education.

. . .

In approaching this problem, we cannot turn the clock back to 1868 when the Amendment was adopted, or even to 1896 when *Plessy* v. *Ferguson* was written. We must consider public education in the light of its full development and its present place in American life throughout the Nation. Only in this way can it be determined if segregation in public schools deprives these plaintiffs of the equal protection of the laws.

Today, education is perhaps the most important function of state and local governments. Compulsory school attendance laws and the great expenditures for education both demonstrate our recognition of the importance of education to our democratic society. It is required in the performance of our most basic public responsibilities, even service in the armed forces. It is the very foundation of good citizenship. Today it is a principal instrument in awakening the child to cultural values, in preparing him for later professional training, and in helping him to adjust normally to his environment. In these days, it is doubtful that any child may reasonably be expected to succeed in life if he is denied the opportunity of an education. Such an opportunity, where the state has undertaken to provide it, is a right which must be made available to all on equal terms.

We come then to the question presented: Does segregation of children in public schools solely on the basis of race, even though the physical facilities and other "tangible" factors may be equal, deprive the children of the minority group of equal educational opportunities? We believe that it does.

In *Sweatt* v. *Painter* . . . in finding that a segregated law school for Negroes could not provide them equal educational opportunities, this Court relied in large part on "those qualities which are incapable of objective measurement but which make for greatness in a law school." In *McLaurin* v. *Oklahoma State Regents*, . . . the Court, in requiring that a Negro admitted to a white graduate school be treated like all other students, again resorted to intangible considerations: ". . . his ability to study, to engage in discussion and exchange views with other students, and, in general, to learn his profession." Such considerations apply with added force to children in grade and high schools. To separate them from others of similar age and qualifications solely because of their race generates a feeling of inferiority as to their status in the community that may affect their hearts and minds in a way unlikely ever to be undone. The effect of this separation on their educational opportunities was well stated by a finding in the Kansas case by a court which nevertheless felt compelled to rule against the Negro plaintiffs:

> Segregation of white and colored children in public schools has a detrimental effect upon the colored children. The impact is greater when it has the sanction of the law; for the policy of separating the races is usually interpreted as denoting the inferiority of the negro group. A sense of inferiority affects the motivation of a child to learn. Segregation with the sanction of law, therefore, has a tendency to retard the educational and mental development of negro children and to deprive them of the benefits they would receive in a racial[ly] integrated school system.

Whatever may have been the extent of psychological knowledge at the time of *Plessy* v. *Ferguson*, this finding is amply supported by modern authority. Any language in *Plessy* v. *Ferguson* contrary to this finding is rejected. We conclude that in a field of public education the doctrine of "separate but equal" has no place. Separate educational facilities are inherently unequal. Therefore, we hold that the plaintiffs and others similarly situated for whom the actions have been brought are, by the reason of the segregation complained of, deprived of the equal protection of the laws guaranteed by the Fourteenth Amendment. This disposition makes unnecessary any discussion whether such segregation also violates the Due Process Clause of the Fourteenth Amendment.

Because these are class actions because of the wide applicability of the decision, and because of the great variety of local conditions, the formulation of decrees in these cases presents problems of considerable complexity. . . . In order that we may have the full assistance of the parties in formulating decrees, the cases will be restored to the docket, and the parties are requested to present further argument on [the appropriate decree]. The Attorney General of the United States is again invited to participate. The Attorneys General of the states requiring or permitting segregation in public education will also be permitted to appear as *amici curiae* upon request to do so by September 15, 1954, and submission of briefs by October 1, 1954.

It is so ordered.

Cases ordered restored to docket for further argument on question of appropriate decrees.

BROWN v. *BOARD OF EDUCATION OF TOPEKA, KANSAS II*
349 U.S. 294; 99 L. Ed. 1083; 75 S. Ct. 753 (1955)

CHIEF JUSTICE WARREN *delivered the opinion of the Court.*

These cases were decided on May 17, 1954. The opinions of that date, declaring the fundamental principle that racial discrimination in public education is unconstitutional, are incorporated herein by reference. All provisions of federal, state, or local law requiring or permitting such discrimination must yield to this principle. There remains for consideration the manner in which relief is to be accorded.

Because these cases arose under different local conditions and their disposition will involve a variety of local problems, we requested further argument on the question of relief. In view of the nationwide importance of the decision, we invited the Attorney General of the United States and the Attorneys General of all states requiring or permitting racial discrimination in public education to present their views on that question. The parties, the United States, and the States of Florida, North Carolina, Arkansas, Oklahoma, Maryland, and Texas filed briefs and participated in the oral argument.

These presentations were informative and helpful to the Court in its consideration of the complexities arising from the transition to a system of public education freed of racial discrimination. The presentations also demonstrated that substantial steps to eliminate racial discrimination in public schools have already been taken, not only in some of the communities in which these cases arose, but in some of the states appearing as *amici curiae*, and in other states as well. Substantial progress has been made in the District of Columbia and in the communities in Kansas and Delaware involved in this litigation. The defendants in the cases coming to us from South Carolina and Virginia are awaiting the decision of this Court concerning relief.

Full implementation of these constitutional principles may require solution of varied local school problems. School authorities have the primary responsibility for elucidating, assessing, and solving these problems; courts will have to consider whether the action of school authorities constitutes good faith implementation of the governing constitutional principles. Because of their proximity to local conditions and the possible need for further hearings, the courts which originally heard these cases can best perform this judicial appraisal. Accordingly, we believe it appropriate to remand the cases to those courts.

In fashioning and effectuating the decrees, the courts will be guided by equitable principles. Traditionally, equity has been characterized by a practical flexibility in shaping its remedies and by a facility for adjusting and reconciling public and private needs. These cases call for the exercise of these traditional attributes of equity power. At stake is the personal interest of the plaintiffs in admission to public schools as soon as practicable on a nondiscriminatory basis. To effectuate this interest may call for elimination of a variety of obstacles in making the transition to school systems operated in accordance with the constitutional principles set forth in our May 17, 1954, decision. Courts of equity may properly take into account the public interest in the elimination of such obstacles in a systematic and effective manner. But it would go without saying that the vitality of these constitutional principles cannot be allowed to yield simply because of disagreement with them.

While giving weight to these public and private considerations, the courts will require that the defendants make a prompt and reasonable start toward full compliance with our May 17, 1954, ruling. Once such a start has been made, the courts may find that additional time is necessary to carry out the ruling in an effective manner. The burden rests upon the defendants to establish that such time is necessary in the public interest and is consistent with good faith compliance at the earliest practicable date. To that end, the courts may consider problems related to administration, arising from the physical condition of the school plant, the school transportation system, personnel, revision of school districts and attendance areas into compact units to achieve a system of determining admission to the public schools on a nonracial basis, and a revision of local laws and regulations which may be necessary in solving the foregoing problems. They will also consider the adequacy of any plans the defendants may propose to meet these problems and to effectuate a transition to a racially nondiscriminatory school system. During this period of transition, the courts will retain jurisdiction of these cases.

The judgments below, except that in the Delaware case, are accordingly reversed and remanded to the District Courts to take such proceedings and enter such orders and degrees consistent with this opinion as are necessary and proper to admit to public schools on a racially non-discriminatory basis with all deliberate speed the parties to these cases. The judgment in the Delaware case—ordering the immediate admission of the plantiffs to schools previously attended only by white children—is affirmed on the basis of the principle stated on our May 17, 1954, opinion, but the case is remanded to the Supreme Court of Delaware for such further proceedings as that court may deem necessary in light of this opinion.

MILLIKEN v. BRADLEY
418 U.S. 717; 41 L. Ed. 2d 1069; 94 S. Ct. 3112 (1974)

MR. CHIEF JUSTICE BURGER *delivered the opinion of the Court.*

We granted certiorari in these consolidated cases to determine whether a federal court may impose a multidistrict, areawide remedy to a single district *de jure* segregation problem absent any finding that the other included school districts have failed to operate unitary school systems within their districts, absent any claim or finding that the boundary lines of any affected school district were established with the purpose of fostering racial segregation in public schools, absent any finding that the included districts committed acts which effected segregation within the other districts, and absent a meaningful opportunity for the included neighboring school districts to present evidence or be heard on the propriety of a multidistrict remedy or on the question of constitutional violations by those neighboring districts.

The action was commenced in August of 1970

by the respondents, the Detroit Branch of the National Association for the Advancement of Colored People and individual parents and students, on behalf of a class . . . to include "all school children of the City of Detroit and all Detroit resident parents who have children of school age." The named defendants in the District Court included the Governor of Michigan, the Attorney General, the State Board of Education, the State Superintendent of Public Instruction, and the Board of Education of the City of Detroit, its members and its former superintendent of schools. The State of Michigan as such is not a party to this litigation and references to the State must be read as references to the public officials, State and local, through whom the State is alleged to have acted. In their complaint respondents attacked the constitutionality of a statute of the State of Michigan known as Act 48 of the 1970 Legislature on the ground that it put the State of Michigan in the position of unconstitutionally interfering with the execution and operation of a voluntary plan of partial high school desegregation, which had been adopted by the Detroit Board of Education to be effective beginning with the fall 1970 semester. The complaint also alleged that the Detroit Public School System was and is segregated on the basis of race as a result of the official policies and actions of the defendants and their predecessors in office, and called for the implementation of a plan that would eliminate "the racial identity of every school in the [Detroit] system and . . . maintain now and hereafter a unitary non-racial school system."

Initially the matter was tried on respondents' motion for preliminary injunction to restrain the enforcement of Act 48 so as to permit the April 7 Plan to be implemented. On that issue, the District Court ruled that respondents were not entitled to a preliminary injunction since at that stage there was no proof that Detroit had a dual segregated school system. On appeal, the Court of Appeals found that the "implementation of

the April 7 Plan was [unconstitutionally] thwarted by state action in the form of the Act of the Legislature of Michigan.". . . The case was remanded to the District Court for an expedited trial on the merits.

On remand the respondents moved for immediate implementation of the April 7 Plan in order to remedy the deprivation of the claimed constitutional rights. In response the School Board suggested two other plans, along with the April 7 Plan, and urged that top priority be assigned to the so-called "Magnet Plan" which was "designed to attract children to a school because of its superior curriculum." The District Court approved the Board's Magnet Plan, and respondents again appealed to the Court of Appeals moving for summary reversal. The Court of Appeals refused to pass on the merits of the Magnet Plan and ruled that the District Court had not abused its discretion in refusing to adopt the April 7 Plan without an evidentiary hearing. The case was again remanded with instructions to proceed immediately to a trial on the merits of respondents' substantive allegations concerning the Detroit School System.

. . . On September 27, 1971, the District Court issued its findings and conclusions on the issue of segregation finding that "Government actions and inaction at all levels, federal, state and local, have combined, with those of private organizations, such as loaning institutions and real estate associations and brokerage firms, to establish and to maintain the pattern of residential segregation throughout the Detroit metropolitan area.". . .

The District Court found that the Detroit Board of Education created and maintained optional attendance zones within Detroit neighborhoods undergoing racial transition and between high school attendance areas of opposite predominant racial compositions. These zones, the court found, had the "natural, probable, foreseeable and actual effect" of allowing White pupils to escape identifiably Negro schools. . . . [T]he District Court concluded, the natural and actual effect of these acts was the creation and perpetuation of school segregation within Detroit.

The District Court found that in the operation of its school transportation program, which was designed to relieve overcrowding, the Detroit Board had admittedly bused Negro Detroit pupils to predominantly Negro schools which were beyond or away from closer White schools with available space. . . .

With respect to the Detroit Board of Education's practices in school construction, the District found that Detroit school construction generally tended to have segregative effect with the great majority of schools being built in either overwhelmingly all Negro or all White neighborhoods so that the new schools opened as predominantly one-race schools. . . .

The District Court also found that the State of Michigan had committed several constitutional violations with respect to the exercise of its general responsibility for, and supervision of, public education. The State, for example, was found to have failed, until the 1971 Session of the Michigan Legislature, to provide authorization or funds for the transportation of pupils within Detroit regardless of their poverty or distance from the school to which they were assigned; during this same period the State provided many neighboring, mostly White, suburban districts the full range of state supported transportation.

The District Court found that the State, through Act 48, acted to "impede, delay and minimize racial integration in Detroit schools.". . .

The District Court also held that the acts of the Detroit Board of Education, as a subordinate entity of the State, were attributable to the State of Michigan thus creating a vicarious liability on the part of the State. . . .

Turning to the question of an appropriate remedy for these several constitutional violations, the District Court deferred a pending motion by intervening parent defendants to join as additional parties defendant some 85 school districts in the three counties surrounding Detroit on the ground that effective relief could not be achieved without their presence. The District Court concluded that this motion to intervene was "premature," since it "has to do with relief" and no reasonably specific desegregation plan was before the court. Accordingly, the District Court proceeded to order the Detroit Board of Education to submit desegregation plans limited to the segregation problems found to be existing within the city of Detroit. At the same time, however, the state defendants were directed to submit desegregation plans encompassing the three-county metropolitan area despite the fact that the school districts of these three counties were not parties to the action and despite the fact that there had been no claim that these outlying counties, encompassing some 85 separate school districts, had committed constitutional violations. An effort to appeal these orders to the Court of Appeals was dismissed on the ground that the orders were not appealable. . . .

. . . On March 7, 1972, the District Court notified all parties and the petitioner school districts seeking intervention, that March 14, 1972, was the deadline for submission of recommendations for conditions of intervention and the date of the commencement of hearings on Detroit-only desegregation plans. On the second day of the scheduled hearings, March 15, 1972, the District Court granted the motions of the intervenor school districts subject, *inter alia*, to the following conditions:

1. No intervenor will be permitted to assert any claim or defense previously adjudicated by the court.
2. No intervenor shall reopen any question or issue which has previously been decided by the court.

. . .

7. New intervenors are granted intervention for two principal purposes: (1) To advise the court, by brief, of the legal propriety or impropriety of considering a metro-

politan plan; (b) To review any plan or plans for the desegregation of the so-called larger Detroit Metropolitan area, and submitting objections, modifications or alternatives to it or them, and in accordance with the requirements of the United States Constitution and the prior orders of this court.

Upon granting the motion to intervene, on March 15, 1972, the District Court advised the petitioning intervenors that the court had previously set March 22, 1972, as the date for the filing of briefs on the legal propriety of a "metropolitan" plan of desegregation and, accordingly, that the intervening school districts would have one week to muster their legal arguments on the issue. . . .

On March 24, 1972, two days after the intervenors' briefs were due, the District Court . . . rejected the state defendants' arguments that no state action caused the segregation of the Detroit schools, and the intervening suburban districts' contention that inter-district relief was inappropriate unless the suburban districts had themselves committed violations. The court concluded:

[I]t is proper for the court to consider metropolitan plans directed toward the desegregation of the Detroit public schools as an alternative to the present intra-city desegregation plans before it and, in the event that the court finds such intra-city plans inadequate to desegregate such schools, the court is of the opinion that it is required to consider a metropolitan remedy for desegregation.

On March 28, 1972, the District Court issued its findings and conclusions on the three "Detroit-only" plans submitted by the city Board and the respondents. It found that the best of the three plans "would make the Detroit system more identifiably Black . . . thereby increasing the flights of Whites from the city and the system." From this the court concluded that the plan "would not accomplish desegregation within the corporate geographical limits of the city." Accordingly, the District Court held that "it must look beyond the limits of the Detroit school district for a solution to the problem," and that "[s]chool district lines are simply matters of political convenience and may not be used to deny constitutional rights."

During the period from March 28, 1972 to April 14, 1972, the District Court conducted hearings on a metropolitan plan. . . . [I]t designated 53 of the 85 suburban school districts plus Detroit as the "desegregation area" and appointed a panel to prepare and submit "an effective desegregation plan" for the Detroit schools that would encompass the entire desegregation area. The plan was to be based on 15 clusters, each containing part of the Detroit system and two or more suburban districts, and was to "achieve the greatest degree of actual desegregation to the end that, upon implementation, no school, grade or classroom [would be] substantially disproportionate to the overall pupil racial composition."

On July 11, 1972, and in accordance with a recommendation by the court-appointed desegregation panel, the District Court ordered the Detroit Board of Education to purchase or lease "at least" 295 school buses for the purposes of providing transportation under an interim plan to be developed for the 1972-1973 school year. The costs of this acquisition were to be borne by the state defendants.

On June 12, 1973, a divided Court of Appeals, sitting *en banc*, affirmed in part, vacated in part and remanded for further proceedings. The Court of Appeals held, first, that the record supported the District Court's findings and conclusions on the constitutional violations committed by the Detroit Board and by the state defendants . . . and that "the District Court was, therefore, authorized and required to take effective measures to desegregate the Detroit Public School System."

The Court of Appeals also agreed with the District Court that "any less comprehensive a solution than a metropolitan area plan would result in an all black school system immediately surrounded by practically all white suburban school systems, with an overwhelming white majority population in the total metropolitan area." The court went on to state that it could "not see how such segregation can be any less harmful to the minority students than if the same result were accomplished within one school district."

Accordingly, the Court of Appeals concluded that "the only feasible desegregation plan involves the crossing of the boundary lines between the Detroit School District and adjacent or nearby school districts for the limited purpose of providing an effective desegregation plan." It reasoned that such a plan would be appropriate because of the State's violations, and could be implemented because of the State's authority to control local school districts. Without further elaboration, and without any discussion of the claims that no constitutional violation by the outlying districts had been shown and that no evidence on that point had been allowed, the Court of Appeals held:

[T]he State has committed *de jure* acts of segregation and ... the State controls the instrumentalities whose action is necessary to remedy the harmful effects of the State acts.

An inter-district remedy was thus held to be "within the equity powers of the District Court.". . .

Ever since *Brown* v. *Board of Education*, 347 U.S. 483 (1954), judicial consideration of school desegregation cases has begun with the standard that:

[I]n the field of public education the doctrine of 'separate but equal' has no place. Separate educational facilities are inherently unequal. 347 U.S., at 495.

This has been reaffirmed time and again as the meaning of the Constitution and the controlling rule of law.

The target of the *Brown* holding was clear and forthright: the elimination of state mandated or deliberately maintained dual school systems with certain schools for Negro pupils and others for White pupils. This duality and racial segregation was held to violate the Constitution in the cases subsequent to 1954, including particularly *Green* v. *County School Board of New Kent County*, 391 U.S. 430 (1968); *Raney* v. *Board of Education*, 391 U.S. 433 (1968); *Monroe* v. *Board of Commissioners*, 391 U.S. 443 (1968); *Swann* v. *Charlotte-Mecklenburg Board of Education*, 402 U.S. 1 (1971); *Wright* v. *Council of City of Emporia*, 407 U.S. 451 (1972); *United States* v. *Scotland Neck Board of Education*, 407 U.S. 484.

The *Swann* case, of course, dealt

with the problem of defining in more precise terms than heretofore the scope of the duty of school authorities and district courts in implementing *Brown I* and the mandate to eliminate dual systems and establish unitary systems at once. . . .

Viewing the record as a whole, it seems clear that the District Court and the Court of Appeals shifted the primary focus from a Detroit remedy to the metropolitan area only because of their conclusion that total desegregation of Detroit would not produce the racial balance which they perceived as desirable. Both courts proceeded on an assumption that the Detroit schools could not be truly desegregated—in their view of what constituted desegregation—unless the racial composition of the student body of each school substantially reflected the racial composition of the population of the metropolitan area as a whole. . . .

In *Swann*, which arose in the context of a single independent school district, the Court held:

If we were to read the holding of the District Court to require as a matter of substantive constitutional right, any particular degree of racial balance or mixing, that approach would be disapproved and we would be obliged to reverse. 402 U.S., at 24.

The clear import of this language from *Swann* is that desegregation, in the sense of dismantling a dual school system, does not require any particular racial balance in each "school, grade or classroom.". . .

The Michigan educational structure involved in this case, in common with most States, provides for a large measure of local control and a review of the scope and character of these local powers indicates the extent to which the inter-district remedy approved by the two courts could disrupt and alter the structure of public education in Michigan. The metropolitan remedy would require, in effect, consolidation of 54 independent school districts historically administered as separate units into a vast new super school district. Entirely apart from the logistical and other serious problems attending large-scale transportation of students, the consolidation would give rise to an array of other problems in financing and operating this new school system. Some of the more obvious questions would be: What would be the status and authority of the present popularly elected school boards? Would the children of Detroit be within the jurisdiction and operating control of a school board elected by the parents and residents of other districts? What board or boards would levy taxes for school operations in these 54 districts constituting the consolidated metropolitan area? What provisions could be made for assuring substantial equality in tax levies among the 54 districts, if this were deemed requisite? What provisions would be made for financing? Would the validity of long-term bonds be jeopardized unless approved by all of the component districts as well as the State? What body would determine that portion of the curricula now left to the discretion of local school boards? Who would establish attendance zones, purchase school equipment, locate and construct new schools, and indeed attend to all the myriad day-to-day decisions that are necessary to school operations affecting poten-

tially more than three quarters of a million pupils?

It may be suggested that all of these vital operational problems are yet to be resolved by the District Court, and that this is the purpose of the Court of Appeals' proposed remand. But it is obvious from the scope of the inter-district remedy itself that absent a complete restructuring of the laws of Michigan relating to school districts the District Court will become first, a *de facto* "legislative authority" to resolve these complex questions, and then the "school superintendent" for the entire area. This is a task which few, if any, judges are qualified to perform and one which would deprive the people of control of schools through their elected representatives.

Of course, no state law is above the Constitution. School district lines and the present laws with respect to local control, are not sacrosanct and if they conflict with the Fourteenth Amendment federal courts have a duty to prescribe appropriate remedies. . . . But our prior holdings have been confined to violations and remedies within a single school district. We therefore turn to address, for the first time, the validity of a remedy mandating cross-district or inter-district consolidation to remedy a condition of segregation found to exist in only one district.

The controlling principle consistently expounded in our holdings is that the scope of the remedy is determined by the nature and extent of the constitutional violation. Before the boundaries of separate and autonomous school districts may be set aside by consolidating the separate units for remedial purposes or by imposing a cross-district remedy, it must first be shown that there has been a constitutional violation within one district that produces a significant segregative effect in another district. Specifically it must be shown that racially discriminatory acts of the state or local school districts, or of a single school district have been a substantial cause of inter-district segregation. Thus an inter-district remedy might be in order where the racially discriminatory acts of one or more school districts caused racial segregation in an adjacent district, or where district lines have been deliberately drawn on the basis of race. In such circumstances an inter-district remedy would be appropriate to eliminate the inter-district segregation directly caused by the constitutional violation. Conversely, without an inter-district violation and inter-district effect, there is no constitutional wrong calling for an inter-district remedy.

The record before us, voluminous as it is, contains evidence of *de jure* segregated conditions only in the Detroit schools. . . . With no showing of significant violation by the 53 outlying school districts and no evidence of any inter-district violation or effect, the court went beyond the original theory of the case as framed by the pleadings and mandated a metropolitan area remedy. To approve the remedy ordered by the court would impose on the outlying districts, not shown to have committed any constitutional violation, a wholly impermissible remedy based on a standard not hinted at in *Brown I* and *II* or any holding of this Court. . . .

The constitutional right of the Negro respondents residing in Detroit is to attend a unitary school system in that district. Unless petitioners drew the district lines in a discriminatory fashion, or arranged for White students residing in the Detroit district to attend schools in Oakland and Macomb Counties, they were under no constitutional duty to make provisions for Negro students to do so. . . .

We conclude that the relief ordered by the District Court and affirmed by the Court of Appeals was based upon an erroneous standard and was unsupported by record evidence that acts of the outlying districts affected the discrimination found to exist in the schools of Detroit. Accordingly, the judgment of the Court of Appeals is vacated and the case is remanded for further proceedings consistent with this opinion leading to prompt formulation of a decree directed to eliminating the segregation found to exist in Detroit city schools, a remedy which has been delayed since 1970.

Reversed and remanded.

MR. JUSTICE MARSHALL, *with whom* MR. JUSTICE DOUGLAS, MR. JUSTICE BRENNAN, *and* MR. JUSTICE WHITE *join, dissenting.*

In *Brown* v. *Board of Education*, 347 U.S. 483 (1954), this Court held that segregation of children in public schools on the basis of race deprives minority group children of equal educational opportunities and therefore denies them the equal protection of the laws under the Fourteenth Amendment. This Court recognized then that remedying decades of segregation in public education would not be an easy task. . . .

After 20 years of small, often difficult steps toward that great end, the Court today takes a giant step backwards. Notwithstanding a record showing widespread and pervasive racial segregation in the educational system provided by the State of Michigan for children in Detroit, this Court holds that the District Court was powerless to require the State to remedy its constitutional violation in any meaningful fashion. Ironically purporting to base its result on the principle that the scope of the remedy in a desegregation case should be determined by the nature and the extent of the constitutional violation, the Court's answer is to provide no remedy at all for the violation proved in this case, thereby guaranteeing that Negro children in Detroit will receive the same separate and inherently unequal education in the future as they have been unconstitutionally afforded in the past.

I cannot subscribe to this emasculation of our constitutional guarantee of equal protection of the laws and must respectfully dissent. Our precedents, in my view, firmly establish that where, as here, state-imposed segregation has been demonstrated, it becomes the duty of the State to eliminate root and branch all vestiges of racial discrimination and to achieve the greatest possible degree of actual desegregation. I agree with both the District Court and the Court of Appeals that, under the facts of this case, this duty cannot be fulfilled unless the State of Michigan involves outlying metropolitan area school districts in its desegregation remedy. Furthermore, I perceive no basis either in law or in the practicalities of the situation justifying the State's interposition of school district boundaries as absolute barriers to the implementation of an effective desegregation remedy. Under established and frequently used Michigan procedures, school district lines are both flexible and permeable for a wide variety of purposes, and there is no reason why they must now stand in the way of meaningful desegregation relief.

The rights at issue in this case are too fundamental to be abridged on grounds as superficial as those relied on by the majority today. We deal here with the right of all of our children, whatever their race, to an equal start in life and to an equal opportunity to reach their full potential as citizens. Those children who have been denied that right in the past deserve better than to see fences thrown up to deny them that right in the future. Our Nation, I fear, will be ill-served by the Court's refusal to remedy separate and unequal education, for unless our children begin to learn together, there is little hope that our people will ever learn to live together.

The great irony of the Court's opinion and, in my view, its most serious analytical flaw may be gleaned from its concluding sentence, in which the Court remands for "prompt formulation of a decree directed to eliminating the segregation found to exist in Detroit city schools, a remedy which has been delayed since 1970." The majority, however, seems to have forgotten the District Court's explicit finding that a Detroit-only decree, the only remedy permitted under today's decision, "would not accomplish desegregation."

Nowhere in the Court's opinion does the majority confront, let alone respond to, the District Court's conclusion that a remedy limited to the city of Detroit would not effectively desegregate the Detroit city schools. I, for one, find the District Court's conclusion well supported by the record and its analysis compelled by our prior cases. . . .

The Court maintains that while the initial focus of this lawsuit was the condition of segregation within the Detroit city schools, the District Court abruptly shifted focus in mid-course and altered its theory of the case. This new theory, in the majority's words, was "equating racial imbalance with a constitutional violation calling for a remedy.". . .

There is simply no foundation in the record, then, for the majority's accusation that the only basis for the District Court's order was some desire to achieve a racial balance in the Detroit metropolitan area. In fact, just the contrary is the case. In considering proposed desegregation areas, the District Court had occasion to criticize one of the State's proposals specifically because it had no basis other than its "particular racial ratio" and did not focus on "relevant factors, like eliminating racially identifiable schools [and] accomplishing maximum actual desegregation of the Detroit public schools." Similarly, in rejecting the Detroit school board's proposed desegregation area, even though it included more all-white districts and therefore achieved a higher white-Negro ratio, the District Court commented:

> There is nothing in the record which suggests that these districts need be included in the desegregation area in order to disestablish the racial identifiability of the Detroit public schools. From the evidence, the primary reason for the Detroit School Board's interest in the inclusion of these school districts is not racial desegregation but to increase the average socio-economic balance of all the schools in the abutting regions and clusters. . . .

Rather than consider the propriety of interdistrict relief on this basis, however, the Court has conjured up a largely fictional account of what the District Court was attempting to accomplish. With all due respect, the Court, in my view, does a great disservice to the District Judge who labored long and hard with this complex litigation by accusing him of changing horses in mid-stream and shifting the focus of this case from the pursuit of a remedy for the condition of segregation within the Detroit school district to some unprincipled attempt to impose his own philosophy of racial balance on the entire Detroit metropolitan area. See *ante.* The focus of this case has always been the segregated system of education in the city of Detroit. The District Court determined that inter-district relief was necessary and appropriate only because it found that the condition of segregation within the Detroit school district could not be cured with a Detroit-only remedy. It is on this theory that the inter-district relief must stand or fall. . . .

. . . [T]he District Court's decision to expand its desegregation decree beyond the geographical limits of the city of Detroit rested in large part on its conclusions (A) that the State of Michigan was ultimately responsible for curing the condition of segregation within the Detroit city schools, and (B) that a Detriot-only remedy would not accomplish this task. In my view, both of these conclusions are well supported by the facts of this case and by this Court's precedents.

To begin with, the record amply supports the District Court's findings that the State of Michigan, through state officers and state agencies, had engaged in purposeful acts which created or aggravated segregation in the Detroit schools. The State Board of Education, for example, prior to 1962, exercised its authority to supervise local school site selection in a manner which contributed to segregation. Furthermore, the State's continuing authority, after 1962, to approve school building construction plans had intertwined the State with site selection decisions of the Detroit Board of Education which had the purpose and effect of maintaining segregation.

The State had also stood in the way of past efforts to desegregate the Detroit city schools. In 1970, for example, the Detroit School Board had begun implementation of its own desegregation plan for its high schools, despite considerable public and official resistance. The State Legislature intervened by enacting Act 48 of the Public Acts of 1970, specifically prohibiting implementation of the desegregation plan and thereby continuing the growing segregation of the Detroit school system. Adequate desegregation of the Detroit system was also hampered by discriminatory restrictions placed by the State on the use of transportation within Detroit. While state aid for transportation was provided by statute for suburban districts, many of which were highly urbanized, aid for intra-city transportation was excepted. One of the effects of this restriction was to encourage the construction of small walk-in neighborhood schools in Detroit, thereby lending aid to the intentional policy of creating a school system which reflected, to the greatest extent feasible, extensive residential segregation. Indeed, that one of the purposes of the transportation restriction was to impede desegregation was evidenced when the Michigan Legislature amended the State Transportation Aid Act to cover intra-city transportation but expressly prohibited the allocation of funds for cross busing of students within a school district to achieve racial balance. . . .

Under Michigan law "a school district is an agency of the State government." It is "a legal division of territory, created by the State for educational purposes, to which the State has granted such powers as are deemed necessary to permit the district to function as a State agency." Racial discrimination by the school district, an agency of the State, is therefore racial discrimination by the State itself, forbidden by the Fourteenth Amendment.

We recognized only last Term in *Keyes* that it was the State itself which was ultimately responsible for *de jure* acts of segregation committed by a local school board. A deliberate policy of segregation by the local board, we held, amounted to "state-imposed segregation." 413 U.S., at 200. Wherever a dual school system exists, whether compelled by state statute or created by a local board's systematic program of segregation, "the *State* automatically assumes an affirmative duty 'to effectuate a transition to a racially nondiscriminatory school system' [and] to eliminate from the public schools within their school system 'all vestiges of state-imposed segregation.'" . . .

Most significantly for present purposes, the State has wide-ranging powers to consolidate and merge school districts, even without the consent of the districts themselves or the local citizenry. . . . Indeed, recent years have witnessed an accelerated program of school district consolidations, mergers, and annexations, many of which were state imposed. . . . Furthermore, the State has broad powers to transfer property from one district to another, again without the consent of the local school districts affected by the transfer. . . .

Whatever may be the history of public education in other parts of our Nation, it simply flies in the face of reality to say, as does the majority, that in Michigan, "No single tradition in public education is more deeply rooted than local control over the operation of schools. . . ." As the State's supreme court has said: "We have repeatedly emphasized that education in this State is not a local concern, but belongs to the State at large." . . .

The continued racial identifiability of the Detroit schools under a Detroit-only remedy is not simply a reflection of their high percentage of Negro students. What is or is not a racially identifiable vestige of *de jure* segregation must necessarily depend on several factors. Foremost among these should be the relationship between the schools in question and the neighboring community. For these purposes the city of Detroit and its surrounding suburbs must be viewed as a single community. Detroit is closely connected to its suburbs in many ways, and the metropolitan area is viewed as a single cohesive unit by its residents. . . .

Under a Detroit-only decree, Detroit's schools will clearly remain racially identifiable in comparison with neighboring schools in the metro-politan community. Schools with 65 percent and more Negro students will stand in sharp and obvious contrast to schools in neighboring districts with less than 2 percent Negro enrollment. Negro students will continue to perceive their schools as segregated educational facilities and this perception will only be increased when whites react to a Detroit-only decree by fleeing to the suburbs to avoid integration. School district lines, however innocently drawn, will surely be perceived as fences to separate the races when, under a Detroit-only decree, white parents withdraw their children from the Detroit city schools and move to the suburbs in order to continue them in all-white schools. The message of this action will not escape the Negro children in the city of Detroit. It will be of scant significance to Negro children who have for years been confined by *de jure* acts of segregation to a growing core of all-Negro schools surrounded by a ring of all-white schools that the new dividing line between the races is the school district boundary. . . .

It is a hollow remedy indeed where "after supposed 'desegregation' the schools are segregated in fact." *Hobson* v. *Hansen*, 269 F. Supp. 401, 495 (D. D. C. 1967). We must do better than "substitute . . . one segregated school system for another segregated school system." *Wright, supra*, 407 U.S., at 456. To suggest, as does the majority, that a Detroit-only plan somehow remedies the effects of *de jure* segregation of the races is, in my view, to make a solemn mockery of *Brown I*'s holding that separate educational facilities are inherently unequal and of *Swann*'s unequivocal mandate that the answer to *de jure* segregation is the greatest possible degree of actual desegregation.

One final set of problems remains to be considered. We recognized in *Brown II*, and have re-emphasized ever since, that in fashioning relief in desegregation cases, "the courts will be guided by equitable principles. Traditionally equity has been characterized by a practical flexibility in shaping its remedies and by a facility for adjusting and reconciling public and private needs."

Though not resting its holding on this point, the majority suggests that various equitable considerations militate against inter-district relief. The Court refers to, for example, financing and administrative problems, the logistical problems attending large-scale transportation of students, and the prospect of the District Court's becoming a "de facto 'legislative authority'" and "'school superintendent' for the entire area." The entangling web of problems woven by the Court, however, appears on further consideration to be constructed of the flimsiest of threads. . . .

Some disruption, of course, is the inevitable product of any desegregation decree, whether it operates within one district or on an inter-district basis. As we said in *Swann*, however,

Absent a constitutional violation there would be no basis for judicially ordering assignment of students on a racial basis. All things being equal, with no history of discrimination, it might well be desirable to assign pupils to schools nearest their homes. But all things are not equal in a system that has been deliberately constructed and maintained to enforce racial segregation. The remedy for such segregation may be administratively awkward, inconvenient, and even bizarre in some situations and may impose burdens on some; but all awkwardness and inconvenience cannot be avoided. . . . 402 U.S., at 28.

Desegregation is not and was never expected to be an easy task. Racial attitudes ingrained in our Nation's childhood and adolescence are not quickly thrown aside in its middle years. But just as the inconvenience of some cannot be allowed to stand in the way of the rights of others, so public opposition, no matter how strident, cannot be permitted to divert this Court from the enforcement of the constitutional principles at issue in this case. Today's holding, I fear, is more a reflection of a perceived public mood that we have gone far enough in enforcing the Constitution's guarantee of equal justice than it is the product of neutral principles of law. In the short run, it may seem to be the easier course to allow our great metropolitan areas to be divided up each into two cities—one white, the other black—but it is a course, I predict, our people will ultimately regret. I dissent.

JONES v. MAYER
392 U.S. 409; 20 L. Ed. 2d 1189; 88 S. Ct. 2186 (1968)

MR. JUSTICE STEWART *delivered the opinion of the Court.*

In this case we are called upon to determine the scope and the constitutionality of an Act of Congress, 42 U.S.C. Sec. 1982, which provides that:

All citizens of the United States shall have the same rights, in every State and Territory, as is enjoyed by white citizens thereof to inherit, purchase, lease, sell, hold, and convey real and personal property.

On September 2, 1965, the petitioners filed a complaint in the District Court for the Eastern District of Missouri, alleging that the respondents had refused to sell them a home in the Paddock Woods community of St. Louis County for the sole reason that petitioner . . . is a Negro. Relying in part upon Sec. 1982, the petitioners sought injunctive and other relief. The District Court sustained the respondents' motion to dismiss the complaint, and the Court of Appeals for the Eighth Circuit affirmed, concluding that Sec. 1982 applies only to state action and does not reach private refusals to sell. . . . [W]e reverse the judgment of the Court of Appeals [and] hold that Sec. 1982 bars *all* racial discrimination, private as well as public, in the sale or rental of property, and that the statute, thus construed, is a valid exercise of the power of Congress to enforce the Thirteenth Amendment.

At the outset, it is important to make clear precisely what this case does *not* involve. Whatever else it may be, 42 U.S.C. Sec. 1982 is not a comprehensive open housing law. In sharp contrast to the Fair Housing Title (Title VIII) of the Civil Rights Act of 1968 . . . the statute in this case deals only with racial discrimination and does not address itself to discrimination on grounds of religion or national origin. It does not deal specifically with discrimination in the provision of services or facilities in connection with the sale or rental of a dwelling. It does not prohibit advertising or other representations that indicate discriminatory preferences. It does not refer explicitly to discrimination in financing arrangement or in the provision of brokerage services. It does not empower a federal administrative agency to assist aggrieved parties. It makes no provision for intervention by the Attorney General. And, although it can be enforced by injunction, it contains no provision expressly authorizing a federal court to order the payment of damages.

Thus, although Sec. 1982 contains none of the exemptions that Congress included in the Civil Rights Act of 1968, it would be a serious mistake to suppose that Sec. 1982 in any way diminishes the significance of the law recently enacted by Congress. . . .

. . . [T]he Civil Rights Act of 1968 . . . underscored the vast differences between, on the one hand, a general statute applicable only to racial discrimination in the rental and sale of property and enforceable only by private parties acting on their own initiative, and, on the other hand, a detailed housing law, applicable to a broad range of discriminatory practices and enforceable by a complete arsenal of federal authority. Having noted these differences, we turn to a consideration of Sec. 1982 itself.

This Court has had occasion to consider the scope of 42 U.S.C. Sec. 1982 in 1948, in *Hurd* v. *Hodge,* 334 U.S. 24. That case arose when property owners in the District of Columbia sought to enforce racially restrictive convenants against the Negro purchasers of several homes in their block. A federal district court enforced the restrictive agreements by declaring void the deeds of the Negro purchasers. It enjoined further attempts to sell or lease them the properties in question and directed them to "remove themselves and all of their personal belongings" from the premises within 60 days. The Court of Appeals for the District of Columbia affirmed, and this Court granted certiorari to decide whether Sec. 1982, . . . barred enforcement of the racially restrictive agreements in that case.

The agreements in *Hurd* covered only two-thirds of the lots of a single city block, and preventing Negroes from buying or renting homes in that specific area would not have rendered them ineligible to do so elsewhere in the city. Thus, if Sec. 1982 had been thought to do no more than grant Negro citizens the legal capacity to buy and rent property free of prohibitions that wholly disabled them because of their race, judicial enforcement of the restrictive covenants at issue would not have violated Sec. 1982. But this Court took a broader view of the statute. Although the covenants could have been enforced without denying the general right of Negroes to purchase or lease real estate, the enforcement of those covenants would nonetheless have denied the Negro purchasers "the same right 'as is enjoyed by white citizens . . . to inherit, purchase, lease, sell, hold, and convey real and personal property.' " 334 U.S., at 34. That result, this Court concluded, was prohibited by Sec. 1982. To suggest otherwise, the Court said, "is to reject the plain meaning of language." *Ibid.*

Hurd v. *Hodge* . . . squarely held, therefore, that a Negro citizen who is denied the opportunity to purchase the home he wants "[s]olely because of [his] race and color," 334 U.S., at 34, has suffered the kind of injury that Sec. 1982 was designed to prevent.... The basic source of the injury in *Hurd* was, of course, the action of private individuals—white citizens who had agreed to exclude Negroes from a residential area. But an arm of the Government—in that case, a federal court—had assisted in the enforcement of that agreement. Thus *Hurd* v. *Hodge*, ... did not present the question whether *purely* private discrimination, unaided by any action on the part of government, would violate Sec. 1982 if its effects were to deny a citizen the right to rent or buy property solely because of his race or color.

The only federal court (other than the Court of Appeals in this case) that has ever squarely confronted that question held that a wholly private conspiracy among white citizens to prevent a Negro from leasing a farm violated Sec. 1982. *United States* v. *Morris,* 125 F. 322. It is true that a dictum in *Hurd* said that Sec. 1982 was directed only toward "governmental action," 334 U.S., at 31, but neither *Hurd* nor any other case has presented that precise issue for adjudication in this Court. Today we face that issue for the first time.

We begin with the language of the statute itself. In plain and unambiguous terms, Sec. 1982 grants to all citizens, without regard to race or color, "the same right" to purchase and lease property "as is enjoyed by white citizens." As the Court of Appeals in this case evidently recognized, that right can be impaired as effectively by "those who place property on the market" as by the State itself. For, even if the State and its agents lend no support to those who wish to exclude persons from their communities on racial grounds, the fact remains that, whenever property "is placed on the market for whites only, whites have a right denied to Negroes." So long as a Negro citizen who wants to buy or rent a home can be turned away simply because he is not white, he cannot be said to enjoy "the *same* right ... as is enjoyed by white citizens ... to ... purchase [and] lease ... real and personal property." 42 U.S.C. Sec. 1982 (Emphasis added.)

On its face, therefore, Sec. 1982 appears to prohibit *all* discrimination against Negroes in the sale or rental of property—discrimination by private owners as well as discrimination by public authorities. Indeed, even the respondents seem to concede that, if Sec. 1982 "means what it says"—to use the words of the respondents' brief—then it must encompass every racially motivated refusal to sell or rent and cannot be confined to officially sanctioned segregation in housing. Stressing what they consider to be the revolutionary implications of so literal a reading of Sec. 1982, the respondents argue that Congress cannot possibly have intended any such result. Our examination of the relevant history, however, persuades us that Congress meant exactly what it said. [Here follows a review of the legislative history of the statute.]

. . .

As we said in a somewhat different setting two Terms ago, "We think that history leaves no doubt that, if we are to give [the law] the scope that its origins dictate, we must accord it a sweep as broad as its language." *United States* v. *Price,* 383 U.S. 787, 801. "We are not at liberty to seek ingenious analytical instruments," *ibid.,* to carve from Sec. 1982 an exception for private conduct —even though its application to such conduct in the present context is without established precedent. And, as the Attorney General of the United States said at the oral argument of this case, "The fact that the statute lay partially dormant for many years cannot be held to diminish its force today."

The remaining question is whether Congress has power under the Constitution to do what Sec. 1982 purports to do: to prohibit all racial discrimination, private and public, in the sale and rental of property. Our starting point is the Thirteenth Amendment, for it was pursuant to that constitutional provision that Congress originally enacted what is now Sec. 1982. The Amendment consists of two parts. Section 1 states:

> Neither slavery nor involuntary servitude, except as a punishment for a crime whereof the party shall have been duly convicted, shall exist within the United States, or any place subject to their jurisdiction.

Section 2 provides:

> Congress shall have power to enforce this article by appropriate legislation.

As its text reveals, the Thirteenth Amendment "is not a mere prohibition of State laws establishing or upholding slavery, but an absolute declaration that slavery or involuntary servitude shall not exist in any part of the United States." *Civil Rights Cases,* 109 U.S. 3, 20. It has never been doubted, therefore, "that the power vested in Congress to enforce the article by appropriate legislation," *ibid.,* includes the power to enact laws "direct and primary, operating upon the acts of individuals, whether sanctioned by State legislation or not."*Id.,* at 23.

Thus, the fact that Sec. 1982 operates upon the unofficial acts of private individuals, whether or not sanctioned by state law, presents no constitutional problems. If Congress has power under the Thirteenth Amendment to eradicate conditions that prevent Negroes from buying and renting property because of their race or color, then no federal statute calculated to achieve that objective can be thought to exceed the constitutional power of Congress simply because it reaches beyond state action to regulate the conduct to private individuals. The constitutional question in this case, therefore, comes to this: Does the authority of Congress to enforce the Thirteenth Amendment "by appropriate legislation" include the power to eliminate all racial barriers to the acquisition of real and personal property? We think the answer to that question is plainly yes.

"By its own unaided force and effect," the Thirteenth Amendment "abolished slavery, and established universal freedom." *Civil Rights Cases,* 109 U.S. 3, 20. Whether or not the Amendment *itself* did any more than that—a question not involved in this case—it is at least clear that the Enabling Clause of that Amendment empowered Congress to do much more. For that clause clothed "Congress with power to pass *all laws necessary and proper for abolishing all badges and incidents of slavery in the United States." Ibid.* [Emphasis added by Justice Stewart.]

. . .

. . . Surely Congress has the power under the Thirteenth Amendment rationally to determine what are the badges and the incidents of slavery, and the authority to translate that determination into effective legislation. Nor can we say that the determination Congress has made is an irrational one. For this Court recognized long ago that, whatever else they may have encompassed, the badges and incidents of slavery—its "burdens and disabilities"—included restraints upon "those fundamental rights which are the essence of civil freedom, namely, the same right . . . to inherit, purchase, lease, sell and convey property, as is enjoyed by white citizens." *Civil Rights Cases,* 109 U.S. 3, 22. Just as the Black Codes, enacted after the Civil War to restrict the free exercise of those rights, were substitutes for the slave system, so the exclusion of Negroes from white communities became a substitute for the Black Codes. And when racial discrimination herds men into ghettos and makes their ability to buy property turn on the color of their skin, then it too is a relic of slavery.

Negro citizens North and South, who saw in the Thirteenth Amendment a promise of freedom—freedom to "go and come at pleasure" and to "buy and sell when they please"—would be left with "a mere paper guarantee" if Congress were powerless to assure that a dollar in the hands of a Negro will purchase the same thing as a dollar in the hands of a white man. At the very least, the freedom that Congress is empowered to secure under the Thirteenth Amendment includes the freedom to buy whatever a white man can buy, the right to live wherever a white man can live. If Congress cannot say that being a free man means at least this much, then the Thirteenth Amendment made a promise the Nation cannot keep.

. . .

The judgment is Reversed.

MR. JUSTICE DOUGLAS, *concurring.*

. . .

Enabling a Negro to buy and sell real and personal property is a removal of one of many badges of slavery. . . .

The true curse of slavery is not what it did to the black man, but what it has done to the white man. For the existence of the institution produced the notion that the white man was of a superior character, intelligence, and morality. The blacks were little more than livestock—to be fed and fattened for the economic benefits they could bestow through their labors, and to be subjected to authority, often with cruelty, to make clear who was master and who slave.

Some badges of slavery remain today. While the institution has been outlawed, it has remained in the minds and hearts of many white men. Cases which have come to this Court depict a spectacle of slavery unwilling to die. We have seen contrivances by States designed to thwart Negro voting, *e.g., Lane* v. *Wilson,* 307 U.S. 268. Negroes have been excluded over and again from juries solely on account of their race, *e.g., Strauder* v. *West Virginia,* 100 U.S. 303, or have been forced to sit in segregated seats in court rooms, *Johnson* v. *Virginia,* 373 U.S. 61. They have been made to attend segregated and inferior schools, *e.g., Brown* v. *Board of Education,* 347 U.S. 483, or been denied entrance to colleges or graduate schools because of their color, *e.g., Pennsylvania* v. *Board of Trusts,* 353 U.S. 230; *Sweatt* v. *Painter,* 339 U.S. 629. Negroes have been prosecuted for marrying whites, *e.g., Loving* v. *Virginia,* 388 U.S. 1. They have been forced to live in segregated residential districts, *Buchanan* v. *Warley,* 245 U.S. 60, and residents of white neighborhoods have denied them entrance, *e.g., Shelley* v. *Kraemer,* 334 U.S. 1. Negroes have been forced to use segregated facilities in going about their daily lives, being excluded from railway coaches, *Plessy* v. *Ferguson,* 163 U.S. 537; public parks, *New Orleans* v. *Detiege,* 358 U.S. 54; restaurants, *Lombard* v. *Louisiana,* 373 U.S. 267; public beaches, *Mayor of Baltimore* v. *Dawson,* 350 U.S. 877; municipal golf courses, *Holmes* v. *City of Atlanta,* 350 U.S. 879; amusement parks, *Griffin* v. *Maryland,* 378 U.S. 130; busses, *Gayle* v. *Browder,* 352 U.S. 903; public libraries, *Brown* v. *Louisiana,* 383 U.S. 131. A state court judge in Alabama convicted a Negro woman of contempt of court because she refused to answer him when he addressed her as "Mary," although she had made the simple request to be called "Miss Hamilton." *Hamilton* v. *Alabama,* 376 U.S. 650.

That brief sampling of discriminatory practices, many of which continue today, stands almost as an annotation to what Frederick Douglass (1817-1895) wrote a century earlier:

Of all the races and varieties of men which have suffered from this feeling, the colored people of this country have endured most. They can resort to no disguises which will enable them to escape its deadly aim. They carry in front the evidence which marks them for persecution. They stand at the extreme point of difference from the Caucasian race, and their African origin can be instantly recognized, though they may be several removes from the typical African race. They may remonstrate like Shylock—"Hath not a Jew eyes? hath not a Jew hands, organs, dimensions, senses, affections, passions? fed with the same food, hurt with the same weapons, subject to the same diseases, healed by the same means, warmed and cooled by the same summer and winter, as a Christian is?"—but such eloquence is unavailing. They are Negroes—and that is enough, in the eye of this unreasoning prejudice, to justify indignity and violence. In nearly every department of American life they are confronted by this insidious influence. It fills the air. It meets them at the workshop and factory, when they apply for work. It meets them at the church, at the hotel, at the ballot-box, and worst of all, it meets them in the jury-box. Without crime or offense against law or gospel, the colored man is the Jean Valjean of American society. He has escaped from the galleys, and hence all presumptions are against him. The workshop denies him work, and the inn denies him shelter; the ballot-box a fair vote, and the jury-box a fair trial. He has ceased to be the slave of an individual, but has in some sense become the slave of society. He may not now be bought and sold like a beast in the market, but he is the trammeled victim of a prejudice, well calculated to repress his manly ambition, paralyze his energies, and make him a dejected and spiritless man, if not a sullen enemy to society, fit to prey upon life and property and to make trouble generally.*

Today the black is protected by a host of civil rights laws. But the forces of discrimination are still strong.

A member of his race, duly elected by the people to a state legislature, is barred from that assembly because of his views on the Vietnam war. *Bond* v. *Floyd,* 385 U.S. 116.

Real estate agents use artifice to avoid selling "white property" to the blacks. The blacks who travel the country, though entitled by law to the facilities for sleeping and dining that are offered all tourists, *Heart of Atlanta Motel* v. *United States,* 379 U.S. 241, may well learn that the "vacancy" sign does not mean what it says, especially if the motel has a swimming pool.

On entering a half-empty restaurant they may find "reserved" signs on all unoccupied tables.

*Excerpt from Frederick Douglass, The Color Line, The North American Review, June 1881, IV The Life and Writings of Frederick Douglass, 343-344 (1955).

The black is often barred from a labor union because of his race.

He learns that the order directing admission of his children into white schools has not been obeyed "with all deliberate speed," *Brown* v. *Board of Education,* 349 U.S. 294, 301, but has been delayed by numerous strategies and devices. State laws, at times, have even encouraged discrimination in housing. *Reitman* v. *Mulkey,* 387 U.S. 369.

This recital is enough to show how prejudices, once part and parcel of slavery, still persist. The men who sat in Congress in 1866 were trying to remove some of the badges or "customs" of slavery when they enacted Sec. 1982. And, as my Brother Stewart shows, the Congress that passed the so-called Open Housing Act of 1968 did not undercut any of the grounds on which Sec. 1982 rests.

MR. JUSTICE HARLAN, *whom* MR. JUSTICE WHITE *joins, dissenting.*

The decision in this case appears to me to be the most ill-considered and ill-advised.

. . .

. . . I believe that the Court's construction of Sec. 1982 as applying to purely private action is almost surely wrong, and at the least is open to serious doubt. The issue of constitutionality of Sec. 1982, as construed by the Court, and of liability under the Fourteenth Amendment alone, also present formidable difficulties. Moreover, the political processes of our own era have, since the date of oral argument in this case, given birth to a civil rights statute embodying "fair housing" provisions which would at the end of this year make available to others, though apparently not to the petitioners themselves, the type of relief which the petitioners now seek. It seems to me that this latter factor so diminishes the public importance of this case that by far the wisest course would be for this Court to refrain from decision and to dismiss the writ as improvidently granted.

I shall deal first with the Court's construction of Sec. 1982, which lies at the heart of its opinion. . . .

The Court's opinion focuses upon the statute's legislative history, but it is worthy of note that the precedents in this Court are distinctly opposed to the Court's view of the statute.

In the *Civil Rights Cases*, 109 U.S. 3, decided less than two decades after the enactment of the Civil Rights Act of 1866, from which Sec. 1982 is derived, the Court said in dictum of the 1866 Act:

> This law is clearly corrective in its character, intended to counteract and furnish redress against State laws and proceedings, and customs having the force of law, which sanction the wrongful acts specified. . . . The Civil Rights Bill here referred to is analogous in its character to what a law would have been under the original Constitution, declaring that the validity of contracts should not be impaired, and that if any person bound by a contract should refuse to comply with it, under color or pretence that it had been rendered void or invalid by a State law, he should be liable in an action upon it in the courts of the United States, with the addition of a penalty for setting up such an unjust and unconstitutional defense. *Id.*, at 16-17.

In *Corrigan* v. *Buckley*, 271 U.S. 323, the question was whether the courts of the District of Columbia might enjoin prospective breaches of racially restrictive convenants. The Court held that it was without jurisdiction to consider the petitioners' argument that the convenant was void because it contravened the Fifth, Thirteenth, and Fourteenth Amendments and their implementing statutes. . . . In *Hurd* v. *Hodge,* 334 U.S. 24, the issue was again whether the courts of the District might enforce racially restrictive convenants. At the outset of the

process of reasoning by which it held that judicial enforcement of such a covenant would violate the predecessor to Sec. 1982, the Court said:

> We may start with the proposition that the statute does not invalidate private restrictive agreements so long as the purpose of those agreements are achieved by the parties through voluntary adherence to the terms. The action toward which the provisions of the statute under consideration is [*sic*] directed is governmental action. . . .

Like the Court, I begin analysis of Sec. 1982 by examining its language. In its present form, the section provides:

> All citizens of the United States shall have the same right, in every State and Territory, as is enjoyed by white citizens thereof to inherit, purchase, lease, sell, hold and convey real and personal property.

The Court finds it "plain and unambiguous," . . . that this language forbids purely private as well as state-authorized discrimination. With all respect, I do not find it so. For me, there is an inherent ambiguity in the term "right," as used in Sec. 1982. The "right" referred to may either be a right to equal status under law, in which case the statute operates only against state-sanctioned discrimination, or it may be an "absolute" right enforceable against private individuals. To me, the words of the statute, taken alone, suggest the former interpretation, not the latter.

Further, since intervening revisions have not been meant to alter substance, the intended meaning of Sec. 1982 must be drawn from the words in which it was originally enacted. Section 1982 originally was a part of Section 1 of the Civil Rights Act of 1866. . . . Sections 1 and 2 of that Act provided in relevant part:

> That all persons born in the United States and not subject to any foreign power . . . are

hereby declared to be citizens of the United States; and such citizens, of every race and color . . . , shall have the same right, in every State and Territory in the United States, . . . to inherit, purchase, lease, sell, hold and convey real and personal property . . . as is enjoyed by white citizens, and shall be subject to like punishments, pains, and penalties, and to none other, any law, statute, ordinance, regulation, or custom, to the contrary notwithstanding.

Sec. 2. . . . That any person who, under color of any law, statute, ordinance, regulation, or custom, shall subject, or cause to be subjected, any inhabitant of any State or Territory to the deprivation of any right secured or protected by this act . . . shall be deemed guilty of a misdemeanor. . . .

It seems to me that this original wording indicates even more strongly than the present language that Sec. 1 of the Act (as well as Sec. 2, which is explicitly so limited) was intended to apply only to action taken pursuant to state or community authority, in the form of a "law, statute, ordinance, regulation, or custom." . . .

[Here follows an examination of the legislative history of the statute to show that the debates do not overwhelmingly support the majority's interpretation.]

. . .

The . . . analysis of the language, structure, and legislative history of the 1866 Civil Rights Act shows, I believe, that the Court's thesis that the Act was meant to extend to purely private action is open to the most serious doubt, if indeed it does not render that thesis wholly untenable. Another, albeit less tangible, consideration points in the same direction. Many of the legislators who took part in the congressional debates inevitably must have shared the individualistic ethic of their time, which emphasized personal freedom and embodied a distaste for governmental interference which was soon to culminate in the era of laissez-faire. It seems to

me that most of these men would have regarded it as a great intrusion on individual liberty for the Government to take from a man the power to refuse for personal reasons to enter into purely private transaction involving the disposition of property, albeit those personal reasons might reflect racial bias. It should be remembered that racial prejudice was not uncommon in 1866, even outside the South. Although Massachusetts had recently enacted the Nation's first law prohibiting racial discrimination in public accommodations, Negroes could not ride within Philadelphia streetcars or attend public schools with white children in New York City. Only five States accorded equal voting rights to Negroes, and it appears that Negroes were allowed to serve on juries only in Massachusetts. Residential segregation was the prevailing pattern almost everywhere in the North. There were no state "fair housing" laws in 1866, and it appears that none has ever been proposed. In this historical context, I cannot conceive that a bill thought to prohibit purely private discrimination not only in the sale or rental of housing but in *all* property transactions would not have received a great deal of criticism explicitly directed to this feature. The fact that the 1866 Act received *no* criticism of this kind is for me strong additional evidence that it was not regarded as extending so far.

In sum, the most which can be said with assurance about the intended impact of the 1866 Civil Rights Act upon purely private discrimination is that the Act probably was envisioned by most members of Congress as prohibiting official, community-sanctioned discrimination in the South, engaged in pursuant to local "customs" which in the recent time of slavery probably were embodied in laws or regulations. . . . Adoption of a "state action" construction of the Civil Rights Act would therefore have the additional merit of bringing its interpretation into line with that of the Fourteenth Amendment, which this Court has consistently held to reach only "state action." This seems especially desirable in light of the Fourteenth Amendment, at least in the minds of its congressional proponents, which was to assure that the rights conferred by the then recently enacted Civil Rights Act could not be taken away by a subsequent Congress.

The foregoing, I think, amply demonstrates that the Court has chosen to resolve this case by according to a loosely worded statute a meaning which is open to the strongest challenge in light of the statute's legislative history.

. . .

The fact that a case is "hard" does not, of course, relieve a judge of his duty to decide it. Since the Court did vote to hear this case, I normally would consider myself obligated to decide whether the petitioners are entitled to relief on either of the grounds on which they rely. After mature reflection, however, I have concluded that this is one of those rare instances in which an event which occurs after the hearing of argument so diminishes a case's public significance, when viewed in light of the difficulty of the questions presented as to justify this Court in dismissing the writ as improvidently granted.

The occurrence to which I refer is the recent enactment of the Civil Rights Act of 1968. . . . Title VIII of that Act contains comprehensive "fair housing" provisions, which by the terms of Sec. 803 will become applicable on January 1, 1969, to persons who, like the petitioners, attempt to buy houses from developers. Under those provisions, such persons will be entitled to injunctive relief and damages from developers who refuse to sell to them on account of race or color, unless the parties are able to resolve their dispute by other means. Thus, the type of relief which the petitioners seek will be available within seven months time under the terms of a presumptively constitutional Act of Congress. In these circumstances, it seems obvious that the case has lost most of its public importance, and I believe that it would be much the wiser course for this Court to refrain from deciding it. I think it particularly unfortunate for the Court to persist in deciding this case on the basis of a highly questionable interpretation of a sweeping, century-old statute which, as the Court acknowledges . . . contains none of the exemptions which the Congress of our own time found it necessary to include in a statute regulating relationships so personal in nature. In effect, this Court, by its construction of Sec. 1982, has extended the coverage of federal "fair housing" laws far beyond that which Congress in its wisdom chose to provide in the Civil Rights Act of 1968. The political process now having taken hold again in this very field, I am at a loss to understand why the Court should have deemed it appropriate or, in the circumstances of this case, necessary to proceed with such precipitous and insecure strides.

I am not dissuaded from my view by the circumstance that the 1968 Act was enacted after oral argument in this case, at a time when the parties and *amici curiae* had invested time and money in anticipation of a decision on the merits, or by the fact that the 1968 Act apparently will not entitle these petitioners to the relief which they seek. For the certiorari jurisdiction was not conferred upon this Court "merely to give the defeated party in the . . . Court of Appeals another hearing," *Magnum Co.* v. *Coty*, 262 U.S. 159, 164, or "for the benefit of the particular litigants," *Rice* v. *Sioux City Cemetery*, 349 U.S. 70, 74, but to decide issues, "the settlement of which is important to the public as distinguished from . . . the parties," *Layne & Bowler Corp.* v. *Western Well Works, Inc.*, 261 U.S. 387, 393. I deem it far more important that this Court should avoid, if possible, the decision of constitutional and unusually difficult statutory questions than that we fulfill the expectations of every litigant who appears before us.

SOUTH CAROLINA v. KATZENBACH

383 U.S. 301; 15 L. Ed. 2d 769; 86 S. Ct. 803 (1966)

MR. CHIEF JUSTICE WARREN *delivered the opinion of the Court.*

By leave of the Court . . . South Carolina has filed a bill of complaint, seeking a declaration that selected provisions of the Voting Rights Act of 1965 violate the Federal Constitution, and asking for an injunction against enforcement of these provisions by the Attorney General. . . .

Recognizing that the questions presented were of urgent concern to the entire country, we invited all of the States to participate in this proceeding as friends of the Court. A majority responded by submitting or joining in briefs on the merits, some supporting South Carolina and others the Attorney General.* Seven of these States also requested and received permission to argue the case orally at our hearing. Without exception, despite the emotional overtones of the proceeding, the briefs and oral arguments were temperate, lawyerlike and constructive. . . .

The Voting Rights Act was designed by Congress to banish the blight of racial discrimination in voting, which has infected the electoral process in parts of our country for nearly a century. The Act creates stringent new remedies for voting discrimination where it persists on a pervasive scale, and in addition the statute strengthens existing remedies for pockets of

*States supporting South Carolina: Alabama, Georgia, Louisiana, Mississippi, and Virginia. States supporting the Attorney General: California, Illinois, and Massachusetts, joined by Hawaii, Indiana, Iowa, Kansas, Maine, Maryland, Michigan, Montana, New Hampshire, New Jersey, New York, Oklahoma, Oregon, Pennsylvania, Rhode Island, Vermont, West Virginia, and Wisconsin.

voting discrimination elsewhere in the country. Congress assumed the power to prescribe these remedies from section 2 of the Fifteenth Amendment, which authorizes the National Legislature to effectuate by "appropriate" measures the constitutional prohibition against racial discrimination in voting. We hold that the sections of the Act which are properly before us are an appropriate means for carrying out Congress' constitutional responsbilities and are consonant with all other provisions of the Constitution. We therefore deny South Carolina's request that enforcement of these sections of the Act be enjoined.

The constitutional propriety of the Voting Rights Act of 1965 must be judged with reference to the historical experience which it reflects. Before enacting the measure, Congress explored with great care the problem of racial discrimination in voting. . . . At the close of . . . deliberations, the verdict of both chambers was overwhelming. The House approved the bill by a vote of 328-74, and the measure passed the Senate by a margin of 79-18.

Two points emerge vividly from the voluminous legislative history of the Act contained in the committee hearings and the floor debates. First: Congress felt itself confronted by an insidious and pervasive evil which had been perpetuated in certain parts of our country through unremitting and ingenious defiance of the Constitution. Second: Congress concluded that the unsuccessful remedies which it had prescribed in the past would have to be replaced by sterner and more elaborate measures in order to satisfy the clear commands of the Fifteenth Amendment. . . .

[Here followed a review of Congressional remedies from 1870 to 1964.]

. . .

Despite the earnest efforts of the Justice Department and of many federal judges, these new laws [enacted in 1956, 1960 and 1964] have done little to cure the problem of voting discrimination. According to estimates by the Attorney General during hearings on the Act, registration of voting-age Negroes in Alabama rose only from 14.2% to 19.4% between 1958 and 1964; in Louisiana it barely inched ahead from 31.7% to 31.8% between 1956 and 1965; and in Mississippi it increased only from 4.4% to 6.4% between 1954 and 1964. In each instance, registration of voting-age whites ran roughly 50 percentage points or more ahead of Negro registration.

The previous legislation has proved ineffective for a number of reasons. Voting suits are unusually onerous to prepare, sometimes requiring as many as 6,000 man-hours spent combing through registration records in preparation for trial. Litigation has been exceedingly slow, in part because of the ample opportunities for delay afforded voting officials and others involved in the proceedings. Even when favorable decisions have finally been obtained, some of the States affected have merely switched to discriminatory devices not covered by the federal decrees or have enacted difficult new tests designed to prolong the existing disparity between white and Negro registration. Alternatively, certain local officials have defied and evaded court orders or have simply closed their registration offices to freeze the voting rolls. The provision of the 1960 law authorizing registration by federal officers has had little impact on local maladministration because of its procedural complexities.

. . .

The Voting Rights Act of 1965 reflects Congress' firm intention to rid the country of racial discrimination in voting. The heart of the Act is a complex scheme of stringent remedies aimed at areas where voting discrimination has been most flagrant. Section 4(a)-(d) lays down a formula defining the States and political subdivision to which these new remedies apply. The first of the remedies, contained in section 4(a), is the suspension of literacy tests and similar voting qualifications for a period of five years from the last occurrence of substantial voting discrimination. Section 5 prescribes a second remedy, the suspension of all new voting regulations pending review by federal authorities to determine whether their use would perpetuate voting discrimination. The third remedy, covered in sections 6(b), 7, 9, and 13(a), is the assignment of federal examiners on certification by the Attorney General to list qualified applicants who are thereafter entitled to vote in all elections.

Other provisions of the Act prescribe subsidiary cures for persistent voting discrimination. Section 8 authorizes the appointment of federal poll-watchers in places to which federal examiners have already been assigned. Section 10(d) excuses those made eligible to vote in sections of the country covered by section 4(b) of the Act from paying accumulated past poll taxes for state and local elections. Section 12(e) provides for balloting by persons denied access to the polls in areas where federal examiners have been appointed.

The remaining remedial portions of the Act are aimed at voting discrimination in any area of the country where it may occur. Section 2 broadly prohibits the use of voting rules to abridge exercise of the franchise on racial grounds. Sections 3, 6(a), and 13(b) strengthen existing procedures for attacking voting discrimination by means of litigation. Section 4(e) excuses citizens educated in American schools conducted in a foreign language from passing English-language literacy tests. Section 10(a)-(c) facilitates constitutional litigation challenging the imposition of all poll taxes for state and local elections. Sections 11 and 12(a)-(d) authorize civil and criminal sanctions against interference with the exercise of rights guaranteed by the Act.

... The only sections of the Act to be reviewed at this time are sections 4(a)-(d), 5, 6(b), 7, 9, 13(a), and certain procedural portions of section 14, all of which are presently in actual operation in South Carolina. We turn now to a ... description of these provisions and their present status.

Coverage Formula

The remedial sections of the Act assailed by South Carolina automatically apply to any State, or to any separate political subdivision such as a county or parish, for which two findings have been made: (1) the Attorney General has determined that on November 1, 1964, it maintained a "test or device," and (2) the Director of the Census has determined that less than 50% of its voting-age residents were registered on November 1, 1964, or voted in the presidential election of 1964. These findings are not reviewable in any court and are final upon publication in the Federal Register.

. . .

South Carolina was brought within the coverage formula of the Act on August 7, 1965, pursuant to appropriate administrative determinations which have not been challenged in this proceeding. On the same day, coverage was also extended to Alabama, Alaska, Georgia, Louisiana, Mississippi, Virginia, 26 counties in North Carolina, and one county in Arizona. Two more counties in Arizona, one county in Hawaii, and one county in Idaho were added to the list on November 19, 1965. Thus far Alaska, the three Arizona counties, and the single county in Idaho have asked the District Court for the District of Columbia to grant a declaratory judgment terminating statutory coverage.

Suspension of Tests

In a State or political subdivision covered by section 4(b) of the Act, no person may be denied the right to vote in any election because of his failure to comply with a "test or device." Section 4(a).

On account of this provision, South Carolina is temporarily barred from enforcing the portion of its voting laws which requires every applicant for registration to show that he:

> Can both read and write any section of [the State] Constitution submitted to [him] by the registration officer or can show that he owns, and has paid all taxes collectible during the previous year on property in this State assessed at three hundred dollars or more. SC Code Ann. section 23-62(4) (1965 Supp.).

The Attorney General has determined that the property qualification is inseparable from the literacy test, and South Carolina makes no objection to this finding. Similar tests and devices have been temporarily suspended in the other sections of the country listed above.

Review of New Rules

In a State or political subdivision covered by section 4(b) of the Act, no person may be denied the right to vote in any election because of his failure to comply with a voting qualification or procedure different from those in force on November 1, 1964. This suspension of new rules is terminated, however, under either of the following circumstances: (1) if the area has submitted the rules to the Attorney General, and he had not interposed an objection within 60 days, or (2) if the area has obtained a declaratory judgment from the District Court for the District of Columbia, determining that the rules will not abridge the franchise on racial grounds. . . .

South Carolina altered its voting laws in 1965 to extend the closing hour at polling places from 6 P.M. to 7 P.M. . . . the Attorney General . . . does not challenge the amendment. There are indications in the record that other sections of the country listed above have also altered their voting laws since November 1, 1964.

Federal Examiners

In any political subdivision covered by section 4(b) of the Act, the Civil Service Commission shall appoint voting examiners whenever the Attorney General certifies either of the following facts: (1) that he has received meritorious written complaints from at least 20 residents alleging that they have been disenfranchised under color of law because of their race, or (2) that the appointment of examiners is otherwise necessary to effectuate the guarantees of the Fifteenth Amendment. In making the latter determination, the Attorney General must consider, among other factors, whether the registration ratio of non-whites to whites seems reasonably attributable to racial discrimination, or whether there is substantial evidence of good-faith efforts to comply with the Fifteenth Amendment. . . .

. . . Any person who meets the voting requirements of state law, insofar as these have not been suspended by the Act, must promptly be placed on a list of eligible voters. . . . Any person listed by an examiner is entitled to vote in all elections held more than 45 days after his name has been transmitted. . . .

On October 30, 1965, the Attorney General certified the need for federal examiners in two South Carolina counties, and examiners appointed by the Civil Service Commission have been serving there since November 8, 1965. Examiners have also been assigned to 11 counties in Alabama, five parishes in Louisiana, and 19 counties in Mississippi. . . .

These provisions of the Voting Rights Act of 1965 are challenged on the fundamental ground that they exceed the powers of Congress and encroach on an area reserved to the States by the Constitution. South Carolina and certain of the amici curiae also attack specific sections of the Act for more particular reasons. They argue that the coverage formula prescribed in section 4(a)-(d) violates the principle of the equality of States, denies due process by employing an invalid presumption and by barring judicial review of administrative findings, constitutes a forbidden bill of attainder, and impairs the separation of powers by adjudicating guilt through legislation. They claim that the review of new voting rules required in section 5 infringes Article III by directing the District Court to issue advisory opinions. They contend that the assignment of federal examiners authorized in section 6(b) abridges due process by precluding judicial review of administrative findings and impairs the separation of powers by giving the Attorney General judicial functions; also that the challenge procedure prescribed in section 9 denies due process on account of its speed. Finally, South Carolina and certain of the amici curiae maintain that sections 4(a) and 5, buttressed by section 14(b) of the Act, abridge due process by limiting litigation to a distant forum.

. . . The objections to the Act which are raised under these provisions may . . . be considered only as additional aspects of the basic question presented by the case: Has Congress exercised its powers under the Fifteenth Amendment in an appropriate manner with relation to the States?

The ground rules for resolving this question are clear. The language and purpose of the Fifteenth Amendment, the prior decisions construing its several provisions, and the general doctrines of constitutional interpretation, all point to one fundamental principle. As against the reserved powers of the States, Congress may use any rational means to effectuate the constitutional prohibition of racial discrimination in voting. . . .

Section 1 of the Fifteenth Amendment declares that "[t]he right of citizens of the United States to vote shall not be denied or abridged by the United States or by any State on account of race, color, or previous condition of servitude." This declaration has always been treated as self-executing and has repeatedly been construed, without further legislative specification, to invalidate state voting qualifications or procedures which are discriminatory on their face or in practice. . . . [S]tates "have broad powers to determine the conditions under which the right of suffrage may be exercised." [However,] [t]he gist of the matter is that the Fifteenth Amendment supersedes contrary exertions of state power. "When a State exercises power wholly within the domain of state interest, it is insulated from federal judicial review. But such insulation is not carried over when state power is used as an instrument for circumventing a federally protected right." *Gomillion* v. *Lightfoot*, 364 U.S., at 347. . . .

South Carolina contends that the [previous] cases are precedents only for the authority of the judiciary to strike down state statutes and procedures—that to allow an exercise of this authority by Congress would be to rob the courts of their rightful constitutional role. On the contrary, section 2 of the Fifteenth Amendment expressly declares that "Congress shall have power to enforce this article by appropriate legislation." By adding this authorization, the Framers indicated that Congress was to be chiefly responsible for implementing the rights created in section 1. "It is the power of Congress which has been enlarged. Congress is authorized to *enforce* the prohibitions by appropriate legislation. Some legislation is contemplated to make the [Civil War] amendments fully effective." *Ex parte Virginia*, 100 U.S. 339, 345. . . . Accordingly, in addition to the courts, Congress has full remedial powers to effectuate the constitutional prohibition against racial discrimination in voting.

Congress has repeatedly exercised these powers in the past, and its enactments have repeatedly been upheld. . . .

The basic test to be applied in a case involving section 2 of the Fifteenth Amendment is the same as in all cases concerning the express powers of Congress with relation to the reserved powers of the States. Chief Justice Marshall laid down the classic formulation, 50 years before the Fifteenth Amendment was ratified:

> Let the end be legitimate, let it be within the scope of the constitution, and all means which are appropriate, which are plainly adapted to that end, which are not prohibited, but consist with the letter and spirit of the constitution, are constitutional. *McCulloch* v. *Maryland*, 4 Wheat 316, 421. . . .

The Court has subsequently echoed his language in describing each of the Civil War Amendments:

> Whatever legislation is appropriate, that is, adapted to carry out the objects the amendments have in view, whatever tends to enforce submission to the prohibitions they contain, and to secure to all persons the enjoyment of perfect equality of civil rights and the equal protection of the laws against State denial or invasion, if not prohibited, is brought within the domain of congressional power. *Ex parte Virginia*, 100 U.S., at 345.

. . .

Congress exercised its authority under the Fifteenth Amendment in an inventive manner when it enacted the Voting Rights Act of 1965. First: The measure prescribes remedies for voting discrimination which go into effect without any need for prior adjudication. This was clearly a legitimate response to the problem, for which there is ample precedent under other constitutional provisions. . . . Congress had found that case-by-case litigation was inadequate to combat widespread and persistent discrimination in voting, because of the inordinate amount of time and energy required to overcome the obstructionist tactics invariably encountered in these lawsuits. After enduring nearly a century of systematic resistance to the Fifteenth Amendment, Congress might well decide to shift the advantage of time and inertia from the perpetrators of the evil to its victims. . . .

Second: The Act intentionally confines these remedies to a small number of States and political subdivisions which in most instances were familiar to Congress by name. This, too, was a permissible method of dealing with the problem. Congress had learned that substantial voting discrimination presently occurs in certain sections of the country, and it knew no way of accurately forecasting whether the evil might spread elsewhere in the future. In acceptable legislative fashion, Congress chose to limit its attention to the geographic areas where immediate action seemed necessary.

. . .

After enduring nearly a century of widespread resistance to the Fifteenth Amendment, Congress has marshalled an array of potent weapons against the evil, with authority in the Attorney General to employ them effectively. Many of the areas directly affected by this development have indicated their willingness to abide by any restraints legitimately imposed upon them. We here hold that the portions of the Voting Rights Act properly before us are a valid means for carrying out the commands of the Fifteenth Amendment. Hopefully, millions of non-white Americans will now be able to participate for the first time on an equal basis in the government under which they live. We may finally look forward to the day when truly "[t]he right of citizens of the United States to vote shall not be denied or abridged by the United States or by any State on account of race, color, or previous condition of servitude."

The bill of complaint is

Dismissed.

MR. JUSTICE BLACK, *concurring and dissenting.*

. . .

Though . . . I agree with most of the Court's conclusions, I dissent from its holding that every part of section 5 of the Act is constitutional. Section 4(a), to which section 5 is linked, suspends for five years all literacy tests and similar devices in those States coming within the formula of section 4(b). Section 5 goes on to provide that a State covered by section 4(b) can in no way amend its constitution or laws relating to voting without first trying to persuade the Attorney General of the United States or the Federal District Court for the District of Columbia that the new proposed laws do not have the purpose and will not have the effect of denying the right to vote to citizens on account of their race or color. I think this section is unconstitutional on at least two grounds.

The Constitution gives federal courts jurisdiction over cases and controversies only. If it can be said that any case or controversy arises under this section which gives the District Court for the District of Columbia jurisdiction to approve or reject state laws or constitutional amendments, then the case or controversy must be between a State and the United States Government. But it is hard for me to believe that a justiciable controversy can arise in the constitutional sense from a desire by the United States Government or some of its officials to determine in advance what legislative provisions a State may enact or what constitutional amendments it may adopt. If this dispute between the Federal Government and the States amounts to a case or controversy it is a far cry from the traditional constitutional notion of a case or controversy as a dispute over the meaning of enforceable laws or the manner in which they are applied. And if by this section Congress has created a case or controversy, and I do not believe it has, then it seems to me that the most appropriate judicial forum for settling these important questions is this Court acting under its original Art. III, section 2, jurisdiction to try cases in which a State is a party. At least a trial in this Court would treat the States with dignity to which they should be entitled as constituent members of our Federal Union.

The form of words and the manipulation of presumptions used in section 5 to create the illusion of a case or controversy should not be allowed to cloud the effect of that section. By requiring a State to ask a federal court to approve the validity of a proposed law which has in no way become operative, Congress had asked the State to secure precisely the type of advisory opinion our Constitution forbids. . . .

My second and more basic objection to section 5 is that Congress has here exercised its power under section 2 of the Fifteenth Amendment through the adoption of means that conflict with the most basic principles of the Constitution. As the Court says the limitations of the power granted under section 2 are the same as the limitations imposed on the exercise of any of the powers expressly granted Congress by the Constitution. . . . Section 5, by providing that some of the States cannot pass state laws or adopt state constitutional amendments without first being compelled to beg federal authorities to approve their policies, so distorts our constitutional structure of government as to render any distinction drawn in the Constitution between state and federal power almost meaningless. One of the most basic premises upon which our structure of government was founded was that the Federal Government was to have certain specific and limited powers and no others, and all other power was to be reserved either "to the States respectively, or to the people." Certainly if all the provisions of our Constitution which limit the power of the Federal Government and reserve other power to the States are to mean anything, they mean at least that the States have power to pass laws and amend their constitutions without first sending their officials hundreds of miles away to beg federal authorities to approve them. Moreover, it seems to me that section 5 which gives federal officials power to veto state laws they do not like is in direct conflict with the clear command of our Constitution that "The United States shall guarantee to every State in this Union a Republican Form of Government."

I cannot help but believe that the inevitable effect of any such law which forces any one of the States to entreat federal authorities in far-away places for approval of local laws before they can become effective is to create the impression that the State or States treated in this way are little more than conquered provinces. And if one law concerning voting can make the States plead for this approval by a distant federal court or the United States Attorney General, other laws on different subjects can force the States to seek the advance approval not only of the Attorney General but of the President himself or any other chosen members of his staff. It is inconceivable to me that such a radical degradation of state power was intended in any of the provisions of our Constitution or its Amendments. Of course I do not mean to cast any doubt whatever upon the indisputable power of the Federal Government to invalidate a state law once enacted and operative on the ground that it intrudes into the area of supreme federal power. But the Federal Government has heretofore always been content to exercise this power to protect federal supremacy by authorizing its agents to bring lawsuits against state officials once an operative state law has created an actual case and controversy. A federal law which assumes the power to compel the States to submit in advance any proposed legislation they have for approval by federal agents approaches dangerously near to wiping the States out as useful and effective units in the government of our country. I cannot agree to any constitutional interpretation that leads inevitably to such a result.

. . .

In this and other prior Acts Congress has quite properly vested the Attorney General with extremely broad power to protect voting rights of citizens against discrimination on account of race or color. Section 5 viewed in this context is of very minor importance and in my judgment is likely to serve more as an irritant to the States than as an aid to the enforcement of the Act. I would hold section 5 invalid for the reasons stated above with full confidence that the Attorney General has ample power to give vigorous, expeditious and effective protection to the voting rights of all citizens.

KIRKPATRICK v. PREISLER
394 U.S. 526; 22 L. Ed. 2d 519; 89 S. Ct. 1225 (1969)

MR. JUSTICE BRENNAN *delivered the opinion of the Court.*

In *Wesberry* v. *Sanders,* 376 U.S. 1 (1964), we held that "[w]hile it may not be possible [for the States] to draw congressional districts with mathematical precision," *id.,* at 18, Art. I, § 2 of the Constitution requires "as nearly as is practicable one man's vote in a congressional election is to be worth as much as another's." We are required in this case to elucidate the "as nearly as practicable" standard.

The Missouri congressional redistricting statute challenged in this case resulted from that State's second attempt at congressional redistricting since *Wesberry* was decided. In 1965, a three-judge District Court for the Western District of Missouri declared that the Missouri congressional districting Act then in effect was unconstitutional under *Wesberry* but withheld any judicial relief "until the Legislature of the State of Missouri has once more had an opportunity to deal with the problem. . . ." Thereafter, the General Assembly of Missouri enacted a redistricting statute, but this statute too was declared unconstitutional. The District Court, however, retained jurisdiction to review any further plan that might be enacted. In 1967, the General Assembly enacted the statute under attack here and the Attorney General of Missouri moved in the District Court for a declaration sustaining the Act and an order dismissing the case.

Based on the best population data available to the legislature in 1967, the 1960 United States census figures, absolute population equality among Missouri's 10 congressional districts would mean a population of 431,981 in each district. The districts created by the 1967 Act, however, varied from this ideal within a range of 12,260 below it to 13,542 above it. In percentage terms, the most populous district was 3.13% above the mathematical ideal, and the least populous was 2.83% below.*

The District Court found that the General Assembly had not in fact relied on the census figures but instead had based its plan on less

*The redistricting effected by the 1967 Act, based on a population of 4,319,813 according to the 1960 census, is as follows:

District No.	Population	% Variation From Ideal
One	439,746	+1.8
Two	436,448	+1.03
Three	436,099	-0.95
Four	419,721	-2.84
Five	431,178	-0.19
Six	422,238	-2.26
Seven	436,769	+1.11
Eight	445,523	+3.13
Nine	428,223	-0.87
Ten	423,868	-1.88

Ideal population per district 431,981
Average variation from ideal 1.6%
Ratio of largest to smallest district . . . . 1.06 to 1
Number of districts within 1.88% of ideal 7
Population difference between largest and
  smallest districts 25,802

accurate data. In addition, the District Court found that the General Assembly had rejected a redistricting plan submitted to it which provided for districts with smaller population variances among them. Finally, the District Court found that the simple device of switching some counties from one district to another would have produced a plan with markedly reduced variances among districts. Based on these findings, the District Court, one judge dissenting, held that the 1967 Act did not meet the constitutional standard of equal representation for equal numbers of people "as nearly as practicable," and that the State had failed to make any acceptable justification for the variances. . . . We affirm.

Missouri's primary argument is that the population variances among the districts created by the 1967 Act are so small that they should be considered *de minimis* and for that reason to satisfy the "as nearly as practicable" limitation and not to require independent justification. Alternatively, Missouri argues that justification for the variances was established in the evidence: it is contended that the General Assembly provided for variances out of legitimate regard for such factors as the representation of distinct interest groups, the integrity of county lines, the compactness of districts, the population trends within the State, the high proportion of military personnel, college students, and other nonvoters in some districts, and the political realities of "legislative interplay."

We reject Missouri's argument that there is a fixed numerical or percentage population variance small enough to be considered *de minimis* and to satisfy without question the "as nearly as practicable" standard. The whole thrust of the "as nearly as practicable" approach is inconsistent with adoption of fixed numerical standards which excuse population variances without regard to the circumstances of each particular case. The extent to which equality may practicably be achieved may differ from State to State and from district to district. Since "equal representation for equal numbers of people [is] the funda-

mental goal for the House of Representatives," *Wesberry* v. *Sanders, supra,* at 18, the "as nearly as practicable" standard requires that the State make a good-faith effort to achieve precise mathematical equality. See *Reynolds* v. *Sims,* 377 U.S. 533, 577 (1964). Unless population variances among congressional districts are shown to have resulted despite such effort, the State must justify each variance, no matter how small.

There are other reasons for rejecting the *de minimis* approach. We can see no nonarbitrary way to pick a cutoff point at which population variances suddenly become *de minimis.* Moreover, to consider a certain range of variances *de minimis* would encourage legislators to strive for that range rather than for equality as nearly as practicable. . . .

Equal representation for equal numbers of people is a principle designed to prevent debasement of voting power and diminution of access to elected representatives. Toleration of even small deviations detracts from these purposes. Therefore, the command of Art. I § 2, that States create congressional districts which provide equal representation for equal numbers of people permits only the limited population variances which are unavoidable despite a good-faith effort to achieve absolute equality, or for which justification is shown.

Clearly, the population variances among the Missouri congressional districts were not unavoidable. Indeed, it is not seriously contended that the Missouri Legislature came as close to equality as it might have come. The District Court found that, to the contrary, in the two reapportionment efforts of the Missouri Legislature since *Wesberry* "the leadership of both political parties in the Senate and the House were given nothing better to work with than a makeshift bill produced by what has been candidly recognized to be no more than . . . an expedient political compromise." . . . Finally, it is simply inconceivable that population disparities of the magnitude found in the Missouri plan were unavoidable. The New York apportionment plan of regions divided into districts of almost absolute population equality described in *Wells* v. *Rockefeller* [394 U.S. 542, 1969] provides striking evidence that a state legislature which tries, can achieve almost complete numerical equality among all the State's districts. In sum, "it seems quite obvious that the State could have come much closer to providing districts of equal population than it did." ...

Missouri contends that variances were necessary to avoid fragmenting areas with distinct economic and social interests and thereby diluting the effective representation of those interests in Congress. But to accept population variances, large or small, in order to create districts with specific interest orientations is antithetical to the basic premise of the constitutional demand to provide equal representation for equal numbers of people. "[N]either history alone, nor economic or other sorts of group interests, are permissible factors in attempting to justify disparities from population-based representation. Citizens, not history or economic interests, cast votes." *Reynolds* v. *Sims, supra,* at 579-580.

We also reject Missouri's argument that "[t]he reasonableness of the population differences in the congressional districts under review must ... be viewed in the context of legislative interplay. ... It must be remembered ... that practical political problems are inherent in the enactment of congressional reapportionment legislation." We agree with the District Court that "the rule is one of 'practicability' rather than political 'practicality.' " Problems created by partisan politics cannot justify an apportionment which does not otherwise pass constitutional muster.

Similarly, we do not find legally acceptable the argument that variances are justified if they necessarily result from a State's attempt to avoid fragmenting political subdivisions by drawing congressional district lines along existing county, municipal, or other political subdivision boundaries. The State's interest in constructing congressional districts in this manner, it is suggested, is

to minimize the opportunities for partisan gerrymandering. But an argument that deviations from equality are justified in order to inhibit legislators from engaging in partisan gerrymandering is no more than a variant of the argument, already rejected, that considerations of practical politics can justify population disparities.

Missouri further contends that certain population variances resulted from the legislature's taking account of the fact that the percentage of eligible voters among the total population differed significantly from district to district—some districts contained disproportionately large numbers of military personnel stationed at bases maintained by the Armed Forces and students in attendance at universities or colleges. There may be a question whether distribution of congressional seats except according to total population can ever be permissible under Art. I, § 2. But assuming without deciding that apportionment may be based on eligible voter population rather than total population, the Missouri plan is still unacceptable. Missouri made no attempt to ascertain the number of eligible voters in each district and to apportion accordingly. At best it made haphazard adjustments to a scheme based on total population: overpopulation in the Eighth District was explained away by the presence in that district of a military base and a university; no attempt was made to account for the presence of universities in other districts or the disproportionate numbers of newly arrived and short-term residents in the City of St. Louis. Even as to the Eighth District, there is no indication that the excess population allocated to that district corresponds to the alleged extraordinary additional numbers of noneligible voters there.

Missouri also argues that population disparities between some of its congressional districts result from the legislature's attempt to take into account projected population shifts. We recognize that a congressional districting plan will usually be in effect for at least 10 years and five congressional elections. Situations may arise where substantial population shifts over such a period can be anticipated. Where these shifts can be predicted with a high degree of accuracy, States that are redistricting may properly consider them. By this we mean to open no avenue for subterfuge. Findings as to population trends must be thoroughly documented and applied throughout the State in a systematic, not an *ad hoc,* manner. . . .

Finally, Missouri claims that some of the deviations from equality were a consequence of the legislature's attempt to ensure that each congressional district would be geographically compact. However, in *Reynolds v. Sims, supra,* at 580, we said, "Modern developments and improvements in transportation and communications make rather hollow, in the mid-1960's, most claims that deviations from population-based representation can validly be based solely on geographical considerations. Arguments for allowing such deviations in order to insure effective representation for sparsely settled areas and to prevent legislative districts from becoming so large that the availability of access of citizens to their representatives is impaired are today, for the most part, unconvincing." . . .

Affirmed.

The concurring opinion of MR. JUSTICE FORTAS *and the dissenting opinion of* MR. JUSTICE HARLAN *(in which* MR. JUSTICE STEWART *joined) are omitted.*

MR. JUSTICE WHITE, *dissenting.*

I have consistently joined the Court's opinions which establish as one of the ground rules for legislative districting that single member districts should be substantially equal in population. I would not now dissent if the Court's present judgment represented a measurable contribution to the ends which I had thought the Court was pursuing in this area, or even if I thought the opinion not very useful but not harmful either. With all due respect, however, I am firmly convinced that the Court's new ruling is an

unduly rigid and unwarranted application of the Equal Protection Clause which will unnecessarily involve the courts in the abrasive task of drawing district lines.

. . . I would not quibble with the legislative judgment if variations between districts were acceptably small. And I would be willing to establish a population variation figure which if not exceeded would normally not call for judicial intervention. As a rule of thumb, a variation between the largest and the smallest district of no more than 10 to 15% would satisfy me, absent quite unusual circumstances not present [here]. At the very least, at this trivial level, I would be willing to view state explanations of the variance with a more tolerant eye.

This would be far more reasonable than the Court's demand for an absolute but illusory equality or for an apportionment plan which approaches this goal so nearly that no other plan can be suggested which would come near. . . . When the Court finds a 3% variation from substantially inexact figures constitutionally impermissible it is losing perspective and sticking at a trifle.

It also seems arbitrary for the majority to discard the suggestion of *Reynolds* v. *Sims,* that if a legislature seeks an apportionment plan which respects the boundaries of political subdivisions, some variations from absolute equality would be constitutionally permissible. Of course, *Reynolds* involved state legislative apportionment and took pains to say that there may be more leeway in that context. But the Court invokes *Reynolds* today and in no way distinguishes federal from state districting.

Reynolds noted that "[i]ndiscriminate districting, without any regard for political subdivision or natural or historical boundary lines, may be little more than an open invitation to partisan gerrymandering." The Court nevertheless now rules that regard for these boundaries is no justification for districts which vary no more than 3% from the norm where another plan which may have no regard for district lines reduces the variation to an even smaller figure. I have similar objections to the Court's rejection of geographical compactness as an acceptable justification for minor variations among congressional districts. This rejection of the virtues of compactness will not be lost on those who would use congressional and legislative districting to bury their political opposition. . . .

Today's decision on the one hand requires precise adherence to admittedly inexact census figures, and on the other downgrades a restraint on a far greater potential threat to equality of representation, the gerrymander. Legislatures intent on minimizing the representation of selected political or racial groups are invited to ignore political boundaries and compact districts so long as they adhere to population equality among districts using standards which we know and they know are sometimes quite incorrect. I see little merit in such a confusion of priorities.

Moreover, today's decision will lead to an unnecessary intrusion of the judiciary into legislative business. It would be one thing if absolute equality were possible. But, admittedly, it is not. The Court may be groping for a clean-cut, *per se* rule which will minimize confrontations between courts and legislatures while also satisfying the Fourteenth Amendment. If so, the Court is wide of the mark. Today's result simply shifts the area

of dispute a few percentage points down the scale; the courts will now be engaged in quibbling disputes over such questions as whether a plan with a 1% variation is "better" than one with a larger variation, say 1.1% or even 2%. If county and municipal boundaries are to be ignored, a computer can produce countless plans for absolute population equality, one differing very little from another, but each having its own very different political ramifications. Ultimately, the courts may be asked to decide whether some families in an apartment house should vote in one district and some in another, if that would come closer to the standard of apparent equality. Using the spacious language of the Equal Protection Clause to inject the Courts into these minor squabbles is an unacceptable pre-emption of the legislative function. Not only will the Court's new rule necessarily precipitate a new round of congressional and legislative districting, but I fear that in the long run the courts, rather than the legislatures or nonpartisan commissions, will be making most of the districting decisions in the several States. Since even at best, with compact and equal districts, the final boundary lines unavoidably have significant political repercussions, the courts should not draw district lines themselves unnecessarily. I therefore dissent.

GRIGGS v. DUKE POWER COMPANY
401 U.S. 424; 28 L. Ed. 2d 158; 91 S. Ct. 849 (1971)

MR. CHIEF JUSTICE BURGER *delivered the opinion of the Court.*

We granted the writ in this case to resolve the question whether an employer is prohibited by the Civil Rights Act of 1964, Title VII, from requiring a high school education or passing of a standardized general intelligence test as a condi-

tion of employment in or transfer to jobs when (a) neither standard is shown to be significantly related to successful job performance, (b) both requirements operate to disqualify Negroes at a substantially higher rate than white applicants, and (c) the jobs in question formerly had been filled only by white employees as part of a longstanding practice of giving preference to whites.

Congress provided, in Title VII of the Civil Rights Act of 1964, for class actions for enforcement of provisions of the Act and this proceeding was brought by a group of incumbent Negro employees against Duke Power Company.... At the time this action was instituted, the Company had 95 employees at the Dan River Station, 14 of whom were Negroes; 13 of these are petitioners here.

The District Court found that prior to July 2, 1965, the effective date of the Civil Rights Act of 1964, the Company openly discriminated on the basis of race in the hiring and assigning of employees at its Dan River plant. The plant was organized into five operating departments: (1) Labor, (2) Coal Handling, (3) Operations, (4) Maintenance, and (5) Laboratory and Test. Negroes were employed only in the Labor Department where the highest paying jobs paid less than the lowest paying jobs in the other four "operating" departments in which only whites were employed. Promotions were normally made within each department on the basis of job seniority. Transferees into a department usually began in the lowest position.

In 1955 the Company instituted a policy of requiring a high school education for initial assignment to any department except Labor, and for transfer from the Coal Handling to any "inside" department (Operations, Maintenance, or Laboratory). When the Company abandoned its policy of restricting Negroes to the Labor Department in 1965, completion of high school also was made a prerequisite to transfer from Labor to any other department. From the time the high school requirement was instituted to the time of trial, however, white employees hired before the time of the high school education requirement continued to perform satisfactorily and achieve promotions in the "operating" departments. Findings on this score are not challenged.

The Company added a further requirement for new employees on July 2, 1965, the date on which Title VII became effective. To qualify for placement in any but the Labor Department it became necessary to register satisfactory scores on two professionally prepared aptitude tests, as well as to have a high school education. Completion of high school alone continued to render employees eligible for transfer to the four desirable departments from which Negroes had been excluded if the incumbent had been employed prior to the time of the new requirement. In September 1965 the Company began to permit incumbent employees who lacked a high school education to qualify for transfer from Labor or Coal Handling to an "inside" job by passing two tests—the Wonderlic Personnel Test, which purports to measure general intelligence, and the Bennett Mechanical Aptitude Test. Neither was directed or intended to measure the ability to learn to perform a particular job or category of jobs. The requisite scores used for both initial hiring and transfer approximated the national median for high school graduates.

The District Court had found that while the Company previously followed a policy of overt racial discrimination in a period prior to the Act, such conduct had ceased. The District Court also concluded that Title VII was intended to be prospective only and, consequently, the impact of prior inequities was beyond the reach of corrective action authorized by the Act.

The Court of Appeals was confronted with a question of first impression, as are we, concerning the meaning of Title VII. After careful analysis a majority of that court concluded that a subjective test of the employer's intent should govern, particularly in a close case, and that in this case there was no showing of a discriminatory purpose in the adoption of the diploma and test requirements. On this basis, the Court of Appeals concluded there was no violation of the Act.

The Court of Appeals reversed the District Court in part, rejecting the holding that residual discrimination arising from prior employment practices was insulated from remedial action. The Court of Appeals noted, however, that the District Court was correct in its conclusion that there was no finding of a racial purpose of invidious intent in the adoption of the high school diploma requirement or general intelligence test and that these standards had been applied fairly to whites and Negroes alike. It held that, in the absence of a discriminatory purpose, use of such requirements was permitted by the Act. In so doing, the Court of Appeals rejected the claim that because these two requirements operated to render ineligible a markedly disproportionate number of Negroes, they were unlawful under Title VII unless shown to be job-related. . . .

The objective of Congress in the enactment of Title VII is plain from the language of the statute. It was to achieve equality of employment opportunities and remove barriers that have operated in the past to favor an identifiable group of white employees over other employees. Under the Act, practices, procedures, or tests neutral on their face, and even neutral in terms of intent, cannot be maintained if they operate to "freeze" the status quo of prior discriminatory employment practices.

The Court of Appeals' opinion, and the partial dissent, agreed that, on the record in the present case, "whites fare far better on the Company's alternative requirements" than Negroes. This consequence would appear to be directly traceable to race. Basic intelligence must have the means of articulation to manifest itself fairly in a testing process. Because they are Negroes, petitioners have long received inferior education in segregated schools and this Court expressly recognized these differences in *Gaston County* v. *United States,* 395 U.S. 285 (1969). There, because of the inferior education received by Negroes in North Carolina, this Court barred the institution of a literacy test for voter registration on the ground that the test would abridge the right to vote indirectly on account of race. Congress did not intend by Title VII, however, to guarantee a job to every person regardless of qualifications. In short, the Act does not command that any person be hired simply because he was formerly the subject of discrimination, or because he is a member of a minority group. Discriminatory preference for any group, mi-

nority or majority, is precisely and only what Congress has proscribed. What is required by Congress is the removal of artificial, arbitrary, and unnecessary barriers to employment when the barriers operate invidiously to discriminate on the basis of racial or other impermissible classification.

Congress has now provided that tests or criteria for employment or promotion may not provide equality of opportunity only in the sense of the fabled offer of milk to the stork and the fox. On the contrary, Congress has now required that the posture and condition of the job seeker be taken into account. It has—to resort again to the fable—provided that the vessel in which the milk is proffered be one all seekers can use. The Act proscribes not only overt discrimination but also practices that are fair in form, but discriminatory in operation. The touchstone is business necessity. If an employment practice which operates to exclude Negroes cannot be shown to be related to job performance, the practice is prohibited.

On the record before us, neither the high school completion requirement nor the general intelligence test is shown to bear a demonstrable relationship to successful performance of the jobs for which it was used. Both were adopted, as the Court of Appeals noted, without meaningful study of their relationship to job-performance ability. Rather, a vice president of the Company testified, the requirements were instituted on the Company's judgment that they generally would improve the overall quality of the work force.

The evidence, however, shows that employees who have not completed high school or taken the tests have continued to perform satisfactorily and make progress in departments for which the high school and test criteria are now used. The promotion record of present employees who would not be able to meet the new criteria thus suggests the possibility that the requirments may not be needed even for the limited purpose of preserving the avowed policy of advancement within the Company. . . .

The Court of Appeals held that the Company

had adopted the diploma and test requirements without any "intention to discriminate against Negro employees." We do not suggest that either the District Court or the Court of Appeals erred in examining the employer's intent; but good intent or absence of discriminatory intent does not redeem employment procedures or testing mechanisms that operate as "built-in headwinds" for minority groups and are unrelated to measuring job capability. . . .

The facts of this case demonstrate the inadequacy of broad and general testing devices as well as the infirmity of using diplomas or degrees as fixed measures of capability. History is filled with examples of men and women who rendered highly effective performance without the conventional badges of accomplishment in terms of certificates, diplomas, or degrees. Diplomas and tests are useful servants, but Congress had mandated the common-sense proposition that they are not to become masters of reality.

The Company contends that its general intelligence tests are specifically permitted by section 703(h) of the Act. That section authorizes the use of "any professionally developed ability test" that is not "designed, intended, or used to discriminate because of race . . . ."

The Equal Employment Opportunity Commission, having enforcement responsibility, has issued guidelines interpreting section 703(h) to permit only the use of job-related tests. The administrative interpretation of the Act by the enforcing agency is entitled to great deference. . . . Since the Act and its legislative history support the Commission's construction, this affords good reason to treat the Guidelines as expressing the will of Congress. . . .

Nothing in the Act precludes the use of testing or measuring procedures; obviously they are useful. What Congress has forbidden is giving these devices and mechanisms controlling force unless they are demonstrably a reasonable measure of job performance. Congress has not commanded that the less qualified be preferred over the better qualified simply because of minority origins. Far from disparaging job qualifications as such, Congress has made such qualifications the controlling factor, so that race, religion, nationality, and sex become irrelevant. What Congress has commanded is that any tests used must measure the person for the job and not the person in the abstract.

The judgment of the Court of Appeals is, as to that portion of the judgment appealed from, reversed.

MR. JUSTICE BRENNAN *took no part in the consideration or decision of this case.*

WYMAN v. JAMES
400 U.S. 309; 27 L. Ed 2d 408; 91 S. Ct. 381 (1971)

MR. JUSTICE BLACKMUN *delivered the opinion of the Court.*

This appeal presents the issue whether a beneficiary of the program for Aid to Families with Dependent Children (AFDC) may refuse a home visit by the caseworker without risking the termination of benefits.

The New York State and City social services commissioners appeal from a judgment and decree of a divided three-judge District Court holding invalid and unconstitutional in application section 134 of the New York Social Services Law, section 175 of the New York Policies Governing the Administration of Public Assistance, and sections 351.10 and 351.21 of Title

18 of the New York Code of Rules and Regulations, and granting injunctive relief. . . .

The District Court majority held that a mother receiving AFDC relief may refuse, without forfeiting her right to that relief, the periodic home visit which the cited New York statutes and regulations prescribe as a condition for the continuance of assistance under the program. The beneficiary's thesis, and that of the District Court majority, is that home visitation is a search and, when not consented to or when not supported by a warrant based on probable cause, violates the beneficiary's Fourth and Fourteenth Amendment rights.

Judge McLean, in dissent, thought it unrealistic to regard the home visit as a search; felt that the requirement of a search warrant to issue only upon a showing of probable cause would make the AFDC program "in effect another criminal statute" and would "introduce a hostile arm's length element into the relationship" between worker and mother, "a relationship which can be effective only when it is based upon mutual confidence and trust"; and concluded that the majority's holding struck "a damaging blow" to an important social welfare program. 303 F. Supp., at 946.

. . . The pertinent facts . . . are not in dispute. Plaintiff Barbara James is the mother of a son, Maurice, who was born in May 1967. They reside in New York City. Mrs. James first applied for AFDC assistance shortly before Maurice's birth. A caseworker made a visit to her apartment at that time without objection. The assistance was authorized.

Two years later, on May 8, 1969, a caseworker wrote Mrs. James that she would visit her home on May 14. Upon receipt of this advice, Mrs. James telephoned the worker that, although she was willing to supply information "reasonable and relevant" to her need for public assistance, any discussion was not to take place at her home. The worker told Mrs. James that she was required by law to visit in her home and that refusal to permit the visit would result in the termination of assistance. Permission was still denied.

On May 13 the City Department of Social Services sent Mrs. James a notice of intent to discontinue assistance because of the visitation refusal. The notice advised the beneficiary of her right to a hearing before a review officer. The hearing was requested and was held on May 27. Mrs. James appeared with an attorney at that hearing. They continued to refuse permission for a worker to visit the James home, but again expressed willingness to cooperate and to permit visits elsewhere. The review officer ruled that the refusal was a proper ground for the termination of assistance. . . . A notice of termination was issued on June 2.

Thereupon, without seeking a hearing at the state level, Mrs. James, individually and on behalf of Maurice, and purporting to act on behalf of all other persons similarly situated, instituted the present civil rights suit under 42 U.S.C. section 1983. She alleged the denial of rights guaranteed to her under the First, Third, Fourth, Fifth, Sixth, Ninth, Tenth, and Fourteenth Amendments, and under Subchapters IV and XVI of the Social Security Act and regulations thereunder. She further alleged that she and her son have no income, resources, or support other than the benefits received under the AFDC program. She asked for declaratory and injunctive relief. A temporary restraining order was issued on June 13, *James* v. *Goldberg,* 302 F. Supp. 478 (SDNY 1969), and the three-judge District Court was convened.

The federal aspects of the AFDC program deserve mention. They are provided for in Subchapter IV, Part A, of the Social Security Act of 1935, 49 Stat. 627, as amended, 42 U.S.C. sections 601-610 (1964 ed. and Supp. V). Section 401 of the Act, 42 U.S.C. section 601 (1964 ed., Supp. V), specified its purpose, namely, "encouraging the care of dependent children in their own homes or in the homes of relatives by enabling each State to furnish financial assistance and rehabilitation and other services . . . to needy dependent children and the parents or relatives with whom they are living to help maintain and strengthen family life. . . ." The same section authorizes the federal appropriation for payments to States that qualify. Section 402, 42 U.S.C. section 602 (1964 ed., Supp. V), provides that a state plan, among other things, must "provide for granting an opportunity for a fair hearing before the State agency to any individual whose claim for aid to families with dependent children is denied or is not acted upon with reasonable promptness"; . . . and must "provide that where the State agency has reason to believe that the home in which a relative and child receiving aid reside is unsuitable for the child because of the neglect, abuse, or exploitation of such child it shall bring such condition to the attention of the appropriate court or law enforcement agencies in the State. . . ."

When a case involves a home and some type of official intrusion into that home, as this case appears to do, an immediate and natural reaction is one of concern about Fourth Amendment rights and the protection which that Amendment is intended to afford. Its emphasis indeed is upon one of the most precious aspects of personal security in the home: "The right of the people to be secure in their persons, houses, papers, and effects. . . ." This Court has characterized that right as "basic to a free society.". . .

This natural and quite proper protective attitude, however, is not a factor in this case, for the seemingly obvious and simple reason that we are not concerned here with any search by the New York social service agency in the Fourth Amendment meaning of that term. It is true that the governing statute and regulations appear to make mandatory the initial home visit and the subsequent periodic "contacts" (which may include home visits) for the inception and continuance of aid. It is also true that the caseworker's posture in the home visit is perhaps, in a sense, both rehabilitative and investigative. But this latter aspect, we think is given too broad a character and far more emphasis than it deserves if it is

equated with a search in the traditional criminal law context. We note, too, that the visitation in itself is not forced or compelled, and that the beneficiary's denial of permission is not a criminal act. If consent to the visitation is withheld, no visitation takes place. The aid then never begins or merely ceases, as the case may be. There is no entry of the home and there is no search.

If however, we were to assume that a caseworker's home visit, before or subsequent to the beneficiary's initial qualification for benefits, somehow (perhaps because the average beneficiary might feel she is in no position to refuse consent to the visit), and despite its interview nature, does possess some of the characteristics of a search in the traditional sense, we nevertheless conclude that the visit does not fall within the Fourth Amendment's proscription. This is because it does not descend to the level of unreasonableness. It is unreasonableness which is the Fourth Amendment's standard. . . .

There are a number of factors that compel us to conclude that the home visit proposed for Mrs. James is not unreasonable:

1. The public's interest in this particular segment of the area of assistance to the unfortunate is protection and aid for the dependent child whose family requires such aid for that child. . . . The dependent child's needs are paramount, and only with hesitancy would we relegate those needs, in the scale of comparative values, to a position secondary to what the mother claims as her rights.

2. The agency, with tax funds provided from federal as well as from state sources, is fulfilling a public trust. The State, working through its qualified welfare agency, has appropriate and paramount interest and concern in seeing and assuring that the intended and proper objects of that tax-produced assistance are the ones who benefit from the aid it dispenses. Surely it is not unreasonable, in the Fourth Amendment sense or in any other sense of that term, that the State have at its command a gentle means, of limited

extent and of practical and considerate application, of achieving that assurance.

3. One who dispenses purely private charity naturally has an interest in and expects to know how his charitable funds are utilized and put to work. The public, when it is the provider, rightly expects the same. . . .

4. The emphasis of the New York statutes and regulations is upon the home, upon "close contact" with the beneficiary, upon restoring the aid recipient "to a condition of self-support," and upon the relief of his distress. The federal emphasis is no different. . . .

5. The home visit, it is true, is not required by federal statute or regulation. But it has been noted that the visit is "the heart of welfare administration"; that it affords "a personal, rehabilitative orientation, unlike that of most federal programs"; and that the "more pronounced service orientation" effected by Congress with the 1956 amendments to the Social Security Act "gave redoubled importance to the practice of home visiting." . . . The home visit is an established routine in States besides New York.

6. The means employed by the New York agency are significant. Mrs. James received written notice several days in advance of the intended home visit. The date was specified. . . . Privacy is emphasized. The applicant-recipient is made the primary source of information as to eligibility. Outside informational sources, other than public records, are to be consulted only with the beneficiary's consent. Forcible entry or entry under false pretenses or visitation outside working hours or snooping in the home are forbidden. . . . All this minimizes any "burden" upon the homeowner's right against unreasonable intrusion.

7. Mrs. James, in fact, on this record presents no specific complaint of any unreasonable intrusion of her home and nothing that supports an inference that the desired home visit had as its purpose the obtaining of information as to criminal activity. She complains of no proposed visitation at an awkward or retirement hour. She suggests no forcible entry. She refers to no snooping. She describes no impolite or reprehensible conduct of any kind. She alleges only, in general and nonspecific terms, that on previous visits and, on information and belief, on visitation at the home of other aid recipients, "questions concerning personal relationships, beliefs and behavior are raised and pressed which are unnecessary for a determination of continuing eligibility." Paradoxically, this same complaint could be made of a conference held elsewhere than in the home, and yet this is what is sought by Mrs. James. The same complaint could be made of the census taker's questions. . . . What Mrs. James appears to want from the agency that provides her and her infant son with the necessities of life is the right to receive those necessities upon her own informational terms, to utilize the Fourth Amendment as a wedge for imposing those terms, and to avoid questions of any kind.

8. We are not persuaded, as Mrs. James would have us be, that all information pertinent to the issue of eligibility can be obtained by the agency through an interview at a place other than the home, or, as the District Court majority suggested, by examining a lease or a birth certificate, or by periodic medical examinations, or by interviews with school personnel. Although these secondary sources might be helpful, they would not always assure verification of actual residence or of actual physical presence in the home. . . .

9. The visit is not one by police or uniformed authority. It is made by a caseworker of some training whose primary objective is, or should be, the welfare, not the prosecution, of the aid recipient for whom the worker has profound responsibility. . . . The caseworker is not a sleuth but rather, we trust, is a friend to one in need.

10. The home visit is not a criminal investigation, does not equate with a criminal investigation, and despite the announced fears of

Mrs. James and those who would join her, is not in aid of any criminal proceeding. . . .

. . . Mrs. James is not being prosecuted for her refusal to permit the home visit and is not about to be so prosecuted. Her wishes in that respect are fully honored. We have not been told, and have not found, that her refusal is made a criminal act by any applicable New York or federal statute. The only consequence of her refusal is that the payment of benefits ceases. Important and serious as this is, the situation is no different than if she had exercised a similar negative choice initially and refrained from applying for AFDC benefits. . . .

Our holding today does not mean, of course, that a termination of benefits upon refusal of a home visit is to be upheld against constitutional challenge under all conceivable circumstances. . . .

We therefore conclude that the home visitation as structured by the New York statutes and regulations is a reasonable administrative tool; that it serves a valid and proper administrative purpose for the dispensation of the AFDC program; that it is not an unwarranted invasion of personal privacy; and that it violates no right guaranteed by the Fourth Amendment.

Reversed and remanded with directions to enter a judgment of dismissal.

It is so ordered.

MR. JUSTICE WHITE *concurs in the judgment and joins the opinion of the Court with the exception of Part IV thereof.*

MR. JUSTICE DOUGLAS, *dissenting.*

We are living in a society where one of the most important forms of property is government largesse which some call the "new property." . . .

The question in this case is whether receipt of largesse from the government makes the *home* of the beneficiary subject to access by an inspector of the agency of oversight, even though the Fourth Amendment's procedure for access to one's *house* or *home* is not followed. The penalty here is not, of course, invasion of the privacy of Barbara James, only her loss of federal or state largesse. That, however, is merely rephrasing the problem. Whatever the semantics, the central question is whether the government by force of its largesse has the power to "buy up" rights guaranteed by the Constitution. But for the assertion of her constitutional right, Barbara James in this case would have received the welfare benefit. . . .

These cases are in the tradition of *United States* v. *Chicago, M., St. P. & P.R. Co.,* 328-329, where Mr. Justice Sutherland, writing for the Court, said:

[T]he rule is that the right to continue the exercise of a privilege granted by the state cannot be made to depend upon the grantee's submission to a condition prescribed by the state which is hostile to the provisions of the federal Constitution.

What we said in those cases is as applicable to Fourth Amendment rights as to those of the First. . . .

Is a search of her home without a warrant made "reasonable" merely because she is dependent on government largesse?

Judge Skelly Wright has stated the problem succinctly:

Welfare has long been considered the equivalent of charity and its recipients have been subjected to all kinds of dehumanizing experiences in the government's effort to police its welfare payments. In fact, over half a billion dollars are expended annually for administration and policing in connection with the Aid to Families with Dependent Children program. Why such large sums are necessary for administration and policing has never been adequately explained. No such sums are spent policing the government subsidies granted to farmers, airlines, steamship companies, and junk mail dealers, to name but a few. The truth is that in this subsidy area society has simply adopted a double standard, one for aid to business and the farmer and a different one for welfare. Poverty, Minorities, and Respect for Law, 1970 Duke L. J. 425, 437-438.

If the welfare recipient was not Barbara James but a prominent, affluent cotton or wheat farmer receiving benefit payments for not growing crops, would not the approach be different? Welfare in aid of dependent children, like social security and unemployment benefits, has an aura of suspicion. There doubtless are frauds in every sector of public welfare whether the recipient be a Barbara James or someone who is prominent or influential. But constitutional rights—here the privacy of the *home*—are obviously not dependent on the poverty or on the affluence of the beneficiary. . . .

I would place the same restrictions on inspectors entering the *homes* of welfare beneficiaries as are on inspectors entering the *homes* of those on the payroll of government, or the *homes* of those who contract with the government, or the *homes* of those who work for those having government contracts. . . .

The bureaucracy of modern government is not only slow, lumbering, and oppressive; it is omnipresent. It touches everyone's life at numerous points. It pries more and more into private affairs, breaking down the barriers that individuals erect to give them some insulation from the intrigues and harassments of modern life. Isolation is not a constitutional guarantee; but the sanctity of the sanctuary of the home is such—as marked and defined by the Fourth Amendment. . . . What we do today is to depreciate it.

I would sustain the judgment of the three-judge court in the present case.

The Court's assertion that this case concerns no search "in the Fourth Amendment meaning of that term" is neither "obvious" nor "simple." I should have thought that the Fourth Amend-

ment governs all intrusions by agents of the public upon personal security. . . .

Even if the Fourth Amendment does not apply to each and every governmental entry into the home, the welfare visit is not some sort of purely benevolent inspection. No one questions the motives of the dedicated welfare caseworker. Of course, caseworkers seek to be friends, but the point is that they are also required to be sleuths. . . .

Actually, the home visit is precisely the type of inspection proscribed by *Camara* and its companion case, *See* v. *City of Seattle,* 387 U. S. 541 (1967) except that the welfare visit is a more severe intrusion upon privacy and family dignity. Both the home visit and the searches in those cases may convey benefits to the householder. Fire inspectors give frequent advice concerning fire prevention, wiring capacity, and other matters, and obvious self-interest causes many to welcome the fire or safety inspection. Similarly, the welfare caseworker may provide welcome advice on home management and child care. Nonetheless, both searches may result in the imposition of civil penalties—loss or reduction of welfare benefits or an order to upgrade a housing defect. The fact that one purpose of the visit is to provide evidence that may lead to an elimination of benefits is sufficient to grant appellee protection since *Camara* stated that the Fourth Amendment applies to inspections which can result in only civil violations, 387 U.S., at 531. But here the case is stronger since the home visit, like many housing inspections, may lead to criminal convictions. . . . Appellants offer scant explanation for their refusal even to attempt to utilize public records, expenditure receipts, documents such as leases, non-home interviews, personal financial records, sworn declaration, etc.—all sources that governmental agencies regularly accept as adequate to establish eligibility for other public benefits. In this setting, it ill behooves appellants to refuse to utilize informational sources less drastic than an invasion of the privacy of the home. . . .

Although the Court does not agree with my conclusion that the home visit is an unreasonable search, its opinion suggests that even if the visit were unreasonable, appellee has somehow waived her right to object. Surely the majority cannot believe that valid Fourth Amendment consent can be given under the threat of the loss of one's sole means of support. Nor has Mrs. James waived her rights. Had the Court squarely faced the question of whether the State can condition welfare payments on the waiver of clear constitutional rights, the answer would be plain. The decisions of this Court do not support the notion that a State can use welfare benefits as a wedge to coerce "waiver" of Fourth Amendment rights. . . .

In deciding that the homes of AFDC recipients are not entitled to protection from warrantless searches by welfare caseworkers, the Court declines to follow prior case law and employs a rationale that, if applied to the claims of all citizens, would threaten the vitality of the Fourth Amendment. This Court has occasionally pushed beyond established constitutional contours to protect the vulnerable and to further basic human values. I find no little irony in the fact that the burden of today's departure from principled adjudication is placed upon the lowly poor. . . . I am not convinced; and, therefore, I must respectfully dissent.

JAMES v. VALTIERRA
402 U.S. 137, 28 L. Ed. 2d 678; 91 S. Ct. 1331 (1971)

MR. JUSTICE BLACK *delivered the opinion of the Court.*

These cases raise but a single issue. It grows out of the United States Housing Act of 1937 which established a federal housing agency authorized to make loans and grants to state agencies for slum clearance and low-rent housing projects. In response, the California Legislature created in each county and city a public housing authority to take advantage of the financing made available by the federal Housing Act. . . . At the time the federal legislation was passed the California Constitution had for many years reserved to the State's people the power to initiate legislation and to reject or approve by referendum any Act passed by the state legislature. . . . The same section reserved to the electors of counties and cities the power of initiative and referendum over acts of local government bodies. In 1950, however, the State Supreme Court held that local

authorities' decisions on seeking federal aid for public housing projects were "executive" and "administrative," not "legislative," and therefore the state constitution's referendum provisions did not apply to these actions. Within six months of that decision the California voters adopted Article XXXIV of the state constitution to bring public housing decisions under the State's referendum policy. The Article provided that no low-rent housing project should be developed, constructed, or acquired in any manner by a state public body until the project was approved by a majority of those voting at a community election.

The present suits were brought by citizens of San Jose, California, and San Mateo County, localities where housing authorities could not apply for federal funds because low-cost housing proposals had been defeated in referendums. The plaintiffs, who are eligible for low-cost public housing, sought a declaration that Article

XXXIV was unconstitutional because its referendum requirement violated: (1) the Supremacy Clause of the United States Constitution; (2) the Privileges and Immunities Clause; and (3) the Equal Protection Clause. A three-judge court held that Article XXXIV denied the plaintiffs equal protection of the laws and it enjoined its enforcement.... We noted probable jurisdiction.... For the reasons that follow, we reverse.

The three-judge court found the Supremacy Clause argument unpersuasive, and we agree. By the Housing Act of 1937 the Federal Government has offered aid to state and local governments for the creation of low-rent public housing. However, the federal legislation does not purport to require that local governments accept this or to outlaw local referendums on whether the aid should be accepted. We also find the privileges and immunities argument without merit.

While the District Court cited several cases of this Court, its chief reliance plainly rested on *Hunter* v. *Erickson,* 393 U.S. 385 (1969). The first paragraph in the District Court's decision stated simply: "We hold Article XXXIV to be unconstitutional. *See Hunter* v. *Erickson....*" The court below erred in relying on *Hunter* to invalidate Article XXXIV. Unlike the case before us, *Hunter* rested on the conclusion that Akron's referendum law denied equal protection by placing "special burdens on racial minorities within the governmental process." ... In *Hunter* the citizens of Akron had amended the city charter to require that any ordinance regulating real estate on the basis of race, color, religion, or national origin could not take effect without approval by a majority of those voting in a city election. The Court held that the amendment created a classification based upon race because it required that laws dealing with racial housing matters could take effect only if they survived a mandatory referendum while other housing ordinances took effect without any such special election. The opinion noted:

Because the core of the Fourteenth Amendment is the prevention of meaningful and unjustified official distinctions based on race, [citing a group of racial discrimination cases] racial classifications are "constitutionally suspect" ... and subject to the "most rigid scrutiny".... They "bear a far heavier burden of justification" than other classifications.

The Court concluded that Akron had advanced no sufficient reasons to justify this racial classification and hence that it was unconstitutional under the Fourteenth Amendment.

Unlike the Akron referendum provision, it cannot be said that California's Article XXXIV rests on "distinctions based on race." ... The Article requires referendum approval for any low-rent public housing project, not only for projects which will be occupied by a racial minority. And the record here would not support any claim that a law seemingly neutral on its face is in fact aimed at a racial minority. Cf. *Gomillion* v. *Lightfoot,* 364 U.S. 339 (1960). The present case could be affirmed only by extending *Hunter,* and this we decline to do.

California's entire history demonstrates the repeated use of referendums to give citizens a voice on questions of public policy. A referendum provision was included in the first state constitution, Cal. Const. of 1849, Art. VIII, and referendums have been a commonplace occurrence in the State's active political life. Provisions for referendums demonstrate devotion to democracy, not to bias, discrimination, or prejudice. Nonetheless, appellees contend that Article XXXIV denies them equal protection because it demands a mandatory referendum while many other referendums only take place upon citizen initiative. They suggest that the mandatory nature of the Article XXXIV referendum constitutes unconstitutional discrimination because it hampers persons desiring public housing from achieving their objective when no such roadblock faces other groups seeking to influence other public decisions to their advantage. But of course a lawmaking procedure that "disadvantages" a particular group does not always deny equal protection. Under any such holding, presumably a State would not be able to require referendums on any subject unless referendums were required on all, because they would always disadvantage some group. And this Court would be required to analyze governmental structures to determine whether a gubernatorial veto provision or a filibuster rule is likely to "disadvantage" any of the diverse and shifting groups that make up the American people.

Furthermore, an examination of California law reveals that persons advocating low-income housing have not been singled out for mandatory referendums while no other group must face that obstacle. Mandatory referendums are required for approval of state constitutional amendments, for the issuance of general obligation long-term bonds by local governments, and for certain municipal territorial annexations. . . . California statute books contain much legislation first enacted by voter initiative, and no such law can be repealed or amended except by referendum. . . .

The people of California have also decided by their own vote to require referendum approval of low-rent public housing projects. This procedure ensures that all the people of a community will have a voice in a decision which may lead to large expenditures of local governmental funds for increased public services and to lower tax revenues. It gives them a voice in decisions that will affect the future development of their own community. This procedure for democratic decision-making does not violate the constitutional command that no State shall deny to any person "the equal protection of the laws."

The judgment of the three-judge court is reversed and the cases are remanded for dismissal of the complaint.

Reversed and remanded.

MR. JUSTICE DOUGLAS *took no part in the consideration or decision of these cases.*

MR. JUSTICE MARSHALL, *whom* MR. JUSTICE BRENNAN *and* MR. JUSTICE BLACKMUN *join, dissenting.*

By its very terms, the mandatory prior referendum provision of Art. XXXIV applies solely to

any development composed of urban or rural dwellings, apartments or other living accommodations for persons of low income, financed in whole or in part by the Federal Government or a state public body or to which the Federal Government or a state public body extends assistance by supplying all or part of the labor, by guaranteeing the payment of liens, or otherwise.

Persons of low income are defined as

persons or families who lack the amount of income which is necessary . . . to enable them, without financial assistance, to live in decent, safe and sanitary dwellings, without overcrowding.

The article explicitly singles out low-income persons to bear its burden. Publicly assisted housing developments designed to accommodate the aged, veterans, state employees, persons of moderate income, or any class of citizens other than the poor, need not be approved by prior referenda.

In my view, Art. XXXIV on its face constitutes invidious discrimination which the Equal Protection Clause of the Fourteenth Amendment plainly prohibits. "The States, of course, are prohibited by the Equal Protection Clause from discriminating between 'rich' and 'poor' *as such* in the formulation and application of their laws." *Douglas* v. *California,* 372 U.S. 353, 361 (1963) (HARLAN, J., dissenting). Article XXXIV is neither "a law of general applicability that may affect the poor more harshly than it does the rich," nor an "effort to redress economic imbalances." It is rather an explicit classification on the basis of poverty—a suspect classification which demands exacting judicial scrutiny. . . .

The Court, however, chooses to subject the article to no scrutiny whatsoever and treats the provision as if it contained a totally benign, technical economic classification. Both the appellees and the Solicitor General of the United States as *amicus curiae* have strenuously argued, and the court below found, that Art. XXXIV, by imposing a substantial burden solely on the poor, violates the Fourteenth Amendment. Yet after observing that the article does not discriminate on the basis of race, the Court's only response to the real question in these cases is the unresponsive assertion that "referendums demonstrate devotion to democracy, not to bias, discrimination, or prejudice." It is far too late in the day to contend that the Fourteenth Amendment prohibits only racial discrimination; and to me, singling out the poor to bear a burden not placed on any other class of citizens tramples the values that the Fourteenth Amendment was designed to protect.

I respectfully dissent.

SAN ANTONIO INDEPENDENT SCHOOL DISTRICT v. RODRIGUEZ
411 U.S. 1; 36 L. Ed. 2d 16; 93 S.Ct. 1278 (1973)

MR. JUSTICE POWELL *delivered the opinion of the Court.*

This suit attacking the Texas system of financing public education was initiated by Mexican-American parents whose children attend the elementary and secondary school in the Edgewood Independent School District, an urban school district in San Antonio, Texas. They brought a class action on behalf of school children throughout the State who are members of minority groups or who are poor and reside in school districts having a low property tax base. . . . In December 1971 [a three-judge federal district court held] the Texas school finance system unconstitutional under the Equal Protection Clause of the Fourteenth Amendment. The State appealed, and . . . [f]or the reasons stated in this opinion we reverse the decision of the District Court.

I

. . .

Until recent times Texas was a predominantly rural State and its population and property wealth were spread relatively evenly across the State. Sizable differences in the value of assessable property between local school districts became increasingly evident as the State became more industrialized and as rural-to-urban population shifts became more pronounced. The location of commercial and industrial property began to play a significant role in determining the amount of tax resources available to each school district. These growing disparities in population and taxable property between districts were responsible in part for increasingly notable differences in levels of local expenditure for education.

In due time it became apparent to those concerned with financing public education that contributions from the Available School Fund were not sufficient to ameliorate these disparities. . . .

Recognizing the need for increased state funding to help offset disparities in local spending and to meet Texas' changing educational requirements, the state legislature in the late 1940's undertook a thorough evaluation of public education with an eye toward major reform. In 1947 an 18-member committee, composed of educators and legislators, was appointed to explore alternative systems in other States and to propose a funding scheme that would guarantee a minimum of basic educational offering to each child and that would help overcome interdistrict disparities in taxable resources. The Committee's efforts led to the passage of ... bills ... establishing the Texas Minimum Foundation School Program. Today this Program accounts for approximately half of the total educational expenditures in Texas. ...

The design of this complex system was two-fold. First, it was an attempt to assure that the Foundation Program would have an equalizing influence on expenditure levels between school districts by placing the heaviest burden on the school districts most capable of paying. Second, the Program's architects sought to establish a Local Fund Assignment that would force every school district to contribute to the education of its children but that would not by itself exhaust any district's resources. Today every school district does impose a property tax from which it derives locally expendable funds in excess of the amount necessary to satisfy its Local Fund Assignment under the Foundation Program. ...

The school district in which appellees reside, the Edgewood Independent School District, has been compared throughout this litigation with the Alamo Heights Independent School District. This comparison between the least and most affluent districts in the San Antonio area serves to illustrate the manner in which the dual system of finance operates and to indicate the extent to which substantial disparities exist despite the State's impressive progress in recent years. Edgewood is one of seven public school districts in the metropolitan area. Approximately 22,000 students are enrolled in its 25 elementary and secondary schools. The district is situated in the core-city sector of San Antonio in a residential neighborhood that has little commercial or industrial property. The residents are predominantly of Mexican-American descent: approximately 90 percent of the student population is Mexican-American and over 6 percent is Negro. The average assessed property value per pupil is $5,960—the lowest in the metropolitan area—and the median family income ($4,686) is also the lowest. At an equalized tax rate of $1.05 per $100 of assessed property—the highest in the metropolitan area—the district contributed $26 to the education of each child for the 1967-1968 school year above its Local Fund Assignment for the Minimum Foundation Program. The Foundation Program contributed $222 per pupil for a state-local total of $248. Federal funds added another $108 for a total of $356 per pupil.

Alamo Heights is the most affluent school district in San Antonio. Its six schools, housing approximately 5,000 students, are situated in a residential community quite unlike the Edgewood District. The school population is predominantly Anglo, having only 18 percent Mexican-Americans and less than 1 percent Negroes. The assessed property value per pupil exceeds $49,000 and the median family income is $8,001. In 1967-1968 the local tax rate of $.85 per $100 of valuation yielded $333 per pupil over and above its contribution to the Foundation Program. Coupled with the $225 provided from that Program, the district was able to supply $588 per student. Supplemented by a $36 per pupil grant from federal sources, Alamo Heights spent $594 per pupil.

Although the 1967-1968 school year figures provide the only complete statistical breakdown for each category of aid, more recent partial statistics indicate that the previously noted trend of increasing state aid has been significant. For the 1970-1971 school year, the Foundation School Program allotment for Edgewood was $356 per pupil, a 62 percent increase over the 1967-1968 school year. Indeed, state aid alone in 1970-1971 equaled Edgewood's entire 1967-1968 school budget from local, state, and federal sources. Alamo Heights enjoyed a similar increase under the Foundation Program, netting $491 per pupil in 1970-1971.* These recent figures also reveal the extent to which these two districts' allotments were funded from their own required contributions to the Local Fund Assignment. Alamo Heights, because of its relative wealth, was required to contribute out of its local property tax collections approximately $100 per pupil, or about 20 percent of its Foundation grant. Edgewood, on the other hand, paid only $8.46 per pupil, which is about 2.4 percent of its grant. It does appear then that, at least as to these two districts, the Local Fund Assignment does reflect a rough approximation of the relative taxpaying potential of each.

Despite these recent increases, substantial interdistrict disparities in school expenditures found by the District Court to prevail in San Antonio and in varying degrees throughout the State still exist. And it was these disparities, largely attributable to differences in the amounts of money collected through local property taxation, that led the District Court to conclude that Texas' dual system of public school finance

*Although the Foundation Program has made significantly greater contributions to both school districts over the last several years, it is apparent that Alamo Heights has enjoyed a larger gain. The sizable difference between the Alamo Heights and Edgewood grants is due to the emphasis in the State's allocation formula on the guaranteed minimum salaries for teachers. Higher salaries are guaranteed to teachers having more years of experience and possessing more advanced degrees. Therefore, Alamo Heights, which has a greater percentage of experienced personnel with advanced degrees, receives more State support. . . . Because more dollars have been given to districts that already spend more per pupil, such Foundation formulas have been described as "anti-equalizing." The formula, however, is anti-equalizing only if viewed in absolute terms. The percentage disparity between the two Texas districts is diminished substantially by State aid. Alamo Heights derived in 1967-1968 almost 13 times as much money from local taxes as Edgewood did. The State aid grants to each district in 1970-1971 lowered the ratio to approximately two to one, *i.e.,* Alamo Heights had a little more than twice as much money to spend per pupil from its combined State and local resources.

violated the Equal Protection Clause. The District Court held that the Texas system discriminates on the basis of wealth in the manner in which education is provided for its people. Finding that wealth is a "suspect" classification and that education is a "fundamental" interest, the District Court held that the Texas system could be sustained only if the State could show that it was premised upon some compelling state interest. On this issue the court concluded that "not only are defendants unable to demonstrate compelling state interests . . . they fail even to establish a reasonable basis for these classifications."

Texas virtually concedes that its historically rooted dual system of financing education could not withstand the strict judicial scrutiny that this Court has found appropriate in reviewing legislative judgments that interfere with fundamental constitutional rights or that involve suspect classifications. If, as previous decisions have indicated, strict scrutiny means that the State's system is not entitled to the usual presumption of validity, that the State rather than the complainants must carry a "heavy burden of justification," that the State must demonstrate that its educational system has been structured with "precision" and is "tailored" narrowly to serve legitimate objectives and that it has selected the "least drastic means" for effectuating its objectives, the Texas financing system and its counterpart in virtually every other State will not pass muster. The State candidly admits that "no one familiar with the Texas system would contend that it has yet achieved perfection." Apart from its concession that educational finance in Texas has "defects" and "imperfections," the State defends the system's rationality with vigor and disputes the District Court's finding that it lacks a "reasonable basis."

This, then, establishes the framework for our analysis. We must decide, first, whether the Texas system of financing public education operates to the disadvantage of some suspect class or impinges upon a fundamental right explicitly or implicitly protected by the Constitution, thereby requiring strict judicial scrutiny. If so, the judgment of the District Court should be affirmed. If not, the Texas scheme must still be examined to determine whether it rationally furthers some legitimate, articulated state purpose and therefore does not constitute an invidious discrimination in violation of the Equal Protection Clause of the Fourteenth Amendment.

II

The District Court's opinion does not reflect the novelty and complexity of the constitutional questions posed by appellees' challenge to Texas' system of school finance. In concluding that strict judicial scrutiny was required, that court relied on decisions dealing with the rights of indigents to equal treatment in the criminal trial and appellate processes, and on cases disapproving wealth restrictions on the right to vote. Those cases, the District Court concluded, established wealth as a suspect classification. Finding that the local property tax system discriminated on the basis of wealth, it regarded those precedents as controlling. It then reasoned, based on decisions of this Court affirming the undeniable importance of education, that there is a fundamental right to education and that, absent some compelling state justification, the Texas system could not stand.

We are unable to agree that this case, which in significant aspects is *sui generis*, may be so neatly fitted into the conventional mosaic of constitutional analysis under the Equal Protection Clause. Indeed, for the several reasons that follow, we find neither the suspect classification nor the fundamental interest analysis persuasive.

A

[1] The wealth discrimination discovered by the District Court in this case, and by several other courts that have recently struck down school financing laws in other States, is quite unlike any of the forms of wealth discrimination heretofore reviewed by this Court. Rather than focusing on the unique features of the alleged discrimination, the courts in these cases have virtually assumed their findings of a suspect classification through a simplistic process of analysis: since, under the traditional systems of financing public schools, some poorer people receive less expensive educations than other more affluent people, these systems discriminate on the basis of wealth. This approach largely ignores the hard threshold questions, including whether it makes a difference for purposes of consideration under the Constitution that the class of disadvantaged "poor" cannot be identified or defined in customary equal protection terms, and whether the relative—rather than absolute—nature of the asserted deprivation is of significant consequence. Before a State's laws and the justifications for the classifications they create are subjected to strict judicial scrutiny, we think these threshold considerations must be analyzed more closely than they were in the court below.

The case comes to us with no definitive description of the classifying facts or delineation of the disfavored class. Examination of the District Court's opinion and of appellees' complaint, briefs, and contentions at oral argument suggests, however, at least three ways in which the discrimination claimed here might be described. The Texas system of school finance might be regarded as discriminating (1) against "poor" persons whose incomes fall below some identifiable level of poverty or who might be characterized as functionally "indigent," or (2) against those who are relatively poorer than others, or (3) against all those who, irrespective of their personal incomes, happen to reside in relatively poorer school districts. Our task must be to ascertain whether, in fact, the Texas system has been shown to discriminate on any of these possible bases. . . .

[Here follows an examination of the Court's

precedents that consider discrimination against indigents.]

Only appellees' first possible basis for describing the class disadvantaged by the Texas school finance system—discrimination against a class of definably "poor" persons—might arguably meet the criteria established in [our] prior cases. Even a cursory examination, however, demonstrates that neither of the two distinguishing characteristics of wealth classifications can be found here. First, in support of their charge that the system discriminates against the "poor," appellees have made no effort to demonstrate that it operates to the peculiar disadvantage of any class fairly definable as indigent, or as composed of persons whose incomes are beneath any designated poverty level. Indeed, there is reason to believe that the poorest families are not necessarily clustered in the poorest property districts. A recent and exhaustive study of school districts in Connecticut concluded that "[i]t is clearly incorrect . . . to contend that the 'poor' live in 'poor' districts."... [T]he Connecticut study found, not surprisingly, that the poor were clustered around commercial and industrial areas—those same areas that provide the most attractive sources of property tax income for school districts. Whether a similar pattern would be discovered in Texas is not known, but there is no basis on the record in this case for assuming that the poorest people—defined by reference to any level of absolute impecunity—are concentrated in the poorest districts.

Second, neither appellees nor the District Court addressed the fact that . . . lack of personal resources has not occasioned an absolute deprivation of the desired benefit. The argument here is not that the children in districts having relatively low assessable property values are receiving no public education; rather, it is that they are receiving a poorer quality education than that available to children in districts having more assessable wealth. Apart from the unsettled and disputed question whether the quality of education may be determined by the amount of

money expended for it, a sufficient answer to appellees' argument is that at least where wealth is involved the Equal Protection Clause does not require absolute equality or precisely equal advantages. Nor indeed, in view of the infinite variables affecting the educational process, can any system assure equal quality of education except in the most relative sense. Texas asserts that the Minimum Foundation Program provides an "adequate" education for all children in the State. By providing 12 years of free public school education, and by assuring teachers, books, transportation and operating funds, the Texas Legislature has endeavored to "guarantee, for the welfare of the state as a whole, that all people shall have at least an adequate program of education. This is what is meant by 'A Minimum Foundation Program of Education.'" The State repeatedly asserted in its briefs in this Court that it has fulfilled this desire and that it now assures "every child in every school district an adequate education." No proof was offered at trial persuasively discrediting or refuting the State's assertion.

For these two reasons—the absence of any evidence that the financing system discriminates against any definable category of "poor" people or that it results in the absolute deprivation of education—the disadvantaged class is not susceptible to identification in traditional terms.

[A]ppellees and the District Court may have embraced a second or third approach, the second of which might be characterized as a theory of relative or comparative discrimination based on family income. Appellees sought to prove that a direct correlation exists between the wealth of families within each district and the expenditures therein for education. That is, along a continuum, the poorer the family the lower the dollar amount of education received by the family's children.

The principal evidence adduced in support of this comparative discrimination claim is an affidavit submitted by Professor Joele S. Berke of Syracuse University's Educational Finance

Policy Institute. The District Court, relying in major part upon this affidavit and apparently accepting the substance of appellees' theory, noted, first, a positive correlation between the wealth of school districts, measured in terms of assessable property per pupil, and their levels of per-pupil expenditures. Second, the court found a similar correlation between district wealth and the personal wealth of its residents, measured in terms of median family income.

If, in fact, these correlations could be sustained, then it might be argued that expenditures on education—equated by appellees to the quality of education—are dependent on personal wealth. Appellees' comparative discrimination theory would still face serious unanswered questions, including whether a bare positive correlation or some higher degree of correlation is necessary to provide a basis for concluding that the financing system is designated to operate to the peculiar disadvantage of the comparatively poor, and whether a class of this size and diversity could ever claim the special protection accorded "suspect" classes. These questions need not be addressed in this case, however, since appellees' proof fails to support their allegations or the District Court's conclusions. . . .

This brings us, then, to the third way in which the classification scheme might be defined—*district* wealth discrimination. Since the only correlation indicated by the evidence is between district property wealth and expenditures, it may be argued that discrimination might be found without regard to the individual income characteristics of district residents. Assuming a perfect correlation between district property wealth and expenditures from top to bottom, the disadvantaged class might be viewed as encompassing every child in every district except the district that has the most assessable wealth and spends the most on education. Alternatively, as suggested in Mr. Justice Marshall's dissenting opinion, the class might be defined more restrictively to include children in districts with assessable property which falls below the statewide average, or median, or below some other artificially defined level.

However described, it is clear that appellees' suit asks this Court to extend its most exacting scrutiny to review a system that allegedly discriminates against a large, diverse, and amorphous class, unified only by the common factor of residence in districts that happen to have less taxable wealth than other districts. The system of alleged discrimination and the class it defines have none of the traditional indicia of suspectness: the class is not saddled with such disabilities, or subjected to such a history of purposeful unequal treatment, or relegated to such a position of political powerlessness as to command extraordinary protection from the majoritarian political process.

[4] We thus conclude that the Texas system does not operate to the peculiar disadvantage of any suspect class. But in recognition of the fact that this Court has never heretofore held that wealth discrimination alone provides an adequate basis for invoking strict scrutiny, appellees have not relied solely on this contention. They also assert that the State's system impermissibly interferes with the exercise of a "fundamental" right and that accordingly the prior decisions of this Court require the application of the strict standard of judicial review. It is this question—whether education is a fundamental right, in the sense that it is among the rights and liberties protected by the Constitution—which has so consumed the attention of courts and commentators in recent years.

B

. . .

The lesson of [our] cases in addressing the question now before the Court is plain. It is not the province of this Court to create substantive constitutional rights in the name of guaranteeing equal protection of the laws. Thus the key to discovering whether education is "fundamental" is not to be found in comparisons of the relative societal significance of education as opposed to subsistence or housing. Nor is it to be found by weighing whether education is as important as the right to travel. Rather, the answer lies in assessing whether there is a right to education explicitly or implicitly guaranteed by the Constitution. . . .

Education, of course, is not among the rights afforded explicit protection under our Federal Constitution. Nor do we find any basis for saying it is implicitly so protected. As we have said, the undisputed importance of education will not alone cause this Court to depart from the usual standard for reviewing a State's social and economic legislation. It is appellees' contention, however, that education is distinguishable from other services and benefits provided by the State because it bears a peculiarly close relationship to other rights and liberties accorded protection under the Constitution. Specifically, they insist that education is itself a fundamental personal right because it is essential to the effective exercise of First Amendment freedoms and to intelligent utilization of the right to vote. In asserting a nexus between speech and education, appellees urge that the right to speak is meaningless unless the speaker is capable of articulating his thoughts intelligently and persuasively. The "marketplace of ideas" is an empty forum for those lacking basic communicative tools. Likewise, they argue that the corollary right to receive information becomes little more than a hollow privilege when the recipient has not been taught to read, assimilate, and utilize available knowledge.

A similar line of reasoning is pursued with respect to the right to vote. . . .

We need not dispute any of these propositions. The Court has long afforded zealous protection against unjustifiable governmental interference with the individual's rights to speak and to vote. Yet we have never presumed to possess either the ability or the authority to guarantee to the citizenry the most *effective* speech or the most *informed* electoral choice. That these may be desirable goals of a system of freedom of expression and a representative form of government is not to be doubted. These are indeed goals to be pursued by a people whose thoughts and beliefs are freed from governmental interference. But they are not values to be implemented by judicial intrusion into otherwise legitimate state activities. . . .

We have carefully considered each of the arguments supportive of the District Court's finding that education is a fundamental right or liberty and have found those arguments unpersuasive. . . .

C

We need not rest our decision, however, solely on the inappropriateness of the strict scrutiny test. A century of Supreme Court adjudication under the Equal Protection Clause affirmatively supports the application of the traditional standard of review, which requires only that the State's system be shown to bear some rational relationship to legitimate state purposes. This case represents far more than a challenge to the manner in which Texas provides for the education of its children. We have here nothing less than a direct attack on the way in which Texas has chosen to raise and disburse state and local tax revenues. We are asked to condemn the State's judgment in conferring on political subdivisions the power to tax local property to supply revenues for local interests. In so doing, appellees would have the Court intrude in an area in which it has traditionally deferred to state legislatures. This Court has often admonished against such interferences with the State's fiscal policies under the Equal Protection Clause. . . .

Thus we stand on familiar grounds when we continue to acknowledge that the Justices of this Court lack both the expertise and the familiarity with local problems so necessary to the making of wise decisions with respect to the raising and disposition of public revenues. . . . No scheme of taxation, whether the tax is imposed on property, income, or purchases of goods and services, has yet been devised which is free of all discriminatory impact. In such a complex arena in which no perfect alternatives exist, the Court does well not to impose too rigorous a standard of scrutiny lest all local fiscal schemes become subjects of criticism under the Equal Protection Clause.

In addition to matters of fiscal policy, this case also involves the most persistent and difficult questions of educational policy, another area in which this Court's lack of specialized knowledge and experience counsels against premature interference with the informed judgments made at the state and local levels. Education, perhaps even more than welfare assistance, presents a myriad of "intractable economic, social, and even philosophical problems." The very complexity of the problems of financing and managing a statewide public school system suggest that "there will be more than one constitutionally permissible method of solving them," and that, within the limits of rationality, "the legislature's efforts to tackle the problems" should be entitled to respect. . . . In such circumstances the judiciary is well advised to refrain from interposing on the States inflexible constitutional restraints that could circumscribe or handicap the continued research and experimentation so vital to finding even partial solutions to educational problems and to keeping abreast of ever changing conditions. . . .

III

. . .

Appellees further urge that the Texas system is unconstitutionally arbitrary because it allows the availability of local taxable resources to turn on "happenstance." They see no justification for a system that allows, as they contend, the quality of education to fluctuate on the basis of the fortuitous positioning of the boundary lines of political subdivisions and the location of valuable commercial and industrial property. But any scheme of local taxation—indeed the very existence of identifiable local governmental units—

requires the establishment of jurisdictional boundaries that are inevitably arbitrary. It is equally inevitable that some localities are going to be blessed with more taxable assets than others. Nor is local wealth a static quantity. Changes in the level of taxable wealth within any district may result from any number of events, some of which local residents can and do influence. For instance, commercial and industrial enterprises may be encouraged to locate within a district by various actions—public and private.

Moreover, if local taxation for local expenditure is an unconstitutional method of providing for education then it may be an equally impermissible means of providing other necessary services customarily financed largely from local property taxes, including local police and fire protection, public health and hospitals, and public utility facilities of various kinds. We perceive no justification for such a severe denigration of local property taxation and control as would follow from appellees' contentions. It has simply never been within the constitutional prerogative of this Court to nullify statewide measures for financing public services merely because the burdens or benefits thereof fall unevenly depending upon the relative wealth of the political subdivisions in which citizens live.

In sum, to the extent that the Texas system of school finance results in unequal expenditures between children who happen to reside in different districts, we cannot say that such disparities are the product of a system that is so irrational as to be invidiously discriminatory. . . . We are unwilling to assume for ourselves a level of wisdom superior to that of legislators, scholars, and educational authorities in 49 States, especially where the alternatives proposed are only recently conceived and nowhere yet tested. The constitutional standard under the Equal Protection Clause is whether the challenged state action rationally furthers a legitimate state purpose or interest. We hold that the Texas plan abundantly satisfied this standard. . . .

Reversed.

[The concurring opinion of JUSTICE POT-
TER STEWART *and the dissenting opinions of*
JUSTICES WILLIAM J. BRENNAN *and* BYRON
WHITE *are not reprinted here.*]

MR. JUSTICE MARSHALL, *with whom* MR.
JUSTICE DOUGLAS *concurs, dissenting.*

The Court today decides, in effect, that a
State may constitutionally vary the quality of
education which it offers its children in accordance with the amount of taxable wealth located
in the school districts within which they reside.
The majority's decision represents an abrupt
departure from the mainstream of recent state
and federal court decisions concerning the unconstitutionality of state educational financing
schemes dependent upon taxable local wealth.
More unfortunately, though, the majority's holding can only be seen as a retreat from our historic
commitment to equality of educational opportunity and as unsupportable acquiescence in a
system which deprives children in their earliest
years of the chance to reach their full potential
as citizens. The Court does this despite the
absence of any substantial justification for a
scheme which arbitrarily channels educational
resources in accordance with the fortuity of the
amount of taxable wealth within each district.

In my judgment, the right of every American
to an equal start in life, so far as the provision of
a state service as important as education is
concerned, is far too vital to permit state
discrimination on grounds as tenuous as those
presented by this record. Nor can I accept the
notion that it is sufficient to remit these appellees to the vagaries of the political process which,
contrary to the majority's suggestion, has proven
singularly unsuited to the task of providing a
remedy for this discrimination. I, for one, am
unsatisfied with the hope of an ultimate "political" solution sometime in the indefinite future
while, in the meantime, countless children un-
justifiably receive inferior educations that "may
affect their hearts and minds in a way unlikely

ever to be undone." I must therefore respectfully
dissent.

I

The Court acknowledges that "substantial inter-
district disparities in school expenditures" exist
in Texas. . . . But instead of closely examining
the seriousness of these disparities and the
invidiousness of the Texas financing scheme, the
Court undertakes an elaborate exploration of the
efforts Texas has purportedly made to close the
gaps between its districts in terms of levels of
district wealth and resulting educational funding.
Yet, however praiseworthy Texas' equalizing
efforts, the issue in this case is not whether Texas
is doing its best to ameliorate the worst features
of a discriminatory scheme, but rather whether
the scheme itself is in fact unconstitutionally
discriminatory in the face of the Fourteenth
Amendment's guarantee of equal protection of
the laws. When the Texas financing scheme is
taken as a whole, I do not think it can be
doubted that it produces a discriminatory impact
on substantial numbers of the schoolage children
of the State of Texas. . . . .

A

It is clear . . . that the disparity of per pupil
revenues cannot be dismissed as the result of lack
of local effort—that is, lower tax rates—by
property poor districts. To the contrary,
. . . data . . . indicate that the poorest districts
tend to have the highest tax rates and the richest
districts tend to have the lowest tax rates. Yet,
despite the apparent *extra* effort being made by
the poorest districts, they are unable even to
begin to match the richest districts in terms of
the production of local revenues. . . . Without
more, this state imposed system of educational
funding presents a serious picture of widely
varying treatment of Texas school districts, and
thereby of Texas school children, in terms of the
amount of funds available for public education. . . .

The majority continually emphasizes how much state aid has, in recent years, been given to property poor Texas school districts. What the Court fails to emphasize is the cruel irony of how much more state aid is being given to property rich Texas school districts on top of their already substantial local property tax revenues. Under any view, then, it is apparent that the state aid provided by the Foundation School Program fails to compensate for the large funding variations attributable to the local property tax element of the Texas financing scheme. And it is these stark differences in the treatment of Texas school districts and school children inherent in the Texas financing scheme, not the absolute amount of state aid provided to any particular school district, that are the crux of this case. There can, moreover, be no escaping the conclusion that the local property tax which is dependent upon taxable district property wealth is an essential feature of the Texas scheme for financing public education. . . .

B

. . .

At the very least, in view of the substantial interdistrict disparities in funding and in resulting educational inputs shown by appellees to exist under the Texas financing scheme, the burden of proving that these disparities do not in fact affect the quality of children's education must fall upon the appellants. . . .

. . . [T]he appellants and the majority may believe that the Equal Protection Clause cannot be offended by substantially unequal state treatment of persons who are similarly situated so long as the State provides everyone with some unspecified amount of education which evidently is "enough." The basis for such a novel view is far from clear. It is, of course, true that the Constitution does not require precise equality in the treatment of all persons. . . . But this Court has never suggested that because some "adequate" level of benefits is provided to all,

discrimination in the provision of services is therefore constitutionally excusable. The Equal Protection Clause is not addressed to the minimal sufficier cy but rather to the unjustifiable inequalities of state action. It mandates nothing less than that "all persons similarly circumstanced shall be treated alike." . . .

In my view, then, it is inequality—not some notion of gross adequacy—of educational opportunity that raises a question of denial of equal protection of the laws. I find any other approach to the issue unintelligible and without directing principle. Here appellees have made a substantial showing of wide variations in educational funding and the resulting educational opportunity afforded to the school children of Texas. This discrimination is, in large measure, attributable to significant disparities in the taxable wealth of local Texas school districts. This is a sufficient showing to raise a substantial question of discriminatory state action in violation of the Equal Protection Clause. . . .

C

. . .

I believe it is sufficient that the over-arching form of discrimination in this case is between school children of Texas on the basis of the taxable property wealth of the districts in which they happen to live. To understand both the precise nature of this discrimination and the parameters of the disadvantaged class it is sufficient to consider the constitutional principle which appellees contend is controlling in the context of educational financing. In their complaint appellees asserted that the Constitution does not permit local district wealth to be determinative of educational opportunity. This is simply another way of saying, as the District Court concluded, that consistent with the guarantee of equal protection of the laws, "the quality of public education may not be a function of wealth, other than the wealth of the state as a whole." Under such a principle, the children of a district are excessively advantaged if that district has more taxable property per pupil than the average amount of taxable property per pupil considering the State as a whole. By contrast, the children of a district are disadvantaged if that district has less taxable property per pupil than the state average. The majority attempts to disparage such a definition of the disadvantaged class as the product of an "artificially defined level" of district wealth. But such is clearly not the case, for this is the definition unmistakably dictated by the constitutional principle for which appellees have argued throughout the course of this litigation. And I do not believe that a clearer definition of either the disadvantaged class of Texas school children or the allegedly unconstitutional discrimination suffered by the members of that class under the present Texas financing scheme could be asked for, much less needed. Whether this discrimination, against the school children of property poor districts, inherent in the Texas financing scheme is violative of the Equal Protection Clause is the question to which we must now turn.

II

. . .

A

To begin, I must once more voice my disagreement with the Court's rigidified approach to equal protection analysis. The Court apparently seeks to establish today that equal protection cases fall into one of two neat categories which dictate the appropriate standard of review—strict scrutiny or mere rationality. But this Court's decisions in the field of equal protection defy such easy categorization. A principled reading of what this Court has done reveals that it has applied a spectrum of standards in reviewing discrimination allegedly violative of the Equal Protection Clause. This spectrum clearly comprehends variations in the degree of care with which the Court will scrutinize particular classifications, depending, I believe, on the constitutional and societal importance of the interest adversely affected and the recognized invidiousness of the basis upon which the particular classification is drawn. I find in fact that many of the Court's recent decisions embody the very sort of reasoned approach to equal protection analysis for which I previously argued—that is, an approach in which "concentration [is] placed upon the character of the classification in question, the relative importance to the individuals in the class discriminated against of the governmental benefits that they do not receive, and the asserted state interests in support of the classification."

I therefore cannot accept the majority's labored efforts to demonstrate that fundamental interests, which call for strict scrutiny of the challenged classification, encompass only established rights which we are somehow bound to recognize from the text of the Constitution itself. To be sure, some interests which the Court has deemed to be fundamental for purposes of equal protection analysis are themselves constitutionally protected rights. . . . But it will not do to suggest that the "answer" to whether an interest is fundamental for purposes of equal protection analysis is *always* determined by whether that interest "is a right . . . explicitly or implicitly guaranteed by the Constitution." . . .

C

. . . We are told that in every prior case involving a wealth classification, the members of the disadvantaged class have "shared two distinguishing characteristics: because of their impecunity they were completely unable to pay for some desired benefit, and as a consequence, they sustained an absolute deprivation of a meaningful opportunity to enjoy that benefit." I cannot agree. . . .

This is not to say that the form of wealth

classification in this case does not differ significantly from those recognized in the previous decisions of this Court. Our prior cases have dealt essentially with discrimination on the basis of personal wealth. Here, by contrast, the children of the disadvantaged Texas school districts are being discriminated against not necessarily because of their personal wealth or the wealth of their families, but because of the taxable property wealth of the residents of the districts in which they happen to live. The appropriate question, then, is whether the same degree of judicial solicitude and scrutiny that has previously been afforded wealth classifications is warranted here.

As the Court points out, no previous decision has deemed the presence of just a wealth classification to be sufficient basis to call forth "rigorous judicial scrutiny" of allegedly discriminatory state action. That wealth classifications alone have not necessarily been considered to bear the same high degree of suspectness as have classifications based on, for instance, race or alienage may be explainable on a number of grounds. The "poor" may not be seen as politically powerless as certain discrete and insular minority groups. Personal poverty may entail much the same social stigma as historically attached to certain racial or ethnic groups. But personal poverty is not a permanent disability; its shackles may be escaped. Perhaps, most importantly, though, personal wealth may not necessarily share the general irrelevance as basis for legislative action that race or nationality is recognized to have. While the "poor" have frequently been a legally disadvantaged group, it cannot be ignored that social legislation must frequently take cognizance of the economic status of our citizens. Thus, we have generally gauged the invidiousness of wealth classifications with an awareness of the importance of the interests being affected and the relevance of personal wealth to those interests.

When evaluated with these considerations in mind, it seems to me that discrimination on the basis of group wealth in this case likewise calls for careful judicial scrutiny. First, it must be recognized that while local district wealth may serve other interests, it bears no relationship whatsoever to the interest of Texas school children in the educational opportunity afforded them by the State of Texas. Given the importance of that interest, we must be particularly sensitive to the invidious characteristics of any form of discrimination that is not clearly intended to serve it, as opposed to some other distinct state interest. Discrimination on the basis of group wealth may not, to be sure, reflect the social stigma frequently attached to personal poverty. Nevertheless, insofar as group wealth discrimination involves wealth over which the disadvantaged individual has no significant control, it represents in fact a more serious basis of discrimination than does personal wealth. For such discrimination is no reflection of the individual's characteristics or his abilities. And thus—particularly in the context of a disadvantaged class composed of children—we have previously treated discrimination on a basis which the individual cannot control as constitutionally disfavored. . . .

In the final analysis, then, the invidious characteristics of the group wealth classification present in this case merely serves to emphasize the need for careful judicial scrutiny of the State's justifications for the resulting interdistrict discrimination in the educational opportunity afforded to the school children of Texas. . . .

FRONTIERO v. RICHARDSON
411 U.S. 671; 36 L. Ed. 2d 583; 93 S. Ct. 1764 (1973)

MR. JUSTICE BRENNAN *announced the judgment of the Court and an opinion in which* MR. JUSTICE DOUGLAS, MR. JUSTICE WHITE, *and* MR. JUSTICE MARSHALL *join.*

The question before us concerns the right of a female member of the uniformed services to claim her spouse as a "dependent" for the purposes of obtaining increased quarters allowances and medical and dental benefits under 36 U.S.C. sections 401, 403 and 10 U.S.C. sections 1072, 1076 on an equal footing with male members. Under these statutes, a serviceman may claim his wife as a "dependent" without regard to whether she is in fact dependent upon him for any part of her support. A servicewoman, on the other hand, may not claim her husband as a "dependent" under these programs unless he is in fact dependent upon her for over one-half of his support. Thus, the question for decision is whether this difference in treatment constitutes an unconstitutional discrimination against servicewomen in violation of the Due Process Clause of the Fifth Amendment. A three-judge District Court for the Middle District of Alabama, one judge dissenting, rejected this contention and sustained the constitutionality of the provisions of the statutes making this distinction. . . . .

In an effort to attract career personnel through re-enlistment, Congress established . . . a scheme for the provision of fringe benefits to members of the uniformed services on a competitive basis with business and industry. Thus, . . . a member of the uniformed services with dependents is entitled to an increased "basic allowance for quarters" and . . . a member's dependents are provided comprehensive medical and dental care.

Appellant Sharron Frontiero, a lieutenant in the United States Air Force, sought increased quarters allowances, and housing and medical benefits for her husband, appellant Joseph Frontiero, on the ground that he was her "dependent." Although such benefits would automatically have been granted with respect to the wife of a male member of the uniformed services, appellant's application was denied because she failed to demonstrate that her husband was dependent on her for more than one-half of his support. Appellants then commenced this suit, contending that, by making this distinction, the statutes unreasonably discriminate on the basis of sex in violation of the Due Process Clause of the Fifth Amendment. In essence, appellants asserted that the discriminatory impact of the statutes is two-fold: first, as a procedural matter, a female member is required to demonstrate her spouse's dependency, while no such burden is imposed upon male members; and second, as a substantive matter, a male member who does not provide more than one-half of his wife's support receives benefits, while a similarly situated female member is denied such benefits. Appellants therefore sought a permanent injunction against the continued enforcement of these statutes and an order directing the appellees to to provide Lieutenant Frontiero with the same housing and medical benefits that a similarly situated male member would receive.

Although the legislative history of these statutes sheds virtually no light on the purposes underlying the differential treatment accorded male and female members, a majority of the three-judge District Court surmised that Congress might reasonably have concluded that, since the husband in our society is generally the "bread-winner" in the family—and the wife typically the "dependent" partner—"it would be more economical to require married female members claiming husbands to prove actual dependency than to extend the presumption of dependency to such members." Indeed, given the fact that approximately 99% of all members of the uniformed services are male, the District Court speculated that such differential treatment might conceivably lead to a "considerable saving of administrative expense and manpower." *Ibid.*

II

At the outset, appellants contend that classifications based upon sex, like classifications based upon race, alienage, and national origin, are inherently suspect and must therefore be subjected to close judicial scrutiny. We agree and, indeed, find at least implicit support for such an approach in our unanimous decision only last Term in *Reed* v. *Reed,* 404 U.S. 71 (1971).

In *Reed,* the Court considered the constitutionality of an Idaho statute providing that, when two individuals are otherwise equally entitled to appointment as administrator of an estate, the male applicant must be preferred to the female. Appellant, the mother of the deceased, and appellee, the father, filed competing petitions for appointment as administrator of their son's estate. Since the parties, as parents of the deceased, were members of the same entitlement class, the statutory preference was invoked and the father's petition was therefore granted. Appellant claimed that this statute, by giving a mandatory preference to males over females without regard to their individual qualifications, violated the Equal Protection Clause of the Fourteenth Amendment.

The Court noted that the Idaho statute "provides that different treatment be accorded to the applicants on the basis of their sex; it thus establishes a classification subject to scrutiny under the Equal Protection Clause." Under

"traditional" equal protection analysis, a legislative classification must be sustained unless it is "patently arbitrary" and bears no rational relationship to a legitimate governmental interest. . . .

In an effort to meet this standard, appellee contended that the statutory scheme was a reasonable measure designed to reduce the workload on probate courts by eliminating one class of contests. Moreover, appellee argued that the mandatory preference for male applicants was in itself reasonable since "men [are] as a rule more conversant with business affairs than . . . women." Indeed, appellee maintained that "it is a matter of common knowledge, that women still are not engaged in politics, the professions, business or industry to the extent that men are." And the Idaho Supreme Court, in upholding the constitutionality of this statute, suggested that the Idaho Legislature might reasonably have "concluded that in general men are better qualified to act as an administrator than are women."

Despite these contentions, however, the Court held the statutory preference for male applicants unconstitutional. . . . The Court . . . held that, even though the State's interest in achieving administrative efficiency "is not without some legitimacy," "[t]o give a mandatory preference to members of either sex over members of the other, merely to accomplish the elimination of hearings on the merits, is to make the very kind of arbitrary legislative choice forbidden by the [Constitution] . . . ." This departure from "traditional" rational basis analysis with respect to sex-based classifications is clearly justified.

There can be no doubt that our Nation has had a long and unfortunate history of sex discrimination. Traditionally, such discrimination was rationalized by an attitude of "romantic paternalism" which, in practical effect, put women not on a pedestal, but in a cage. Indeed, this paternalistic attitude became so firmly rooted in our national consciousness that, exactly 100 years ago, a distinguished member of this Court was able to proclaim:

Man is, or should be, a woman's protector and defender. The natural and proper timidity and delicacy which belongs to the female sex evidently unfits it for many of the occupations of civil life. The constitution of the family organization, which is founded in the divine ordinance, as well as in the nature of things, indicates the domestic sphere as that which properly belongs to the domain and functions of womanhood. The harmony, not to say identity, of interests and views which belong, or should belong, to the family institution is repugnant to the ideas of a woman adopting a distinct and independent career from that of her husband. . . .

. . . The paramount destiny and mission of woman are to fulfill the noble and benign offices of wife and mother. This is the law of the Creator. Bradwell v. Illinois, 83 US [16 Wall] 130 (Bradley, J., concurring).

As a result of notions such as these, our statute books gradually became laden with gross, stereotypical distinctions between the sexes and, indeed, throughout much of the 19th century the position of women in our society was, in many respects, comparable to that of blacks under the pre-Civil War slave codes. Neither slaves nor women could hold office, serve on juries, or bring suit in their own names, and married women traditionally were denied the legal capacity to hold or convey property or to serve as legal guardians of their own children. . . .

It is true, of course, that the position of women in America has improved markedly in recent decades. Nevertheless, it can hardly be doubted that, in part because of the high visibility of the sex characteristic, women still face pervasive, although at times more subtle, discrimination in our educational institutions, on the job market and, perhaps most conspicuously, in the political arena. . . .

Moreover, since sex, like race and national origin, is an immutable characteristic determined solely by the accident of birth, the imposition of special disabilities upon the members of a particular sex because of their sex would seem to violate "the basic concept of our system that legal burdens should bear some relationship to individual responsibility. . . ." And what differentiates sex from such nonsuspect statutes as intelligence or physical disability, and aligns it with the recognized suspect criteria, is that the sex characteristic frequently bears no relation to ability to perform or contribute to society. As a result, statutory distinctions between the sexes often have the effect of invidiously relegating the entire class of females to inferior legal status without regard to the actual capabilities of its individual members.

We might also note that, over the past decade, Congress has itself manifested an increasing sensitivity to sex-based classifications. In Title VII of the Civil Rights Act of 1964, for example, Congress expressly declared that no employer, labor union, or other organization subject to the provisions of the Act shall discriminate against any individual on the basis of "race, color, religion, *sex,* or national origin." Similarly, the Equal Pay Act of 1963 provides that no employer covered by the Act "shall discriminate . . . between employees on the basis of *sex.*" And section 1 of the Equal Rights Amendment, passed by Congress on March 22, 1972, and submitted to the legislatures of the States for ratification, declares that "[e]quality of rights under the law shall not be denied or abridged by the United States or by any State on account of sex." Thus, Congress has itself concluded that classifications based upon sex are inherently invidious, and this conclusion of a coequal branch of Government is not without significance to the question presently under consideration. . . .

With these considerations in mind, we can only conclude that classifications based on sex, like classifications based upon race, alienage, or national origin, are inherently suspect, and must therefore be subjected to strict judicial scrutiny. Applying the analysis mandated by that stricter standard of review, it is clear that the statutory scheme now before us is constitutionally invalid. . . .

III

... [T]he Government concedes that the differential treatment accorded men and women under these statutes serves no purpose other than mere "administrative convenience." In essence, the Government maintains that, as an empirical matter, wives in our society frequently are dependent upon their husbands, while husbands rarely are dependent upon their wives. Thus, the Government argues that Congress might reasonably have concluded that it would be both cheaper and easier simply conclusively to presume that wives of male members are financially dependent upon their husbands, while burdening female members with the task of establishing dependency in fact.

The Government offers no concrete evidence, however, tending to support its view that such differential treatment in fact saves the Government any money. In order to satisfy the demands of strict judicial scrutiny, the Government must demonstrate, for example, that it is actually cheaper to grant increased benefits with respect to *all* male members, than it is to determine which male members are in fact entitled to such benefits and to grant increased benefits only to those members whose wives actually meet the dependency requirement. Here, however, there is substantial evidence that, if put to the test, many of the wives of male members would fail to qualify for benefits. And in light of the fact that the dependency determination with respect to the husbands of female members is presently made solely on the basis of affidavits, rather than through the more costly hearing process, the Government's explanation of the statutory scheme is, to say the least, questionable.

In any case, our prior decisions make clear that, although efficacious administration of governmental programs is not without some importance, "the Constitution recognizes higher values than speed and efficiency." ... And when we enter the realm of "strict judicial scrutiny," there can be no doubt that "administrative convenience" is not a shibboleth, the mere recitation of which dictates constitutionality.... On the contrary, any statutory scheme which draws a sharp line between the sexes, *solely* for the purpose of achieving administrative convenience, necessarily commands "dissimilar treatment for men and women who are ... similarly situated," and therefore involves the "very kind of arbitrary legislative choice forbidden by the [Constitution]...." We therefore conclude that, by according differential treatment to male and female members of the uniformed services for the sole purpose of achieving administrative convenience, the challenged statutes violate the Due Process Clause of the Fifth Amendment insofar as they require a female member to prove the dependency of her husband.

Reversed.

MR. JUSTICE STEWART *concurs in the judgment, agreeing that the statutes before us work an invidious discrimination in violation of the Constitution.* Reed v. Reed, *404 U.S. 71.*

MR. JUSTICE REHNQUIST *dissents for the reasons stated by Judge Rives in his opinion for the District Court,* Frontiero v. Laird, *341 F. Supp. 201 (1972).*

MR. JUSTICE POWELL, *with whom the* CHIEF JUSTICE *and* MR. JUSTICE BLACKMUN *join, concurring in the judgment. The opinion is not reprinted here.*

ROE v. WADE
410 U.S. 113; 35 L. Ed. 2d 147; 93 S. Ct. 705 (1973)

MR. JUSTICE BLACKMUN *delivered the opinion of the Court.*

This Texas federal appeal and its Georgia companion, *Doe* v. *Bolton,* present constitutional challenges to state criminal abortion legislation. The Texas statutes under attack here are typical of those that have been in effect in many States for approximately a century. The Georgia statutes, in contrast, have a modern cast and are a legislative product that, to an extent at least, obviously reflects the influences of recent attitudinal change, of advancing medical knowledge and techniques, and of new thinking about an old issue. . . .

The Texas statutes that concern us . . . make it a crime to "procure an abortion," as therein defined, or to attempt one, except with respect to "an abortion procured or attempted by medical advice for the purpose of saving the life of the mother." Similar statutes are in existence in a majority of the States. . . .

[Appellant] Roe alleged that she was unmarried and pregnant; that she wished to terminate her pregnancy by an abortion "performed by a competent, licensed physician, under safe, clinical conditions"; that she was unable to get a "legal" abortion in Texas because her life did not appear to be threatened by the continuation of her pregnancy; and that she could not afford to travel to another jurisdiction in order to secure a legal abortion under safe conditions. She claimed that the Texas statutes were unconstitutionally vague and that they abridged her right of personal privacy, protected by the First, Fourth, Fifth, Ninth, and Fourteenth Amendments. . . .

. . . On the merits, the District Court held that the "fundamental right of single women and married persons to choose whether to have children is protected by the Ninth Amendment, through the Fourteenth Amendment," and that the Texas criminal abortion statutes were void on their face because they were both unconstitutionally vague and constituted an overbroad infringement of the plaintiffs' Ninth Amendment rights. The court then held that abstention was warranted with respect to the requests for an injunction. It therefore dismissed the Doe complaint, declared the abortion statutes void, and dismissed the application for injunctive relief.

The plaintiffs . . . have appealed to this Court from that part of the District Court's judgment denying the injunction. . . .

The principal thrust of appellant's attack on the Texas statutes is that they improperly invade a right, said to be possessed by the pregnant woman, to choose to terminate her pregnancy. Appellant would discover this right in the concept of personal "liberty" embodied in the Fourteenth Amendment's Due Process Clause; or in personal, marital, familial, and sexual privacy said to be protected by the Bill of Rights or its penumbras, see *Griswold* v. *Connecticut,* . . . or among those rights reserved to the people by the Ninth Amendment. . . . Before addressing this claim, we feel it desirable briefly to survey, in several aspects, the history of abortion, for such insight as that history may afford us, and then to examine the state purposes and interests behind the criminal abortion laws.

[The Court here reviews the history of abortion in terms of Ancient Attitudes, The Hippocratic Oath, The Common Law, The English Statutory Law, and The American Law.

The Court also summarizes the positions of the American Medical Association, the American Public Health Association, and the American Bar Association.]

It is thus apparent that at common law, at the time of the adoption of our Constitution, and throughout the major portion of the 19th century, abortion was viewed with less disfavor than under most American statutes currently in effect. Phrasing it another way, a woman enjoyed a substantially broader right to terminate a pregnancy than she does in most States today. At least with respect to the early stage of pregnancy, and very possibly without such a limitation, the opportunity to make this choice was present in this country well into the 19th century. Even later, the law continued for some time to treat less punitively an abortion procured in early pregnancy. . . .

Three reasons have been advanced to explain historically the enactment of criminal abortion laws in the 19th century and to justify their continued existence.

It has been argued occasionally that these laws were the product of a Victorian social concern to discourage illicit sexual conduct. Texas, however, does not advance this justification in the present case, and it appears that no court or commentator has taken the argument seriously. The appellants and *amici* contend, moreover, that this is not a proper state purpose at all and suggest that, if it were, the Texas statutes are overbroad in protecting it since the law fails to distinguish between married and unwed mothers.

A second reason is concerned with abortion as a medical procedure. When most criminal abortion laws were first enacted, the procedure was a hazardous one for the woman. . . . Thus it has been argued that a State's real concern in enacting a criminal abortion law was to protect the pregnant woman, that is, to restrain her from submitting to a procedure that placed her life in serious jeopardy.

Modern medical techniques have altered this situation. Appellants and various *amici* refer to medical data, indicating that abortion in early pregnancy, that is, prior to the end of first trimester, although not without its risk, is now relatively safe. Mortality rates for women undergoing early abortions, where the procedure is legal, appear to be as low as or lower than the rates for normal childbirth. Consequently, any interest of the State in protecting the woman from an inherently hazardous procedure, except when it would be equally dangerous for her to forego it, has largely disappeared. Of course, important state interests in the area of health and medical standards do remain. The State has a legitimate interest in seeing to it that abortion, like any other medical procedure, is performed under circumstances that insure maximum safety for the patient. . . . The prevalence of high mortality rates at illegal "abortion mills" strengthens, rather than weakens, the State's interest in regulating the conditions under which abortions are performed. Moreover, the risk to the woman increases as her pregnancy continues. . . .

The third reason is the State's interest—some phrase it in terms of duty—in protecting prenatal life. Some of the argument for this justification rests on the theory that a new human life is present from the moment of conception. The State's interest and general obligation to protect life then extends, it is argued, to prenatal life. Only when the life of the pregnant mother herself is at stake, balanced against the life she carries within her, should the interest of the embryo or fetus not prevail. Logically, of course, a legitimate state interest in this area need not stand or fall on acceptance of the belief that life begins at conception or at some point prior to live birth. In assessing the State's interest, recognition may be given to the less rigid claim that as long as at least *potential* life is involved, the State may assert interests beyond the protection of the pregnant woman alone. . . .

It is with these interests and the weight to be attached to them, that this case is concerned.

The Constitution does not explicitly mention any rights of privacy. In a line of decisions, however, . . . the Court has recognized that a right of personal privacy, or a guarantee of certain areas or zones of privacy, does exist under the Constitution. In varying contexts the Court or individual Justices have indeed found at least the roots of that right in the First Amendment, *Stanley* v. *Georgia,* (1969); in the Fourth and Fifth Amendments, *Terry* v. *Ohio,* (1968), *Katz* v. *United States* (1967); . . . in the penumbras of the Bill of Rights, *Griswold* v. *Connecticut,* (1965); in the Ninth Amendment, or in the concept of liberty guaranteed by the first section of the Fourteenth Amendment, see *Meyer* v. *Nebraska* (1923). These decisions make it clear that only personal rights that can be deemed "fundamental" or "implicit in the concept of ordered liberty," *Palko* v. *Connecticut* (1937), are included in this guarantee of personal privacy. They also make it clear that the right has some extension to activities relating to marriage, *Loving* v. *Virginia,* procreation. *Skinner* v. *Oklahoma,* contraception, *Eisenstadt* v. *Baird,* family relationships, *Prince* v. *Massachusetts,* and child rearing and education, *Pierce* v. *Society of Sisters, Meyer* v. *Nebraska.*

This right of privacy, whether it be founded in the Fourteenth Amendment's concept of personal liberty and restrictions upon state action, as we feel it is, or, as the District Court determined, in the Ninth Amendment's reservation of rights to the people, is broad enough to encompass a woman's decision whether or not to terminate her pregnancy. The detriment that the State would impose upon the pregnant woman by denying this choice altogether is apparent. Specific and direct harm medically diagnosable even in early pregnancy may be involved. Maternity, or additional offspring, may force upon the woman a distressful life and future. Psychological harm may be imminent. Mental and physical health may be taxed by child care. There is also the distress, for all concerned, associated with the unwanted child, and there is the problem of bringing a child into a family already unable, psychologically and otherwise, to care for it. In other cases, as in this one, the additional difficulties and continuing stigma of unwed motherhood may be involved. All these are factors the woman and her responsible physician necessarily will consider in consultation.

On the basis of elements such as these, appellants and some *amici* argue that the woman's right is absolute and that she is entitled to terminate her pregnancy at whatever time, in whatever way, and for whatever reason she alone chooses. With this we do not agree. Appellants' arguments that Texas either has no valid interest at all in regulating the abortion decision, or no interest strong enough to support any limitation upon the woman's sole determination, is unpersuasive. The Court's decisions recognizing a right of privacy also acknowledge that some state regulation in areas protected by that right is appropriate. As noted above, a state may properly assert important interests in safeguarding health, in maintaining medical standards, and in protecting potential life. At some point in pregnancy, these respective interests become sufficiently compelling to sustain regulation of the factors that govern the abortion decision. The privacy right involved, therefore, cannot be said to be absolute. In fact, it is not clear to us that the claim asserted by some *amici* that one has an unlimited right to do with one's body as one pleases bears a close relationship to the right of privacy previously articulated in the Court's decisions. The Court has refused to recognize an unlimited right of this kind in the past. *Jacobson* v. *Massachusetts,* (1905) (vaccination); *Buck* v. *Bell* (1927) (sterilization).

We therefore conclude that the right of personal privacy includes the abortion decision, but that this right is not unqualified and must be considered against important state interests in regulation. . . .

Where certain "fundamental rights" are involved, the Court has held that regulation limiting these rights may be justified only by a "compelling state interest," . . . and that legislative enactments must be narrowly drawn to express only the legitimate state interests at stake. . . .

The District Court held that the appellee failed to meet his burden of demonstrating that the Texas statute's infringement upon Roe's rights was necessary to support a compelling state interest, and that, although the defendant presented "several compelling justifications for state presence in the area of abortions," the statutes outstripped these justifications and swept "far beyond any areas of compelling state interest." Appellant and appellee both contest that holding. Appellant, as has been indicated, claims an absolute right that bars any state imposition of criminal penalties in the area. Appellee argues that the State's determination to recognize and protect prenatal life from and after conception constitutes a compelling state interest. As noted above, we do not agree fully with either formulation.

The appellee and certain *amici* argue that the fetus is a "person" within the language and meaning of the Fourteenth Amendment. In support of this they outline at length and in detail the well-known facts of fetal development. If this suggestion of personhood is established, the appellant's case, of course, collapses, for the fetus' right to life is then guaranteed specifically by the Amendment. The appellant conceded as much on reargument. On the other hand, the appellee conceded on reargument that no case could be cited that holds that a fetus is a person within the meaning of the Fourteenth Amendment.

The Constitution does not define "person" in so many words. Section 1 of the Fourteenth Amendment contains three references to "person." The first, in defining "citizens," speaks of "persons born or naturalized in the United States." The word also appears both in the Due Process Clause and in the Equal Protection Clause. "Person" is used in other places in the Constitution. . . . But in nearly all these instances, the use of the word is such that it has application only postnatally. None indicates, with any assurance, that it has any possible prenatal application.

All this, together with our observation, supra, that throughout the major portion of the 19th century prevailing legal abortion practices were far freer than they are today, persuades us that the word "person," as used in the Fourteenth Amendment, does not include the unborn. . . .

This conclusion, however, does not of itself fully answer the contentions raised by Texas, and we pass on to other considerations.

The pregnant woman cannot be isolated in her privacy. She carries an embryo and, later, a fetus, if one accepts the medical definitions of the developing young in the human uterus. . . . The situation therefore is inherently different from marital intimacy, or bedroom possession of obscene material, or marriage, or procreation, or education, with which *Eisenstadt, Griswold, Stanley, Loving, Skinner, Pierce,* and *Meyer* were respectively concerned. As we have intimated above, it is reasonable and appropriate for a State to decide that at some point in time another interest, that of health of the mother or that of potential human life, becomes significantly involved. The woman's privacy is no longer sole and any right of privacy she possesses must be measured accordingly.

Texas urges that, apart from the Fourteenth Amendment, life begins at conception and is present throughout pregnancy, and that, therefore, the State has a compelling interest in protecting that life from and after conception. We need not resolve the difficult question of when life begins. When those trained in the respective disciplines of medicine, philosophy, and theology are unable to arrive at any consensus, the judiciary, at this point in the development of man's knowledge, is not in a position to speculate as to the answer. . . .

In areas other than criminal abortion the law has been reluctant to endorse any theory that life, as we recognize it, begins before live birth or to accord legal rights to the unborn except in narrowly defined situations and except when the rights are contingent upon live birth. . . . [T]he unborn have never been recognized in the law as persons in the whole sense.

In view of all this, we do not agree that, by adopting one theory of life, Texas may override the rights of the pregnant woman that are at stake. We repeat, however, that the State does have an important and legitimate interest in preserving and protecting the health of the pregnant woman, whether she be a resident of the State or a non-resident who seeks medical consultation and treatment there, and that it has still *another* important and legitimate interest in protecting the potentiality of human life. These interests are separate and distinct. Each grows in substantiality as the woman approaches term and, at a point during pregnancy, each becomes "compelling."

With respect to the State's important and legitimate interest in the health of the mother, the "compelling" point, in the light of present medical knowledge, is at approximately the end of the first trimester. This is so because of the now established medical fact . . . that until the end of the first trimester mortality in abortion is less than mortality in normal childbirth. It follows that, from and after this point, a State may regulate the abortion procedure to the extent that the regulation reasonably relates to the preservation and protection of maternal health. Examples of permissible state regulation in this area are requirements as to the qualifications of the person who is to perform the abortion; as to the licensure of that person; as to the facility in which the procedure is to be performed, that is, whether it must be a hospital or may be a clinic or some other place of less-than-hospital status; as to the licensing of the facility; and the like.

This means, on the other hand, that, for the period of pregnancy prior to this "compelling" point, the attending physician, in consultation with his patient, is free to determine, without regulation by the State, that in his medical judgment the patient's pregnancy should be terminated. If that decision is reached, the judgment may be effectuated by an abortion free of interference by the State.

With respect to the State's important and legitimate interest in potential life, the "compelling" point is at viability. This is so because the fetus then presumably has the capability of meaningful life outside the mother's womb. State regulation protective of fetal life after viability thus has both logical and biological justifications. If the State is interested in protecting fetal life after viability, it may go so far as to proscribe abortion during that period except when it is necessary to preserve the life or health of the mother.

Measured against these standards, the Texas Penal Code, in restricting legal abortions to those "procured or attempted by medical advice for the purpose of saving the life of the mother," sweeps too broadly. The statute makes no distinction between abortions performed early in pregnancy and those performed later, and it limits to a single reason, "saving" the mother's life, the legal justification for the procedure. The statute, therefore, cannot survive the constitutional attack made upon it here. . . .

Affirmed in part and reversed in part.

The concurring opinion of MR. JUSTICE STEWART *is omitted here.*

MR. JUSTICE REHNQUIST, *dissenting.*

The Court's opinion brings to the decision of this troubling question both extensive historical fact and a wealth of legal scholarship. While its opinion thus commands my respect, I find myself nonetheless in fundamental disagreement with those parts of it which invalidate the Texas statute in question, and therefore dissent. . . .

. . . I have difficulty in concluding, as the Court does, that the right of "privacy" is involved in this case. Texas by the statute here challenged bars the performance of a medical abortion by a licensed physician on a plaintiff such as Roe. A transaction resulting in an operation such as this is not "private" in the ordinary usage of that word. Nor is the "privacy" which the Court finds here even a distant relative of the freedom from searches and seizures protected by the Fourth Amendment to the Constitution which the Court has referred to as embodying a right of privacy.

If the Court means by the term "privacy" no more than that the claim of a person to be free from unwanted state regulation of consensual transactions may be a form of "liberty" protected by the Fourteenth Amendment, there is no doubt that similar claims have been upheld in our earlier decisions on the basis of that liberty. I agree with the statement of Mr. Justice Stewart in his concurring opinion that the "liberty," against deprivation of which without due process the Fourteenth Amendment protects, embraces more than the rights found in the Bill of Rights. But that liberty is not guaranteed absolutely against deprivation, but only against deprivation without due process of law. The test traditionally applied in the area of social and economic legislation is whether or not a law such as that challenged has a rational relation to a valid state objective. The Due Process Clause of the Fourteenth Amendment undoubtedly does place a limit on legislative power to enact laws such as this, albeit a broad one. If the Texas statute were to prohibit an abortion even where the mother's life is in jeopardy, I have little doubt that such a statute would lack a rational relation to a valid state objective under the test stated *supra*. But the Court's sweeping invalidation of any restrictions on abortion during the first trimester is impossible to justify under that standard, and the conscious weighing of competing factors which the Court's opinion apparently substitutes for the established test is far more appropriate to a legislative judgment than to a judicial one.

The Court eschews the history of the Fourteenth Amendment in its reliance on the "compelling state interest" test. But the Court adds a new wrinkle to this test by transposing it from the legal considerations associated with the Equal Protection Clause of the Fourteenth Amendment to this case arising under the Due Process Clause of the Fourteenth Amendment. Unless I misapprehend the consequences of this transplanting of the "compelling state interest test," the Court's opinion will accomplish the seemingly impossible feat of leaving this area of the law more confused than it found it.

While the Court's opinion quotes from the dissent of Mr. Justice Holmes in *Lochner* v. *New York* (1905), the result it reaches is more closely attuned to the majority opinion of Mr. Justice Peckham in that case. As in *Lochner* and similar cases applying substantive due process standards to economic and social welfare legislation, the adoption of the compelling state interest standard will inevitably require this Court to examine the legislative policies and pass on the wisdom of these policies in the very process of deciding whether a particular state interest put forward may or may not be "compelling." The decision here to break the term of pregnancy into three distinct terms and to outline the permissible restrictions the State may impose in each one, for example, partakes more of judicial legislation than it does of a determination of the intent of the drafters of the Fourteenth Amendment.

The fact that a majority of the States, reflecting after all the majority sentiment in those States, have had restrictions on abortions for at least a century seems to me as strong an indication there is that the asserted right to an abortion is not "so rooted in the traditions and conscience of our people as to be ranked as fundamental." Even today, when society's views on abortion are changing, the very existence of the debate is evidence that the "right" to an abortion is not so universally accepted as the appellants would have us believe.

To reach its result the Court necessarily has had to find within the scope of the Fourteenth

Amendment a right that was apparently completely unknown to the drafters of the Amendment. As early as 1821, the first state law dealing directly with abortion was enacted by the Connecticut legislature. Conn. Stat. Tit. 22, sections 14, 16 (1821), By the time of the adoption of the Fourteenth Amendment in 1868 there were at least 36 laws enacted by state or territorial legislatures limiting abortion. While many States have amended or updated their laws, 21 of the laws on the books in 1868 remain in effect today. Indeed, the Texas statute struck down today was, as the majority notes, first enacted in 1857 and "has remained substantially unchanged to the present time."

There apparently was no question concerning the validity of this provision or of any of the other state statutes when the Fourteenth Amendment was adopted. The only conclusion possible from this history is that the drafters did not intend to have the Fourteenth Amendment withdraw from the States the power to legislate with respect to this matter. . . .

SELECTED REFERENCES

Barker, Lucius J., "Black Americans and the Burger Court: Implications for the Political System," 1973 Wash. Univ. L.Q. 747 (Fall, 1973).

_____,"Third Parties in Litigation: A Systemic View of the Judicial Function," 29 *Journal of Politics* 41 (1967).

Bell, Derrick, *Race, Racism, and American Law* (Boston: Little Brown and Co., 1973). (Includes extensive references to problems of race and racism, see especially pp. XXXV–XXXVIII.)

_____,"School Litigation Strategies for the 1970's: New Phases in the Continuous Quest for Quality Schools," 1970 *Wisconsin Law Review* 257 (1970).

Burkey, Richard, *Racial Discrimination and Public Policy in the United States* (Lexington, Mass.: Heath Lexington Books, 1971).

Cary, Eve, "Pregnancy Without Penalty," 1 *The Civil Liberties Review* 31 (1973).

Erikson, Robert, "The Partisan Impact of State Legislative Reapportionment," 15 *Midwest Journal of Political Science* (Feb., 1971).

Grier, William H., and Price M. Cobbs, *Black Rage* (New York: Basic Books, Inc., 1968).

Kanowitz, Leo M., *Sex Roles in Law and Society* (Albuquerque: University of New Mexico Press, 1972).

_____, *Women and the Law,* rev. ed. (Albuquerque: University of New Mexico Press, 1969).

Matthews, Donald R., and James W. Prothro, *Negroes and the New Southern Politics* (New York: Harcourt Brace Jovanovich, Inc., 1966).

Miller, Loren, *The Petitioners: The Story of the Supreme Court of the United States and the Negro* (Cleveland: The World Publishing Company, 1966).

Peltason, Jack W., *Fifty-eight Lonely Men: Southern Federal Judges and School Desegregation* (New York: Harcourt Brace Jovanovich, Inc., 1961).

Polsby, Nelson, ed., *Reapportionment in the 70s* (Berkeley: University of California Press, 1971).

Pritchett, C. Herman, "Equal Protection and the Urban Majority," 58 *American Political Science Review* 869 (1964).

Report of the National Advisory Commission on Civil Disorders (Washington: U.S. Government Printing Office, 1968).

Ryan, Phillip Scott, "Decent Housing as a Constitutional Right—42 U.S.C. Sec. 1983—Poor People's Remedy for Deprivation," 14 *Howard Law Journal* 338 (1968).

Steel, Lewis M., "A Critic's View of the Warren Court—Nine Men in Black Who Think White," *New York Times Magazine* (Oct. 13, 1968), pp. 56ff.

Symposium "Anatomy of a Riot: An Analytical Symposium of the Causes and Effects of Riots," 45 *Journal of Urban Law* 499 (1968).

United States Commission on Civil Rights, Periodic Reports of the Commission (Washington: U.S. Government Printing Office, 1959-1973.)

Van Loon, Eric E., "Representative Government and Equal Protection," 5 *Harvard Civil Rights—Civil Liberties Review* 472 (1970).

Index of Cases